Ethics in Canada

Ethics in Canada

Ethical, Social, and Political Perspectives

Edited by
Karen Wendling

OXFORD
UNIVERSITY PRESS

OXFORD
UNIVERSITY PRESS

Oxford University Press is a department of the University of Oxford. It furthers the University's objective of excellence in research, scholarship, and education by publishing worldwide. Oxford is a registered trade mark of Oxford University Press in the UK and in certain other countries.

Published in Canada by
Oxford University Press
8 Sampson Mews, Suite 204,
Don Mills, Ontario M3C 0H5 Canada

www.oupcanada.com

Library and Archives Canada Cataloguing in Publication

Ethics in Canada : ethical, social, and political perspectives / edited by Karen Wendling.

Includes bibliographical references and index.
ISBN 978-0-19-544320-2 (pbk.)

1. Ethics—Canada. 2. Social ethics—Canada. 3. Political ethics—Canada. 4. Globalization—Moral and ethical aspects—Canada. I. Wendling, Karen, 1956–, editor

BJ402.E847 2015 170.971 C2015-900378-4

Cover image: igor kisselev/Shutterstock

Oxford University Press is committed to our environment. Wherever possible, our books are printed on paper which comes from responsible sources.

Printed and bound in the United States of America

1 2 3 4 — 18 17 16 15

Contents

Preface

Most of the applied ethics textbooks in North America follow a pretty standard pattern: perhaps prefaced by a chapter or section on ethical theories and moral argumentation, they have a series of chapters that present a range of philosophical views on controversial moral issues, occasionally supplemented with non-philosophical material such as court decisions or excerpts from works of fiction. One of the things these books lack is a sense of what ties the moral or ethical issues together and how students might use the readings and their reflections on them to develop a coherent set of ethical, social, and political views. They do not encourage students to locate their own views on the map of philosophical perspectives on each topic, to see how their views about environmental ethics mesh with their views about abortion, multiculturalism, or health care, and to fit them all together into a unified ethical and political philosophical perspective.

Ethics for Canadians is a different sort of textbook. Its premise is that different views about applied ethics or social issues are undergirded by consistent ethical and political perspectives, and that these perspectives are reflected in contemporary Canadian society, institutions, and policies. *Ethics for Canadians* will not only help students develop reasoned, coherent views on particular topics; it will also help them help them see how their views fit together into an overall ethical and political perspective, and where this perspective fits on a philosophical map of reasonable views. The book is designed to help students make their views coherent and consistent both within and across the topics. In addition, it helps them learn what is distinctive about Canadian perspectives on the issues. Our students grow up steeped in media dominated by the US, and often they do not know even that (and much less why) Canadian policies and laws differ from American ones. This text is designed to remedy some of those misconceptions, and to help students decide who they think we are or should be as Canadians, while they are learning philosophy. Ultimately, the goal of *Ethics for Canadians* is to help students become more reflective citizens who have a better understanding of the philosophical grounding of their views; who can explain why they hold a certain perspective on a particular issue to people who do not necessarily agree with them; who have a better understanding of and respect for views with which they disagree; and who are eager for further courses in philosophy.

The Book's Structure

Ethics for Canadians begins with a primer on moral and political theories and the Canadian legal system, followed by a moral and political preferences indicator to show them where their current views fit on the spectrum of Canadian views. The main part of the book invites students to think about what it means to be Canadian. Part I, Who Are We?, contains chapters on Aboriginal rights, Quebec nationalism, multiculturalism, and English-speaking Canadians—the main components of our political identities as Canadians. Part II, Who Are "We"?, asks who is a member of the moral community. Whose interests must we consider in our moral decision-making? Part III, What Do We Owe Each Other?, is designed to help students develop their ethical and political views on our rights and obligations as citizens. Part IV, Living in a Global World, helps students round out their views by considering Canada's role internationally.

Wherever possible in the text, I have chosen readings from books or articles by Canadians. This was actually quite easy; many fine Canadian philosophers have written on these issues. On three topics (abortion, animal rights, and climate change) Canadian views are strongly influenced by what has been written and what has happened elsewhere, so in these chapters I have included non-Canadian perspectives. Overall, *Ethics for Canadians* contains 86 per cent Canadian material (37 of 43 readings)—more than any comparable applied ethics or social issues textbook on the market today.

Introduction: The Short Primer

The short primer covers moral and political theories and presents a short overview of the Canadian legal system. The reason for including the moral theories is obvious: this is an applied ethics/contemporary moral issues textbook, so beginning with a grounding in moral theories is important. In addition, since many of the readings in parts I through IV refer to utilitarianism, deontology, virtue theory, and care ethics, it is helpful if students learn something about these theories before they tackle the issues.

Ethical theories provide the deep justification for political philosophy and applied ethics. Political philosophy puts flesh on the bones of ethical theory, and applied ethics animates it. Political philosophy and applied ethics ask higher-level questions about the good society and particular policies or practices within it that cannot be answered by ethics alone. One of the premises of the book is that political philosophy is theoretically closer to applied ethics than ethical theory is, because theories of the good society are closer to theories of social practices (which is what applied ethics considers) than are theories of the good, the right, the virtues, or relationships. The section on political philosophy in the short primer helps students decide what their own views are on particular topics, and helps them explain their views to others who do not necessarily agree with them.

I have included material on the Canadian legal system to help students understand the background of some of the readings, particularly the Supreme Court decisions, as well as the relation between law and morality. Supreme Court decisions often are a form of public philosophy, in which the Court carefully articulates the reasons why, in its judgment, a particular law or public policy upholds or violates the rights and freedoms guaranteed in the *Charter*. Because our constitution is so young, the Supreme Court has been particularly explicit about the moral principles on which its judgments are based. Of course law and morality do not overlap completely, any more than political philosophy and morality do. But large areas of the law, especially the criminal law and tort law, do overlap with morality. Crimes are a subset of moral wrongs a society considers so serious that it punishes and even imprisons people who commit them. Torts are a further subset of wrongs that a society says deserve compensation rather than punishment. The section on the Canadian legal system will help students understand how morality and the law fit together, and why we have particular laws and policies in Canada. It will round out their views of what it means to be Canadian by helping them think about whether—and if so, how—some of our basic moral and political principles ought to be codified in law.

The short primer ends with a section on reading and understanding philosophy. This teaches students to see the structure of an author's argument (also aided in the readings by annotations), how to unpack a complicated argument, how to unpack a complicated sentence, and then how to re-compose the pieces to gain a coherent understanding of the argument.

The introduction ends with a moral and political preferences indicator. Here students are asked questions about their views on some Canadian social issues. The pattern of their answers shows them where they fit, at least initially, on the spectrum of moral and political views in Canada. Throughout the text, they are invited to revisit their initial answers, to see whether (and if so, how) their moral and political views have solidified, shifted, or even changed in response to their views on contemporary moral issues.

Part I: Who Are We?

Part I contains chapters on the building-blocks of contemporary Canadian identity: Aboriginal peoples, Quebec nationalism, multiculturalism, and English-speaking Canadians. The chapters in this part introduce students to some of our defining characteristics as a nation and help them understand what philosophers and other theorists have said about who we are as a people or peoples. Questions of identity have significant historical as well as philosophical dimensions; who we are as a nation is in great part a function of who we have been. Aboriginal rights, Quebec nationalism, multiculturalism, and English-speaking Canada cannot be understood in isolation from the particular histories of Aboriginal peoples, French and British colonization, Quebec as a francophone society in an ocean of anglophones, Canada as a loyalist colony, and the successive waves of immigration that have made Canada what it is today. Part I, Who Are We?, helps students develop and deepen their views on what it means to be Canadian. This will orient them for the material in the remainder of the text. What we think about contemporary moral issues—who "we" includes and excludes, what we think we owe fellow Canadians and distant others—depends at least in part on how we conceptualize ourselves, on who we consider to be part of "us" and who is "them."

Part II: Who Are "We"?

In Part I we look at who we are as Canadians. Part II examines who counts as a member of the moral community, by looking at two hard cases: abortion and animal rights. In the chapter on abortion, views range from the claim that morally relevant human life begins at conception to the claim that abortion is really about reproductive control, not the personhood of the fetus. The next chapter examines animal rights. Here we consider what we can do to non-human animals, what sorts of protection they deserve, and whether they should be included in the moral community. Part II, Who Are "We"?, asks students to think about what it means to be a member of a moral community, and the grounds for inclusion in or exclusion from that community.

Part III: What Do We Owe Each Other?

Part III gets students to think about what it means to live in a political community, and what sorts of guarantees and protections we owe our fellow citizens. The first chapter in this section, on the role of government, is the practical application of the moral and political theories in the introduction. It asks students to think about the justification of government action or inaction in various spheres, about the minimal guarantees a society owes its citizens and the maximal restrictions it may put on them. This will help them develop their views on the other topics in this part. Chapter 8, on health and health care, applies ideas from the previous chapter to what many Canadians consider to be one of our defining features: health care. It asks students to think about what a just health care system should look like—whether the system should be purely public, purely private, or a mixture of the two, and what it should cover and exclude. It also examines some philosophical issues in public health, which focuses on the health of populations rather than individuals. The last chapter in this section examines euthanasia and assisted suicide, a moral and political issue on which public opinion has been shifting for several decades. Twenty-five years ago most Canadians opposed assisted suicide, while today most favour it. Clearing up some conceptual confusions on various sides of the issue will help students develop better reasoned and more clearly articulated views.

Part IV: Living in a Global World

Part IV deals with international threats and obligations. It encourages students to think about what it means to live in a global community—whether, for example, we should focus on human rights, prosperity through international trade, preventing climate change, or something else, and how we as a nation ought to respond to local and global threats such as terrorism. The first chapter examines war and its aftermath, including peacekeeping—perhaps Canada's most important contribution to international relations, in spite of its abysmal failure in Rwanda. Here the questions surround when it is just to go to war, how we should end a war justly, and how we should respond to failed states, human rights abuses, and genocide. The next chapter discusses terrorism, focussing on Canadian examples such as the FLQ crisis, the Air India disaster, and the years-long detainment of several men on security certificates, as ways of thinking about how we as a society ought to deal with threats to our security. The last chapter examines Canada's response to global warming. It asks how we as a middle-sized, wealthy nation ought to respond to a global threat that requires global cooperation for its solution, in the absence of that global cooperation.

Other Features

A Broader Range of Views

Most textbooks attempt to sample the range of philosophical issues on each topic. This has the advantage of giving students a sense of the breadth of philosophical inquiry. But it also has the disadvantage of making them think that each of the readings is *the* philosophical view on that issue, when of course philosophers have a range of views on every issue. In addition, most ethicists' and political philosophers' views are on the egalitarian (centre to left) end of the political spectrum, whereas our students' views span the whole spectrum. In my experience, students who do not see their views represented in the readings often shut down rather than examine their views.

In *Ethics for Canadians* I have aimed to present a range of views on a single topic or closely related topics. (I discuss the wider range of philosophical views on the topic in the introductions to each chapter.) This gives students a better view of the ways that different philosophers approach a topic and the range of solutions they present. In addition, the chapters include a wider range of political views than most philosophy textbooks do. While of course I prefer that everyone agree with me politically, as a philosopher and educator, I would rather that my students have intelligent, coherent views, whatever they are. They may learn that some of their views are incoherent, and in that case, they will have learned something important. But there are intelligent voices across the political and philosophical spectrum. Presenting them makes for better and deeper discussions, and allows students to learn how to defend their views intelligently.

Some of the chapters contain a somewhat narrower range of views. This is deliberate: there are not two sides to every issue. Most of the time there are several sides, but occasionally all the reasonable arguments are on one side. So in the chapter on climate change, for example, there are no readings that deny climate change is happening, because that is not a reasonable position. Bjørn Lomborg argues the danger of climate change has been exaggerated and there are global problems that are at least as pressing, but he acknowledges that climate change is real. In the chapter on animal rights, there are no readings that deny animals have any rights at all. No reasonable person believes it is permissible to torture cats, cows, or even rats. The question is not whether animals have rights but rather what rights they have. There are no arguments against multiculturalism because, again, they are not reasonable arguments. We can argue about what sort of policy we should have, but not whether there should be any multicultural accommodation. (And, in fact, the vast majority of Canadians agree. In 2003, eighty-five per cent of Canadians said multiculturalism was important to their identity, which is much stronger than mere approval of multiculturalism as a policy.[1]) Finally, there are only centrist and social democratic views in the chapter on English-speaking Canadians. This is not because conservative views are unreasonable, but rather because conservative Canadians do not tend to wax philosophical about the nature of Canadian citizenship or identity.

The chapters on Aboriginal rights and Quebec nationalism present a narrower range of views for different reasons. The average non-Aboriginal and non-Québécois Canadian is woefully ignorant—and worse, misinformed—about the history and philosophical issues regarding Aboriginal peoples and Quebec. (Mention Aboriginal issues in an average college or university class and the first thing that most non-Aboriginal students bring up is free tuition. They don't know, however, that an Aboriginal person is more likely to go to prison than to graduate from high school.[2] Nor would most of non-Aboriginal people be willing to trade places with an Aboriginal person. We have to combat misunderstanding, ignorance, and bad thinking before we can even begin discussing the issues.) I decided it was better to address misconceptions in the chapter introductions and present some of the best arguments in favour of Aboriginal rights and Quebec nationalism in the readings. Once students have more accurate information, they can make up their own minds about what they think on the topic.

Aids for Students

Philosophy may be the only discipline in which introductory textbooks consist of primary source material—articles and selections from books written by philosophers for their peers. My experience is that this material is too difficult for most first- and second-year undergraduates. Most of them understand the readings poorly, if at all. The majority glean what they can from lectures, tutorials, and the editor's introductions, and either ignore the readings or search them only for quotations in their essays. The primary sources, the bedrock of our discipline, might as well be written in runes.

Although I believe there are problems with assigning material we write for each other to students straight out of high school, doing so does afford important opportunities for learning that can benefit students in any program. Given sufficient aids and instruction, most students who are willing to work can learn to read and understand the complex arguments and language of philosophers. This will help them in whatever they do. Most white-collar jobs require the ability to read and understand complex material, and to write briefs or memos that aim to convince others to do something or take a particular position. Philosophy hones all of these skills. In addition, learning about issues in ethics, political philosophy, and applied ethics helps students develop well-reasoned views on important moral, social, and political issues, and prepares them to participate reflectively in Canadian society. And, we hope, it makes them want to take further philosophy courses.

So *Ethics for Canadians* brings the readings to students. I have used standard primary sources, but added numerous aids and supplementary material to help students understand and contextualize the readings. First, the introduction includes a section on reading and understanding philosophy. Some of the authors write very clearly, but others are more difficult to understand. This section teaches students to slow down, unpack difficult sentences and ideas, read and re-read, and string the ideas together to understand the author's argument. Second, most of the readings have been abridged. Introductory students really need to understand the main point of the readings. All the nitty-gritty details of an argument that interest professional philosophers and upper-year students usually only confuse first- and second-year students. The abridgements preserve each author's main points but leave the finer details for future courses. The readings in each chapter are also more or less the same length, which makes choosing which readings to include easier for instructors.

Most of the readings have been annotated. In many cases I (and my capable assistant, Max Degaust) broke papers into sections and subsections and added headings to aid students' understanding. This allows students to skim the article quickly to see the structure of the author's argument before they settle down to unpack it. We have also pointed out when authors are discussing their own views (AV for "author's view") and when they are discussing views they disagree with (~AV for "not the author's view"). Introductory students often have difficulty with the fact that philosophers carefully lay out views that are not their own, and then even more carefully explain why those views are mistaken. Frequently students think an objection the author addresses is really the author's own position. Marking the text allows students to focus on the author's actual arguments, rather than getting derailed at the outset by misunderstanding the author's point.

Each chapter ends with six or seven discussion questions. In addition, the companion website associated with this volume (www.oupcanada.com/Wendling) includes more questions aimed at different levels of understanding. Some questions are designed to aid students' understanding of the particular reading, others to prod them to analyze the reading critically and compare it with other readings, and yet others to encourage them to form their own opinions. These questions will help students understand and think philosophically about the material. They also may give instructors ideas for test or essay questions.

Each chapter ends with a list of suggested readings and websites, with short explanations of the author's argument or the website's position. These will point students and instructors to further useful information. Finally, the text includes an extensive glossary of philosophical terms plus the odd unusual or arcane word. Defined words are indicated in boldface, and the glossary gives context-sensitive definitions to aid students' understanding.

Notes

1. Will Kymlicka, "The Current State of Multiculturalism in Canada and Research Themes on Canadian Multiculturalism 2008–2010" (Ottawa: Minister of Public Works and Government Services Canada, 2010): 7–8.
2. Assembly of First Nations Chief Shawn Atleo, "There is an election on, isn't it time we talked?", CBC News, 13 April 2011, www.cbc.ca/news/canada/story/2011/04/13/cv-election-atleo-oped.html.

Acknowledgements

I have incurred many debts while working on this textbook. My extremely capable research assistants, Max Degaust and Hannah Peck, made my work a lot easier. Max abridged and annotated most of the readings in this book, and wrote many of the definitions in the Glossary. Hannah helped me choose many of the readings, abridged some of them, and co-translated "Two Ways to Politicize Identity" in Chapter 2, Quebec Nationalism. I could not have completed the book without their help.

Helen Prinold steered me towards excellent background material, suggested two of the authors in Part IV, and helped me work through blocks when I was writing. Heather Dean, Melissa Dean, Karyn Freedman, Maya Goldenberg, John Hacker-Wright, Jean Harvey, John Lundy, and Omid Payrow-Shabani commented on the prospectus or parts of the manuscript. Matthew Furlong, Jennica Grimshaw, Kelly Jones, Aaron Massecar, and Rachel Wallace provided additional research assistance. Monique Lanoix pointed me towards the rich Québécois feminist literature. Diane Lamoureux clarified some points in the translation of "Two Ways to Politicize Identity." Several anonymous reviewers provided excellent suggestions that made this a better book. I thank them all for their help. Any errors that remain are my responsibility.

My former chair, Andrew Bailey, put me in contact with Ryan Chynces, then acquisitions editor at Oxford University Press, who solicited the book and sent the prospectus out for review. Stephen Kotowych took over from there and ably shepherded the book to completion. Mary Wat, Mark Thompson, and Tamara Capar, developmental editors extraordinaire, provided just the right balance of encouragement and firmness. Serene Ong ably copyedited the manuscript.

My greatest debt is to my partner, Louise Stuart, who brainstormed with me, read and commented on most of the manuscript, encouraged me throughout the writing and editing process, and who reminds me that there is life outside academia. It is a much better life because she is in it.

Karen Wendling
December 2014

A Short Primer on Ethics, Political Philosophy, and the Canadian Legal System

This textbook is designed to help you figure out what it means to you to be Canadian. You will do this by examining various topics about who Canadians are (Part I, Who Are We?), who we ought to include in our moral and political decision-making (Part II, Who Are "We"?), what we think governments should and should not do (Part III, What Do We Owe Each Other?), and what we think our global responsibilities are (Part IV, Living in a Global World). By no means does it cover every aspect of what it means to be Canadian, but it is a start. You will learn that your views on one topic, such as animal rights, are connected to your views on another seemingly unconnected topic, like assisted suicide—at least, they should be if they are consistent. My goal is to help you develop good reasons for your views, whatever they are. Many—probably most—times this will involve learning good or better arguments in favour of them. This will deepen your views and strengthen your underlying moral and political convictions. Sometimes it will involve modifying or even changing your views. The arguments may make you realize that your previous views had unwanted consequences that you do not like or contradicted deeper convictions that you hold. Whether your views remain the same or change, you will learn some important things about yourself and about morality and democracy:

- reasonable moral and political views must be supported by good reasons;
- you must be able to explain your views to others who do not agree with you;
- you must seriously consider others' objections to your views;
- responding adequately to others' objections deepens your view or, if you cannot respond adequately, indicates that you ought to change your mind;
- reasonable people disagree, in good faith and with good reasons, about many important and contentious issues; and
- it is possible to disagree with others yet still respect and get along with them.

Democracies function best when citizens are well informed and actively engaged in their societies. I hope you will use what you learn to become a better citizen.

Ethics, Political and Legal Philosophy, and Applied Ethics

This book covers topics in **applied ethics**, which is the philosophical study of real-world moral and/or political issues like multiculturalism, assisted suicide, and animal **rights**. However, it cannot be understood well without a grounding in ethics, which provides the foundations of ethical principles and concepts, and political and legal philosophy,[1] which provide mid-level grounding. (Note: I use "ethics" and "morality," and "ethical" and "moral," interchangeably.)

We can compare the levels of generality and specificity in ethics, political and legal philosophy, and applied ethics, to those in a world map, a map of Canada, and a map of a city. The world map gives us the big-picture view. It does not show anything in much detail, but we see things in relation to the whole world. A map of Canada zooms in to show more detail—we see provinces and territories, major cities, and so on. A map of a city shows details at an even higher level of resolution. Here we see relatively fine-grained details, like streets, highways, and parks.

Ethics is analogous to the world map: it involves the broadest and most general analysis. Philosophers call such big-picture views "foundational." At this level we discuss the meaning and nature of value, whether one sort of value (such as the good) grounds another (such as virtue), and to whom value applies. Political and legal philosophies are analogous to the map of Canada: they are still quite broad and general, but less so than ethics. At this level we discuss the justification of government and law, whether one form of government or law is preferable to another, and to whom their benefits and responsibilities apply. While sometimes ethicists and political and legal philosophers discuss particular values, governments, or laws to show how their principles apply to real-world cases, the focus is on principles and not particulars.

Applied ethics is analogous to the city map: it involves the most fine-grained level of ethical analysis. Like these maps, it is still general—all philosophy is conceptual, including applied philosophy—but it is more focused on particular details than ethics or political and legal philosophy. Applied ethicists combine abstract ethical, political and legal principles with context-specific ones, such as the principles embodied in codes of ethics and concepts like "personhood" or "the environment." They then use these abstract and context-specific principles to examine ethical and political issues like abortion and Quebec nationalism, and policies like multiculturalism and health care.

Applied ethicists assume their readers have at least a basic understanding of foundational (ethics) and mid-level (political and legal) principles, so this is where we will begin.

Normative Ethics

Philosophers divide ethics into three branches. **Metaethics** examines the presuppositions and beliefs of ethical thought and practice, such as what the moral terms "good" or "right" mean, and whether moral judgments are objective or relative. **Normative ethics** examines the moral rules or principles we use to guide our conduct (e.g., "do what creates the most good" or "respect rights"), develop our character (e.g. by practising virtues of honesty and integrity), and maintain our relationships (e.g. by caring knowledgeably and appropriately). Applied ethics applies moral, political, and legal principles to real-world issues like abortion or war.

There are three main theories in normative ethics:

1. **consequentialism**, which focuses on consequences;
2. **deontology**, which focuses on duties or principles; and
3. **virtue ethics**, which focuses on motives and character.

We will also examine a relatively new form of normative ethics, **care ethics**, which focuses on the norms and standards of caring relationships, such as those between friends or between parents and children.

Consequentialism: Good Acts

Consequentialists say that what matters, morally, are consequences; we should do whatever creates the best overall consequences. For example, in Canada all motor vehicle drivers and passengers must wear seatbelts. Seatbelt laws are justified because they save thousands of lives a year (a good consequence) at the cost of minor inconveniences to drivers and passengers and very small increases in the price of cars (bad consequences).[2]

What makes consequences "good" or "bad"? We will discuss only the most famous form of consequentialism, **utilitarianism**. Contemporary utilitarians define something as "good" if it improves **welfare** (literally, how *well* individuals *fare*, that is, do), and "bad" if it reduces welfare. Most utilitarians consider welfare to be a measure of how well individuals' preferences are satisfied, as reported by the individuals themselves. Utilitarians say that, subject to a few conditions—such as that individuals' preferences must not be caused by coercion, serious pain, or brainwashing—satisfying individuals' preferences is good and frustrating them is bad. (What about preferences for things that harm others, such as theft or assault? Utilitarians say these preferences almost always will be outweighed by others' preferences that they not be harmed.)

Utilitarianism is a **maximizing** theory: it says we should do whatever creates the most overall—the maximum—welfare; that is, we should aim to create "the greatest good for the greatest number." This principle has two parts: "the greatest good," which we should maximize, and "the greatest number." The second part tells us that the benefits and burdens of our actions should fall on people relatively equally. Suppose an institution is choosing between two programs. Program A provides a smaller amount of service to 5000 people a year. Program B provides a greater amount of service to 1000 people a year, but each person served benefits roughly five times as much as those in Program A. Both provide the same total amount of welfare. Assuming equal costs, utilitarians would favour Program A, because it creates the same amount of good for a greater number of people.

Given a sufficiently detailed list of criteria, utilitarians say we can, in principle, assign values to utilities and rank consequences. Economists use money as a measure of utility. That may be fine for the market but not for morality; it is not possible to put a price on some important things like love, health, or freedom. So while exact measures of utility are almost never possible in philosophy, we can still use the idea of utility ranking to discuss the relative merits of different actions or policies and to decide between them.

Utilitarianism applies to all levels of moral and political decision-making, from individual decisions to the decisions of friends, strangers, citizens, governments, and even the international community. It is an **impartial** theory—individuals may not give more weight to their own, their friends' and their family members' interests than to the interests of strangers. Because it treats everyone's interests equally, it is also an **egalitarian** theory.

Objections to Utilitarianism

Some critics claim utilitarianism requires people to sacrifice their interests for the greater good, which ignores the fundamental importance of individuals. Utilitarians respond that sometimes we voluntarily put aside our interests for the greater good: we do so in disasters, and friends and family members often make sacrifices for each other. A related criticism is that utilitarianism is too demanding: for example, the requirement to always maximize the good appears to forbid leisure because we could be doing something else that would create more good, like working for a charity. Some utilitarians accept this conclusion and claim that we ought to do a lot more to make the world a better place. Other utilitarians distinguish what we *should* do from what we *must* do, and say that we must do something only if (a) doing it will maximize utility, and (b) not doing it is so bad that we should punish people who fail to do it. Since punishing people reduces utility, probably more than relaxing rather than doing good work does, some leisure is permitted, utilitarians say—though we still ought to do much more to improve the world.

Other critics accuse utilitarianism of injustice: it permits a majority to impose extreme burdens on a minority if the overall utility is greater than a more equal distribution. For example, it could justify enslaving ten per cent of the population if the increased welfare of the free ninety per cent were great enough to outweigh the misery of the enslaved minority, or it could justify killing healthy people and distributing their organs to several others who will die without transplants. Utilitarians respond to this criticism by arguing that these examples count short term and not long term benefits; in the long run, it is not clear that enslaving a minority or killing healthy people to harvest their organs is beneficial. (In the latter case, in fact, it is clear that it is not—people would avoid doctors and hospitals, and no one would agree to be an organ donor.)

Some philosophers criticize utilitarianism's impartiality; they claim that sometimes we ought to weigh the interests of friends or family members more heavily than we do strangers' interests. Utilitarians respond that giving more weight to our own, our friends' or our families' interests implies that some people are worth more than others, an idea which they deny. They say moral partiality leads to hypocrisy (for instance, believing that our interests matter more to us than others' interests do to them) and corruption (such as politicians giving contracts to their friends rather than to the best or lowest bidder). Both hypocrisy and corruption involve treating people unequally when they should be treated equally. According to utilitarians, impartiality is necessary for moral equality.

Deontology: Good Principles

According to deontologists (from the Greek *deon*, meaning necessity), actions are required, permitted, or prohibited by moral principles (such as "do not harm others" and "tell the truth") that apply regardless of consequences. Of course deontologists may allow some exceptions, such as telling a lie if the truth would hurt innocent people, but there are few such exceptions. Moral principles are analogous to laws. (In fact, most criminal laws are based on morality.) The law against murder, for example, forbids almost all killing, but it does allow a few carefully circumscribed exceptions, such as killing in self-defence or causing death in an accident that was not your fault. Similarly, moral principles apply in almost all cases, with very few exceptions.

The deontological ethics you are most likely to be familiar with are the Golden Rule ("Do unto others . . .") and religious ethics. But religion is not the only source of deontological principles. All societies need moral rules to function—not only rules against murder, assault and theft, but also rules about telling the truth, keeping promises, being fair to others, and so on. Since members of society hold differing religious or other beliefs, deontologists (and ethicists in general) give justifications that can be accepted by anyone. Most contemporary forms of deontological ethics are **secular** (non-religious).

While most people agree that some moral principles are necessary, there is less agreement about which principles are necessary and what justifies them. The philosopher Immanuel Kant focused on duties (actions required or forbidden by morality). He said all duties have a similar form: they apply in every case without exception, and they can be **universalized** (that is, they apply to everyone, always and everywhere). He called the general form of duties the **categorical imperative** (categorical = "without exceptions," imperative = "command"), which states that an action is permitted only if we can make a general rule from our conduct that would always apply to everyone in similar circumstances. The categorical imperative is a philosophical version of the question, "What if everyone did that?" Suppose you are tempted to lie because it would be inconvenient if another person knew the truth. Ask yourself, "What if everyone lied when it was convenient?" You can see that truth would lose all meaning, and no one would be able to trust anyone. Next ask yourself, "What if everyone told the truth, even when it was inconvenient?" You can easily see that this rule can be universalized. Thus lying is wrong, and we ought to tell the truth. All duties can be determined in the same way, Kantians say, by asking whether everyone should do the same thing under the same circumstances.

Other deontologists focus on **rights** rather than duties. A right is a valid, enforceable claim, either against everyone (your right not to be assaulted) or against a specific person (your right to have others keep their promises to you). **Natural rights** theorists claim rights are **natural** (they exist regardless of whether they are recognized politically or legally) and **universal** (they apply to all people in all times and places). **Human rights** theories are a version of natural rights theories that ground rights in the inherent dignity or worth of humans. Natural rights theories have the advantage that they apply universally, but the disadvantage that the claim that rights are natural is difficult to justify. Natural rights theorists generally say that the natural faculty of reason justifies rights. However, different theorists disagree about which rights exist, which suggests that reason alone cannot justify natural rights.

Positive rights theorists deny that rights are natural; they say the only rights we have are those that our society recognizes and upholds. We may argue that our society *ought* to recognize and protect a right, they say, but we cannot say that the right exists or appeal to it for justification if our society refuses to recognize it. Positive rights theories have the advantage that their foundations are clear—rights are social creations—but the disadvantage that rights are not universal. (We usually think moral theories apply universally, but positive rights do not exist in every society.)

Like consequentialism, deontology is impartial, that is, moral principles apply equally to everyone. We may not give special consideration to the claims of ourselves or our friends and family members. If it is wrong to lie, it wrong for everyone; if others must keep their promises to you, then you must keep your promises to others. To claim otherwise is hypocrisy.

Objections to Deontology

Some critics contend that deontology is either dogmatic or empty: either it requires following principles even when the consequences are disastrous, or its principles have so many exceptions that they lose their moral force. Deontologists reply that principles can be drawn carefully to allow only a few carefully circumscribed exceptions, thus avoiding the worst consequences while still retaining the principles' moral content. For example, while most of the time we should tell the truth, in a very few cases, telling a lie is permitted (if not required) if it upholds a more important principle. For instance, lying would be permitted to prevent someone from being murdered, because the moral requirement to tell the truth is outweighed by the requirement to prevent wrongful killing. Determining which exceptions should be allowed and why occupies many deontologists.

Other critics say that deontological principles either are too general to guide action (how does the categorical imperative apply to assisted suicide?), or they multiply like rabbits (people claim rights to things that cannot be enforced, such as rights to happiness or to bear children). Deontologists respond that fully fleshing out the moral principles gives them sufficient content both to be action-guiding and to distinguish between central, peripheral, and frivolous principles.

Others accuse deontology of providing little guidance when its principles conflict. Suppose, for example, you are deciding whether to tell a friend a painful truth. The principle "tell the truth" counsels honesty, while the principle "be kind to others" counsels the opposite in this case. Deontologists reply that moral principles are rules, not invariant laws; they must be applied as judges apply the law, balancing respect for the rules with sensitivity to the particulars of situations and people.

Some philosophers criticize deontology's impartiality. We owe some things to our friends because they are who they are, the critics say, not because of abstract rules of friendship. Deontologists, like consequentialists, argue that partiality implies that some people are more important than others, which is a form of moral corruption.

Virtue Ethics: Good Character

Contemporary virtue ethicists say consequentialists and deontologists focus too much on acts and not enough on character. They say an act is only truly ethical if it is done with the proper moral attitude. Even if an act's consequences are good or it follows a sound moral principle, it is not *ethical* without the appropriate attitude. Take people who behave decently to members of other races in public but make fun of them in private. Of course it is better that they behave well to others' faces than that they behave rudely, but we would not say that such people deserve praise—in fact, we would say they deserve blame for both their disrespect and racism. They may not harm or violate the rights of members of other races, but their behaviour shows that they do not respect them as equals. Contrast this with people who treat everyone well, both publicly and privately, because they have the virtue of respect for others. These people deserve praise and, according to virtue ethicists, only their behaviour is truly ethical.

Virtues are character traits that are necessary for humans to live together and flourish. They are multifaceted; they include not only beliefs ("respect others") but also values (assuming the best about others unless there are good reasons not to) and emotions (feeling pleasure when others show respect and displeasure when they do not). Virtues also involve choices (preferring to associate with other respectful people, and encouraging others to be respectful too), attitudes (listening and learning before acting or judging), interests (disliking entertainment that expresses disdain or disrespect for others), and so on. They are stable: virtuous people behave well consistently, over time and in a variety of situations. People can be more or less virtuous: they may possess some virtues but not others, they may lack the courage of their convictions, or they may have insufficient control over some of their vices. Virtuous people are likely to behave ethically, even in unfamiliar situations or under duress. They do not necessarily behave well in every situation, but rather in most of them, particularly the most important ones. They make relatively few mistakes, and the ones they do make are generally minor. Virtue ethics is not only for moral saints.

Moral virtues are not purely intellectual; they cannot be learned as academic subjects are. However, this is not to say that virtues do not require thought. Philosophers call this sort of moral thought **practical wisdom**. A person who has developed practical wisdom understands the virtues and knows how to apply them properly. Practical wisdom must be practised extensively before people are good at it. In this respect, learning to be virtuous is more like learning to play hockey, make violins, or perform surgery than it is like learning mathematics or geography. Becoming a hockey player, a violin maker, or a surgeon requires not just (or even primarily) intellectual knowledge. Hockey players, violin makers, and surgeons must practise day in and day out to become even proficient, much less good, at what they do. You probably would not pay to see a hockey player's first game, nor would you buy a violin maker's first violin—and you almost certainly would not want to be a heart surgeon's first patient. Similarly, people must practise the virtues for a long time to become virtuous. Contrast this with both utilitarianism and deontology. In those theories, anyone who knows the rules ("maximize utility" or "respect duties or rights") and applies them properly behaves ethically, whether or not that person understands how the rules fit together or is able to apply them consistently and with sensitivity to particular contexts. It's a bit like people who are good at solving problems in mathematics or science without understanding the background concepts—they might get good grades, but we would not say they really comprehend the material. Similarly, virtue ethicists say, it is possible for utilitarians and deontologists to do well or right without being ethical people—and that is an incomplete view of morality.

Objections to Virtue Ethics

The most common objection to virtue ethics is that it is not action-guiding—it focuses on moral character and does not tell us what to do in moral situations. Virtue ethicists respond by arguing that virtue ethics *does* tell people what to do: people should do whatever would be honest, generous, fair, kind, and whatever else is required in a particular situation. In addition, they point out that utilitarianism and deontology generally do not provide clearer answers in moral situations—weighing utilities and balancing principles are hardly exact sciences.

A second objection, related to the first, is that virtue ethics cannot tell us what to do when virtues conflict. A virtue ethicist could face the same dilemma as the deontologist above, about whether to tell a painful truth to a friend; here the virtues of honesty and kindness appear to conflict. Once again, virtue ethicists have two responses: first, that someone with practical wisdom has learned how to balance the virtues in this and other situations, and second, that deontology and utilitarianism give no clearer answers.

Some critics say the concept of virtue is vague and unspecified; they argue that what we call virtues are only the traits we approve of in this time and place, not enduring moral traits. Virtue ethicists acknowledge that specific traits are given different names or are classified in different ways in different cultures, but they say all virtues are similar at their core: they are character traits that are necessary for humans to flourish. Virtues make it possible for us to live well together.

Other critics claim that virtue ethics is a theory for **egoists** (self-centred people, concerned only with their own interests), because it focuses on individuals' character traits and not on other people. Virtue ethicists reply that virtues are clearly social and not self-centred—we can only be generous, honest, benevolent, or fair *to* and *with* others.

Care Ethics: Good Relationships

Utilitarianism, deontology and virtue ethics all focus on the individual. Utilitarians and deontologists examine the morality of individual action, while virtue ethics examines individual moral character. In contrast, care ethicists focus on caring relationships. Care ethicists say that, by focusing on individuals, mainstream ethics (utilitarianism, deontology, and virtue ethics) miss the fundamentally relational nature of morality. There are no ethical issues without other people (and possibly animals, but let's put them aside for now), and most ethical issues arise within relationships. Thus ethics should focus on relationships, not individual actions or character. Care ethicists examine the normative requirements of caring relationships such as friendships and relationships within families, provide theoretical grounding for them, and propose changes or alternatives to problematic relationships.

Utilitarianism and deontology require that ethical decisions be impartial. Care ethicists say this eliminates the possibility that caring relationships have any special ethical significance, and thus these theories handle ethical issues in caring relationships poorly, if at all. For example: a man runs into a burning house containing his daughter and her friend. He can save only one of them. Who should he save? For mainstream ethicists, it's a toss-up. His daughter's life is no more valuable than her friend's; presumably the friend too has parents who love her. But we all *know* he should save his daughter; in fact, we would criticize him severely if he did not. Care ethicists say that the man's relationship with his daughter gives her priority in this situation. They claim that either mainstream ethicists cannot explain why the daughter has priority, or their explanations are forced and convoluted.

We do not want family members, friends, caregivers, or lawyers to behave impartially towards us, care ethicists say; we want and need them to care about us as individuals and to promote our interests. Nor are we always equal, independent, or adult, as mainstream ethical theories assume. Humans are born completely dependent; none of us would have survived infancy if one or more adults had not cared for us for a long time. Even as adults, people move in and out of relationships of inequality and dependence—they are patients, clients of professionals with specialized knowledge, students, and so on. They often encounter ethical issues in these relationships. Yet until recently, mainstream ethicists routinely dismissed the ethics of caring relationships as "natural morality," based on instinct and not reason.

Care ethics begins with relationships that are caring and not necessarily voluntary, involving people who may not be equals. This requires significant shifts in ethical perspectives: from individuals to relationships, impartiality to partiality, voluntariness to involuntariness, and equality to inequality. This is uncharted ethical territory, and we must ask new ethical questions. What are the features of good caring relationships? What are their social requirements? ("It takes a village to raise a child," an African proverb says.) What are the standards of good care? How should we balance care receivers' and caregivers' interests? Which emotions, intentions, attitudes, values, perspectives, and so on do different caring relationships require?

Most caring relationships contain both formal and informal rules for caregivers, and sometimes also for care receivers. Parents have legal duties to their children, plus extensive socially enforced obligations, such as that they love their children and treat them equally. Professional caregivers also have legal as well as socially enforced obligations, such as that they care about those they care for. We evaluate caring relationships by more stringent criteria than we use for interactions between strangers; for example, someone who does no more than what the rules require may be a good enough citizen but is not a good enough caregiver.

Good caring relationships require emotional connections between caregivers and care receivers. Good caregivers understand and pay attention to care receivers' needs and desires, know how and when—and when not—to fulfil them, put care receivers' needs above their own most of the time, and view care receivers as valuable individuals, not burdens. When possible and appropriate, caregivers help care receivers become independent. They also must be fair to others under their care, which may require weighing and balancing competing interests. Good caring relationships are hardly "natural"; producing and maintaining relationships requires caregivers, and often care receivers, to develop a great deal of specialized moral perception and intelligence.

Objections to Care Ethics

Some critics claim that care ethics is not action-guiding, and that it cannot handle conflicts between care and justice. Care ethicists reply out that they do have rules. Suppose a patient tells her therapist that she has committed a crime. The therapist–client relationship is privileged, meaning that therapists must keep what clients say confidential; the caring relationship trumps justice in this case. (Most professions have codes of ethics that specify conduct, and there is also a great deal of case law concerning professional–client relationships.) In many cases, care ethics handles these cases better than mainstream ethics, care ethicists say.

Other critics say the scope of care ethics is too narrow. We do not have caring relationships with the vast majority of people, including most of our fellow citizens, people in other countries, and future generations. Care ethicists deny that caring relationships require face-to-face contact. Care ethics *begins* with face-to-face caring relationships, but it does not end with them. People do care about fellow citizens, fellow humans, non-humans, and future generations, even without personal contact. Care ethics handles these more abstract relationships at least as well as mainstream theories handle caring relationships, its proponents say.

Finally, critics charge that the emotions involved in caring relationships bias moral reasoning; impartiality is necessary to maintain fairness and avoid corruption. Care ethicists reply that sometimes impartiality is neither desirable nor possible in caring relationships, but we still need ethical guidance. For example, fairness in caring relationships requires at least some partiality. Good parents know that sometimes fairness requires identical treatment (the same rules apply to all their children), but other times it requires making distinctions based on the children's interests, abilities, and needs (one gets music lessons while another plays hockey). Good parents cannot be completely impartial even among their own children, much less among people in general. While care ethicists acknowledge that caring sometimes leads to unfairness and moral corruption, they say impartiality may ignore established relationships, which is a different form of unfairness and moral corruption.

Which Theory Should You Choose?

Many ethicists employ a single theory—utilitarianism, deontology, virtue ethics, or care ethics—in their writings. This approach has theoretical clarity on its side; we decide all moral issues according to a single standard. Proponents of this approach say using only one theory makes us more likely to be consistent in our moral judgments, which is important in ethics. Other ethicists take a **pluralist** approach, combining parts of some or all of the theories. This approach is theoretically much messier, but in fact its proponents consider this an advantage. Real life is messy, they say; no single theory captures all moral issues well. Each has its advantages and can address certain kinds of moral issues better than the others, so we ought to include them all in our moral deliberations. You will decide for yourself which approach you prefer.

Political Philosophy: Liberalism

Ethics is the foundation of the principles used by applied ethicists. Concepts and principles from political philosophy also feature prominently in applied ethicists' writings, and we turn to them now.

Political philosophy examines the nature and justification of the **state** (government or political society) and **institutions** within the state, such as the market, education, and immigration and citizenship. (In this chapter, I use "the state" and "government" interchangeably.) In Canada all mainstream political views are variants of **liberalism**, a political philosophy that advocates rights, freedom, equality, and democracy. (Note: Someone who espouses liberalism is a *liberal*, and that person holds *liberal* views. "Liberalist" is incorrect.) Liberalism focuses on (1) individuals who are (2) free and (3) equal, each of whom has (4) the capacity for self-determination, and (5) a unique set of interests.

(1) Liberalism focuses on individuals, as opposed to classes, social statuses, families, ethnic groups, and so on. To liberals, it is not enough to say that a particular social arrangement is best for the family, the group, or even the nation; if it is not best for individuals then it is not justified. Liberals justify the state and society in terms of individuals.

(2) Free individuals exercise choice and **agency**. Liberals say people's choices are not entirely determined, whether by divine law, evolution, or socialization; there is a significant sphere within which individuals exercise free will. Society ought to be arranged to support and enhance their free choices. Freedom of thought and action are the central freedoms for liberal individuals, limited only by the similar freedoms of others—or to put it in plainer language, liberals say people may do whatever they want, as long as they don't harm others.

(3) There are no natural political statuses among equal individuals. Many political philosophers, from Plato and Aristotle to the present day, have claimed that natural characteristics such as class, sex, race, or intelligence make some people unequal to others. Liberal political philosophers say only two natural characteristics are relevant to political equality: the **age of majority** (the age at which a person legally becomes an adult) and **mental competence** (roughly, the capacity to reason, deliberate, and choose). Every mentally competent adult is equal to all others.

(4) Free and equal individuals possess the capacity for self-determination—the ability to run their own lives. This capacity makes them able to make voluntary and reasoned choices to cooperate with others. That is, they have sufficient mental capacities and self-control to participate in choosing the kind of society they want to live in, and they can reflect on their choices, make decisions, and change their minds, given sufficient reasons.

(5) Liberals say every individual has a unique set of interests. Liberals interpret interests subjectively, that is, from the perspective of each individual. By hypothesis, no two individuals have identical sets of interests. Of course people share many or even most interests—everyone has an interest in a stable and safe society, food and shelter, love and friendship, a clean environment, and good health. Liberals assume individuals have other interests that everyone does not share, though—in their particular families, religious and political beliefs, careers, pastimes, and so on. Moreover, liberals assume that people seek to further their own interests. Thus a liberal society should be arranged so individuals can pursue their interests, whatever they are, as long as this does not harm others.

Because individuals possess and pursue their unique interests, liberal societies are characterized by **pluralism**, by citizens and groups with diverse interests, identifications, and worldviews regarding themselves and others. These interests vary widely and sometimes conflict with others' interests. Liberals consider pluralism an **asset**, not a drawback. The nineteenth-century liberal philosopher John Stuart Mill said diversity is the lifeblood of societies, without which they stagnate.

Liberals say people with such diverse interests, identifications, and worldviews will choose to live in **democratic** societies that guarantee them liberty and equality, and that enshrine some of these guarantees in rights. Some philosophers distinguish between **liberty rights**, on the one hand, and **equality rights**, on the other. Liberty rights are rights to basic freedoms necessary for self-determination, such as freedom of thought and action, and safety from arbitrary detention or torture. Equality rights are rights to social goods that improve citizens' welfare, such as education, old age pensions, or health care; thus they are sometimes called **welfare rights**.

Some philosophers say liberty rights require only that citizens be left alone to pursue their interests, without interference from the state or other individuals; they call these **negative rights**, because upholding them requires nothing from others except that they leave individuals alone. Equality rights, on the other hand, require the state and citizens to actively promote individuals' welfare; they call these **positive rights**, because upholding them requires that others do specific things for individuals. However, this distinction is not as sharp as it may initially appear. For example, the right to freedom of expression—a negative right—requires:

- laws and court cases that spell out the few cases where expression may be limited (e.g., no one may lie under oath or yell "Fire!" in a crowded theatre);
- access to legal representation if the right has been infringed;
- courts to decide whether someone's right has or has not been violated;
- courts that operate with adequate speed;
- legislators, police, and court officers trained to uphold citizens' rights, and paid well enough to avoid corruption;
- a free press that publicizes wrongs;
- citizens who care about others' rights; and so on.

Liberty rights are empty without at least a mostly fair state, a free press, and active citizens who care about others' rights. If no one else knows and/or cares about rights violations, then liberty rights are meaningless. They require much more than simply being left alone.

Varieties of Liberalism

Liberalism has two core principles: freedom and equality. Liberal views range from those that always prioritize liberty over any other value, except for merely **formal equality** (libertarianism), to those that give roughly equal weight to liberty and equality (social democracy). Views that prioritize equality over liberty are not liberal views.

Libertarianism (conservative) and social democracy (egalitarian) are the two ends of the liberal spectrum in Canada. Does that make them "extreme" views? No. Both fit squarely within the liberal tradition, and liberalism has not been an extreme philosophy for centuries. You might consider one or both views wrong, but that does not make them extreme. Nor can we say that centrism combines the best of conservatism and egalitarianism. It might, but it might equally adopt the worst of one or both views, or it might simply be cobbled together in an unprincipled way. You will decide which you prefer.

There are three main forms of liberalism in Canada, which I will call conservative, centrist, and egalitarian.[3] They differ primarily in the weights they give to freedom and equality, and how—and how much—they think governments should promote citizens' welfare. Another difference is their relative pessimism or optimism about human nature. I will discuss conservatives and egalitarians first, because they have theoretically distinct positions. Centrist views blend conservative and egalitarian perspectives.

A note on terminology: "conservative," "egalitarian," and "centrist" have different meanings at different times and in different places. Conservative centrists were considered simply conservative thirty years ago, and would have been considered egalitarian in nineteenth-century Canada, as well as in the US today. Social democrats—egalitarians—would be considered centrist or even conservative in contemporary Sweden. The distinctions sketched below describe conservatives, egalitarians, and centrists in contemporary Canadian terms.

Conservative Liberalism

Conservative liberals focus on private property and freedom. They define freedom as freedom from interference; people are most free when they can do as they wish (as long as they do not harm others), without interference from others. In general, conservatives consider economic freedom the most important freedom. They believe the state's primary or only purpose is to protect private property and ensure the free market runs smoothly. Taxation is justified to protect property and maintain the free market; this includes police and military protection, a fair system of courts, and democratic government. Beyond this, most conservatives believe people ought to be left alone to manage their own affairs. In general, conservatives believe governments should regulate as little as possible because regulations limit freedom, and the free market does most things better than government.

Conservatives believe in **formal equality**, according to which the same rules apply to everyone. They consider the distribution of income and social benefits irrelevant, as long as fair rules are applied even-handedly to all. They believe citizens must be equal before and under the law, and that there should be **formal equality of opportunity**—places in society should be assigned according to merit in fair competitions open to everyone. They oppose government promotion of equality through **employment equity** or social programs to lessen existing inequalities, because such policies and programs interfere with individual freedom and the free market.

In principle, conservatives oppose using the government to uphold equality rights, as this poses unjust limitations on individuals' liberty. In practice, however, almost all conservatives in Canada support a number of equality rights: at a minimum, most support progressive taxation (taxing wealthier people at higher rates than poorer people) and rights to public education, health care, disability, old age pensions, and employment insurance. (Welfare for able-bodied recipients is a contentious issue.) Opposing any of these equality rights, particularly health care, is political suicide in Canada. But conservative liberals do not think governments should extend equality rights beyond those we already have.

Conservatives tend to be pessimists about human nature; they think most or at least too many people will violate others' rights if they can, and therefore we need the state to protect us and our property. But they also think we need to protect ourselves against the state, because governments limit liberty. Some conservatives think governments are necessary evils—necessary because they provide services we would be unable to maintain on our own (police, courts, roads, etc.), but evil because they limit our freedoms.

Varieties of Conservative Liberalism

Conservative liberalism has the most positions because liberalism is more than two hundred years old, and yesterday's progressives become today's conservatives. They have had the longest time to develop their views and distinguish themselves from each other.

Libertarians believe the state's sole justification is protecting private property and individual freedom. They believe government should ensure fair procedures (the free market, fair civil and criminal courts, and police and military protection) and treat all citizens equally. Any more unjustly limits liberty; the state has no right to tell individuals or businesses how to conduct their affairs unless they harm others. Libertarians oppose all equality rights as limitations on individuals' freedom. For example, they oppose public pensions, public education, and publicly funded health care on the grounds that no one should be required to support anyone except their own children. People may choose to give to charities that support the elderly, schools, health care, or classical music, but this should not be mandatory. Libertarians also oppose federal and provincial human rights codes, which forbid discrimination in services, housing, and employment, as unjust restrictions on freedom. The state has no more business regulating business than it does free speech. Very few Canadians are libertarians, but libertarianism is popular in the US and among a few Canadian philosophers.

Neo-conservatives support a greater role for the state than libertarians do, but they too believe that government should do much less than it currently does. They believe the government's main function is to support and promote private enterprise. Neo-conservatives may endorse limited social programs such as public schools and health care, but they believe social programs can be provided more cheaply and efficiently by the free market than by government. They favour laws and programs that support businesses, and they oppose restrictions on corporations' abilities to earn money, including environmental protection laws, minimum wage laws, and programs that promote equality. They believe taxes should be cut dramatically to eliminate waste; they believe most social programs such as pensions or health care, and government-owned corporations such as the CBC, should be privatized or scrapped. Governments should support individual freedoms, the market, and no more.

Social conservatives believe the state should promote religious values and the traditional family. The state should not interfere with religion or the family, as it did when it legalized same-sex marriage. Government also should not promote social equality, particularly of women or gays and lesbians, because this undermines the traditional family. However, social conservatives' views may conflict with liberal principles of freedom and equality. For example, some social conservatives have opposed making divorce easier to obtain because they say divorce erodes the traditional family. But stricter divorce laws limit people's liberty, especially when both parties want the divorce. Thus, a social conservative who consistently favours traditional values over liberty or equality is not a liberal. While there are social conservatives in the Conservative and Liberal parties in Canada, both parties have explicitly liberal platforms that, in cases of conflict, support liberty and formal equality over traditional values.

Egalitarian Liberalism

Egalitarians differ from conservatives in four main ways. First, egalitarians define freedom substantively, in terms of the ranges of meaningful choices available to individuals. Second, they believe liberalism should give equal weight to liberty and equality, which they also define substantively. Third, egalitarians think that, in addition to protecting citizens' rights and freedoms, the state must promote their well-being. And fourth, they are optimists about human nature.

Egalitarians say freedom is not just freedom from interference; it is a positive value, similar to substantive rather than formal equality. Societies in which most people have equal abilities to exercise their freedoms are better than societies in which some people have effective access to much more freedom than others. Freedom means everyone can choose among a range of actions and social roles that they and their society consider meaningful. Like all liberals, egalitarians believe people should have as much freedom as possible, given similar freedoms for others. In societies with large differences in status and income, however, high-status and rich people are freer than low-status or poor people because they can do much more and take on more roles. Greater equality is necessary for substantive liberty, egalitarians say.

But freedom without equality is exploitation—of the weak by the strong, the poor by the rich, minorities by majorities, and so on. And equality without freedom is totalitarianism (think North Korea). Liberty and equality must be kept in balance, or neither is meaningful.

Egalitarians believe equality involves more than simply applying the same rules to everyone. They support **substantive equality**, which involves eliminating undeserved barriers to equality and creating a level playing field. How well people do in life is significantly influenced by things like their sex, race, and parents' education and income, and where they were born,[4] they say, yet none of those things could be chosen or deserved. Such inequalities are particularly unfair because people are denied access to desirable social positions based on factors they cannot control and/or that are irrelevant to the positions. Hence egalitarians support laws and social programs that promote greater equality. Government must ensure that substantively equal opportunities exist and that all citizens have genuinely equal access to social goods and benefits. (The Supreme Court has used a substantive view of equality in cases involving section 15 of the *Charter*, the equality section.) Some egalitarians think social programs promoting equality should be expanded, for example by including prescription medicines in provincial health care plans, or eliminating college and university tuition. Other egalitarians think governments should be more involved in the market, such as by promoting employment equity or regulating the prices of necessities like rent, hydro, and food, so everyone can afford them.

Egalitarians believe balancing liberty and equality requires governments to play a significant role in society. They support state intervention to lessen economic inequalities, including **progressive taxation** and social programs like education and health care. Many support creating new social programs, such as universal daycare and including prescriptions in provincial health care plans. Egalitarians think government's role extends beyond the economic sphere; it also should promote what the twentieth-century philosopher John Rawls called "the social basis of self-respect"—a society in which all citizens view themselves and others as equals in worth and dignity. Equality rights are necessary for well-being and self-respect, and they demonstrate citizens' respect for each other.

Egalitarians believe no one in a wealthy country like Canada should lack necessities like food, education, and health care; the state should ensure everyone has realistic opportunities to attain necessities, through employment at a living wage, reduced or free tuition, or subsidies.

Egalitarians tend to be optimists about human nature, government, and society. Think of Jack Layton's letter to Canadians: "My friends, love is better than anger. Hope is better than fear. Optimism is better than despair. So let us be loving, hopeful and optimistic. And we'll change the world." Egalitarians believe most people are decent and will follow reasonable rules under fair circumstances; they believe fairer societies help bring out the best in people. They support government's active role in society because they believe many government regulations and services enhance citizens' freedom by limiting their risks (workplace and highway safety) and expanding their opportunities (public schools and laws against discrimination). Citizens benefit a great deal from government action, policies, and programs, and they should pass on at least as many benefits to future generations.

Varieties of Egalitarian Liberalism

Egalitarian liberalism is the newest form of liberalism; most of its philosophical defences were written after 1970. Because of its newness, there is only one distinct egalitarian liberal position in Canada, **social democracy**. Social democrats believe the state should work actively to reduce economic and social inequalities. They criticize inequalities permitted by conservatives and centrists that allow some individuals, corporations, and groups to gain unequal access to government, because this undermines freedom and democracy. Social democrats also criticize conservatives' and centrists' reduction of freedom to economic freedom, because there is much more to freedom than what individuals buy and how they earn their incomes. People enjoy nature, spend time with family and friends, volunteer for charities or political causes, play games and sports, play and listen to music; these activities involve freedom as much as monetary interactions do. Social democrats believe the state should promote all forms of liberty, and it should ensure, as much as possible, that all citizens have the means to live good, worthwhile lives. This requires robust governments that are much more active in the economy and society than they are now. Governments should, for example, provide everyone with prescription drugs, glasses, dental care, universal childcare, generous maternity and paternity leave, and reduced or no college and university tuition; promote tolerance and work actively to end discrimination; and regulate the prices of or own some necessities of life, such as energy and water, so they remain affordable for everyone. We are freest when we are most equal, social democrats say.

Centrist Liberals

Centrist liberalism mixes conservative and egalitarian elements. Centrists believe liberty requires a free market, but equality requires limits on the market. Conservatives and egalitarian centrists differ primarily in whether they consider the market or equality primary.

Conservative centrists are economically conservative but socially egalitarian. They agree with other conservatives that government should protect private property, but they also believe citizens have responsibilities to each other, and that government should fulfill some of these responsibilities. Inequalities between citizens must not become too great, they think, because this leads to injustice. They support existing social programs and laws that lessen widespread inequality, such as progressive taxation, human rights codes, public schools, health care, old age pensions, welfare, and disability. They also believe governments must be economically conservative to protect these programs. Conservative centrists sometimes support new demands for equality, but they prefer to do so in ways that do not increase taxes or create greater costs for businesses. Legal and social changes to increase equality should be introduced slowly, they think, so people have time to adjust to the changes. In general, conservative centrists prioritize the market over equality in cases of conflict.

Egalitarian centrists support a largely free market economy, but with more limits than conservative centrists do. They believe government must ensure that no citizen falls below some minimum—a welfare "floor"—so they support programs such as employment insurance, pensions, workers' compensation, disability, and welfare. They also support laws and policies like progressive taxation, workplace safety regulations, minimum wage laws, publicly funded schooling, and prohibitions on discrimination and child labour, because such policies enhance the effectiveness of liberty for citizens. (A truly free market contains no such laws or policies, because all of them limit economic freedom.) The state must ensure that social and economic inequalities do not become too great. In a **welfare state** individuals and businesses may compete, succeed, and fail, and some people may become rich while others remain poor. However, governments must intervene economically and socially to limit the gap between rich and poor, to avoid undermining both freedom and equality. In general, egalitarian centrists prioritize equality over the market if the two conflict.

Non-liberal Views

Non-liberal political theories reject one or more of the basic **tenets** (principles) of liberalism, particularly individualism, freedom, and equality. Some non-liberal theories, such as Confucianism, are based on families or groups, not individuals. Non-liberal theories may deny humans are fundamentally free (some religious views and all slave societies) or equal (monarchies and class or caste societies). Non-liberal societies may be democratic, though; examples include contemporary Botswana and ancient Athens. Non-liberal democracies usually reject individualism and the assumption of unique interests. Instead, a group such as the nation, an ethnic group, or the family is considered the basic unit of society, and members are assumed to share a common and/or ultimate goal, such as improving the group's fortunes or following a particular religion.

Canada's Legal System

We have covered basic concepts in ethics, at the highest level of generality, and political philosophy, at the next most general level. The principles underlying Canada's legal system bring us yet closer to the issues dealt with in applied ethics. Every topic in this book has legal aspects, from the place of Aboriginal peoples and Quebec in Canadian law and the *Charter*, to the constitutional status of the *Anti-terrorism Act* and assisted suicide. We turn now to some of the principles that ground Canadian law.

Law is a public, codified system of rules that helps citizens attain the benefits of cooperating with others and penalizes rule-breaking. It creates and authorizes social institutions such as courts, departments of government, social programs, charitable organizations, marriage and the family, clubs, schools, and corporations. It fosters and regulates interactions between citizens, social institutions, and/or government. Law differs from other public systems of rules, such as by-laws or the rules of professional sports, because its rules are the highest secular level of authority in the society: all individuals, groups, and social institutions must conform to the law.

(You might wonder how the law "creates" marriage and the family. The law decides which individuals it recognizes as married and which groups it recognizes as families, and it assigns legal rights, responsibilities, and benefits to married people, families, and family members that unmarried people and those who are not family members do not have. Thus it creates marriage and the family as legal categories with social and political consequences for married people and family members.)

Canada is a democracy governed by the **rule of law**, which means that every person, institution, and official, public or private, as well as the government itself, is subject to the law. Laws must be publicized by the legislature, enforced equally by the **executive power**, and applied fairly by an independent judiciary. Courts must be independent of Parliament because judges must be free to make decisions based on the law and principle that might be unpopular with the government of the day.

In a **representative democracy**, as we have in Canada, elected representatives and judges have the authority to make law. Canadian law is made in three ways: through the *Canadian Charter of Rights and Freedoms*, through legislation, and through the common law. All legislation must conform to the *Charter*, and all common law decisions must conform to both legislation and the *Charter*.

The Common Law

The **common law** originated in England but is now the form of law in most English-speaking countries, including Britain, Canada, and the US. The common law is made by judges, based on **precedent** and custom. A precedent is a legal decision, grounded on a particular set of facts and evidence, that determines how all similar cases must be decided in the future. It ensures that judges do not have to reinvent the wheel each time they try a case, and that judicial decisions are consistent and predictable, so citizens can know how the law will be interpreted. Custom in the common law includes the changing laws, rules, and practices of the society, which keeps the common law relevant to current circumstances. It also includes principles of **natural justice**, which come from the ancient Roman view that some legal principles are part of the natural order and thus self-evident to anyone with good judgment and practical wisdom. (Notice the similarity to natural rights, discussed above in the section on deontology.) The best-known principles of natural justice are the right to be heard (the right to present one's case in court) and the rule that one cannot judge in one's own case (judges must be unbiased and must not have conflicts of interest).

In the common law, decisions made at one level are binding on courts at the same level or lower. A higher court can overrule, affirm, or modify a decision made by a lower court, and that decision binds all lower courts as well as future similar cases at that level. A higher court also can refuse to hear an appeal from a lower court, which has the effect of affirming the lower court's decision.

Legislation

Canada has a **federal** system of government, in which legislative powers are split between two or more levels of government. The federal (national) government has jurisdiction over matters of national interest, including citizenship, defence, Aboriginal people and reserves, the criminal law, marriage and divorce, regulation of trade and commerce, taxation, and employment insurance. Provincial and territorial governments have jurisdiction over matters of provincial interest, including education, health care, municipalities, property and civil rights, provincial taxation, and the administration of justice. The federal and provincial governments share jurisdiction over old age pensions, immigration, and agriculture.

Provincial and territorial governments delegate some of their powers to municipal (e.g., regional, city, and township) governments to make laws and regulations concerning matters under their jurisdiction, including responsibility for zoning, waste collection, public transit, libraries, and water. The federal government delegates some of its power to the military and Aboriginal people to make laws and regulations to govern soldiers, military bases, and reserves. In addition, some Aboriginal peoples have negotiated self-government agreements that give them powers to make laws and regulations concerning matters such as land use, education, child welfare, health care, housing, and economic development.

Legislation is legally superior to the common law. If a court interprets the law in a way that legislators do not like, they can rewrite the law or write a new law that overrides the court's decision.

The *Charter*

A political constitution such as the *Charter* spells out the principles on which a nation is grounded and by which it is to be governed. The *Charter* is the supreme law of Canada; all court decisions and legislation must conform to its principles (unless a government invokes the "notwithstanding" clause, discussed below). It guarantees rights and freedoms that neither the federal nor the provincial/territorial governments can legislate away. While it can be amended, changes to the *Charter* usually require the unanimous consent of the federal government and the consent of at least two-thirds of the provincial governments that represent at least fifty per cent of the population. (There are a few exceptions, but we can put these aside for now.) This ensures that *Charter* protections cannot be changed easily, such as in an atmosphere of political hysteria after a terrorist attack.

The *Charter* applies to decisions, laws, and regulations made by federal, provincial, and territorial governments and their "delegated decision-makers," such as health care and educational administrators. It does not apply to the actions of private individuals or private institutions such as charitable groups, clubs, and corporations. However, the actions of private individuals and institutions are governed by federal, provincial, and territorial laws, policies, and human rights codes, so the *Charter* may apply to them indirectly. If individuals or institutions believe a law or policy was applied or interpreted in a way that violates one of their *Charter* rights, they may bring a *Charter* challenge against that law or policy.

Sometimes legislators or civil servants do not foresee that a law or regulation will restrict rights or freedoms or treat members of a group unfairly. Sometimes a law is over-inclusive (it includes people it should leave out) or under-inclusive (it leaves out people it should have included). If the Supreme Court rules that there is a Charter violation, then the law or regulation will be **struck down** or modified to remove the injustice. A law or regulation that is struck down ceases to have effect. Sometimes, however, the Court decides that only part of the legislation in question violates the Charter. It can sever the wrongful portion of the law, **read down** a wrongful inclusion (interpret the law in a way that restricts its scope of application), or **read in** a wrongful exclusion (interpret the law in a way that broadens its scope of application).

Striking down a law or regulation requires a two-step process under the *Charter*. First, the court determines that the law or regulation violates a *Charter* guarantee. Next, it must consider the violation in light of section 1 of the *Charter*, which states, "The *Canadian Charter of Rights and Freedoms* guarantees the rights and freedoms set out in it subject only to such reasonable limits prescribed by law as can be demonstrably justified in a free and democratic society." The court must ask itself whether the law is a "reasonable limit" and whether it can be "demonstrably justified." To do this, it applies the **Oakes test** (named after the case in which the Supreme Court first used a section 1 analysis). The Oakes test requires answering four questions, in order:

1. Does the law fulfill a "pressing and substantial objective"?
2. Is the law rationally connected to this objective?
3. Does the law impair the right as little as possible?
4. Are the effects of the law proportionate to its objective?

The law is saved only if the Court answers "yes" to all four questions. A negative answer to any question stops the process; the law is not a reasonable limit, and the remaining questions need not be answered.

The *Charter* is not *quite* the supreme law of Canada, however. Section 33, the so-called notwithstanding clause, allows a federal or provincial government to retain a law that violates section 2 (the fundamental freedoms) or sections 7 to 15 (individual rights), notwithstanding (that is, in spite of) what the Charter says in those sections. Such a law is valid for five years, after which it expires if the government does not re-enact the legislation. This clause was added to maintain **the supremacy of Parliament**—to ensure that there is no higher law-making authority than federal and provincial legislatures. The "notwithstanding" clause makes the rights and freedoms guaranteed by sections 2 and 7 through 15 almost untouchable, but gives federal or provincial/territorial governments the final say if they want. The federal government has never invoked (put into use) section 33. Some provincial or territorial governments have threatened to invoke it, but so far only Quebec has. In 1987, the Supreme Court ruled that some sections of the Quebec language law violate the freedom of expression guarantees in section 2(b) of the *Canadian Charter* and section 3 of the *Quebec Charter of Human Rights and Freedoms*. The government of Quebec used the "notwithstanding" clause to override the Supreme Court's ruling, and has renewed it every five years since.

Court Decisions as "Public Philosophy"

Philosophers refer to court decisions much more often than to legislation. This is because philosophers are interested in reasons for and against claims, and courts, particularly the Supreme Court, tend to be more careful and explicit in their reasoning than legislators. Legislation is often preceded by statements of principles and definitions, but rarely do legislators lay out all the reasons for a law. In precedent-setting judgments, however, the court gives explicit reasons for its decision, and it examines arguments against the decision as well. Such judgments frequently discuss the history, purpose, and goals of the law in question; social issues addressed or ignored by the law; the effects of the law; and how these considerations fit with other laws and with the *Charter*. Supreme Court decisions often refer to works by philosophers and legal theorists; several authors in this book have been cited in their judgments. For applied ethicists and social and political philosophers, court decisions are a form of public philosophy in which abstract principles get put into concrete practice. While philosophers do not always agree with Supreme Court decisions, they are a rich source of arguments.

The Connection between Ethics, Political and Legal Philosophy, and Applied Ethics

The connections between political and legal philosophy and applied ethics are fairly straightforward. Conservatives' and egalitarians' views on, say, abortion tend to be consistent with their views on terrorism and multiculturalism. (If they are not, the inconsistency can be cured with a dose of philosophy.) However, the connections between ethical theories, on the one hand, and political and legal philosophy and applied ethics, on the other, is less clear. In fact, ethicists agree on almost all moral issues. All moral theories **prescribe** (require) truth-telling, gratitude, and respect (most if not all the time), and **proscribe** (forbid) murder, rape, and assault (let's hope all the time). We would not recognize a theory as a *moral* theory if it did not make these prescriptions. Furthermore, almost every reasonable moral decision, spanning the range of views on a topic, can be justified by each of the ethical theories. So how is ethics connected to political and legal philosophy and applied ethics?

Ethical theories examine values in general and provide their deep justification. Ethics is connected to applied ethics through political and legal philosophy, whose analyses are closer to real-life moral issues. Applied ethicists use selected ethical, political, and legal principles, combined with principles specific to particular disciplines or cases, to discuss what we should do in real-world situations that arise in imperfect societies made up of fallible human beings.

(This might be a good time to go to the Moral and Preferences Indicator on the website for this book, to see where your current views fit on a spectrum of Canadian views. Later in the course, you can see if your views have changed, and if so, how.)

Reading and Understanding Philosophy

What Do Philosophers Do?

Philosophers argue. Now, by "argue" we don't mean "fight"; rather, we use "argue" in a more reasoned, contemplative sense. For a philosopher, to argue means *to give good reasons for believing something*. For example, we take stands on various issues, and provide good reasons for our views. In addition, we often give reasons why alternative views are faulty, or at least not as good as our own. Furthermore, we generalize from our viewpoints; we search for principles underlying our arguments that could be applied in other cases. We may begin with a particular principle (such as "respect people's rights" or "create the most good overall") and examine the meaning and implications of this principle. Frequently we examine the meanings of contentious or muddled terms, such as "freedom" or "quality of life," and give reasons to favour one definition over others.

One of the most frustrating things for some beginning philosophy students is that there appear to be no right answers in philosophy. For the most part, they're right—there rarely is a single right or true answer in philosophy. However, this does not mean that philosophers just say whatever we think and call it philosophy. We use arguments to convince others that a particular answer or set of answers is better than another. What makes a philosophical answer better or worse? Since our method is making arguments—that is, giving good reasons for believing something—then better answers must provide better reasons for accepting them than worse answers do. For example, a better answer might show us what is really at stake in the issue; be more clearly focused on the problem at hand; make clearer, more careful, or more useful distinctions; apply to a broader range of cases; appeal to deeper or more plausible principles; better account for the facts at hand; provide better answers to possible objections, and so on.

Reading what others have to say on a particular issue can help you develop and deepen your own views. There is no reason to re-invent the wheel if others have already laid the groundwork for us, or pointed out traps in arguments that we might consider. But reading will not tell you what "the right answer" is. What you will discover is that there is a great deal of disagreement, even among those who have thought deeply about the issues. That in itself is worth knowing. It is worth reading and listening to people with different views. You can see what others have to say for themselves, figure out what you think of their arguments and conclusions, and why you think what you do. That will help you clarify and deepen your views. It might help you make your views on one subject, like climate change, consistent with your views on another subject, say, the role of government. It might point out some unforeseen consequences of your beliefs. It might challenge your views. Perhaps most importantly, it might teach you to respect different viewpoints. It is worth knowing that intelligent, thoughtful, informed people disagree in good faith about many important questions. It is worth understanding those people's viewpoints, even if you disagree with them. Understanding is the basis of mutual respect, which is necessary for a democracy to function well.

Understanding Precedes Criticism

You probably have strong views on at least some of the issues in this book. Almost certainly you will disagree with some of the readings. You might find yourself criticizing a particular reading from the outset. In that case, try to put your criticisms aside until you are sure you understand the argument correctly. Why? Because it is easy to misread an argument you disagree with. If you write an essay on that argument, you might present a caricature of it rather than an accurate view. This is a common **fallacy** (mistake of reasoning) known as the **straw man fallacy**. It means that you did not criticize the real argument, but rather a pushover version of it—you knocked down a straw figure (a weak argument) rather than the actual argument.

How do you avoid this? Approach the material with an open mind. Apply what philosophers call the principle of charity; that is, interpret the author's arguments as charitably as possible. (The principle of charity can also be called the "no dope" rule: Assume that none of the authors in this book is a dope. If an argument looks stupid to you, remember the author is not a dope, and keep looking until you find a less stupid interpretation of the argument.) Sometimes, no matter how charitably you interpret an argument, you will disagree with it. That's fine. The point is not to agree with every author. They often disagree with each other, so agreeing with all of them would mean you held contradictory views, which is a serious problem in philosophy. The point is to understand the authors on their own terms. Then and only then should you decide whether you agree or disagree with them, and why.

Aids to Help You Understand the Readings

Philosophy is perhaps the only subject that asks beginning students to read material written by professionals in the field for other professionals in the field. We do this because what really matters in philosophy is not so much what someone claims but rather the reasons given in favour of those claims, and no one can present those arguments better than the person who developed them. But reading this material can be very difficult going for first- or second-year students, so this book contains a lot of aids to help you understand the readings.

My research assistant Max Degaust and I have added explanatory notes and markings to most of the readings. In some cases we broke the readings into sections and subsections and gave them titles, to help you understand the arguments better. We also explained references that you might not understand in endnotes. I know that most undergraduates do not read endnotes, but it is a good idea to look at the ones in this book. Here's a way to make it easier: Mark the page the endnotes are on with a paper clip or a sticky note so you can find the notes easily. Glance at the endnotes before you start reading. Ignore the ones that only give references; those are there mostly for academics, who often want to look up the original sources. Find the first endnote that contains explanatory material, and write down its number or note it in your head. Ignore all the endnote numbers in the text until you get to that number, and then read the endnote. While you're there, find the number of the next explanatory endnote. Read until you get to that number, and read that endnote. Continue that way to the end. That way you will not waste time looking up references you do not need, but you will get the benefit of the explanations.

There is a glossary of philosophical terms and phrases, plus the odd obscure word, at the back of the book. Mark this with a paper clip or sticky note as well. Words that are defined in the glossary are indicated by **boldface**. Notice that some words have technical meanings in philosophy that differ from the way the words are used in ordinary language. For example, "welfare" refers to what is best for people overall, not social assistance. Be sure you understand and use all technical terms correctly. Note too that the glossary does not give every possible meaning of a word or phrase. Rather, it gives the meaning as the word or phrase is used in the text. A good dictionary can give you other meanings.

There are discussion questions at the end of each chapter that ask you to evaluate part of an author's argument or compare it to another author's argument. There are more questions on the website associated with this course, including questions intended to guide your understanding of the readings. They will help you see what is important in the reading and understand the author's reasoning. Other questions will ask you to evaluate particular arguments or the author's overall argument, or to compare this argument with the argument in another reading. These questions will help you understand the arguments better, and decide what your own views are on the issue.

Know What Is and Is Not the Author's View

Philosophers give reasons for believing a claim, but we also frequently anticipate possible objections to our views and respond to those objections. We lay out criticisms of our views carefully, in ways that those who do not agree with us would recognize as accurate descriptions of their views. This can be very confusing to beginning philosophy students. Why do we do it? Because responding adequately to criticisms provides further evidence in favour of our view, or at least shows that alternative views have serious problems. But it can be difficult for introductory students to distinguish what is our own view and what we argue against. So I have marked in the readings with (AV) for "author's view" and (~AV) for "not the author's view" to make this clearer. Here is an example:

> Torture is always wrong. (~AV) Someone may claim torture is justified if it prevents a much worse wrong, such as a terrorist attack that kills hundreds or thousands

of people. That sounds plausible: harming one guilty person seems less bad than allowing that person to harm many innocent people. AV But think about it for a minute. Notice that allowing torture, even only selectively, assumes that the person being tortured really is a terrorist who has planned an attack. What if we are wrong? That would be a terrible wrong with no possible benefits to outweigh it. ~AV The objector may argue that we would only torture people we *know* are terrorists. AV But determining guilt and innocence falls under courts' **jurisdiction**, not the police's or military force's. (See the discussion of Maher Arar in the Introduction to Chapter 11, Real and Suspected Terrorism.) Torturing a suspected terrorist violates the **presumption of innocence**, the assumption that an accused person is innocent until proven guilty in a court of law. Our criminal system is based on the principle that it is better to let many guilty people go free than to falsely imprison (or here, torture) one innocent person. This is a bedrock principle of our legal system, and eroding it could have very serious consequences for the entire system. Finally, why do we believe that people tell the truth when they are tortured? Movies and television shows may make it look like torture works, but they promote a dangerous fiction. The evidence from military and intelligence experts strongly suggests that torture provides bad information.[5] Apparently, suspects who are tortured will say anything to make the torture stop. Therefore, on both principled and empirical grounds, torture is always wrong.

When you see ~AV, the author disagrees with everything that follows, until you see AV again. Generally we did not mark the text until the first argument appeared that was not the author's view; anything before that is the author's own view. Sometimes an author develops objections across more than one section. In those cases, we put an ~AV mark at the beginning of the section, so you can be sure that this is still not the author's view. These marks should help you understand the readings accurately and avoid one of the most common errors in beginning students' writing—claiming an author believes something that in fact he or she argues against.

Doing the Readings

Philosophy requires slow and repeated reading. Expect to read each of the readings at least two or three times if you want to understand it. Here is a method that should help you:

1. First, skim the reading. Find out what the author's main point is. Sometimes this will be obvious; the author might say something like "I will argue that . . ." in the first few paragraphs. Other times you will have to figure out the main point from the context. On this first skim-read, notice the headings and subheadings. These will give you the skeleton of the author's argument.
2. Next, you should go through the reading *s-l-o-w-l-y*.
    a. See what the author's arguments are in favour of his or her argument, which objections are addressed, and how the author responds to them. Use the headings and the markings to help you keep your place in the argument. What reasons does the author give? What evidence does the author present

in favour of her or his view, or against opposing views? Use the "Questions of Understanding" on the website to guide your reading.

b. Take notes *in your own words*. Don't use quotes. A quote is the philosophical equivalent of pointing: "That's what the author says." When you write an essay, your instructor will want to know that you understand the author's arguments, and a quote alone does not demonstrate understanding. A quote should always be followed by an explanation of what it means. It's faster to go straight to the explanation by putting the ideas in your own words.

Doing this detailed work will put flesh on the bones of the argument.

3. Read the selection again, along with your notes, and put the argument together. How do the reasons fit with each other to support the overall argument? There are three general ways to do this, visually, verbally, and mathematically; choose the one that fits your learning style best.

a. Sometimes it's helpful to diagram the argument's structure. Look again at the indented argument under "Know What Is and Is Not the Author's View" above. It gives three reasons in favour of the claim that torture is always wrong: (A) we might torture an innocent person, (B) torture undermines the presumption of innocence, and (C) it does not work. It concludes that (D) torture is always wrong. In this argument, the reasons operate separately, thus:

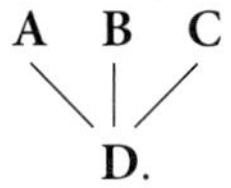

That is, the truth of reason A does not depend on the truth of reason B or C. In other arguments, however, two or more of the reasons may be linked. For example, two reasons may work together, but the third may be separate:

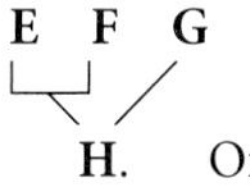

Or all may work together:

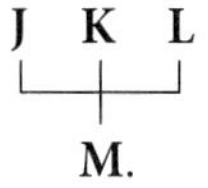

Or they may work like links in a chain, where the first leads to the second, then the third, and thus to the conclusion:

Why does this matter? Because we evaluate different structures differently. In figure 1, if reason A is problematic, the author still has two independent reasons in favour of the argument. In figure 2, however, if E is problematic, then E and F together can't be a good reason, so the author is left with only one reason for the conclusion, H. In figures

3 and 4, if any reason is problematic, the whole argument falls apart. This method is most useful if you are a visual thinker—if you think in primarily pictures.

b. You might think of the reasons as part of an argument in a trial. Sticking with our argument in "Know What Is and Is Not the Author's View," if the author were a lawyer arguing against torture, how would the author fit the reasons together to make the overall case? If you were an attorney on the other side, what might you say in response to the author's arguments? How do you think the author would reply? If you were a second attorney on the author's side, how would you suggest the author reply to objections from opposing counsel? This method of analysis is most useful if you are a verbal thinker—if you think primarily in words.

c. You might think of the argument as steps in a proof, much like solving a math problem where you show all your work. Think again of the argument against torture. How has the author arranged these reasons so they result in his or her conclusion? Would the formula be $A + B + C \rightarrow D$, or $(A \rightarrow D) + (B \rightarrow D) + (C \rightarrow D)$? Perhaps it's $(A + B) + C \rightarrow D$, or $A \rightarrow (B + C) \rightarrow D$. Do the reasons fit together coherently to support the author's claim? Has the author missed any crucial steps—the equivalent of not showing all of the author's work—or made mistakes in reasoning—the equivalent of making mistakes in calculation? Has missing a step led to a mistake in reasoning? Notice that these are different sorts of problems. Think about what could be done to shore up the proof or show its faults. This method of analysis is most useful if you are a mathematical thinker—if you think in symbols and abstract operations.

However you do this—visually, verbally, mathematically, or some combination—the point is to determine whether the author's reasons support the conclusion. If you believe they do not, remember two things: First, most of the readings have been abridged, so the missing arguments may be in the larger work. And second, the "no dope" rule should tell you that a mistake you see is at least as likely to be yours as the author's, so be charitable and re-examine the author's reasons.

I think of philosophy as a conversation that has been going on for over two thousand years; when we do philosophy we join the conversation. Think of the readings in this book as part of the ongoing conversation about how we should live with and act toward others. Philosophers read widely and think deeply before we express our views on a subject. If you went somewhere and people who knew a lot more than you were discussing an issue, it would be smart to listen for a while and understand what they were saying, and why, before you jumped in with your own views. Going through each of the readings several times, slowly and carefully, is the equivalent of carefully listening to and understanding arguments by people who have thought a lot about these issues. Then decide which arguments you agree or disagree with, and why. That's when you begin to do philosophy.

Welcome to the conversation.

Readings: Moral Theories

🍁 = Canadian source or author

Utilitarianism

🍁 Braybrooke, David. *Utilitarianism: Restorations, Repairs, Renovations*. Toronto: University of Toronto Press, 2004.

Mill, John Stuart. *Utilitarianism*. Original text: www.utilitarianism.com/mill1.htm.

🍁 Sumner, L.W. *Welfare, Happiness and Ethics*. New York: Oxford University Press, 1996.

Deontology

🍁 Brennan, Samantha. "The Liberal Rights of Feminist Liberalism." In *Varieties of Feminist Liberalism. Edited by Amy Baehr. Lanham, MD: Rowman and Littlefield, 2004, 85–102.*

Kant, Immanuel. Groundwork for the Metaphysics of Morals. Thomas Kingsmill Abbott translation: http://ebooks.adelaide.edu.au/k/kant/immanuel/k16prm/.

🍁 Narveson, Jan. "Property Rights." *Social Philosophy and Policy* 27, 1 (2010): 101–34.

🍁 Orend, Brian. *Human Rights: Concept and Context*. Peterborough, ON: Broadview Press, 2002.

Virtue Ethics

Aristotle. *Nicomachean Ethics*. http://classics.mit.edu/Aristotle/nicomachaen.html.

🍁 Hurka, Thomas. *Virtue, Vice, and Value*. New York: Oxford University Press, 200).

Hursthouse, Rosalind. *On Virtue Ethics*. Oxford: Oxford University Press, 1999.

Care Ethics

Baier, Annette. "The Need for More than Justice." *Canadian Journal of Philosophy 17, supplementary vol. 13, "Science, Morality and Feminist Theory"* (1987): 41–56.

Held, Virginia. *"Non-contractual Society: A Feminist View." Canadian Journal of Philosophy 17, supplementary vol. 13, "Science, Morality and Feminist Theory"* (1987): 111–37.

🍁 Koggel, Christine. *Perspectives on Equality: Constructing a Relational Theory*. Lanham, MD: Rowman and Littlefield, 1998.

🍁 Nedelsky, Jennifer. "Reconceiving Rights as Relationship." *Review of Constitutional Studies* 1, 1 (1993): 1–26.

Readings: Political Theories

Liberal Theories: Classic Texts

The Social Contract Tradition

Locke, John. *Second Treatise of Civil Government*. Original text: www.class.uidaho.edu/mickelsen/ToC/Locke%202nd%20ToC.htm.

Nineteenth-Century Liberalism

Mill, John Stuart. *On Liberty*. Original text: http://ebooks.adelaide.edu.au/m/mill/john_stuart/m645o/.

Twentieth-Century Liberalism

Habermas, Jürgen. *Between Facts and Norms: Contributions to a Discourse Theory of Law and Democracy*. William Rehg, trans. Cambridge, MA: MIT Press, 1998.

———. *The Postnational Constellation: Political Essays*. Max Pensky, trans. Cambridge, MA: MIT Press, 2001.

Nozick, Robert. *Anarchy, State, and Utopia*. New York: Basic Books, 1974.

Rawls, John. *A Theory of Justice*. Rev. ed. Cambridge, MA: Harvard University Press, 1999.

———. *Political Liberalism*. New York: Columbia University Press, 1993.

Conservative Liberalism

- Gauthier, David. *Morals By Agreement*. Oxford: Clarendon Press, 1986.
- Narveson, Jan. *The Libertarian Idea*. Philadelphia: Temple University Press, 1988.

Egalitarian Liberalism

- Cohen, G.A. *Rescuing Justice and Equality*. Cambridge, MA: Harvard University Press, 2008.
- Cunningham, Frank. "The Socialist Retrieval of Liberal Democracy." *International Political Science Review* 11, 1 (1990): 99–110.
- Kymlicka, Will. "Left-Liberalism Revisited." In *The Egalitarian Conscience: Essays in Honour of G.A. Cohen. Edited by Christine Sypnowich. Oxford: Oxford University Press, 2006, 9–35.*

Centrist Liberalism

- Ignatieff, Michael. *The Rights Revolution*. Toronto, ON: House of Anansi Press, 2007.
- Aster, Howard, and Thomas S. Axworthy, eds. *Searching for the New Liberalism: Perspectives, Policies, Prospects*. Oakville, ON: Mosaic Press, 2003.

Notes

1. Legal philosophy is usually called philosophy of law. However, "political philosophy and philosophy of law" is awkward, so I refer to them here as political and legal philosophy.
2. Transport Canada, *Seat Belt Sense* (March 2007), p. 3, www.tc.gc.ca/media/documents/roadsafety/TP14646e.pdf.
3. Egalitarians are often referred to as liberals, but that confuses liberalism as a political philosophy with liberal (and Liberal) political positions. It also ignores the difference between centrist liberals, whom I call centrists, and left-wing liberals, whom I call egalitarians (roughly, the distinction between Red Tories, most Liberals, and some Greens, on the one hand, and New Democrats, most Greens, and the Bloc Quebecois on the other).
4. Sex: Statistics Canada, *Women in Canada: A Gender-based Statistical Report*, 5th edition (2006), www.statcan.gc.ca/pub/89-503-x/89-503-x2005001-eng.pdf; race: Feng Hou and Simon Coulombe, "Earnings Gaps for Canadian-Born Visible Minorities in the Public and Private Sectors," *Canadian Public Policy* 36, 1 (2010), pp. 29–43; parents' education and income: Jo Blanden, "Love and Money: Intergenerational Mobility and Marital Matching on Parental Income," Statistics Canada (2005), http://dsp-psd.pwgsc.gc.ca/Collection/Statcan/11F0019MIE/11F0019MIE2005272.pdf; place of birth: Statistics Canada, "Median Total Income, by Family Type, by Province and Territory," www40.statcan.ca/l01/cst01/famil108a-eng.htm.
5. Dexter Filkins, "General Says Less Coercion of Captives Yields Better Data," *New York Times* (7 September 2004), www.nytimes.com/2004/09/07/international/middleeast/07detain.html?_r=0, and David Rose, "Tortured Reasoning," *Vanity Fair* (16 December 2008), www.vanityfair.com/magazine/2008/12/torture200812?currentPage=4.

Part I

Who Are We?

Introduction

If you are reading this book, you are an English speaker. You also are of **Aboriginal**, British, francophone or Québécois, or other immigrant heritage, possibly a mixture of two or more of those heritages. Some of you are landed immigrants, a few of you are visa students, but most of you are Canadian citizens. What does it mean to be Canadian? This book uses readings by mostly Canadian philosophers to examine this question. By reading the material, thinking about it, discussing it, and writing about it, I hope you will decide what it means to *you* to be Canadian.

In Part I we ask: Who are we as Canadians, and what should our relations with each other be like? How do we fit the various parts of our identities together to create a twenty-first-century Canadian identity? Certainly that identity must include our history—Aboriginal peoples,[1] European contact, French and English settlement, the Battle of the Plains of Abraham, Confederation, the railroad, World Wars I and II, and so on. Our identity also should include parts of our history that we are less proud of, such as the decimation of Aboriginal peoples by European diseases, the *Indian Act*, the Chinese Head Tax, the internment of Japanese Canadians during World War II, and the residential schools. We need to remember these things because the past still affects the present, and because we do not want to repeat our mistakes.

The situation of many groups in Canada improved between European contact and the early twentieth century. Most white non-British immigrants, after an initial period of discrimination, assimilated well and thrived in Canadian society. Woman's rights in the nineteenth century and woman's **suffrage** in the twentieth improved the lives and prospects of white women.[2] Unions improved working people's conditions, particularly if they were white.[3] But Aboriginal peoples, francophones, and people of colour did not fare so well. White racism, the *Indian Act*, and white Canadians' attempts to force Aboriginal people to renounce their Aboriginal identities stymied most efforts by Aboriginal peoples to improve their status. British Canadians' attempts to suppress French language and culture, and even to convert francophones to Protestantism, blocked francophones' efforts. White racism blocked efforts by Chinese Canadians, Japanese Canadians, and African Canadians. English Canadians—and Americans, Australians, New Zealanders, and other British colonizers—expected everyone to adopt English language, manners, and practices. If they would not (French Canadians and Aboriginal peoples) or could not (members of other races were unable to become white), they were shoved to the margins of society.

The Human Rights Revolution

For any movement by a minority to gain traction, it must convince a significant part of the majority that its concerns are real and ought to be listened to. There were plenty of intelligent, articulate Aboriginal, francophone, and "of colour" advocates of equality, but white and English-speaking people did not listen. After World War II, however, the human rights revolution that swept the world unplugged white and English-speaking Canadians' ears. Slowly they began to listen to Aboriginal peoples, the Québécois, and people of colour, and take their concerns seriously.

The human rights revolution was a reaction to the Holocaust, which shocked and horrified people around the world. Battle-hardened soldiers who liberated the concentration camps wept when they saw the survivors and realized what had gone on. Newsreels of the camps and survivors were shown worldwide. People in Western countries (western Europe, North America, Australia, and New Zealand) could not dismiss the Holocaust as the product of some foreign or "less civilized" society. Germany was a central part of Western culture. It had produced Bach, Beethoven, Kant, and Einstein. Yet this flower of European civilization had dehumanized, degraded, and slaughtered six million Jews, Roma ("Gypsies"), gays and lesbians, people with disabilities, political opponents, and anyone else the **Nazis** decided were inferior.

The United Nations was founded in 1945 "to keep peace throughout the world . . . to help **nations** work together to improve the lives of poor people, to conquer hunger, disease and illiteracy, and to encourage respect for each other's rights and freedoms."[4] There already had been two world wars in the first half of the twentieth century, with deaths on a scale far exceeding past wars. The founders of the UN wanted to prevent another all-consuming war. A central pillar of the UN is the Universal Declaration of Human Rights. Its Preamble states that "the inherent **dignity** and . . . the equal and inalienable rights of all members of the human family is the foundation of freedom, justice and peace in the world" and that "a common understanding of these rights and freedoms is of the greatest importance for the full realization of this pledge."[5] Eleanor Roosevelt, Chair of the UN Commission of Human Rights, described the Universal Declaration as "the international *Magna Carta* of all men everywhere."[6]

After World War II, people around the world began to ask themselves whether a Holocaust could happen in their countries. That led them to examine their policies towards members of internal groups and races. For the first time, they listened to voices of protest they had long tuned out. Within twenty years of the end of World War II, the **civil rights movement** in the US, **anti-colonial** and independence movements in former European colonies, and other **equality-seeking movements** finally caught the attention of people who did not themselves suffer from these wrongs.[7] All of the movements had been active for decades or longer, but finally the already-equal were willing to listen. The movements began to make real gains.

Philosophical Issues in Part I

Neither Aboriginals peoples nor the Québécois want to assimilate into the white, English-speaking Canadian mainstream. Rather, they want to maintain their separate, unique statuses as nations within—or perhaps, in the case of Quebec, without—Canada. The philosophical questions dealt with in the first two chapters include:

- What is a nation? Generally evidence of nationhood includes a shared tradition, culture, and language, and a complete set of institutions that allow members to live their entire lives within the nation if they choose. Do Aboriginal peoples and Quebec society constitute nations?
- What status and powers should **sub-state** nations have within larger **nation-states**? Most Canadian philosophers favour **asymmetrical federalism**, in which **First Nations** and Quebec have control over some things, such as education and policing for Aboriginal peoples and immigration and pensions for Quebec, in ways that other provinces or political units do not. However,

some people, such as former Prime Minister Pierre Trudeau, oppose different rights for different groups; they believe there should be a single status for all Canadian provinces and citizens.

- Should nations become independent states? In particular, should Quebec separate? (There is no real likelihood of Aboriginal peoples forming separate states.)

Immigrants (other than the British and Québécois) are not considered separate nations within Canada. How should we integrate people from other countries? Canada has chosen **multiculturalism**, a policy that encourages immigrants to maintain their original cultural identities alongside their new Canadian ones. The Québécois, on the other hand, prefer the French model of citizenship, in which there is a single **civil**, **secular** status for all citizens. They believe immigrants' languages, cultures, dress, and religion should be part of the **private sphere**; they do not belong in the **public sphere**, where no one should be marked, or should mark themselves, as different from other citizens. Should English-speaking Canada and Quebec have different multiculturalism policies?

The status of women is central to all these debates. Monique Deveaux discusses the issue of Aboriginal women who lost their Indian status in chapter 1, Aboriginal Peoples. In the pre-*Charter* days, an Aboriginal man who married a non-Aboriginal woman kept his Indian status, but an Aboriginal woman who married a non-Aboriginal man lost her Indian status. Even if she later divorced her non-Aboriginal husband, she remained a non-Indian in the eyes of the *Indian Act* and her band. The readings in chapter 3, Multiculturalism, discuss ways that women's rights and the rights of religious minorities may conflict in a multicultural society. Conflicts may occur not only in newer immigrant groups such as Muslims, but also in longer-established groups such as Christians and Jews.

English-speaking Canadians have re-fashioned our identities, partly in response to Aboriginal rights, Quebec nationalism, and multiculturalism. Most of us are proud of multiculturalism, and have quite happily integrated it into our identities. Most of us are torn, in different directions, about Quebec nationalism. And while most of us support Aboriginal rights in principle, our practice is something else again, in large part because of the **byzantine** legal and institutional structures that govern Aboriginal peoples. Of course there is more to English-speaking Canadian identities than this—we are peacekeepers, hockey champions, enthusiastic supporters of the winter Olympics, and most definitely not Americans. But that is the subject of chapter 4. In the end, you will decide for yourself what it means to be English-speaking Canadian.

Notes

1. I write "Aboriginal peoples," plural, because before European contact, there were many nations living in what we today call Canada. Aboriginal peoples were no more a single people than Europeans were.
2. The *Married Women's Property Act* of 1882 altered British (and Canadian) law, giving white, English-speaking, married women the right to possess and control property in their own names. Prior to this *Act*, marriage permanently transferred a woman's property rights to her husband. The *Act to Confer the Electoral Franchise upon Women* of 1918 gave Canadian women the right to vote on the same terms as Canadian men.

3. Trade unions are organizations of workers whose collective aim is to improve the working conditions and bargaining power of participating members. Trade unions have existed in Canada as early as 1812, but were outlawed until the *Trade Unions Act* of 1872. Among other things, the *Act* reduced the work day from twelve to nine hours. Unfortunately, the *Act* was not uniformly enforced. For example, "bunkhouse men," foreign, non-English-speaking men who provided unskilled labour in frontier work camps, continued to work twelve-hour days, seven days a week, under harsh conditions, well until the 1930s.
4. UN at a Glance, www.un.org/en/aboutun/index.shtml.
5. Preamble of the Universal Declaration of Human Rights, www.un.org/en/documents/udhr/.
6. Eleanor Roosevelt, "Adoption of the Declaration of Human Rights," 9 December 1948, www.udhr.org/history/ergeas48.htm. The *Magna Carta* (Latin for "Great Charter") is an ancient English political charter drafted in 1215. It is important because it is the first legal document of its kind to set limits to the exercise of political power. For example, it prohibited punishment and imprisonment without **due process**.
7. In the US, the civil rights movement was a series of social and political events that eventually led to equal civil rights for African American citizens. Two famous results of the struggle were the *Civil Rights Act of 1964*, which outlawed discrimination against racial, ethnic, and religious minorities and women in the workplace and public facilities, and the *Voting Rights Act of 1965*, which prohibited discrimination of the same kind in political elections. The civil rights movement had a positive ripple effect throughout the world, boosting the efforts of other equality-seeking movements that dealt with the unfair treatment of marginalized groups. In 1962 the UN passed a resolution condemning **apartheid** policies. In 1969, Canada decriminalized same-sex sex. In the 1970s, disability rights became a significant force in the US. Anti-colonial movements, which strove for political independence from European colonizers, made significant strides around the same time. For example, Barbados, Botswana, Guyana, and Lesotho all gained independence from England in 1966.

Chapter 1

Aboriginal[1] Peoples

Background

Aboriginal societies in Canada before European contact varied widely, from large settled agricultural societies to small groups of nomadic hunter-gatherers. The largest concentrations of people lived in the Iroquois Confederacy in the northeastern part of the continent, and in the many nations along the northwest coast of British Columbia. Social and political structures ranged from **egalitarian** (all adult members participated in decision-making and had roughly equal wealth and status) to extremely hierarchical (decisions were made by one man or a small group of men, and social ranks ranged from nobles to slaves).

Aboriginal religious beliefs were generally **pantheistic** (they believed everything in the world was a tangible expression of the creator). Thus Aboriginal peoples had familial connections with everything in the world: they had obligations to care for and preserve the land, plants, and animals, as these things cared for and preserved the people, and as the people cared for and preserved their human family members. Europeans, on the other hand, saw—and still see—land, plants, and animals as things that can be bought, owned, and sold, and they believed that owners could, within limits, do as they please with their property. This radical difference in worldviews would be a major source of misunderstandings and conflict between Aboriginal peoples and Europeans.

Contact with Europeans was, quite literally, deadly to Aboriginal people; they had no resistance to European illnesses such as measles, influenza, and smallpox. Roughly half of Aboriginal people died from these diseases within a few years of first contact with Europeans. (The fourteenth-century Black Death, generally considered the worst plague in European history, killed a similar percentage of Europeans.) One hundred and fifty years after first contact, successive waves of European diseases had killed up to ninety per cent of Aboriginal people.[2] Sometimes Europeans even deliberately inflicted their illnesses, practising an early form of germ warfare, by giving smallpox-infested blankets to Aboriginal people.[3]

Separation, "Civilization," and Assimilation

The British considered North America to be unowned and virtually uninhabited. Explorers claimed large areas of land for the Crown and, in the British view, this made the Aboriginal peoples who lived there also subject to the Crown. For example, the *Royal Proclamation of 1763* stated that the "nations or tribes of Indians . . . who live under our protection, should not be molested or disturbed in the possession of such parts of our dominions and territories . . . [that] are reserved to them." Three things are important here. First, the Crown stated that it owned the land in North America ("our dominions and territories"). Second, the Crown said that First Nations were under its "protection," and therefore authority. And third, the Crown stated that land was "reserved to" Aboriginal peoples—it would be kept for them, but they did not own it.

The *British North America Act*, which established Canada as an independent nation in 1867, gave the federal government **jurisdiction** over "Indians, and lands reserved for the Indians." In 1876 the Canadian government passed the *Indian Act*, which has regulated most aspects of the lives of First Nations peoples for over a century. Even today, the *Act* determines who is a "status Indian" and who is not; gives the federal government control over Aboriginal land, resources, money, property, wills, and inheritance; and imposes a form of government on First Nations that often conflicts with traditional and preferred forms. It also recognizes First Nations as distinct peoples (communities with a common culture, history, religion, etc.) and provides some protections and benefits, such as health care and education. Neither the protections nor the benefits First Nations receive are necessarily equal, however. For example, child services on reserves receive twenty-two per cent less funding per child than provincially funded child services that serve primarily non-Aboriginal families, despite the greater cost of delivering services on reserves, especially in remote communities.[4] Infant mortality among Aboriginal people is three times the rate for non-Aboriginal people, education funding for Aboriginal children on reserves averages $2000 a year less per child than education funding for non-Aboriginal children, and an Aboriginal person is more likely to go to prison than to graduate from high school.[5]

Later amendments to the *Indian Act* required Aboriginal people to ask the Indian Agent for passes to leave their reserves, or for permission sell agricultural products; revoked their Indian status if they graduated from university or became doctors, lawyers, or members of the clergy; forbade important cultural practices such as the **Sun Dance** or **potlatch**; allowed Indian Agents to oversee **band council** elections, run council meetings, cast tie-breaking votes, and remove elected councillors from band government; made it illegal for Aboriginal people to hire lawyers to challenge the government in court or even to hold public meetings to discuss their concerns; and gave Indian Agents wide-ranging powers over the personal and family lives of Aboriginal people.

The Canadian government's explicit policy was to separate, "civilize," and assimilate Aboriginal people. They were to be separated from "civilized" (European) society until they got an education, converted to Christianity, and gave up their treaty rights and Indian status. Giving up their Indian status required that they leave their families and reserves though, so most Aboriginal people refused the "benefits" of European civilization. Even if they did attempt to assimilate, they were second-class citizens. They were forbidden to enter certain professions or to advocate on behalf of their former people, nor could they vote or serve on juries. Federal voting rights were not extended to all "status Indians" until 1960, and in 1969 Quebec became the last province to extend provincial voting rights to Aboriginal people.

In the 1960s, the federal government commissioned a report on the social conditions of First Nations in Canada. The Hawthorn Report said Aboriginal people were the most disadvantaged and **disenfranchised** people in Canada; Hawthorn described them as "citizens minus." In response to this report, the Trudeau government produced the 1969 White Paper, which proposed dismantling Indian Affairs, getting rid of the *Indian Act*, reserves, and "Indian status," removing all legal distinctions between Aboriginal and non-Aboriginal people, and transferring services for Aboriginal people from the federal government to the provinces.

The White Paper provoked a storm of protest by Aboriginal people. In their consultations with the government following the Hawthorn Report, members of First Nations had said they wanted the *Indian Act* to be made less discriminatory, and they wanted the federal government to deal with land claims, treaty rights, **self-government**, education, and health care. The White Paper addressed none of these issues; instead, it proposed assimilating Aboriginal people into non-Aboriginal society. Aboriginal people wanted none of that. They had been **sovereign** (independent, **self-governing**) peoples before Europeans arrived in Canada, and they wanted the Canadian government to honour the commitments it had made in treaties and other forms of negotiation with First Nations. Harold Cardinal, then President of the Indian Association of Canada, wrote,

> We do not want the *Indian Act* retained because it is a good piece of legislation. It isn't. It is discriminatory from start to finish. . . . [B]ut we would rather continue to live in bondage under the inequitable *Indian Act* than surrender our sacred rights. Any time the government wants to honour its obligations to us we are more than ready to help devise new Indian legislation.[6]

The *Indian Act* continues to dominate the day-to-day lives of Aboriginal people from birth (determining "status") to death (wills and inheritance). Its most blatantly discriminatory aspects were removed by amendments in 1951 and 1985, but it still imposes an often alien form of government on First Nations, and gives the federal government ultimate control over First Nations governance and most financial aspects of Aboriginal people's lives. Nor is its discriminatory treatment of Aboriginal people simply a relic of the past. Until 2008, Aboriginal people were prevented from using the *Canadian Human Rights Act* to challenge the *Indian Act* or any decision or policy made under it. The Minister of Aboriginal Affairs and Northern Development still has wide-ranging financial and political powers over Aboriginal people's lives. The Minister may appoint executors of an Aboriginal person's will, declare a will void, administer the property of a mentally incompetent Aboriginal person, appoint guardians of children, make regulations concerning how band council meetings are to be run, and revoke a First Nation's right to administer and manage its lands. Government officials ordinarily have no such powers over the lives of non-Aboriginal people or provincial or municipal governments.

Residential Schools

Converting Aboriginal people to Christianity and teaching them European language and manners were central to the government's policy to wipe out "Indianness" and make Aboriginal people like other Canadians (though with fewer rights). Aboriginal children were sent to church-run residential schools, often far from their families, where they were forbidden to speak their first languages or to practise their own traditions. Physical, emotional, and sexual abuse were common. So was death. In 1909, an official for the Department of Indian Affairs reported that, between 1894 and 1908 in western Canada, thirty to sixty per cent of Aboriginal children had died within five years of entry to a residential school. Moreover, the students' education was substandard. Many teachers were unqualified, the children did not learn either English or French well, and they were not taught skills that would help them function in non-Aboriginal society. However, the residential schools were successful in making the children forget their first languages and customs, and feel ashamed of their Aboriginal heritage. Unable to find work in non-Aboriginal society, they would return to their communities, only to find they had lost the skills to function there too.

Residential schools have had a lasting impact on Aboriginal people, both individually and collectively. Many people who attended residential schools still suffer the effects of long term abuse and having been taught to be ashamed of their cultures. Much traditional knowledge and many Aboriginal languages are in danger of being lost because the residential schools deliberately disrupted their transmission from generation to generation. Aboriginal communities' poverty has worsened, and Aboriginal people have much higher drop-out, unemployment, crime, and suicide rates, poorer health, and lower life expectancies than non-Aboriginal people.

Near the end of the twentieth century, churches and the federal government began to make amends for their parts in the abuse of students in residential schools. In 1986 and again in 1998, the United Church apologized for its role in the abuse of students in the residential school system. Apologies came from the Anglican Church in 1993 and the Presbyterian Church in 1994. The Catholic Church has not apologized officially, but in 2009 Pope Benedict XVI expressed his "sorrow" for the abuses at Catholic-run schools. In 1998 the Chrétien government issued a Statement of Reconciliation apologizing for abuses at the residential schools, and set up an Aboriginal Healing Foundation. In 2008, Prime Minister Harper apologized on behalf of the Canadian government for its assimilation and residential schools policies. "Today, we recognize that this policy of assimilation was wrong, has caused great harm, and has no place in our country. The government now recognizes that the consequences of the Indian residential schools policy were profoundly negative and that this policy has had a lasting and damaging impact on aboriginal culture, heritage, and language," Harper said.[7]

Philosophical and Legal Issues

In this section I will discuss only two of the philosophical issues involving Aboriginal peoples in Canada, Aboriginal title in the land (property) and the status of treaties. I can only sketch the legal situation since the **constitution** came into effect in 1982 and some other philosophical issues regarding Aboriginal peoples.

Aboriginal Title in the Land

Some philosophers have asked whether Aboriginal people owned the land in North America before Europeans arrived. John Locke, the most influential writer on property in the English language, argued that when people "mix their labour" with a previously unowned thing, they own it. "[I]n the beginning, all the world was America," he wrote, by which he meant both that the world was originally unowned, and that Aboriginal people did not own the land in America because they had not mixed their labour with it. But Locke was wrong about America. By European standards, most Aboriginal peoples had "mixed their labour" with the land in ways that demonstrated ownership—for example, by farming and building towns or cities. However, that did not stop Europeans from taking their land.

Are European standards of ownership appropriate for Aboriginal people, though? Aboriginal conceptions of property differ significantly from European ones. First, Aboriginal people did not think land was the sort of thing that could be owned, any more than parents or children could be owned. They did have conceptions of property, but these conceptions differed from European ones. Property in Aboriginal societies is based on use, not ownership. Aboriginal conceptions of property follow from their religious belief that the creator exists in everything in the world—all of creation is holy, and holy things must be respected and protected. Even when Aboriginal people destroy or kill something, for example by burning wood or eating animals, they are required to treat the thing with respect and to thank it for allowing itself to be used. In Aboriginal societies, things could be possessed but not owned. An object "belonged" to an individual only when it was being used; when it was not in use, others in the community had the right to use it. (Europeans have similar views about some forms of property. When a vehicle legally occupies a public parking space, no other vehicle can displace it; the space belongs to the person who parked the vehicle. But when that vehicle leaves, the driver no longer has any claim on the parking space—it is open to the next driver who wishes to use the space.) Notice too that the Aboriginal conception of property was communal rather than individual. That is, inasmuch as anything was owned, it was owned by—it was for the use of—the community.

By contrast, the Christian God is entirely separate from his creation, and this influenced European conception of property. Christians believe some objects are holy, but these are a tiny fraction of all the objects in the world. Non-holy objects can be owned, and owners can do almost anything with their property. Someone who owns a horse, for example, can hitch it to a plow, paint it green, or sell it for dog food, as they wish. Someone who owns land can farm it, mine it, or burn it. The only restriction is that they may not harm other people.

When people with such radically different worldviews interact, conflict is inevitable. Now compound those different understandings with mixed or worse motives. Add the British views that North America was unowned and that Aboriginal peoples were inherently inferior and required the Crown's "protection." The result was completely incompatible interpretations of the same events. For example, Europeans arrived bearing beads and blankets, which Aboriginal people accepted. "They've brought us hostess gifts," Aboriginal people thought. "We just bought Upper Canada," Europeans thought. (Was Europeans' interpretation justified, though, even from their own perspective? Suppose I drop in on you unexpectedly, bearing a bottle of wine. You thank me for the wine, invite me in, and feed me dinner. Can I reasonably believe that, by accepting my wine, you just gave me your house?) These different understandings of the same events continue to affect relations between Aboriginal peoples and federal and provincial governments.

Treaties

Long before Europeans arrived, Aboriginal peoples made treaties with each other. Treaties established or normalized relations between First Nations, settled disputes, determined territorial boundaries, and ended wars. But they did not grant or transfer land, because land could not be owned, any more than family members could be owned.

Europeans used treaties for pretty much the same reasons—to settle disputes, end wars, and determine territorial boundaries. But Europeans thought all natural and human-made things could be owned, and that owners could do more or less what they wanted to their property. Thus treaties could transfer land from one country to another, and they could make people on the transferred land subjects of the country that now owned the land. Conquerors could kick people off the land or kill them, even if the people had not participated in the war. (This was a practical matter, not a moral one.) Victors often imposed punitive and one-sided treaties on their defeated opponents.

Aboriginal peoples and the Canadian government have very different interpretations of the treaties between them. Aboriginal peoples view treaties between the Crown and themselves as nation-to-nation agreements between sovereign **states**. The Canadian government, on the other hand, views treaties as agreements between a government and its subjects, which it can change on its own, without consultation. This definition is non-standard—so much so that it gets a separate entry in at least one dictionary. The sixth definition of "treaty" in the *Collins English Dictionary* is "(in Canada) any of the formal agreements between Indian bands and the federal government by which the Indians surrender their land rights in return for various forms of aid."[8] One of the other meanings of "treaty" is "an agreement or contract," but this definition is not usually used when one of the parties is a government. When a government makes an agreement for a service the agreement is called a contract, not a treaty. This is how the Canadian government interprets treaties between itself and Aboriginal peoples, though—as contracts. However, this definition applies only to treaties between the Crown and Aboriginal peoples, not to any other treaties made by the Canadian government. For instance, according to the Treaty Section of the Department of Foreign Affairs, Canada follows the 1969 Vienna Convention on the Law of Treaties, which defines a treaty as "an international agreement concluded between States in written form and governed by international law."[9] The Vienna Convention definition is consistent with Aboriginal peoples' interpretation of Crown–Aboriginal treaties, not the Canadian government's. Acts that First Nations view as violating a nation-to-nation agreement are viewed by the Canadian government as the legitimate exercise of its power.

Large parts of Canada are not covered by any treaty. The Aboriginal peoples in Newfoundland and Labrador, most of Quebec, Nunavut, British Columbia, Yukon, and a small part of the Northwest Territories did not make treaties with either European or Canadian governments. In the Maritime provinces, Aboriginal peoples and the Crown made Peace and Friendship treaties that did not grant or surrender land. Nevertheless, the government of Canada's position is that Aboriginal peoples' title to land was either surrendered to or **extinguished** (nullified) by the Crown, regardless of the existence of treaties.

Legal Rights

In 1973 the Supreme Court recognized for the first time that aboriginal title to land existed, at least in principle.[10] Aboriginal rights were given a firmer foundation in the *Constitution Act, 1982*. In Part I of the *Act*, the *Canadian Charter of Rights and Freedoms*, section 25 states that Aboriginal rights and freedoms are not affected by the *Charter*, and in particular that the *Charter* does not override any rights or freedoms arising from the *Royal Proclamation of 1763* or land claims agreements made before the *Charter* came into effect. Section 35, Part II of the *Constitution Act, 1982*, recognizes the "existing aboriginal and treaty rights of the aboriginal peoples of Canada." The Supreme Court has affirmed Aboriginal title in several post-Constitution decisions and has argued that Aboriginal rights are *sui generis* (one of a kind, unique). The Court characterizes the relationship between the Crown and Aboriginal peoples as a **fiduciary relationship**. (In a fiduciary relationship one party—here, the Crown—is in a position of trust with respect to the other—here, Aboriginal peoples—and is required to use its rights and powers for the benefit of the other.) In interpreting the Crown's responsibilities, the Court wrote, "a generous and liberal interpretation should . . . be given in favour of aboriginal peoples. Any [constitutional] ambiguity . . . must be resolved in favour of aboriginal peoples."[11] In another decision, the Court stated that "the honour of the Crown is at stake in dealings with aboriginal peoples. The special trust relationship and the responsibility of the government vis-a-vis aboriginals must be the first consideration in determining whether the [infringing] legislation or action in question can be justified."[12] The Court has also stated that the fiduciary relationship between the Crown and Aboriginal peoples differs from standard fiduciary relationships in which the fiduciary's sole duty is to the party with whom it has a relationship of trust. In some cases, the Crown must balance Aboriginal peoples' interests against other interests in Canada.

Since 1982, there have been over a dozen Supreme Court cases dealing with Aboriginal and treaty rights and jurisdictional issues. The Supreme Court has ruled that the "existing aboriginal and treaty rights of the aboriginal peoples of Canada" in section 35 includes only Aboriginal practices that pre-dated European contact. According to the Court, section 35 recognizes that Aboriginal societies existed prior to European contact, and thus "the test for identifying the aboriginal rights recognized and affirmed by s. 35(1) must be directed at identifying the crucial elements of those pre-existing distinctive societies. It must, in other words, aim at identifying the practices, traditions and customs central to the aboriginal societies that existed in North America prior to contact with the Europeans."[13] Hence hunting and fishing for Aboriginal peoples' families or bands' own use is permitted and cannot be regulated by federal or provincial codes, but selling game or fish to non-Aboriginals is not protected, nor is trapping (which began only to feed the European desire for furs) or other modern activities like gambling or setting up modern enterprises. John Borrows, one of the authors in this chapter, calls these "frozen rights" (see Suggested Readings and Websites); he says the Supreme Court has "frozen" Aboriginal peoples in time, and does not protect modern practices. Supporters of the Court's decision argue that the Supreme Court has not forbidden modernization—it has just said that modernizing activities are not outside the scope of Canadian law and the *Charter*, but rather are subject to the same rules as non-Aboriginal activities.

The Court has also strengthened Aboriginal peoples' claims to title in land. Evidence that an area was under exclusive regular occupation and use by a First Nation—that is, that it was used solely by the particular First Nation and was not shared or contested by another First Nation—can establish title to the land. In a landmark 1997 decision, *Delgamuukw v. B.C.*,[14] the Court ruled that oral histories could be introduced as evidence of occupation and use of land. This is significant because Aboriginal peoples did not have written documents; rather, they relied on ceremonial objects, oral history, and interpretations. (See Borrows' discussion of the Gus Wen Tah, the two-row wampum belt, in this chapter.) In

Delgamuukw, the Court also said section 35 places the Crown "under a moral, if not a legal, duty to enter into and conduct . . . negotiations [with Aboriginal peoples] in good faith."[15]

Many First Nations have argued for some form of self-government, of control of their own affairs beyond the reach of the Crown and the *Indian Act*. While the Crown often agrees in principle with the idea of self-government, there is a wide gulf between what Aboriginal peoples want and what the Crown is prepared to offer. Roughly, there are three levels of government in Canada: municipalities (cities, towns, or districts), provinces, and the federal government. The Crown has mostly offered municipal-like powers to First Nations—control over things like water and sewage, police and fire services, childcare, social services, and public housing. First Nations, on the other hand, want province-like or nation-like powers, including control over education, policing, courts, and who counts as "Aboriginal." These matters remain to be settled. The one significant exception is the territory of Nunavut, which has province-like power over education, policing, and courts, but not over minerals or natural resources such as oil.

Many Aboriginal people, like many Quebecois and some political philosophers, support **asymmetrical federalism** (in Canada, giving some provinces—in particular, Quebec—powers that other provinces do not have, such as increased control over immigration). For example, they argue that Aboriginal peoples ought to have greater control over education and police, normally provincial powers, as well as criminal law and penalties and Indian status, which are federal powers. Opponents of asymmetrical federalism argue that rules and powers ought to be the same for all provinces or other sub-units, and that giving different powers to some provinces means that all citizens in Canada are not equal.

Other Philosophical Issues

There are significant issues concerning cultural rights and membership with both First Nations and Quebec in Canada. What does the term "nation" mean? Generally nations are defined by language, culture, and institutions, but specifying the concept more than that is difficult. There are **nation-states**, which are political societies in which most of the citizens share a common language, culture, and institutions. However, all nations are not states (governments with supreme power); there are many multi-nation states such as the United Kingdom (consisting of England, Scotland, Wales, and Northern Ireland), Spain (Spanish, Catalan, Galician, Basque, and Aranese peoples), and of course Canada (English-speaking Canada, Quebec, and First Nations). The term "First Nations" is an explicit assertion of nationhood—a claim that, because Aboriginal peoples were self-governing nations before European contact, they ought to have more rights over their own affairs. There are also significant discussions about the meaning and importance of cultural membership. Empirical evidence indicates that a sense of belonging is necessary for well-being, and that people who lack a firm sense of belonging have multiple social problems, including poverty, unemployment, poorer health, shorter lifespans, and high rates of imprisonment. There are also significant issues concerning what should be done about past wrongs to Aboriginal peoples. Many Aboriginal and non-Aboriginal Canadians were happy when Prime Minister Harper apologized for the residential schools' policy of assimilation. Former Prime Minister Trudeau thought apologies for past wrongs were a serious mistake, however; he said "we can only be just in our time." Others argue that apologies are not enough, and that reparations are due to Aboriginal people, in the form of money, institutions such as the Aboriginal Healing Foundation, policies to promote Aboriginal programs or businesses, and so on.

The Readings

In the first reading, James Tully argues against the colonial relationship that the Canadian government imposes on Aboriginal peoples. He argues that a just relationship between Aboriginal and non-Aboriginal peoples must rest on five principles: mutual recognition (each side recognizing the other as equal and self-governing), intercultural negotiation (a form of dialogue aimed at mutual understanding and unforced agreements for cooperation), mutual respect (including public respect for the other's cultures), sharing (which involves acknowledging the generosity of Aboriginal peoples in helping Europeans survive when they first landed in North America, and the Canadian government sharing legal and economic powers), and mutual responsibility (seeing ourselves as caretakers of the land and our cultures who must preserve them for future generations).

John Borrows, an Aboriginal law professor, proposes a thought experiment: imagine what Canada would be like if Aboriginal people controlled Canadian affairs, from the Prime Minister and Supreme Court to CEOs, union leaders, doctors, scientists, activists, and so on. Even if Aboriginal people participated in institutions such as government, universities, and businesses proportionately to their representation in the population, Borrows says, their influence in Canada would be much greater than it is today. Borrows has several points in this paper: to get non-Aboriginal Canadians to think about what it might be like to be peripheral rather than central, what meaningful participation by Aboriginal people in Canada would look like, and to show that Aboriginal cultures are not static or "frozen"—that Aboriginal people already blend traditional and modern, and Aboriginal and non-Aboriginal, ideas and ways of being in their lives.

Monique Deveaux examines an issue that is a theme in Part I: the possible clash between cultural rights and women's rights to equality, and between group rights and liberal individual rights. She examines three possible approaches to reconciling "individual sex equality rights and cultural group rights": the view that traditional values are most important and are best protected by giving group rights precedence over individual equality rights; the view that both group rights and individual equality rights are important, but that cultural minorities should work out for themselves how to protect individual equality rights; and the view that group rights for cultural minorities must be subject to individual equality protections such as the *Charter* rights. Deveaux argues that only the third view adequately protects women's rights.

Why Do All the Readings Support Aboriginal Rights?

The quick answer to this question is that the *Charter* refers explicitly to Aboriginal rights, so some form of differential rights for Aboriginal peoples is the law of the land. Between the 1969 White Paper and the repatriation of the *Charter* in 1982, Aboriginal peoples changed even the Trudeau government's ideas about assimilating them into European-Canadian culture. (I say "even" because Pierre Trudeau was the best-known opponent of special status for anyone in Canada. See chapter 2, Quebec Nationalism, and chapter 3, Multiculturalism.) Any plan to eliminate Aboriginal rights is a complete non-starter in Canada. Aboriginal peoples oppose it virtually unanimously, there is no real desire among European Canadians to make such a change, and it clearly would not stand up to a *Charter* challenge.

The Moral and Political Preferences Indicator

Aboriginal rights do not fit neatly on the conservative-egalitarian spectrum. In general, people who support Aboriginal rights tend to be on the egalitarian end of the spectrum. However, there are significant exceptions. Prime Minister Harper, who is a **neo-conservative** or a **libertarian**, apologized to Aboriginal people on behalf of the Canadian government for the abuses at the residential schools and the failed policy of assimilation—more than any Liberal prime minister had done. On the other hand, former Prime Minister Trudeau, who was an egalitarian centrist, advocated assimilating Aboriginal people in the larger culture in the 1969 White Paper, and firmly refused to apologize for past wrongs to Japanese Canadians, Aboriginal peoples, or any other group. Harper's view fits with his larger view that provinces ought to have more power and the federal government less; it would be consistent for him to see Aboriginal peoples as similar in some respects to provinces or territories. Trudeau's view, on the other hand, was consistent with his staunch opposition to any special status for Quebec or any subgroup, his view that Canadian citizenship must be the same for everyone, and his view that "we can only be just in our time." Perhaps the most that can be said is that conservatives generally favour policies regarding Aboriginal peoples that do not cost (much) money, and generally oppose expensive policies. Egalitarians, on the other hand, are more willing to enact policies that will cost money.

Notes

1. I use "Aboriginal" to refer to First Nations people, the Métis, and the Inuit. "First Nations" is a Canadian term that applies to people defined as **status** and **non-status Indians** in the *Indian Act*; it does not include the Métis or Inuit.
2. Noble David Cook, *Born to Die: Disease and New World Conquest, 1492–1650* (Cambridge: Cambridge University Press, 1998), p. 206.
3. For one example, see Peter d'Errico, "Jeffrey Amherst and the Smallpox Blankets," which contains photocopies of letters between General Amherst and several other officials about distributing smallpox blankets: www.umass.edu/legal/derrico/amherst/lord_jeff.html.
4. "No More Stolen Sisters," Amnesty International Canada (2009), 16, www.amnesty.ca/amnestynews/upload/AMR200122009.pdf.
5. Assembly of First Nations Chief Shawn Atleo, "There is an election on, isn't it time we talked?," CBC News, 13 April 2011, www.cbc.ca/news/canada/story/2011/04/13/cv-election-atleo-oped.html.
6. Harold Cardinal, *The Unjust Society: The Tragedy of Canada's Indians* (Edmonton: MG Hurtig, 1969), p. 140.
7. "PM cites 'sad chapter' in apology for residential schools," CBC News, 11 June 2008, www.cbc.ca/news/canada/story/2008/06/11/aboriginal-apology.html.
8. *Collins English Dictionary—Complete & Unabridged*, 10th Edition. HarperCollins Publishers. http://dictionary.reference.com/browse/treaty.
9. Canada Treaty Information, www.treaty-accord.gc.ca/procedure.asp.
10. *Calder et al. v. Attorney-General of British Columbia*, [1973] S.C.R. 313.
11. *R. v. Van der Peet*, [1996] 2 S.C.R. 507, p. 3.
12. Cited in Mary C. Hurley, "The Crown's Fiduciary Relationship with Aboriginal Peoples," Parliamentary Research Branch of the Library of Parliament (2000; revised 2002), p. 3.

13. *Van der Peet*, para. 44.
14. [1997] 3 S.C.R. 1010.
15. Hurley, p. 4.

James Tully

A Just Relationship between Aboriginal and Non-Aboriginal Peoples of Canada

[This is a very complex reading. Here are the headings in outline form to help you understand the structure of the argument and know where you are in it.—Editor]

1. Introduction
   a. The Treaty Relationship
   b. Criticism of the Colonial Relationship
      i. The "Stages" View of the Colonial Relationship
      ii. Analysis: The Colonial Relationship in the Twentieth Century
2. Proposing a New Relationship
   a. Mutual Recognition
      i. The Historical Justification for Mutual Recognition
   b. Intercultural Dialogues of Negotiation
   c. Mutual Respect
      i. The Aboriginal Tradition of Respect
      ii. The European Tradition of Respect
      iii. Public Respect for Each Other's Cultures
   d. Sharing
      i. The Historical Ground for Sharing
      ii. A Postcolonial Conception of Sharing
   e. Mutual Responsibility

Conclusion: Aboriginal Self-Government and **Liberal Democracy**

AV = author's view; ~AV = not the author's view

[Introduction]

. . . Aboriginal peoples in Canada . . . are engaged in three . . . types of struggles: a struggle to free themselves from **internal colonization** by the Canadian . . . governments, to govern themselves democratically by their own laws and ways on their territories, and to establish a just relationship between Aboriginal and non-Aboriginal peoples of Canada. . . . Moreover, they have a long history of struggle stretching back to when Europeans arrived, reduced their population by 90 per cent, took their territories, and subjected them to colonial rule. This history provides a profound narrative in terms of which they understand their task today and imagine a future when they will be free and equal to the peoples who have dominated them for half a millennium.

. . . Of the three types of struggle Aboriginal peoples are engaged in—struggles for **decolonization**, **self-rule**, and a just relationship—I wish to take up only the third. . . . I will describe two major types of relationship between Aboriginal peoples and (non-Aboriginal) Canadians[1] over the last four centuries and argue that one of these should be the prototype for a new and just relationship between them. . . .

A note of caution. Any generalization about the relations between Aboriginal peoples and Canadians is fraught with danger. There are several hundred Aboriginal peoples or nations on the northern half of North America whose histories and cultures over the last ten thousand years are diverse. The length of time and the manner in which they have had to interact with Canadians are also varied. The visions of different Aboriginal peoples of a just relationship with Canadians are also diverse and in a continuous process of reinterpretation. My sketch of two major types of relationship and of arguments for one of them is not comprehensive or definitive. It constitutes an opening and fallible attempt to articulate an *intermediate* description that is not too dissimilar to the ways many Aboriginal people express their relationship with Canadians, on the one hand, yet that is understandable to non-Aboriginal readers on the other. . . .

[The Treaty Relationship]

The relationships between Aboriginal peoples and Canadians have varied over the last four centuries from mutually beneficial association to war, dispossession, and extermination; from consensual negotiations between equal nations to the coercive imposition of a structure of domination. Whenever relations have passed from consent to coercion, Aboriginal peoples have refused to submit and have resisted in a number of ways: with tactical compliance in residential schools and prisons, substance abuse and suicide on reserves, open confrontation and battle, and legal and political challenges.

In this complex history of interaction, two main types of relationship have persisted. The first is the treaty relationship. In it, Aboriginal peoples and Canadians recognize each other as equal, coexisting, and self-governing nations and govern their relations with each other by negotiations based on procedures of reciprocity and consent that lead to agreements that are then recorded in treaties or treaty-like accords of various kinds, to which both parties are subject. Treaty-making developed in the early modern period as a way of settling differences and governing trade, military, and land-sharing arrangements by means of discussion and consent, without interfering in the internal government of either society. Treaty relations were surrounded by a sea of strategic relations of pressure, force, and fraud, and the treaty system itself was constantly abused. Nevertheless, from the first recorded treaties in the seventeenth century to the land-base and off land-base agreements of the Metis from 1870 to the present, the Nunavut Agreement with the Inuit of the eastern Arctic in 1993, and treaty negotiations with the Nisga'a nation of the Pacific Northwest today, the treaty relationship has survived and evolved, comprising over five hundred treaties and other treaty-like agreements. For most Aboriginal peoples, including those who live off Aboriginal reserves, it provides the **normative prototype** of the just relationship they aim to achieve by their struggles. Let us set it aside for a moment and turn to the second type of relationship.

[Criticism of the Colonial Relationship]

During the nineteenth century a different relationship was imposed over the Aboriginal peoples without their consent and despite their active resistance. Their status as equal, coexisting, and self-governing nations was denied. Their governments were displaced, and they were forcibly subjected to the Canadian political system by the establishment of a structure of domination administered through a series of Indian acts. This colonial regime has gone through several phases. Aboriginal peoples have been treated as obstacles to Canadian settlement and expansion who could be removed from their territories, relocated on Crown reserves, and governed by the Indian Act; they have been treated as primitive wards incapable of consent whose religions, languages, cultures, and governments could be eliminated and who could be coerced into the superior Canadian ways by their civilized guardians; they have been treated as disappearing races who could be marginalized and left to die out; and they have been treated as burdens on the Crown who could be off-loaded and assimilated to Canadian citizenship by **extinguishing** or **superseding** their **Aboriginal and treaty rights**. More recently, they have been treated as minorities with a degree of legal **autonomy**, **self-government**, and claims to land within the Canadian political system. What has remained constant through these phases is the colonial assumption that Aboriginal peoples are subordinate and subject to the Canadian government, rather than equal, self-governing nations subject to the agreements reached through the treaty system. . . .

The colonial relationship was set in place as the settler population increased and spread across Aboriginal America in the nineteenth century, changing the demographic balance and disrupting Aboriginal ways of subsistence. The end of the British and French wars rendered the military alliances with the First Nations irrelevant. The shift from trade to settled agriculture and manufacture caused the trading treaties to decline, and the new technologies led to the over-exploitation of wildlife, undermining Aboriginal economies and forcing Aboriginal peoples into relations of dependency. These factors and others upset the balance of power that underlay the rough equality of the treaty relationship.

[The "Stages" View of the Colonial Relationship]

~AV The prevailing view of the world of (English and French) Europeans and European-Canadians in the nineteenth century served to legitimate the colonial relationship. This "stages" view ranked cultures and peoples hierarchically in accord with their stage in a purported process of world historical development. Modern European nations were taken to be at the highest and most developed stage, and their institutions and cultures provided the **norm** against which all others could be ranked. As the process of modernization spread around the world from the European centre, the colonies and lower nations would develop into uniform nations like those in Europe. Aboriginal peoples were ranked at the lowest and most primitive stage, in a **state of nature** without governments or territorial rights, and thus beneath, or earlier than, relations of nation-to-nation equality and consent on which the treaty system had mistakenly been founded. Rather, they were taken to be under the **sovereignty** of the superior **imperial** power that discovered them and established effective control. . . . Since Aboriginal people were assumed to be subject to the Crown, the treaties were reinterpreted as domestic contracts to settle them on land the Crown reserved for them, to grant them hunting, gathering and fishing rights under Canadian law—subject to the pleasure of the Crown—and to extinguish whatever **precontact** rights they might have had.

[Analysis: The Colonial Relationship in the Twentieth Century]

AV In the twentieth century, the **Eurocentric** biases of the stages view that legitimated the colonial relationship in the heyday of European **imperialism** have been exposed by scholars in the human sciences as the imperial system has been partially dismantled in practice. Former European colonies have gained their freedom and equality as self-governing nations. In the case of Canada, it was only in 1982 that the last vestiges of British colonial rule were removed by the **patriation of the Constitution** (until then, amendment of the constitution was still subject to Imperial consent). In their many struggles, the **indigenous** peoples of the world are demanding that the process of decolonization be extended to them, and for the same reasons. As a **postcolonial** attitude spreads, Aboriginal peoples are beginning to be seen, not as lower and subordinate, but as contemporary and equal; not to be ranked in Eurocentric stages but to be seen for what they are—as "diverse": that is, as exhibiting cultural similarities and dissimilarities. These monumental changes are beginning to have effects in court cases, constitutional negotiations, international law, the United Nations, and in the attitude and behaviour of citizens who wish to free their society from the disgraceful vestiges of internal colonialism and to recognise Aboriginal peoples as equals.

At the present time, this enlightened trend is confronted by a powerful backlash that seeks to reassert the colonial relationship and justify it by uncritically repeating the discredited assumptions of the stages view and court rulings based on them and by playing on the fears of the consequences of equality. If this dangerous confrontation is to be overcome, two questions need to be answered: "what is the just form of **recognition** of Aboriginal peoples," and "what is the practical form of accommodation of this recognition by the former colonizing society"? I would like to argue now that Aboriginal peoples should be recognized as equal, coexisting, and self-governing nations and accommodated by renewing the treaty relationship.

[Proposing a New Relationship]

From the discussions between Aboriginal and non-Aboriginal people over the last fifteen years, as well as from the extensive research and dialogue carried out under the auspices of the Canadian Royal Commission on Aboriginal Peoples,[2] a relationship that would meet the demands of justice and **utility** on both sides appears to consist of the following five principles: mutual recognition, intercultural negotiation, mutual respect, sharing, and mutual responsibility. Mutual recognition means that Aboriginal peoples and Canadians recognize and relate to each other as equal, coexisting, and self-governing peoples throughout their many relations together. Once mutual recognition is achieved, they engage in intercultural negotiations with the aim of reaching agreements on how they will redress past injustices and associate together in the future. Mutual respect, sharing, and mutual responsibility inform the relations of association and interdependence to which they agree. These principles constitute an Aboriginal-Canadian **charter** that should govern relations between Aboriginal and non-Aboriginal peoples. If they were adhered to, the distrust and confrontation would give way to trust and **civility**.

. . .

[Mutual Recognition]

The first and most difficult question in engaging in a just relationship is for the participants to agree on how they should recognize each other at the outset and relate to each other throughout. The first principle of mutual recognition as equal, coexisting, and self-governing peoples and cultures answers this initial question. It means that Canadians recognize the distinctive presence of First Peoples in Canadian life and, at the same time, that Aboriginal people recognize that non-Aboriginal people are also of this land by birth and adoption, with histories, institutions, rights, and enduring interests having their equal legitimacy. This form of mutual recognition replaces the unilateral recognition of the colonial relationship, where Canadians recognized themselves as self-governing and Aboriginal peoples as subject to Canadian governments as either a persisting or **extinguishable** minority.

Mutual recognition consists of two steps: the acceptance of this form of recognition by both peoples, and its public affirmation in the basic institutions and symbols of Canada. When people enter into a relationship, they always recognize each other under some description. Recognition is usually habitual and unreflective, part of one's customary cultural understanding of, and attitude towards, self and others. The taken-for-granted form of recognition sets the **horizon** within which one envisions and relates to oneself and others. Up to the 1960s the stages view provided the unquestioned horizon of recognition for many Canadians, and it was **inscribed** in the institutions of Canadian society. Since then, it has been called into question and criticized, and the movement to a mutually acceptable form of recognition initiated through public discussions, court challenges, curriculum reform, constitutional negotiations, and film-making.

The transformation in the way Canadians and Aboriginal peoples recognize and relate to one another is difficult because it involves freeing oneself, and each other, from deep-seated prejudices and habits of thought and behaviour inherited from the imperial past. However, the change can be put in its proper perspective if placed in the wider context of analogous changes in self-understanding that Canadians are undergoing as they free themselves from captivity to other **inegalitarian** relations of the imperial age. Over the last sixty years Canadians have learned to recognize themselves, not as **colonials** subordinate to the British people, but as members of a self-governing **confederation**, different but equal to the peoples of the world. This new form of postcolonial recognition has been publicly affirmed by a Canadian flag and the patriation of the Constitution. European Canadians have recently learned to recognize non-European Canadians, not as inferiors unfit for the rights of citizenship, but as citizens equal to themselves with cultures worthy of preservation and to affirm this recognition in the Constitution.

. . .

[The Historical Justification for Mutual Recognition]

What, then, are the justifications for this form of mutual recognition? Why should Aboriginal and non-Aboriginal peoples accept and affirm this self-description as equal, coexisting, and self-governing peoples as the basis of their acting together? The form of recognition I recommend can be justified . . . by the arguments that justify the recognition of any self-governing nation: the basic principles of political theory, international law, the **common law** of the Commonwealth and former Commonwealth countries, and the conventions of the Canadian and American constitutions.

Aboriginal people were the first inhabitants of this continent. As the result of long use and occupation they have continuing rights to the land, unless they are properly **relinquished**. Further, they have the status of independent, self-governing nations, in virtue of prior sovereignty, grounded in the practice of governing themselves by their own laws and ways and of entering into international relations with other Aboriginal nations and with Europeans when they arrived. Their status as self-governing nations was acknowledged in many early relations, and it was not surrendered by the establishment of settler governments or by treaties. . . .

When Europeans arrived, the Aboriginal peoples they encountered were independent, self-governing nations equal in status to European nations. Their status as self-governing nations rested on exactly the same criteria in international law, then and now, as the status of European nations: the proven ability to govern themselves on a territory over time and to enter into international relations with other nations. These are the universal criteria of the inherent right of self-government on which nationhood rests in the modern world. The Aboriginal peoples had every right to recognize the Europeans as immigrants subject to their laws (perhaps granting them some sort of minority status), as nations did then and do now. The only valid way, therefore, in which Canada and the United States could acquire sovereignty in North America, was by gaining the consent of the sovereign nations that were already here, as would be the case anywhere else in the world. The Aboriginal peoples agreed to recognize the settlers as coexisting, self-governing nations equal in status to themselves, with the right to acquire land from them over which the settler governments could then exercise **jurisdiction** and sovereignty by means of nation-to-nation treaties based on mutual agreement. This is the basis of the treaty relationship.

. . .

Therefore, the international legitimacy of Canada as a self-governing **federation** actually rests on its recognition by the Aboriginal peoples, not the other way round. Their consent to recognize Canada is, in turn, conditional, first, on Canada's acknowledgement of the Aboriginal peoples' equal yet prior status as nations, and, second, on Canada conducting relations with the First Nations by consent gained through the treaty system. There is no other valid justification of Canada as a sovereign federation and no way of avoiding this one. The other purported justifications reduce to might makes right, which is no justification at all; to **specious misrecognitions** of the status of the Aboriginal peoples at the time of contact, such as the imperial fiction of a state of nature; or to **begging the question** by presupposing the sovereignty of the Crown, as in the colonial relationship.

If Canadian governments fail to recognize the status of the Aboriginal peoples as equal yet prior nations, then they violate the inherent right of self-government, [which is] the ground on which the legitimacy of the global system of nations rests. Canada would then be an illegitimate state, founded on **usurpation**. . . .

[Intercultural Dialogues of Negotiation]

Once the way Aboriginal and non-Aboriginal peoples should recognize each other has been established, the next question will be how should they work out their relations together. The answer is through dialogues of negotiation in which they meet as equals.

Dialogue is the form of human relationship in which mutual understanding and agreement can be reached and, hence, consent can replace coercion and confrontation. Between Aboriginal and non-Aboriginal people, it is an intercultural dialogue in which the partners aim to reach mutual understanding and uncoerced agreements by contextually appropriate forms of negotiation and reciprocal questioning on how they should cooperate and review their relations of cooperation over time. Specific types of relations are agreed to, written down as treaties, put into practice, and reviewed and renewed. It is not a once-and-for-all agreement, as in **social contract theories**, nor an accord frozen in a constitutional document—it is a conversation between the members of Aboriginal and non-Aboriginal cultures in all walks of life over the time they live together and share this land.

An intercultural dialogue is different from a dialogue within Aboriginal or non-Aboriginal cultures. Here the participants discuss and act in the customary practices of their culture. They acquire the abilities to think and act in these customary ways, and to reflect on and revise them, by growing up in their cultures. . . .

When Aboriginal and non-Aboriginal partners engage in a dialogue to reach agreement on something or other, they unavoidably bring their cultural understandings with them, yet they enter a space where their cultures overlap—a middle ground. The dialogue is therefore intercultural, and more difficult for that reason. All sorts of misunderstandings arise just because the partners act implicitly in accordance with their different cultural understandings and expectations. There is a temptation for the more powerful to overcome these difficulties by forcing their cultural ways of speaking and acting on the other and to justify this by their presumed superiority. This was the role of the stages view discussed earlier.

The new relationship has no place for the injustice of non-Aboriginal people speaking for Aboriginal people, either in the **imperial** monologue of command and obedience or in the more subtle injustice of permitting Aboriginal people to speak, but only in the languages, traditions, and institutions of the dominant society. Justice demands a democratic dialogue in which partners listen to and speak with, rather than for, each other. Each speak in their own languages and customary ways, on equal footing, in order to reach fair agreements. This principle of self-identification, of listening to the voices of others in their own terms and traditions, is now widely recognized as the first step in a just dialogue.

This seems like an impossible task only because of another false assumption of the imperial age: that cultures are independent, closed, and internally homogeneous. As we have learned over the last sixty years, cultures are interdependent, overlapping, and internally complex. Cultures exist in dynamic processes of interaction, negotiation, internal challenge, and reinterpretation and transformation. As a result, humans are always members to varying degrees of more than one culture. They experience misunderstandings and differences within their first cultures—such as between genders, generations, and classes—that are not completely different in kind from misunderstandings and differences across cultures. Cultural understanding and identity is thus enormously more complex, open-textured, interactive, and dynamic than the old vision of closed and homogeneous cultures presupposed.

. . .

[Mutual Respect]

Once Aboriginal and non-Aboriginal peoples recognize each other as equals, it is necessary that they go on to show respect for each other—for their languages, cultures, laws, and governments—in their dialogue and in their conduct together if their relations are to be harmonious.

[The Aboriginal Tradition of Respect]

Respect has a somewhat different significance in Aboriginal and non-Aboriginal cultures. In many Aboriginal groups, particularly those adhering to traditional ways, great respect is shown to an elder who has lived long and acquired wisdom. Here respect is accorded in virtue of the specific worthiness of the individual person. This kind of respect relative to specific worth is common in many Aboriginal relations. However, there is another sense of respect in which it is bestowed on all members of the circle of life just in virtue of their *being* members of the circle of life: to animals, plants, waters, spirits, as well as to human beings. Failure to show respect to humans or other-than humans means violating spiritual law and is likely to bring retribution in some form or other.

[The European Tradition of Respect]

Respect is a valued aspect of relationships in non-Aboriginal cultures as well. Respect is often thought to be earned by personal effort and is therefore withheld from someone who fails to meet society's standards of behaviour. Demonstration of respect can also be demanded by persons and institutions of authority. However, there is another sense of respect that is similar to the circle of life sense in Aboriginal culture. Here, human beings are said to **warrant** a certain respect just in virtue of being human, of being of equal dignity and of being **ends rather than means**. This general sense of respect is often extended beyond the human species to all living things, to god's creatures, and to nature.

[Public Respect for Each Other's Cultures]

There is also a kind of mutual cultural respect that is akin to the more general, circle-of-life sense of respect in both Aboriginal and non-Aboriginal ethics. This kind of respect needs to be cultivated if mutual recognition of the two partners is to be effective and their relations harmonious. It is a public attitude of mutual respect for each other's cultures that undergirds individual self-respect, and so the ability to act freely and responsibly in public and private life. One can say that the well-being of members of both cultures is dependent on each other's attitude of cultural respect.

If a public attitude of mutual cultural disrespect prevails, as with the colonial relationship, then cultural difference is seen as a deficiency or disability. The child who enters an exclusively English- or French-language school speaking only Cree is treated as linguistically deficient. The industrial worker who goes hunting to help provide food for his extended family is treated as a delinquent worker. The teacher and boss see the attachment of the pupil and worker to their cultural differences as a sign of disrespect towards their culture and authority. Each thinks the other a bigot, intolerance and racism escalate, commands and the giving of orders replace dialogue. The sense of the pupil's and worker's self-worth is undercut, the strength of their conviction in learning and working dissipates, and self-abuse and dependency follow. This result is then pointed to by the teacher and boss to warrant and reinforce their initial disrespectful attitude, thereby closing the vicious circle. Of course, the other members of Aboriginal cultures can and do seek to shore up the self-confidence of the pupil and worker by affirming the respectability of their language and hunting. But because non-Aboriginal Canadians outnumber them to such an extent, their public attitude of cultural disrespect corrodes their cultural self-assurance as a whole.

Therefore, a public attitude of mutual cultural respect needs to accompany the mutual recognition and public acknowledgement of the equality of Aboriginal and non-Aboriginal peoples and governments. This attitude includes respect on both sides, in virtue of the membership of all Canadians in the circle of life. The justification for this attitude is partly economic self-interest, the realization that it will provide the social basis for lives of individual initiative and economic self-sufficiency. There is also a dimension of moral consistency in extending to Aboriginal people the same kind of culture respect that European Canadians have enjoyed in their own case and that has always been the unacknowledged spring of their self-respect and initiative.

. . .

[Sharing]

The relations of interdependency between Aboriginal and non-Aboriginal peoples are also characterized by the principle of sharing. For relationships between the partners to evolve and develop, they must involve an element of sharing, the giving and receiving of benefits. Although sharing sustains all relations, I want to discuss its application to economic, political, and legal relations, since these are the most important and the most contested.

[The Historical Ground for Sharing]

The practice of sharing is at the centre of many Aboriginal cultures. The harmony and balance among all living things is sustained by a chain of **benevolence** and gratitude. . . .

Canada is founded on an act of sharing that is almost unimaginable in its generosity. The Aboriginal peoples shared their food, hunting, and agricultural techniques, practical knowledge, trade routes, and geographic knowledge with the needy newcomers. Without this sharing the first immigrants would have been unable to survive. As we have seen, the Aboriginal peoples formalized the relation of sharing in the early treaties in the following form: they agreed to share this land with the newcomers on the agreement that the newcomers would neither attempt to govern them nor use their land without their consent. The treaties involved other exchanges as well, such as trade, military, educational, and medical benefits, and political and legal interrelations, but the sharing of land and trade on this understanding was at the heart of the relationship.

. . .

~AV When the colonial system was erected in the nineteenth century, government was imposed and land taken without Aboriginal consent. The original sharing of their goods and knowledge, the gift of the land, and their contribution to the trade and settlement economy were eliminated from most history books and Canada's collective memory. . . . Aboriginal people were said to waste and squander their goods and to have contributed little if anything to Canada's growth. If they remained faithful to their ethic of sharing, this was taken as proof of their backwardness and the justification for policies of forced removal and assimilation.

. . .

[A Postcolonial Conception of Sharing]

AV The great question now is, how can sharing be built into a new, postcolonial relationship in order to generate mutually beneficial economic interdependence and ecologically benign forms of resource management? The answer is that, first, as in any modern cooperative relation, the partners must recognize and respect the rights of each—their rights of self-government and equality as peoples—and they must acknowledge and manifest mutual cultural respect. Under the heading of sharing, there must be a recognition and public acknowledgement of the presently unacknowledged and suppressed relation of sharing at the foundation of the Canadian confederation and economy, in our histories, narratives, and public institutions. As a long-overdue act of justice and gratitude to initiate the new relationship, Aboriginal peoples should have access to the ancestral lands that were unjustly taken from them. They should be assisted in developing economic self-reliance through new relations of economic cooperation, resource development, and the sharing of knowledge and technologies, just as they once helped non-Aboriginal people.

. . .

The second dimension of sharing is a just means of sharing legal and political powers. Aboriginal nations vary greatly in their ability and desire to govern themselves by their own laws. Some wish to delegate several of their powers to the federal or a provincial government and voluntarily subject themselves to those laws. Others wish to **repatriate** many of their legal and political powers and to govern themselves in accord with their own laws and traditions. Aboriginal peoples living off the reserves require another form of relation. One of the immense advantages of the treaty relationship over any other possible system is that it can handle this range of **interdelegation** of powers in a way that is responsive to local differences.

. . .

At the present time many laws are applied to Aboriginal peoples without their consent, many treaties have been violated, and in some cases, such as that of British Columbia, treaties have never been made. While Aboriginal peoples protest this, very few are in a position to govern themselves immediately. This dilemma is at the centre of the current expensive and destructive impasse. Aboriginal and non-Aboriginal people have a strong interest in establishing a system that is acceptable to both sides, flexible, and dependable.

. . .

[Mutual Responsibility]

The final principle of a just relationship is that the partners act responsibly towards one another and towards the habitat they share. Aboriginal Elders explain that the identity of their people is related to the places they live in; that the Creator has placed them here with the responsibility to care for all the ecologically interrelated forms of life in all their harmonious diversity. This timeless responsibility involves looking back to the wisdom of one's ancestors and forward to the seventh generation in the future. This unshakeable sense of responsibility to the source and network of life is at the core of Aboriginal identity. As noted earlier, it is coupled with a strong sense of self-, or individual, responsibility. . . .

It would be idealistic to hold that this two-fold ethic of responsibility finds perfect expression in the organization and administration of the everyday affairs of Aboriginal peoples. Still, the Elders who emphasize responsibility more than rights to do as one pleases are speaking from an ancient and powerful understanding of the nature of humankind and its place in the larger community of life on this planet. . . .

Non-Aboriginal people of European extraction have their own cultural understanding of responsibility. A high value is placed on individual responsibility, and individual freedom is associated with responsibility in many traditions. The sense of individual responsibility extends out to care for one's family and friends and care for the common good of one's communities, from local associations to the Canadian federation, and to a sense of responsibility for endangered peoples and species around the globe.

. . . There is a dawning awareness of the environment as a living system of interdependency in which humans, as one member among millions, have responsibilities of caretaking for its delicately balanced ecological diversity. In this view, we should be responsible for the caretaking of ecological diversity for the same reason that we should be responsible for cultural diversity, as the very condition of our existence and well-being.

The change in attitude from the earlier, exploitative stance is even deeper than this for many Canadians. It is the sense that the diverse ways of life of Canadian peoples have their history and their being in this encompassing and awe-inspiring ecological diversity. To act irresponsibly is not just short-sighted but a spiritual failure; an act of sacrilege and desecration against the source of being of the peoples we are.

This broader vision of Canada as a harmonious confederation of cultural and ecological diversity and of Canadians as caretakers of this irreplaceable dwelling place of endless beauty can be understood to some extent in the spiritual traditions of non-Aboriginal Canadians. However, there is something distinctively Canadian about this emerging sense of identity, as if Canadians have finally freed themselves from their colonial habit of defining themselves in traditions derived from Europe and have taken responsibility for defining themselves. It is not surprising, therefore, that many have turned to the indigenous Canadian wisdom of Aboriginal Elders for guidance and cooperation in working out an ethic of responsibility appropriate to this new vision of Canada. Mutual responsibility, then, provides the final fibre for weaving a just and inspiring partnership between Aboriginal and non-Aboriginal peoples.

. . .

[Conclusion: Aboriginal Self-Government and Liberal Democracy]

Aboriginal and non-Aboriginal peoples expect a political association to provide the basis for the individual freedom and dignity of its members in both the **public** and **private spheres**. It should enable them to participate freely and with equal dignity in governing their society and to live their private lives in accordance with their own choices and responsibilities. The first good, **civic** participation, cannot be achieved by seeking to assimilate Aboriginal peoples to non-Aboriginal forms of government. This is not only unjust, for the reasons given, it is the cause of the **alienation**, **anomie**, and defiance that come to any free people who are forcibly governed by **alien** laws and ways. Self-government enables Aboriginal peoples, just as it enables non-Aboriginal peoples, to participate in governing their societies in accord with their own laws and cultural understanding of democracy, to overcome alienation, and to regain their dignity as equal and active citizens. This, in turn, generates a strong sense of pride in, and allegiance to, the Canadian confederation as a whole, because it is the protector, rather than the destroyer, of self-government and citizen participation.

. . .

Aboriginal peoples, with their smaller societies, tend to place greater emphasis on direct participation and government by consensus. In many cases, political authority rests on the ability of the person or council to sustain the actual consent of each citizen over time. When ongoing consent is lacking, the people often form sovereign bodies, such as healing circles, to reform defective practices. The inequalities of rule imposed through the Indian Act, such as that of men over women, are being dissolved as the colonial system is dismantled and these democratic forms are revitalized and renovated, in a way analogous to the reform of gender inequalities in non-Aboriginal governments. Although these forms of face-to-face self-government have always been an ideal in Western traditions, non-Aboriginal governments, due to their size and degree of **institutionalization**, place more emphasis on representative government and majority rule, with compulsory obedience even if citizens dissent from the outcomes. And, alas, reform is not as easy in these large forms as in the smaller and more consensual Aboriginal governments.

The second good, individual freedom and responsibility, is equally important. It too is understood in slightly different ways in both cultures. Aboriginal peoples in general have a strong sense of responsibility to their communities, combined with an equally strong commitment not to interfere with but only to provide suggestive role models for the freedom of the individual in taking up these responsibilities in an autonomous way. As a result, there is in general a larger commitment to individual freedom in parenting, friendship, and work than in non-Aboriginal societies, where a greater degree of intervention and conformity are seen to be necessary and valuable.

The protection and enhancement of both civic and individual freedom and responsibility has always been the primary concern of **liberalism**. In recent years **liberal** theorists have asked how these values can be preserved in the more culturally diverse, postcolonial societies of today. They have argued that the social condition of being able to exercise civic and individual freedom in pursuing and revising one's life plans is that people should be members of **viable** cultures that provide the necessary and partly **constitutive** context for individual autonomy and choice. Consequently, viable cultures are now seen as a **primary good** of a liberal society.

. . .

. . . Thus, if a liberal democratic society is to provide the basis for its two most important liberties, civic and personal liberty, it must protect the cultures of its members and engender the public attitude of mutual respect for cultural diversity that self-respect requires.

There are many ways this can be done: by protecting all Canadian cultures from Americanization, by accepting each province's right to govern in accordance with its distinct laws and ways, and by recognizing official language minorities, **multiculturalism**, and the special role of Quebec in protecting its culturally diverse, predominantly French-speaking society. For Aboriginal cultures there is only one just way this can be done: by recognizing their inherent right to govern themselves in accordance with their own cultures and engendering among both Aboriginal and non-Aboriginal people respect for each other's cultures. Consequently, the mutual recognition of Aboriginal and non-Aboriginal peoples as equal, coexisting and self-governing peoples is not only just but also preserves and enhances the values of liberal democracy in a manner appropriate to a culturally diverse and postcolonial age.

Notes

1. I often use the term "Canadian" to stand for "non-Aboriginal Canadians" for reasons of brevity. This is not to suggest that Aboriginal people are not Canadian. In the section on mutual recognition I explain in what sense Aboriginals peoples are members of Aboriginal nations and "Canadians." . . .
2. The Royal Commission on Aboriginal Peoples was established by the federal government in 1991. Its guiding question was "What are the foundations of a fair and honourable relationship between the Aboriginal and non-Aboriginal people of Canada?" (Highlights from the Report of the Royal Commission on Aboriginal Peoples, A Word from Commissioners, www.aadnc-aandc.gc.ca/eng/1100100014597/1100100014637#chp2). The Commission released its five-volume report in 1996. [Editor]

John Borrows

"Landed" Citizenship: Narratives of Aboriginal Political Participation

AV = author's view; ~AV = not the author's view

My grandfather was born in 1901 on the western shores of Georgian Bay, at the Cape Croker Indian reservation. Generations before him were born on the same soil. Our births, lives, and deaths on this site have brought us into citizenship with the land. We participate in its renewal, have responsibility for its continuation, and grieve for its losses. As citizens with this land, we also feel the presence of our ancestors, and strive with them to have the relationships of our polity respected. Our loyalties, allegiance, and affection are related to the land. The water, wind, sun, and stars are part of this **federation**. The fish, birds, plants, and animals also share this union. Our teachings and stories form the constitution [make-up] of this relationship, and direct and nourish the obligations this citizenship requires. The Chippewas of the Nawash have struggled to sustain this citizenship in the face of the diversity and **pluralism** that has become part of the land. This has not been an easy task. Our codes have been disinterred, disregarded, and repressed. What is required to re-inscribe these laws, and once again invoke a citizenship with the land?

[Introduction]

More than thirty years have passed since Harold Cardinal wrote an influential book entitled *The Unjust Society*.[1] His work catalogued the troubling conditions Indians found themselves in during the late 1960s. He described the denial of Indian citizenship, and wrote as a response to the Trudeau government's plan to eliminate Indian rights. His message captured the feelings of Aboriginal people everywhere. He chronicled a disturbing tale of how Indians were marginalized in Canada through bureaucratic neglect, political indifference, and societal ignorance. He labelled Canada's treatment of Indians as "cultural genocide," and in the process gave widespread literary presence to the absence of Indian rights. In convincing tones he outlined thoughtful solutions to overcome threats to our underlying citizenship, organized around the central theme of Indian control of Indian affairs. He called for action to protect special Aboriginal connections with the land. He advocated the strengthening of Indian organizations, the abolition of the Department of Indian Affairs, educational reform, restructured social institutions, broad-based economic development, and the "immediate recognition of all Indian rights for the re-establishment, review and renewal of all existing Indian treaties." Cardinal's ideas resonated throughout Indian country and parallel proposals became the mainstay of Indian political **discourse** for the next three decades. He articulated a revolutionary message in a transformative time.

Fast-forward to the massive five-volume *Report of the Royal Commission on Aboriginal Peoples* released in 1996. Same story: an account of the violation of Aboriginal rights, and a call for their immediate recognition and renewal. The report records the continued excision [surgical removal] of Aboriginal relationships with their lands. It demonstrates that the problems Cardinal profiled stubbornly remain. Despite some notable achievements in the intervening years, such as constitutional recognition and affirmation of Aboriginal rights, it illustrates how **indigenous** citizenship with the land is increasingly tenuous. In their broad outlines, Cardinal and the commission's messages are notable for their similarity. Aboriginal people are suffering, their rights are being abrogated, and the answer to this challenge is Aboriginal control of Aboriginal affairs. Like Cardinal, though more elaborately and expansively, the commission recommended a series of legislative and policy goals such as the strengthening of Aboriginal nations, the abolition of the Department of Indian Affairs, educational reform, restructured social institutions, broad-based economic development, and the immediate recognition of all Aboriginal rights for the reestablishment, review, renewal, and creation of treaties. Same story, same solutions. A revolutionary message in a reactionary time.

Why the same approach? If the message didn't have the desired effect the first time, why repeat it? Does the call for Aboriginal control of Aboriginal affairs stand a greater chance in the spirit of the late 1990s than it did in the late 1960s? While there are hopeful signs on the horizon, there is also cause for concern. Despite the wisdom of the message, so far the reaction to the commission has been as feeble as the response to Cardinal. All the while, Aboriginal citizenship with the land is being slowly diminished. The disenfranchisement of our people (and our spirits) from the land, water, animals, and trees continues at an alarming rate. Do we need a new story, new solutions? We do. We no longer need a revolutionary message in a transformative time; we need a transformative message in a reactionary time.

[The Thought Experiment: Aboriginal Control of Canada]

To preserve and extend our participation with the land, it is time to talk also of Aboriginal control of Canadian affairs. Aboriginal people must work individually and as groups beyond their communities to enlarge and increase their influence over matters that are important to them. We need an Aboriginal prime minister, Supreme Court judge, and numerous indigenous CEOs. We need people with steady employment, good health, and entrepreneurial skill. They should be joined by Indian scientists, doctors, lawyers, and educators; and be coupled with union leaders, social activists, and conservative thinkers. We need these people to incorporate indigenous **ideologies** and perspectives into their actions, including ideas about the **federalism** we should enjoy with the earth. These people could join with compatible existing groups, or they could form new political organizations, research institutions, and corporate enterprises to expand Aboriginal influence. These people should stand beside reserve-based teachers such as Aboriginal elders, chiefs, grandmothers, aunties, hunters, fishers, and medicine people as bearers and transmitters of culture. For too long the burden of cultural transmission has been placed on reserve-based teachers and leaders. While their knowledge will always remain vitally important in the expansion of ideas, other Aboriginal people in different settings within Canada also have to shoulder some of this responsibility. Aboriginal people must transmit and use their culture in matters beyond "Aboriginal" affairs. Aboriginal citizenship must be extended to encompass other people from around the world who have come to live on our land.

After all, this is *our* country. Aboriginal people have a right and a legal obligation as a prior but ongoing indigenous citizenship to participate in its changes. We have lived here for centuries, and will for centuries more. We will continue to influence the land's resource utilization, govern its human relationships, participate in trade, and be involved in all of its relations—as we have done for millennia. Fuller citizenship requires that this be done in concert with other Canadians—as well as on our own, in our own communities. Aboriginal control of Aboriginal affairs is a good message, and it has to be strengthened—but it is also limiting. It is not consistent with holistic notions of citizenship that must include the land, and all the beings upon it. When we speak of Aboriginal control of Aboriginal affairs, it is evident that Canadians feel they do not have much of a stake in that message, except maybe what "they" think "we" take from "them" in the process. Canada's stake in Aboriginal peoples, in the land, has to be raised: at radical, liberal, and conservative levels.

Our world is bigger than the First Nation, reserve, or settlement. Approximately half of the Aboriginal population live outside these boundaries. Certainly our traditional lands and relationships lie outside these boundaries. Even if the reserve is where we live, national and international forces influence even the most "remote" or seemingly local time-honoured practice. In fact, an **autonomous** Aboriginal nation would encounter a geography, history, economics, and politics that requires participation with Canada and the world to secure its objectives. Aboriginal control through Canadian affairs is an important way to influence and participate in our lands. Without this power we are left outside significant decision-making structures that have the potential to destroy our lands. This is a flawed notion of citizenship. Canadians must participate with us, and in the wider view of polity that sustained our relations for thousands of years.

[Extending Aboriginal Citizenship]

If we pursue this notion of citizenship, what will this new narrative sound like? How will its constituent stories be arranged? How does this new narrative relate to the former? What is lost, and what is gained? ~AV The development of another narrative may severely undermine those who have invested their aspirations and energies in the former [narrative], even if the message is complementary. Some have spent a tremendous amount of time and effort developing messages of an exclusive citizenship and measured separatism for Indians, through a form of self-government. AV These real human interests need recognition. But that approach, while appropriate and helpful, is not rich enough to encompass the wide variety of relationships we need to negotiate in order to live with the hybridity, displacement, and positive potential that our widening circles represent. The extension of Aboriginal citizenship into Canadian affairs is a developing reality because of their increasingly complex social, economic, and political relations. Intercultural forces of education, urbanization, politics, and intermarriage each have a significant influence in drawing indigenous people into closer relationship with Canadian society. The impulse behind the call for this refocused narrative is suggested by these changing dynamics in the Indian population. Since 1961 our populations have quadrupled, rates of urban residency have climbed to 50 per cent of the total Aboriginal population, and one in every two Aboriginal people marries a non-Aboriginal person. Moreover, our health has improved, and incomes have increased. While these indicators hide the continuing individual and collective pain of too many Aboriginal people, numerous Aboriginal people frequently interact with Canadians in a very significant way.

I have taught at three of Canada's larger universities in the past seven years, and my experience at each of them indicates that an increasing number of Aboriginal people are graduating from them prepared to contribute at the First Nation, provincial, national, and in some cases the international level. Over 150,000 Aboriginal people now have or are in post-secondary education. That is a significant development, since in 1969 there were fewer than 800 Aboriginal post-secondary graduates. When 150,000 is measured against our overall population of approximately 1 million, it is apparent that Aboriginal citizenship is expanding—and that Aboriginal control of Aboriginal affairs, while necessary, is not enough to reflect the simultaneous cultural participation occurring. I have directly supervised and watched graduate 100 Aboriginal law students, and have spoken to and visited with hundreds more. I have watched them fill jobs as entrepreneurs, managers, lawyers, teachers, politicians, researchers, and public servants. In the wider university setting I have witnessed a similar phenomenon. In May 1997 I watched the graduation of the top medical student at the University of British Columbia (UBC), who was an Ojibway woman. A few months earlier I was an **external reviewer** of the Native Indian Teacher Education program at UBC and discovered that some of the province's most respected educators, and a good number of principals, graduated from this program. UBC also has similar programs in forestry, business, health, engineering, and arts that demonstrate similar success. These deep changes that can be statistically and anecdotally noted show that Aboriginal narratives on citizenship have to be transformed.

Yet, I have also witnessed the struggles some of these same students experience. Racism, cultural alienation, family tragedy, poor academic preparation, insensitive teachers, and unresponsive **curricula** conspire to rob many Aboriginal people of the benefits education can bring. Furthermore, I know that there are many more who could be participating who are not; some out of choice but most do not because of the **colonial** pathologies that continue to resonate within our communities. The backdrop of these and other continued challenges may generate a cool reaction to assertions of Aboriginal control of Canadian affairs. As such, I anticipate that the account I am suggesting will meet with some resistance.

[The Aim Is Not Assimilation]

~AV For example, it may be thought that I am advocating assimilation. AV I am not. Assimilation implies a loss of political control, culture, and difference. Aboriginal control of Canadian affairs has the potential to facilitate the acquisition of political control, the continued development of culture, and respect for difference because it could change contemporary notions of Canadian citizenship. Citizenship under Aboriginal influence may generate a greater attentiveness to land uses and cultural practices that are preferred by many Aboriginal peoples. Canadian notions of citizenship might not only develop to include greater scope for people's involvement in sustenance activities, but these ideas of citizenship might also further reduce the tolerance for land uses which extirpate [wipe out] these pursuits. A recognition of the importance of these objectives could thus shield Aboriginal peoples from assimilation by ensuring sufficient space for the pursuit of preferred Aboriginal activities.

[The Land as Citizen]

Moreover, Canadian citizenship under Aboriginal influence may expand to recognize the land as a party to Confederation in its own right. Many Aboriginal groups have well-developed notions in their philosophies and practices about how to recognize the land as citizen. They may be able to influence other Canadians to consider the adverse impact of their activities on the land itself, as an entity in its own right. Aboriginal values and traditions could help shape these changes and reframe the relationships within our polity. Aboriginal peoples would resist assimilation with such a recognition because their values concerning land could be entrenched in Canada's governing ideas and institutions, and help to reconfigure Canada in an important way.

[Participation Fosters a Living Tradition]

Tradition can be the dead faith of living people, or the living faith of dead people. If indigenous traditions are not regarded as useful in tackling these present concerns, and applying in current circumstances, then these traditions are the dead faith of living people. On the other hand, if our people, institutions, and ideologies are relevant for participation beyond our boundaries, this marks the living faith of our ancestors—the living traditions of dead people. Aboriginal peoples can resist assimilation by applying their traditions to answer the questions they encounter in the multifaceted, **pluralistic** world they now inhabit.

When my great-great-grandfather placed his name and **totemic symbol** on a treaty that surrendered 1.5 million acres in southern Ontario, he did not assent to assimilation. He sought control over his life amidst changing cultural circumstances. He knew that Chippewa-Anishinabe culture could benefit from the promises of non-Aboriginal education, employment, housing, and medicine. These were pledged to us in return for other people participating in citizenship with our land. We have fulfilled our part of the agreement: other people enjoy our land; it is now time for Aboriginal peoples to access promises related to Canadian affairs. This is not to extinguish Aboriginal culture through its interaction with Canada; it is to enrich it by allowing for its development and application to our current needs. There is contemporary worth in indigenous traditions which consider all the constituent parts of the land related. While I regard this knowledge as imperfect and incomplete, it is also insightful and wise. There is much to be gained by applying this knowledge—within Aboriginal communities—and within Canada. Our intellectual, emotional, social, physical, and spiritual insights can simultaneously be compared, contrasted, rejected, embraced, and intermingled with others. In fact, this process has been operative since before the time that Indians first encountered others on their shores.

[Aboriginal Identity and Traditions Are Not Fixed]

-AV Concerns about assimilation may not be the only grounds on which others may object to a narrative of Aboriginal control of Canadian affairs. Participation within Canada may not sound or appear to be "Aboriginal." It may be said that this notion violates sacred treaties and compromises traditional cultural values. AV Yet, it should be asked: what does it mean to be Aboriginal or traditional? Aboriginal practices and traditions are not "frozen." Aboriginal identity is constantly undergoing renegotiation. We are traditional, modern, and **postmodern** people. Our values *and* identities are constructed and reconstructed through local, national, and sometimes international experiences. The meaning of Aboriginal is not confined to some pristine moment prior to the arrival of Europeans in North America. Similarly, the notion of Canadian, or any other cultural identifier, is not fixed. As Edward Said observed about identity and culture:

> No one today is purely *one* thing. Labels like Indian, or woman, or Muslim or American are not more than starting points, which if followed into actual experience for only a moment are quickly left behind. Imperialism consolidated the mixture of cultures and identities on a global scale. But its worst and most paradoxical gift was to allow people to believe they were only, mainly, exclusively, white, or Black, or Western, or Oriental. Just as human beings make their own history, they also make their cultures and ethnic identities. No one can deny the persisting continuities of long traditions, sustained habitations, national languages and cultural geographies, but there seems no reason except fear and prejudice to keep insisting on their separation and distinctiveness, as if that was all human life was about.[2]

As Said implies, the formation of culture and identity is contingent on our interactions with others. This insight makes it difficult to object to the point that an assertion of Aboriginal control of Canadian affairs is not "Aboriginal." Aboriginal values and identity develop in response to their own *and* other cultures' practices, customs, and traditions. As such, "Aboriginality" is extended by Aboriginal control of *both* Canadian and Aboriginal affairs. Since important aspects of Aboriginal identity are influenced by Canada, Aboriginal control of Canadian affairs is one way to assert more control over what it means to be Aboriginal. In the process, such assertions may even shape what it means to be Canadian.

[Aboriginal Citizenship Does Not Violate Tradition]

-AV Some, however, may not be impressed with this more fluid notion of what it means to be Aboriginal. There may be objections that I have gone too far, that the idea that Aboriginal citizenship could include non-Aboriginal people inappropriately stretches tradition. For example, it might be claimed that Aboriginal control of Canadian affairs violates sacred cultural traditions such as the two-row wampum belt. The Gus Wen Tah, as the belt is called, was first adhered to by my people, the Ojibway, in 1764, when the British made an alliance with the Indians of the upper Great Lakes. The belt consists of three parallel rows of white beads, separated by two rows of purple. To some, the belt suggests a separate nation-to-nation relationship between First Nations and the Crown that prohibits

Aboriginal participation in Canadian affairs. This interpretation flows from a focus on the purple rows. One purple row symbolizes the British going down a river, politically navigating their ship of state; while the other purple row represents the Indians going down their river, politically controlling their own ship of state. Some have said "these two rows never come together in that belt, and it is easy to see what that means. It means that we have two different paths, two different people."[3] This reading of the belt centres on the **autonomy** of each party, as the parallel purple lines are thought to signify that neither party was to interfere in the political organization of the other. In this symbolism is rooted the idea of Aboriginal control of Aboriginal affairs. In fact, according to this description Aboriginal control of Canadian affairs seems to violate a fundamental **tenet** of the Gus Wen Tah.

AV In considering the potential of the Gus Wen Tah for embracing a notion of citizenship that includes non-Aboriginal people, two important observations deserve attention. First, the Gus Wen Tah contains more than two purple rows. The three rows of white beads represent a counter-balancing message that signifies the importance of sharing and interdependence. These white rows, referred to as the bed of the agreement, stand for peace, friendship, and respect. When these principles are read together with those depicted in the purple rows, it becomes clear that ideas of citizenship also have to be rooted in notions of mutuality and interconnectedness. The ecology of contemporary politics teaches us that the rivers on which we sail our ships of state share the same waters. There is no river or boat that is not linked in a fundamental way to the others; that is, there is no land or government in the world today that is not connected to and influenced by others. This is one reason for developing a narrative of Aboriginal citizenship that speaks more strongly to relationships that exist beyond "Aboriginal affairs." Tradition, in this case represented by the Gus Wen Tah, can support such an interpretation.

A second observation that speaks to the Gus Wen Tah's potential to encompass Aboriginal control of Canadian affairs is that its interpretation must be made by reference to other belts exchanged in the same period. The Gus Wen Tah cannot be read in isolation from these other instruments, which clarify the meaning of the two-row wampum. Just as one should not read a treaty according to its written words alone, one should not interpret the Gus Wen Tah solely according to its woven characters. For example, at the time the Gus Wen Tah was exchanged at Niagara in 1764, another belt accompanied it which emphasized the interdependence between the Indians of the Great Lakes and the nascent settler population. A ship was woven into one end of the belt with its bow facing towards Quebec. At the other end of the belt is an image of Michilimackinac, a place in the centre of the Great Lakes regarded as the heart of the Chippewa-Anishinabe homelands. Between the two objects were woven twenty-four Indians holding one another's hands, with the person furthest to the right holding the cable of the ship, while the one on the extreme left has his foot resting on the land at Quebec. Representatives of the twenty-two First Nations assembled at Niagara in 1764 touched this "Belt of Peace" as a symbol of friendship and as a pledge to become "united." This strong imagery conveys the connection between Aboriginal and non-Aboriginal peoples and the lands they occupied. In fact, in this belt the Indians are holding onto the ship to pull it over to receive and participate in the benefits from the non-indigenous population. These wider understandings demonstrate that tradition can support a notion of citizenship that encourages autonomy, and at same time unifies and connects us to one another and the lands we rely on.

[Citizenship, Inclusion, and Fairness]

~AV Concerns about Aboriginal control of Canadian affairs, however, will probably not end at borders of Indian reserves, Inuit lands, and Metis settlements. The idea may also cause some concern among the broader Canadian public. The radical approach to Aboriginal control of Canadian affairs could be troublesome as some wonder about the potentially wrenching nature of this kind of action. If Aboriginal people are going to participate in Canadian and global politics, this will require a great deal of change within the country. An assertive and aggressive stance for control may bring to mind ethnic and racial strife in other countries where groups are attempting to seize control of the state. Canadians have already in a small measure experienced such conflict where, in select instances, Aboriginal peoples have taken direct action to maintain their place with the land. Some Aboriginal peoples may be willing to pursue this challenging course to control Canadian affairs if their underlying concerns about their continuing relationships with the land are not respected. AV However, even more conciliatory liberal or conservative approaches could create difficulties, as some within the current establishment will not be prepared to cede or share power. There is a need to overcome this near-exclusivity. The chairs, corridors, and halls of legislatures, universities, courts, law societies, unions, and corporate boards of directors have been sluggish in responding to the influx of Aboriginal people. To my knowledge, though this needs to be supplemented with further research, there are approximately ten Aboriginal legislators, twenty tenured Aboriginal professors, seventeen Aboriginal judges, one law society bencher, no national Aboriginal union executives, and no Aboriginal members of boards of directors in Canada's twenty-five largest corporations. These levels of representation have to change. Indeed, it is required if Canada is ever to enjoy an inclusive citizenship.

Such a change would not require the grant of any special numeric weight to Aboriginal peoples participating in these institutions beyond their proportionate representation of 5 per cent of the general population. If Aboriginal peoples were to have their proportionate participation reflected in national institutions, there could potentially be over fifty Aboriginal legislators, 1700 tenured Aboriginal professors, 100 Aboriginal judges, and hundreds of Aboriginal union and corporate executives. Participation at this level could result in significant changes to the way land in Canada is treated and allocated. Aboriginal people could bring their views of land, formed through contemporary and centuries-long teachings about its place in community citizenship, to the attention of Canada's institutions. There is no doubt that the exercise of Aboriginal participation in decision-making power in these settings would result in the control of Canadian affairs being different from what it is today. While I appreciate that not all Aboriginal peoples working in these positions would adhere to the notions of citizenship outlined in this chapter, my experience and knowledge in dealing with Aboriginal peoples across the country convinces me that their participation would enfold many of the ideas developed here. Many of these people would help to reformulate ideas about the place of land in our conceptions of citizenship. While some would function without attentiveness to the values formed through interactions with the people who hold the philosophies and values described herein, others certainly would, because such ideas and experiences have a central place in many Aboriginal communities. As such, Aboriginal participation even at a level proportionate to their population in Canada would have an unparalleled effect on the functioning of our society and our conceptions of citizenship.

[Extending Aboriginal Influence to Off-Reserve Affairs]

~AV Yet, in accomplishing this change, there could be another concern among the broader Canadian public about the equity and fairness of Aboriginal control of Canadian affairs. After all, if Aboriginal peoples represent approximately 5 per cent of Canada's population, and have exclusive control of land on their reserves, it may be asked why they should have any interest and influence over land use outside of their reserves. It may be said that Aboriginal peoples cannot expect both to control their own affairs and also to exercise significant influence over others. The seeming inequality in this approach to citizenship may cause some concern because it may appear as if Aboriginal peoples would enjoy rights in Canada that others do not possess. AV One response to this matter may rest on Aboriginal people's legal status under Canadian property and constitutional law. Most Canadians do not demonstrate great concern over the law's recognition of property and civil rights; in fact, such guarantees are an important part of the country's most cherished values. An argument can be made that the protection of Aboriginal off-reserve property and civil rights merely (and belatedly) extends the benefits of Canadian property and civil rights law to Aboriginal peoples. Simply speaking, Aboriginal peoples may not have surrendered these rights over land outside their reserves. For example, in those areas of the country where Aboriginal peoples never entered into agreements with the Crown, they maintain a relationship with land outside their reserves that flows from their pre-existing use and occupation of that land. Furthermore, in those areas of the country where Aboriginal peoples entered into treaties with the Crown, the oral history and text of these agreements often contains guarantees of Aboriginal land use outside reservation boundaries for numerous livelihood purposes. These examples illustrate that many Aboriginal peoples have never consented to sever all relations with the land outside their reservations. Thus, on equitable and legal principles Canadian law may support the notion that Aboriginal peoples have a right to influence decisions outside their reserves, on their traditional lands, even if they have control over their own affairs.

Another response to concern about the fairness of Aboriginal peoples having exclusive control over their own lands—and at the same time participating in the control of lands outside their boundaries—involves the recognition that federalism as a political system should operate to encourage the simultaneous integration and separation of communities. An exclusive focus on Aboriginal control of Aboriginal affairs does not equally facilitate these principles in the relationships Aboriginal peoples have with others. Aboriginal control of Aboriginal affairs focuses on the idea of autonomy to the exclusion of interdependence. The concurrent assertion of Aboriginal control of Canadian affairs rebalances interdependence with autonomy. Other Canadians have long enjoyed autonomy *and* interdependence through their participation in provincial and national communities that somewhat represent both their local and nationwide concerns. Aboriginal peoples have never participated with other Canadians in this way. At the local level their position has been largely ignored, and at the national level their interests have been repressed by centuries-long colonial control. Thus, the notion that Aboriginal peoples should control

Canadian affairs is, at some levels, a claim for Aboriginal peoples to enjoy the same rights as other Canadians, and participate as citizens in the country with appropriate federal structures and representation. There is no unfairness in such a claim; in fact, it would be unfair to prevent Aboriginal peoples from participating in Canada's federal structures in a manner similar to other regional and national communities. While from this perspective it may hardly seem transformative to speak of Aboriginal control of Canadian affairs given the well-entrenched notions about federalism in Canada, sadly, this discourse is ground-breaking when dealing with Aboriginal peoples. Their historical treatment and recent narratives have focused ideas of citizenship on principles that facilitate autonomy, to the exclusion of other more interdependent models of citizenship.

[Aboriginal Citizenship Can Include Non-Aboriginals]

~AV However, even if Aboriginal peoples do have rights concerning land outside of their reservations through the application of legal rights and the principles of federalism, non-Aboriginal people may still wonder about the fairness of Aboriginal peoples qualifying for citizenship in their political system, when they cannot qualify as citizens in Aboriginal peoples' systems. This question may be especially poignant when other institutions of federalism guarantee mobility rights between various jurisdictions, as membership in other federal structures is not restricted by ethnicity. In response to this question many Aboriginal peoples would argue that their circumstances are different, and that they must be able to place restrictions on citizenship based on ethnicity to preserve the existence and survival of the group. AV While I think restrictions on Aboriginal citizenship are necessary to maintain the social and political integrity of the group, I must admit that I am troubled by ideas of Aboriginal citizenship that may depend on blood or genealogy to support group membership. Scientifically, there is nothing about blood or descent alone that makes an Aboriginal person substantially different from any other person. While often not intended by those who advocate such criteria, exclusion from citizenship on the basis of blood or ancestry can lead to racism and more subtle forms of discrimination that destroy human dignity.

However, while I do not favour limits on citizenship on racialized grounds, it may be appropriate to have rigorous citizenship requirements on other grounds, to protect and nurture these communities. Aboriginal peoples are much more than kin-based groups. They have social, political, legal, economic, and spiritual ideologies and institutions that are transmitted through their cultural systems. These systems do not depend exclusively on ethnicity and can be learned and adapted by others with some effort. Therefore, Aboriginal peoples could consider implementing laws consistent with these traditions to extend citizenship in Aboriginal communities to non-Aboriginal people. If non-Aboriginal people met certain standards that allowed for the creation and reproduction of these communities' values, then these people should have a way to become Aboriginal citizens. The extension of this responsibility would respect the autonomy of Aboriginal communities, while at the same time recognizing the need to consider our interdependence as human beings. Thus, it is possible to develop answers to concerns people may have about Aboriginal control of Canadian affairs.

In the end, however, perhaps the most profound concern in adopting the discourse outlined in this essay is the multidimensional nature of the power imbalance Aboriginal peoples experience. Control in Canada is not exercised merely through people and institutions. Both are governed by deep-seated global and national **tenets** that animate and direct the "acceptable" bounds within which people and institutions can exercise power. Aboriginal notions of citizenship with the land are not among these accredited ideologies. Assertions of Aboriginal control of Canadian affairs will encounter a matrix of power that works to exclude notions of "land as citizen." This will be especially evident when its economic implications are understood. In some cases the application of indigenous traditions might require that Aboriginal people share the wealth from the land with other Canadians; in others it may mean that a proposed use would have to be modified or terminated. A reorientation of this magnitude is not likely to occur without substantial opposition from those who benefit from the prevailing ideologies currently allocating power. To surmount this challenge Aboriginal people must employ many complementary discourses of control. This is the reason that Aboriginal control of Canadian affairs must join prevailing narratives of Aboriginal control of Aboriginal affairs in preserving and extending citizenship with the land.

Conclusion

There exists a "special bond" between Aboriginal peoples and the lands they have traditionally occupied. These bonds should be reflected in the discourses of Aboriginal citizenship. To only speak of Aboriginal control of Aboriginal affairs would disfranchise most Aboriginal peoples from their traditional lands. Measured separatism would separate many from places they hold dear. Why should an artificial line drawn around my reserve prevent me from participating in the vast areas my ancestors revered? This focus could prevent the acknowledgement and strengthening of the continuing Aboriginal reliance, participation, and citizenship with the lands they use outside these lines. Aboriginal peoples still honour the places made meaningful by an earlier generation's encounters. They still travel through these places and rely on them for food, water, medicine, memories, friends, and work. Many are hesitant to relinquish their relationship with them in the name of Aboriginal self-government merely because non-Aboriginal people now live there and also rely on this land.

Aboriginal control of Canadian affairs provides a discourse which simultaneously recognizes the meaningful participation of Aboriginal people with one another, and with their non-Aboriginal neighbours. It contains a deeper commitment to preserve and extend the special relationship Aboriginal peoples have with the land. It does not abandon age-old territorial citizenships merely because non-Aboriginal people are now necessary to preserve the land's ancient relations.

In 1976 my grandfather died on the same shores he was born on seventy-five years earlier. He did not live his whole life there, however. His life's experiences were not completely bounded by the artificial borders of a colonial department's Indian reserve. As a young boy he hunted with his father in traditional territories recently made into rich, fertile farmlands. As a young man he worked in Wiarton, Owen Sound, Windsor, and Detroit as a plasterer and labourer. At the same time he fished in the waters of Georgian Bay and Lake Huron (and, in later years, taught his grandson about this practice when I was growing up). He then went on to Hollywood, California, acted in hundreds of films, and married a non-Aboriginal woman from this state while he was there. As a middle-aged man he came back to the reserve when Pearl Harbor was bombed and resumed his practice of working off-reserve as a labourer, and hunting off-reserve to support his family. He received an honorary doctorate from the University of Kentucky because of his knowledge of plants and medicines throughout the 1.5 million acres of land his grandfather treatied over. Everywhere he went, including California, there were always people around with whom he could speak Ojibway, fluently. During the last twenty-five years of his life he alternatively lived on the reserve with my grandmother in their old cabin, on our hunting grounds north of the reserve, or with some of his eight children, who lived off the reserve in non-Aboriginal towns throughout the traditional territory. Discourses of Aboriginal citizenship must be enriched to reflect this fuller range of relationships with the land. Aboriginal culture is not static and, at least in southern Ontario, develops and redevelops through a wider variety of interactions than is recognized in conventional narratives of citizenship. Narratives of Aboriginal political participation should be transformed to reflect this fact.

Notes

1. Harold Cardinal, *The Unjust Society* (Edmonton: Hurtig, 1969). Cardinal's title was meant as a deliberate contrast to then-Prime Minister Trudeau's "Just Society." [Editor]
2. Edward Said, *Culture and Imperialism* (New York: Knopf, 1993), p. 336.
3. Haudenosaunee Confederacy, *Minutes and Proceedings and Evidence of the Special Committee on Indian Self-Government* (Ottawa: The Committee, 1983).

Monique Deveaux

Conflicting Equalities? Cultural Group Rights and Sex Equality

(AV) = author's view; (~AV) = not the author's view

Could special rights and arrangements for cultural minority groups in **liberal democratic** states reinforce the subordination of women? Tensions between the goal of **gender** equality and calls for greater accommodation for ethnic, religious and national minorities have become increasingly apparent in recent years. Many worry that the practices of recent immigrants from so-called traditional societies—customary marriages, polygamy, segregated schooling for girls and boys, and **female circumcision**, are frequently cited examples—may violate liberal sensibilities and laws. However, a different and in some ways more pressing source of concern has received much less attention. This is the uneasy relationship between claims for collective group rights by certain national minorities—including demands for forms of **self-government**—and liberal, individual rights, which are critical to the protection of sex equality. Below, I explore this tension as it relates to a recent case in Canadian politics in which Aboriginal (or native) women activists sought to preserve constitutional sex equality protections alongside proposals for self-government in public defiance of native leaders. Their story reveals the challenges faced by communities seeking to move to a framework of self-government based on collective rights and responsibilities, and may also gesture towards some possible ways to reconcile the demands of group and individual rights.

In the period leading up to the referendum on proposed changes to Canada's constitutional arrangements in 1992—known as the **Charlottetown Accord**—native women's groups expressed their support for the goal of self-government for Aboriginal peoples but insisted that they were not prepared to relinquish formal protection of their sex equality rights as guaranteed by the 1982 *Canadian Charter of Rights and Freedoms*. Leaders of the main Aboriginal associations countered that native people required full independence from the legal **paradigms** and political structures of the liberal Canadian state, and that future native governments would find their own ways of protecting their individual members. Concerned that future Aboriginal group rights might not adequately protect them, native women demanded that their leaders and politicians negotiating the constitutional settlement take steps to secure their sex equality rights.

Focusing on the tensions between individual sex equality rights and cultural group rights as evinced by the Canadian case, I discuss three **normative** approaches to this problem which, while by no means exhaustive, correspond roughly to the position articulated by native peoples during the 1992 constitutional dispute. One perspective calls for a return to traditional values and social arrangements and insists that collective, cultural rights provide the best framework for securing balance and harmony within native communities. A second approach also endorses claims for collective, cultural rights and treats the individual rights framework of liberal democracies with suspicion, but accepts international human rights as morally binding on all governments. A third view concedes the legitimacy of collective rights for certain national minorities (such as Aboriginal peoples) but attaches the **proviso** that self-governing groups must also respect comprehensive individual rights and freedoms, such as those guaranteed by the constitutions of many liberal democracies. Only this third approach, I suggest, gives adequate attention to the need for safeguards and protections that apply to women in both their public and private lives.

Gender Equality and Multiculturalism: Three Conflicts in One?

. . .

. . . [The] central concerns at stake in the case of national minorities seeking **self-determination** [involve] . . . tension between the cultural, collective rights required for self-government and the desire by women in the collective to preserve their sex equality rights as protected by individual rights legislation. Native women in Canada, as I shall show below, sought gender equality protections because they feared that newly self-governing native communities might actively seek to discriminate against women, for reasons that will shortly become clear. Yet far from rejecting the norms, values and beliefs of traditional Aboriginal society, native women emphasized that the discrimination they most feared was rooted in specifically *contemporary* forms of inequality and oppression within native society. At the same time, native women cautioned that hasty attempts to return to customary values and forms of social and political organization might have the effect of reinforcing existing sex discrimination and oppression.

Collective Rights and Sex Equality: Aboriginal Canadians

Canada's Aboriginal peoples comprise a diverse population of native Indians (known as "First Nations" peoples), Metis, and Inuit across the country, with different languages, customs, values and forms of **governance**. Native or First Nations peoples are especially diverse in this respect, encompassing diverse nations with distinct identities and ancestries. First Nations members are further differentiated by region and by whether they live on or off Indian reserves. Despite their diversity, Aboriginal peoples in Canada have long been unified in their quest for formal, constitutional recognition of their intrinsic right to self-government. While self-government could take many forms, constitutional recognition of this right would in principle **accord** Aboriginal communities as much political and legal **autonomy** as they require to govern themselves according to their own values and traditions. Nor is this an unrealistic goal in the context of recent Canadian politics, particularly since **Aboriginal and treaty rights** are already recognized by the state's 1982 *Constitution Act* (section 35(2)). The 1992 Charlottetown Accord would have strengthened these claims, and paved the way for greater powers of self-government for Aboriginal peoples as well as for the province of Quebec. However, dissatisfaction with aspects of the agreement and with the political processes surrounding the **accord** led Canadians to vote against the proposed amendments, including a surprising majority rejection of the accord by Aboriginal peoples living on reserves.

[Rejection of the Accord by Aboriginal Leaders]

Agreement amongst Aboriginal peoples in Canada on the objective of constitutional recognition of the right to self-government has frequently been accompanied by serious disagreement on the form that self-government should take and the best political means of securing it. Both the processes of constitutional negotiation and the proposals and accords pertaining to **sovereignty tabled** in 1992 elicited diverse responses from native peoples and leaders, with some supporting and some rejecting the proposed amendments. One critical area of dispute was the precise relationship to Canadian law which Aboriginal peoples should seek to maintain within the framework of self-government. In negotiations with federal officials, it became clear that native leaders wanted their communities to have extensive powers of self-rule unfettered by Canadian law, including the *Canadian Charter of Rights and Freedoms*. The main associations were in accord on this point: the Assembly of First Nations (AFN)—the largest native organization, representing status Indians across Canada—the Native Council of Canada—representing non-status Indians—the Metis National Council, and the Inuit Tapirisat of Canada, all sought reassurance that future Aboriginal governments would not be answerable to Canadian law.

The reasons for seeking independence or indeed immunity from the *Charter* had more to do with the perceived inappropriateness of liberal democratic **norms** and principles[1] and with the genesis of the document than with any explicit desire to challenge specific individual rights. One of the best summaries of the central concerns of many Aboriginal leaders appeared in an article published three years after the failure of the Charlottetown Accord:

> Aboriginal leaders, and particularly the First Nations leadership, have expressed reservations about the applications of the *Charter* to Aboriginal governments. The reason is two-fold. First, the *Charter* was developed without the involvement or consent of Aboriginal peoples and does not accord with Aboriginal culture, values and traditions. Second, the *Charter* calls for an **adversarial** approach to the resolution of rights conflicts before Canadian courts and there is a concern that this confrontational mode will undermine Aboriginal approaches to conflict resolution. . . . This is not to say that Aboriginal peoples have no concern for individual rights and individual security under Aboriginal governments. The concern rests more with the *Charter's* elevation of guaranteed legal rights over unguaranteed social and economic rights,[2] the emphasis on rights rather than responsibilities, the failure to emphasize collective rights, and the **litigation** model of enforcement.[3]

The rights-based orientation of the *Charter* and the assumption of the superiority of an elected representative democracy are viewed by many as significantly at odds with native philosophy. As Ovide Mercredi, then Grand Chief of the AFN, wrote, "Canada's idea of democracy is majority rule. Our idea of running governments is consensus by the people. Who is to say that Canada's principles are better than ours?"[4] Aboriginal leaders insisted that they sought the suspension of the *Charter vis-a-vis* Aboriginal governments primarily "to keep options open for traditional forms of government such as those based on clans, **confederacy**, or hereditary chiefs."[5]

It remains unclear whether the Charlottetown Accord would have given future Aboriginal governments *de facto* **immunity** from the Canadian *Charter* in the absence of a formal agreement specifying such exemption. Section 32 of the *Charter* states that the document is meant to apply to "the Parliament and government of Canada" as well as all provincial governments; yet no mention is made of the applicability or inapplicability of the *Charter* to Aboriginal governments, as it predates the era of negotiations for native sovereignty. Some legal scholars have suggested that "[d]espite the silence of section 32 on Aboriginal governments, it is probable that a court would hold that Aboriginal governments are bound by the *Charter*."[6] Predicting this, native leaders sought to include specific language in the Charlottetown Accord that promised that future Aboriginal governments would not be bound by the *Charter* provisions. Federal government negotiators, unwilling to grant such full exemption from the *Charter*, proposed a compromise solution whereby Aboriginal governments would be granted access to section 33 of the *Constitution Act* (known as the "**notwithstanding clause**"), which the province of Quebec had already successfully negotiated on the grounds of its status as a "distinct society." Access to this clause would effectively enable Aboriginal governments to suspend those parts of the *Charter* that posed obstacles to self-rule and collective rights. Native leaders agreed to this concession, and the change was duly included in the final draft of the *Consensus Report on the Constitution*, or the Charlottetown Accord.

[Rejection of the Accord by Aboriginal Women's Advocates]

In striking contrast to the position of male chiefs, many Aboriginal women . . . feared losing existing protections of their sex equality rights as guaranteed by federal Canadian law, specifically by the *Charter*. They expressed concern that Aboriginal governments might decide to suspend precisely those sections of the constitution designed to protect women's equality rights in order to override a controversial piece of legislation known as Bill C-31, which was opposed by many native leaders. Passed in 1985, Bill C-31 overturned a discriminatory provision in the Indian Act responsible for **disenfranchising** tens of thousands of native or First Nations women (and their children), who routinely forfeited their Indian status if they married non-status Indian men or non-Indian men. The **converse** was not true of men, whose white or non-Indian wives and children automatically gained full Indian status and privileges upon marriage. Without formal Indian status, native women and their children lost their **treaty rights** and numerous associated benefits, such as inheritance rights and permission to reside on reserve land. The practice of removing women's Indian status as a penalty for marrying non-Indian status men was not a long-standing native tradition, but rather a function of Canada's 1869 *Indian Act*, which introduced a number of **patriarchal** conceptions and arrangements into Aboriginal communities. Nonetheless, **band council** leaders used this legal device to prevent women and their non-Indian status husbands and children from sharing in the resources of native communities, and were among the staunchest [toughest] opponents of the legislation that finally overturned the practice in 1985. The *Charter* was instrumental in defending Bill C-31, which was introduced in Parliament after a **disenfranchised** native woman, Sandra Lovelace, successfully brought her case before the United Nations justice committee, which deemed that removing a person's Indian status was discriminatory under international law. In the years since this decision, an estimated 57,000 persons—the vast majority women and their children—have applied to be reinstated as full status Indians, but many band councils have refused to offer these individuals land, housing, and other benefits. Some of the wealthiest bands are also the biggest offenders in this respect: oil-rich band councils in the province of Alberta have managed to resist recognizing and re-settling fewer than two per cent of persons who obtained legal reinstatement using the 1985 amendment.

In light of entrenched forms of discrimination against them by leaders of their own communities, some women argued that they could not trust their local band chiefs or indeed national leaders to guarantee their sex equality rights at the local reserve level or to include such protections in proposed Aboriginal constitutions. The question whether the *Charter* should continue to apply to self-governing native communities thus sparked a much-publicized rift between some native women's groups and mainstream Aboriginal bodies, and ultimately may have served to erode support for the Charlottetown Accord. In locking horns with the main Aboriginal associations over the issue of protections for women, native women's groups brought into sharp relief some tensions between cultural, collective rights, and individual sex equality rights. As the president of the Native Women's Association of Canada (NWAC), the group leading the fight for equality protections, commented:

> Our Aboriginal leadership does not favour the application of the Canadian *Charter of Rights and Freedoms* to self-government. The opinion is widely held

> that the *Charter* is in conflict with our notions of sovereignty, and further that the rights of Aboriginal citizens within their communities must be determined at the community level. As women, we can look at nations around the world which have placed collective and cultural rights ahead of women's sexual equality rights. Some nations have found that sexual equality interferes with tradition, custom and history. There are many, many nations around the world which have refused to implement United Nations guarantees of sexual equality . . . Canada cannot exempt itself.[7]

Suggestions by mainstream Aboriginal leaders that the *Charter* was merely a remnant of Canada's colonial relationship with native peoples and stood in conflict with the values and practices of traditional self-government were met with skeptical responses by native women's lobbyists, who demanded a serious review of the *Charter* issue. Led by NWAC—representing Indian or First Nations women—and supported by several provincial native women's groups and the newly formed National Metis Women of Canada, Aboriginal women pressed for **assurances** that their equality rights would be guaranteed in any constitutional settlement pertaining to Aboriginal self-government. Since the Charlottetown Accord seemed initially likely to succeed—it was, after all, supported by the main native organizations—NWAC argued that the accord should require future Aboriginal governments to be bound by the *Charter*. The group also demanded a place at the constitutional negotiating table for a representative of native women, so that women's perspectives could be heard. Not all who spoke out insisted on permanent *Charter* protection: some women left open the possibility that eventually adequate sex equality protections might be included in Aboriginal constitutions, and even proposed an Aboriginal Charter of Rights. However, NWAC leaders, recognizing that Aboriginal governments could overturn or eliminate sex equality guarantees in their own constitutions with relative ease—in contrast to the constitutional amendments required to alter the Canadian *Charter*—argued for irreversible *Charter* protection.

In defending the continued application of the *Charter*, NWAC cited ongoing discrimination against native women by Indian band councils and the political quietude of national Aboriginal chiefs on sex equality issues as ample justification for their mistrust of the "wait and see" approach urged by native leaders. As women who had themselves been reinstated to Indian status by Bill C-31, it is unsurprising that NWAC leaders were reluctant to trust that women's equality rights would be safeguarded by Aboriginal governments in the absence of federal laws requiring them to do so. Moreover, some band councils readily admitted that they were looking for legal ways to override Bill C-31 and so disenfranchise recently reinstated persons of their Indian status, as well as forestalling future claims for reinstatement. Another reason many native women were skeptical of assurances that their equality rights would be respected in the context of self-government was that the dramatic increase in violence and sexual abuse in their communities had not been given the serious attention by native leaders that women felt it urgently required. Reports of rates of domestic assault against native women living on and off First Nations reserves that were several times the rate for non-Aboriginal women began to emerge in the early 1980s, and the lack of a sustained, institutional response by band councils angered and **alienated** many women from mainstream native politics. While not necessarily seeking a constitutional solution to the problem of violence, many native women viewed their leaders' poor track record on this issue as further reason to worry that access to the override section [the "notwithstanding" clause] of the *Charter* for Aboriginal governments could mean a setback for women's equality rights. In consultations with members of the Royal Commission on Aboriginal Peoples—announced amidst the ashes of the defeated Charlottetown Accord—native women spoke of male leaders urging them not to discuss publicly with commissioners their communities' problems of domestic violence, alcoholism and sexual abuse, in part because of fears that this would detract from critical negotiations on questions of self-government. Commissioners meeting ***in camera*** with native women across the country were told of pressure tactics employed by band council leaders and chiefs to dissuade women from speaking out.

A further reason for concern about *Charter* exemption for Aboriginal governments concerned the male-dominated character of the main native organizations, which groups like NWAC felt had the effect of blocking serious discussion of issues of sexual equality (and sexual violence). In connection with this concern, a pivotal part of NWAC's strategy was the group's launching of a legal challenge in the Federal Court of Canada in January 1992. To punctuate their opposition to the proposed exemption of Aboriginal communities and governments from the *Charter* to publicize the unwillingness of national native organizations to listen to their concerns, NWAC representatives charged that federal agencies had failed to fund their association and other national Aboriginal women's groups while funding mainstream, male-dominated groups. NWAC claimed that the discrepancy in support for native associations prevented their dissenting views from being heard, especially on the *Charter* issue. On the eve of major political talks with Aboriginal leaders and provincial premiers on Canada's future, NWAC also sought formal participant status at the constitutional negotiating table. At the trial level, NWAC's case failed (in March 1992): the judge rejected the association's charges that government funding of the main native associations and denial of equal financial support to native women's groups compromised their freedom of speech or constituted sex discrimination. However, NWAC appealed to the Federal Court of Appeals, which ruled in August 1992 that native women's rights of political participation were negatively impacted by unfair government funding practices. Despite their initial moral victory, NWAC spokeswomen did not succeed in getting invited to the constitutional talks along with other Aboriginal leaders, because the issue of participation was deemed outside the court's power. The implications of the continued exclusion of women's groups from constitutional negotiations were far-reaching: the draft Charlottetown Accord barely made mention of native women's concerns, stating that "the issue of gender equality should be on the agenda of the first First Minister's Conference on Aboriginal Constitutional matters," and granted future Aboriginal governments access to the controversial "notwithstanding clause" (section 33).[8] Ironically, native women's demand to be included in constitutional talks was eventually heeded, albeit several months after the defeat of the Charlottetown Accord: in early 1993, NWAC was finally invited to participate in talks at an inter-governmental conference on constitutional issues.

Native women were by no means unanimous in their call for formal constitutional protection of their individual equality rights by means of the *Charter*, and disagreement continues today. Chief Wendy Grant, vice-chief of the Assembly of First Nations at the time of the original dispute, spoke out against NWAC's position and argued in favor of

Aboriginal self-government free from the constraints of Canadian law. Like other native leaders, Grant characterized the conflict as fundamentally about different, even **incommensurable** legal and political systems, not about disparate commitments to women's equality: "Your governments and laws are set up in such a way that it is a hierarchical government and—justifiably so—you've got to put protection in for the individual. But when you look at a traditional [native] government, it's the other way: the collective is the driving force and the individuals rights are enhanced and protected by the collective which looks after those individual rights."[9] Some native women legal scholars, including Mary Ellen Turpel, also disagreed strongly with NWAC's arguments. However, a significant number of native women went on record as supporting continued *Charter* protection for Aboriginal peoples precisely because they feared the erosion of women's rights. This is reflected not only in the positions taken by NWAC and provincial native women's groups, but also in the rejection (in the referendum vote) of the Charlottetown Accord by two thirds of native peoples on reserves. NWAC's position was considered sufficiently representative of native women to earn endorsement from mainstream national women's groups, including the largest and most influential organization, the National Action Committee on the Status of Women (NAC). Although NWAC and its supporters were only one of several interests opposed to the Charlottetown Accord, the publicity surrounding this lobby's objections and the sense that it exposed a serious rift among Aboriginal associations was not insignificant to the accord's ultimate defeat.

The Clash between Sex Equality Rights and Collective Rights

To some extent, the conflict over whether the *Charter* should apply to future self-governing Aboriginal communities reflected the already strained relationship between native women's groups and organizations with more political clout, especially the AFN. The different political priorities and strategies of these associations intensified the disagreement over the *Charter*'s relevance to native peoples. Some who watched the debate unfold suggested that NWAC's demands for guarantees for sex equality rights was mostly a manifestation of growing schism between disenfranchised, disempowered members of native communities—a disproportionate percentage of whom are women—and the male elite leadership of band councils and national associations.

While not minimizing the significance of antagonisms within Aboriginal communities and between different native organizations, it seems undeniable that NWAC's challenge represented a more fundamental clash in political values and legal frameworks. In particular, the debate over whether the *Charter* should apply to future Aboriginal governments highlights two critical normative tensions which I suggest arise from competing commitments to gender equality and special arrangements for cultural minorities. The first of these dilemmas concerns conflicting interpretations and evaluations of the **norm** of *equality* held by women's rights advocates and cultural groups. This in turn derives in part from a second tension, namely, that between collective rights and individual rights.

Native women activists and leaders of the main Aboriginal associations disagreed and continue to disagree on both the nature of social equality and the proper political priorities as concerns the goal of equality. Native leaders perceive self-government as the key equality objective, understood as the goal of securing formal recognition of First Nations, Inuit, and Metis peoples as self-determining; the political relationship to the rest of Canada which Aboriginal negotiators sought to establish in the early 1990s was expected to instantiate such equality. Individual equality and the ideal of sexual equality are viewed by some as an appropriate goal for native peoples. As native legal scholar Mary Ellen Turpel writes, "Equality is simply not the central organizing principle in our communities. It is frequently seen by our Elders as a suspiciously selfish notion, as individualistic and alienating from others in the community. It is incongruous to apply this notion to our communities. We are committed to what would be termed a '**communitarian**' notion of responsibilities to our peoples, as learned through traditional teachings and our life experiences."[10] In response to their dissenting rank-and-file members and NWAC lobbyists, spokesmen for the AFN argued that sexual equality was a matter for native peoples themselves to work out in their own communities, altogether separate from issues of Aboriginal sovereignty. By contrast, NWAC and other native women's groups supported a broadly (but not exclusively) feminist conception of sexual equality and of the importance of legal protection for their individual rights.

The asymmetry between the account of equality advocated by many native women and that endorsed by mainstream Aboriginal associations was also a reflection of the tension between individual rights—which supply formal guarantees for women's sex equality rights—and collective rights, which form the basis of proposals for Aboriginal self-government. Collective rights are also invoked in calls for policies aimed at the preservation of cultural minorities' distinct identities, such as protective language laws, provisions for first-language education, and special dispensation for religious minorities. Native leaders and band council chiefs lost no time in characterizing the rift between their associations and native women's groups as one of clashing legal systems and political norms. Not only did they try to convey the message that traditional native social, legal, and political institutions were best protected by a framework of collective rights, but some suggested that NWAC's sex equality concerns were proof of the extent to which European concepts and thinking had influenced native society. Arguing in [this] vein, Mercredi, then AFN Chief, stated that many native people "challenge the *Charter*'s interpretation of rights as weapons to be used against governments; we tend to see rights as collective responsibilities instead of individual rights—or at least see the strong link between the two." Moreover, Mercredi argued that the legal system imposed by the *Charter* posed tensions with aspects of Aboriginal justice—"it doesn't include our communal vision"[11]—and could pose obstacles to the authority of the traditional clan system and other institutions which Aboriginal communities might seek to reintroduce.

Despite the possible perils of collective rights for native women, NWAC and its provincial counterparts were somewhat less inclined than were Aboriginal leaders to portray the disagreement over the *Charter* as a conflict between collective rights and individual rights, for in principle they supported both. NWAC spokeswomen did however feel they needed to respond to attempts by national leaders to characterize collective rights as the only "authentic" form of Aboriginal rights. To this end, they emphasized the importance of formal recognition of individual and human rights, which they warned should not be eclipsed by the quest for Aboriginal sovereignty. Rejecting intimations by native traditionalists that individual rights and collective rights were in some sense incompatible, native women argued that explicit protection of their individual rights could and should go hand in hand with the collective rights intrinsic to Aboriginal self-government.

Reconciling Gender Equality and Cultural Self-Determination

The political impasse created by disputes over the meaning of equality and the relationship between individual and collective rights was not adequately resolved during the 1992 constitutional crisis, and disagreement persists today. However, at least three different strategies for reconciling conflicting conceptions of equality and tensions between collective rights and individual rights emerged in the course of the Canadian constitutional debate. I suggest that these broadly reflect the main choices facing (autonomy-seeking) national minority communities as they grapple with the problem of how to accommodate competing commitments to sex equality and collective rights.

The View from Tradition

One initial response to NWAC's insistence on *Charter* protection for women's equality rights was the appeal by some native leaders to traditional Aboriginal models of family and society. In particular, some Aboriginal spokespeople invoked what is sometimes called the "traditional Indian motherhood ideal" to suggest ways of reconciling demands for sex equality (whether internal or external to the community) with native cultural norms and social arrangements. Typically, proponents of this view offer reassurances that women are respected and valued in their capacities as wives and mothers, and as full members of the community; different roles, on this view, need not mean unequal ones. Moreover, customary Aboriginal family roles for men and women are thought to contribute to social harmony and the preservation of communities' traditional identities. By contrast, liberal democratic social and legal norms are seen to pose dangers to the Aboriginal peoples' aspirations for cultural self-determination. This thought was voiced by some native spokespeople during the 1992 debates, including one high-ranking woman leader, Chief Wendy Grant (then vice-president of the AFN), who commented that "divisions between First Nations people based upon the non-native fascination with extreme individualism simply support the assimilation of our people into the non-native culture."[12] As this remark suggests, the "view from tradition" rejects liberal notions of individual rights in favor of a reassertion of native cultural values and forms of social organization. While this approach clearly reflects native peoples' desire to direct the social, cultural and political life of their communities, it may also represent a backlash against dissenting members who demand social and political reform.

The Collective Rights/Human Rights Approach

A second strategy for reconciling individual sex equality rights with cultural group rights that emerged in the course of the debate on Aboriginal sovereignty and the *Charter* is what we might call the "collective rights/human rights model." Proponents of this view support the principle of self-government based on collective cultural rights, but concede that such governments are in turn morally bound to respect the basic human rights of their members, as specified by international **covenants**. Since the idea that "women's rights are human rights" is gradually becoming a key aspect of human rights **discourse**, some protection for women's basic rights could be expected to follow from the collective rights/human rights model. However, extensive and legally binding sex equality rights are best secured by a state's own formal constitution, rather than by international human rights covenants, which are not always easy to enforce. But since those who support the collective rights/human rights approach maintain that self-governing cultural minorities should not be answerable to liberal democratic laws and norms, this model provides little assurance that female members will enjoy comprehensive equality protections.

During the 1992 constitutional negotiations, many heads of the main Aboriginal associations and band council chiefs espoused views about the legal and political requirements and constraints of native sovereignty that could best be characterized as fitting the collective rights/human rights model. Moreover, their position was later adopted by Canada's Royal Commission on Aboriginal Peoples, whose final report contains perhaps the best articulation of this perspective; the commissioners endorse an approach which

> [A]ccepts that Aboriginal governments are subject to international human rights standards in their dealings with people under their **jurisdiction**. However, it argues that an Aboriginal government cannot be held accountable in Canadian courts for alleged violations of the Canadian *Charter of Rights and Freedoms* unless the Aboriginal nation in question has previously consented to the application of the *Charter* in a binding constitutional instrument.[13]

Although Aboriginal leaders eventually accepted the federal government's compromise solution during the 1992 negotiations—access to the notwithstanding clause of the *Charter* as part of the native sovereignty package—they would have preferred complete amnesty from Canada's constitution. Native spokespeople however were careful to couch their claims for sovereignty with reassurances that they acknowledged the value of individual human rights protections.

The Equality View

AV A third approach to the dilemma of reconciling sex equality rights with collective, cultural rights is encapsulated by the stance taken by many native women . . . from the sidelines of the constitutional negotiations, and advanced with considerable force by NWAC. This view endorses the goal of self-determination for native peoples but emphasizes the importance of sexual equality protections and other individual rights provisions. Some versions of this perspective regard women's equality rights and cultural self-determination as equal in importance. In the Canadian case, native women activists emphatically rejected suggestions that women should even temporarily set aside their equality concerns for the purpose of forming a united front for native sovereignty. Yet nor do advocates of the "equality view" accept traditionalists' claim that individual rights and collective rights are incompatible, though they acknowledge numerous tensions between them. Fears that the application of the *Charter* to Aboriginal governments would merely prolong the colonial relationship between native peoples and the rest of Canada and obstruct traditional native forms of self-governance may well have been justified; however, Native spokeswomen and NWAC leaders argued that these were risks that native peoples should be willing to take in order to secure the protection of the rights of all of their members, women included.

Of the different approaches to reconciling sex equality rights and calls for collective, cultural rights discussed here, only the final of these takes sexual justice claims seriously enough to consider the full range of ramifications for women of proposals for self-government. Moreover, it appears that the third approach alone challenges the assumption (central, I suggest, to struggles for cultural rights and self-determination) that legal and political protections should mainly protect cultural groups against the wider liberal society, and indeed protect individuals as members of the collective, but *not* extend that protection to individuals in their status as private citizens. This may seem a curious point to raise in connection with Canadian Aboriginal peoples, whose extensive social infrastructure of clans, tribes, and nations stresses the importance of family kinship and harmonious social life. However, many native communities today are struggling with the breakdown of social support systems and the erosion of traditional ways of life, identities, and languages. These dramatic changes have resulted in problems of high unemployment, alcoholism, suicide, and violence. Just as the *Charter* did not magically resolve these issues for native communities, it is not yet clear to what extent self-government based on collective rights and traditional native law could reverse these trends, or help to revive more harmonious and **equitable** social relationships in native communities.

Conclusion

. . .

Native women's challenge to Aboriginal leaders on sex equality issues serves as a dramatic illustration of the ways in which the political priorities and strategies of women's equality advocates may differ from those of proponents of collective, cultural rights. The Canadian example is of special interest because it reveals the difficult decisions and trade-offs which those who advocate *both* equality rights and collective rights must make, and the far-reaching political effects of their choices. The defeat of the Charlottetown Accord in October 1992 in **referenda** in Quebec and the rest of Canada was by all accounts a steep price to pay to protest the deferral of political and legal guarantees for native women's equality rights. Yet the support these women garnered from other citizens and advocacy groups suggests that many Canadians, women in particular, were concerned about the possible implications of collective rights for gender equality. As such, this case serves as a poignant reminder that less powerful members of national minority groups—especially women—have good reason to press for explicit recognition of their equality rights amidst the struggle for collective cultural rights and self-government.

Notes

1. In a **liberal democracy**, individual freedom and equality under the law are fundamental principles which support and make possible the pursuit of each person's conception of the good life, and each person's participation in democratic decision-making. All people are free to make up their own

minds, and free to act on their beliefs, as long as they do not harm others. Legal protections are designed to ensure that everyone can enjoy these freedoms and has an equal opportunity to contribute to and benefit from the public. Some Aboriginal peoples reject individual freedom and legal equality as fundamental principles. They still recognize the equal **moral standing** of community members, and the importance of collective decision-making, but believe the welfare of the community, not the individual, is fundamental. [Editor]

2. Social and economic rights are rights to certain socially provided goods, such as public education, pensions, and universal health care. [Editor]
3. P Hogg and ME Turpel, "Implementing Aboriginal Self-government: Constitutional and Jurisdiction Issues," *The Canadian Bar Review*, 74, 2 (1995): 213.
4. O Mercredi and ME Turpel, *In the Rapids: Navigating the Future of First Nations* (Toronto: Viking/Penguin, 1993), p. 102.
5. Government of Canada, *Overview of the First Round Royal Commission on Aboriginal Peoples: Public Hearings* (1992), p. 41.
6. Hogg and Turpel, p. 214.
7. G Stacey-Moore, "Aboriginal Women, Self-Government, the Canadian *Charter of Rights and Freedoms*, and the 1991 Canada Package on the Constitution," Unpublished manuscript (address to the Canadian Labor Congress, Ottawa, December 3, 1991), p. 7.
8. Government of Canada, *Consensus Report on the Constitution (Charlottetown Accord).*
9. Quoted in R Platiel, "Gender issue sparks native disunity: women's group charges constitutional proposals will undermine female equality," *Globe and Mail*, 20 July 1992.
10. ME Turpel, "Patriarchy and paternalism: the legacy of the Canadian State for First Nations Women," *Canadian Journal of Women and the Law* 6, 1 (1993): 180.
11. Mercredi and Turpel.
12. Quoted in R. Platiel, "Aboriginal women divide on constitutional protection," *Globe and Mail* (13 July 1992).
13. Government of Canada, *Report of the Royal Commission on Aboriginal Peoples* (1996), p. 228.

Discussion Questions

1. Tully distinguishes between treaty and colonial relationships. What does he mean by these terms? Which does he favour, and why?
2. Tully argues that Canada's legitimacy as a nation requires recognizing the prior sovereignty of Aboriginal peoples and treaties as nation-to-nation agreements. What is his argument for this claim? Do you agree with him?
3. What is the point of Borrows' suggestion that "it is time to talk also of Aboriginal control of Canadian affairs"? What does his thought experiment show?
4. Would Borrows agree with Tully's argument for a just relation between Aboriginal and non-Aboriginal people? Why or why not?
5. How, according to Deveaux, do group rights and individual equality rights conflict for Aboriginal women?
6. Deveaux argues that Aboriginal people ought to have greater control over their own affairs, but their policies should be subject to the *Charter*. Do you think Tully would agree? Why or why not?

Suggested Readings and Websites

✦ = Canadian source or author

✦ Assembly of First Nations, www.afn.ca/. [The national organization that represents First Nations in Canada.]

✦ Borrows, John. "Frozen Rights in Canada: Constitutional Interpretation and the Trickster." *American Indian Law Review* 22, 1 (1997–8): 37–64. [Borrows, an Aboriginal lawyer, argues against four 1996 Supreme Court decisions that ruled that the only activities protected by the Constitution are those that Aboriginal people practised before European contact.]

✦ Hurley, Mary C. "The *Indian Act*." Parliamentary Information and Research Service, PRB 09-12E. Ottawa: Parliamentary Information and Research Service, Library of Canada, 23 November 2009, www.parl.gc.ca/Content/LOP/ResearchPublications/prb0912-e.htm. [A non-partisan discussion of issues and developments involving the *Indian Act* between 1996 and 2009.]

✦ Hurley, Mary C. and Jill Wherrett. Summary of The Report of the Royal Commission on Aboriginal Peoples, PRB 99-24E. Ottawa: Parliamentary Information and Research Service, Library of Canada, 2 August 2000, www.parl.gc.ca/Content/LOP/ResearchPublications/prb9924-e.htm. [A non-partisan summary and commentary on the Report.]

✦ Inuit Tapiriit Kanatami, www.itk.ca/. [The national Inuit organization in Canada.]

✦ Native Women's Association of Canada, www.nwac.ca/. [Represents First Nations and Métis women in Canada.]

✦ Tully, James. *Strange Multiplicity: Constitutionalism in an Age of Diversity*. Cambridge: Cambridge University Press, 1995. [An examination of constitutional democracy and cultural diversity that draws on both European and non-European traditions, with special attention to Aboriginal peoples.]

✦ Turner, Dale. *This Is Not a Peace Pipe: Towards a Critical Indigenous Philosophy*. Toronto: University of Toronto Press, 2006. [Turner, an aboriginal philosopher, argues that Aboriginal worldviews and understandings must be included in discussions of Aboriginal and non-Aboriginal relations.]

Chapter 2

Quebec Nationalism

Quebec nationalism has been one of the most contentious features of Canadian politics for the last fifty years. Most English Canadians do not understand why the Québécois consider themselves a separate **nation**, and why many of them want to separate from Canada. Most English-speaking Canadians are woefully ignorant of the issues, something I hope to dispel in this chapter. You might well still believe what you believe, but you will believe it for good reasons. Before we can begin, though, we need to define some terms.

- A nation can be defined, loosely, as a people who share common language, history, culture, and **institutions**.
- All nations are not necessarily **states** (governments with supreme power); there are **multinational** states composed of two or more nations, such as Canada (Aboriginal peoples, the Québécois, and English-speaking Canadians) and Belgium (the Belgians and the Flemish).
- **Nationalism** is loyalty or commitment to the interests of one's nation, where those interests are seen to differ from other nations' interests. Patriotism is a form of nationalism.
- **Separatists** are those who advocate that their nation **secede** (formally withdraw) from a state and become **sovereign** (independent, **self-governing**).
- **Sovereigntists** (a Canadian term) are those who advocate that Quebec secede from Canada, but still maintain some joint undertakings such as defence and currency.

"Nationalist" is broader than "sovereigntist" or "separatist." All sovereigntists and separatists are nationalists, but all nationalists are not necessarily sovereigntists or separatists. Someone can be a nationalist and a **federalist** (someone who advocates a **federal** union in which there is a central government and several subordinate sub-units). In Canada, a person believes that Quebec's national aspirations are best protected by staying in Canada, as long as the federal government recognizes Quebec's distinct status. Nationalist federalists support **asymmetrical federalism**, a form of federalism in which different provinces have different powers.

Almost all francophones in Quebec are nationalists; they think that Quebec is a separate nation within Canada whose interests sometimes differ from English-speaking Canada's interests, and that Quebec's interests currently are not always met, or met well, within Canada. Many Quebec nationalists are also sovereigntists and/or separatists.

Background

The history of Quebec nationalism can be dated to the conquest of New France by the British in 1760, and the 1763 Treaty of Paris that ended the Seven Years' War (known in Quebec as the Conquest) between France and Great Britain. The Treaty of Paris granted most of France's North American holdings to the British, and guaranteed freedom of religion to Roman Catholics in Quebec. The British government attempted to assimilate the French-speaking occupants of Quebec and convert them to Protestantism, but they were never successful. Quebec remained French-speaking and Roman Catholic, unique among Britain's North American colonies.

For the better part of two centuries, French Canadian nationalism was maintained through the "three pillars of survival": the Catholic faith, the French language, and French Canadian institutions. The most important pillar was the Church, which was the dominant organization in French Canadians' lives. English was not only the language of the conquerors; it was also the language of almost all Canadian Protestants, while French was the language of almost all Canadian Catholics. Hence, holding fast to the Church was also a way of holding fast to the French language. In addition, the Church ran most schools in Quebec, which were important protectors of French Canadian language and culture. Other important institutions were the French **civil law** and the **seigneurial system**. Any attempt by the English to abolish either would rouse French Canadians to action, and they would prevent the loss of one of their pillars of survival.

The Catholic Church was very conservative in both France and Quebec. In France, the Church was allied with the monarchy and the aristocracy against the progressive forces in the French Revolution (1789–99), the July Revolution of 1830 and the 1848 Revolution, which [all] advocated a **secular** society (one not allied with any particular religion). In Quebec, the Church was allied with "the established social order in which the Roman Catholic Church dominated, agriculture was lauded as society's material and moral foundation, parish and family were the basic social institutions, commercial and industrial pursuits were disdained, and foreign influences were shunned."[1] This conservatism did maintain French Canadians' faith, language, and institutions, but it also worked to English Canadians' advantage, making it much easier for them to dominate commerce and industry in Quebec. Hence the preservation of the French Canadian nation came at the cost of increasing the political and financial gap between francophones and anglophones in Quebec and the rest of Canada.

While of course many French Canadians were unhappy with the dominance of *les Anglais*, the conservatism of Quebec society focused their attention on preserving their culture rather than overcoming English domination. But the winds of change that swept across the world after World War II (see the Introduction to Part I, Who Are We?) began to blow across Quebec as well. From 1944 to 1959 Quebec was ruled by the conservative

Union Nationale Party headed by Maurice Duplessis. In 1959 Duplessis died, and the next year Quebec citizens elected the Liberals under Jean Lesage, who ran on a reform platform.

The years the Lesage Liberals were in power, 1960 to 1966, was a time of intense social change. Perhaps most significant was Québécois' rejection of "the three main components of French Canadian thought: agriculturalism, anti-statism, and messianism."[2] First, although most French Canadians already lived in cities, agriculture had an almost mythical status in Québécois consciousness—as it did, perhaps to a lesser extent, in English Canadians' minds. During this time, French Canadians began to view Quebec as a modern, vibrant, urban society. Second, rather than opposing the state, French Canadians began to see—and use—the Quebec government as an instrument to realize their nationalist goals. The government also took an increasingly active role in French Canadian society: among other things, it nationalized private electricity companies, changed ridings to better reflect Quebec's increasing urbanization, created a department of education not run by the Catholic Church, and revised the labour code. And third, after more than two centuries of identifying the French difference with the Catholic Church, Quebec became a secular society that defined its difference by its language, culture, and institutions. Culture replaced faith while language became the central pillar of the now Québécois identity. A writer from the *Globe & Mail* described what was going on in Quebec as "nothing short of a revolution, albeit a quiet one."[3] Thus this period came to be known as the Quiet Revolution.

Many English Canadians and some French Canadians worried about the growing nationalist sentiment in Quebec. One of them was Pierre Trudeau, who was elected to Parliament in 1965 and who served as Prime Minister from 1968 to 1979 and 1980 to 1984. Trudeau was a charismatic leader who became a central figure in the debate about the role of Quebec in Canada. He was a fierce federalist who believed all Canadians should be treated identically, and who staunchly opposed special status or protection for any group. Historian Claude Bélanger writes that Trudeau

> challenged the assumption that Quebec was the national government of French Canadians and contended that the protection and development of the French culture in Canada was as much the task of the federal government as that of the government of Quebec; he believed that all of Canada was the homeland of French Canadians and not only Quebec. To the emerging concept of a French Quebec, Trudeau opposed the idea of a French Canada which could live side-by-side with an English Canada. Consequently, more powers were not necessary for Quebec, but French Canadians had to play a stronger role in the federal government if they were to achieve equality and develop their culture.[4]

On the other side were Québécois nationalists, who disagreed with all of Trudeau's claims and argued that justice required a different status and federal policies for Quebec. The battle that has defined Canadian politics for the last fifty years commenced.

In 1969, in response to a recommendation of the Royal Commission on Bilingualism and Biculturalism, the federal government passed the *Official Languages Act*. It made English and French the official languages of Canada and required that all federal services and communication be provided in both languages. The *Official Languages Act* was popular in Quebec, but the federal government's 1971 multiculturalism policy was not. Trudeau rejected the idea that either French or English should be given primacy in Canadian policies. In his speech to the House of Commons announcing multiculturalism, Trudeau said, "There is no official culture, nor does any ethnic group take precedence over any other. No citizen or group of citizens is other than Canadian, and all should be treated fairly."[5] Many Québécois saw multiculturalism as an attempt to treat them as no more than another ethnicity in a multicultural state dominated by anglophones. They believed that, unless Québécois language, culture, and institutions were given precedence in Quebec, they would be engulfed by the enormous anglophone population of North America.

In 1976 the Parti Québécois, an explicitly separatist party, formed the government in Quebec. One of their campaign promises had been that if they were elected, they would hold a referendum on separation. In 1980 they made good on their promise. The question before the Québécois was whether the PQ should negotiate a "**sovereignty association**" with Canada. Trudeau opposed the referendum, promising that, if sovereignty association failed, he would interpret it as a mandate for a renewed federalism. There was a great deal of confusion about what sovereignty association meant, and in particular whether it meant **secession** (the political equivalent of divorce) or a renegotiated federalism. The PQ did not manage to clear up the confusion, and the referendum failed. 59.5 per cent of Quebec citizens voted "no" to sovereignty association and 40.5 per cent voted "yes."

Trudeau soon began negotiations to **patriate** (bring home) the **constitution**. When the *British North America Act* was passed in 1867, it was a piece of British legislation, and it had remained so for over a century. This meant that any amendments to the *Act* required the British Parliament's approval. In that sense Canada was not a truly **sovereign** state. Trudeau's promise of a renewed federation in the lead-up to the referendum required British approval. That was unacceptable; Trudeau, a Canadian nationalist, believed that control over Canadian affairs ought to reside with Canadians. (Notice Chaput's sharp criticism of this view in the first reading.) Trudeau solicited proposals for constitutional reform from across the country. After eighteen months of fevered negotiations, the premiers of nine of the ten provinces agreed to the proposed constitution and its patriation. Quebec held out for, among other things, constitutional recognition of its distinct status and a veto over any constitutional amendments. Trudeau rejected these demands. He ended the negotiations and patriated the constitution without Quebec's agreement. The *Canadian Charter of Rights and Freedoms* (one part of the constitution) has been very popular in anglophone Canada, and has become a significant part of the English-speaking Canadian identity. The Québécois, however, view the constitution and the *Charter* as the undemocratic imposition of rules that undermine Quebec's ability to determine its own future.

In the 1984 election the federal Liberals lost Quebec's support, and the Conservatives under Brian Mulroney formed the federal government. Mulroney, like Trudeau, was a fluently bilingual Canadian federalist from Quebec, and he promised to bring Quebec back into Confederation "with honour and enthusiasm." The Mulroney government tried and failed twice, first with the 1987 Meech Lake Accord and then with the 1992 Charlottetown Accord. Meech Lake required the approval of Parliament and of all ten provincial legislature by 1990, but it was unsuccessful. The Charlottetown Accord was put to a national referendum, where it failed by a vote of fifty-five to forty-five per cent.

The failure of the Meech Lake and Charlottetown Accords increased support for separatism in Quebec. In the 1993 election the Bloc Québécois, a separatist federal party, sent more than fifty MPs from Quebec to Ottawa. The Parti Québécois regained power in Quebec in 1995, and they promised to hold another referendum on separation. The question asked in this referendum was, "Do you agree that Quebec should become sovereign, after having made a formal offer to Canada for a new economic and political partnership, within the scope of the Bill respecting the future of Quebec and of the agreement signed on 12 June 1995?" Every household in Quebec received a package outlining the question, the Bill on the future of Quebec, the June 1995 agreement, and the government's reasons for advocating sovereignty. The PQ was not going to lose another referendum because voters did not understand their proposal. The referendum failed by the narrowest of margins: 50.5 to 49.5 per cent.

In 1998, the Supreme Court considered a **reference question** from the federal government concerning Quebec secession. (A reference question comes from the federal or a provincial government, asking the Court's opinion on a legislative matter.) The federal government asked whether the constitution or international law would permit Quebec to secede **unilaterally** (on its own, without the agreement of the rest of Canada). The Court ruled that Quebec did not have the **right** to secede unilaterally, but it did say that "A clear majority vote in Quebec on a clear question in favour of secession would confer democratic legitimacy on the secession initiative which all of the other participants in Confederation would have to recognize."[6] That is, the Court said that Quebec has no legal right to secede, but it does have a democratic right to do so. Both the federal and Quebec governments were happy with the Supreme Court's decision. However, in 2000 the federal government passed the *Clarity Act*, based on the Supreme Court's ruling. The *Clarity Act* gives the federal government the power to decide if a question on secession is clear and if there is a clear majority in favour of secession, as well as to refuse to negotiate if it decides either standard has not been met. Unsurprisingly, Quebec rejects the *Clarity Act*, arguing that the law interferes with its right to **self-determination** (the right of an individual or group to determine its future on its own without outside interference).

Philosophical Issues

We have already examined several philosophical issues concerning nationalism. Here I will sketch a few more that are relevant to Canada and Quebec.

The first set of arguments concerns the grounds of separatist nationalism. The most prominent defence of nationalism "depicts the community as the deep source of value or as the unique transmission device that connects the members to some important values."[7] Proponents of this view claim, first, that some morally valuable goods such as personal identity or a sense of meaning can develop and be maintained best—or only—in a nation (defined by a set of characteristics such as language, culture, history, and institutions). Second, they argue that nations can best maintain their members' identities and preserve their own identities as nations by becoming sovereign states. Thus nations have the right to become states. Critics say this view is based on an implausible **metaphysics** (a view about the nature of existence or reality). It treats nations as if their characteristics were uncontroversial and fixed, when in fact they are always contested—from inside and outside—and fluid, changing in response to members' demands, external influences, internal criticism, and so on. In addition, they say this conception is unable to explain emigration and immigration. If identities are formed only by and within particular nations, how do some people voluntarily give up one nationality and take on another?

Other philosophers ground support for nationalism in politics rather than metaphysics. The most prominent proponent of this view is the Canadian philosopher Will Kymlicka, who argues that nationalism can be justified on egalitarian grounds. Take Quebec. There are roughly 7.5 million French speakers in an ocean of over 300 million English speakers in North America. Without protections for the French language and Quebec culture, the Québécois will be overwhelmed by an anglophone tsunami. Thus, if we take seriously

- the liberal claim that everyone's interests count equally,

and combine it with empirical evidence for the claims that

- people's lives go better if they have a particular community that they identify with and feel at home in, and
- it is difficult and disruptive for people to drop their allegiance to their home communities,

it follows that

- it is wrong for a state to coerce its citizens to change their ethnic, racial, and national identifications,
- national minorities have a right to protect their members' interests, and
- the liberal state ought to protect national minorities' interests against the majority.

More practically, philosophers discuss ways that **multinational states** (states made up by two or more nations) ought to deal with national minorities like the Québécois. What should their relationship be? Answers range from Trudeau's view that all citizens ought to have to same status (which is essentially a denial of minority nations' existence), to the view that the federal government ought to accommodate the minority nation (most likely through some form of asymmetrical federalism), to partial or complete separation of the minority nation. Most Canadian philosophers agree the Trudeau solution will not work: it will not meet the needs of the Québécois or of French Canadians outside Quebec, and it virtually guarantees that Quebec will separate. Most anglophone Canadian philosophers support asymmetrical federalism, while francophone and Québécois philosophers are split between asymmetrical federalism and separation.

Quebec separatism has not been a prominent issue in Canada for nearly a decade, but no one thinks the issue has been resolved. The battle that has defined Canada since the Quiet Revolution shows few signs of dying out.

The Readings

The first reading was published at the beginning of the Quiet Revolution. In it, Marcel Chaput discusses reasons for advocating an independent Quebec and responds to objections to Quebec separatism. He begins by locating Quebec separatism in the human rights revolution that was sweeping the world. He continues by laying out arguments, considering objections, developing the arguments, answering more objections, and so on. Chaput's arguments in favour of separatism do not recite the litany of Quebec's grievances against English Canada; rather, he focuses on basic liberal concepts such as human dignity and the rights to freedom and self-determination, which can be found in the American Declaration of Independence, the French Declaration of the Rights of Man and of the Citizen, and the Universal Declaration of Human Rights.

In the second reading, Diane Lamoureux argues that both feminism and nationalism have politicized the concept of "identity." She discusses similarities and differences between feminism and nationalism regarding three aspects of identity construction. First, the movements constructed a politicized identity that was open to new developments and changes. Second, the movements developed a vision of an alternative community to replace the current, problematic one. In feminism, this initially took the form of sisterhood between women. However, it quickly became apparent that this relied on the problematic assumption that women were all the same. This led to critiques of single fixed identities by **postmodernists** and the search for a more adequate, complex conception of unity. Third, the movements imagined what relations with others (men and people outside Quebec) would be like in a world where feminists and nationalists had achieved their goals. (This is a difficult and complex reading. While Lamoureux is a professor, this excerpt comes from a book published by a popular non-academic press in Quebec—which says a lot about how sophisticated political discussion is among ordinary citizens in Quebec.)

The third reading by Charles Taylor discusses differences and similarities in the values of Quebec and "Canada outside Quebec" (COQ). The first question we need to ask, he says, is "What is a country for?" or, more specifically, "Why Canada?" and "Why Quebec?" Taylor's answer to the "Why Canada?" question discusses five features of Canadian identity: (a) Canada is less violent and has fewer conflicts than the US; (b) the Canadian commitment to "collective provision," the belief that we owe certain things to our fellow Canadians; (c) "the equalization of life conditions and life chances between the regions"; (d) multiculturalism; and (e) the *Charter*. In his answer to the "Why Quebec?" question, Taylor proposes a sixth condition, (f) preserving and promoting *la nation canadienne-française*. This in turn requires bilingualism plus some degree of autonomy for Quebec (asymmetrical federalism, though Taylor does not use the term). He then turns to the question of whether COQ can accept this sixth condition. Taylor says the differences between COQ and Quebec are due to the fact that each employs a different version of liberalism, and asks whether they can be reconciled. His answer is a provisional yes, if COQ can be convinced that its version of liberalism is not the only possible one.

Why Are There No Arguments against Quebec Nationalism?

Here we need to distinguish between Quebec nationalism and Quebec separatism. Chaput clearly favours Quebec separatism, and Lamoureux may also favour some form of separation. Taylor favours asymmetrical federalism. The authors present a range of views on the question of separation. But there is little disagreement among philosophers or even most politicians on the question of Quebec nationalism; that is, whether Quebec constitutes a sub-state nation within Canada and whether the federal government ought to recognize its nationhood. In 2006 Prime Minister Harper proposed a motion in Parliament, "That this

House recognize that the Québécois form a nation within a united Canada." It passed 265 to 16. Arguing against Quebec nationalism is a non-starter in Canada today.

The Moral and Political Preferences Indicator

Views on Quebec nationalism, like views on Aboriginal peoples, do not fit neatly on a political spectrum, particularly in Quebec. In general, English-speaking Canadians who are egalitarians are more likely to believe that Quebec's demands for asymmetrical federalism are justified than are conservative English-speaking Canadians. But there are significant exceptions. Mulroney, who was a neo-conservative on economic issues and a conservative centrist on social justice issues, fought hard to change the constitution to permit asymmetrical federalism, whereas Trudeau, who was an egalitarian centrist on some issues and a social democrat on others, was a committed opponent of asymmetrical federalism. Both the Meech Lake and Charlottetown Accords were supported by the Progressive Conservative, Liberal, and New Democratic parties, though not by the Reform Party. (This was before Reform and the Progressive Conservatives merged and became the Conservative Party.) The vast majority of Québécois, wherever they stand on the political spectrum, support either asymmetrical federalism or separation.

Notes

1. Richard Jones, "French Canadian Nationalism," The Canadian Encyclopedia, www.thecanadianencyclopedia.ca/en/article/french-canadian-nationalism/.
2. Michel Brunet, cited in Claude Bélanger, Quebec History > Events, Issues and Concepts of Quebec History > The Quiet Revolution, http://faculty.marianopolis.edu/c.belanger/quebechistory/events/quiet.htm.
3. Bélanger, "The Quiet Revolution."
4. Bélanger, Quebec History > Readings in Quebec History > Pierre Elliott (E.) Trudeau, Quebec and the Canadian Constitution.
5. Prime Minister Trudeau, speech in Parliament (8 October 1971), announcing Canada's multiculturalism policy, Canada History > Documents > Leaders > Trudeau > Multiculturalism, www.canadahistory.com/sections/documents/leaders/Trudeau/On%20Multiculturalism.html.
6. *Reference re Secession of Quebec* [1998] 2 S.C.R.: 220.
7. Nenad Miscevic, Nationalism > 3. The Moral Debate > 3.1 Classical and liberal nationalisms, Stanford Encyclopedia of Philosophy, http://plato.stanford.edu/entries/nationalism/.

Marcel Chaput
Why I Am a Separatist

AV = author's view; ~AV = not the author's view

The world is made up of Separatists; the man who is master of his home is a Separatist. Each of the hundred nations striving to maintain its national identity is Separatist. France and

England are mutually Separatist, even in relation to the Common Market.[1] And you who long for a real Canadian **Constitution**, you are a Separatist. The only difference between you and me is that you want Canada to be free in relation to England and the United States, and I want Quebec to be free in relation to Canada. In mathematical terms, Quebec's independence is to Canada as Canada's independence is to the United States and England. But Quebec is far more justified than English Canada in asserting its individuality, since of the four territories, Quebec alone has a distinct culture, whereas English Canada, the United States and England tend to be very similar.

In spite of this, Separatism has always received a poor press in Quebec. The very term Separatism is certainly responsible in part. It is negative and doesn't seem to encourage a constructive approach.

And yet, for anyone who pauses to reflect on it, Separatism leads on to great things: to Independence, Liberty, Fulfillment of the Nation, French Dignity in the New World.

It has become fashionable in some quarters to treat Separatists as dreamers. Thank heaven that there are still men and women in French Canada capable of dreaming! But to grasp the distinction between a practical dream and a utopia, you must at least be able to put aside the sort of subjective dogmatism, which immediately rejects the idea of independence for Quebec without a thought.

It is true that independence is a matter of character rather than of logic. Everyone is not capable of being independent. A feeling of pride is even more essential than having a reasonable claim.

If you possess this pride of which free men are made, if you can shake off all preconceived notions about the subject and bring a sincere, discerning attitude to the discussion, then, and only then, should we sit down and talk. . . .

Most of all, you would be wrong to think that I consider independence the solution to all of Quebec's problems; on the contrary, I believe that it would create many more new ones.

Why independence then?

Because it is highly desirable that a normal man or nation be free.

I just don't believe, as do certain MPs, that the bilingualism of French-Canadians is an indication of their superiority, but rather a proof of their enslavement. I cannot stand by silently, as others seemingly can, and watch the day-by-day extermination of my people, even if by our own foolishness we are more to blame than the "damned English."

The six million French-Canadians are no longer obliged to accept this minority position, which makes of us a people without a future, shut up in the vicious circle of destructive bilingualism.

Since I naturally owe my first allegiance to French Canada, before the **Dominion**, I must ask myself the question: which of two choices will permit French-Canadians to attain the fullest development—**Confederation**, in which they will forever be a shrinking minority, doomed to subjection?—or the independence of Quebec, their true native land, which will make them masters of their own destiny?

But judging by the reaction of some of my compatriots to this basic question, it seems to me that truly free French-Canadians are even harder to find than you would think, which is after all normal for a people in bondage.

Faced with Separatism, some smile ironically, others hide their eyes, the established well-to-do have proved to themselves that independence isn't necessary to the Good Life, the **bourgeois** have other things on their minds, and the **petty workers** are afraid of losing their jobs.

And then, after all, we aren't so badly off. Actually, we are quite well off. Who do these Separatist people think they are, coming along to disturb our serenity? Do they want to shut themselves up in the "Quebec reservation"?

And so on through the whole list of current objections.

But let's not get ahead of ourselves. Let us start at the beginning. . . .

The Historical Dimension

A World-Wide Trend to Independence

We of the mid-twentieth century are living [in] historic years. Since World War II more than thirty former colonies have liberated themselves from foreign domination to attain national and international **sovereignty**. In 1960 alone, seventeen African colonies, fourteen of them French-speaking, have obtained their independence. And now it is the turn of the French-Canadian people to arise and claim their rightful place among free nations.

Why Independence? We Are Free

Why independence? you may ask. What is this Separatism that is making so much fuss? We French-Canadians are free. We are free to speak our language, to practice our religion. We have the right to vote, even the right to be elected. Is not the very presence of a French-Canadian as Governor-General an outright refutation of Separatist claims? And what of the two French-Canadian Prime Ministers? And the head of the Supreme Court? And the generals? Are the Separatists trying to compare the French-Canadians to the African tribes who have recently won their independence? These [Africans], often illiterate, sometimes deprived of the most basic rights, exploited, living in under-developed countries, had a right to claim the independence they lacked. But as for us French-Canadians, the situation is quite different.

Similarity and Difference

It is true that our situation in French Canada is not identical with that of the [Africans]. It is true that we have enjoyed rights for a long time which these people have only recently acquired. But we are not assured of total independence by the mere fact that we have certain rights which give us a partial control of our national affairs, even if this control be much greater in practice than that held by the newly **decolonized** countries. You may be closer to your goal than a neighbour is, without having reached the goal.

In the rise of people toward independence, no two cases are identical. But French Canada *is* like all these new **sovereign** nations in that she too has been taken by force, occupied, dominated, exploited, and in that even today, her destiny rests to a great extent in the hands of a nation which is foreign to her. . . .

Confederation: The Lesser of Two Evils

To affirm, as some do, that Confederation was freely accepted by the French-Canadians of the time, is to play with words, to distort the meaning of liberty. First of all, the **BNA Act** was never put to the vote. It was imposed by a decree of parliament at Westminster,[2] and by a majority vote of twenty-six to twenty-two among the Canadian representatives.

For Confederation to have been labeled the free choice of the French-Canadians, it would have been necessary to have given them the freedom of choice between Confederation or total sovereignty. And this freedom was not granted, either by the London parliament or by the English-speaking colonies of America.

In 1867, French Canada, Lower Canada, old Canada in short, was a British colony, and the alternatives offered her did not include independence. She was a colony and was to remain so, inside or outside Confederation. If there was any freedom of choice, it was that of the convicted man who is allowed to choose between a fine and prison. Just as the prisoner chooses the fine, if he can afford it, French Canada entered Confederation. It was, in her opinion, the lesser of two evils. . . .

What About the Canadian Nation?

There is no Canadian **nation**. We cannot have a Canadian nation and a French-Canadian nation at the same time. There is a Canadian **State**.

Certain groups, invariably English, would like to see a genuine Canadian nation. But this would involve the negation of the French-Canadian group as such.

The Canadian State is a purely political and artificial entity formed originally by armed force and maintained by a submission of the French-Canadians to the federal government.

On the contrary, the French-Canadian nation is a natural entity whose bonds are those of culture, flesh and blood.

If the American army were to invade Mexico and force its amalgamation with the United States, there would still be a Mexican nation. In the same way there is still a French-Canadian nation.

The Confrontation of Two Nationalisms

The Separatists also urge French-Canadians to make their presence felt everywhere in Canada, in America, in the world. But we feel just as strongly that French-Canadians must be *in control* somewhere, in a country of their own, specifically in Quebec.

That is why modern Separatism constitutes an irreconcilable opposition to traditional nationalism. Whereas the latter is employed to uphold rights in a vast Canada in which French-Canada is a minority group, Separatists, the Freedom Fighters of Quebec, are aspiring to set up the French-Canadians as masters of their own destiny.

It has nothing whatsoever to do with Anglophobia, chronic discontent, or vengefulness. The removal of each individual injustice suffered by the French-Canadians will not cause the idea of an independent Quebec to disappear.

We want independence for a totally different reason. It is because dignity requires it. It is because of the idea that minorities, like absentees, are always wrong. . . .

A Pact between Two Great Races

French Canada is unfortunately populated with people who, for want [lack] of reality, like to tell themselves stories. One of the dangerous ones is that Confederation is a sacred pact between two great races, French and English. It is a poetic idea. It inspires you. But the fact remains that it is an illusion. For you can search in vain, in the texts and especially in the facts, without finding a single word or action to justify it.

All political decisions of importance in Canada are made by the Parliament or the Cabinet, where the French-Canadians are in a minority. Proof? Newfoundland's entrance to Confederation, Canada's membership in the UN, in NATO or in NORAD, had no need of French-Canada's approval. Even if we had been consulted, we couldn't have done anything because of our minority position.

You may retort that French is still an official language, but you would be wrong—or at least you would be only partly right. French is, along with English, official in Quebec—this makes us the *only* bilingual province in our dealings with the Ottawa Parliament and the Federal Courts of Justice. This limitation puts French on an unequal footing with the English from the outset.

In Parliament, nine per cent of the speeches have been given in French since the installation of simultaneous interpretation. Are the members from Quebec less talkative than their English colleagues? Or perhaps they simply want to show off their "bilingual superiority"? Nonsense! It is nothing but a minority reflex, conditioned by two hundred years of subjection.

The final result is that, internally, Canada is a predominantly English country and, from the outside, Canada is also an English country, a country in which, they say, English and French live in perfect harmony for the edification of humanity.

The Economic Dimension

After All, We're Not So Badly Off

-AV For many people, not only French-Canadians, the economic aspect of a problem is always the most important. Faced with the prospect of Quebec's independence, they invariably say that they will support the idea as soon as they see proof that Quebec would gain economically.

AV This subsection was not written to prove that an independent Quebec would be an economically sound proposition. We shall discuss this later. My only purpose for the moment is to remind you that the French-Canadians have gained nothing from Confederation; on the contrary, they are losing continuously.

Perhaps the relative comfort you enjoy makes you fear a lowering of your standard of living, a serious change in your habits, a prolonged economic recession. After all, the French-Canadians aren't so badly off, no matter what they say.

Let me hasten to remind you that individual liberty is not under discussion here. Certainly there are rich men, even millionaires, among the French-Canadians, which seems to show that a French-Canadian can make a lot of money, even under Confederation. But we are discussing French-Canadians as a people, as a nation, in their province of Quebec. The French-Canadian nation is economically weak and economically under-developed, living in economic bondage. . . .

A People in Bondage

There is no need to be an economist, statistician or informed industrialist to realize that the French-Canadians are not the masters, are not the proprietors of their own province or cities. You have only to take a stroll through any city in Quebec with your eyes open, to seize at a glance our economic insignificance. Our contribution is limited to furnishing cheap raw materials, cheap manpower and five million docile consumers. All this for the sake of a few crumbs.

We French-Canadians made up twenty-nine per cent of Canada's population in 1951, but our participation in the economy was limited to five or ten per cent, closer to five than to ten. In Quebec we are eighty-three per cent of the population, but less than twenty per cent of the economy is in our hands. At the Montreal Stock Exchange (you rarely hear it called *la Bourse de Montreal*), it is said that one per cent of the business is based on French-Canadian capital—in a city containing at least a million French-Canadians! Scarcely a month goes by that you don't learn in the papers or by word of mouth that another French-Canadian enterprise has sold out to a big American or Anglo-Canadian firm. It is a well-known fact, appearing in the papers every year, that Quebec has the greatest number of bankruptcies in Canada. The corner grocery, which used to be our own, has been supplanted, or rather, strangled, by the supermarkets, all of which are under foreign control. And the small grocer who has managed to survive has done so only by joining some *chain*, and the main link of this chain is invariably in the hands of foreign control as well.

The Labour Market

On the labour market, the French-Canadians are at the bottom of the ladder. You may insist that it is their own fault, that all they have to do is get more education to prepare themselves for better positions. But I insist that I am not attempting an assessment of commendation and rebuke—I am establishing facts.

For equal labour, workers in Quebec are paid less than in Ontario. If there is an economic recession or unemployment, Quebec always has the longest list of unemployed. If anyone receives a good salary, he is almost certain to be in the employ of a foreign company. But at the higher levels of these foreign companies, at directorship level, French-Canadians are no longer found. Even in the Federal corporations our compatriots are significantly rare. Out of the seventeen directors of the Bank of Canada, one is a French-Canadian; out of the seventeen vice-presidents of the CNR, none is French-Canadian. Out of the seven top officials in the new Federal ministry of forests, none is French-Canadian, although Quebec has twenty-five per cent of Canada's commercial forest area. In public office, the higher you go, the fewer French-Canadians you meet. The situation is the same in the armed forces. We are good enough when it comes to paying taxes, or playing the role of consumer and soldier, but we are not good enough to take our rightful place on the well-paid levels of Canadian life.

Quebec—Ottawa's Private Treasure Chest

If only Quebec got back in service what it gave to Ottawa. But far from it—it pays to have itself Anglicized and to maintain its state of bondage.

Quebec pays two billion dollars a year to Ottawa in taxes. It gets back only five hundred million dollars per year, twenty-five per cent of its contribution. . . .

English, Language of Labour and Thought

Any country in the world must have its bilinguals. Interpreters and translators are required in diplomatic service, transport, communications, hotels, the army, even in the civil service. But in what proportion? That is the problem. Let us be generous and say five per cent.

But in French-Canada, at least half the workers must know English to earn their living. Of these, at least half must, like me, throw off their native language with their overcoats at the office or factory entrance each morning—their native language, French, an international language, used by one hundred and fifty million people.

For the majority of French-Canadian workers, even in Quebec, English is the language of labour and thought. French? It is used in translations, in the family, in folklore. In his own language, the French-Canadian leads a fairytale existence. Active life, the life of earning enough to keep bread on the table, the life of entertainment, the life of the mind, is carried on in English as often as not. . . .

You think you are going to a French show—if you can find one at all. Two times out of three you will see the French version of a Hollywood hit. You open your French newspaper and read the French translation of an English translation of a speech given in French by General de Gaulle.[3] The Canadian Press (there is no such thing as *la Presse Canadienne*) has not even passed on the original, and this in a country where they say French is an official language. You subscribe to a Canadian magazine of genuinely French content, only to find that it has recently been bought out by Anglo-American capital. You pass by a large building, even in Montreal—you will find three words of French on a bronze plaque and a bilingual elevator-boy. Seek no further. That is the extent of the French. "Patrons are requested to leave their tongue in the umbrella rack."

What About the Schools?

Why should our schools teach French, real French, if the language is of so little use here? It is English that we need, and more and more of it. Really, can you imagine a more absurd situation than the one in which you and I have found ourselves? Six, eight, ten, twelve years of French studies, when this language, which is supposedly so beautiful, is of no use in earning your daily bread. So many long years spent learning a language when English is what you really need when you leave school. As a result, parents demand more English, and those parents are right. Far be it from me to criticize them, for their logic is impeccable. Parents see things in their true light, and children too. They realize quite well that without English you might not be able to earn your keep in Canada, that without English you run the risk of swelling the ranks of Quebec's unemployed.

But what is the result of these repeated demands, which are heard today more than yesterday, and tomorrow more than today? The more bilingual our children become, the more they will use English; the more they use English, the less use they will get from French; and the less use they get from French, the more they will use English: *It is a paradox of French-Canadian life: the more bilingual we become, the less need there is to be bilingual.* This is a path which can lead us only to Anglification. Moreover, we have already come such a long way in this direction that we would be better off to know only English—so let's get on with the process and speak no more about it. . . .

Bilingualism—a Sign of Bondage or Superiority?

It may seem strange to some people that a French-Canadian like me, who earns his living in English, should not appreciate the benefits of bilingualism.

Well, I do; I am very happy that I know English, and if I didn't know it yet, I would learn it. I derive satisfaction from knowing English, just as I should like to do with several more languages, English even more than other languages because it is the most widespread in North America. But it is not a question of deciding whether it is useful or not for French-Canadians to know English, but of discovering what this knowledge and its constant use is costing them.

They learn English to the detriment of their native language which is deteriorating, their French culture which is wilting away, their dignity which is being insulted.

I didn't learn English out of intellectual curiosity. I learned it because it was the language of the stronger side, because I needed it to earn my living. Perhaps a man who knows two languages is worth two men, but a man who is forced to speak the Other Fellow's language in order to eat is worth only half a man. The misfortune of the French-Canadian people is to mistake the fetters of its bilingualism for a sign of superiority. Just as a little boy afraid of the dark will whistle to bolster his courage, the brow-beaten French-Canadian prides himself on his bilingualism to hide his inferiority complex. . . .

The Social Dimension

We Are Inferior to Ourselves

As in other spheres, or perhaps even more here than elsewhere, French-Canadians are inferior to themselves. You often hear it said: What have we to complain about? We have accomplished a great deal. Haven't we produced two prime ministers, a governor-general, a chief justice [of the Supreme Court]? Don't we have our artists, our scientists, our writers?

It is true that, in spite of serious difficulties, French-Canadians have nevertheless produced a lot. But, for nations, just as for men, it isn't enough to know whether they have produced; we must ask whether they have produced enough—whether they have produced as much as their **capabilities** permit. This is the parable of the talents.[4]

Far be it from me to excuse my compatriots by blaming the "damned English" for our inferiority. But all the same we must recognize the fact that the French-Canadians have not had the same history as the English-speaking Canadians during the past two hundred years, not even in the ninety-four years of Confederation. Armed with **abundant** capital, political authority and numerical superiority, the English Canadians had an easier time of it than we. We had the talents—and we still have—but we lacked the financial boost and political favour, so that, socially, we are second-rate citizens.

In the Workaday World

In the workaday world of industry and commerce, we are on the bottom rung of the ladder. Quebec is the place to go for cheap labour; in times of crisis or economic recession, Quebec always has the greatest number of unemployed. This was obvious in the winter of 1960–61. Across the country, eleven per cent of the working force was idle in March, according to the papers; in Quebec, the figure was fourteen per cent. . . .

All you have to do is open your eyes: all the large industries in Quebec make excessive use of the English to the detriment of the French. In so doing, they are merely following the example of those around them, but this marked predominance of English places the French-Canadian worker in an inferior position from the start. That is obvious. There is a dividing line between the management and the labour force. The first is English, the second French. . . .

But in the face of the imminent dangers confronting the French-Canadian nation, I fear that the outgrown methods of this noble society are no longer sufficient. Confederation, **pan-Canadianism**, bilingualism, and the whole Canadian way of life have depersonalized the French-Canadian, have even robbed him, over the years, of his capacity for indignation. At his most brash, he is no more than a beggar. The schools have forgotten about **nationalist** education, and life in Quebec doesn't even teach us our language. Something better than the repetition of the same old reports must be found if we are going to change things. . . .

Independence of Quebec

The Rejection of Liberty

You have just read, a few pages back, that a minority which wishes to live cannot hand over the control of its affairs to a foreign majority. That is the simple reason why the Separatists want Quebec to be independent. As long as the French-Canadians form a linguistic and cultural minority, they will be doomed to subjection and mediocrity. It is not because of hostility or a desire for revenge against the English; it is not a way of finding an alibi for all our stupidities and cowardly acts; it is not a way of excusing men by blaming the **institutions**. On the contrary, it is based on a purely mathematical truth of democracy—the majority prevails over the minority. Either we must bow to the decisions of the majority and stop complaining, or withdraw from Confederation. The desire to stick with Confederation at all costs is a search for excuses to justify the rejection of liberty.

Commonwealth and Crown

Why should we kid ourselves any longer? For two hundred years the French-Canadians have been trying to free themselves from the British Crown, the symbol of foreign domination. All the French-Canadian nationalist movements of the past have embodied this subconscious or avowed [acknowledged] refusal to submit. It is high time that English Canada realized the fact that, outside of a few rare politicians, the French-Canadians have *never* accepted subjection to British Royalty. They simply endured it. We had to submit to it under force of arms; you can't reproach us all the same if we want to free ourselves from it now.

The formation of a new confederation with English Canada can only mean continued domination for the French. It is normal that English Canada should be attached to the British Crown and all its symbols—the Union Jack, the Red Ensign,[5] **protocol**, etc., and they cannot be reproached for it, but nothing holds the French Canadians to these things.

In the year 1961, the British Crown can mean only one thing: the free, voluntary and intentional acceptance of a tie, on the part of a people which has the right to turn down this tie. If the British Crown is imposed where it is not wanted, then it becomes **imperialistic**. . . .

Well, we French-Canadians *do* form a nation, simply by possessing all necessary **attributes**. We are certainly large enough—five or six million is more than necessary for the foundation of an independent nation. Half of the members of the UN are smaller.

But the population figure alone does not make us a nation. We have numerous institutions—we have a territory which we have occupied for almost four centuries, Quebec, which belongs to us by virtue of Article 109 of the BNA Act; we speak the same language,

French; above all, we have maintained a collective will to live unbroken even by the events of the past two centuries.

A nation we certainly are, all the more since our ties are those of flesh and blood and spirit, whereas our membership in what some people call the Canadian nation is a merely political one imposed by circumstances. . . .

In practice, this situation is at our throats every day. Every day we have to choose between being French-Canadian or Canadian because there is no longer any equivalence or conciliation [dispute resolution] possible between the two. Nowadays, if you want to be *Canadian*, you must be English. . . .

Nevertheless, the theory of Quebec's independence has other claims to desirability than that of being normal. As surely as Confederation has kept us in an unfavourable position by making us into a minority group, Quebec's independence will ensure our advancement by handing over to us the control of our own destiny.

Quebec's independence is therefore desirable for the same reasons that Confederation, in which we are the minority, is not.

Historically, Quebec's independence would allow the French-Canadians to enjoy liberty. History intended that there should be a free French people on American soil. By claiming independence for Quebec, we are merely leading our people back to its historic destiny. After being conquered by armed might, dominated by a foreign nation, after having fought the hard battle for survival, French Canada, by leaving Confederation, will be doing nothing more than leaving behind it one further stage in its long march toward full sovereignty.

Politically, Quebec's independence is desirable because it would take the French-Canadians out of their position of numerical helplessness. In politics as in everything else, for the French-Canadians as for all people, numerical balance is essential to the smooth running of affairs. Starting with our Independence Day, Quebec will negotiate on equal terms with other countries, including the rest of Canada. Once it has become the recognized master of its destiny, a sovereign Quebec can then approve any **unions**, sign any treaties, practise any amount of friendly relations, [and] set up any plans for helping under-developed countries or Canadian provinces that are dictated by its own responsibilities and interests.

Independence is politically desirable because it is always good for people to be free, and because no nation has ever become great by leaving the political control of its destiny in the hands of another.

Economically, political independence is desirable for Quebec because, without control over political power, economic independence remains a sweet daydream. . . .

There will always be some who assert that the economy has nothing to do with **nationalistic** spirit, but this is only true for the man without a country. It is also true, however, that nationalistic spirit is not something you can acquire at will. It is something permanent which penetrates into all realms of activity and which springs from a deeper feeling—that of a nation that is well-defined, and quite capable of conducting its own affairs.

Culturally, independence would be the nation's salvation. Do you realize what life would be like in a **unilingual** country? Morning to night you would hear the same language, the national language.

It would mean the end of the absurd and deadly situation, economically and culturally, for the majority of French-Canadians, the situation of working in English after having gone to French schools.

It would mean the end of this noxious co-existence of two languages and two systems of thought which makes French-Canadian bilingualism into the *doubtful art of speaking two languages at once.*

Do not misunderstand me; I consider English to be a beautiful language, when spoken properly. It is the mutual penetration of two languages, of two thought-patterns, which is harmful. And Quebec's independence would separate them—not by raising a cultural wall around Quebec, which would be impossible and undesirable. Since it is geographically part of America, a totally French Quebec will obviously have to open its doors to Anglo-American culture.

But as in everything, it is a question of balance. A French Quebec can make no cultural progress unless it feeds principally on French cultural traditions, in lesser proportions on traditions from English Canada, America and elsewhere.

At present, under Confederation, Anglo-American language and culture are weighing down too heavily on the French consciousness. . . .

Basing our case on the United Nations Charter which stipulates—Article 1, paragraph 2—that all peoples have the right of **self-determination**, we will then begin negotiations with Ottawa. And Ottawa, which has also signed this Charter, cannot do other than agree.

Notes

1. The European Common Market was the precursor to the European Union. [Editor]
2. The British Parliament meets in London in the Palace of Westminster. [Editor]
3. General Charles de Gaulle (1890–1970) was the leader of the Free French Forces who resisted Nazi rule over France during World War II. He served as President of France from 1959 to 1969. [Editor]
4. The parable of the talents is a story told by Jesus in the New Testament. Three servants are each given some money to manage while their master is away travelling. (A "talent" was a kind of ancient money.) Returning home, the master rewards the two servants who increased the amount of money they were given through investment and business, but the third, who failed to increase the amount he was given, is punished by his master. [Editor]
5. The Union Jack is the flag of the United Kingdom. The Red Ensign was the Canadian flag at the time Chaput wrote this; the maple leaf became the official Canadian flag in 1965. [Editor]

Diane Lamoureux

Two Ways to Politicize Identity

AV = author's view; ~AV = not the author's view

[This is an important but very difficult reading, which is why it is so short. You should read the Notes if you want to understand it.—Editor]

If we want to understand the relationship that Québécoise feminists have (and that they try to maintain) with the Québécois state, we cannot rely on a general analysis of the **welfare state** and the possibility of politically regulating social relations between the sexes—even if such an analysis does explain the sometimes tense relationship between feminists and the state. We also must understand how, by politicizing "identity," feminism and nationalism can be reunited.

In order to examine the relationship between feminism and nationalism, I will begin with two quite different texts that allow us to draw analogies that we must then analyze. These are an article by Ti-Grace Atkinson concerning what she calls the "nationalization" of feminism,[1] and an article by Brian Walker that extends the concept of "nation" to groups that are not **ethnocultural** in kind.[2]

Atkinson criticizes feminism for behaving like nationalism—that is, for fitting women into the model of the "in itself" and the "for itself" (an approach pioneered by Simone de Beauvoir in *The Second Sex*)[3]—and consequently for aiming to develop a political project only for women, instead of one for all people. Atkinson is especially critical of the idea of female separatism. She distinguishes five steps in the development of second-wave feminism that, she says, have more or less condemned the movement to ineffectiveness.

The first step is [1] tactical nationalism, that is, separating from mixed organizations. Tactical nationalism became [2] strategic nationalism: the oppression of women was supposed to allow us to understand all forms of oppression, but this made developing the movement [rather than ending oppression] feminism's main goal. Strategic nationalism then evolved into [3] cultural nationalism, by "reclaiming" and **valorizing** the feminine and by postulating the existence of a women's culture. Cultural nationalism quickly turned into [4] territorial nationalism, which aimed to construct a women's subculture within **patriarchal** culture. Finally, the appearance of lesbian separatism [in the 1970s] produced, for certain parts of the movement, [5] the equivalent of a nation-state project.

Walker's view is quite different. He targets what he calls nationalist-culturalist arguments like those of Taylor or Kymlicka which claim, from a liberal perspective, that state intervention is necessary to protect minority cultures, because they provide a "**context of choice**" for the individuals who compose them. Walker says that, by limiting their discussions to ethnocultural groups, Taylor and Kymlicka do not see that other groups also qualify as nations, because they too provide a context of choice for their members. He cites the lesbian and gay community (which he considers to be a single community) as an example.

Walker argues that there is a distinct **queer** culture [that is analogous to ethnic and national cultures]. It provides a refuge from the pervasive **homophobia** in mainstream society. It also offers models for individuals to orient themselves in the world (coming out, ways of relating to others, sites for socialization), which provide a context of choice unique to the formation of individual identity. Finally, queer culture makes possible the development of **solidarity** and forms of identification.

Atkinson's and Walker's arguments focus on the concepts of (1) identity, (2) community, and (3) relations with others. These concepts allow us to discern similarities as well as differences between nationalism and feminism.

[Identity]

The concept of identity leads us to question the justification of political movements and the existence of political subjects. Recently there has been a renewed interest in the question of identity among political theorists.

. . .

In modernity, personal identity is a reflexive process.[4] That is, the "subject" constitutes itself through a series of experiences that it integrates into a narrative. In large part, we construct our identities from the choices available to us. We build our ways of life by trying to make our various options coherent, based on our choices and whether we can change them. However, our identities are not purely the product of choice or will. Indeed, the possibilities available to us vary according to the circumstances of our development: whether we are rich or poor, a man or a woman, white or of colour, are all relevant. But we are not entirely determined by our circumstances, either; in part, we shape them.

Feminists have distinguished at least three levels in the development of [feminist] identity. On the first level, the woman refuses her assigned identity by refusing to correspond to the "ideal" patriarchal woman. The second involves her relationship to a radical identity: she is not the patriarchal woman, but neither is she solely a radical. Finally, on the third level, feminism opens up the possibility of constructing a female subject that **transcends** the previous dimensions of her existence. She can aim to construct her identity by integrating/surpassing it, that is, by **subverting** what it means to be a woman.

Similarly, from the national perspective, we begin with the definition of "nation." In the case of Quebec, this definition involves the trilogy of language, culture, and institutions. But it is also true that nations transform themselves; they are not born from the abstract concept of "the nation." There is continuity in the Québécois nation despite the fact that the language spoken today is a standardized and normalized version of the written language, rather than the diverse regional dialects that existed before public education and television homogenized them. Similarly, for a long time most cultural **referents** were rural, while today urban referents dominate. Mainstream institutions have also changed. All this means that contemporary national [Québécois] identity is substantially different from, yet is still historically continuous with, national identity in the eighteenth century.

We can see that Quebec nationalism's receptivity to feminism since the 1970s—a receptivity that conflicts with the tendencies to **machismo** inherent in nationalist thought—is partly due to the chronological overlap between their two processes of identity formation, overlap in which feminists have played a role in several respects. Feminism has been the ground not only of the demands for equality and independence, but also of the interconnected demands for liberation from assigned identities, as in the popular slogan "No Free Quebec Without the Liberation of Women, No Liberation of Women Without a Free Quebec."

[Community]

The second element, the vision of community, derives in large part from identity formation. Feminist and nationalist movements simutaneously construct a collective and an individual identity, neither of which is reducible to the other.

~AV The fictional unity of women as a group is constructed in a classic way: first find an enemy, a principle of opposition—men. Next define social relations as binary,[5] and reclaim and **valorize** femininity. Then, women who had defined themselves mostly in opposition to femininity suddenly "discover" they are female; this corresponds to the cultural nationalism phase discussed by Atkinson.

Next comes dogmatism, along with the denial of reality and the pressure to conform: a real feminist is—my reflection [that is, someone identical to me]. The much-criticized [patriarchal] One[6] turns into a radical One that is just as oppressive. At this point the movement fragments into many separate communities, and it becomes difficult to share and talk among ourselves because discussion or debate requires us to first admit that we are not all "the same." The community simultaneously censors individuals and undermines their accountability to each other. It becomes a **normative** ideal.

AV The presumed sameness of early feminism has since been reconceptualized to understand the relations between women better. The concept of sisterhood was criticized and replaced with the idea of a political community of women. The analysis took two directions: on the one hand the critique of identity, done mostly by **postmodernists**; on the other, the search for a complex yet non-homogenizing unity.

[The Critique of Identity]

Postmodernists have focused on the necessity of rupturing fixed identities.[7] These imply some distance from contemporary, and thus sexist, social expectations of the category "woman," and from the place assigned to women in social relations. And, in fact, one of feminism's major accomplishments has been to broaden what we mean by the word "woman."

Putting fluid identities[8] into practice (and performing them[9]) requires that we question the logic of feminist action and its theoretical grounding. Most important, at the political level, is maintaining a capacity for action that is not based on the fiction of sameness and transparency in the world of women.

[The Search for a Complex Unity]

~AV In the beginning, feminism operated rather like nationalism, with its saga of oppression, its **valorization** of the feminine, its focus only on women. This "nationalist" logic conjured up a new idealized model of the family in which there were only sisters (sometimes with mean phallic mothers[10] to reinforce the bonds between the sisters). The sisterhood claimed that in the world of women all divisions would disappear, and we would enter into a universe of openness in which there would be no estrangement among us.

AV As a counterpart to this utopian fantasy, some theorists envision the women's movement as a coalition. For example, Butler argues that, to maintain feminism's effectiveness, we must recognize the differences that separate us and treat them politically—that is, our practices must both acknowledge our differences and reflect them.[11]

Young approaches the problem of sameness and diversity in a different way.[12] Her goal is to define women in a way that does not oppose "women" and "feminism." She also wants to account, socially and politically, both for women's shared condition under patriarchy and for the socially significant differences between them. She uses Sartre's concept of the "series"[13] to explain the external unity of women and their internal diversity. This allows her to envision feminism as taking a political stand on behalf of women, without needing the fiction of unity among women to be effective.

The same phenomenon of homogenization occurs in Québécois nationalism. The main difference between it and feminism is that nationalism did not arise solely from an imagined community,[14] despite its attempt to evolve from ethnic to civic nationalism.[15] . . .

[Relations with Others]

Finally, identity and identity-construction are central to the **emancipatory** movements that have **animated** modern democracies. These movements can be seen as liberating individuals or groups from constraints that hinder their self-realization. Liberation has two dimensions: on the one hand, there is the attempt to throw off the shackles of the past, thus making it possible to shape the future, primarily by putting an end to statuses, to assigned identities; on the other hand, there is the desire to overturn the illegitimate domination of individuals or groups.

Thus emancipatory politics involves criticizing the concept of power based on hierarchy, which becomes **exploitation**, inequality, and oppression. Unjustly **monopolizing** resources—especially money or political power—is exploitation. The systematically differential access to these resources[16] is inequality. The illegitimacy of these differences is oppression. An emancipatory politics contrasts the principles of exploitation, inequality, and oppression with those of justice, equality, and mutual recognition.[17]

This focusses on what we should eliminate rather than what we should strive for. Hence the distrust of utopias, although emancipatory projects all contain at least a dash of utopianism, if only because they claim that things could be otherwise. Furthermore, emancipatory politics emphasize the concept of **autonomy**. This presupposes that social life is organized so individuals are free and able to act on their environment—that is, that the environment actually provides the resources they need to act freely. "Freedom" here is not the projection of the individual's will but rather the capacity to act responsibly, in the Kantian sense of the term.[18]

The emancipatory dimension animates "old" social movements as well as the "new" ones. ~AV The "old" social movements aim to transform society, consistent with their vision of social unity, AV whereas the "new" ones promote the construction of subjects, in a time when we are no longer sure that the subject is the centre of the world.

What makes identity a political problem is that it is a process of building awareness. ~AV In fact, if our identities were not problematic, we could simply "discover" and acknowledge them. AV But the dynamic of the new social movements is quite different: a good part of their job is precisely to define the new identity that also causes them to exist. . . .

~AV In nationalism and feminism, political action is directed more toward the self than outward. The movement allows the formation of the political subject and, in certain periods, it even gets bogged down in a completely narcissistic **solipsism**. Its coherence comes less from outside, from opposition, than from the internal work of homogenization that it performs on itself.

AV As a result, both nationalism and feminism partly drop the third element, relations with others. This is clear enough in feminism, which has tended to target sexism rather than men. As for nationalism—at least the kind that, like Québécois nationalism, is both liberal and democratic—it is more concerned with defining "us" than with seeking an opponent. This does not mean the image of the other is never treated as an enemy, as it was in [Jacques Parizeau's] insidious claim that "money and the ethnic vote" stole victory from the **sovereigntists** in the [1995] referendum.[19] However, we know we must find a reasonable compromise with the other—hence the idea of **sovereignty association** to describe future Canada–Quebec relations [in the 1980 referendum], or the offer of partnership in the 1995 referendum question.[20]

Notes

1. Ti-Grace Atkinson, "Le nationalisme féminin," *Nouvevlles questions féministes* 6–7 (1984).
2. Brian Walker, "Une critique du nationalisme culturaliste: l'idée d'une nation gaie," in François Blais, Guy Laforest and Diane Lamoureux, eds., *Libéralismes et nationalismes* (Sainte-Foy: Presses de l'Université Laval, 1995).
3. Roughly, the "in itself" is object-like or sub-human existence and the "for itself" is human existence. Some oppressed groups and colonized nations claim they have been forced to live as objects for others rather than as equal human beings. The concepts come originally from the 19th-century German philosopher GWF Hegel, who used them to explain the development of self-consciousness. De Beauvoir uses them to explain the condition of women. [Editor]
4. A reflexive process is one in which people's actions and ideas affect the very actions or ideas they are developing. In this case, Lamoureux is saying that the process of identity-formation changes the identities we form. [Editor]
5. In Western cultures, many things are defined as binary opposites—man and woman, mind/soul and body, reason and emotion, human and animal, strong and weak, etc. Feminists have criticized this way of thinking for several reasons. First, it tends to privilege the first item of each pair and define the second in terms of the it (e.g., women are not men, bodies are not transcendent, emotions are unreasonable), as if the second item has no existence apart from the first. Second, the privileged items tend to be associated with each other—men are associated with the mind/soul, reason, humanity, and strength, and women with the body, emotions, animality, and weakness—which is false in many cases (all men are not reasonable or strong and all women are not emotional or weak). Third, the privileged items are viewed as nobler or better than their supposed opposites, which is also false in many cases. Fourth, it mis-describes reality; there may well be more than two possibilities (e.g., many races), the possibilities may exist along a continuum (as "masculine" and "feminine" do), or the two may be mutually necessary rather than opposites (there is good psychological evidence that reason is impossible without emotions). [Editor]
6. The One and the Other are concepts from *The Second Sex*. Roughly, the One is the universal or standard, while the Other is the particular or the exception, defined only in relation to the standard. De Beauvoir argues that men have defined themselves as the standard and women as non- or sub-standard, with no existence apart from men. [Editor]
7. To "rupture fixed identities" means to bring the identities to consciousness and examine them critically, at which point their inconsistencies become obvious and they burst, showing they are not really fixed. [Editor]
8. Fluid identities are not fixed, but change over time in response to different circumstances, conditions, relations, and so on. [Editor]
9. Judith Butler argues that gender is "real only to the extent that it is performed"—that is, there are no "true" male and female genders or identities, just **socially constructed** ones. See "Performative Acts and Gender Constitution: An Essay in Phenomenology and Feminist Theory," *Theatre Journal* 40, 4 (1988): 519–31. [Editor]
10. In psychoanalysis, a phallic mother is a boy's fantasy of a mother with both breasts and a penis. Here, Lamoureux uses the term to signify women who identify with patriarchy. [Editor]
11. See, for example, the first part of Butler's *Gender Trouble* (New York: Routledge, 1990).
12. Iris Young, "Gender as Seriality," *Signs* 19, 3 (1994).
13. For Sartre, a series is a group of people who are unified passively rather than actively. He gives as examples people waiting in line for a bus, listening to a radio broadcast or watching street theatre.

Being "someone in line," "a radio listener," or "a street theatre viewer" is an accidental membership, a byproduct of social conditions that both permit and constrain individuals' behaviour (e.g., etiquette about waiting in lines, the availability of a variety of radio shows, appropriate responses to street theatre). There are groups that people consciously choose to join, like clubs, teams, and political parties, but they do not consciously choose to join a series. [Editor]

14. "Imagined communities" is a term coined by Benedict Anderson to refer to communities that cannot be face-to-face. We identify with our fellow citizens not as because we actually know them but because we share similar ideas of what it means to be Québécois, Canadian, or Bolivian. See his *Imagined Communities: Reflections on the Origin and Spread of Nationalism* (London: Verso, 1983; revised edition 1991). Lamoureux's point here is that while Quebec began as a face-to-face society where people were linked by blood, it is no longer face-to-face or defined by blood. Women and feminists, on the other hand, never were part of a face-to-face society comprised only of female blood relatives. [Editor]
15. Ethnic nationalism is based on ties of blood, while civic nationalism is based on political identification with a community. [Editor]
16. Access to resources such as money and political power is "systematically differential" if members of some groups consistently have fewer resources than others. [Editor]
17. "Mutual recognition" means seeing and treating each other as equals. The term comes originally from Hegel. [Editor]
18. For Kant, **autonomous** individuals act in accordance with reason rather than desire. Desire makes us its slaves; only reason can make us truly free. Reason tells individuals what their duties are, and autonomous individuals do their duty. [Editor]
19. After losing the 1995 sovereignty referendum by a very narrow margin (50.56% No to 49.44% Yes), former PQ Premier Jacques Parizeau claimed that "money and the ethnic vote" cost sovereigntists the election. Most sovereigntists disagree with Parizeau's claim. [Editor]
20. In 1995, the Parti Québécois held a referendum on sovereignty. The question before voters was, "Do you agree that Quebec should become sovereign after having made a formal offer to Canada for a new economic and political partnership within the scope of the bill respecting the future of Quebec and of the agreement signed on June 12, 1995?" The "bill respecting the future of Quebec" gave the Quebec National Assembly the power to declare Quebec sovereign. The "agreement signed on June 12, 1995" was an agreement between the leaders of the Parti Québécois, the Bloc Québécois, and the Action démocratique du Québec to negotiate a partnership with Canada "so that we can manage our common economic space together, particularly by means of joint institutions, including institutions of a political nature." A copy of this agreement was sent to every household in Quebec several weeks before the referendum. The referendum failed by the narrowest of margins (50.56% No to 49.44% Yes). [Editor]

Charles Taylor

Shared and Divergent Values

Are there divergences of value between the different regions of Canada? In a sense, these are minimal. There appears to be a remarkable similarity throughout the country and across the French-English difference when it comes to the things in life that are important. Even when it comes to the values that specifically relate to political culture, there seems to be broad agreement about equality, non-discrimination, the **rule of law**, the **mores** of

representative democracy, about social provision, about violence and firearms, and a host of other issues.

This was not always the case. Half a century ago, it seemed that there were serious differences between the two major groups as far as political culture was concerned. . . .

. . .

Ironically, at the very moment when we agree upon so much, we are close to breakup. We have never been closer to breakup in our history, although our values have never been so uniform. . . .

Why Canada?

So what is the problem? It emerges when you ask another kind of question, which also is in the realm of values in some broad sense. Not "What do people cherish as good?" but "What is a country for?" That is, what ought to be the basis of unity around which a **sovereign** political entity can be built? . . .

In Canada outside Quebec (COQ) the alternatives have been two: the country or bits of it could join together or could join the United States; also, the bits might have failed to join together—or, having joined, might one day deconfederate. So there are two **existential** questions for COQ which we can call the unity and distinctness questions, respectively. For Quebec there is one big question, which is too familiar and too much on the agenda today to need much description. It is the issue of whether to be part of Canada or not; and if so, how. I stress that neither of the existential alternatives may be strong options in COQ today, but that does not stop them functioning as reference points for self-definition, as ways of defining the question "What do we exist for?" . . .

So what are the answers? It will be easier to set out the problem by taking "English" Canada first. The answer here used to be simple. Way back when it really fitted into our official name of British North America, the distinctness question answered itself; and unity seemed to be the **corollary** of the drive for distinctness in face of the American colossus. But as the Britishness, even "Englishness," of non-Quebec Canada declines, this becomes less and less **viable** as an answer. . . . What binds Canada together outside Quebec is thus no longer a common provenance [place of origin], and less and less is it a common history. But people find the bonding elements in political **institutions** and ways of being. This is not a total break from the old identity, because Britishness also defined itself largely in terms of political institutions: parliamentary government, a certain **juridical** tradition, and the like. . . .

Canadians feel that they are different from the Americans, because (a) they live in a less violent and conflict-ridden society. This is partly just a matter of luck. We do not have a history that has generated an undeclared, low-level race war continually feeding itself in our cities. It is also a matter of political culture. From the very beginning, Americans have put a value on energetic, direct defence of rights and therefore are ready to mitigate their condemnation of violence. . . . Canadians tend to put more value on "peace, order, and good government." At least, this is how we see ourselves, which is perhaps what is important for our purposes; but there seems to be some truth in the perception.

As a consequence, there is more tolerance here of rules and restrictions that are justified by the need for order. With it, there is more of a favourable prejudice (at least in

English Canada) and a free gift of the benefit of the doubt to the police forces. Hence the relative absence of protest when the War Measures Act was invoked in 1970[1]. . . .

Related to this first point is a second point (b) that Canadians see their political society as more committed to collective provision, over against an American society that gives greater weight to individual initiative. Appeals for reduced government can be heard from the right of the political spectrum in both countries, but the idea of what reduced government actually means seems to be very different. There are regional differences in Canada, but generally Canadians are proud of and happy with their social programs, especially health insurance, and find the relative absence of these in the United States disturbing. The fact that poverty and destitution have been left to proliferate in American cities as they did during the Reagan years is generally seen here as a black mark against that society. Canadian practice may not be as much better as many of us believe, but the important point is that this is seen as a difference worth preserving.

Thus these two answers—(a) law and order, and (b) collective provision—help to address the distinctness question. They explain why we are a distinct political unit and why we want to remain so. But what answers the unity question? Why be a single country, and what common goals ought to animate this country? In one sense (a) and (b) can serve here as well if we think (as many Canadians instinctively do) that we need to hang together in order to maintain this alternative political culture as a viable option in North America. Moreover (b) can be logically extended into one of the **principal** declared common objectives of the Canadian **federation** in recent decades, namely (c) the equalization of life conditions and life chances between the regions. The **solidarity** of collective provision, which within each regional society generates such programs as Medicare, can be seen as finding its logical expression in a solidarity of mutual help between regions.

So Canadian **federalism** has generated the practices of large-scale redistribution of fiscal resources through equalization payments, and attempts have been made at regional development. . . . We perhaps owe the drive to equality to the fact that we have been confronted with existential questions in a way that our neighbours have not since 1865. The Canadian federal **union** has been induced to justify itself, and greater interregional solidarity may be one of the fruits of this underlying *angst.*

. . .

. . . Over the decades English Canada has been becoming more and more diverse and less and less "English." The fact that it has always been an immigrant society (that is, one that functions through admitting a steady stream of new arrivals), on top of the fact that it could not aspire to make immigrants over to its original mould, has meant that it has **de facto** become more and more **multicultural** over the years. It could not aspire to assimilate the newcomers to an existing mould, because this mould was originally British, hence ethnic . . . . It was never as clear what the Canadian identity amounted to in political terms, and insofar as it was conceived as British it could not be considered **normative** for new arrivals. First, it was only the identity of one part of the country and, second, it could not but come to be seen as one ethnic background among others.

Canadians have seen their society as less of a melting pot than the United States; . . . people have spoken of a Canadian "mosaic." So this has even become, for some, a new facet of their answer to the distinctiveness question, under the rubric (d) **multiculturalism**. This is also far from trouble-free. Questions are being posed in both the major cultures about the pace and even goals of integration, or assimilation of immigrants into the larger anglophone or francophone society. This is particularly troubling in Quebec, which has much less historic experience of assimilating immigrants and a much higher proportion of whose francophone population is *pure laine*.[2]

This makes even more acute the need for a further point of unity, a common reference point of identity, which can rally people from many diverse backgrounds and regions. In a quite astonishing way (e) the ***Charter of Rights and Freedoms*** has come to fill this role in English Canada in the past few years. It is astonishing, because as recently as 1980 it [the *Charter*] did not exist. Nor was there that much of a groundswell of support demanding its introduction before it became a bone of contention between federal and provincial governments in the run-up to the patriation of 1981–82. . . . For many people, it has come in the space of a few years to define in part the Canadian political identity. And since in COQ the national identity has to be defined in terms of political institutions (for reasons rehearsed above), this has been a fateful development.

Why Quebec?

How about Quebec? How can it go about answering its existential question? The terms are very different. In Quebec, there is not a distinctness issue. The language and culture by themselves mark us off from Americans, and also from other Canadians. Much of (a) to (e) is seen as a "good thing" in Quebec. Regarding (a)—law and order—people do not compare themselves a lot with the United States, but there is no doubt that Quebeckers are spontaneously on the side of law and order and are even more horrified by **internecine** [mutually destructive] conflict than other Canadians are. The members of the FLQ utterly and totally relegated themselves to irrecoverable history as soon as they murdered Pierre Laporte[3]. . . . The reaction to the massacre of the women at Montreal's Ecole Polytechnique in 1989[4] is also eloquent on this score. Quebec society reacted more like a wounded family than like a large-scale, impersonal political unit.

Regarding (b)—collective provision—it goes without saying that people are proud of their social programs in the province and want to keep them. Point (d)—multiculturalism—is more problematic. As a federal policy, multiculturalism is sometimes seen as a device to deny French-speaking minorities their full **recognition**, or even to reduce the importance of the French in Canada to that of an outsized ethnic minority. Meanwhile, within Quebec itself, the growing diversity of francophone society is causing much heartburn and anxiety. Point (c)—regional equality and mutual self-help—is generally supported in Quebec, and even (e)—the Charter—was viewed favourably until it came to be perceived as an instrument for the advancement of the uniformity of language regimes across the country. Even now its other provisions are widely popular.

But these do not go very far to answer the question "What is a country for?" There is one obvious answer to this question, which has continued down through the decades for over two centuries, namely (f) that one needs a country in order to defend or promote the **nation**. The nation here was originally *la nation canadienne-française*. Now, without entirely abandoning the first formulation, it tends to be put as *la nation québécoise*. This does not betoken any change in ethnic identity, of course. Rather, it reflects a sense, which presents itself as realistic but may be too pessimistic, that the really survivable elements of *la nation canadienne-française* are to be found only in Quebec. But the real point here is that (f) makes the survival and/or flourishing of this nation/language one of the prime goals of political society. No political entity is worth allegiance that does not contribute to this. The issue, independent Quebec versus remaining in Canada, turns simply on different judgments about what does contribute to this.

Put in terms of a possible formula for Canada, this means that from a Quebec perspective (a) to (e) may be attractive features, but the absolutely crucial one that Canada must have in order to possess a *raison d'être* is that it contribute to the survival and/or furtherance of *la nation canadienne-française.* This means in practice some kind of **dualism**. It was this, of course, that successive Quebec leaders always gave expression to when they described Canada as a pact between two nations, or two founding peoples. Dualism in turn had to exist at two levels: (i) It meant that French had to be recognized as a language along with English in the **federation**; that is, French had to be given a status clearly different from that of an ethnic immigrant language, even if it was the most important among these; and (ii) it meant that *la nation canadienne-française,* or its major part, had to have some **autonomy**, some ability to act as a unit. Both these features were built to some degree into the original **Confederation** pact, but in the case of (i)—bilingualism—in partial and somewhat grudging form. Bilingualism (i) and Quebec autonomy (ii) are separate requirements, but they are also in a sense related. There is a certain degree of complementarity in that the more freely and completely (i) is granted, in theory the less need will be felt for **autonomous** action. It is perhaps the tragedy of Canada that (i) was eventually granted too late and too grudgingly, and that this established a high and irreversible pattern of demands on (ii).

Both these requirements have been a source of difficulty. The extension of (i) beyond its original limits raised a problem, because COQ in its developing multiculturalism was naturally led to **accord** English the status of a common language and to split language from culture. That English was the main language was not meant to imply that people of English descent had **privileges** or were somehow superior. The **hegemony** of English had to be justified in purely **utilitarian** terms. Within this framework, the case for putting French alongside English was impossible to make. Outside Quebec, a special status for French was rarely justified by numbers, and certainly not by its indispensability as a medium of communication. It seemed like indefensible favouritism. . . .

It has been one of the remarkable achievements of the last thirty years, and particularly of the Trudeau government, to have established bilingualism (i) almost integrally. There has been a certain cost in resentment in some areas, and this may be fateful in forthcoming negotiations. I want to return to this below. But there is no doubt that a big change has been brought about. On Quebec autonomy (ii) as well, great progress has been made. First, the Canadian federation has proven a very flexible instrument, giving lots of powers to the provinces. And second, where Quebec's needs have been different from the other provinces, a large de facto special status has been developed. Quebec has its own pension plan, levies its own income tax, has a special immigration regime, and so on.

But it is the formal recognition of Quebec's autonomy that has been blocked. Giving Quebec the autonomy it needs, without disbalancing the Canadian federation, would involve giving Quebec a different kind of relation to the **federal government** and institutions. Although this has been worked de facto to a remarkable extent, there is powerful resistance to according it recognition in principle. This is because there is a deep clash of purpose between the two sides of Canada. Where the old clash of values seems to have disappeared, a new conflict of purposes—of answers to the question "What is a country for?"—has surfaced.

The demands of (ii), of a special status for Quebec, run against those of regional equality (c) as these are conceived by many in COQ, and against a widespread understanding of the Charter (e). Point (c) has come to be defined for some as entailing an equality of the provinces. The great moral force of the principle of **equity** between regions has been mobilized behind the rather abstract juridical issue of the relative **constitutional** status of provinces. Regional equity seems to be flouted if all provinces are not placed on the same footing. A special status can be presented as a breach in this kind of equality. More grievously, the special status for Quebec is plainly justified on the grounds of the defence and promotion of *la nation canadienne-française* (f). But this is a collective goal. The aim is to ensure the flourishing and survival of a community. The new patriotism of the Charter has given an impetus to a philosophy of **rights** and of non-discrimination that is highly suspicious of collective goals. It can only countenance them if they are clearly subordinated to individual rights and to provisions of non-discrimination. But for those who take these goals seriously, this subordination is unacceptable. The Charter and the promotion of the nation, as understood in their respective constituencies, are on a collision course. . . .

This difficulty arises with the concept of Quebec autonomy (ii), where it did not for bilingualism (i). The provisions for bilingualism in federal legislation can be justified in terms of individual rights. They concern the guarantee that francophones can be dealt with and obtain government services in their own language. Once French is given this status along with English, what is protected are the rights of individuals. The collective goal goes beyond this. The aim is not only that francophones be served in French but that there still be francophones there in the next generation; this is the objective of (f). It cannot be translated into an **assurance** of rights for existing francophones. Indeed, pursuing it may even involve reducing their individual freedom of choice, as Bill 101 does in Quebec, where francophone parents must send their children to French-language schools.

So the two halves of Canada have come onto a collision course because of the conflict between their respective answers to the question "What is a country for?"—in particular, a conflict between regional equality and the Charter, on one hand, and Quebec **autonomy**, on the other. Other difficulties have been raised about special status—in particular, the problem of participation of Quebeckers in a federal **parliament** if the matters it deals with for other Canadians come to diverge greatly from the matters it deals with affecting Quebec. But I think this difficulty is exaggerated. The two areas of concern have to come very far apart for this to be a real problem.

. . .

Rights and Nations

Can these demands be reconciled? Let us take the conflicts one at a time. First, that between the Charter and Quebec's collective goals. Our Charter follows the trend of the last half of the twentieth century and gives a basis for **judicial** review on two basic scores.

First, it protects the rights of the individual in a variety of ways. Second, it guarantees equal treatment of citizens in a variety of respects; or, put another way, it defends against discriminatory treatment on a number of irrelevant grounds, such as race and sex. There is a lot else in our Charter, including provisions for linguistic rights and **aboriginal** rights, that could be understood as according powers to collectivities, but the two themes I have singled out dominate in the public consciousness.

. . .

[The] sense that the Charter clashes with basic Quebec policy was one of the strong grounds of opposition to the Meech Lake Accord[5] in COQ. The worry here concerned the "distinct society" clause,[6] and the common demand for amendment was that the Charter be "protected" against this clause or take precedence over it. . . . [T]here are two kinds of serious points. First, there is a genuine difference in philosophy concerning the bases of a **liberal** society. Second, there is a difference in view about the basis for national unity.

Let us take the philosophical difference first. Those who take the view that individual rights must always come first and, along with non-discrimination provisions, must take precedence over collective goals, are often speaking out of a view of a liberal society that has become more and more widespread in the Anglo-American world. Its source is, of course, the United States, and it has recently been elaborated and defended by some of the best philosophical and legal minds in that society. . . . There are various formulations of the main idea, but perhaps the one that encapsulates most clearly the point that is relevant to us is Dworkin's way of putting things in his short paper entitled "**Liberalism**."[7]

Dworkin makes a distinction between two kinds of moral commitment. We all have views about the **ends** of life, about what constitutes a good life that we and others ought to strive for; but we also acknowledge a commitment to deal fairly and equally with one another, regardless of how we conceive our ends. We might call the latter "**procedural**" commitments, while those that concern the ends of life are "**substantive**." Dworkin claims that a liberal society is one which, as a society, adopts no particular substantive view about the ends of life. Rather, the society is united around strong procedural commitments to treat people with equal respect. The reason why the polity as such can espouse no substantive view—why it cannot, for instance, allow that one of the goals of legislation should be to make people virtuous in one or the other meaning of that term—is that this would involve a violation of its procedural **norm**; for, granted the diversity of modern societies, it would unfailingly be the case that some people and not others would be committed to the favoured conception of virtue. They might be in a majority; indeed, it is very likely that they would be, for otherwise a **democratic** society would probably not espouse their view. Nevertheless, this view would not be everyone's, and in espousing this substantive outlook the society would not be treating the dissident minority with equal respect. In effect, it would be saying to them, "Your view is not as valuable, in the eyes of this polity, as the view of your more numerous **compatriots**."

. . .

But a society with collective goals like Quebec's violates this model. It is **axiomatic** for Quebec governments that the survival and flourishing of French culture in Quebec is a good. Political society is not neutral between those who value remaining true to the culture of our ancestors and those who might want to cut loose in the name of some individual goal of self-development. It might be argued that one could after all capture a goal like *survivance*[8] for a **proceduralist** liberal society. One could consider the French language, for instance, as a collective resource that individuals might want to make use of, and act for its preservation, just as one does for clean air or green spaces. But this cannot capture the full thrust of policies designed for cultural survival. It is not just a matter of having the French language available for those who might choose it (which might be seen to have been the goal of some of the measures of federal bilingualism over the last twenty years). It is also a matter of making sure that there is a community of people here in the future that will want to avail itself of this opportunity. Policies aimed at survival actively seek to create members of the community—for instance, in assuring that the rising generations go on identifying as French speakers, or whatever. There is no way that they could be seen as just providing a facility to already existing people.

Quebeckers therefore, and those who give similar importance to this kind of collective goal, tend to opt for a rather different model of a liberal society. On this view, a society can be organized around a definition of the good life, without this being seen as a depreciation of those who do not personally share this definition. Where the nature of the good requires that it be sought in common, this is the reason for its being an object of public policy. According to this conception, a liberal society singles itself out as such by the way in which it treats minorities, including those who do not share public definitions of the good; and, above all, by the rights it accords to all its members. In this case, the rights in question are conceived to be the fundamental and crucial ones that have been recognized as such from the very beginning of the liberal tradition: the right to life, liberty, **due process**, free speech, free practice of religion, and the like. On this model, there is something exaggerated, a dangerous overlooking of an essential boundary, in speaking of fundamental rights to such things as commercial signage in the language of one's choice. One has to distinguish between, on the one hand, the fundamental liberties—those which should never at any time be infringed and which therefore ought to be unassailably entrenched—and, on the other hand, the privileges and immunities which are important but can be revoked or restricted for reasons of public policy (although one needs a strong reason to do so).

A society with strong collective goals can be liberal, on this view, provided it is also capable of respecting diversity, especially when this concerns those who do not share its goals, and provided it can offer adequate safeguards for fundamental rights. There will undoubtedly be tensions involved, and difficulties, in pursuing these objectives together, but they are not uncombinable, and the problems are not in principle greater than those encountered by any liberal society that has to combine liberty and equality, for example, or prosperity and justice.

Here are two incompatible views of liberal society. One of the great sources of our recent disunity has been that they have come to square off against each other in the last decade. The resistance to the distinct society which called for precedence to be given to the Charter came in part from a spreading procedural outlook in English Canada. From this point of view, attributing the goal of promoting Quebec's distinct society to a government was to acknowledge a collective goal, and this move had to be neutralized by being subordinated to the existing Charter. From the standpoint of Quebec, this attempt to impose a procedural model of liberalism not only would deprive the "distinct society" clause of some of its force as a rule of interpretation, but it bespoke a rejection of the model of liberalism on which this society had come to be founded. There was a lot of misperception by each society of the other throughout the Meech Lake debate, as I mentioned above. But here both saw something right about the other—and did not like it. COQ saw that the "distinct society" clause legitimated collective goals. And Quebec saw that the move to give the Charter precedence imposed a form of liberal society that was **alien** and to which Quebec could never accommodate itself without surrendering its identity. In this context, the protestations by Charter patriots that they were not "against Quebec" rang hollow.

...

But if the Charter is really serving as common ground, it is hard to accept that its meaning and application may be modulated in one part of the country, by something like the "distinct society" clause, differently from the way it applies in others. The resistance to this clause of the Meech Lake Accord came partly from the sense that the Charter of all things had to apply in the same way to all Canadians. If the procedural bond is the only thing that can hold us together without ranking some above others, then it has to hold without exception.

Can this conflict be arbitrated? In a sense, no. One side insists on holding the country together around a model of liberalism which the other cannot accept. If there is to be agreement, this first side has to give way. But in another sense, the possible common ground is obvious. Procedural liberals in English Canada just have to acknowledge, first, that there are other possible models of liberal society and, second, that their francophone compatriots wish to live by one such alternative. That the first is true becomes pretty evident once one looks around at the full gamut of contemporary free societies in Europe and elsewhere, instead of attending only to the United States. The truth of the second should be clear to anyone with a modicum of knowledge of Quebec history and politics.

But once you accept both, it is clear that the attempt to make procedural liberalism the basis of Canadian unity is both illegitimate and doomed to failure. For it represents an imposition of one society's model on another, and in the circumstances of late-twentieth century Canadian **democracy** this cannot succeed. The only way we can coexist is by allowing ourselves to differ on this. Does this mean that we can only coexist as two independent societies, perhaps loosely linked by **supranational** institutions? This is the **thesis** of Quebec sovereigntists.[9] But this has never seemed to me to be self-evident. It becomes true only to the extent that procedural liberals stand so firmly on principle that they cannot stand sharing the same country with people who live by another model. Rigidity of this kind began to be evident during the Meech Lake debate. If this were to be COQ's last word, then indeed the independentists[10] are right and there is no solution short of sovereignty association.[11]

Equality of What?

The second great area of conflict is between the demands of a special status for Quebec and those of regional equality, once this is interpreted as requiring equality between the provinces. But whereas over the two models of liberalism there is really a genuine philosophic difference underlying all the misunderstanding, here there is still much mutual misperception and cross purposes. For, in fact, the two demands come out of quite different agendas, as has often been remarked. The demand for special status is usually one for assuming a wider range of responsibilities and hence for greater autonomy. The call for regional equality comes generally from those who feel that their interests have been given insufficient weight in federal policy making, and hence aim for more clout in this process. One side wants to take a greater distance from the central government and legislature. The other wants a weightier place within them. That is why it has taken the form in recent years of a call for reform in federal institutions, notably the Senate.

So understood, these demands are not logically opposed. Of course, they can at many points get in each other's way. There has been a fear among provinces that look to a more active federal government to equalize conditions across the regions, that excessive powers to Quebec might end up weakening the power of the centre to act. This may indeed occur, but it is not fated to do so. It is not the reflection of a logical conflict, such as that between equality of all provinces, on the one hand, and special powers for one of them, on the other. The demands for special status and strong central government can possibly be made compatible. What has made this difficult in practice has been precisely the refusal to depart from uniformity. This has meant that any "concession" to Quebec has had to be offered to all the provinces. Fortunately, these have not always been taken up, and so we have evolved quite a considerable de facto special status for Quebec, as I remarked above. But it has never been possible to proceed in that direction openly and explicitly, because of the pressure for uniformity. In the Meech Lake Accord itself, which was designed to address the difficulties of Quebec, most of what was accorded to Quebec had to be distributed to all the others.

The language of "equality" between provinces has in fact been a source of confusion, screening the reality of what is at stake and making solution more difficult. Equality is a notoriously difficult concept to apply and depends on the respect one makes **salient**. It could be argued that Quebec needs powers that other provinces do not, to cope with problems and a vocation that other provinces do not have. Accordingly, this point could be seen as a move towards equality (to each province according to its tasks), not away from it. Moreover, the special status has nothing to do with having more clout at the centre. It involves something quite different.

All of this should encourage us to think that it may not be beyond human wit to discover a way to satisfy these different demands together. There are (a) provinces which want more say in the decisions of the federal government. There are others which, while not disinterested in this first goal, are mainly concerned with (b) maintaining an active federal government as a force for economic and social equalization between regions. Then there is Quebec, which (c) wants the powers it thinks essential to the preservation and promotion of its distinct society. To this we now have to add the aboriginal dimension. This means that our arrangements have to accommodate the need for forms of **self-government** and self-management appropriate to the different **First Nations**. This may mean in practice allowing for a new form of **jurisdiction** in Canada, perhaps weaker than the provinces, but, unlike municipalities, not simply the creatures of another level of government.

Putting all this together will be very difficult. It will take much ingenuity and good will—perhaps more of either than we possess . . . . But it will also require that we see each other's aspirations for what they are, as free as possible from the **rhetoric** of resentment.

Levels of Diversity

Various solutions can be glimpsed beyond the present stalemate. One set would be based on a dualism in which Quebec would no longer be a federal unit just like the others. The other possible range would have as its basis a four- or five-region federalism that was decentralized enough to accommodate Quebec as a member on all fours with [equal to] the rest. Either type of solution would have to accommodate difference in a way we have not yet succeeded in doing—at least openly and admittedly. Can we do it? It looks bad, but I would like to close by saying a few words about what this might mean.

In a way, accommodating differences is what Canada is all about. Many Canadians would concur in this. That is why the mutual suspicion and ill will that has so often accompanied the constitutional debate has been so painful to many of our compatriots. It is not just that the two sources of difference I have been describing are becoming more salient. Old questions may be reopened. To some extent, Trudeau's remarkable achievement in extending bilingualism was made possible by a growing sympathy towards the French fact among political and social elites in COQ. The elites pushed the bilingual process at a pace faster than many of their fellow citizens wanted. For many people lower down in the hierarchy, French was being "stuffed down their throats"; but because of the elite-run nature of the political accommodation process in this country, they seemed to have no option but to take it.

. . .

To build a country for everyone, Canada would have to allow for . . . "deep" diversity, in which a **plurality** of ways of belonging would also be acknowledged and accepted. Someone of, say, Italian extraction in Toronto or Ukrainian extraction in Edmonton might indeed feel Canadian as a bearer of individual rights in a multicultural mosaic. His or her belonging would not "pass through" some other community, although the ethnic identity might be important to him or her in various ways. But this person might nevertheless accept that a Québécois or a Cree or a Dene might belong in a very different way, that these persons were Canadian through being members of their national communities. Reciprocally, the Québécois, Cree, or Dene would accept the perfect legitimacy of the "mosaic" identity.

. . .

. . . The world needs other models to be legitimated in order to allow for more humane and less constraining modes of political cohabitation. Instead of pushing ourselves to the point of break-up in the name of the uniform model, we would do our own and some other peoples a favour by exploring the space of deep diversity. To those who believe in according people the freedom to be themselves, this would be counted a gain in civilization. In this exploration we would not be alone. Europe watchers have noticed how the development of the European Community has gone along with an increased breathing space for regional societies—Breton, Basque, Catalan[12]—which were formerly threatened with the steamroller of the national **state**.

. . .

Notes

1. In 1970 the Front de libération du Québec (or FLQ; in English, Quebec Liberation Front) kidnapped James Cross, the British trade commissioner, and Pierre Laporte, Minister of Immigration and Minister of Labour. (The FLQ was a Québécois nationalist movement whose stated goal was the political independence of Quebec.) The Quebec government formally requested help from the Canadian Armed Forces. Prime Minister Pierre Trudeau invoked the *War Measures Act*, which gave the federal government wide-ranging power to maintain security and order in case of war or insurrection. Trudeau suspended civil liberties in Quebec and give the military broad powers of search and seizure. Over 450 people were detained without charges; most of them were eventually released without being charged with anything. James Cross was eventually released, but Pierre Laporte was killed by his captors. [Editor]
2. *Pure laine* is a French term (literally "pure wool") that refers to the idea of a population composed exclusively of people of French-Canadian ethnicity or ancestry. [Editor]
3. Pierre Laporte was the former Minister of Labour for the Province of Quebec. He was kidnapped and murdered by members of the FLQ during the October (FLQ) Crisis. His kidnapping was motivated by an anti-government protest and the desired release of "political prisoners." According to his captors, his death was an accident. [Editor]
4. The Ecole Polytechnique Massacre, or the Montreal Massacre, occurred on 6 December 1989. At the Ecole Polytechnique, an engineering school affiliated with the Université de Montréal, a twenty-five-year-old man shot twenty-eight people, killing fourteen women and injuring ten other women and four men. Then he killed himself. His actions, the content of his suicide letter, and his statements during the shooting indicate that his motives were anti-feminist. [Editor]
5. The Meech Lake Accord was the predecessor of the Charlottetown Accord, and contained many similar and identical proposals. [Editor]
6. One of the five main modifications to the Canadian constitution proposed by the Meech Lake Accord was the recognition of Quebec as a "distinct society," which many in English Canada saw as granting Quebec privileges beyond those enjoyed by the other provinces. [Editor]
7. Ronald Dworkin, "Liberalism," in *Public and Private Morality*, ed. Stuart Hampshire (Cambridge: Cambridge University Press, 1978).
8. *La Survivance* is a French phrase that refers to the meager survival of French culture in spite of Anglo-Canadian and Anglo-American cultural pressures. [Editor]
9. Sovereigntists are separatists who support sovereignty association (see note 12). [Editor]
10. Independentists are separatists who support sovereignty association (see note 12). [Editor]
11. Sovereignty association is a proposal for the political independence of Quebec that would involve sovereignty on matters of taxation, legislation, and signing treaties, but would also maintain some political and economic ties with Canada in order to protect Quebec from possible economic threats, such as tariffs or other barriers to trade imposed by Canada, the United States, or other countries. The idea of sovereignty association was first popularized by former Premier of Quebec René Lévesque in his 1968 essay "Option Québec." [Editor]
12. The Bretons, Basques, and Catalans are each ethnically, linguistically, and culturally distinct groups with their own indigenous geographic localities that are annexed to larger political bodies. The Bretons predominantly inhabit the region of Brittany in France, the Basque in portions of France and Spain, and the Catalans in Northern Spain. [Editor]

Discussion Questions

1. Chaput argues that "it is highly desirable that a normal man or nation be free." What are his reasons for this claim? Why did he think French Canadians were not free? Do you think this was true in 1961? Do you think this is still true today? Why or why not?
2. Chaput describes bilingualism as a sign of bondage for French Canadians. What are his arguments for this claim? Do you think this is still true today? Why or why not?
3. How are feminist and nationalist identities similar, according to Lamoureux? Do you agree with her? Why or why not?
4. What is the postmodernist critique of identity? How have feminism and nationalism responded to this critique?
5. Why does Taylor think the question "What is a country for?" is so important? Do you agree with his analysis? Why or why not?
6. What are the two versions of liberalism that Taylor discusses? What are his reasons for saying they can be reconciled? Do you agree with him? Why or why not?
7. Do you think Chaput would agree with Taylor's analysis of liberalism? Why or why not?

Suggested Readings and Websites

♣ = Canadian source or author

♣ Bélanger, Claude. "Quebec Nationalism." Readings in Quebec History, 2000. http://faculty.marianopolis.edu/c.belanger/quebechistory/events/nat-all.htm. [A long essay by a nationalist professor at Marianopolis College, a CEGEP (*Collège d'enseignement général et professionnel*) in Westmount, Quebec.]

♣ Bélanger, Claude. "Pierre Elliott (E.) Trudeau, Quebec and the Canadian Constitution." Readings in Quebec History, 2000. http://faculty.marianopolis.edu/c.belanger/quebechistory/readings/trudeau.htm.

♣ Bélanger, Claude. "The Quiet Revolution." Readings in Quebec History, 2000. http://faculty.marianopolis.edu/c.belanger/quebechistory/events/quiet.htm.

♣ Carens, Joseph H. *Is Quebec Nationalism Just? Perspectives from Anglophone Canada*. Montréal: McGill-Queen's University Press, 1995. [Essays on the relationship between liberalism and nationalism in Canada and Quebec.]

♣ Dufour, Christian. "Trudeau's Canadian Legacy from a Quebec Perspective: New Canadian Nationalism Weakens Canada." *London Journal of Canadian Studies* 18 (2002/3): 5–13. [Argues that "the legacy of Trudeau, the enemy of all nationalisms, is paradoxically a new Canadian nationalism based on the denial of the Québécois heart of Canada."]

♣ Gauthier, David. "Breaking Up: An Essay on Secession." *Dialogue* 24, 3 (1994): 357–72. [A contractarian argument in favour of "no-fault" secession, analogous to no-fault divorce.]

♣ Jones, Richard. "French Canadian Nationalism." *The Canadian Encyclopedia*, 2012. www.thecanadianencyclopedia.com/articles/french-canadian-nationalism.

♣ Jones, Richard. "Separatism." *The Canadian Encyclopedia*, 2012. www.thecanadianencyclopedia.com/articles/separatism.

- O'Neal, Brian. "Distinct Society: Origins, Interpretations, Implications." Parliamentary Research Branch PRB 408E. Ottawa: Library of Parliament, 1995. [A non-partisan discussion of the concept of a "distinct society."]
- Quebec: Francophone Nation of the Americas. Policy Statement of the Bloc Québécois. http://fjbq.bloc.org/document.aspx?doc=4F54DEE5-BCC6-4A8E-A790-E7752A7C1D8D. [A policy statement by the Bloc.]
- Taylor, Charles. *Reconciling the Solitudes: Essays on Canadian Federalism and Nationalism.* Montréal: McGill-Queen's University Press, 1993.

Chapter 3

Multiculturalism

The previous chapters covered two of the three founding peoples of Canada, Aboriginal people and the Québécois, and the next will discuss the third, the English. But while the original European settlers came from France and England, others soon followed. Today, Canada is populated by people from all over the world. We have one of the highest rates of immigration in the world as a percentage of our population and we also have one of the most successful multiculturalism programs in the world.

Background

Canadians like to say that we had the world's first multiculturalism policy, and that Canada is one of the world's most successful multicultural nations. But while we may have had the first multiculturalism *policy*, we certainly didn't have the first multicultural *practice*. Multiculturalism as a practice is far older than Canada, and far older than European civilization.

The roots of multiculturalism lie in conquest and toleration: expansionist civilizations conquered neighbouring societies and absorbed them. Some of those societies, such as Rome, feudal China, medieval India, and the medieval Ottoman Empire, imposed their government but not their languages, cultures, and religions on those whom they conquered. Sometimes there were philosophical justifications of toleration,[1] but by and large the practices were based on practical considerations and not philosophically justified: as a matter of fact, conquered people accepted being conquered better if they were allowed to keep their languages and religions. For example, feudal China was officially Confucian, but Buddhists, Taoists, Muslims, Christians, and members of other religions thrived and were tolerated. The Chinese tolerated anyone who had a moral system. And the Islamic Ottoman Empire tolerated "people of the Book" (Jews and Christians). Both Jews and Christians thrived in the Ottoman Empire during the time of the Inquisition in Europe.

For example, the Jewish philosopher Maimonides left Europe for the Ottoman Empire in the twelfth century because of the horrible persecution of Jews in Europe.

India is undoubtedly the most multicultural nation in the world, and it has been multicultural for well over a thousand years. Its 1.2 billion citizens speak sixteen official languages, and more than one hundred languages and dialects in total. They are members of four major religions—Hinduism, Islam, Christianity, and Sikhism—as well as dozens of smaller religions. India manages its cultural diversity by setting state boundaries according to language and ethnicity, and by a system of **asymmetrical federalism** (a form of **federalism** in which the central government grants different powers to different states, provinces, or territories). While there are some significant ethnic and religious tensions in India, it has remained a democracy since independence in 1947—a feat accomplished by only a few ex-colonies worldwide, most of which, unlike India, are relatively wealthy.

Brazil is another contemporary multicultural society that differs from both Canada and India in its policies and practices concerning diversity. Like the Spanish and the French, the Portuguese sent men but not women to govern and exploit the resources of their colonies. Since the men would be in the colony for years, they were encouraged to marry local women. Add in slaves imported from Africa, immigration from other European countries and from east and south Asia, especially India, et voila!—Brazil, like other South and Central American countries, is one of the most racially diverse countries in the world. Brazilians speak proudly of their racial harmony. While of course it is not perfect, it is a significant accomplishment.

Canadian Multiculturalism

Canada's multiculturalism policy has its roots in the human rights revolution that followed World War II. (See the Introduction to Part II for an explanation of its significance for Aboriginal rights, Quebec nationalism, and multiculturalism.) After World War II, the federal government dismantled some of the most discriminatory parts of the *Indian Act* (1951) and extended federal voting rights to all status Indians (1960; see Chapter 1, Aboriginal Peoples). It also began, slowly, to change its immigration policies, which had been discriminatory and racist even by early twentieth-century European and North American standards. These laws and policies included:

- the *Chinese Head Tax and Exclusion Act* of 1885 which, having recruited thousands of Chinese labourers to work—and often die—on the Canadian Pacific Railway, restricted further immigration by imposing a large tax on any Chinese immigrant (the Chinese were the only group explicitly excluded by Canadian legislation);
- the 1919 *Immigration Act* that excluded people of colour, southern and eastern Europeans, Doukhobors, Mennonites, and Hutterites (small Protestant groups), and labour organizers and other socialists;
- the 1923 *Chinese Immigration Act*, which excluded all Chinese nationals except diplomats, students, children of Canadian citizens, and investors;
- the Liberal government's refusal to admit Jews fleeing Nazi oppression in the 1930s and 40s (Canada admitted many fewer Jews per capita than the US

or any western European nation), which continued even after the war; for example, when asked how many Jewish refugees Canada would admit, an unidentified immigration official replied, "None is too many."[2]

The federal government gradually removed restrictions on immigration. In 1947, it repealed the *Chinese Immigration Act*. In 1962 it announced regulations that eliminated most of the discriminatory immigration criteria: henceforth, anyone with sufficient education, skill, or other qualifications would be eligible for immigration, regardless of race or national origin. In 1967, the "white Canada" policy was officially put to rest when the federal government introduced a points system for immigrants that was based on qualifications rather than characteristics like race, religion, or national origin.

In 1963, the Royal Commission on Bilingualism and Biculturalism (a.k.a. the B&B Commission) was established. Its original mandate, as the name implies, was to inquire into bilingualism and biculturalism in Canada, in part to deal with the growing tide of nationalism in Quebec. Other ethnic groups, particularly Ukrainian Canadians, petitioned the government to consider the contributions of groups other than the English and French, so the B&B Commission's mandate was broadened. The Commission produced six volumes between 1965 and 1970: official languages, education, work, multiculturalism, the role of the federal capital (Ottawa) in Canadian life, and voluntary associations.

Royal Commissions' recommendations often go unfulfilled for years or longer. Not so the B&B Commission. The Parti Québécois had formed in 1968, and Prime Minister Trudeau wanted to nip Quebec separatism in the bud. In 1969 the federal government passed the *Official Languages Act*, which made English and French the official languages of Canada and required all federal institutions to provide service in either official language, at the citizen's or customer's request. And in 1971, Canada announced the first multiculturalism policy in the world. Its objectives were "to assist cultural groups to retain and foster their identity; to assist cultural groups to overcome barriers to their full participation in Canadian society; . . . to promote creative exchanges among all Canadian cultural groups; and to assist immigrants in acquiring at least one of the official languages."[3] (Many Québécois believe that the federal policy was developed to undercut Quebec's distinct status and instead treat Québécois culture like an ethnicity. While this never was one of the policy's explicit aims, given Trudeau's well-known belief in a single status for all Canadians and his strong opposition to Quebec nationalism, the belief is at least plausible.) Canada's multiculturalism policy was soon copied by Australia and other countries. In the twenty-six years since the end of World War II, Canada's immigration and settlement policies had been transformed from some of the most discriminatory and racist in the West to some of the fairest and most open.

In the intervening years, multiculturalism has become more and more firmly a part of Canadian institutions and culture. It is enshrined in the *Charter*; section 27 states, "This *Charter* shall be interpreted in a manner consistent with the preservation and enhancement of the multicultural heritage of Canadians." In 1988, the *Canadian Multiculturalism Act* became the first national multiculturalism law in the world. This is significant for several reasons. First, Parliament explicitly affirmed the *Charter's* protection of multiculturalism, turning section 27's guarantee into the law of the land. Second, Parliament made promoting multiculturalism a responsibility of all branches of the federal government, and required that the Multiculturalism Directorate report every year on how the various branches are doing (or not doing) this. Third, the *Act* makes explicit part of what section 27 of the *Charter* requires—for example, the federal government must promote "full and equitable participation" in Canadian society and help eliminate "any barrier to that participation."

Multiculturalism has been both celebrated and criticized since it was first proposed in 1971. It supporters say it makes immigrants feel more welcome and smooths their integration into Canadian society, which leads to a stronger sense of belonging and identification with Canadian values. Critics say multiculturalism's focus on differences between groups rather than a shared Canadian identity leads to the formation of ethnic ghettos that foster crime, social unrest, and even home-grown terrorists such as the Toronto 18 (eighteen Muslim men and youth who were charged in 2006 with planning terrorist attacks on Canada; see chapter 11, Real and Suspected Terrorism).

Both the pro- and anti-multiculturalism claims are empirical, and thus they can be settled (at least in principle) with evidence. On this question, the evidence points much more strongly to the "pro" than to the "anti" side. In 2003, eighty-five per cent of Canadians believed that multiculturalism is important to Canadian identity, up from seventy-four per cent in 1997.[4] Immigrants identify strongly with Canada and with Canadian values, especially freedom, democracy, and multiculturalism.[5] They become citizens at much higher rates than do immigrants to most other nations: "According to a 2005 study, 84 per cent of eligible immigrants were Canadian citizens in 2001; in contrast, the rate was 56 per cent in the UK, 40 per cent in the US, and lower still in many European states."[6] While immigrants often do live in ethnic neighbourhoods, these are not ghettos characterized by poverty, lack of social mobility, and apathy; they are "a stepping stone to integration, not a prison that impedes immigration."[7] Furthermore, the evidence indicates that Canada's multiculturalism policies have played a significant role in the integration of immigrants. Countries that have multiculturalism policies integrate immigrants better, and immigrants feel a stronger sense of connectedness, than they do in countries that do not have such policies. On most of these measurements, Canada does better than almost any other Western country.

The success of Canada's multiculturalism policy stands in stark contrast to the backlash against multiculturalism in western Europe. The Netherlands, which had one of the strongest multiculturalism programs in Europe in the 1980s, dropped it in the 2000s in favour of a policy of "civic integration." In 2004 France banned the **hijab** (headscarves worn by some Muslim women) in schools, and in 2011 it banned the **niqab** (the full veil, which exposes only the eyes) in public. In 2005 a Danish newspaper sparked an international controversy when it published twelve cartoons depicting the prophet Mohammed, most of them connecting him to terrorism. In 2009 the Swiss voted to ban minarets (tall spires on mosques, from which the call to prayer is made). Former Pope Benedict XVI opposed Turkey's admission to the European Union because, he said, Europe is fundamentally Christian, and he urged Europe not to forget its Christian roots. In 2010 German Chancellor Angela Merkel declared that multiculturalism had "utterly failed" in Germany. In 2011 a Norwegian right-wing extremist who hated immigrants killed ninety-one people, most of them teenagers, at a camp sponsored by the Norwegian ruling party. Later that year, British Prime Minister David Cameron and French President Nicolas Sarkozy also expressed their opposition to multiculturalism.

Why has multiculturalism been embraced in Canada but thoroughly rejected in Europe? Of course the answer is complicated. Much of it is almost certainly due to different historical conceptions of citizenship. In Canada, citizenship (at least for people of European descent) has been based on residence; after living in Canada for a certain period, immigrants are eligible to become citizens. By contrast, until recently citizenship in European states was based on blood, passing from parents (especially fathers) to their children, sometimes even if the children were not born in and had never lived in the parents' country. Immigrants who lacked the blood connection could not become citizens, no matter how long they lived in the country, nor could their children become citizens, even if they were born in and had lived their entire lives in the new country. As a result, European countries tended to be quite homogeneous, unlike Canada, which has been relatively heterogeneous for over a century. In recent years European countries have adopted a residence-based model of citizenship and thus are allowing immigrants who previously were excluded to become citizens. However, this change is still fairly recent and has not been fully accepted by all Europeans—quite the opposite, in fact. By contrast, a society like Canada that is already relatively heterogeneous is likely to accept immigrants more readily than one with a long tradition of relative homogeneity.

Some Philosophical Issues

Almost all philosophers today reject basing citizenship on blood. While everyone agrees that immigrants should be integrated into their new societies, they do not agree about the best form of integration. Should immigrants be encouraged or even forced to give up their ethnic identities and think of themselves simply as French, American, or Canadian? How much, if anything, should they be encouraged to retain from their ethnic origins? The French argue that there should be a single civil status in the public sphere that is the same for everyone. They believe cultural practices such as non-official languages, religion, customs, dress, and so on are parts of the private sphere and so should not intrude on the civic realm. In Canada, by contrast, immigrants are encouraged to maintain their ethnic identities alongside their new Canadian identities, in the public as well as the private sphere. The underlying question that both policies seek to address is: What does it mean to be French, Canadian, or whatever? Clearly there must be some common features by which we can distinguish the French from the British or Canadians from Americans. But how "thick" a political identity must be—or how "thin" it can be—is the subject of much debate.

Most philosophers agree that immigrant cultures should not have the same status as Aboriginal peoples and national minorities such as the Québécois. But how a country should combine a majority culture, Aboriginal peoples, a national minority, and immigrant groups is hotly debated. As the philosopher Will Kymlicka points out, Canada is unusual in having all four kinds of diversity.[8] Australia and the US, for example, have majority populations, indigenous peoples (Aborigines in Australia and Aboriginal peoples in the US), and large immigrant populations, but no national minorities. Spain and Belgium have majority populations and national minorities (the Basques and the Flemish, respectively), but no indigenous people and little immigration. How we should combine the various parts of our multinational and multicultural state is still being debated and decided.

Some philosophers reject multiculturalism not because they believe we all should have the same identity as Canadians or Brazilians, but rather because they have a **cosmopolitan** (international, belonging to the whole world) view of culture. According to this view, people should have access to cultures, plural, not just to a particular culture, singular. In a globalized world, identities are formed by many cultures, they say; the mono- or bicultural view is both empirically false and politically undesirable. Supporters of multiculturalism agree that multicultural identities are politically desirable, but such identities must be grounded in a particular cultural identity that is the individual's source of meaning. People fare poorly in societies in which their cultural identities are denigrated and destroyed, they say. They point to the social breakdown of Aboriginal peoples caused by the residential school system in Canada, and to social breakdowns experienced by formerly nomadic peoples, such as the Roma in Europe and the Kurds in the Middle East, who have been forced by various states to settle down. Cosmopolitan identities without a firm cultural foundation are as insubstantial as smoke after a flame has gone out.

Philosophers also discuss what citizens share that immigrants need to learn or believe. What makes us Canadian? Many people point to values embodied in the *Charter* and Canadian institutions such as health care. Others criticize this view, arguing that the values of one liberal culture do not differ significantly from those of another liberal culture. Many Canadians believe our health care system makes us distinct. But this view is based on a single comparison group, the US. If we compare ourselves to other Western liberal democracies like Sweden or Greece, it is clear that our health care system does not make us unique. In fact, there is almost certainly no particular characteristic or small set of characteristics that citizens share and that defines a nation. Rather, it is our shared history, ideals, and projects that make us who we are. Those who were born here were born into an ongoing society, and part of their education involved learning about Canada's history, ideals, and projects so they can participate in shaping our future. Those who came from other countries must learn about Canadian history, ideals, and projects so they too can become full participants in Canada's present and future.

The Readings

The readings in this chapter focus on one of the most contentious issues in multiculturalism: How should a liberal society handle conflicts between cultural practices and individual rights? (Notice the similarity between them and the reading by Deveaux in Chapter 1, Aboriginal Rights, which discusses ways to reconcile women's equality rights with cultural group rights.)

In the first reading, Ayelet Shachar discusses what she calls "privatized diversity," which involves demands by religious minorities for alternative institutions, outside of secular mainstream institutions, that will support and maintain their religious practices. For example, observant religious women who get divorced may want a religious as well as a civil divorce, so they can remarry within their faith and remain part of their religious community. However, conservative religions tend to assign unequal rights to men and women, most often to the detriment of women. Because of the separation of religion and the state in liberal societies, courts are often unwilling to impose secular standards on religious practices, leaving observant women who wish to assert their rights and stay in their religious communities with few options. Shachar discusses two alternatives to a hands-off approach by the state: engaging in democratic deliberation and intercultural dialogue, and changing the background conditions of the problematic situations.

In the second reading, Benjamin Berger argues that clashes between religion and the law are "an instance of cross-cultural encounter." However, according to both the law and multicultural theory, the law is actually outside the cross-cultural relationship. On this view, the "encounter" is actually between religion and culture, and the law acts as referee or adjudicator. This puts religion at a disadvantage, Berger says, because it must always translate its concerns into the language of liberal legalism, whereas the law does not have an analogous obligation to translate its terms into the language of religion. He suggests intercultural dialogue as a solution (similar to Tully's discussion of a just relationship between Aboriginal and non-Aboriginal peoples in Canada in Chapter 1, Aboriginal Peoples), but says such a dialogue cannot begin unless the law perceives itself as a participant in rather than a referee of the "encounter."

In the third reading, Joseph Carens and Melissa Williams discuss the integration and accommodation of Muslim immigrants in liberal societies. They focus on three questions: (1) Does the centrality of Islam in the lives of believers conflict with democratic citizenship? (2) Do Muslim beliefs conflict with women's equality? (3) Do Muslims have a right to be recognized as a cultural group whose claims should be accommodated, within reason? They answer "no" to the first question; there is no inherent conflict between Islamic beliefs and democratic citizenship. In response to the second question, they acknowledge that some fundamentalist interpretations of Islam do conflict with women's equality. However, they point out that this is equally true of fundamentalist interpretations of Judaism and Christianity, though most people do not consider this a reason not to tolerate Jewish and Christian fundamentalism. And they answer "yes" to the third question: Islamic communities should be given the same sorts of multicultural accommodations that other groups receive.

Why Are There No Arguments against Multiculturalism?

As with chapter 1, Aboriginal Peoples, the quick answer is that the *Charter* explicitly refers to multiculturalism. Section 27 states that the *Charter* "shall be interpreted in a manner consistent with the preservation and enhancement of the multicultural heritage of Canadians." It is the law of the land. But even more, it is enormously popular with Canadians, and it is becoming more and more popular and more and more part of our identity as Canadians. The issue in Canada is not *whether* we should have a multiculturalism policy, but what kind of policy we should have. On this latter question there is reasonable disagreement, some of which the readings express.

The Moral and Political Preferences Indicator

The lines between conservative and egalitarian liberals are much sharper on the topic of multiculturalism than they are on Aboriginal peoples and Quebec nationalism. While both conservative and egalitarian liberals are proud of the multicultural character of Canada, most conservative liberals either oppose multiculturalism as a policy or prefer that government support for non-founding cultures be minimal. In particular, conservatives tend to worry about Muslim immigrants' attachment to Canadian values and practices, and to believe that women are fundamentally unequal in Islam. (Many egalitarian liberals accuse them of hypocrisy, pointing out that conservatives rarely worry about women's inequality when it comes to other issues such as wages, childcare, foreign aid, or violence against women.) Egalitarian liberals generally support multiculturalism laws and policies and believe that immigrant cultures should be recognized and accommodated. As usual, conservative and egalitarian centrists fall somewhere in the middle, though they generally lean fairly heavily towards accommodation rather than assimilation.

Notes

1. See, for example, Amartya Sen, "Human Rights and Asian Values," Sixteenth Morgenthau Memorial Lecture on Ethics and Foreign Policy (NY: Carnegie Council on Ethics and International Affairs, 1997).
2. Irving Abella and Harold Troper, *None Is Too Many: Canada and the Jews of Europe, 1933–1948* (Toronto: Lester and Orpen Dennys, 1982).
3. Michael Dewing, "Canadian Multiculturalism," Parliamentary Information and Research Services (2009), p. 4.
4. Will Kymlicka, "The Current State of Multiculturalism in Canada and Research Themes on Canadian Multiculturalism 2008–2010" (Ottawa: Minister of Public Works and Government Services Canada, 2010), p. 7.
5. Kymlicka, p. 8.
6. Keith Banting and Will Kymlicka, "Canadian Multiculturalism: Global Anxieties and Local Debates," *British Journal of Canadian Studies* 23, 1 (2010): 56.
7. Kymlicka, p. 9.
8. See Will Kymlicka, "Being Canadian," Chapter 4, Being English-Speaking Canadian.

Ayelet Shachar

Faith in Law? Diffusing Tensions between Diversity and Equality

AV = author's view; ~AV = not the author's view

How should a **democratic state** and its public law system respond to claims by members of religious minorities seeking to establish private faith-based arbitration tribunals to resolve family disputes? **Classic liberals** and **civic republicans** would have had a quick response to such a query. They favoured a strict separation between state and religion, as part of their support for drawing a plain and clean line between the public and private spheres. Be a citizen in public, a Jew (or a Catholic or a Muslim, and so on) in private, remains the favoured mantra, dating back to as early as the 1791 French National Assembly's[1] decree admitting Jews as individuals to the **rights** of citizenship, after they had "freed" themselves from any communal semi-autonomous governance institutions.

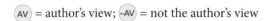

But the world now is a very different place. My aim in this article is to highlight the centrality of women, **gender** and the family in renewed state and religion contestations that inject new meanings into the traditional categories of "private" and "public." The article focuses exclusively on the situation of members of minority religions living in otherwise **secularized** societies. My interest, more specifically, lies in exploring how different legal arrangements between **secular** and religious **jurisdictions** shape and affect women's rights to religious freedom and equality. Of special interest here are those situations in which renegotiated relations between state and religion intersect and interact with public concerns about power disparities between men and women in the resolution of family-law disputes.

At present, the bulk of the theoretical literature on citizenship and **multiculturalism** engages in intricate attempts to delineate the boundaries of *public*, state-sponsored accommodation of diversity, as exemplified by the veiling controversies. As if these charged dilemmas currently playing out in the courts do not present enough of a hurdle, we are also starting to see a new type of challenge on the horizon: the request by members of religious minorities to *privatize diversity*. By this I refer to the recent proposals raised by self-proclaimed "guardians of the faith" to establish private arbitration tribunals in which consenting members of the group will have their legal disputes resolved in a binding fashion—according to religious principles—under the secular umbrella of alternative dispute resolution ("ADR"). While formally deploying the logic of ADR, this new development is potentially far-reaching: the main claim raised by advocates of privatized diversity is that respect for religious freedom or cultural integrity does not require inclusion in the **public sphere**, but *exclusion* from it. This leads to a demand that the state adopt a hands-off, non-interventionist approach, placing **civil** and family disputes with a religious or cultural aspect "outside" the official realm of equal citizenship. This potential storm must be addressed head on. This is the case because privatized diversity mixes three inflammatory components in today's political environment: religion, gender and the rise of a **neo-liberal** state. The volatility of these issues is undisputed; they require a mere spark to ignite.

Privatized diversity's potentially dramatic alterations to the legal system increasingly revolve around the regulation of women and the family, placing them at the centre of larger debates about citizenship and identity. These challenges cannot be fully captured by our existing legal categories; they require a new vocabulary and a fresh approach. I will begin to sketch here the contours of such an approach by asking what is owed to women whose legal dilemmas (at least in the family law arena) arise from the fact that their lives have already been affected by the interplay between overlapping systems of identification, authority, and belief: in this case, religious and secular law.

~AV The standard legal response to this challenge is to seek shelter behind a formidable "wall of separation" between state and religion, even if this implies turning a blind eye to the concerns of religious women—especially those caught in the uncoordinated web of secular and religious marriage bonds. AV I will advance a different approach. By placing these once-ignored agents at the centre of analysis, this article explores the idea of permitting a degree of *regulated interaction* between religious and secular sources of obligation, so long as the baseline of citizenship-guaranteed rights remains firmly in place. Despite the understandable desire to "disentangle" law from religion by metaphorically "caging" each in its appropriate sphere or domain, it is worth contemplating whether a carefully regulated recognition of multiple legal affiliations (and the subtle interactions among them) can allow devout women to benefit from the protections offered by the state to other citizens—yet without abandoning the **tenets** of their faith. I will demonstrate the possibility of implementing such a vision by reference to a recent decision of the Supreme Court of Canada, *Bruker v. Marcovitz*, which breaks new ground.

Finally, I will revisit an acrimonious controversy that broke out in Canada following a proposal by a communal Muslim organization in Ontario to establish a private "Islamic court of justice" (*darul qada*) to resolve family law disputes among consenting adults, known as the "Shari'a tribunal" debate. I will reflect on the government's chosen policy to ban any type of family arbitration by such faith-based tribunals, thus reaffirming the classic secular-religious divide. While this decision is politically defensible and symbolically astute, it does not necessarily provide adequate protection for those individuals most vulnerable to their community's formal and informal pressures to push them to accept "unofficial" dispute-resolution forums in resolving marital issues. The decision may instead thrust these tribunals underground where no state regulation, coordination, or legal recourse is made available to those who may need it most.

Privatized Diversity

Before we turn to alternative remedies, it is important first to articulate the privatized diversity challenge in greater detail. -AV In discussions about citizenship, we repeatedly come across the **modernist** and **liberal** schema of separate spheres: we are expected to act as citizens in the public sphere, but remain free to express our distinct cultural or religious identities in the private domain of family and communal life. AV Yet multiple tensions have exposed cracks in this separate-spheres formula. For example, where precisely does the "private" end and the "public" begin? Who is to bear the burdens if the modern state's desire to keep religion out of the public sphere indirectly inspires calls to limit access to citizenship, or, conversely, to create unregulated "islands of jurisdiction" that immunize the practices of certain religious communities because they occurred under the cover of privatized diversity? By focusing on these topical issues, we are faced with a larger puzzle: what might the new engagement between state and religion in the 21st century look like? Would it permit a path to accommodating diversity *with* equality? . . .

Family Law and Religious Minority Women

Family law serves as an excellent illustration to these simmering gender and religion tensions. It demonstrates that for some observant women, the claim for achieving greater equality and legal protection as female citizens may in part be informed by their claim for religious recognition and accommodation. Consider, for example, the situation of observant religious women who may wish (or feel bound) to follow their faith community's divorce requirements in addition to the rules of the state that remove barriers to remarriage. Without the removal of such barriers, women's ability to build new families, if not their very membership status (or that of their children), may be adversely affected. This is particularly true for observant Jewish and Muslim women living in secular societies who have entered marriage through a religious ceremony—as permitted by law in many jurisdictions. For them, a civil divorce . . . is simply part of the story; it does not, and cannot, dissolve the religious aspect of the relationship. Failure to recognize their "split-status" position—of being legally divorced according to state law, but still married according to their faith tradition—may leave these women prone to abuse by recalcitrant husbands. These men are often well aware of the adverse effect this split-status situation has on their wives. . . .

Add to this the recognition that, for a host of complex historical, political and **institutional** path-dependency reasons, family law has become crucial for minority religions in maintaining their definition of membership. Religious minorities in secularized **democracies** are typically non-territorial entities. . . . They have no semi-autonomous sub-unit in which they constitute a majority, nor have they power to define the public symbols that manifest, and in turn help preserve, their distinctive national or linguistic heritage. . . . [A]s non-territorial communities, [they] are thus forced to find other ways to sustain their distinct traditions and ways of life. With no authority to issue formal documents of membership, regulate mobility, or hold the power to collect mandatory taxes, religious personal laws that define marriage, divorce and lineage have come to serve an important role in regulating membership boundaries. These laws demarcate a pool of individuals endowed with the collective responsibility to maintain the group's values, practices, and distinct ways of life (if they maintain their standing as members in that community). I have elsewhere labeled this as family law's *demarcating* function. . . . It delineates who is legally affiliated to the community and thus strengthens the bonds of continuity between past and future by identifying who is considered part of the tradition. This is why gaining control over the religious aspects of entry into (or exit from) marriage matters greatly to these communities; it is part of a membership demarcation and intergenerational project. At the same time, family law is also the area in which women have historically and traditionally been placed at a disadvantage both by states and by religious communities, in part because the recognition of female members plays a crucial role in "reproducing the collective"—both literally and figuratively. Although this core contribution to the collective could, in theory, have empowered them, in most places and legal traditions, it led to tight control and regulation of women, treating them, by law, as less than equal.

A Rejected Proposal

With this background in mind, we can now see more clearly why the Shari'a tribunal controversy in Canada has provoked such an unwieldy storm of response. . . . In Ontario, a bitter debate erupted after a small and relatively conservative organization, the Canadian Society of Muslims, declared in a series of press releases its intention to establish a faith-based tribunal that would operate as a forum for binding arbitration on consenting parties. The envisioned tribunal (which never came into operation) would have permitted consenting parties not only to enter a less adversarial, out-of-court, dispute resolution process, but also to use choice of law provisions to apply religious norms to resolve family disputes, according to the "laws (*fiqh*)" of any Islamic school, e.g. *Shiah* or *Sunni*. . . .

The proposal to establish a tribunal of this kind was perceived as challenging the **normative** and **juridical** authority, not to mention legitimacy, of the secular state's asserted mandate to represent and regulate the interests and rights of *all* its citizens in their family matters, irrespective of communal affiliation. In this respect, it raised profound questions concerning hierarchy and **lexical order** in the contexts of law and citizenship: which norms should prevail, and who, or what entity, ought to have the final word in resolving any value-conflicts between equality and diversity. No less significant for our discussion is the recognition that the proposal to establish a non-state arbitration tribunal of this kind does not by itself provide a conclusive answer to determining how secular and religious norms should interact in governing the family. To the contrary, it serves to provoke just such a debate. As an **analytical** matter, secular and religious norms may stand in tension with one another, point in different directions, lead to broadly similar results, or directly contradict one another. It is the latter outcome that is seen to pose the greatest challenge to the superiority of secular family law by its old adversary: religion.

If the only choice on offer were between rejecting or accepting such a tribunal . . . I would strongly oppose it. I would hold this position even if we accept the force of the argument for non-intervention on the grounds of allowing communities as much associational freedom as possible to pursue their own visions of the good in a diverse society. The reason is as simple as it is powerful: hardly anyone suggests that religious liberty is absolute; it may be overridden or restricted by other liberties or compelling state interests. Without such limitations in place, the state becomes an implicit accomplice in potentially tolerating infringements of women's basic citizenship protections in the name of respecting a static interpretation of cultural and religious diversity.

Furthermore, the privatized diversity framework relies on an artificial and oversimplified distinction between private and public, culture and citizenship, contractual and moral obligation. This vision is not only inaccurate on a descriptive level; it is **normatively** unattractive as well. It is blind to the intersection of overlapping affiliations in individuals' lives. These parallel "belongings" are often the significant source of meaning and value for religious women; at the same time, they may also make them vulnerable to a double or triple disadvantage, especially in a legal and governance system that permits little interaction and dialogue between their overlapping sources of obligation. Women situated in minority religious communities are often especially hard hit by the privatized diversity framework and are left to fend for themselves under structurally unfavourable conditions.

The Predicament Facing Vulnerable Members of Religious Communities

~AV The established strict-separation approach asks religious women to adhere to the civil rules on the dissolution of marriage and divorce, leaving it up to each individual woman to somehow negotiate a termination of the religious aspect of the relationship—a task that may prove extremely difficult if the husband is recalcitrant. Another response, often presented by well-meaning philosophers and political theorists, is to recommend that these members simply "exit" their home communities if they experience injustice within. AV However, this recommendation provides little solace. If pious women wanted to leave their communities, the central legal dilemmas that haunt them—the challenge of adhering both to secular and to non-state religious requirements of forming and dissolving marriage—would not have arisen in the first place.

~AV Into this vacuum enters the privatized diversity approach. It takes a diametrically opposed path to that of strict separation, placing the need to address the religious side of the marriage at the heart of . . . [its] response: for instance, by recommending that parties move the "full docket" of their disputes from public state-provided courtrooms to private faith-based tribunals that may (or may not) . . . [protect the] rights and obligations that citizens hold as members of the larger political community. Blanket acceptance of privatized diversity would thus amount to a dramatic redefinition of the relationship between state and religion under the guise of mere **procedural** reliance on private alternative dispute resolution mechanisms. The price to be paid for such a move might prove dangerously high: forfeiting the hard-won protections that women won through democratic and **equity**-enhancing legislation, itself achieved as a result of significant social mobilization by women's groups and other justice-seeking individuals and communities. While offering opposing solutions, [both] the strict-separation and privatized-diversity approaches . . . [deny] their *shared* responsibility and obligation to assist women whose marriage regulation is grounded in an uneasy amalgam of secular and religious traditions. Between them, the two approaches compel devout women to make an all-or-nothing choice between these sources of law and identity.

AV This punishing dilemma can be avoided if the option of regulated interaction is contemplated. The core issue for us to assess is whether, and under what conditions, women's freedom and equality can be promoted (rather than inhibited) by law's recognition of certain faith-based obligations that structure marriage and divorce for religious citizens. The additional challenge is to develop a legal approach that can foster **viable** institutional paths for cooperation that begin to match the actual complexity of women's lived experience. Instead of assuming that gender equality and religious **pluralism** inevitably pull in contrasting directions, the recognizing of the actual dilemmas and claims raised by women embedded in religion . . . calls for new approaches that incorporate state and communal input into the regulation of faith-based processes as an opportunity both to empower women and to encourage transformation from within the tradition and by its authorized interpreters. This kind of regulated interaction promotes the intersection of religion with state oversight, ideally encouraging the participation of those long excluded from the "temple" of formal religious knowledge and the work of interpreting the faith's sacred texts. This is done with an eye to increasing new voices and rereadings of the tradition in a more **egalitarian** and inclusive fashion, but still within its permissible decision-making and interpretative techniques.

~AV The standard legal response to such dilemmas is of course different. It tends to relegate civil and family disputes with certain religious aspects *beyond* the reach of the secular courts—and thus outside the realm of provision of the safeguards provided by the state to other **litigants** or vulnerable parties. AV This need not, however, be the sole or even primary response to such dilemmas, especially when "non-intervention" effectively translates into immunizing wrongful behaviour by more powerful parties. In the deeply gendered world of intersecting religious and secular norms of family law, these more powerful parties are often husbands who may refuse to remove barriers to religious remarriage . . . or who may seek to retract a financial commitment undertaken as part of the religious marriage contract. . . . Such retaliation impairs the woman's ability to build a new family or establish financial independence after divorce. The broader concern here is that while their multiple affiliations might offer religious women a significant source of meaning and value, they may also make them vulnerable to a double or triple disadvantage, especially in a legal system that **categorically** denies cooperation between their overlapping sources of obligation.

Is it possible to find a more fruitful engagement that overcomes this predicament by placing the interests of these historically marginalized participants at the centre of the analysis? . . . From the perspective of women caught in the web of overlapping and potentially competing systems of secular and sacred law, the almost automatic rejection of any attempt to establish a forum for resolving standing disputes that address the religious dimension of their marriage might respect the protection-of-rights dimension of their lived experience, but unfortunately does little to address the cultural or religious affiliation issue. The latter may well be better addressed by attending to the removal of religious barriers to remarriage, obstacles that do not automatically disappear following a civil divorce. This is particularly true for observant women who have solemnized marriage according to the requirements of their religious tradition, and who may now wish—or feel obliged—to receive the blessing of this tradition for the dissolution of that relationship.

In the Canadian debate, this constituency also reflected a *transnational* element. In families with roots in more than one country, a divorce agreement that complies with the demands of the faith (as a non-territorial identity community)—in addition to those of the state of residence—is perceived as more "transferable" across different Muslim jurisdictions. In technical terms, this need not be the case—private international law norms are based on the laws of states, *not* of religions. But what matters here is the perception that a faith-based tribunal may provide a valuable legal service to its potential clientele, a service that the secular state, by virtue of its formal divorce from religion, simply cannot provide.

I believe we also face the urgent task of investigating and highlighting the importance of state action (or *in*action) in shaping, through law and institutional design, the context in which women can pursue their claims for equity and justice. Viewed through this perspective, the rise of privatized diversity mechanisms to implement religious principles should rightly be perceived with a healthy dose of skepticism, particularly if the parties lose the background protections and bargaining chips they are otherwise entitled to under secular law. One may well wonder whether this development represents a whole new and convenient way for the neo-liberal state (and its "rolled-back" public institutions) to avoid taking responsibility for protecting the rights of more vulnerable parties precisely in that arena of social life, the family, that is most crucial for realizing both gender equality and collective identity.

In order to militate against such a result, it is high time to search for new terms of engagement between the major players. They have a stake in finding a viable path that accommodates diversity *with* equality, a path that includes the faith community, the state and the individual. Any tractable [manageable] solution, however, must do so in ways that will benefit religious women, while duly acknowledging they are members of intersecting (and potentially conflicting) identity- and law-creating jurisdictions.

Forging a New Path

Any new path requires a delicate balance. On the one hand, it demands vigilance to address the serious communal pressures that make "free consent" to arbitration a code name for thinly veiled coercion. On the other hand, it requires avoidance of any hasty conclusion that the answer to such complex legal and identity challenges lies in turning a blind eye to the severe implications of the split-status problem confronting women who wish to maintain good standing both in their religious and in their non-religious communities. A number of alternative ideal-type responses present themselves. I will discuss just two promising alternatives: democratic deliberation and intercultural dialogue in civil society; and changing the background conditions that influence such **intra**- and **inter**-cultural negotiations.

The democratic deliberation path emphasizes the importance of dialogue in civil society and involves formal and informal intercultural exchanges. This route permits revealing the internal diversity of opinions and interpretations of the religious and secular family law traditions in question. Deliberation and contestation can also promote agency and direct empowerment through political participation and social mobilization.

While I fully endorse and support these civil society avenues, something else might be required in terms of institutional design to address situations of negotiation breakdown, imbalance of power, and restoration or establishment of rights. That "something else" translates into a focus on legal-institutional remedies that respond to the fact that erosion of women's freedom and autonomy is increasingly the "collateral damage" of charged state-religious "showdowns." To avert this disturbing result, I will briefly explore how, despite the fact that the strict-separation approach still remains the standard or default response, courts and legislatures have recently broken new ground by adopting what we might refer to as "intersectionist" or "joint governance" remedies.

One example is . . . *Bruker v. Marcovitz*, in which the Canadian Supreme Court explicitly rejected the simplistic "your culture or your rights" formula. Instead, it ruled in favour of "[r]ecognizing the enforceability by civil courts of agreements to discourage religious barriers to remarriage, addressing the gender discrimination those barriers may represent and alleviat[ing] the effects they may have on extracting unfair concessions in a civil divorce." In the *Marcovitz* case, a Jewish husband made a promise to remove barriers to religious remarriage in a negotiated, settled agreement, which was incorporated into the final divorce decree between the parties. He said he would give his wife a *get*, a bill of divorcement. This contractual obligation thus became part of the terms that enabled the civil divorce to proceed. Once the husband had the secular divorce in hand, however, he failed to honour the signed agreement to remove the religious barriers to his wife's remarriage, claiming that he had undertaken a moral rather than legal obligation. The Supreme Court was not in a position to order specific performance (forcing the husband to grant a *get*); instead, the court ordered the husband to pay monetary damages for breach of the contractual promise, a breach that had harmed the wife personally and the public interest generally. What *Marcovitz* demonstrates is the possibility of employing a standard legal remedy (damages for breach of contract, in this example) in response to specifically gendered harms that arise out of the intersection between multiple sources of authority and identity—religious and secular—in the actual lives of women.

The significance of the *Marcovitz* decision lies in its recognition that both the secular and religious aspects of divorce matter greatly to observant women if they are to enjoy gender equality, articulate their religious identity, enter new families after divorce, or rely on contractual ordering just like any other citizen. This joint-governance framework offers us a vision in which the secular law may be invoked to provide remedies for religious women to protect them from husbands who might otherwise "cherry-pick" their religious and secular obligations. This is a clear rejection of a punishing "either/or" approach, and instead it offers a more nuanced and context-sensitive analysis that begins from the "ground up." It identifies who is harmed and why, and then proceeds to find a remedy that matches, as much as possible, the need to recognize the (indirect) intersection of law and religion that contributed to the creation of the very harm for which legal recourse is now sought.

Regulated Interaction

The last set of issues that I wish to address relates to the thorny challenge of tackling the potential conflict between secular and religious norms governing family disputes. The fear that religious law represented a rival normative system that resisted and challenged the paramount constitutional principle of the rule of law clearly played a significant part in the anxiety surrounding the Shari'a tribunal debate in Canada. Given the deference typically afforded to out-of-court arbitration procedures, critics of the proposal charged that nothing less than an attempt to use a technique of privatized diversity to redefine the relationship between state and religion was under way. This posed an existential threat that no secular state authority was likely to accept with indifference—not even in tolerant, multicultural Canada. And so, after much contemplation, the chosen response to the challenge was to quash the proposed tribunal with all the legal force the authorities could muster. This took the shape of an **absolutist** solution: prohibiting by decree the operation of any religious arbitration process in the family law arena. This response, which relies on imposition by state fiat, sends a strong symbolic message of unity, although it is a unity achieved by prohibition instead of dialogue. This universal ban effectively shuts down, rather than encourages, coordination between civil and religious authorities.

A less heavy-handed approach might have been worth exploring, especially once the idea of granting unrestricted **immunity** in the name of religious freedom to *any* kind of dispute resolution forum is rejected. The alternatives include a range of options that permit . . . regulatory oversight in the service of human rights protections, mandatory provisions that no party is permitted to waive, and enhanced access to whatever public-sponsored resources are normally available to anyone facing a family breakdown. Regulated interaction envisions a new way of allocating and sharing jurisdiction between states and religious minorities.

The major insight here is that today's most contested social arenas—family law, education, criminal justice, and immigration, to mention but a few key examples—are internally divisible into parts or "sub-matters": multiple, separable yet complementary, legal components. Existing legal and normative models rarely recognize that most contested social arenas encompass multiple functions, or diverse sub-matters. Rather, they operate on the misguided assumption that each social arena is internally *indivisible* and thus should be under the full and exclusive jurisdiction of one authority, either the state or faith community. On this account, there is always a winner and a loser in the jurisdictional contest between state and religion. But if power can be divided into sub-matters within a single social activity, it becomes possible to have a more creative, nuanced and context-sensitive basis for coordination.

Take marriage. Here at least two sub-matters should be identified. There is a *demarcating* function mentioned earlier, which regulates, among other things, the change of one's marital status or one's entitlement to membership in a given community. And then there is a *distributing* function, which covers, among other things, the definition of the rights and obligations of married spouses, together with a determination, in the event of divorce or death, of the property and economic consequences of this change in marital status. These demarcation and distributive sub-matters parallel the two key legal aspects of marriage and divorce rules: status and property relations. This division permits ample room for legal creativity. Recent studies have shown, for example, that Muslim women in

Britain have turned to non-state institutions in order to gain a religious-authorized release from a dead marriage, one that, in certain cases, no longer legally existed because a state divorce decree had already been granted. For these women, the religious councils were performing the crucial communal demarcating function of removing religious barriers to remarriage. These "end users" were seeking specialized religious-oriented divorce services that the secular state is, by definition, barred from supplying. At the same time, the women who turned to these local, faith-based councils expressed no interest in (and indeed, some explicitly rejected) the idea of delegating control over the distributive components of their fractured marriage. They did not want their post-divorce property relations (controlling matters such as the rights and obligations owed by each former spouse to the other, to the children, if any, and to various third parties) determined by these non-state institutions. Such division of responsibility fits well with the idea of sub-matter jurisdictions. It rejects transferring the "full docket" or "package" to privatized-diversity entities and, instead, demands that some degree of coordination occur between religious and civil institutions in any initial allocation of shared responsibility and its subsequent implementation.

In addition to the recommended division of authority according to component functions, the literature on institutional design distinguishes between different forms or techniques of oversight. The classic approach envisages minimal oversight: the rationale here is that the consenting parties intentionally removed their dispute from the public system, preferring instead an out-of-court process. In the case of severe breaches of procedural or substantive justice, however, laws governing alternative dispute resolution routinely permit the arbitrating parties to seek judicial review. This is characterized in the literature as the "fire alarm" response (a . . . [case-by-case, after the fact] review initiated by individual complainants or public interest groups) as opposed to "police control" (a more centralized, governmental . . . [before the fact] mode of oversight). These combined protections are designed to assist individuals by reducing information asymmetries and power imbalances, as well as providing a check on the exercise of authority by arbitrators or any other independent third-party decision-makers. However, just like any other legal measure that respects individual choice, they may fall short of providing a *full* guarantee that no communal (or other) pressure was imposed on those utilizing an alternative dispute-resolution forum. To address these real concerns, any principled scheme of regulation must also include a robust commitment to ensure that women are not dispossessed of whatever equal rights and protections they have as citizens when they raise a legal claim that incorporates the religious dimension as well. The possibility of implementing precisely such an "intersectionist" commitment was exemplified by the *Marcovitz* ruling.

With these conditions firmly in place, we can appreciate the dynamism and behaviour-alteration potential of the regulated interaction approach. For instance, communal decision-makers (ideally trained in *both* civil and religious law) have the opportunity to enjoy the benefits of state recognition of their decisions—including the coveted public enforcement of their awards—when dissolving a religious marriage in accordance with the tenets of the relevant faith. The state retains the power to issue a civil divorce and to define the thresholds or default rules in matters such as the post-divorce distribution of matrimonial and other property, matters that inevitably concern *all* citizens facing a marriage breakdown. These safeguards typically establish a minimal baseline or "floor" of protection, above which significant room for variation is permitted. These protections were designed, in the first place, to address concerns about power and gender inequities in family relations—concerns that are not absent from religious communities either. If anything, these concerns probably apply with equal force in the religious context as in the individualized, secular case.

This then is the regulated interaction model, one that offers an alternative to the "top-down" prohibition model that was eventually chosen by the government in the Canadian debate. Provided the resolution by a non-state "arbitration" body falls within the reasonable margin of **discretion** permitted a family-law judge or secular arbitrator, there is no reason to discriminate against that tribunal *solely* for the reason that it was guided by, and applied, religious norms and principles. The operative assumption here is that, in a diverse society, we can safely assume that at least some individuals might wish to turn to their "communal" institutions, knowing that their basic state-backed rights are still protected by these alternative **fora**.

Under these conditions, the option of turning to a *regulated* non-state tribunal may, perhaps paradoxically, nourish the development of a more dynamic, context-sensitive and moderate interpretation of the faith tradition. Why? Because it may transform the standing of non-state sources of authority from the realm of unofficial, non-binding advice to that of potentially compelling decisions over consenting parties. The proviso that comes with such revamped jurisdictional authority is that actors cannot breach the basic protections to which each woman is entitled by virtue of her equal citizenship status. If they ignore these entitlements, religious authorities risk depriving themselves of the ability to provide relevant legal services to the very members of the community they most dearly care about. If they wish to see their faith community survive (and indeed, flourish), and if they wish to continue to define who belongs within the faith community's membership boundaries, these basic protections cannot be spurned.

As we have seen earlier, religious marriage and divorce rules play a crucial role in fulfilling this identity-demarcating function. The obligation to comply with minimal standards defined by the larger community in governing the distributive obligations between the separated or divorced parties (and toward relevant third parties) does not have to cripple the new-found authority gained by the religious community and its tribunals. They may maintain their identity through control over the demarcating aspect of marriage and divorce (for those members who desire such an affiliation). By ensuring that incidents of "split status" are reduced within a diverse plural society (one that retains the option of secular divorce), both the community at large and the specific women involved benefit by having all barriers to remarriage removed in a conclusive and non-ambivalent manner. Such processes could plant the seeds for meaningful reform that falls within the interpretative margins and methodologies for innovation permitted by the religious tradition and improves women's bargaining position and rights protection. This creates an alignment of interests between the group, the state and the individuals at risk. In this fashion, regulated interaction can address the multiple aspects of marriage and its breakdown, generating conditions that permit an effective, non-coercive encouragement of more egalitarian and reformist changes from *within* the tradition itself. The state system, too, is transformed from strict separation by regulated interaction. It is no longer permitted to categorically relegate competing sources of authority to the realm of unofficial, exotic, if not outright dangerous, "non-law." The regulated interaction approach discourages an underworld of unregulated religious tribunals. It offers a path to transcend the "either/or" choice between culture and rights, family and state, citizenship and islands of "privatized diversity." . . .

Note

1. Prior to the French Revolution, Jews, Muslims, and other non-Christians in France were excluded from citizenship. In 1791, during the Revolution, the French National Assembly granted the political rights of citizenship to non-Christians. [Editor]

Benjamin L. Berger

The Cultural Limits of Legal Tolerance

AV = author's view; ~AV = not the author's view

[Berger spends most of this reading arguing against the dominant legal view of the law and religion. Think of this form of argument as a response to the "If it ain't broke, don't fix it" claim—Berger first has to show that the dominant view is "broke" before he can say how he thinks we should fix it. Thus he only gets to his positive claim near the end.—Editor]

. . . The success of the rhetoric of legal **multiculturalism** has clouded our capacity to see clearly the true nature of the relationship between religious conscience and the **constitutional rule of law.** ~AV Legal multiculturalism has held that, in a society characterized by deep cultural **pluralism**, the role of the law is to operationalize a political commitment to multiculturalism by serving as custodian and wielder of the twin key tools of tolerance and accommodation. In the context of religious difference in Canada, this commitment has translated into a prevailing **juridical** wisdom that freedom of religion is a hallmark of the **liberal** constitutional order and that the mechanism by which religious culture can be harmonized with the **state** is through the **rights**-based use of these legal tools.

. . .

AV But when this approach is applied to instances in which the law comes face to face with pronounced cultural difference it also creates a deeply flawed story about the relationship between religious difference and the constitutional rule of law.

. . .

. . . [L]egal multiculturalism . . . obscures the fact that the contemporary encounter between religion and the constitutional rule of law is a cross-cultural encounter. This means that the concepts and tools used by . . . conventional theories are not understood as components of a cultural system and as producing profound cultural impacts for those subject to them. This being so, whenever religious groups find themselves before the bar of the law the terms of the debate are, in important ways, always already settled—certain commitments and assumptions of the culture of **constitutionalism** are not up for grabs or open to debate because they are seen as solutions to, not aspects of, the underlying tension. When this is the case, the rhetoric of pluralism, tolerance, and accommodation can be experienced as a language of power, coercion and enforced transformation. This is the felt cultural force of the law.

. . .

Law's Approach [to Tolerance]

. . . The starting point for understanding law's posture when it encounters religion is the fountainhead [original source] case on religious liberties in Canada, *R. v. Big M. Drug Mart.*[1] In it, Justice Dickson (as he then was) linked the notion of religious freedom to the very nature of a free society, stating that such a society "is one which can accommodate a wide variety of beliefs, diversity of tastes and pursuits, customs and codes of conduct."[2] The concept of freedom of religion, then, is centrally concerned with permitting the free and unconstrained expression of religious belief and conduct. Freedom of religion is, in the **jurisprudence**, an ideal that revolves around the notion of tolerance. The Court has explained its view that "respect for and tolerance of the rights and practices of religious minorities is one of the hallmarks of an enlightened **democracy**,"[3] going so far as to declare that "mutual tolerance is one of the cornerstones of all **democratic** societies."[4] It has characterized Canada as "a diverse and multicultural society, bound together by the values of accommodation, tolerance and respect for diversity."[5] The story that law tells about its encounter with religion is generally shot through with the language of tolerance. Law should be a mechanism of repelling the state from interference with religion and should itself be parsimonious in its interventions with religious beliefs and practice.

The Court explains that this commitment to tolerance is directly linked to the fact of living in a "multiethnic and multicultural country such as ours, which accentuates and advertises its modern record of respecting cultural diversity and human rights and of promoting tolerance of religious and ethnic minorities."[6] Our policy of multiculturalism produces the commitment to religious tolerance and the constitutional manifestation of this commitment is the protection of religious freedom in section 2 of the *Charter*.[7] This, then, is the first plank in law's approach to religion: given the multicultural character of the state, tolerance is the guiding feature of law's engagement with religion, giving a margin of freedom for a broad diversity of pursuits, tastes, beliefs, and practices. Section 2(a) of the *Charter*, thus, asserts an aspiration of religious tolerance within a multicultural society and surely holds out substantial comfort to communities of religious belief.

Two Features of Legal Tolerance in Canada

On closer inspection, however, the picture becomes rather more complex and intricate. In *Big M.*, Justice Dickson explains that the **corollary** of freedom of religion is freedom *from* religion. If the basis for religious freedom is, in the first place, respect for the **autonomy** and freedom of each person, then it is equally antithetical to our commitments to allow the religious beliefs of one individual or group to be imposed upon the unwilling or the non-believing. This . . . gestures towards the potential—not infrequently actualized in contemporary issues of religious freedom—of the conflicts of rights: "respect for religious minorities is not a stand-alone absolute right; like other rights, freedom of religion exists in a matrix of other correspondingly important rights that attach to individuals."[8] The issue is not solely one of the parallel individual rights of others; rather, the tolerance of religious difference takes place within a society with its own concerns, needs, and imperatives. Otherwise put, "[r]espect for minority rights must also coexist alongside societal values that are central to the make-up and functioning of a free and democratic society."[9]

In recognition of this embeddedness within a context of other rights and other pressing societal interests and needs, the Canadian legal story adds to its aspiration of tolerance a second feature: limits on freedom of religion may be justified in order to protect broad social interests or preserve the rights of others. Since *Big M.*, there has been some ambiguity and debate . . . as to whether the right to religious freedom found in s. 2(a) may be internally—or "definitionally"—limited by certain powerful public interests, such as public safety and order, or by the rights and freedoms and others. Recently, however, the Court has expressed a strong preference for managing such conflicts not by declaring that the religious practice falls outside the protection of section 2(a), but by recognizing a breach of religious freedoms and then moving on to assess whether a limit on that right is reasonable. In *Multani*[10] as well as the *Same Sex Marriage Reference*[11] the Court explained that the most appropriate means of dealing with such conflict is to balance religious freedom against these other rights and interests under the rubric of section 1 of the *Charter*, which asks whether a limit on a right can be "demonstrably justified in a free and democratic society."[12] Section 1 is, in essence, a means-ends proportionality review.[13] The rhetorical **rendering** of a successful limitation of religious liberties is a declaration that, "although we have limited your religious liberties and, in this sense, failed to be as tolerant as we would otherwise aspire to be, that we have done so is justified in light of the core commitments [of] our free and democratic society." . . .

This doctrinal framework serves as the **rules of engagement** for law's cross-cultural encounter with religion. . . . [T]hese principles suggest the posture that the Canadian constitutional rule of law assumes in its encounter with religion. . . . On the surface, law begins firmly in the milieu of tolerance and **laissez-faire liberalism**. The law claims that our society is firmly dedicated to multiculturalism and this commitment demands tolerance of the ways that people choose to live their lives, including the free expression and manifestation of beliefs and cultural practices. AV However, there is no assumption that religious cultures might offer something valuable from which the legal culture might borrow. Law and religion are certainly not engaging in a conversation as relative equals, one that may result in the transformation of either. Law's formal encounter with religion is neither an instance of cultural borrowing nor of dialogic engagement. Neither, though, is there an attempt—at this point—to subordinate difference by means of the kind of **ideological** force that characterizes conversion or assimilation. ~AV Instead, the law affirms diversity, but at arm's length. Religious cultures are entitled to the benefit of a liberal philosophy of ***modus vivendi*** tolerance.[14]

AV The difficulty with tolerance, as Bernard Williams has argued, "is that it seems to be at once necessary and impossible."[15] Tolerance takes its place as a robust virtue at those points at which the tolerating group "thinks that the other is blasphemously, disastrously, obscenely wrong."[16] A virtuous toleration that will "accommodate a wide variety of beliefs, diversity of tastes and pursuits, customs and codes of conduct"[17] must be one that finds it difficult to accept these practices and beliefs within its own system of meaning and commitments. As Williams explains, "[w]e need to tolerate other people and their ways of life only in situations that make it really difficult to do so. Toleration, we may say, is required only for the intolerable. That is its basic problem."[18] The doctrinal structure of Canadian constitutional law as I have described it reflects this "basic problem" and, in so doing, points to important characteristics of law's mode of cross-cultural engagement with religion.

The Conversionary Mode of Legal Tolerance

AV . . . That which has come before the law is nominally "religion" and religious difference should be tolerated. Yet if the religious conduct or beliefs in question are arguably "intolerable," the law moves to a means-end proportionality analysis that asks whether the limit on legal tolerance is justified. With this move, the law quickly collapses into a conversionary mode of cross-cultural encounter. A particular instance of religious pluralism has been deemed problematic and the law now asks whether the limit imposed on the tolerance of this religious culture is justified. When asking if a limit on religious freedom is justified, the question is assessed within the values, assumptions, and symbolic commitments of the rule of law itself. In particular, law's conception of religion comes strongly into play. The law assesses whether the religious expression in question has deviated—and if so, how much—from acceptable religion. Here, the relevant questions include whether the **controverted** practice is closely linked to individual flourishing, whether it was merely private or **encroached** on the public, and whether it limited the autonomy or equality of another. These are the criteria that determine if this instance of cultural difference will be tolerated or not. Crucially, these criteria are drawn from inside the culture of Canadian constitutionalism itself. The more that a given religious culture or practice **accords** with law's understanding of religion, the less abrasive and challenging to law's commitments it will be and, hence, the more likely it is that it will fall within the limits of legal tolerance. When, however, a claim to religious freedom begins to grate or put pressure on the law, it appears legally intolerable. The deeming of a particular manifestation of religion as "intolerable"—and, hence, the limitation of religious freedom as "justified"—can always be read as the product of a misfit between the **claimant**'s religion or religious practice and what law understands as "acceptable religion." Law's religion is tolerable religion.

If the limit on tolerance is justified, it is justified owing to its fidelity to the commitments, values, and overarching objectives of the rule of law. If the limit on tolerance is not justified, *the reason is the same*. It is not justified because we erred in thinking that the practice *actually* offended the basic commitments of law's rule. The limitation was unduly onerous or we did not appreciate that, in fact, the religious practice or belief in question could be viewed as or rendered consonant with these commitments—commitments such as autonomy, the protection of individuals, and the maintenance of a **private sphere** characterized by personal values and a **public sphere** cleansed of the influences of choice and taste. Within this **analytic** structure, law always vindicates its own cultural understandings.

With this, law's encounter with religion . . . [resembles] the conversionary/assimilationist mode of cross-cultural encounter. (This experience of an encounter with law as an experience of **cultural imperialism** or as conversion/assimilation is, of course, something all too familiar for the Indigenous peoples of Canada. . . .) Most significantly, there is an underlying repudiation of the diversity and difference recognized, from a distance, in the minimal engagement posture. Law tolerates that which is different only so long as it is not *so different* that it challenges the organizing **norms**, commitments, practices and symbols of the Canadian constitutional rule of law. As such, the denial is an ethical one; it inheres in both the assertion that there is a single and indissoluble package of criteria that is appropriate to judging the result of such conflicts of rights and interests and in the fact that these criteria are all drawn from within the culture of the rule of law itself. Once this move has taken place, there is only one of two possibilities: the courts will either deem the conduct intolerable and require the religious group or individual to conform to the norms and commitments of the rule of law, or the courts will conclude that the state was wrong in limiting this instance of religious diversity *because this instance of cultural pluralism is itself consistent with the values and commitments of the rule of law*. In either instance, there is the kind of **universalism** and, characteristic of conversionary and assimilationist modes of cross-cultural encounter, an ultimate denial of difference. In the final analysis, you are either required to conform your way of life to the symbols, values, and meanings of the rule of law, or permitted to carry on without interference *because the law recasts the meaning of your practices and beliefs as already consistent with* those cultural commitments. In either instance, the law spreads a cultural pattern or way of life that has, at its base, "the insistence on a common or identical human nature."[19] In either instance, the religionist is sent the message that, despite the values at stake for him or her at this analytic moment, what really matters is the set of values and commitments held by the rule of law and, whether by **proscribing** certain behaviour or by re-casting the meaning of that behaviour, you will be made to conform to the culture of law's rule.

Two Examples of Legal Decision-Making about Religious Tolerance

Consider two examples drawn from the jurisprudence, one in which religion "wins" and one in which religion "loses." What is the message about the nature of legal tolerance expressed in each of these cases? The case of *Multani* is an interesting example of apparent legal tolerance, in part because it also contains a passionate plea by the Court for the importance of religious tolerance in Canadian society and the need to teach this value to Canadian youth. *Multani* involved an Orthodox Sikh boy who felt that his faith required him to wear a *kirpan*, a small ceremonial dagger, at all times. His school issued an absolute prohibition on wearing the *kirpan* at school on the basis of its policy that prohibited students from carrying any "weapons and dangerous objects." Given that it was the product of a sincerely held religious belief, the Court had no difficulty finding that the policy offended Multani's section 2(a) right. The bulk of the analysis turned on section 1. Although the school board argued that the prohibition was justified as a safety measure and that the *kirpan*'s presence could have an adverse impact on the school environment, the Court concluded that this absolute prohibition was not a proportional limit on Multani's religious right. Dismissing the safety concern as ill-founded, the Court noted that there was no history of *kirpan*-related violence and that Multani had already agreed to wear the *kirpan* under his clothes and in a wooden sheath, itself wrapped and sewn in a cloth envelope. Contrary to the school board's submissions that the presence of a *kirpan* would damage the school environment, the Court explained that it was, in fact, the absolute prohibition that would have this [adverse] effect:

> A total prohibition against wearing a kirpan to school undermines the value of this religious symbol and sends students the message that some religious practices do not merit the same protection as others. On the other hand, accommodating Gurbaj Singh and allowing him to wear his kirpan under certain conditions demonstrates the importance that our society attaches to protecting freedom of religion and to showing respect for its minorities.[20]

So this religious practice is entitled to legal tolerance. The Court even emphasizes that "[r]eligious tolerance is a very important value of Canadian society."[21] But note that before arriving at this conclusion, the Court has cast the meaning of Multani's religious expression in a form consistent with law's understanding of religion, whether that comports with his understanding or not. The logic of the section 2(a) analysis says that Mr. Multani's religious expression is constitutionally cognizable because it is an aspect of an "individual's self-definition and fulfilment and is a function of personal autonomy and choice."[22] Although it takes place at school, this religious practice is an expression of individual difference, does not touch the domain of public reason, and does not threaten the autonomy, choice, or equality of any others. Sheathed, sealed, and tucked away inside the folds of young Multani's clothing, religion does not threaten any of the values or structural commitments of the rule of law.[23] *Multani* holds that this religious difference will be "tolerated," but the underlying message is that it will be tolerated because it conforms to law's understanding of religion and does not meaningfully grate upon any of the central cultural commitments of the culture of Canadian constitutionalism.[24] In this way, even as it tolerates, law asserts its cultural superiority and performs the dominance of public norms. The message sent is that Multani's religion should be tolerated because it ought not to be of genuine public concern.

What, on the other hand, is the message sent when the law trumps religious freedom? In *B.R.*,[25] the religious freedom issue was whether the government of Ontario had interfered with parents' religious liberties by overriding their decision not to permit a blood transfusion for their infant child, a decision motivated by their Jehovah's Witness faith. The majority of the Court accepted that this decision was an expression of the parents' religious freedom as protected by section 2(a). When, however, the judges turned to the section 1 analysis, they reasoned that the state's actions were justified limitations on this religious freedom. The Court explained that the child had "never expressed any agreement with the Jehovah's Witness faith" and that respect for the child's autonomy demanded that she be allowed to "live long enough to make [her] own reasoned choice about the religion [she] wishes to follow,"[26] if any. The parents had found the limit of legal tolerance at the border of individual autonomy and choice. There was simply no way that the Canadian constitutional rule of law would cede the necessary territory to make room for the parents' sincerely-held ethical and **epistemological** commitments. The message sent in *B.R.* is that, in the presence of a religious difference that actually challenges the fundamental commitments of the Canadian constitutional rule of law, tolerance is at an end.

. . .

AV A common dynamic appears in these cases: To the extent that religion can be contained within the structural commitments of the rule of law, interpreted as comporting with its values, and read as consistent with its understanding of religion, tolerance is the mode of cross-cultural engagement. The grant of tolerance is based on the implicit judgment that the cultural differences found in the "tolerated" really ought not to bother the law. The point at which religion transgresses these commitments and defies these conceptions is the point at which tolerance gives way to the forceful imposition of the culture of Canadian constitutionalism.

. . .

Legal Tolerance as Indifference

~AV In his essay "Tolerating the Intolerable," Bernard Williams refers to an apparent form of tolerance in history of the relationship among various churches and denominations within the Christian world. One means of managing this pluralism was to assert that, despite seeming differences, all of these brands of Christianity were, in essence, the same. Since all were ultimately concerned with the same goals, one need not care much about the details of what the other believed. Although he recognizes this as a solution with certain practical political goods, AV Williams cautions against an excessively **sanguine** evaluation of this state of affairs, stating that "as an attitude, it is less than toleration. If you do not care all that much what anyone believes, you do not need the attitude of toleration, any more than you do with regard to other people's tastes in food."[27] Instead, the attitude being relied upon beneath the language of toleration is, in truth, indifference.

~AV What I have described above is a tolerance of indifference. Insofar as religious culture either produces no apparent conflicts with what centrally matters to the law or the basic ways in which law understands the world, toleration is the mode of engagement. This kind of tolerance ends at the point at which the religious culture genuinely begins to grate on the values, practices, and ways of knowing of Canadian constitutionalism. When religious practice actually starts to *matter* to the law by challenging something central to the culture of law's rule, we begin to see the depth and force of law's commitments. Legal tolerance of religion re-enacts the public/private divide that is so central to law's culture. The law is able to tolerate those religious beliefs and practices that exert little pressure on the public norms and commitments of Canadian constitutionalism. . . . When the law can no longer be indifferent—when the religious belief or practice begins to trouble the law—we encounter the cultural limits of legal toleration.

. . .

AV Law's tolerance of indifference is not a simple one, nor is it entirely without virtue. Recall the constitutional logic employed when analyzing whether an aspect of religious culture that might appear to chafe on the commitments of the liberal rule of law ought to be tolerated: before limiting the right, the courts should carefully consider whether the religious expression that is producing the apparent conflict can actually be satisfyingly digested within the values and commitments of the rule of law. This reflective process demands a continual refinement and perhaps even expansion of the realm of indifference. Law asks itself to reconsider and reconfigure the geography of indifference using its own categories, like the private/public, and its own values, like autonomy and choice. Perhaps what we thought, on first glance, was objectionable is actually something that we can convince ourselves we shouldn't really mind after all . . . [because] the belief [is] sufficiently private so as not to trouble the law. . . .

Seen in this way, modern legal tolerance takes place within the margins set by . . . [the cultural assumption] of **incommensurability** between law and religion at which law will move to a posture of enforcement or "conversion." Although very much consistent with the roots of liberal thinking about the nature of political tolerance of religion, this is a more modest practice than that presented in the modern story of legal multiculturalism. But by imposing the reflective demand to learn about the nature and contours of the religious practice or commitment appearing before it and asking whether it should *really* matter that much to the law, there is the abiding prospect that the law will stay its violent hand in more cases than it might absent this demand for the refinement of indifference. In this sense, the tacit or express declaration that a particular religious expression is "not intolerable" is a kind of political intervention with virtues and significance that it would be a mistake to ignore. There is real liberty within this margin created by an expanded and continually refined indifference. An assiduously cultivated liberal "tolerance as indifference" is a meaningful virtue.

Nevertheless, when toleration of a given religious commitment would require the law to actually cede **normative** or symbolic territory, law trumps it in the name of procedural fairness, choice, autonomy, or the integrity of the public sphere; with this, tolerance gives way to conversion. Like religion, the rule of law is concerned with shaping meaning and it is not modest in its claims. Living within the Canadian constitutional rule of law is living within a culture that makes claims about the relevance of space and time, about the source and nature of authority, and about what is of value about the human subject. So, too, does religion. Law and religion are, in this sense, **homologous**; both constitute meaningful worlds. Within a liberal democratic rule of law, however, the tacit but powerful assumption is that law's meaning must "win" at points of conflict; perhaps this is to be expected—every culture assumes that its way of seeing is basically correct and, as I will argue, law is a uniquely positioned and equipped culture, equally committed to this sense of its own centrality. Thus, when religion makes a claim upon the law that is not digestible within legal frameworks, this **homology** means that the claim is in competition with law's vision of the world. At this point law asserts its dominance and law's asserted dominance is experienced as a conversionary effort for those committed to the religious culture's way of being in the world. These are the unacknowledged cultural stakes of law's encounter with religion.

"Once we see that the rule of law is a way of being in the world that must compete with other forms of social and political perception, a range of questions about the actual forms and character of this competition open up. We need to study the places at which conflict emerges and the ways in which law has succeeded or failed in these conflicts."[28] Studying the points of conflict between the culture of law's rule and religious forms of being in the world has revealed an unacknowledged complexity. Law's self-understanding speaks of multiculturalism, toleration and accommodation as the key principles. Yet, as I have shown, this brand of toleration depends upon a kind of indifference (no matter how cultivated) and at precisely the points at which the law can no longer be indifferent—tellingly, often at the points at which the stakes for the religious culture concerned have themselves become the highest—its conversionary aspirations appear. The simplified story about the demands and ethics of tolerance and accommodation in a multicultural society is far more comforting but far less satisfying. In Mannheim's sense of [**ideology**]—a way of thinking that "obscures the real condition of society both to itself and to others and thereby stabilizes it"[29]—legal tolerance is ideology.

The Limits of Theory

. . . What other forms of legal tolerance of religious difference can be imagined? ~AV One of the distinctive features of law's rule is that it is, in a very particular and practical respect, never wrong. This is not, of course, to say that law never admits error and makes changes accordingly; it surely does this. The point, rather, is that the ultimate authority and correctness of the law is never in question for itself. Even when it accepts that the application of its principles were misguided in a given case or that certain rules should adjust to account for changes in society, there is a permanent conservation of law's authority and, contrary to the dialogic demand to be open to the risk of self-decentring, a structurally permanent affirmation of its place at the centre of the management of all public dispute. Paul Kahn puts the issue as follows:

> Any failure at all will appear to threaten the whole of the rule of law. Law does not win localized victories over action; it cannot tolerate defeats as long as they are balanced by victories. . . . Law never explicitly concedes defeat; it never admits powerlessness. A partial rule of law is not the rule of law at all. The rule of law must always claim that no one is above the law.[30]

Thus, although it might, in a given case, concede that the line between the private and public was incorrectly drawn in the past, we cannot imagine Canadian constitutional rule of law disavowing the organizing significance of . . . [the public-private distinction]. Similarly, although the legal configurations necessary to protect individual autonomy and choice might be hotly debated in the law, the normative primacy of these values is never itself at stake. The rule of law is a way of understanding the world; when law asserts its ultimate authority, it asserts the dominance of its basic understandings. If this is true, it leaves little room for dialogic engagement.

AV When religious cultures claim the protection of rights that are a part of modern legal multiculturalism, there is no openness to the possibility that the law might not be the ultimate arbiter of the terms and conditions that will settle this dispute. Another way of seeing this very particular feature of the culture of contemporary Canadian constitutionalism is in linguistic terms. In his plea for a form of dialogic constitutionalism[31] that can better serve the needs of deep diversity, Tully argues as follows:

> if there is to be a **post-imperial** dialogue on the just **constitution** of culturally diverse societies, the dialogue must be one in which the participants are recognized and speak in their own language and customary ways. They do not wish either to be silenced or to be recognized and constrained to speak within the institutions and traditions of interpretation of the **imperial** constitutions that have been imposed over them.[32]

Yet once cast as a claim about legal tolerance or accommodation within contemporary Canadian constitutional culture, the possibility of the use of a language other than law's own is foreclosed. The language becomes the language of rights constitutionalism, privileging the terms "autonomy," "equality," and "choice." The salient concepts are those of the public and the private, jurisdiction, and standing. The ways become the way of legal process and the matter is firmly set within the institutions and traditions of interpretation of the culture of law's rule. Tully sees this point, noting that a central defect of modern liberal constitutionalism's engagement with difference is that "[w]hen the defenders of modern constitutionalism take up claims for recognition, they assume that to comprehend (understand) what the claimants are saying consists in comprehending it within an inclusive language or conceptual framework in which it can then be **adjudicated**."[33] Indeed, this recognition of the dialogic limitations of the liberal constitutional rule of law impels his search for a means of entirely reconceiving and reconstructing modern constitutionalism.

The meaningful form that law gives to experience is not the only form imaginable; indeed, law's meanings are always and essentially in competition with other ways of imagining the world—other cultures. This is what makes the dialogic form of cross-cultural encounter so attractive. But, in a liberal constitutional democracy, the law is privileged among such possible interpretations and it is this feature of legal culture that seems to put this more promising form of cross-cultural encounter out of reach. Once cultural conflict is embedded within the language of rights and legal accommodation, by its very nature the rule of law exerts a kind of structural dominance **immiscible** with dialogic forms of cross-cultural encounter. So, in the end, whereas blindness to *the fact* of the culture of contemporary Canadian constitutionalism consigns legal multiculturalism to a form of cultural assimilation, seeing the precise nature of this contemporary legal culture forecloses the possibility of the promising dialogic form of cross-cultural engagement.

Conclusion: The Challenges of Seeing Culture

. . . The conceptual core of this article is the suggestion that the conventional story about the relationship between the rule of law and religious cultures depends upon the conceit of law's autonomy from culture, a conceit that hides the fact that law is not merely an overseer or instrumental force in the politics of multiculturalism. When analyzed as a cultural force in its own right, the boundaries of legal doctrines of tolerance and the nature of the cross-cultural encounter between religion and law become more transparent. Yet what is thereby revealed is that legal tolerance involves a more modest posture towards religious pluralism than the rhetoric of multiculturalism would suggest. In the end, law's tolerance is a form of cultivated and continually refined indifference towards religious cultures. . . . [T]his posture of tolerance collapses into one that is assimilationist or conversionary . . . [and] it becomes clear that . . . law's rule is . . . very much prepared to assert its dominance.

Understanding the meeting of law and religion as a cross-cultural encounter breaks down our complacencies about what it means for law to accommodate strong forms of religious pluralism and exposes the cultural limits of legal toleration. It is a more honest account of what is occurring between law and religion under the rubric of legal multiculturalism. . . . [I]f viewing . . . the interaction of law and religion as a cross-cultural encounter causes us to see this interaction as decidedly fraught and durable, then . . . [this] account . . . has served us well because it has helped us to see better.

Notes

1. [1985]1 S.C.R. 295 (*Big M.*).
2. *Big M.*, para. 295.
3. *Syndicat Northcrest v. Amselem*, [2004] 2 S.C.R. 551: para. 1 (*Amselem*).
4. *Amselem*, para. 87.
5. *Chamberlain v. Surrey School District No. 36*, [2002] 4 S.C.R. 710: para. 21 *Chamberlain*).
6. *Amselem*, para. 87.
7. Section 2 of the *Charter* secures "fundamental freedoms" for Canadian. The four fundamental freedoms specified in the *Charter* are: "(a) freedom of conscience and religion; (b) freedom of thought, belief, opinion and expression, including freedom of the press and other media of communication; (c) freedom of peaceful assembly; and (d) freedom of association." [Editor]
8. *Amselem*, para. 1.
9. *Amselem*, para. 1.
10. *Multani v. Commission scolaire Marguerite-Bourgeoys*, [2006]1 S.C.R. 256 (*Multani*). Orthodox Sikh men are required to wear a *kirpan*, a ceremonial dagger. Multani's school forbade him to wear the *kirpan* because of its policy against "weapons and dangerous objects." The Supreme Court ruled that the school's policy violated Multani's right to freedom of religion. [Editor]
11. *Reference re: Same-Sex Marriage*, [2004]3 S.C.R. 698. One of the questions the Court was asked in the *Same Sex Marriage Reference* was whether broadening the definition of marriage to include same-sex marriage would infringe the rights of religious groups that do not support same-sex marriage. The Court said it would not. [Editor]
12. Section 1 of the Charter reads as follows: "The *Canadian Charter of Rights and Freedoms* guarantees the rights and freedoms set out in it subject only to such reasonable limits prescribed by law as can be demonstrably justified in a free and democratic society." [Editor]
13. A means-ends proportionality review is a method for analyzing the constitutionality of a law. This method requires courts to identify a legal objective (an end) and decide whether this objective can be justified in light of the interference or harm it will impose on the citizenry (the means). The definition of proportionality will vary depending on the constitution, laws, and objectives in question. In the Canadian context, the Oakes test is an example of a means-ends proportionality review. [Editor]
14. "*Modus vivendi*" is Latin for "way of life." "*Modus vivendi* tolerance" refers to a practice and policy of accepting all ways of life that do not conflict with liberal values. [Editor]
15. Bernard Williams, "Tolerating the Intolerable," in Susan Mendes, ed., *The Politics of Toleration in Modern Life* (Durham, NC: Duke University Press, 1999), p. 65.
16. Williams, p. 65.
17. *Big M.*, para. 336.
18. Williams, p. 65.
19. Fred Dallmayr, *Beyond Orientalism: Essays on Cross-Cultural Encounter* (Albany: SUNY Press, 1996), pp. 9–10.
20. *Multani*, para. 79.
21. *Multani*, para. 76.
22. *Amselem*, para. 42.
23. A structural commitment is a duty imposed by an external source. The structural commitments of Canadian law are the constitutionally protected rights of Canadian citizens, and the values (liberty and equality) that these rights presuppose. [Editor]
24. Berger identifies Canadian constitutionalism as a "culture" because it is a shared value of Canadian society. The "cultural commitments" of Canadian constitutionalism require citizens to recognize the *Charter* as the supreme law of Canada, and to live in accordance with the values protected by the *Charter*. Canadian courts and legislature must conform their actions and decisions to the principles set forth in the *Charter*, and citizens must obey the law, respect the rights of their fellow citizens, and be tolerant of diversity and pluralism. [Editor]

25. *B.(R.) v. Children's Aid Society of Metropolitan Toronto*, [1995] 1 S.C.R. 315 (*B.R.*).
26. *B.R.*, para. 437.
27. Williams, p. 67.
28. Paul W. Kahn, *The Cultural Study of Law: Reconstructing Legal Scholarship* (Chicago, IL: University of Chicago Press, 1999), pp. 84–5.
29. Karl Mannheim, *Ideology and Utopia* (New York: Harcourt, Brace, and Co., 1936), p. 40.
30. Paul W. Kahn, *The Reign of Law: Marbury v. Madison and the Construction of America* (New Haven, CT: Yale University Press, 1997), p. 167.
31. "Dialogic constitutionalism" promotes a rule of law, in which rules and decisions arise from the equal participation of all involved parties. For Tully, dialogic constitutionalism demands that courts and legislatures allow cultural minorities to reference their own traditions in justifying their own actions and in questioning the actions of others. [Editor]
32. James Tully, *Strange Multiplicity: Constitutionalism in an Age of Diversity* (Cambridge: Cambridge University Press, 1995), p. 24.
33. Tully, p. 56.

Joseph H. Carens and Melissa S. Williams

Islam, Immigration, and Group Recognition

AV = author's view; ~AV = not the author's view

Muslim Migrants and the "Clash of Civilizations"

Over the past three decades immigrants from Asia, Africa, and Latin America have settled in Europe and North America in much larger numbers than in previous eras. Their arrival has brought questions about cultural difference and **liberal democracy** to the fore. In what ways may receiving states expect immigrants to adapt to the dominant culture and way of life in their new home? In what ways should the receiving states recognize the **cultural commitments** and group identities of the immigrants?

These questions are often seen as particularly urgent with regard to the social and political integration of immigrants of Islamic faith. Muslims have featured prominently in a number of recent political conflicts. In Britain, there was the Salman Rushdie affair; in France, *l'affaire des foulards*; in Germany, the debate over the status of the descendants of the Turkish guest workers.[1] In all these cases and others, questions about the relation of Muslim immigrants to the states where they have settled have provoked public debates about the meaning of citizenship and the requirements of liberal democratic principles.[2] ~AV Some people speak almost apocalyptically about a "clash of civilizations" between Islam and the West. Much of this alleged clash involves relations between states, but immigrants of Islamic faith are often constructed as a kind of **fifth column** in this struggle, because they live in the West yet (supposedly) carry with them these threatening values and alien ways of life. Thus, some people argue, it is particularly important to identify the conflicts between Islamic beliefs and practices and those that undergird the liberal democratic **institutions** of the West and to limit the capacity of Muslim immigrants to pass on their **norms** and values to others, including their children.

AV We think that this stance is wrong, both in the way it portrays Muslim migrants as a threat and in the way it fails to respect their legitimate concerns. While it is reasonable to ask questions about the kinds of cultural adaptation receiving states can expect of immigrants, any serious commitment to liberal democratic principles requires a much greater openness to Islam and to Muslim migrants than those allegedly concerned with defending Western civilization seem prepared to acknowledge. The article develops our view in three stages. First we consider whether the centrality of Islam in the lives of Muslims conflicts with the requirements of democratic citizenship. In the second section, we critically examine common **critiques** of Islamic practice and doctrine among would-be defenders of liberal democracy and **gender** equality, and attempt to show the ways in which these views tend to mischaracterize the **normative** issues that particular practices raise, wrongly attribute objectionable practices to Islam as such, or employ a double standard by ignoring parallel issues within religious traditions that liberal democratic cultures already accept. Finally, we step back from particular practices in Islam to assess the strength of Muslim claims to special forms of **group recognition** in the light of their status as immigrants.

Islam as a Communal Identity in Liberal Society

~AV One question that one encounters frequently, either implicitly or explicitly, is whether Muslims can be full members of liberal democratic societies given the strength of their communal identity. In the view of some democratic theorists, membership in the democratic process requires a capacity to distance oneself from one's identity, in order to put oneself in the position of another. On this view, this capacity for reflective distance from one's commitments is a prerequisite for genuine dialogue. But both Muslims and non-Muslims have argued that Islam constitutes, for many of its members, a communal identity which is . . . thoroughly constitutive of their identity as individuals, something from which they cannot and do not wish to distance themselves. . . . Does this pose a problem for the position of Muslims in liberal democracies?

AV In considering this question, we should first draw attention to the variability among Muslims. Muslims do not all fit a single mold. We should not suppose that they all have exactly the same understanding of Islamic doctrine and its implications for social life, the same unqualified and unambivalent commitment to Islam, and so on. In fact, there is enormous variability among Muslims as there is among Christians, Jews, and other religious groups, with respect to doctrine, practice, and ways of life. For some immigrants, Islam may be primarily a cultural marker, a symbolic locus of identity that has little bearing on the norms that guide their actions in public and private life. For others, the commitment to Islam is at the centre, guiding every activity and choice. For many, it is something in between.

Second, if we focus only on those Muslims who do have a powerful sense of communal identity as described, we have to consider whether the same questions would be raised about Christians or Jews with comparably strong senses of religious identification. Anyone who reads the anti-immigrant literature from the nineteenth and early twentieth centuries is bound to be struck by the similarity between the doubts and fears expressed with respect to Catholics and Jews then and the doubts and fears expressed with respect to Muslims now. One finds the same rhetoric about alien invasions, with Catholics and Jews portrayed as threatening and unassimilable because of their **illiberal** and undemocratic values. Nobody today would defend those earlier views (or at least nobody should). Nobody today would question whether Christians or Jews could be full members of a liberal democratic society, whatever their religious beliefs, although many committed Jews and Christians would reject the idea that they are obliged to distance themselves from their own religious identities to engage in the democratic process. One of the recurring and largely justifiable complaints of Muslims is that the standards used to evaluate their behavior and beliefs are different from those used with respect to other members of society.

Finally, we might ask whether the problem here lies not with the Muslims but with an understanding of democracy that would exclude or require fundamental changes from not only many Muslims but many other people as well, at least if applied consistently. This model of **deliberative democracy** requires that people **abstract** themselves from their identities. But there is an alternative model of democracy that simply requires that people listen and engage with each other. To treat other people with respect—which is a requirement of deliberative democracy—does not necessarily require that one suspend one's own commitments or distance oneself from one's own identity. Indeed conversations are often most fruitful when people speak from their deepest selves.

~AV Someone might object that religious beliefs can have no standing in a **pluralist** society that must be committed to respect for all religions. AV But consider the case of Martin Luther King, Jr, whose effective leadership of the civil rights struggle in the US, a struggle for democratic justice, was inextricably linked to his religious rhetoric. King's understanding of justice was rooted in his Christian convictions, and he could not have articulated it adequately without reference to them. Of course, other Christians were staunch defenders of segregation, while many of those who supported the civil rights struggle were not Christian. But that does not make King's method of communication inappropriate. To be sure, religious rhetoric can often be abused and manipulated. But so can a purely **secular** rhetoric. So Muslims, too, should be free to bring their religious views to the democratic dialogue, recognizing, of course, that to be effective in persuading others they will have to find a way (as King did) to communicate their convictions in ways that resonate with people who do not share their religion.

Assuredly, there may be a point at which the claims of religious community become **incommensurable** with the claims of democratic citizenship. This seems especially likely at the point where religious communities seek to reshape the public sphere in their own image and at the expense of other religious or moral conceptions. An inquiry into the deeper question of what liberal democracies may in general claim of religious communities would take us far beyond the scope of this paper. Our point here is simply that it is wrong to make allowances for Christian and Jewish communities and to refuse to make them for Muslim communities.

Islam and Gender Equality

To acknowledge the right of Muslims to participate in the democratic dialogue without abandoning their fundamental convictions is not to say how non-Muslims should respond to them. In the next section of this essay we will focus on one particular area where the beliefs and practices of Muslims are often alleged to be in fundamental conflict with the values and practices of liberal democratic societies: the issue of gender equality.

We begin by articulating views critical of Islam that we wish to challenge. ~AV According to the critics, Islamic practices and conceptions of women's role in society are incompatible with the liberal democratic commitment to equal citizenship. The critics say that Islam authorizes the genital mutilation of young girls, that it legitimates **patriarchal** authority and even wife-beating, that it permits polygamy, and that it requires women to dress in restrictive ways that limit their capacity to act in the public sphere. From the critics' perspective, rather than accommodating these practices as a way of respecting the cultural commitments of Muslim immigrants, liberal democratic states should challenge and constrain these practices as much as possible, prohibiting some of them and insisting on a legal regime and an educational system based on principles of gender equality.

AV In our view, the critics' account is inaccurate both with respect to Islam and with respect to the requirements of liberal democracy. Some of the practices mentioned above are deeply objectionable and should be prohibited, but it is wrong or at least deeply misleading to describe them as Islamic practices. Some of the practices are Islamic but are less in conflict with gender equality than the critics suppose. Finally, liberal democracies do and must tolerate some departures from gender equality in the name of respect for religious freedom.

Let us begin with the last point. As we noted above in discussing the issue of communal identification, it is unreasonable to make demands of Muslims that are not made of adherents of other religions with comparable views and practices. The overall claim that women are subordinated within Islam is a claim that can also be made about Christianity and Judaism. Both Christianity and Judaism have deeply patriarchal elements in their religious traditions. Some versions of both religions, as they are understood and practiced today, have very negative views of female sexuality, teach that women's primary responsibilities are in the home, assert the authority of the husband within the household, and so on. Yet no reasonable person suggests that traditional Catholics or fundamentalist Protestants or orthodox Jews should be required to modify these religious beliefs and practices as a condition of full membership in liberal democratic societies.

~AV Some might object that there is a tremendous range of theological views within Christianity and Judaism and that this deep **patriarchalism** is characteristic of only a small part of each. AV But there is great variability within Islam as well, both in practice and in theological interpretation. Muslim feminists argue that there is nothing in Islam properly understood that requires the subordination of women. The question here, however, is how to respond to those elements in a religious tradition—whether Islam or Christianity or Judaism—that see patriarchalism (in some form) as religiously mandated.

Why are patriarchal versions of Christianity and Judaism tolerated? Perhaps because the commitment to gender equality in liberal democratic states is not as deep in practice as is alleged when **ideological** contrasts are drawn between Islam and the West, but also because, even at the level of principle, the commitment to gender equality stands in some tension with other liberal democratic commitments. Liberal democratic principles entail a deep commitment to freedom of religion, of conscience, of thought and of opinion. For that reason, a liberal democratic state cannot require intellectual or moral conformity, not even to its own ideals, although the state may legitimately try to inculcate key elements of the public democratic culture through the educational system and may establish a legal order [constitution, laws, and courts] that reflects its basic principles. Furthermore, a commitment to individual **autonomy** entails the recognition of some sort of private or personal sphere that the state may not regulate, including much of the activity within the family sphere. At a minimum then, any liberal democratic state will have to leave untouched some beliefs and practices that conflict with gender equality, and it is unreasonable to demand more of Muslims in this respect than of the adherents of other faiths.

How then should we respond to the specific practices that critics claim are characteristic of Islam and in conflict with gender equality? Consider first the charge that Islam authorizes the genital mutilation of young girls. We will argue that the most prevalent forms of the practice to which the critics object should indeed be prohibited, but that modified forms might be permissible and that it is misleading and harmful to claim that Islam authorizes the practice. We consider first the question of how to respond to the practice, assuming that some immigrants want to continue it for cultural and religious reasons. Then we turn to questions about the relation of this practice to Islam.

In a number of countries in Africa, Asia, and South America—mainly in twenty countries in the middle belt of Africa—girls commonly undergo some form of circumcision. The procedure ranges from what is sometimes called "circumcision proper" (**incision** or removal of the **prepuce** of the **clitoris**), to **clitoridectomy** or **excision** (removing part or all of the clitoris and often part or all of the **labia minora** as well) to **infibulation** (removing the clitoris, the labia minora and part of the **labia majora** and sewing together the two sides of the **vulva**, leaving only a small opening for menstrual blood and urine). The most common version appears to be some form of excision. In the mid-1980s, it was estimated that 75–80 million females in Africa were affected. This is an ancient practice whose origins are unclear. The (overlapping) reasons offered for continuing the practice of female circumcision are that it is traditional, that it is connected to cultural norms regarding sexuality and reproduction, that it is religiously required or at least encouraged, and that girls will not be accepted as eligible marriage partners and full members of the community unless they have been circumcised. These reasons continue to have weight for some immigrants who have their daughters circumcised either in the West (usually covertly) or in their countries of origin while visiting on vacation, although most immigrants from countries where female circumcision is common do not continue the practice after they have arrived in the West and some people leave their countries of origin (even seeking refugee status) precisely to avoid having their daughters subjected to circumcision.

~AV Suppose someone argued that female circumcision should be permitted in liberal democratic states because it is clearly an important social practice for some people and immigrants cannot reasonably be expected simply to abandon their preexisting cultural and religious commitments. That sort of argument would have considerable weight with respect to some issues, as we shall see later. How does it work here?

AV Our basic answer is this. The respect due to particular cultural and religious commitments must be assessed in the context of their implications for other fundamental human interests. Female circumcision as normally practiced has horrific physical and psychological consequences that have been well documented. Even the mildest form of clitoridectomy is painful, permanent, debilitating, and devoid of health benefits. One crucial responsibility of any liberal democratic state is to protect the physical safety and bodily integrity of its inhabitants, including children. This responsibility obliges the state to set strict limits to the authority of parents over their children, regardless of the parents' motives (i.e., even if they believe themselves to be acting in the best interests of the child). Thus it is proper for the state to restrict or prohibit cultural and religious practices that cause serious harm to children. Given the consequences of female circumcision, any liberal democratic state not only may but should regard the practice as genital mutilation and prohibit it from being performed upon young girls.

This general line of argument is subject to two important qualifications, the first focusing on the involuntary nature of the procedure, the second on the degree of harm it causes. So far, we have described female circumcision as it is most widely practiced, that is, upon girls who are usually not consulted and who are too young to consent even if they were. But suppose it were a question of an adult woman voluntarily undergoing circumcision? . . .

Would it still be obligatory or even permissible for a liberal democratic state to ban the practice for adults? Every liberal regime must grant considerable latitude to individuals to lead their lives and even to treat their bodies however they choose. Liberal states permit women to undergo a wide variety of cosmetic surgeries (breast enlargement and reduction, liposuction, facelifts, etc.) and bodily alterations (tattooing, body piercing) in order to meet cultural norms regarding beauty and sexuality. On the one hand, feminists rightly criticize many of these practices for the ways in which they reflect, serve, and reinforce problematic ideals of the female body. These practices, too, could be described as forms of bodily mutilation. But feminists also insist on the rights of women to control their own bodies and are wary of granting state authorities the power to restrict women's choices. Criticism is one thing, prohibition and control another. Why should female circumcision be treated differently from these other forms of bodily mutilation?

. . . We find the practice of clitoridectomy abhorrent, and we would want to challenge anyone who would defend it. But should an adult woman . . . be legally prohibited from undergoing such a procedure in a licensed medical facility? We think not. Our tentative view is that such a ban interferes too much with the right people ought to have to conduct their lives in accordance with their own convictions and cultural commitments.

~AV What should we think of what has been called "circumcision proper" (i.e., removal only of the prepuce of the clitoris)? Some discussions of female circumcision seem to dismiss altogether the cultural and religious dimensions of the practice, as though these should carry no weight at all, at least in deciding whether infants and children may be subjected to circumcision. AV But on such a view it seems hard to understand why the practice of male circumcision should be tolerated either, at least in the absence of evidence about its health benefits. Medical views of male circumcision have varied over the years, and we are not in a position to assess them. At a minimum, it seems safe to say that there have been times when the prevailing view was that there was no medical justification for circumcising all males. Nevertheless, so far as we know, no liberal democratic state in recent times has tried to prevent people from having their male children circumcised for cultural and religious reasons. . . .

If female circumcision were culturally important and caused no more harm than male circumcision, we think that it would be appropriate to permit it, too, even for children.

Would "circumcision proper" fall into this category? That requires information about its health consequences that we do not have. At the least though, we can say that it seems possible to imagine a form of female circumcision in which the health risks were small enough that it should be permitted for cultural or religious reasons. This is not merely a hypothetical possibility. On one account that we have read, a woman who wanted her daughter to maintain the cultural ties and communal standing that come with passage through this rite of initiation into womanhood but did not want her to suffer the physical consequences of mutilation persuaded the relevant actors in her community (themselves female) to accept a pinprick of blood from the clitoris as a satisfactory performance of the ritual.[3] It may be objected that this is not the traditional practice, but traditions can evolve without disintegrating. If a particular community were to find that this sort of ritual played an important cultural role, it is hard to see why it should be prohibited.

Let us turn now to the question of the relation between Islam and female circumcision. Female circumcision is practiced by Muslims in some countries, but it is not practiced by Muslims in other countries including Saudi Arabia, Algeria, Iran, Iraq, Libya, Morocco, and Tunisia, all of which have predominantly Islamic populations. We have not been able to find any estimates of the overall percentage of Muslims who practice female circumcision, but judging from the relative populations of countries in which it is and is not practised, it would appear to be a minority practice within Islam. Furthermore, in those countries in Africa where female circumcision is most common, it is practised by Christians, **animists**, and others besides Muslims and it clearly predates Islam. . . .

. . .

. . . This makes it descriptively misleading, though not entirely inaccurate, to describe female circumcision as an Islamic practice. But how is this relevant to the question of how liberal democratic states should respond to Muslim immigrants? After all, it is not the business of political authorities in a liberal democratic state to pass judgments on what is authentically Islamic.

. . .

The problem with characterizing female circumcision as an Islamic practice is . . . [that] this characterization contributes to the construction of a negative image of Islam and of Muslim immigrants. Popular discussions of Islam frequently identify female circumcision as an Islamic practice and use it to illustrate and define the nature of the presumed conflict of values between Islam and the West. . . .

Imagine a comparable attempt to discredit Christianity. The people who engage in violent opposition to abortion (bombing abortion clinics, murdering doctors who perform abortions, and so on) frequently describe themselves as acting out of a sense of Christian religious duty. In most cases, there is no reason to doubt the sincerity of these claims, and, in any event, state officials (such as judges in a criminal trial) should not try to assess the doctrinal merits of their beliefs, at least under normal circumstances. They need only conclude that such actions are not legally permissible, regardless of their religious foundations. But most Christians (even among those opposed to abortion) would object strenuously if such activities were described as Christian practices, because they do not engage in these activities themselves and do not wish to be associated with them. Similarly, most Muslim immigrants do not practise female circumcision and do not wish to be identified with the practice. Of course, the construction of public **discourse** is multi-sided, and Muslims can contribute to a dissociation between Islam and female circumcision by criticizing the practice publicly as unIslamic, just as, for example, some Catholic bishops in the United States recently criticized violence against abortion clinics as unChristian.

~AV Consider now, much more briefly, the claim that Islam legitimates patriarchal authority within the household, including the right of the husband to beat his wife under certain circumstances. AV Interpretations of religious traditions are always subject to contestation. Muslims disagree among themselves, to some extent, about the correct understanding of Islamic teaching on the family and relations between spouses. . . . Apart from physical violence, in addressing the issue of Islamic legitimation of patriarchal authority, we encounter the problem, discussed above, that liberal democratic commitments to religious freedom and personal autonomy preclude any attempt to regulate directly the character of relationships between spouses or between parents and children, even where some cultural tradition **prescribes** patterns of authority and deference within the household that are quite at odds with equality of the sexes.

Physical violence is, however, another matter. As we noted above, protection of physical security is a core task of any liberal democratic government. Cultural and religious commitments cannot provide a ground for exemptions from the general prohibitions on violence, including domestic violence. . . .

. . .

. . . ~AV Critics of Islam point to a passage in the Qur'an which allows a husband to strike his wife under certain circumstances. AV But Muslims insist, with good reason, that it is unfair to take the passage out of context. Some argue that the passage should be read as severely restricting the practices prevalent at the time rather than as granting ongoing permission for this sort of behaviour. Even conservative Islamic scholars emphasize the steps that must be taken before the husband may use physical force and the drastic limits on the kind of physical force that may be employed. We would want to challenge even this highly circumscribed legitimation of physical force in relations between spouses, but clearly this cannot be taken as a general legitimation of domestic violence. Spousal abuse is undoubtedly a problem among Muslims as among every group in Western societies, and it may be that some Muslim men seek to justify their actions by appealing to the Qur'an, but both their behaviour and their appeals are contrary to Islam as understood by most Muslims.

In sum, our response to the issue of spousal abuse parallels the one given to female circumcision. The state can and should prohibit domestic violence, but it is deeply misleading and harmful to say that Islam legitimates wife-beating.

~AV What about Islam's endorsement of polygamy? AV First it should be noted that many authors have argued that there are resources within Islam for prohibiting polygamy, based on the Qur'anic injunction that a husband must treat each of his wives justly, and, if unable to treat more than one justly, should marry only one. Furthermore, a legal prohibition of polygamy does not prevent a Muslim man from doing anything required by his religion (provided that he has not yet taken more than one wife) but only limits something that is permitted by Islam.

Polygamy is significantly different from female circumcision and wife-beating in one important respect: it is not obvious why it should be legally prohibited. Every liberal democratic state does forbid it, of course, but it is not clear how that fits with the general principle that adults should normally be able to enter into whatever contracts or personal relationships they choose. If the defense of the prohibition rests on a concern for the well-being of women and children in such relationships, it would seem appropriate to consider the effects of easy divorce as well. Muslim commentators rightly point out that the relative ease of divorce and remarriage in Western states creates a kind of **de facto** serial polygamy, and recent studies show that the economic position of women and children after the breakup of a marriage is usually greatly reduced for a significant period while that of men often improves quite rapidly. If the issue is asymmetry between men and women, that would appear to be remedied by a legal regime that permitted women as well as men to have multiple spouses, even if, among Muslims, only men availed themselves of this opportunity.

Consider finally the issue of Islamic dress. This is a particularly puzzling issue. The right to dress as one chooses—subject only to standards of public decency (themselves highly contestable and often gender biased)—would seem the quintessential liberal right. Indeed, one of the objections against Islamic regimes is that they require all women to conform to a narrow, publicly determined dress code, thus unduly restricting their personal liberty. So, why would anyone object if Muslim women choose to wear the ***hijab*** as a way of expressing their cultural identity or religious convictions?

In some contexts, however, there are norms of dress such that wearing the *hijab* would require an exemption from the norms that others are expected to follow. ~AV For example, in Montreal recently a judge expelled a Muslim woman for refusing to remove her head covering on the grounds that there was a prohibition against wearing anything on one's head in court. AV The judge's action was widely condemned in the press on the grounds that it was insensitive to the cultural and religious significance of the *hijab*. One Muslim critic wondered rhetorically whether the judge would have required a Catholic nun in a traditional habit to remove her head covering. In the Canadian context, with its institutionalized commitment to multiculturalism, it seems obvious that the judge was wrong. A Muslim woman shows no disrespect to the legal system by wearing her *hijab* in court. If the right to do so is considered a special right, it is precisely the sort of special right required by the deeper commitment to equal treatment. It does not privilege Muslim women over other people but merely ensures that their cultural and religious differences from the majority do not become unfair sources of disadvantage.

. . .

The *hijab* has long played a central role in the Western imagination, standing particularly as a symbol of the subordination of women within Islam and hence as a proof of the moral superiority of the West. Precisely for that reason many women in the **anti-colonial movement** who had never worn the *hijab* began to put it on, using it as a symbol of their rejection of Western values. . . . But even if the *hijab* does stand for the subordination of women within Islam, why shouldn't Muslim girls be permitted to wear it if they choose to do so?

. . .

These various examples of alleged conflicts between liberal commitments and the place of women in Islam suggest that, in fact, liberal critiques of Islam often demand more of Muslims than of members of other religious communities. For the most part, a commitment to equality would seem more strongly to support a modification of Western attitudes toward Muslim immigrants than a demand that Muslims modify their practices.

Islam as an Immigrant Culture: Implications for Equality and Difference

. . . The place of Islam in liberal democracies poses a number of problems to the categories of analysis which are typically brought to bear on discussions of group claims for special recognition. In this section we will focus on the fact that, with the exception of the **Nation of Islam** in the US and scattered converts to Islam from the majority cultures, Muslims in liberal democratic societies are immigrants or the children of immigrants. Although the principle of religious toleration—which has come to mean the freedom to practice one's religion in the "**private sphere**" without penalty—would not seem to be affected by a religious group's immigrant status, debates over forms of special group recognition often focus on the nature of the groups whose claims to recognition should be met. Because the benefits conferred in arrangements of **differentiated citizenship** often do impose costs on other groups, and because group claims to recognition may conflict, we need some **criterion** by which to distinguish the groups that **merit** recognition from those that do not. Different criteria have emerged in the literature, but on the face of it many would seem to exclude immigrant communities from at least some forms of differentiated citizenship.

Will Kymlicka,[4] for example, has offered a defence of special rights of **self-government** for minority cultural communities to enable them to protect themselves from gradual dissolution under pressures from the surrounding majority culture. In particular, Kymlicka is concerned to protect the claims of **aboriginal** peoples to self-government. His argument rests on the view that collective or community rights can best be understood and defended as extensions of the rights that we have as individuals. Because our cultures provide the "**context of choice**" in which we, as individuals, can make meaningful choices about the course our lives will take, the security and stability of our culture is a **primary good**, a condition for the exercise of our capacity for autonomy. Members of the majority culture may take the security of this cultural context of choice for granted. Cultural change certainly occurs as a product of changing dynamics *within* the culture, but those dynamics are themselves subject to some degree of control or shaping by members of the culture. In contrast, for members of minority cultures, the *external* sources of cultural change are generally more powerful than the internal powers of cultural maintenance and self-direction. In the interests of the **moral agency** of members of minority cultures, therefore, Kymlicka defends the creation of special **collective rights**, including rights of self-government, to enable minority cultures to protect themselves from the encroachments of the majority culture.

But Kymlicka offers strong reasons why immigrant communities neither do nor should receive the same recognition that **national minorities** should and do receive.

> In deciding to uproot themselves, immigrants voluntarily relinquish some of the rights that go along with their original national membership. For example, if a group of Americans decide to emigrate to Sweden, they have no right that the Swedish government provide them with institutions of self-government or public services in their mother tongue. (Kymlicka, 1995, p. 96)

Kymlicka's argument has much to recommend it. Part of his argument about the claims of aboriginal communities turned on the fact that they did not willingly acquiesce in the absorption of their communities into the majority community, but had no means of preventing it. Absorption was something imposed upon them involuntarily. But immigrants choose voluntarily to enter their host societies, and in so doing we may presume that they consent to the fact that they may not be able to sustain their cultural distinctiveness, at least not on the terms they would prefer. It is true that they have lost the secure culture which provides a meaningful context of choice, but that sacrifice was itself something that they must have (or should have) weighed against the benefits they gained from immigrating.

. . .

Why does it seem unduly harsh to conclude that Muslims, as an immigrant community, have absolutely no claims to special recognition? Well, first, because it too easily justifies host countries' abdication of responsibility for the social consequences of their immigration policies. It is irrational to expect that a substantial influx of a culturally distinct group will place no transformative pressure upon the majority's ways of doing things. We also question whether it is reasonable to ask immigrant groups to give up central features of their religious beliefs and commitments upon entering Western societies, given liberal democratic commitments to individuals' freedom of conscience and of religion.

Even if one concludes that it is, there is the further problem of intergenerational transmission of culture. When the numbers of an immigrant community are large enough, it seems reasonable to predict that they will, as a matter of fact, be able to sustain some of their distinctive cultural beliefs and practices, and to pass on their cultural identity to their children. But what of the children of immigrants? No one can tell them that they consented to relinquish their cultural identity upon entering the country; they did not consent to be born there. They are now, and should be regarded as, full members of the society, and yet remain, like their parents, distinct from the cultural majority.

. . .

. . . [T]he historical condition of Muslims in Western liberal democracies would not seem to warrant the strongest forms of special group recognition, such as enhanced representation in legislative bodies. Although there certainly has been a clear pattern of discrimination against Muslims, most of it is not **sanctioned** by law. Moreover, given that Muslims have been a significant presence in Western liberal democracies for less than two generations, it would be extremely difficult to show that the contemporary material and social inequalities that characterize Muslim immigrant communities are a product of that discrimination rather than the vestige of the fact that most Muslims were quite poor when they arrived. Many immigrants' standard of living remains low for the first generation or so after immigration, a phenomenon which cannot be ascribed solely or even primarily to discrimination against them. In fact, the persistent intergenerational poverty of African-Americans is often contrasted with the rise out of poverty of immigrant groups as a way of demonstrating that poverty itself is not the only force at work in the marginalization of African-Americans.

In sum, then, Muslim immigrant communities' claims to group recognition are perhaps not as strong as some other groups,' but are powerful in their own right. At the least, they have a strong claim that non-Muslims should be attentive to the ways in which majority practices may effectively disadvantage them, or impose burdens on them which are not borne by members of the majority culture. In addition, because the level of trust between Muslims and non-Muslims is currently quite low, a strong argument can be made that Muslim community leaders should be regularly consulted by policy-making bodies on issues that are particularly important to Muslims. Although Muslims would not seem to have a compelling claim to the strongest forms of group recognition, their status as an immigrant community does not altogether **vitiate** their claims to some forms of group recognition.

Conclusion

As we hope is clear from the foregoing, our principal purpose here has been quite modest. We do not offer any settled or determinate view of the mutual obligations between liberal democracies and the Muslim immigrant communities within them. Rather, we have written as non-Muslim political theorists, concerned about the need to reconcile the principle of equality with the fact of social difference, and about the full citizenship of immigrants within liberal democracies. We have been struck by the vehemence of anti-Muslim sentiment not only in Western societies generally, but particularly within the academy [universities], and this was one of our principal sources of motivation to write this article. We have not intended either to defend or to criticize Islam, as such, but rather have hoped to unsettle some of the assumptions that critics of Islam often make. Certainly, we have only scratched the surface of this rich and challenging subject, and are especially aware of the fact that any complete account of the appropriate relationship between Muslim immigrants and their liberal democratic host countries must consult the voices of Muslims themselves.

. . .

Notes

1. Salman Rushdie is a British-Indian novelist. In 1988 his fourth novel, *The Satanic Verses*, ignited a storm of controversy. Many Muslims objected to what they described as a blasphemous portrayal of the Prophet Mohammed and his family in the book. In 1989, Ayatollah Khomeini, the Supreme Leader of Iran, issued a *fatwa* (a legal order based on Islamic law) calling for the death of Rushdie and anyone associated with publishing the book. Several publishers or translators of the book were attacked, and one was killed. Rushdie lived in hiding, under twenty-four-hour guard, for ten years.

   L'affaire des foulards (the scarves affair) was a 1989 controversy in France over women wearing the ***hijab*** (the head scarf that some observant Muslim women wear) in French public schools. Opponents of the *hijab* said it symbolized women's subordination to men and it brought visible religious symbols into what was supposed to be the **secular** public sphere. Critics of *l'affaire des foulards* said opponents of the *hijab* really opposed Islam and multiculturalism.

   Starting in the 1950s, the German economy underwent enormous expansion, and Germany needed labourers. It recruited guest workers (*Gastarbeiter*) from southern European nations and from Turkey. Eventually many guest workers brought their families and settled permanently in Germany. When Carens and Williams wrote this article, children of guest workers who had been born and raised in Germany were not and could not become German citizens. In 1991, Germany allowed children who had been born to foreign parents in Germany to apply for citizenship. In 2000, it passed legislation granting German citizenship to all German-born children of foreigners who were born after 1990 (that is, the children did not have to apply for citizenship).

2. Liberalism focuses on individuals who are free and equal, each of whom has the capacity for self-determination and a unique set of interests. (See the Short Primer in the Introduction, under Political Philosophy: Liberalism.) Liberal-democratic principles combine liberal principles with democratic principles, such as government by and for citizens, equality before and under the law, universal **suffrage** (all adult citizens may vote), free and fair elections at regular intervals, accountable and transparent governments, political toleration, and **the rule of law**.
3. C. Hodge, "Throwing Away the Circumcision Knife," *The Globe & Mail*, 15 January 1994: D2.
4. W. Kymlicka, *Multicultural Citizenship: A Liberal Theory of Minority Rights* (Oxford: Oxford University Press, 1995).

Discussion Questions

1. What does Shachar think is wrong with the "hands off" approach? Do you agree with her? Why or why not?
2. What does Shachar mean by engaging in democratic deliberation and intercultural dialogue? How does it solve the problem for observant women? Do you agree with her analysis? Why or why not?
3. Why does Berger think the clash between the law and religion is "an instance of cross-cultural encounter"? Do you agree with his analysis? Why or why not?
4. How does Berger think intercultural dialogue between law and religion will improve the clash between them? Do you agree with his analysis? Why or why not?
5. Carens and Williams argue that fundamentalism of any kind, not just Islamic fundamentalism, conflicts with liberalism. What are their reasons for this claim? Do you agree with their analysis? Why or why not?
6. Why do Carens and Williams think that Islamic communities should get multicultural accommodations? Does their view imply that any other religions should get similar accommodations? If so, which other religions? Do you agree with them? Why or why not?
7. Do you think Shachar and Carens and Williams would agree with Berger's proposal for an intercultural dialogue between law and religion? Why or why not?

Suggested Readings and Websites

🍁 = Canadian source or author

🍁 Banting, Keith, and Will Kymlicka. "Canadian Multiculturalism: Global Anxieties and Local Debates." *British Journal of Canadian Studies* 23, 1 (2010): 43–72. [Discusses the global backlash against multiculturalism and argues Canada does not fit the European pattern.]

Bennhold, Katrin. "A Veil Closes France's Door to Citizenship." *The New York Times* (19 July 2008). [France's highest administrative court upheld a court's decision to deny citizenship to a *niqab*-wearing woman because the *niqab* is incompatible with women's equality.]

✤ Bouchard, Gérard, and Charles Taylor. *Building the Future, a Time for Reconciliation: Abridged Report*. Montreal: Commission de consultation sur les pratiques d'accomodement reliées aux différences culturelles, 2008. [Abridged version of the Bouchard-Taylor report on multiculturalism and the accommodation of differences in Quebec.]

✤ Coalition for Cultural Diversity, www.cdc-ccd.org/. ["the cultural milieu's main voice in debates on culture and trade."]

✤ Dewing, Michael. "Canadian Multiculturalism." Parliamentary Information and Research Service PRB 09-20E. Ottawa: Library of Parliament, 2009. [A non-partisan overview of multiculturalism as policy and practice.]

✤ *Encyclopedia of Canada's Peoples*, http://multiculturalcanada.ca/Encyclopedia ["provides an overview of people within the geographical and social framework of Canada."]

✤ Mapleleafweb, Immigration Policy in Canada: History, Administration and Debates, www.mapleleafweb.com/features/immigration-policy-canada-history-administration-and-debates [Mapleleafweb is a non-partisan education website; this page contains some good background and beginning-level information.]

Sen, Amartya. "Human Rights and Asian Values." Sixteenth Morgenthau Memorial Lecture on Ethics & Foreign Policy. New York: Carnegie Council on Ethics and International Affairs, 1997. [Argues against the claim that human rights conflict with Asian values.]

✤ Stein, Janet Gross, et al. *Uneasy Partners: Multiculturalism and Rights in Canada*. Waterloo, ON: Wilfrid Laurier Press, 2007. [Contributors examine the conflict between *Charter* equality rights and multiculturalism.]

✤ Taylor, Charles, and Amy Gutmann. *Multiculturalism: Examining the Politics of Recognition*. Princeton, NJ: Princeton University Press, 1994. [Contains Taylor's famous essay on the politics of recognition and commentaries on it.]

Chapter 4

Being English-Speaking Canadian

What does it mean to be an English-speaking Canadian today? By "English-speaking Canadian" I do not mean only Canadians of British background or Canadians whose first language is English. Rather, I mean Canadians who live much of their public lives in English—who use English in school, at work, in stores, and on the street; who buy music with English lyrics, watch movies with English dialogue, and read books or web pages in English; and so on. They might speak a different language at home, they might be bilingual or trilingual or more, but they primarily use English in public.

What Is National Identity?

Will Kymlicka describes nations as "historical societies, more or less **institutionally complete**, occupying a given territory or homeland, sharing a distinct language and societal culture."[1] A **national identity** is a sense of belonging to such a society, of belonging with others who share the same history, language, customs, institutions, and territory. It is like a picture or a story, involving how we appear to others, how we appear to ourselves, the stories we tell about ourselves, as well as mythology, heroes, and hopes. National identity is more like a portrait than a snapshot, though—it is a *composed* picture or narrative that does not show our acne or scars, but is still recognizably "us." It is a story about us as we would like it to be told. By and large, national identities show us to ourselves in a favourable light.

National identities must be learned. Children learn national values, attitudes, characteristics, etc. from many sources, such as their families, schools, the media, and their friends. Immigrants adopt a new identity by living in the new country for some time and (presumably) benefiting from the new country and its opportunities and institutions. Most governments engage in a sort of continuing education in national identity: they remind citizens of contemporary and historical events that are sources of pride, promote national values, support athletes and artists, and so on. Certain public or political events can contribute to an upwelling of nationalism. Sometimes this is positive (Canadian nationalism during the 2010 Winter Olympics), and other times enormously destructive (the descent of many former Balkan states into tribal warfare after the downfall of the USSR).

National identity involves shared values, like fairness or democracy, which usually come from a set of shared experiences—how we responded to war and unrelenting cold, and how we worked to build a better, fairer society. But values are not the whole story. Most **liberal democratic nation-states**—countries founded on freedom, equality, and democracy, such as Canada, the US, and most western European countries—have similar values, yet we do not identify with every nation that shares our nation's values. Learning about a society with values that we prefer to ours usually makes us want to improve Canadian values, not join the other society.

National identity combines a shared history, shared practices, and a sense of belonging to the larger nation and to each other. We might think of national identity as "living with an accent"—we not only speak like Canadians, we also behave like them. National identity makes nations unique, as personal identity makes individuals unique.

Doubts about Canadian Identity

> Canada is the essence of not being. Not English, not American, it is the mathematic of not being. And a subtle flavour—we're more like celery as a flavour.
>
> —comedian Mike Myers

> Canada is the only country in the world that knows how to live without an identity.
>
> —Marshall McLuhan

Type "Is there a Canadian identity?" into your search engine. Scroll quickly through the sites on the first five or so pages, and you will find many prominent and ordinary Canadians weighing in on whether there is a distinctly Canadian identity, and if so, what characterizes it. Now type "Is there a British identity?" and scroll through the sites on the first five pages, and do the same for "Is there an American identity?" Most of the discussions concern what British or American identity is, how it is changing, and what it ought to be. But no one on those sites asks *whether* a British or an American identity exists. Who could deny it in either case?

Canada is one of the few countries in the world whose citizens ask ourselves whether we even have a national identity. Citizens of Britain, the US, or Korea may disagree about what makes them British, American, or Korean, but they do not seriously question that there is something that distinguishes them from everyone else in the world. Yet more than 140 years after Confederation, English-speaking Canadians are still asking whether there is anything distinctively Canadian about ourselves. (As we saw in Chapter 3, this is not true of the Québécois, who have no doubt that a distinct Québécois identity exists.)

It does not help that we live next door to the world's only superpower, a brash country whose citizens know exactly who they are—the best in the world at everything. And there are many similarities between us. The majority of citizens in both countries speak English; both are former British colonies and liberal democracies, with constitutions and common-law legal systems; both countries call their currency the dollar; each is the other country's largest trading partner; both have many of the same chain stores, and so on.

English-speaking Canadians have a love-hate relationship with the US. We watch their movies and televisions programs, envy their lower prices and warmer winters, and think our products and artists have really made it if they break into the US market. At the same time, we resent their domination of Canadian life and policies, and we do not like their ridiculous stereotypes about us. (Think of the "I Am Canadian" rant from the beer commercial: "Hey, I'm not a lumberjack, or a fur trader; I don't live in an igloo . . . ; I have a Prime Minister, not a president. . . . And I pronounce it 'about,' not 'a boot.'") For better or for worse, the US has a significant influence on Canadian politics, policies, and life. Airline passengers to the US go through US Customs in Canada, before they even board their flights; on all other international flights, passengers go through customs when they arrive at their destination, not before they depart. Particularly since 9/11, security at our borders and on airlines has been effectively dictated by the American government. A segment on airport security in *The Rick Mercer Report* in 2010 began with the advice, "Please arrive three days before your flight," and ended with a screen containing the logo of Transport Canada, followed by the words "A division of the US Department of Homeland Security." Anyone who has flown to the US in the last few years knows that there is more than a grain of truth in that segment.

The US dominates Canada's domestic policies too. Our environmental policies tend to follow theirs closely.[2] Even Canadian laws are affected by the US. In 2003, the Liberal government briefly considered decriminalizing the possession of small amounts of marijuana. This proposal had the backing of the Canadian Association of Chiefs of Police, which argued that prosecuting people for possessing small amounts of marijuana was a waste of scarce resources. However, the Chretien government dropped the proposal under intense pressure from the US government.[3] Former Prime Minister Pierre Trudeau once told an American audience, "Living next to you is in some ways like sleeping with an elephant. No matter how friendly and even-tempered is the beast, if I can call it that, one is affected by every twitch and grunt."

As a result of America's proximity and its dominant influence, we define ourselves partly as *not* American: we're not so violent, not so unequal, not so overconfident, not so ignorant of the rest of the world—and oh yes, we have universal health care. Sometimes people in other countries see us the same way. For example, the British newspaper *The Economist* once described Canadians as "Americans with healthcare and no guns."[4] However, defining ourselves as not or not-quite American is hardly a basis for a national identity—we share that feature with everyone in the world except Americans. While it may be necessary to distinguish ourselves from Americans to people from other countries, especially Americans, it cannot be how we identify ourselves as a nation—or at least, it cannot be more than a small part of our identity.

Of course, Canada is more than America-plus-and-minus. We have a parliamentary form of government, two official languages, an anti-revolutionary Loyalist history, and vast natural resources, and we're not at all likely to resort to civil war if Quebec separates. Like other Commonwealth countries, we aim for "peace, order, and good government," which could hardly be more different from America's "life, liberty, and the pursuit of happiness."

What Is English-Speaking Canadian Identity?

English-speaking Canadians today possess a complex identity. It includes the fact that there are three founding peoples in Canada: Aboriginal peoples, the French, and the British. With the exception of Aboriginal peoples, we are a nation of immigrants. We have a Loyalist past. Our separation from Britain was cordial and not complete; we remain a member of the Commonwealth, and new citizens still pledge allegiance to the Queen. We are proud that we beat the Americans in the War of 1812 and that we refused to return escaped slaves to the US before the American Civil War. When we are honest with ourselves, we acknowledge our terrible treatment of Aboriginal peoples, the internment of Japanese Canadians in World War II, and the *Chinese Exclusion Act*. We know the British not only beat the French, but also pushed French Canadians out of Quebec and tried to assimilate the ones who remained.

We are a bilingual, tri-national, multicultural society. Since the 1950s and 60s, we have worked to improve our relations with Aboriginal peoples and Quebec. We have not been perfect, and there has been much anger and misunderstanding on all sides, but that we have tried is part of English-speaking Canadian identity. We are very proud of the *Charter*. (The Québécois do not share our enthusiasm; see Chapter 2, Quebec Nationalism.) English-speaking Canadian identity also includes well-deserved pride in multiculturalism. We probably have the most successful multiculturalism program in the world, and the global backlash against multiculturalism has not happened in Canada. For example, in 2003 85 per cent of Canadians said multiculturalism is important to their identity, up from 74 per cent six years earlier.[5] We have elected a much greater percentage of immigrants to Parliament than any other country.[6] There is less anti-Muslim sentiment in Canada than in most Western democracies; 83 per cent of Canadians say Muslims contribute positively to Canadian society.[7] And we are liked enough in other countries that Canadians travelling abroad are advised to put a Maple Leaf on their luggage. A fair number of Americans do the same; they would rather be considered Canadians than Americans when they are abroad.

And yes, not being American is a big part of our identity. Many English-speaking Canadians believe our health care system is central to our national identity. It is not so much that we think that universal health care makes us unique; we know that most rich countries have it also.[8] But universal healthcare distinguishes us, positively, from the superpower to the south—as does our lack of a gun culture, our "almost complete absence of immigrant or visible or religious minority ghettos,"[9] and our politeness (we say "Excuse me" to someone who steps on our foot). We also know much more about Americans than they know about us. Perhaps the best-known example of this was "Talking to Americans" on *This Hour Has 22 Minutes*. Rick Mercer posed as a reporter, told Americans ludicrous "facts" about Canada, and asked for their opinions or congratulations. For example, he got a Harvard professor to state his opposition to "the seal hunt on the ice floes of Saskatchewan" and the governor of Iowa to congratulate us on adopting the twenty-four-hour day. We may be less powerful than Americans, but we can still pull the wool over their eyes.

In 1971, CBC radio host Peter Gzowski held a contest in which listeners were asked to complete the phrase, "As Canadian as . . . ". Most submissions were predictable: eh?, the RCMP, maple syrup. The winner, Heather Scott, probably captured English-speaking Canadians best of all: "As Canadian as possible under the circumstances."[10]

Philosophical Issues

Some philosophers oppose multiculturalism's hyphenated identities (e.g., Ukrainian-Canadian, Somali-Canadian). These undermine liberalism's greatest strengths, they say: its focus on equal liberty, equal citizenship, and social fairness. Liberalism ended slavery and has improved the status of women and poor people, none of which could have occurred if multiple statuses had been enshrined in law or the *Charter*.[11] Other critics worry that multicultural identities encourage ghettoization, social isolation, stereotyping, and anti-Western radicalism.[12] Some worry that hyphenated identities fragment and weaken the traditional majority culture, leaving nothing for new immigrants to identify with.[13] And some argue that liberal ideas of toleration, freedom of conscience, and freedom of association conflict with the group rights that multiculturalism enshrines. Group rights allow groups to trample on the rights of some of their members, they say. Instead, liberal societies should focus only on individual rights and have a hands-off policy to groups.[14]

The first three criticisms make empirical claims not always supported by the facts. Kymlicka argues that empirical evidence indicates that immigrants to Canada integrate into the mainstream English-speaking society faster and more thoroughly than do immigrants in countries with weaker or no multiculturalism policies. Canadians are more likely than citizens of other countries to view immigration positively, and less likely to see immigrants as sources of social unrest. And immigrants to Canada are more likely to be proud of Canada, especially its values of freedom and democracy, than immigrants to other countries are.[15] In addition, immigrants become Canadian citizens at much higher rates than immigrants in other countries. In 2001, eighty-four per cent of eligible immigrants in Canada had become citizens, compared to fifty-six per cent in the UK, forty per cent in the US, and even fewer in other western European countries.[16] Ironically, the people who feel least connected to Canada are those whose ancestors have been here longest, Aboriginal peoples and the Québécois.[17]

Another philosophical issue involves how we ought to come to terms with our history, with all its warts and pimples. Most English-speaking Canadians are proud of the *Charter*, our military efforts in World Wars I and II, and our role in peacekeeping. However, our treatment of Aboriginal peoples, the internment of Japanese Canadians in World War II, the Head Tax on Chinese people immigrating to Canada,[18] and our treatment of French Canadians in Quebec are not things to be proud of. How do we deal with them?

The Canadian government has begun to acknowledge and address some of those wrongs. Former Prime Minister Brian Mulroney apologized (on separate occasions) for the internment of Japanese Canadians, Ukrainians, and Italians during World War II. Prime Minister Stephen Harper apologized for the Chinese Head Tax and the residential school system.[19] While apologies and reparations[20] do not make everything right and fair, they are a start. And since no democratic government would issue an apology without the support of a substantial majority of voters, these apologies and reparations also indicate that most Canadians are willing to recognize that we have committed serious wrongs.

English-speaking Canadians must forge an identity that integrates the parts of our nation and history that make us justifiably proud with a recognition of the parts that we would not have chosen and a resolution to do better. Doing this involves at least

- making a commitment to changing ourselves and our institutions so we do not repeat those mistakes,
- ending the formal effects of our problematic history, such as discriminatory laws and policies,
- working to end the less formal effects of this history, such as persistent negative stereotypes and victim-blaming, and
- fostering the willing and meaningful participation of members of ostracized groups in Canada, on terms that they and we negotiate together.[21]

(See the readings by Tully in Chapter 1, Aboriginal Peoples, and Taylor in Chapter 2, Quebec Nationalism.)

The Readings

Hugh Segal argues that private purposes do not constitute the "Canadian ideal"; rather, "the social, economic, and communal context" transforms our private goals to a larger ideal. He begins with history—our relationship to the land, our development of tolerance and **pluralism**, and the values and loyalties that we share with people in other countries. Next, he discusses the importance of the balance we strike between economic and social progress, between an economy that performs well and a society that protects its members from "the vicissitudes and cruelties of the international marketplace." We are a pragmatic people, not torn by left-right (egalitarian-conservative) divisions, who learn from other countries' experiences and adapt what we have learned to our own needs. In this way we fashion a uniquely Canadian ideal.

Will Kymlicka begins his argument about English-speaking Canadian identity by distinguishing external and internal dimensions of identity. The external dimensions cover how we see ourselves in the world, while the internal dimensions concern how we see our relations with each other. Canadians see ourselves as citizens of the world, as people who play their part in international negotiations and conflicts. We also see ourselves as part of the West, as a **secular** liberal democracy based on a market economy which has, since the end of World War II, developed a robust **welfare state**. We are members of the New World of North America rather than the Old World of Europe. We are more open to immigration and social mobility than the Old World. Finally, we are not Americans. Kymlicka then turns to the internal dimensions of our identity: Aboriginal peoples as the first inhabitants, the Québécois, and immigrants. Because Aboriginal peoples and the Québécois had separate, institutionally complete societies before conquest, they identify more with their "nations within" than with Canada. Immigrants were originally expected to assimilate into British culture in Canada, but multiculturalism has encouraged them to keep their ethnic identities alongside their new Canadian identities. Kymlicka then turns to the question of Canada's uniqueness. He argues that most of these features can be found in other Western societies as well. What holds us together? He suggests the answer is probably the fairness and trustworthiness of our institutions. Once again, this does not make us unique; it is shared by all modern liberal societies.

The Moral and Political Preferences Indicator

Conservative and egalitarian Canadians probably agree more than they disagree about what it means to be English-speaking Canadian. Pretty much everyone accepts that we have three founding peoples, that our society is a "mosaic," that we need to accept immigrants, and so on. Conservatives are more likely to worry that the British-Protestant or British-French-Christian core of our identity is being diluted, and perhaps even to think it needs official protection. Social conservatives might think immigrants should assimilate to a British and Christian society, but their views get little traction even within the Conservative Party. What conservatives do not like, though, is anything that ties ethnic or cultural identities to group rights. Conservatives believe people should succeed purely on their own merits, and group membership should be irrelevant.

Egalitarians, on the other hand, are more likely to welcome and celebrate the diversity of Canadian society. They enjoy the ways that cultures (and food!) mix in Canadian society. Even those who are British and Christian themselves tend not to worry that their culture and history will be engulfed by a sea of immigrants. They are, after all, optimists about people (see the Introduction, A Short Primer), and more likely to feel confident that change will be positive. Social democrats generally believe that group rights are a good thing. This is particularly true with regards to Aboriginal peoples and the Québécois, whose cultures need protection from the tsunami-like force of nearly four hundred million non-Aboriginal English-speakers in North America.

Conservative centrists and egalitarian centrists are more likely to agree with egalitarians than with conservatives on cultural inclusion. Conservative centrists mostly oppose anything like group rights, as do some but not all egalitarian centrists (such as former Prime Minister Pierre Trudeau).

Notes

1. Will Kymlicka, *Finding Our Way: Rethinking Ethnocultural Relations in Canada* (Don Mills, ON: Oxford University Press, 1998), p. 132.
2. For example, the federal government withdrew from the Kyoto Protocol in 2011; see Chapter 12, Responding to Climate Change.
3. Lisa Khoo, "Up in smoke? Canada's marijuana law and the debate over decriminalization," CBC News Online (25 November, 2004), www.cbc.ca/news2/background/marijuana/marijuana_legalize.html.
4. Cited in Wendy Cukier, "International Perspectives on Gun Control," *New York Law School Journal of International and Comparative Law* 15, 2 & 3 (1995): 253.
5. Will Kymlicka, "The Current State of Multiculturalism in Canada and Research Themes on Canadian Multiculturalism 2008–2010" (Ottawa: Minister of Public Works and Government Services Canada, 2010), 7–8.
6. Kymlicka, "The Current State of Multiculturalism," p. 8.
7. Kymlicka, "The Current State of Multiculturalism," p. 9.
8. See the Introduction to Chapter 8, Health and Health Care, for comparisons of Canadian health care with other countries' health care systems.
9. Kymlicka, "The Current State of Multiculturalism," p. 8.

10. Peter Gzowski, "On the origin of an aphorism," *The Globe and Mail* (24 May 1996): A15.
11. See, for example, Brian Barry, *Culture and Equality: An Egalitarian Critique of Multiculturalism* (Cambridge, MA: Harvard University Press, 2001).
12. See, for example, Allan Gregg, "Identity Crisis: Multiculturalism: A Twentieth-Century Dream Becomes a Twenty-first Century Conundrum," *The Walrus* 3, 2 (2006): 38–47.
13. See, for example, Jeffrey Reitz and Rupa Banerjee, "Racial Inequality, Social Cohesion and Policy Issues in Canada," in Keith Banting, Thomas J. Courchene, and F. Leslie Seidle, eds., *Belonging? Diversity, Recognition and Shared Citizenship in Canada* (Montreal: Institute for Research on Public Policy, 2007).
14. See, for example, Chandran Kukathas, *The Liberal Archipelago: A Theory of Diversity and Freedom* (Oxford: Oxford University Press, 2003).
15. Kymlicka, "The Current State of Multiculturalism," pp. 7–11.
16. Keith Banting and Will Kymlicka, "Canadian Multiculturalism: Global Anxieties and Local Debates," *British Journal of Canadian Studies* 23, 1 (2010): 56.
17. Banting and Kymlicka, p. 54.
18. The Head Tax was a fee charged to every Chinese person entering Canada, meant to discourage Chinese immigration after the Canadian Pacific Railway was finished. It was replaced in 1923 by the *Chinese Immigration Act*, which prevented virtually all Chinese immigration.
19. The residential school system was designed to "kill the Indian in the child" and assimilate Aboriginal children into Canadian culture. See the Introduction to Chapter 1, Aboriginal Peoples.
20. Japanese Canadians people who were interned, Chinese Canadians who paid the Head Tax, and Aboriginal people who went through the residential school system have received some financial reparations.
21. See Karen Wendling, "Choosing the Given," *Public Affairs Quarterly* 17, 1 (2003): 65–82.

Hugh Segal

Advancing the "Canadian Ideal"

We live our lives largely for private purposes; building a home, sustaining a family, studying for a degree, pursuing artistic or scholarly endeavours, falling in love—these have little to do with a nation's purposes or patriotic ideal. But, to a very real extent, the way a country shapes its ideal has a lot to do with the social, economic, and communal context within which we all pursue those things most important to us.

I have never apologized for the romantic response the Canadian ideal has always inspired in me. An ideal, for a country as compelling, humane, and determined as Canada, is not set by any politician or political party. It emerges as an amalgam of the motivating and defining ideas each part of our evolution and history has generated. These ideas have in turn, through intergenerational presence and adaptation, become part of that unspoken Canadian ideal we all sense in varying degrees. And, to some extent, how we move forward as a society is defined by how prepared we are to engage in sustaining the Canadian ideal, understanding full well that every generation will have its own take on the dynamics and breadth of that ideal in their time.

History

The nature of Canada's discovery by the Europeans, the **aboriginal** civilization that preceded their arrival, the way in which religion was a huge determinant of the missionary zeal with which we were explored, the tight relationship of first the fur trade, then lumber and minerals with the will to settle and explore, has always made us a country whose psyche and self-image are tied up with resources and the land. Many of our greatest national debates, such as those over the TransCanada pipeline in the mid-1950s[1] (which led to the demise of a government) or over the energy pricing regime in 1979–80[2] (which led to the demise of a government), reflect how deeply the idea of a land with resources and riches is embedded in our collective experience.

The importance of religion in those early European expeditions to our shores—the way in which religion was imposed on our aboriginal **first nations**, or used to marginalize them—has also created a thought process that, both through some aspect of shame and historical perspective, produced a very Canadian idea of **pluralism**, tolerance, and multinational identity for Canada as a country. This too has defined and broadened the Canadian ideal—in a way that makes our welcome to newcomers, while not yet as supple and unconditional as some may want, still among the warmest in the world.

The way in which Canada emerged from first French and then British colonies in North America—without bloodshed and revolution, but with determination and resolve to be different from our American neighbours yet part of a larger global network then known as the British Empire—contributed broadly to a Canadian ideal which very much arrays networks like the Commonwealth, la Francophonie,[3] the Organization of American States, and the UN as balance points in our dynamic with our American ally and economic partner. And, in the post-9/11 context, I will always be grateful to John Manley[4] for reminding Canadians that while officials and his boss in Ottawa scurried around trying to ensure, perhaps in a rather contrived way, that we looked and sounded different from the United States, he remembered that Canadians were buried in battlefields around the world where we had stood with our allies against tyranny in two world wars, and we were not about to cut and run on our allies now. It was his finest moment in public life and hopefully not his last. But it was a moment that reminded us that part of our Canadian ideal has been a series of loyalties that moved our parents and grandparents and their parents to engage fully and with uncommon courage in support of abstract ideas like freedom and democracy, and that they were prepared to—and did—lay their lives down for freedoms we now share.

Balancing Economic and Social Progress

The postwar period saw the construction of the **liberal welfare state**, and while the UK and the US built their own versions during the same period, we built ours in our own way. Public education, pensions, family allowances, universal health insurance, and employment insurance were all part of a rubric whereby our collective resources would protect individuals at vulnerable points in their lives from the **vicissitudes** and cruelties of the international marketplace—as did **tariffs** and relatively restrictive trade practices. And that core idea of *l'État-providence* [the welfare state] required the rents and royalties and revenues of our resource exports to finance [it], which only fed into the Canadian ideal already tied to the importance of those resources. And as our economic and industrial capacity grew, spurred on by two world wars and our role as both a breadbasket for the world and foundry for democracy, it became apparent that our relatively small domestic market could not buy enough to generate the revenues essential to sustaining the very European social safety net we sought to sustain.

That increased the **salience** of trade, bringing us back full circle to the early lumber and fur trade days so vital to our initial development. The imperative around trade leads right back to the requirement for social justice and equality of opportunity that made the Canadian frontier so different from the American. Our "Peace, Order, and Good Government" are not only different from America's "Life, Liberty, and the Pursuit of Happiness," but reflect a Canadian ideal that is just as tolerant of individual freedom—perhaps more so—yet embraces our responsibility for and to one another in a much more brazen and affectionate way. It is where the Canadian and American ideals differ from one another most directly.

And the challenge going forward is very much the social and political challenge of adapting our policies to sustain these two compelling elements of the Canadian ideal—the collective will to encourage, protect, and support our common heritage of peace, order, and good government—to wit, the balance between economic performance and social progress, and the capacities and revenues necessary to do so effectively.

This is not about the old left-right **dialectic**, about which Canadians have been and remain encouragingly unimpressed. However much **ideologues** of the far right or the mind-numbing "**solidarity** forever" left have chanted, organized, and hectored, Canadians have been, quite consistent with our **pragmatic** Canadian ideal, utterly unattracted to either siren call. Our **socialist** parties are remarkably moderate; our conservative parties succeed when they embrace the balance and sanity of moderation, and our dominant political party is determined resolutely never to choose between right or left. And Canadians' response to excess in either direction is that of vague disengagement—as if we sense viscerally that in the same way excessive patriotism is the refuge of the scoundrel, so too is **ideology** a conceit behind which can be found politicians who have little else but empty slogans or hollow cant [insincere talk] to offer.

It strikes me that Canadians want to make choices and embrace leadership that define in realistic terms the balance going forward between economic performance and social progress, within a thoughtful framework of decisions we must ponder individually and pursue collectively. And in this regard the people appear to be somewhat ahead of our political class. They know that—as former NDP finance minister of Saskatchewan Janice MacKinnon has argued—the core arithmetic of health simply does not work, and cannot without key change and modernization. They know that our armed forces lack the capacity to protect or advance the Canadian ideal without serious reinvestment, which is as much about our independence from our American allies as it is about our capacity to stand with our allies, including the Americans. They know that a divide has grown between the governed and those who govern, in ways that seem less than right for our democracy and our values; they know that the Canadian ideal requires the architecture of economic performance and social civility to prosper and advance.

And at some level we all understand that our ability to go about our own lives as students, parents, scholars, artists, business owners, employers and employees, farmers, teachers, and the rest is genuinely affected by a smaller world where the terrorist and biological threats seem more proximate, more readily on our personal radar screens. We know too the state apparatus we have come to depend on in simpler times is puffing and wheezing to catch up with these threats in a way that will allow us to live our own personal lives largely unoppressed by the scourges and evil that are out there.

Sustaining the Canadian ideal may require some new courage on our part—to look at the Europe whose social programs we admire, and reflect on how their continental union, which maximized collective benefit and individual mobility, may offer lessons for America, Mexico, and our country; courage to try new ways of delivering health care under the public universal insurance umbrella; courage to let universities pursue excellence and universal access for the truly qualified rather than government-imposed dilution of excellence; courage to re-engage parliamentary control of our spending at the expense of the ease with which the apparatus of the state can spend and intervene.

Whatever it takes, I have little doubt that the "Canadian Ideal" will be sustained. We are a **pluralist** multinational country with a strong sense of how our individual freedoms require collective responsibility for and to each other. We have taken centuries to get here, and millions want to come to our shores. The "Canadian Ideal" has never mattered more.

Notes

1. Construction of a TransCanada pipeline was proposed in 1951 in response to energy shortages throughout Eastern Canada. Two different plans for construction were submitted to the Government of Canada for approval. One was an all-Canadian route, and the other proposed branching off into the United States. Although the all-Canadian route was calculated to be more costly and less profitable, it was given the go-ahead. Debate in Parliament was restricted by the then-majority Liberal government in order to speed up construction. This scandal contributed to the defeat of the Liberal Party. [Editor]
2. During their 1979 election campaign, the Progressive Conservative Party had promised to cut taxes to stimulate the economy. When elected that same year, the party raised taxes on gas in order to reduce the government's budget deficit. This led to a vote of non-confidence in Parliament, and the defeat of the Progressive Conservative government in a 1980 federal election. [Editor]
3. La Francophonie is an international political organization in which over fifty member states participate in the common interest of political cooperation and the promotion of French culture. [Editor]
4. A former Liberal Member of Parliament. [Editor]

Will Kymlicka

Being Canadian

AV = author's view; ~AV = not the author's view

When questions are raised about the nature of Canadian identity, they tend to focus on how "being Canadian" relates to various **sub**-state group identities, such as Québécois, Aboriginal, and immigrant groups. It is often said that there is a distinctively or uniquely

Canadian way of reconciling or accommodating these identities, as a "**multicultural**," "**multination**," or "**postmodern**" state. I think that perceptions of Canadian uniqueness on issues of internal diversity are much exaggerated, and I shall return to that point in the second half of this paper. But Canadian identity, like all identities, has an external as well as an internal dimension. Canada is situated within certain larger regional or geopolitical contexts—for example, it is part of the New World, part of the West, part of the global community—and each of these strongly shapes Canadian identities. Canadian identity is continually being renegotiated not only in relation to internal sub-group identities, but also in relation to these external international or **transnational** identities.

These external dimensions of Canadian identity are, I believe, quite important. Canadians tend to have a particular view of the role they play in the larger world, and attach importance to how they are perceived by other countries. Indeed, concerns about Canada's status in the world often affect the way the internal dimensions of Canadian identity are negotiated. In this article, therefore, I shall start by examining the external dimensions of Canadian identity, before turning to the more familiar debates about internal diversity.

[The External Dimensions of Canadian Identity]

People have political identities at various levels from the local to the global. In one sense, "being Canadian" is just one identity within this larger set of identities. Yet, for most people, being Canadian has implications for these other identities. Part of what it means to be Canadian (or at least to be a "good Canadian") is to accept certain roles or responsibilities with respect to these other forms and levels of human society. In this section, I shall discuss how "being Canadian" affects three such larger identities.

Canadians as Citizens of the World

One of the most powerful aspects of Canadian identity is the belief that Canadians are good citizens of the world. Canadians think of themselves as having played a useful and constructive role in international affairs, as UN peacekeepers, as "honest brokers" in various international negotiations or conflict resolutions, and as supporters of virtually every important international legal or political initiative, such as the recent International Criminal Court or the international convention against landmines.

It is important to emphasize that this is seen as a national character trait, part of the national identity, and as an obligation of national citizenship. Many "**cosmopolitan**" political theorists have argued that people's national identities—i.e., their identities as citizens of particular **nation-states**—interfere with the recognition of their obligations as "citizens of the world," and that the former must be downplayed or transcended in order to promote the latter. Yet the link between national identities and cosmopolitan responsibilities is more complicated than that. In Canada, to be indifferent to our obligations as citizens of the world is seen as "unCanadian." We find the same situation in many other Western democracies. Norway is a good example: there is nothing more characteristically Norwegian than being active in international diplomacy and international aid. Indeed, Canadians rather envy and resent the fact that Norway has become the preferred "honest broker" in places like the Middle East or Sri Lanka. This is the sort of role that Canadians feel that they are uniquely qualified as a country to perform.

In this sense, Canadians distinguish themselves from Americans, who are seen as prone to isolationism, **unilateralism**, and excessive suspicion of international agencies like the UN or UNESCO (the United Nations Educational, Scientific, and Cultural Organization). When Canadians participate in international affairs, it is seen as reflecting and reinforcing our distinctiveness as a nation from our neighbours to the south.

Like most aspects of national identity, this idea of "Canadians as good citizens of the world" is more mythology than fact. Canada's contribution to foreign aid is abysmally low compared to most Western European countries, and Canada's negotiating position on some international treaties—like the Kyoto climate change treaty—is embarrassingly selfish and self-serving. And even Canada's **vaunted** contribution to peacekeeping—singled out by the UN for a special honour—has been dramatically eroded by scandal (Canadian peacekeepers in Somalia tortured a boy to death) and budget cuts.

But national identities are matters of perception, and it is clear that Canadians perceive themselves as good citizens of the world. (According to a 1997 survey, ninety-four per cent of Canadians agreed with the statement that "Canada is a world leader in working for peace and human rights around the world.") Canadians also like to believe that this perception is widely shared around the world, and that Canadians are respected and trusted internationally. This aspect of Canadian self-identity is reinforced in countless ways. Teenagers are told that when they travel abroad they should put a Canadian flag on their backpack, to help ensure a friendly welcome. They are also told, in passing, that they may encounter some Americans who have put Canadian flags on their backpacks, as a safeguard against anti-Americanism.

Advertisers often are able to capture a national identity better than any scholarly description. A recent television ad in Canada showed a group of astronauts walking on a desolate planet who are suddenly surrounded by menacing aliens pointing their guns directly at the astronauts. The astronauts slowly turn around to point out the Canadian flag on the pack attached to their uniforms. The aliens then drop their guns, give the "thumbs-up" signal, and embrace the Canadian astronauts. This is almost a perfect expression of "being Canadian." Canadians would like to think that no matter where they go, in this world or other worlds, their good reputation will proceed them, and a Canadian flag will ensure a warm welcome.

Similar sentiments attach to a Canadian passport. Canadians were outraged to learn that Mossad, the Israeli secret service, uses forged Canadian passports when on missions in other countries to kidnap or assassinate its enemies. But I suspect that the outrage was mixed with a degree of silent satisfaction, since part of the reason why Mossad uses Canadian passports is that people carrying them are more likely to be respected, trusted, and helped by state officials around the world. Indeed, I think that Canadians might have been disappointed if Mossad had judged that some other passport was now more respected internationally.

In all of these ways, Canadians nurture and cherish an identity as good citizens of the world, and view their flag and passport as internationally recognized symbols of that goodness. And part of what it means to be a (good) Canadian is to protect this reputation, and to pass it on to the next generation of Canadians as a kind of national heritage. One is a good Canadian nationalist by being a good internationalist.

Canadians as Part of the West

While Canadians think of themselves as honest brokers in world affairs, mediating between East and West, North and South, the reality is that Canada is firmly embedded within "the West" economically, politically, militarily, and culturally. Like all Western countries, Canada is a **secular** constitutional **liberal democracy**, with a market economy and a **welfare state**, and is linked with other Western democracies through a dense set of alliances and agreements. That this Western model of economics and politics should be adopted is completely undisputed in Canada. Few Canadians doubt that this model is the recipe for a successful country, and most would applaud the adoption of this model elsewhere.

However, the reality is that Western-style liberal democracy has not spread that widely or quickly around the world, and there have always been various international forces that see themselves in conflict with Western liberal-democratic values, whether it be Nazis, communists, tribal warlords or religious fundamentalists. Canadians do not generally talk about these conflicts . . . [as] a "clash of civilizations," or as a matter of "the West versus the rest." It would be considered arrogant to talk openly about the superiority of Western civilization, and entirely unacceptable to talk about the superiority of Christianity or the white race. In part because of ideas of being an honest broker, and in part because of internal diversity, Canadians attempt to avoid explicit or aggressive assertions of "Westernness."

However, deep down, I think most Canadians would agree that being Canadian includes "being Western," and this aspect of the Canadian identity arises particularly in times of global crises, like September 11th. I suspect that most Canadians believe that there is a core set of Western countries that are more or less successful, surrounded by countries to the east and south that are in varying degrees corrupt, poor, repressive, and unstable. Canadians might be less likely than Americans to blame this state of affairs on developing countries themselves, and more likely to accept that the West itself is partly responsible for creating or perpetuating these problems. However, Canadians conveniently attribute this responsibility to either European **imperialism** or American multinational corporations and American foreign policy, and so tend to think of Canada itself as relatively blameless.

Canada as Part of the "New World"

While part of the West, Canada strongly differentiates itself from the "Old World" of Europe. Canada has largely been built by settlers and immigrants who have left the constraints of the old world behind, to start a new life in a new land. Of course, Canada was not a *terra nullius* [an unowned land], and the process of colonization and settlement in Canada involved many injustices to the **indigenous** peoples. I shall return to that issue below. But Canadians think of their country as a young, modern society, free from the old hierarchies, cultural prejudices and embedded traditions of the Old World. It is, Canadians like to think, a classless, **meritocratic** and democratic society, open to newcomers and to new ideas. (. . . Openness to immigrants is reflected in Canada's policy of admitting one per cent of its population each year as new immigrants—the highest per capita immigration rate in the world alongside Australia. Surveys show that many Canadians think this is "too many," and one political party, the Canadian Alliance, has campaigned on the platform of cutting the intake to 0.5 per cent a year. This is often described as an "anti-immigration" platform, but 0.5 per cent is roughly equivalent to the American level of immigration. In other words, the debate between "pro-immigration" and "anti-immigration" parties in Canada is a debate between those who think Canada should be tied with Australia for first in the world in per-capita immigration and those who think Canada should be tied with the US for second in the world in per-capita immigration. Even the "anti-immigrant" section of the Canadian populace is more welcoming of immigrants than most European citizens.)

The flip side of this self-image of Canada as a young New World country is the acknowledgement that our society and cultural life lack the historic depth of old-world European countries. Canadians who travel to Europe inevitably talk about "the sense of history" one gets walking in many European cities or driving through the countryside. They also admire the artistic and cultural treasures that **abound** [are plentiful] in Europe. But Canadians also typically get frustrated with the closed nature of European societies, where it seems one has to have lived there for many years (if not generations) in order to figure out how things work. Since Canadian institutions have had to make themselves understandable to waves of immigrants over the past 150 years, the "rules of the game" tend to be pretty clear and simple, and not dependent on the sort of dense local cultural knowledge that many European institutions seem to presuppose.

Much of this "new world/old world" contrast is of course mythical. Immigrants to Canada find much of Canadian society baffling, and many European institutions have become more open in recent years to accommodate the needs of immigrants and EU integration. Yet the perception persists. Canadians cherish a self-image of a young and open society—open to mobility, to newcomers and to new ideas—where the weight of history is lighter and less stifling of individual initiative or cultural diversity.

Canadians as Non-Americans

So Canadians are citizens of the world, the West, and the New World. In all three of these respects, Canadians are like Americans. Indeed, looked at objectively, the two national identities have much in common. And yet what defines being Canadian, perhaps above all else, is precisely not being an American.

This contrast with America goes back to the American Revolution, although the character of the contrast has changed dramatically over the years. Historically, the first contrast was precisely over the revolution. Despite several attempts by Americans to cajole or force the British colonies in Canada to join the revolution against Britain, the settlers in what is now Canada remained loyal to the Crown. And this Loyalist streak was reinforced by the huge numbers of Loyalist refugees from the United States who fled to Canada after losing the War of Independence.

For much of Canadian history, therefore, it has been common to distinguish a "deferential" and "**communitarian**/conservative" Canadian identity from a "revolutionary" and "liberal/individualist" American identity. This contrast persisted perhaps even up to the Second World War. Some scholars argue that it persists to this day.

In fact, however, the liberal/conservative positions have largely been reversed. Surveys suggest that Americans are more conservative and deferential to authority on many issues, such as gay rights, the rights of prisoners, racial intermarriage and gender equality. Scholars have written extensively about the "decline of deference" in Canada, and the rise of a very liberal and individualist outlook.

. . .

Perhaps the most common contrast that is drawn today, however, is the idea that Canada is a "kinder and gentler" country. Canada and the US share the same basic ideals of liberal **constitutionalism**, but Canadians view their society as less violent, more caring for the sick or disadvantaged, less punitive, more environmentally responsible, and more confident that government policies can actually make a difference in people's lives. Canadians like to think they have a better balance between public services and private markets. It is perhaps no coincidence that *The Affluent Society*—John Kenneth Galbraith's influential critique of the US for its obsessive focus on private wealth to the neglect of public goods like schools, roads, and parks—was written by an expatriate Canadian. The same contrast is nicely captured in the title of a recent best-selling book: *The Efficient Society: Why Canada Is as Close to Utopia as It Gets*. The idea of Canada as a utopia is a stretch, but this perception of having found the right balance of public and private has been reinforced by the fact that Canada has had the highest score on the annual UN Human Development Index for three of the past five years.[1] Needless to say, this UN ranking is always widely reported in newspapers and loudly trumpeted by politicians.

As always, ideas of Canada as a "kinder, gentler" country are partly mythical. For example, while Canadians have for a generation prided themselves on the idea that we have liveable cities, unlike the decaying inner cities of the US, the reality is that Americans have recently invested huge amounts in revitalizing their city centres, while the infrastructure of Canadian cities has been deteriorating. And Canada's environmental laws are often worse than their American counterparts. (Forty-eight out of fifty states in the US have a better environmental record than Ontario, Canada's largest province.) It is striking how Canadians are able to overlook any such embarrassing facts that contradict their preferred self-image.

In all of these respects, "being Canadian" is seen as different from, and morally superior to, "being American." To an outside observer, this Canadian tendency to make moralizing comparisons with the US must seem rather tiring and pathetic. And indeed much of it is. But we could find similar tendencies in all countries. This is "nation-work"—the ongoing work of producing and reproducing national identities and allegiances—and one can find it in all countries. It is not a pretty sight in any country.

In the Canadian case, however, it also serves another function. Much of this moralizing contrast serves as a compensation for an even deeper-seated sense of Canadian inferiority *vis-à-vis* the US. Canadian attitudes towards the US are not only tinged with envy of its power and wealth, but also chastened by the knowledge that many talented Canadians emigrate to the US to pursue their careers in film, music, academia, and business. Canadians know that the US is "where the action is," and that Canada simply cannot compete with the US in terms of the resources it can provide for gifted scientists, entrepreneurs, artists or scholars. . . . This "brain drain" is perceived to be so powerful that it is difficult for people who remain in Canada to be recognized as world-class in their field. After all, if they are so good, why aren't they in the States? At times, then, being Canadian means "being not quite good enough or ambitious enough to play in the big leagues in the US."

All of this may help to explain the Canadian tendency to make moralizing contrasts with the US. Winning a few moral victories provides a salving compensation for deeper feelings of inferiority. (It also soothes some of the resentment that comes from the fact that the US seems to take Canada's support for granted on international issues, without asking for Canada's advice, and without showing much gratitude for the support. This is a sore point, but it seems that most of America's allies feel the same way.) Whatever the explanation, the tendency to define "Canadian" as "non-American" has important effects on Canadian public debate. There is a nearly universal assumption that the state has the responsibility to preserve "the Canadian way," which by definition is different from "the American way." As a result, public policy proposals are often debated, not on their own merits, but rather in terms of whether they would lead to the "Americanization" of Canada.

. . .

These, then, are some of the international dimensions of Canadian identity. "Being Canadian" is to be a good citizen of the world; to be committed to Western values and anxious about possible threats to them, but hesitant to talk about a clash of civilizations; to celebrate the self-consciously modern and classless society that is possible in the New World, open to newcomers and new ideas; and to have a tortured relationship with the US, asserting moral superiority as a kinder and gentler country, but tacitly acknowledging that Canada cannot compete with the US for the development and exercise of talents and skills.

These international aspects of being Canadian are, I think, largely shared across ethnic and linguistic lines in Canada. (It should be noted, however, that Canada is a regionalized country, and there are regional variations in these attitudes. There is a strand of right-wing **populism** in Western Canada, particularly Alberta, that does not share some of the attitudes I have just described, particularly regarding the international community—towards which it is more sceptical—and the United States—towards which it is more friendly.) As I discuss below, it may indeed be something that helps keep the country together. This is a useful corrective to the view, often repeated, that there is no such thing as a shared Canadian identity, and that there is just the "masochistic" celebration of difference.

Diversity Within Canada

However, this commonality in views about Canada's place within the larger world is counterbalanced, if not outweighed, by deep disagreements about the management of diversity within Canada. . . . Learning how to accommodate this internal diversity, while still maintaining a stable political order, has always been one of the main challenges facing Canada, and remains so today.

These struggles have resulted in a number of legal and institutional reforms, from official bilingualism to multiculturalism to Aboriginal rights. ~AV These are often lumped together under the heading of "the Canadian model" of diversity, and are sometimes said, both by defenders and critics, to be unique. According to *The Economist*, for example:

> The "Canadian model"—whether of disintegration or of holding together in some new, postmodern version of the nation-state—is going to be an example to avoid or follow for all but a few **federations**, for all multicultural societies, especially immigrant ones, for countries whose borders reflect conquest more than geography, and for all states riven [torn apart] or driven by nationalism.[2]

AV My own view, however, is that Canada's approach to internal diversity is not so different from that of other Western democracies. On the contrary, the Canadian approach is best understood as an outgrowth or application of the same basic **liberal-democratic values** that are shared by all Western democracies. And, as a result, the way in which national and sub-state identities are negotiated and accommodated in Canada is, in many respects, [the same] as in other Western countries.

To explain this, I need to say a few words about Canada's ethnic diversity. Canada is a "British settler society," in the sense that Canada emerged from the union of four British colonies, and it was the British colonists and colonial administrators who established many of the dominant institutions that still govern us. But the British have never been alone on this territory, and they have become an ever-decreasing percentage of the population. We can divide Canada's increasing **ethnocultural** diversity into two broad categories.

The first source of ethnocultural diversity in Canada is the peoples who were here before the British—namely, the Aboriginal peoples and French-Canadians. They formed complete and functioning societies, long-settled on their own territory, with their own institutions operating in their own language, prior to being incorporated into British North America. This incorporation was involuntary—the result of colonization and conquest. However, efforts have been made to turn this involuntary incorporation into a more voluntary federation of peoples, either through the signing of treaties with Aboriginals, or the negotiation of Confederation with French-Canadians. But neither group is satisfied with its current status within Canada, and both have sought greater powers of **self-government** so as to maintain their status as culturally distinct and self-governing societies within the larger state.

The other major source of ethnocultural diversity in Canada is immigration. This too has been a long-standing feature of Canadian history, going back to the Irish immigrants in the 1840s, and occurring in waves ever since. As a result, Canada now contains people whose ancestral roots lie in all four corners of the world. These immigrant groups have a very different history from the "nations within." They are the result, not of the involuntary incorporation of complete societies settled on their historic homeland, but rather of the decision of individuals and families to leave their original homeland for a new life. This choice was more or less voluntary, at least in the sense that many of their friends and family chose to stay, and it was made by people who knew that they were entering a new society with its own established laws and institutions.

I will refer to these groups as "immigrant groups," since their origins in Canada lie in the act of immigration. But for some groups, particularly those from Northern Europe, these origins lie quite far in the past, so that the bulk of the group's members today are not immigrants, but rather the children, grandchildren or even great-grandchildren of the original immigrant. It seems slightly odd, therefore, to describe German-Canadians or Ukrainian-Canadians as "immigrant groups." Many people use the term "ethnic group" instead, and I too will use that term in places. But the fact that these groups were formed initially through immigration is pivotal in understanding their status in Canada, and in understanding how and why they differ from our "nations within."

How then does being Canadian relate to these subgroup identities? I shall start with immigrant ethnic groups, and then consider the Aboriginal peoples and French Canadians.

Immigrant Groups

In the past, Canada had an assimilationist approach to immigration. Immigrants were encouraged and expected to assimilate to the pre-existing society, with the hope that over time they would become indistinguishable from native-born Canadians in their speech, dress, recreation, and way of life generally. Any groups that were seen as incapable of this sort of cultural assimilation were prohibited from emigrating to Canada, or from becoming citizens. (This was reflected in rules excluding Asians and Africans in the first half of the twentieth century.)

However, since the late 1960s, we have seen a dramatic reversal in this approach. There were two related changes: first, the adoption of race-neutral admissions criteria (the "points system"), so that immigrants to Canada are increasingly from non-European (and often non-Christian) societies; and secondly, the adoption of a more "multicultural" conception of integration, one which expects that many immigrants will visibly and proudly express their ethnic identity, and which accepts an obligation on the part of public institutions (like the police, schools, media, museums, etc.) to make reasonable accommodations for these ethnic identities.

These two changes have dramatically changed Canadian society, but it is important to realize that the same two-fold change has occurred in all of the other traditional countries of immigration, like Australia, New Zealand, the United States, or Britain. All of them have shifted from discriminatory to race-neutral admissions and naturalization policies. And all of them have shifted from an assimilationist to a more multicultural conception of integration. Of course, there are differences in how official or explicit this shift to multiculturalism has been. In Canada, as in Australia and New Zealand, this shift was formally and officially marked by the declaration of a multicultural policy by the central government. By contrast, the US does not have an official policy of multiculturalism at the federal level. Yet if we look at lower levels of government in America, such as states or cities, we will find a broad range of multiculturalism policies. If we look at state-level policies regarding the education curriculum, for example, or city-level policies regarding policing or hospitals, we shall find that they are often indistinguishable from the way provinces and cities in Canada deal with issues of immigrant ethnocultural diversity. . . . Similarly, in Britain, while there is no nation-wide multiculturalism policy, the same basic ideas and principles are pursued through their race relations policy. All of these countries have accepted the same two-fold change at the heart of the Canadian model: i.e., adopting race-neutral admissions and naturalization policies, and imposing on public institutions a duty to accommodate immigrant ethnocultural diversity.

Indigenous Peoples

In the past, Canada had the goal and expectation that its indigenous peoples (the Indians, Inuit and Metis) would eventually disappear as distinct communities, as a result of dying out, or intermarriage, or assimilation. Various policies were adopted to speed up this process, such as stripping indigenous peoples of their lands, restricting the practice of their traditional culture, language and religion, and undermining their institutions of self-government.

However, there has been a dramatic reversal in these policies, a change which in Canada started in the early 1970s. Today, the Canadian government accepts, at least in principle, the idea that Aboriginal peoples will exist into the indefinite future as distinct societies within Canada, and that they must have the land claims, treaty rights, cultural rights, and self-government rights needed to sustain themselves as distinct societies. Key events here included the repudiation of the assimilationist 1969 White Paper on Indian Policy, the Supreme Court's recognition of Aboriginal land title in the *Calder* decision,[3] the revalidation of older treaties, the signing of new treaties, such as the James Bay and Nunavut agreements with the Inuit and Cree,[4] and the constitutional entrenchment of Aboriginal rights in the 1982 Constitution.

These changes have dramatically affected the status of indigenous peoples in Canada. But here again, Canada is not unique in this shift. We see the same pattern in all of the other Western democracies that contain indigenous peoples. Consider the revival of treaty rights through the Treaty of Waitangi in New Zealand; the recognition of land rights for Aboriginal Australians in the Mabo decision; the creation of the Sami Parliament in Scandinavia; the evolution of "Home Rule" for the Inuit of Greenland; and the laws and court cases upholding self-determination rights for American Indian tribes (not to mention the flood of legal and constitutional changes recognizing indigenous rights in Latin America). In all of these countries, there is a gradual but real process of **decolonization** taking place, as indigenous peoples regain their lands and self-government.

The Québécois

The Québécois are Canada's main example of a sub-state nationalist movement. Other examples in the West include the Scots and Welsh in Britain, the Catalans and Basques in Spain, the Flemish in Belgium, the German-speaking minority in South Tyrol in Italy, or the Hispanics in Puerto Rico in the United States. In all of these cases, we find a regionally-concentrated group that conceives of itself as a nation within a larger state, and mobilizes behind nationalist political parties to achieve recognition of its nationhood, either in the form of an independent state or through territorial autonomy within the larger state.

In the past, all of these countries . . . have attempted to suppress these forms of sub-state nationalism. To have a regional group with a sense of distinct nationhood was seen as a threat to the state. In the Canadian case, various efforts were made in the eighteenth and nineteenth centuries to erode this sense of distinct French-Canadian nationhood, including restricting minority language rights, abolishing earlier forms of autonomous self-government, and encouraging anglophones to settle in the French-Canadians' traditional territory, so that the minority would become a minority even in its homeland. Similar stories apply to most of the other Western cases of sub-state nationalism.

However, these policies have gradually been repudiated. Today, all of the countries I have just mentioned have accepted the principle that these sub-state national identities will endure into the indefinite future, and that their sense of nationhood and nationalist aspirations must be accommodated in some way or other. This accommodation has typically taken the form of what we can call "multination **federalism**": that is, creating a federal or quasi-federal sub-unit in which the minority group forms a local majority, and so can exercise meaningful forms of self-government. Moreover, the group's language is typically recognized as an official state language, at least within their federal sub-unit, and perhaps throughout the country as a whole.

At the beginning of the twentieth century, only Switzerland and Canada had adopted this combination of territorial autonomy and official language status for sub-state national groups. Since then, however, virtually all Western democracies that contain sizeable sub-state nationalist movements have moved in this direction. . . . Here again, the Canadian model of accommodating sub-state nationalism falls within the usual patterns of Western democracies.

Canadian Exceptionalism?

In all three of these areas, therefore, Canada's shift to accommodating diversity is simply one manifestation of a much larger trend throughout the West. In all of these countries, including Canada, these changes have been strongly contested, and remain controversial. Yet the overall trends are fairly consistent throughout the West towards greater recognition of diversity.[5]

I emphasize this because it is often seen as a distinctively Canadian characteristic to tolerate and accommodate diversity. For some, this is a distinctive virtue of Canadians' national character, for others it is a distinctive failing. But in reality, it is not distinctively Canadian at all. It reflects underlying sociological and political factors that affect all Western democracies. Canadians who are exposed to Spanish debates over the accommodation of Catalan nationalism, or to Australian debates about immigrant multiculturalism, or to New Zealand's debates about the place of indigenous peoples, will find much that is familiar. In all of these cases there are the same powerful forces pushing for greater recognition of diversity, resisted by the same entrenched interests and by the same fears of fragmentation and instability, with broadly similar outcomes.

Canada is distinctive in having to deal with all three forms of diversity at the same time. Australia and New Zealand, for example, have been grappling with issues of immigration and indigenous peoples, but have no sub-state nationalist movements. Belgium, Switzerland, Spain and Britain, by contrast, have been grappling with issues of both sub-state nationalism and immigration, but have no indigenous peoples. Canada is unusual in having to confront all three issues at the same time.

Also, Canada is distinctive in the extent to which it has not only legislated, but also *constitutionalized*, practices of accommodation. Canada's commitment to multiculturalism is enshrined not only in statutory legislation, but also in section 27 of the Constitution. No other Western country has **constitutionalized** multiculturalism. Canada's commitments to Aboriginal and treaty rights are similarly constitutionalized, in section 35, in a stronger or more explicit fashion than most Western countries. And so too with Canada's commitments to federalism and official language rights.

This decision to constitutionalize these practices of accommodation is one example of a more general feature of the Canadian experience: namely, the decision to highlight these practices in Canada's national narratives. While the actual practices of accommodation in Canada are not unique, Canada is unusual in the extent to which it has built these practices into its symbols and narratives of nationhood. Canadians tell each other that accommodating diversity is an important part of Canadian history, and a defining feature of the country. This is unlike the United States, for example. In practice, as already noted, the US does accord self-government and treaty rights to American Indians, regional autonomy and language rights to Puerto Rico, and multicultural accommodations to immigrant groups. But these are peripheral to the self-conception of many Americans, and are not considered defining features of the American identity or its national narrative. Americans accommodate diversity in practice, but they do not shout that fact from the rooftop, as Canadians sometimes do.

In other words, accommodating diversity has a symbolic **salience** in Canada that is not matched in most other Western countries. This is probably a mixed blessing. The self-conscious affirmation of diversity at the symbolic and constitutional levels has probably helped provide members of various groups in Canada with a stronger sense of security and comfort, and given them the courage and conviction to fight more effectively for changes in their public institutions. On the other hand, the preoccupation with symbols has also probably heightened opposition to these changes. The experience of other countries suggests that it is sometimes easier to push through changes to accommodate minorities if it is done quietly, with as little fanfare as possible.

The "Unity" Question

The trend towards recognizing diversity in Canada raises a puzzle: what turns this crazy quilt of ethnocultural diversity into a coherent functioning country? What is the nature of the "social glue" that binds the country together?

Many commentators assume that for the country to function, citizens must have a strong sense of identification with Canada as a political community, an identification that stands over and above their more particularistic sub-group identities. They must have a strong feeling of "being Canadian," in addition to their feelings of belonging to sub-groups.

Constructing such a **pan-Canadian** sense of identity has required dramatic changes to Canada's historic self-images and traditions. For much of its history, Canada was seen by its rulers as essentially a (white) British country, an outpost of British culture and civilization in the New World. Non-British groups, including French, Aboriginal, and immigrant groups, were at best tolerated, at worst excluded entirely. This was reflected in the predominance of the English language over French within the federal government, the adoption of British symbols and holidays, and in rules that excluded Asians and Africans from emigrating to Canada, and that excluded Aboriginals from citizenship. Needless to say, many minority groups had difficulty feeling Canadian when it was defined in this narrowly white/British way.

Since the 1950s, however, concerted efforts have been made to construct a "made-at-home" Canadian identity that essentially severs the connection with Britain, while reaching out to minority groups within Canada. This is reflected in the adoption of a new flag in place of the **Union Jack**, a new national anthem and national holidays, a new made-at-home constitution, as well as the adoption of official bilingualism, official multiculturalism and a race-neutral admissions policy and other forms of anti-discrimination policy. All of these have dramatically changed the look of Canadian institutions, to make them appear more open and inclusive of Canada's diversity.

These attempts at redefining Canadian identity to accommodate internal diversity have had some unexpected results. Some commentators worried that these changes would alienate Canadians of British origin, who remain the single largest group in Canada. In reality, however, no matter how much they complain about minorities being "coddled" in Canada, Canadians of British origin remain steadfastly patriotic. Indeed, their attachment to Canada has actually grown since the 1960s, and they are more likely than ever to identify themselves as Canadians rather than in terms of any sub-state provincial or ethnic identity.

These changes have also had some success in instilling a pan-Canadian identity amongst immigrant groups. These groups often doubt the sincerity of the dominant society's commitment to multiculturalism, which they sometimes see as purely rhetorical. But most immigrants nonetheless appreciate the symbolism, and acknowledge that many institutions like the schools or media have in fact made serious efforts to accommodate immigrant ethnicity. Indeed, studies show that many highly-skilled immigrants who could have gone to Britain or Germany, and probably made more money, nonetheless chose to come to Canada because it was seen as a more welcoming country for immigrants. (On the other hand, if immigrants have a choice between Canada and the United States, they typically choose the US.)

However, attempts to construct a pan-Canadian identity have failed at their main goal—namely, to strengthen Canadian identity amongst the Québécois. After all, these efforts at building a pan-Canadian identity were instigated by the rise of a separatist movement in Quebec in the 1960s, and were primarily aimed at nurturing Quebeckers' feelings of identification with Canada. Since the 1960s, however, the number of Quebeckers who identify themselves as "Canadian" rather than "Québécois" has steadily dropped. Constructing a new pan-Canadian identity was primarily intended to displace the centrality of Britishness in Canada, to make room for the Québécois. Yet, ironically, it has had the opposite effect. It has strengthened Canadian identity amongst British-origin Canadians, while reducing the feeling of Canadianness amongst the Québécois.

. . .

. . . In the past forty years, we have seen a clear convergence between English and French on basic political values, such that political values are virtually identical in the two communities (e.g. regarding freedom of speech, women's rights, the rights of defendants, etc.). Yet in precisely the same time, as we have seen, the number of Quebeckers who identify themselves as "Canadian" rather than "Québécois" has significantly dropped. (We can find similar examples within the Aboriginal community. The increasing influence of Western values and Western education within Aboriginal communities has not guaranteed that Aboriginals "feel Canadian." While some Aboriginal leaders reject Western liberal values, even those who generally accept them do not always identify themselves as Canadian.)

This should not be a surprise, since there is no reason why Quebeckers could not pursue these common political values in their own constitution adopted for their own separate state. The fact that 30 million people in Canada, or 300 million people in Europe, generally agree on the political values that should be respected in any constitution does not yet tell us whether they should form one country, or two, or twenty.

Since common political principles seem too "thin" a basis for an overarching Canadian identity, some commentators have argued that we need to find a "thicker" source of common identity, like a sense of common history. A feeling of being Canadian, on this view, would be tied up with common feelings of pride or shame about various events in Canadian history. Unfortunately, French and English often have quite different views on Canadian history. It is even more difficult to persuade immigrants that being Canadian should be defined by one's feelings towards events that predated their arrival in Canada.

Charles Taylor suggests another possible basis for an overarching Canadian identity: namely, the value of diversity itself. He expresses the hope that Canadians could come to see the management of deep diversity as an "exciting" collective endeavour. [See the reading by Taylor in Chapter 2, Quebec Nationalism.] A more crass version of this argument, much trumpeted lately by the federal government, is that being a bilingual multicultural country gives Canada a competitive advantage in the global marketplace, and thereby increases our **GNP**. But it seems unlikely that most Canadians feel this way about diversity. For most Canadians, I suspect, diversity is an ineradicable fact about Canada that needs to be accommodated, but they find the endless issues it raises to be painful and tiring rather than exciting or enriching. And even if people did find diversity to be exciting, the fact is that even if Quebec separates, each of the resulting states [Canada and Quebec] would still be very ethnically and linguistically diverse, and so would still presumably offer the excitement or economic benefits that flow from diversity.

So we have a variety of theories about the sources of pan-Canadian identity, including common political principles, shared history, and the aesthetic or economic value of diversity itself. I suspect that while each of these has resonance with some Canadians, none of them provides a secure foundation for constructing or maintaining a strong feeling of Canadian identity amongst all Canadians, particularly amongst the Québécois. As we have seen, the evidence of declining Canadian identification in Quebec suggests that these factors are insufficient.

Yet this focus on constructing a strong sense of pan-Canadian identity amongst all citizens may be misplaced. The ability of Canada to function as a country may not depend on such an identity. After all, the basic functioning of the Canadian state has not been adversely affected by the gradual decline in Canadian identity amongst Quebeckers. Indeed, on many criteria, like the UN Human Development index, Canada has actually outperformed many Western democracies over the past ten to fifteen years.

It seems that having a strong Canadian identity is not a precondition for citizens to cooperate in the functioning of pan-Canadian institutions. Indeed, there is interesting evidence that feelings of trust and legitimacy in Canadian institutions have remained strong in Quebec even when Canadian identity has diminished. There are many people for whom being Canadian is becoming a less and less important part of their identity, yet who remain willing to participate actively in Canadian institutions, to accept the legitimacy of their decisions, and to do their fair share to uphold those institutions.

Why would people who do not feel a strong sense of being Canadian nonetheless continue to trust and participate in Canadian institutions? There are probably several overlapping factors here, including inertia, risk aversion, economic self-interest, personal bonds. Part of the explanation may even lie in Canada's international reputation. Surveys show that support for **secession** drops considerably when it is made clear that this would mean Quebeckers would no longer have Canadian citizenship and Canadian passports. (Some defenders of "**sovereignty association**" . . . implied that a sovereign Quebec could still enjoy Canadian citizenship and passports.) Even people who lack a feeling of Canadian identity can nonetheless see the international benefits that flow from being recognized as a Canadian.

But here again, perhaps we are looking in the wrong place for our explanations. Why would people who do not feel a strong sense of Canadian identity nonetheless trust pan-Canadian institutions? Perhaps because those institutions are in fact trustworthy: they operate according to fairly high standards of the **rule of law**, human and minority rights, democratic accountability, constitutional safe-guards, an impartial police force and independent **judiciary**, and so on. Even Quebec nationalists who do not feel a strong sense of Canadian identity acknowledge that francophones are generally treated fairly in federal decisions about government contracts, civil service hiring, public service delivery, economic development plans, or urban infrastructure projects. More generally, pan-Canadian institutions help to guarantee the basic freedom and security of individuals, and to provide reasonably good and efficient public services, for both English and French, while also supporting a prosperous economy. Quebec nationalists cooperate in the successful functioning of pan-Canadian institutions because those institutions do in fact function successfully for both English and French: they enable Quebeckers to lead good lives as individuals, and to thrive as a community.

Of course, most Quebeckers think that an independent Quebec state could also operate according to the same high standards of legitimacy and efficiency. Some think it could even do a better job, and so support **secessionist** political parties. They look forward to the day when Quebec exists outside the Canadian state. But in the meantime, their lack of a strong sense of Canadian identity does not prevent them from recognizing that Canadian institutions are generally trustworthy and effective, and hence worthy of cooperation.

The success of political institutions in the modern age depends heavily on the active and willing cooperation of citizens. Commentators have typically assumed that this sort of active and willing cooperation will only arise if citizens have a strong sense of identification with the country. But this assumption may be mistaken. Perhaps citizens will cooperate whenever they view political institutions as trustworthy (i.e. even-handed between individuals and groups) and effective (i.e., providing good services). The same dynamic would almost certainly exist in reverse if Quebec were to **secede**. Even if a clear majority in Quebec voted to secede, there would still be many anglophone and immigrant Quebeckers who identify more with Canada than Quebec, and who would therefore have trouble identifying with their new country. Yet so long as the new Quebec state operated in accordance with high standards of the rule of law, human and minority rights, impartiality, democratic accountability, and so on, then these people would almost certainly cooperate to ensure the successful functioning of Quebec institutions. Their lack of a strong sense of Quebec identity would not prevent them from recognizing and participating in trustworthy and legitimate institutions.

The strength of identification with the country may not be the crucial variable. Russia provides some confirming evidence from the opposite direction. There are very high levels of national identification with the Russian political community, but very little willingness to cooperate with the institutions of the state, which are seen as neither impartial nor effective. Strong identification does not guarantee active cooperation; weak identification does not preclude active cooperation.

Many will find this an unsatisfactory account of the "social glue" that enables diverse countries like Canada to function. It may seem too provisional or contingent. No doubt there is more to be said about the sources of social unity. However, whatever the answer to this question of social unity, it is unlikely to be distinctive to Canada. The factors that explain how Canada functions, despite its rich diversity, will almost certainly be the same factors that explain why other multination states like Britain, Belgium or Switzerland continue to function successfully. In all of these cases, the sense of "being British," "being Belgian" or "being Swiss" is becoming less important to some people's identities, supplanted by either sub-state or **supra**-state identities. Yet they all continue to function more or less successfully as prosperous democracies, reproducing the public institutions and generating the public services that enable most individuals and groups to thrive. If this seems a mystery, it is not a uniquely Canadian mystery.

Conclusion: The Banality of Identity Politics

What general lessons, if any, does the Canadian experience with **identity politics** hold? I would say that the Canadian story confirms one familiar view about modern identities, while challenging another. It is often said that identities today are multi-level, fluid, relational, porous, constructed, contested and overlapping. The complex and changing relationships that I have described between sub-state, national and international identities in Canada clearly attest to all of these attributes of modern identities. None of the identities I have described is unchanging or uncontroversial, and none can be understood outside its connections to (and reciprocal influence on) the other wider or narrower identities that coexist in Canada.

This . . . approach to identity has become a platitude in the literature, so I shall not belabour the point. However, there is one aspect of the Canadian story which challenges one of the received wisdoms of the literature. ~AV According to many commentators, "identity politics" involve a fundamentally different political dynamic from "interest politics." In particular, identity claims are said to be less subject to democratic deliberation and negotiation than interest claims, and hence a greater threat to democracy.

AV . . . Nothing could be further from the truth in the Canadian context. Minority group leaders in Canada offer innumerable arguments in the media, the courts, and the legislature in the hope of persuading members of the larger society to recognize their claims. Indeed, this is precisely why minorities seek political representation in the legislature or on government advisory and regulatory bodies (and also greater access to the media). If . . . [identity politics' critics] were correct, there would be no point in minority groups seeking representation on decision-making bodies in which they would be a numerical minority. If their claims are non-arguable, they would have no hope of persuading others of their views, and no hope of affecting the ultimate outcome. In reality, minority groups believe that, even though they lack the votes or vetoes needed to win by themselves, they can use their presence to persuade members of other groups of their position.

Similarly, identity claims are eminently "negotiable." Identity politics in Canada is an unending series of such democratic negotiations. Consider a typical example regarding official language rights: Francophones start by claiming that all public services should be available in their mother tongue wherever they live in Canada. The state starts by limiting French-language provision to a few public services in a few regions. They then discuss, argue, negotiate, and bargain, and the result is some provisional compromise which provides a significant level of French-language services (but not all services) in significant regions of Canada (but not all). This is normal, everyday democratic politics, no different in its structure from decision-making about taxes or environmental regulation.

Or consider demands by indigenous peoples in Canada regarding the development of natural resources on their traditional territory. Indians and Inuit in Canada start by demanding the right to make all of the development decisions and keep all the royalties; the state starts by demanding the right to control resource development and to keep all the revenue. They discuss and negotiate, and arrive at some provisional agreement to share decision-making control and royalties.

Or consider indigenous land claims. Indigenous groups start by demanding that all of the land taken from them historically be returned; the state starts by saying that indigenous title is null and void. They then discuss and bargain, and the result is a provisional agreement that returns some but not all of the land wrongfully taken from indigenous peoples.

I could go on and on listing such examples. Consider policies to enhance the political representation of minorities, or affirmative action, or the division of powers between Ottawa and Quebec, or the accommodation of minority religious holidays. All of these issues have been (provisionally) settled in Canada through normal processes of democratic debate and negotiation, in which all sides give reasons and make compromises. The demands of identity groups are no different in this respect from other political **actors** or movements. In short, identity politics in Canada is simply everyday democratic politics.

For those who have been raised on fears about the inherently explosive and irrational nature of identity politics, what is perhaps most striking about identity politics in Canada is its utter banality. (By saying it is banal, I do not mean to imply that it is trivial or benign. On the contrary, the process of publicly negotiating identities occurs within a field of power relations that construct and sustain various forms of assimilation, inequality, oppression, hierarchies and expertise. Powerful actors seek to contain or shape this process of negotiation, including both state actors and corporate actors. . . .) The ebb and flow of political mobilizations around immigrant multiculturalism, Québécois nationalism and indigenous decolonization barely raise an eyebrow anymore. It is as predictable, peaceful and indeed (for most Canadians) boring as mobilizations around tariff barriers, transportation policy, or tax cuts.

Here again, I don't think this is unique to Canada. Identity politics throughout the West have become routinized and domesticated as part of everyday processes of democratic deliberation and negotiation. This may make the topic of identity politics less interesting for scholars and citizens, but is arguably a good sign for the maturity of our political culture and the robustness of our democratic institutions.

Notes

1. In 2010 and 2011, Canada's ranked slipped to sixth. [Editor]
2. "Survey of Canada," *The Economist* (29 June 1991) p. 3.
3. In 1973 the Supreme Court recognized for the first time that Aboriginal title to land existed, at least in principle. [Editor]
4. In 1971, the construction of hydroelectric power plants began in northern Quebec without the consent of the Cree and Inuit who inhabited the region. The Cree and Inuit took the Quebec government to court. The James Bay Cree and Inuit exchanged territorial rights for money and greater rights of self-government. This was the first treaty signed by an Aboriginal people and a Canadian government since the early twentieth century. [Editor]
5. This is no longer true. Many northern European countries, including the Netherlands, Germany, France, and Great Britain, have backtracked furiously on multiculturalism policies. See the Introduction to Chapter 3, Multiculturalism. [Editor]

Discussion Questions

1. What does Segal mean by the "Canadian ideal"? What does he think this ideal looks like, and why? Do you agree with him? Why or why not?

2. Kymlicka says our sense of ourselves as global citizens does not make us unique. What are his reasons for this claim? Do you agree with him? Why or why not?
3. According to Kymlicka, what difference does being part of the New World make to Canadian identity? Do you agree with him? Why or why not?
4. Over and over, Kymlicka argues that most features of English-speaking Canadian identity can be found in other Western liberal democracies. Is there anything that makes us uniquely Canadian, according to Kymlicka? Do you agree with him? Why or why not?
5. Do you think Segal would agree with Kymlicka that most features of our Canadian identity are not unique to Canadians? Why or why not?
6. Do you think Kymlicka would agree with Tully (Chapter 1, Aboriginal Peoples) on the relationship between Aboriginal and non-Aboriginal Canadians? Why or why not?
7. Would he agree with Taylor (Chapter 2, Quebec Nationalism) about the relationship between the Québécois and English Canadians? Why or why not?

Suggested Readings and Websites

🍁 = Canadian source or author

🍁 Banting, Keith, and Will Kymlicka. "Canadian Multiculturalism: Global Anxieties and Local Debates." *British Journal of Canadian Studies* 23, 1 (2010): 43–72. [Argues that European criticisms of multiculturalism have not gained traction in Canada.]

🍁 Blake, Raymond B. "Standing on Guard: Canadian Identity, Globalization, and Continental Integration." Regina: Saskatchewan Institute of Public Policy Paper, Public Policy Paper 25 (2004). [Argues that "Canadian nationalism and identity [will] not only . . . survive but thrive in the 21st Century," despite "the forces of North American economic and cultural integration and globalization."]

🍁 Historica-Dominion Institute. www.historica-dominion.ca/. ["The Historica-Dominion Institute is the largest, independent organization dedicated to Canadian history, identity, and citizenship."]

🍁 Kymlicka, Will. "The Current State of Multiculturalism in Canada and Research Themes on Canadian Multiculturalism 2008–2010." Ottawa: Minister of Public Works and Government Services Canada, 2010. [A report "commissioned by the Department of Citizenship and Immigration to determine which multiculturalism issues are important nationwide and require the development of further research."]

🍁 Kymlicka, Will. *Finding Our Way: Rethinking Ethnocultural Relations in Canada*. Don Mills, ON: Oxford University Press, 1998. [When he wrote this, shortly after the 1995 Quebec referendum, Kymlicka was more pessimistic about the future of Canada than he is in his more recent work.]

Miscevic, Nenad. "Nationalism." *Stanford Encyclopedia of Philosophy* 2010. [See section 3, The Moral Debate, for defences and criticisms of nationalism and national identity.]

🍁 Peace, order, and good government, eh? Who promised you democracy would be easy? www.pogge.ca/ [A blog about Canadian politics, roughly centrist politically.]

🍁 Revolutionary Moderation. http://revmod.blogspot.ca/ [Another blog about Canadian politics, also roughly centrist.]

Part II

Who Are "We"?

Introduction

In Part I, Who Are We?, we looked at who we are as Canadians. What does it mean to be Canadian? What does being Canadian stand for? Unpacking that involved looking at our past, our present, and our plans for our future, because who we are involves both who we have been and who we hope to become.

Part II asks a similar question, but its scope is broader. In this part we are not asking who we are as citizens, but rather who we consider to be members of our moral community. This is partly a **metaphysical** question. (Metaphysics is the branch of philosophy that deals with the nature of existence or reality.) But it is not a **foundational** metaphysical question that asks what it means for anything at all to exist, or what **consciousness** (awareness of one's own existence) is. Ethicists and social and political philosophers assume the answers to foundational questions are either settled or irrelevant to their concerns, so they can ask higher-order questions about humans and their communities. In Part II, we are interested in moral and political existence: the nature of the beings who figure, or ought to figure, in our moral and political deliberations. When we are making ethical and political decisions, whose interests, needs, rights, welfare, virtues, and relationships must we consider? Who is capable of acting morally—that is, who is a **moral agent**? Who is owed moral treatment despite their inabilities to act morally—that is, who is a **moral patient**? Who, or what, is neither? Who has rights? Which rights? To whom do we owe duties? With whom, or what, do we have relationships? Whose behaviour and character can we praise or blame, and to whom, or what, does it make no sense to assign praise or blame? Whose welfare counts, and whose does not? Who do we consider part of "us," and who do we exclude?

Most people in liberal societies believe all humans are moral equals. That alone is a substantial achievement. Two centuries ago, most liberal citizens—admittedly a small, narrowly defined group—thought women, poor people, non-Europeans, Aboriginal peoples, and slaves were lesser forms of humans who mattered sometimes (for example, if they committed crimes, and sometimes if they were victims of crimes), but most times not at all (for example, if their **interests** conflicted with those of European men or if, like slaves, legally they had no interests). For three hundred years many political movements—women's rights, **abolitionism**, **civil rights**, labour organizing, independence movements in colonies, Aboriginal rights, rights of people with disabilities, lesbian/gay/bisexual/**transgendered/queer** etc. rights, and so on—have worked to broaden membership in the moral and political community. In liberal societies today, there is widespread agreement that all people are equal members of the moral community, and all competent adults are members of the political community.

But what is it that qualifies us and only us for moral status? Many criteria have been suggested—the soul, consciousness, **self-consciousness** (self-awareness), the capacity for love and relationships, the capacity for **autonomy** (independence or freedom), etc. But for each **criterion**, there are some human beings who lack the feature, such as people with severe intellectual disabilities who lack the capacities for autonomy and self-consciousness, and some animals that appear to possess it as well, such as primates and **cetaceans** (the biological order that includes dolphins and whales) that appear to possess both autonomy and self-consciousness.

The readings in Part II examine the claim that all and/or only humans count morally. The readings in Chapter 5, Abortion, discuss whether all humans matter morally. Should fetuses/unborn children be considered part of the moral community? If so, are they members from conception, or from a later stage of development? Why? How should their interests be protected and balanced with the interests of other humans, particularly the pregnant women who carry them? The readings in Chapter 6, Animal Rights, discuss whether only humans matter morally. Do some or all animals have interests that we ought to consider in our moral deliberations? If so, which ones, and why? How should their interests be protected and balanced with the interests of humans? You will decide for yourself.

Chapter 5

Abortion

Abortion is one of the most politically charged issues in Canada. It involves questions about rights (the pregnant woman's, the male partner's, the fetus/unborn child's[1]), politics (women's rights, the status of the fetus/unborn child in law, fathers' rights, the health care system, the interests of the state), metaphysics (when life begins, what makes us "us," religious v. **secular** views of the person), medicine (**viability**, codes of ethics), and sexuality (sanctioned and unsanctioned sex, women's roles, fathers' responsibilities). It is a bubbling cauldron.

Every culture has rules about pregnancy, childbirth, and parenting, since this is the main way that new citizens are produced. (Immigration is another, but much less common, way.) And almost every culture has laws or rules about abortion, ranging from a total ban on abortions to abortion on demand. Canada and China (and possibly North Korea) are the only countries in the world that have no laws at all regarding abortion.[2]

According to the World Health Organization, of the roughly 210 million pregnancies that occur every year, forty-six million (twenty-two per cent) end in abortion. Of those forty-six million abortions, approximately forty per cent are illegal.[3] Surprisingly, whether a country has restrictive, permissive, or no laws on abortion makes very little difference in the rates of abortions performed.[4] That is, more restrictive laws do not lower the numbers of abortions; they merely make them illegal. What *does* lower abortion rates is the availability and cost of contraception. Countries where contraceptives are widely available and affordable have significantly lower abortion rates than countries with poorer access to contraception.[5] For example, in the 1960s Chile permitted abortions only to save the life of the pregnant woman, but surveys indicated that a quarter of all Chilean women had had an abortion. The government began to promote family planning, and in fifteen years deaths from illegal abortions (often used to estimate the total number of illegal abortions) declined by eighty per cent. In 1989, however, the military dictatorship in Chile prohibited abortion even to save the life of the pregnant woman.[6] Despite this, a 1994 study estimated that thirty-five per cent of pregnancies in Chile ended in abortion—higher than in Brazil,

Colombia, Mexico, and the Dominican Republic, all of which at least permitted abortions to save the life of the pregnant woman.[7]

Women seek abortions because they do not want or cannot afford a (or another) child. So why do they get pregnant, then? Sometimes contraception is unavailable or the woman cannot afford it. Sometimes contraceptives fail, even when used properly; no method of contraception is completely effective. (The World Health Organization estimates that even if all women used contraception perfectly, there would still be six million unplanned pregnancies every year.[8]) A woman also may become pregnant involuntarily because of improper or inconsistent use of contraception. Some women feel unready to become mothers. Some who are already mothers cannot afford another child. Some women are pressured by their male partners to have abortions. Sometimes a relationship breaks down, and the woman no longer wants or can afford to have a child. Some women become pregnant as a result of rape or incest. Some find out the child would be born with a disability, and they do not want or cannot afford a child with special needs. Some want a child of a particular sex, and this will not be that child. Some women have medical conditions that make pregnancy life-threatening. Some have **ectopic** (outside the uterus) pregnancies that will kill them before the fetus/unborn child is **viable** (capable of living outside the uterus); the only choices in such cases are one death—the fetus/unborn child's—or two—both the woman's and the fetus/unborn child's.

That some women want abortions does not make them right, of course. Many people cheat on their taxes, take illegal drugs, steal, rape, and murder, but this does not make these things even permissible, much less right. Pro-life advocates say that the fetus/unborn child is morally the same as an adult human being, and thus abortion is murder. Moreover, the criminal law does not exist only to punish criminals; it also is intended to prevent crimes and to express social disapproval of them. Laws prohibiting abortion are necessary to express the wrongness of taking innocent human life, they say. Of course such laws should be enforced, but even if it turns out that they are largely unenforceable, as they are in countries like Chile, it is still important that society expresses its strong disapproval of abortion.

The Legal Situation in Canada

Prior to 1969, both abortion and contraception were illegal in Canada. In 1969 the Trudeau government passed a massive rewrite of the *Criminal Code*, which, among other things, permitted contraception and abortion in some circumstances. Section 251 of the *Criminal Code* was amended to allow a woman to get an abortion if a hospital's Therapeutic Abortion Committee, composed of three doctors, ruled that pregnancy was a threat to her life or physical or mental health. Hospitals were not required to set up Therapeutic Abortion Committees, and only about one-third of hospitals did. As a result, access to abortion was uneven across Canada; it was available almost on demand in some places, such as major cities, and unavailable in other places, especially rural areas. Furthermore, some Therapeutic Abortion Committees often took weeks to make a decision, giving Canada one of the highest second-trimester abortion rates in the world. Some committees put strict limits on the numbers of abortions they would permit, some approved no abortions, and some never met.

Enter Dr Henry Morgentaler. He was one of the first Canadian doctors to provide vasectomies, insert IUDs, and prescribe the pill to unmarried women. In the 1970s, he began to defy the law and perform abortions at his clinic—not in a hospital—and without the approval of a Therapeutic Abortion Committee. In 1973 he stated publicly that he had performed five thousand abortions outside of hospitals and without committee approval. The Quebec government charged him with violating section 251 of the *Criminal Code*. At his trial, Morgentaler freely admitted doing what he was accused of. His defence was "necessity": he said he performed abortions because they were necessary to the life or health of women.[9] A jury found him not guilty, but in an unprecedented decision, the Quebec Court of Appeal overturned the jury's verdict and sentenced Morgentaler to eighteen months in prison.[10] The public was outraged. In response to public pressure, the federal government passed an amendment to the *Criminal Code* which removed appeals courts' power to overturn jury acquittals and impose guilty sentences.[11]

While Morgentaler was still in prison, the Quebec government laid further charges against him. Once again he was acquitted by a jury, and once again the government appealed the acquittal. This time, though, the Quebec Court of Appeal unanimously upheld the verdict. After the federal government removed courts' power to overturn jury acquittals and impose sentences, the Quebec government reversed Morgentaler's conviction and ordered a new trial. For the third time a jury refused to convict Morgentaler. In 1976 Quebec elected the Parti Québécois, which decided it was pointless to lay charges if juries would not convict. They dropped the remaining charges and announced that abortions could be permitted in free-standing clinics (not attached to hospitals).

Morgentaler then decided to challenge the abortion law by opening private abortion clinics in other provinces, in clear and open violation of the law. In 1983 Toronto police charged Morgentaler and two colleagues with providing illegal abortions. At trial, the jury acquitted all three doctors. The Crown appealed the acquittal. The Ontario Court of Appeals overturned the acquittal and ordered a new trial. Morgentaler and his colleagues **cross-appealed** (appealed the Crown's appeal), and the case went to the Supreme Court. In 1988 the Court, by a five-to-two majority, **struck down** (declared unconstitutional and therefore of no force or effect) section 251 of the *Criminal Code*, the abortion law, on the grounds that it violated section 7 of the *Charter*, which guarantees "life, liberty, and security of the person." All five justices in the majority said that section 251 violated the "security of the person" clause of section 7. Chief Justice Brian Dickson wrote, "Forcing a woman, by threat of criminal sanction, to carry a fetus to term unless she meets certain criteria unrelated to her own priorities and aspirations, is a profound interference with a woman's body and thus an infringement of security of the person" (p. 5). The state does have a legitimate interest in protecting the fetus, he said, but pregnant women's rights were infringed more than was necessary to protect that interest.

Justice Bertha Wilson agreed with the other justices in the majority, but thought they did not go far enough. She argued that the abortion law also violated women's rights to liberty in section 7 of the Charter. Citing previous decisions in which the Supreme Court had said that human **dignity** is central to the right to liberty, she argued that women's rights to dignity were central to this case. Giving a committee rather than the pregnant woman the power to decide whether she could *end* her pregnancy was as bad giving a committee rather than the pregnant woman the power to decide whether she could *continue* her pregnancy. "Both these arrangements violate the woman's right to liberty by deciding for her something that she has the right to decide for herself," she wrote (para. 241).

Justice William McIntyre, writing in **dissent** (disagreement with the majority opinion), denied that section 251 raised any constitutional issues. He argued that section 251 did not grant "any general right to have or to procure an abortion. On the contrary, the provision is aimed at protecting the interests of the unborn child and only lifts the criminal sanction where an abortion is necessary to protect the life or health of the mother" (para. 184). Nor could a right to abortion be found in the *Charter*. He said "the courts must not, in the guise of interpretation, postulate rights and freedoms which do not have a firm and a reasonably identifiable base in the *Charter*" (para. 186). Since no right to abortion could be found in the *Charter*, section 251 could not infringe on them.

None of the justices except Wilson addressed the question of the fetus/unborn child's **moral status** (whether an individual or class of individuals counts morally). Wilson cited the Canadian philosopher L.W. Sumner, who argues that moral status is acquired gradually, from conception to birth. (See the reading by Sumner in this chapter.) "A developmental view of the fetus . . . supports a permissive approach to abortion in the early stages of pregnancy and a restrictive approach in the later stages," Wilson wrote (para. 258). All seven justices agreed, however, that Parliament and not the courts should decide when and how the fetus/unborn child should be protected by the law.

In their judgment, the Supreme Court made it clear that a different law regulating abortion could be constitutional, as long as it did not violate pregnant women's *Charter* rights. The federal government proposed two laws to regulate abortion. The first failed in a vote in Parliament. The second passed in Parliament but failed in the Senate (the vote was a tie, and tie votes do not pass). No other laws regulating abortion have been passed.

The Real-World Debate

One of the things that makes abortion such a difficult issue is that an acceptable compromise is impossible. If someone believes that, from the moment of conception, a fetus/unborn child is morally the same as an adult human, there can be no room for compromise, just as there is no room for compromise on killing adult humans. There are a few carefully circumscribed exceptions to the rule that deliberately killing adult humans is murder, such as killing in self-defence, but the vast majority of deliberate killings are murder or at least manslaughter. So, for example, pro-life advocates may say that abortion is permissible if both the pregnant woman and the fetus/unborn child will die without it, as is the case in an ectopic pregnancy. The fetus/unborn child cannot survive in any case, so saving the life of the pregnant woman by aborting the fetus/unborn child may be allowed.

Some people justify a very small number of abortions using the **doctrine of double effect**, according to which an ordinarily wrong consequence may be permitted even though normally it would be considered wrong, if (a) the act, under normal circumstances, is morally permitted; (b) the immoral consequence is an unintended effect of the permitted act; and (c) the good of the act outweighs the immorality of the consequence. Abortion to save a pregnant woman's life sometimes may be permissible, then, even if the pregnancy could be continued until the fetus/unborn child became viable. For example, some women have forms of uterine cancer that progress much more rapidly if they become pregnant—rapidly enough to kill the woman if the pregnancy continues until viability. In this case a hysterectomy might be permitted even though it will kill the fetus/unborn child, because the death of the fetus/unborn child is a foreseen but unintended consequence of the goal of saving the woman's life, and that goal is at least as important as saving the fetus/unborn child's life.

No other exceptions are possible for a consistent pro-life advocate. If a fetus/unborn child has full moral status from the moment of conception, then permitting abortion in any other cases is the same as permitting murder. The physical or mental health of the pregnant woman is irrelevant, because it is not permissible to kill one person to preserve another's physical or mental health. That a fetus/unborn child will have a disability is irrelevant. It is wrong to kill a newborn with a disability, and since the fetus/unborn child is morally the same as a newborn, aborting it because it will have a disability is also murder. Whether a fetus/unborn child was conceived by incest or rape, including rape in war, is also irrelevant, because how a person came into existence has nothing to do with his or her moral status. It would be wrong to kill a two-year-old who was conceived as a result of rape or incest. Since a fetus/unborn child and a two-year-old are morally identical, it cannot be permissible to abort a fetus/unborn child who was conceived as a result of rape.

While there is only one consistent pro-life position—abortion is always wrong, with the possible exception of abortion to save the life of the pregnant woman—there are many consistent pro-choice positions. What they all share is the view that, at some points or for some reasons, the fetus/unborn child has less moral status than humans who have been born. Anyone who thinks abortion should be permitted in cases of incest or rape, to save the physical or mental health of the pregnant woman, or because another child will (further) impoverish the family, necessarily thinks the rights, interests, or welfare of some pregnant women matter more than the rights, interests, or welfare of some fetuses/unborn children. They are pro-choice in at least these cases.

Most pro-choice advocates believe that, at conception, the fetus/unborn child has no independent moral status. Moral status develops gradually, becoming morally significant somewhere between conception and birth. The most common pro-choice view is that the fetus/unborn child has no independent moral status in the first trimester, so a pregnant woman should be able to get an abortion for any reason during that time. Gradually the fetus/unborn child begins to develop key features of moral status, such as **sentience** (the capacity to feel pleasure or pain), **consciousness** (awareness of our own existence), **rationality** (the ability to reason), **autonomy** (being able to run one's own life), or the capacity for moral relationships. Somewhere between the middle of the second trimester and the beginning of the third, the moral status of the fetus/unborn child becomes almost equal to that of a newborn.[12] At this point very good moral reasons need to be given to justify a late abortion, usually involving the life or health of the pregnant woman.

Some of the readings in this chapter discuss what the authors call the "liberal" position, according to which abortion is permissible until birth. In fact no one but a philosopher takes this view seriously or advocates it politically. It is a logically possible position, but not an actual one.

Philosophical Issues

Most of the philosophical debate on abortion focuses on the moral status of the fetus/unborn child, and most philosophers think the answer to the question of whether the fetus/unborn child has moral status or rights determines the rightness or wrongness of abortion. Pro-life philosophers argue that the fetus/unborn child is morally the same as any other human from the moment of conception. Since killing a human is wrong, and since abortion kills the fetus/unborn child, abortion is wrong. Pro-choice philosophers argue that at conception, and for some time afterward, the fetus/unborn child has no independent moral status, and therefore abortion is permissible in at least some cases. Both sides discuss criteria for having moral status, and when, if ever, a fetus/unborn child develops this status. They agree that if something has moral status, killing it is wrong, with a very few exceptions such as self-defence.

Feminist philosophers deny that the moral status of the fetus/unborn child settles the issue of whether abortion is right or wrong. Fetuses/unborn children are not separate individuals; they cannot survive outside the pregnant woman's body for at least twenty weeks, and they do not have even a fifty per cent chance of survival until the twenty-fourth week. A mother who does not want to continue being a mother can, in principle, give her children up for adoption. (I say "in principle" because, as a matter of fact, social pressures make this virtually impossible; she will be viewed as a moral monster.) But a pregnant woman cannot give a fetus/unborn child to anyone else; it is literally part of her. Thus women and their social status are central to the abortion debate, feminists say. The right to determine when or if they will bear children is a key aspect of women's equality. Access to safe and effective contraception is key to that right, and since no method of contraception is completely effective, abortion must be available as a back-up.

The Readings

Judith Jarvis Thomson begins by assuming that pro-life advocates are right, that the fetus has moral status (is a person) from the moment of conception. Even so, she argues that abortion is justified under some circumstances. She uses an example involving an unconscious violinist to argue that abortion is permissible in the case of rape. She discusses the right of self-defence to argue that abortion is permissible to save the life of a pregnant woman. She argues that the right to life does not include the right to use another's body, and that abortion may be permissible even if a woman engaged in voluntary intercourse knowing it might result in pregnancy. And she argues that, while the law normally does not require us to provide lifesaving aid to another person, laws criminalizing abortion do precisely that to pregnant women.

Don Marquis begins by asking what makes killing wrong. It is wrong, he says, because losing one's life is one of the greatest harms that can happen to someone—it deprives that person of a future. He calls this the "future-like-ours" account. One of its implications is that abortion is wrong, because fetuses have the same sorts of future possibilities as infants, who it is wrong to kill. He considers two alternative accounts, that killing is wrong because people desire to live, and that it is wrong because they want to continue experiencing life. He rejects the desire account because it implies that killing someone who is depressed, suicidal, or perhaps even sleeping is permissible. The second account, which he calls the "discontinuation account," depends on the value of the experiences someone may have, which reduces to the future-like-ours account. Finally, he considers the objection that something cannot be valuable to someone unless that person actually values it, and fetuses do not value anything. But this view also cannot account for the wrongness of killing infants, he says.

L.W. Sumner argues that clarifying the moral status of the fetus will settle the question of abortion. He begins by discussing what he calls the "liberal" and "conservative" views. According to the liberal view, the fetus has no moral status, so abortion is always permissible. The liberal view sets the bar for moral status fairly high, such as rationality or consciousness. But such a view excludes some adults with intellectual disabilities and all newborns. On the conservative view, a fetus acquires moral standing at the moment of conception. However, there is nothing morally relevant about being human. The problem with both views, he says, is that they present a uniform account of the moral status of the fetus. He offers a "moderate" view in which fetuses develop moral standing gradually. He says the **criterion** for moral standing should be sentience, the capacity to experience pleasure and pain. Fetuses develop this capacity sometime during the second trimester of pregnancy. Before this time, abortion is morally equivalent to contraception, and after it, abortion is morally equivalent to infanticide (that is, murder).

Susan Sherwin argues that feminist pro-choice arguments differ significantly from non-feminist arguments. Feminists believe many social practices and institutions still subordinate women, such as family expectations and rape. Abortion rights are part of a long-running feminist campaign to help women avoid unwanted pregnancies that began with birth control and ends with access to abortions. As a result, feminist discussions of abortion focus on the pregnant woman. Non-feminist accounts that focus on the fetus tend to make pregnant women secondary, if they consider them at all. They treat the fact that fetuses inhabit women's bodies as morally irrelevant. (Thomson does not.) Sherwin says the status of the fetus is necessarily relational; unlike a newborn, it cannot be separated from the woman who carries it. She also points out that most opponents of abortion also want to maintain a social system that subordinates women.

The Moral and Political Preferences Indicator

This is a make-or-break issue for social conservatives. Many people who are pro-life are also social conservatives, and all social conservatives are pro-life. Some other conservatives and some centrists are pro-life, but usually their views on abortion play a relatively small part in their larger political views. Those who are pro-choice range from libertarians to social democrats, holding every political view except social conservatism.

Roughly three-quarters of Canadians believe abortion should be allowed at least some of the time. Even more believe that abortion should be available in cases of rape and where a pregnancy that threatens woman's life. Most pro-choice Canadians view the moral status of the fetus as Sumner does—it is unlike a newborn at the beginning of pregnancy, and much like one at the end. The further towards egalitarianism someone's views are, the more likely it is that they will be pro-choice; virtually all social democrats are pro-choice.

Abortion also is a make-or-break issue for feminists: to be a feminist in North America is to be pro-choice. The movement for abortion rights grew out of the feminist movement for birth control. Feminists see control over reproduction, including abortion, as a **necessary condition** for women's autonomy.

People born with disabilities are more likely to be pro-life than members of the general population, even if they are not social or any other kind of conservative. Most pro-choice supporters think a woman who gets an abortion because she is carrying a fetus/unborn child with a disability is justified. Many think she is doing the right thing, and some even think she *ought* to have an abortion. This worries people with disabilities, who already are told by strangers that they should never have been born.[13] They worry that, if most people see disabilities as calamities that ought to be prevented, the lives of people with disabilities will go even less well than they do today. Even feminists with disabilities tend to be conflicted about abortion in ways that non-disabled feminists are not; their feminism and their disability rights views pull them in different directions.

Notes

1. Since there is no neutral term—pro-choice advocates prefer "fetus" while pro-life advocates prefer "unborn child"—I use both unless the context dictates otherwise.
2. Department of Economic and Social Affairs Population Division, *Abortion Policies: A Global Review* (New York: United Nations, 2001), vol. I, pp. 83–5, 94–6, 120–1.
3. World Health Organization, *Safe Abortion: Technical and Policy Guidance for Health Systems* (Geneva: World Health Organization, 2003) p. 12.
4. Siegrid Tautz, "(Un)Safe Abortion," Deutsche Gesellschaft für Technische Zusammenarbeit (German Society for Technical Cooperation), Sector Project Reproductive Health, 2004: 3.
5. Tautz, p. 2; *Abortion Policies*, vol. I, p. 5.
6. *Abortion Policies*, vol. I, pp. 92–3.
7. Cited in Lidia Casas-Becerra, "Women Prosecuted and Imprisoned for Abortion in Chile, *Reproductive Health Matters* 9 (1997): 35, note 3.
8. *Safe Abortion*, p. 12.
9. The defence of necessity may be used if a defendant broke a law to avoid a significant harm, if there was no adequate way to avoid the harm without breaking the law, and if the harm avoided was greater than the harm of breaking the law. Suppose some people are hiking in the mountains and a storm comes up suddenly. If they break into an unoccupied cabin to avoid freezing to death, they may use the defence of necessity against trespassing charges.
10. Appeals courts did not normally overturn juries' acquittals because this undermined the very purpose of trying an accused person by a jury of his or her **peers** (equals): the common law is supposed to make common sense to common people.
11. Appeals courts can overturn jury acquittals and order new trials, but they can no longer find defendants guilty and impose sentences. Courts can, however, overturn juries' verdicts of *guilt* and either order new trials or acquit defendants outright, because this upholds the **presumption of innocence** (the assumption that an accused person is innocent until proven guilty beyond a reasonable doubt).
12. Why "almost equal"? Because the fetus/unborn child does not yet exist independently of the pregnant woman.
13. Personal communication with a friend who has been blind since birth.

Judith Jarvis Thomson
A Defence of Abortion

AV = author's view; ~AV = not the author's view

Most opposition to abortion relies on the premise that the fetus is a human being, a person, from the moment of conception. The premise is argued for, but, as I think, not well. Take, for example, the most common argument. ~AV We are asked to notice that the development of a human being from conception through birth into childhood is continuous; then it is said that to draw a line, to choose a point in this development and say "before this point the thing is not a person, after this point it is a person" is to make an arbitrary choice, a choice for which in the nature of things no good reason can be given. It is concluded that the fetus is, or anyway that we had better say it is, a person from the moment of conception. AV But this conclusion does not follow. Similar things might be said about the development of an acorn into an oak tree, and it does not follow that acorns are oak trees, or that we had better say they are. . . .

I am inclined to agree, however, that the prospects for "drawing a line" in the development of the fetus look dim. . . .

I propose, then, that we grant that the fetus is a person from the moment of conception. How does the argument go from here? Something like this, I take it: ~AV Every person has a right to life. So the fetus has a right to life. No doubt the mother has a right to decide what shall happen in and to her body; everyone would grant that. But surely a person's right to life is stronger and more stringent than the mother's right to decide what happens in and to her body, and so outweighs it. So the fetus may not be killed; an abortion may not be performed.

AV It sounds plausible. But now let me ask you to imagine this. You wake up in the morning and find yourself back to back in bed with an unconscious violinist. A famous unconscious violinist. He has been found to have a fatal kidney ailment, and the Society of Music Lovers has canvassed all the available medical records and found that you alone have the right blood type to help. They have therefore kidnapped you, and last night the violinist's circulatory system was plugged into yours, so that your kidneys can be used to extract poisons from his blood as well as your own. The director of the hospital now tells you, "Look, we're sorry the Society of Music Lovers did this to you—we would never have permitted it if we had known. But still, they did it, and the violinist now is plugged into you. To unplug you would be to kill him. But never mind, it's only for nine months. By then he will have recovered from his ailment, and can safely be unplugged from you." Is it morally incumbent on you to accede to this situation? No doubt it would be very nice of you if you did, a great kindness. But do you *have* to accede to it? What if it were not nine months, but nine years? Or longer still? What if the director of the hospital says, "Tough luck, I agree, but you've now got to stay in bed, with the violinist plugged into you, for the rest of your life. Because remember this. All persons have a right to life, and violinists are persons. Granted you have a right to decide what happens in and to your body, but a person's right to life outweighs your right to decide what happens in and to your body. So you cannot ever be unplugged from him." I imagine you would regard this as outrageous, which suggests that something really is wrong with that plausible-sounding argument I mentioned a moment ago.

In this case, of course, you were kidnapped; you didn't volunteer for the operation that plugged the violinist into your kidneys. Can those who oppose abortion on the ground I mentioned make an exception for a pregnancy due to rape? Certainly. ~AV They can say that persons have a right to life only if they didn't come into existence because of rape; or they can say that all persons have a right to life, but that some have less of a right to life than others, in particular, that those who came into existence because of rape have less. AV But these statements have a rather unpleasant sound. Surely the question of whether you have a right to life at all, or how much of it you have, shouldn't turn on the question of whether or not you are the product of a rape. And in fact the people who oppose abortion on the ground I mentioned do not make this distinction, and hence do not make an exception in case of rape.

. . . ~AV Some won't even make an exception for a case in which continuation of the pregnancy is likely to shorten the mother's life; they regard abortion as impermissible even to save the mother's life. AV Such cases are nowadays very rare, and many opponents of abortion do not accept this extreme view. All the same, it is a good place to begin: a number of points of interest come out in respect to it.

1. [The Extreme View of Abortion]

Let us call the view that abortion is impermissible even to save the mother's life "the extreme view." I want to suggest first that it does not issue from the argument I mentioned earlier without the addition of some fairly powerful premises. Suppose a woman has become pregnant, and now learns that she has a cardiac condition such that she will die if she carries the baby to term. What may be done for her? The fetus, being a person, has a right to life, but as the mother is a person too, so has she a right to life. Presumably they have an equal right to life. How is it supposed to come out that an abortion may not be performed? . . .

~AV The most familiar argument here is the following: We are told that performing the abortion would be directly killing the child, whereas doing nothing would not be killing the mother, but only letting her die. Moreover, in killing the child, one would be killing an innocent person, for the child has committed no crime, and is not aiming at his mother's death. And then there are a variety of ways in which this might be continued. (1) But as directly killing an innocent person is always and absolutely impermissible, an abortion may not be performed. Or, (2) as directly killing an innocent person is murder, and murder is always and absolutely impermissible, an abortion may not be performed. Or, (3) as one's duty to refrain from directly killing an innocent person is more stringent than one's duty to keep a person from dying, an abortion may not be performed. Or, (4) if one's only options are directly killing an innocent person or letting a person die, one must prefer letting the person die, and thus an abortion may not be performed.

Some people seem to have thought that these are not further premises which must be added if the conclusion is to be reached, but that they follow from the very fact that an innocent person has a right to life. (AV) But this seems to me to be a mistake, and perhaps the simplest way to show this is to bring out that while we must certainly grant that innocent persons have a right to life, the theses in (1) through (4) are all false. Take (2), for example. (~AV) If directly killing an innocent person is murder, and thus is impermissible, then the mother's directly killing the innocent person inside her is murder, and thus is impermissible. (AV) But it cannot seriously be thought to be murder if the mother performs an abortion on herself to save her life. It cannot seriously be said that she must refrain, that she must sit passively by and wait for her death. . . .

I should perhaps stop to say explicitly that I am not claiming that people have a right to do anything whatever to save their lives. I think, rather, that there are drastic limits to the right of self-defence. If someone threatens you with death unless you torture someone else to death, I think you have not the right, even to save your life, to do so. But the case under consideration here is very different. In our case there are only two people involved, one whose life is threatened, and one who threatens it. Both are innocent. . . . For this reason we may feel that we bystanders cannot intervene. But the person threatened can.

In sum, a woman surely can defend her life against the threat to it posed by the unborn child, even if doing so involves its death. And this shows not merely that the theses in (1) through (4) are false; it shows also that the extreme view of abortion is false, and so we need not canvass any other possible ways of arriving at it from the argument I mentioned at the outset.

2. [Others May Perform Abortions]

(~AV) The extreme view could of course be weakened to say that while abortion is permissible to save the mother's life, it may not be performed by a third party, but only by the mother herself. (AV) But this cannot be right either. For what we have to keep in mind is that the mother and the unborn child are not like two tenants in a small house which has, by an unfortunate mistake, been rented to both: the mother *owns* the house. . . .

We should really ask what it is that says "no one may choose" in the face of the fact that the body that houses the child is the mother's body. It may be simply a failure to appreciate this fact. But it may be something more interesting, namely the sense that one has a right to refuse to lay hands on people, even where it would be just and fair to do so, even where justice seems to require that somebody do so. . . . This, I think, must be granted. But then what should be said is not "no one may choose," but only "I cannot choose," and indeed not even this, but "*I* will not *act*," leaving it open that somebody else can or should, and in particular that anyone in a position of authority, with the job of securing people's rights, both can and should. So this is no difficulty. I have not been arguing that any given third party must accede to the mother's request that he perform an abortion to save her life, but only that he may. . . .

3. [The Right to Life Does Not Include the Right to Use Another's Body]

(~AV) Where the mother's life is not at stake, the argument I mentioned at the outset seems to have a much stronger pull. "Everyone has a right to life, so the unborn person has a right to life." And isn't the child's right to life weightier than anything other than the mother's own right to life, which she might put forward as ground for an abortion?

AV This argument treats the right to life as if it were unproblematic. It is not, and this seems to me to be precisely the source of the mistake.

For we should now, at long last, ask what it comes to, to have a right to life. In some views having a right to life includes having a right to be given at least the bare minimum one needs for continued life. . . .

~AV Some people are rather stricter about the right to life. In their view, it does not include the right to be given anything, but amounts to, and only to, the right not to be killed by anybody. AV But here a related difficulty arises. If everybody is to refrain from killing that violinist, then everybody must refrain from doing a great many different sorts of things. Everybody must refrain from slitting his throat, everybody must refrain from shooting him—and everybody must refrain from unplugging you from him. But does he **have a right against** everybody that they shall refrain from unplugging you from him? To refrain from doing this is to allow him to continue to use your kidneys. ~AV It could be argued that he has a right against us that we should allow him to continue to use your kidneys. . . . AV But certainly the violinist has no right against you that you shall allow him to continue to use your kidneys. . . .

The difficulty I point to here is not peculiar to the right to life. It reappears in connection with all the other **natural rights**; and it is something which an adequate account of rights must deal with. . . . I am arguing only that having a right to life does not guarantee having either a right to be given the use of or a right to be allowed continued use of another person's body—even if one needs it for life itself. So the right to life will not serve the opponents of abortion in the very simple and clear way in which they seem to have thought it would.

4. [Rights and Injustice]

AV There is another way to bring out the difficulty. In the most ordinary sort of case, to deprive someone of what he has a right to is to treat him unjustly. Suppose a boy and his small brother are jointly given a box of chocolates for Christmas. If the older boy takes the box and refuses to give his brother any of the chocolates, he is unjust to him, for the brother has been given a right to half of them. But suppose that, having learned that otherwise it means nine years in bed with that violinist, you unplug yourself from him. You surely are not being unjust to him, for you gave him no right to use your kidneys, and no one else can have given him any such right. But we have to notice that in unplugging yourself, you are killing him; and violinists, like everybody else, have a right to life, and thus in the view we were considering just now, the right not to be killed. So here you do what he supposedly has a right you shall not do, but you do not act unjustly to him in doing it. . . .

~AV But it might be argued that there are other ways one can have acquired a right to the use of another person's body than by having been invited to use it by that person. Suppose a woman voluntarily indulges in intercourse, knowing of the chance it will issue in pregnancy, and then she does become pregnant; is she not in part responsible for the presence, in fact the very existence, of the unborn person inside her? No doubt she did not invite it in. But doesn't her partial responsibility for its being there itself give it a right to the use of her body? If so, then her aborting it would be more like the boy's taking away the chocolates, and less like your unplugging yourself from the violinist—doing so would be depriving it of what it does have a right to, and thus would be doing it an injustice.

And then, too, it might be asked whether or not she can kill it even to save her own life: If she voluntarily called it into existence, how can she now kill it, even in self-defence?

AV The first thing to be said about this is that it is something new. Opponents of abortion have been so concerned to make out the independence of the fetus, in order to establish that it has a right to life, just as its mother does, that they have tended to overlook the possible support they might gain from making out that the fetus is *dependent* on the mother, in order to establish that she has a special kind of responsibility for it, a responsibility that gives it rights against her which are not possessed by any independent person—such as an ailing violinist who is a stranger to her.

On the other hand, this [objection] would give the unborn person a right to its mother's body only if her pregnancy resulted from a voluntary act, undertaken in full knowledge of the chance a pregnancy might result from it. It would leave out entirely the unborn person whose existence is due to rape. . . .

. . . It seems to me that the argument we are looking at can establish at most that there are some cases in which the unborn person has a right to the use of its mother's body, and therefore *some* cases in which abortion is unjust killing. There is room for much discussion and argument as to precisely which, if any. But I think we should sidestep this issue and leave it open, for at any rate the argument certainly does not establish that all abortion is unjust killing.

5. [Rights and Moral Indecency]

~AV There is room for yet another argument here, however. We surely must all grant that there may be cases in which it would be morally indecent to detach a person from your body at the cost of his life. Suppose you learn that what the violinist needs is not nine years of your life, but only one hour: all you need do to save his life is to spend one hour in that bed with him. Suppose also that letting him use your kidneys for that one hour would not affect your health in the slightest. Admittedly you were kidnapped. Admittedly you did not give anyone permission to plug him into you. Nevertheless it seems to me plain you *ought* to allow him to use your kidneys for that hour—it would be indecent to refuse.

Again, suppose pregnancy lasted only an hour, and constituted no threat to life or health. And suppose that a woman becomes pregnant as a result of rape. Admittedly she did not voluntarily do anything to bring about the existence of a child. Admittedly she did nothing at all which would give the unborn person a right to the use of her body. All the same it might well be said, as in the newly emended [changed] violinist story, that she *ought* to allow it to remain for that hour—that it would be indecent in her to refuse.

Now some people are inclined to use the term "right" in such a way that it follows from the fact that you ought to allow a person to use your body for the hour he needs, that he has a right to use your body for the hour he needs, even though he has not been given that right by any person or act. They may say that it follows also that if you refuse, you act unjustly toward him. AV This use of the term is perhaps so common that it cannot be called wrong; nevertheless it seems to me to be an unfortunate loosening of what we would do better to keep a tight rein on. . . .

So my own view is that even though you ought to let the violinist use your kidneys for the one hour he needs, we should not conclude that he has a right to do so. . . . And similarly, that even supposing a case in which a woman pregnant due to rape ought to allow the unborn person to use her body for the hour he needs, we should not conclude that he has a right to do so; we should conclude that she is self-centered, callous, indecent, but not unjust, if she refuses. The complaints are no less grave; they are just different. However, there is no need to insist on this point. . . .

6. [Good and Minimally Decent Samaritans]

We have in fact to distinguish between two kinds of Samaritan: the Good Samaritan and what we might call the Minimally Decent Samaritan. The story of the Good Samaritan, you will remember, goes like this:

> A certain man went down from Jerusalem to Jericho, and fell among thieves, which stripped him of his raiment [clothing], and wounded him, and departed, leaving him half dead.
>
> And by chance there came down a certain priest that way; and when he saw him, he passed by on the other side.
>
> And likewise a Levite, when he was at the place, came and looked on him, and passed by on the other side.
>
> But a certain Samaritan, as he journeyed, came where he was; and when he saw him he had compassion on him.
>
> And went to him, and bound up his wounds, pouring in oil and wine, and set him on his own beast, and brought him to an inn, and took care of him.
>
> And on the morrow, when he departed, he took out two pence, and gave them to the host, and said unto him, "Take care of him; and whatsoever thou spendest more, when I come again, I will repay thee." (Luke 10:30–35)

The Good Samaritan went out of his way, at some cost to himself, to help one in need of it. We are not told what the options were, that is, whether or not the priest and the Levite could have helped by doing less than the Good Samaritan did, but assuming they could have, then the fact they did nothing at all shows they were not even Minimally Decent Samaritans, not because they were not Samaritans, but because they were not even minimally decent.

These things are a matter of degree, of course, but there is a difference, and it comes out perhaps most clearly in the story of Kitty Genovese, who, as you will remember, was murdered while thirty-eight people watched or listened, and did nothing at all to help her.[1] A Good Samaritan would have rushed out to give direct assistance against the murderer. Or perhaps we had better allow that it would have been a Splendid Samaritan who did this, on the ground that it would have involved a risk of death for himself. But the thirty-eight not only did not do this, they did not even trouble to pick up a phone to call the police. Minimally Decent Samaritanism would call for doing at least that, and their not having done it was monstrous. . . .

Indeed, with one rather striking class of exceptions, no one in any country in the world is *legally* required to do anywhere near as much as this for anyone else. The class of exceptions is obvious. . . . [I]n most states in this country women are compelled by law to be not merely Minimally Decent Samaritans, but Good Samaritans to unborn persons inside them.[2] This doesn't by itself settle anything one way or the other. . . . But it does show that there is a gross injustice in the existing state of the law. And it shows also that the groups currently working against **liberalization** of abortion laws, in fact working toward having it declared **unconstitutional** for a state to permit abortion, had better start working for the adoption of Good Samaritan laws generally, or earn the charge that they are acting in bad faith.

. . . What we should ask is not whether anybody should be compelled by law to be a Good Samaritan, but whether we must accede to a situation in which somebody is being compelled—by nature, perhaps—to be a Good Samaritan. We have, in other words, to look now at third party interventions. I have been arguing that no person is morally required to make large sacrifices to sustain the life of another who has no right to demand them, and this even where the sacrifices do not include life itself; we are not morally required to be Good Samaritans or anyway Very Good Samaritans to one another. But what if a man cannot **extricate** himself from such a situation? What if he appeals to us to extricate him? It seems to me plain that there are cases in which we can, cases in which a Good Samaritan would extricate him. There you are, you were kidnapped, and nine years in bed with that violinist lie ahead of you. You have your own life to lead. You are sorry, but you simply cannot see giving up so much of your life to the sustaining of his. You cannot extricate yourself, and ask us to do so. . . . There is no injustice to the violinist in our doing so.

7. [Rights and Responsibility]

. . . ~AV But of course there are arguments and arguments, and it may be said that I have simply fastened on the wrong one. It may be said that what is important is not merely the fact that the fetus is a person, but that it is a person for whom the woman has a special kind of responsibility issuing from the fact that she is its mother. And it might be argued that all my analogies are therefore irrelevant—for you do not have that special kind of responsibility for that violinist. . . . And our attention might be drawn to the fact that men and women both are compelled by law to provide support for their children.

AV I have in effect dealt (briefly) with this argument in [Rights and Injustice] above; but a (still briefer) recapitulation now may be in order. Surely we do not have any such "special responsibility" for a person unless we have assumed it, explicitly or implicitly. If a set of parents do not try to prevent pregnancy, do not obtain an abortion, and then at the time of birth of the child do not put it out for adoption, but rather take it home with them, then they have assumed responsibility for it, they have given it rights, and they cannot now withdraw support from it at the cost of its life because they now find it difficult to go on providing for it. . . . I am suggesting that if assuming responsibility for it would require large sacrifices, then they may refuse. A Good Samaritan would not refuse—or anyway, a Splendid Samaritan, if the sacrifices that had to be made were enormous. But then so would a Good Samaritan assume responsibility for that violinist. . . .

8. [Conclusion]

. . . [W]hile I do argue that abortion is not impermissible, I do not argue that it is always permissible. There may well be cases in which carrying the child to term requires only

Minimally Decent Samaritanism of the mother, and this is a standard we must not fall below. I am inclined to think it a merit of my account precisely that it does *not* give a general yes or a general no. It allows for and supports our sense that, for example, a sick and desperately frightened fourteen-year-old schoolgirl, pregnant due to rape, may *of course* choose abortion, and that any law which rules this out is an insane law. And it also allows for and supports our sense that in other cases resort to abortion is even positively indecent. It would be indecent in the woman to request an abortion, and indecent in a doctor to perform it, if she is in her seventh month, and wants the abortion just to avoid the nuisance of postponing a trip abroad. The very fact that the arguments I have been drawing attention to treat all cases of abortion, or even all cases of abortion in which the mother's life is not at stake, as morally on a par ought to have made them suspect at the outset.

... At this place, however, it should be remembered that we have only been pretending throughout that the fetus is a human being from the moment of conception. A very early abortion is surely not the killing of a person, and so is not dealt with by anything I have said here.

Notes

1. In 1964 in New York City, Kitty Genovese was raped and stabbed to death near her home. Between twelve and thirty-eight nearby people heard or saw at least some of the attack, which lasted approximately thirty minutes. The *New York Times* published a scathing article claiming that thirty-eight people watched Genovese die. One bystander apparently yelled at the attacker to stop and another said he called the police, who did nothing. Even so, between ten and thirty-six people were aware of the attack and did nothing at all. [Editor]
2. When this paper was originally published, abortion was illegal in the US. [Editor]

Don Marquis

Why Abortion Is Immoral

(AV) = author's view; (~AV) = not the author's view

... This essay sets out an argument that purports to show, as well as any argument in ethics can show, that abortion is, except possibly in rare cases, seriously immoral, that it is in the same moral category as killing an innocent adult human being.

The argument is based on a major assumption. Many of the most insightful and careful writers on the ethics of abortion ... believe that whether or not abortion is morally permissible stands or falls on whether or not a fetus is the sort of being whose life it is seriously wrong to end. The argument of this essay will assume, but not argue, that they are correct....

... Passions in the abortion debate run high. There are both plausibilities and difficulties with the standard positions. Accordingly, it is hardly surprising that partisans of either side embrace with fervor the moral generalizations that support the conclusions they pre-analytically favour, and reject with disdain the moral generalizations of their opponents as being subject to inescapable difficulties. It is easy to believe that the counterexamples to one's own moral principles are merely temporary difficulties that will dissolve in the wake of further philosophical research, and that the counterexamples to the principles of one's opponents are as straightforward as [logical contradictions]. . . . This might suggest to an impartial observer (if there are any) that the abortion issue is unresolvable.

There is a way out of this apparent dialectical quandary. The moral generalizations of both sides are not quite correct. The generalizations hold for the most part, for the usual cases. This suggests that they are all **accidental** generalizations; that the moral claims made by those on both sides of the dispute do not touch on the **essence** of the matter.

This use of the **distinction between essence and accident** is not meant to invoke obscure **metaphysical** categories. Rather, it is intended to reflect the rather **atheoretical** nature of the abortion discussion. If the generalization . . . [someone] adopts were derived from the reason why ending the life of a human being is wrong, then there could not be exceptions to that generalization unless some special case obtains in which there are even more powerful **countervailing** reasons. Such generalizations would not be merely accidental generalizations; they would point to, or be based upon, the essence of the wrongness of killing, what it is that makes killing wrong. All this suggests that a **necessary condition** of resolving the abortion controversy is a more theoretical account of the wrongness of killing. After all, if we merely believe, but do not understand, why killing adult human beings such as ourselves is wrong, how could we conceivably show that abortion is either immoral or permissible?

[Why Murder Is Wrong]

In order to develop such an account, we can start from the following unproblematic assumption concerning our own case: it is wrong to kill us. Why is it wrong? ~AV Some answers can be easily eliminated. It might be said that what makes killing us wrong is that a killing brutalizes the one who kills. AV But the brutalization consists of being **inured** to the performance of an act that is hideously immoral; hence, the brutalization does not explain the immorality. ~AV It might be said that what makes killing us wrong is the great loss others would experience due to our absence. AV Although such hubris is understandable, such an explanation does not account for the wrongness of killing hermits, or those whose lives are relatively independent and whose friends find it easy to make new friends.

A more obvious answer is better. What primarily makes killing wrong is neither its effect on the murderer nor its effect on the victim's friends and relatives, but its effect on the victim. The loss of one's life is one of the greatest losses one can suffer. The loss of one's life deprives one of all the experiences, activities, projects, and enjoyments that would otherwise have constituted one's future. Therefore, killing someone is wrong, primarily because the killing inflicts (one of) the greatest possible losses on the victim. To describe this as the loss of life can be misleading, however. The change in my biological state does not by itself make killing me wrong. The effect of the loss of my biological life is the loss to me of all those activities, projects, experiences, and enjoyments which would otherwise have constituted my future personal life. These activities, projects, experiences, and enjoyments are either valuable for their own sakes or are means to something else that is valuable for its own sake. Some parts of my future are not valued by me now, but will come to be valued by me as I grow older and as my values and capacities change. When I am killed, I am deprived both of what I now value which would have been part of my future personal life, but also what I would come to value. Therefore, when I die, I am deprived of all of the value of my future. Inflicting this loss on me is ultimately what makes killing me wrong. This being the case, it would seem that what makes killing any adult human being **prima facie** seriously wrong is the loss of his or her future. . . .

. . . The claim that what makes killing wrong is the loss of the victim's future is directly supported by two considerations. In the first place, this theory explains why we regard killing as one of the worst of crimes. Killing is especially wrong, because it deprives the victim of more than perhaps any other crime. In the second place, people with AIDS or cancer who know they are dying believe, of course, that dying is a very bad thing for them. They believe that the loss of a future to them that they would otherwise have experienced is what makes their **premature** death a very bad thing for them. A better theory of the wrongness of killing would require a different **natural property** associated with killing which better fits with the attitudes of the dying. What could it be?

The view that what makes killing wrong is the loss to the victim of the value of the victim's future gains additional support when some of its implications are examined. In the first place, it is incompatible with the view that it is wrong to kill only beings who are biologically human. It is possible that there exists a different species from another planet whose members have a future like ours. Since having a future like that is what makes killing someone wrong, this theory entails that it would be wrong to kill members of such a species. Hence, this theory is opposed to the claim that only life that is biologically human has great moral worth, a claim which many anti-abortionists have seemed to adopt. This opposition, which this theory has in common with **personhood** theories, seems to be a merit of the theory.

In the second place, the claim that the loss of one's future is the wrong-making feature of one's being killed entails the possibility that the futures of some actual nonhuman mammals on our own planet are sufficiently like ours that it is seriously wrong to kill them also. Whether some animals do have the same right to life as human beings depends on adding to the account of the wrongness of killing some additional account of just what it is about my future or the futures of other adult human beings which makes it wrong to kill us. No such additional account will be offered in this essay. Undoubtedly, the provision of such an account would be a very difficult matter. Undoubtedly, any such account would be quite controversial. Hence, it surely should not reflect badly on this sketch of an elementary theory of the wrongness of killing that it is indeterminate with respect to some very difficult issues regarding animal rights.

In the third place, the claim that the loss of one's future is the wrong-making feature of one's being killed does not entail, as **sanctity of human life theories** do, that **active euthanasia** is wrong. Persons who are severely and incurably ill, who face a future of pain and despair, and who wish to die will not have suffered a loss if they are killed. It is, strictly speaking, the value of a human's future which makes killing wrong in this theory. This being so, killing does not necessarily wrong some persons who are sick and dying. Of course, there may be other reasons for a prohibition of active euthanasia, but that is another matter. Sanctity-of-human-life theories seem to hold that active euthanasia is seriously wrong even in an individual case where there seems to be good reason for it independently of public policy considerations. This consequence is most implausible, and it is a plus for the claim that the loss of a future of value is what makes killing wrong that it does not share this consequence.

In the fourth place, the account of the wrongness of killing defended in this essay does straightforwardly entail that it is prima facie seriously wrong to kill children and infants, for we do presume that they have futures of value. Since we do believe that it is wrong to kill defenseless little babies, it is important that a theory of the wrongness of killing easily account for this. ~AV Personhood theories of the wrongness of killing, on the other hand, cannot straightforwardly account for the wrongness of killing infants and young children.[1] Hence, such theories must add special **ad hoc** accounts of the wrongness of killing the young. AV The plausibility of such ad hoc theories seems to be a function of how desperately one wants such theories to work. The claim that the primary wrong-making feature of a killing is the loss to the victim of the value of its future accounts for the wrongness of killing young children and infants directly; it makes the wrongness of such acts as obvious as we actually think it is. This is a further merit of this theory. Accordingly, it seems that this value of a future-like-ours theory of the wrongness of killing shares strengths of both sanctity-of-life and personhood accounts while avoiding weaknesses of both. In addition, it meshes with a central intuition concerning what makes killing wrong.

The claim that the primary wrong-making feature of a killing is the loss to the victim of the value of its future has obvious consequences for the ethics of abortion. The future of a standard fetus includes a set of experiences, projects, activities, and such which are identical with the futures of adult human beings and are identical with the futures of young children. Since the reason that is sufficient to explain why it is wrong to kill human beings after the time of birth is a reason that also applies to fetuses, it follows that abortion is prima facie seriously morally wrong.

This argument does not rely on the invalid **inference** that, since it is wrong to kill persons, it is wrong to kill potential persons also. The category that is morally central to this analysis is the category of having a valuable future like ours; it is not the category of personhood. The argument to the conclusion that abortion is prima facie seriously morally wrong proceeded independently of the notion of person or potential person or any equivalent. ~AV Someone may wish to start with this analysis in terms of the value of a human future, conclude that abortion is, except perhaps in rare circumstances, seriously morally wrong, infer that fetuses have the right to life, and then call fetuses "persons" as a result of their having the right to life. AV Clearly, in this case, the category of person is being used to state the conclusion of the analysis rather than to generate the argument of the analysis. . . .

[Two Alternative Accounts of the Wrongness of Killing]

. . . How complete an account of the wrongness of killing . . . does the value of a future-like-ours account have to be in order that the wrongness of abortion is a consequence? This account does not have to be an account of the necessary conditions for the wrongness of killing. Some persons in nursing homes may lack valuable human futures, yet it may be wrong to kill them for other reasons. Furthermore, this account does not obviously have to be the sole reason killing is wrong where the victim did have a valuable future. This analysis claims only that, for any killing where the victim did have a valuable future like ours, having that future by itself is **sufficient** to create the strong presumption that the killing is seriously wrong.

~AV One way to overturn the value of a future-like-ours argument would be to find some account of the wrongness of killing which is at least as intelligible and which has different implications for the ethics of abortion. Two rival accounts possess at least some degree of plausibility. One account is based on the obvious fact that people value the experience of living and wish for that valuable experience to continue. Therefore, it might be said, what makes killing wrong is the discontinuation of that experience for the victim. Let us call this the *discontinuation account*. Another rival account is based upon the obvious fact that people strongly desire to continue to live. This suggests that what makes killing us so wrong is that it interferes with the fulfillment of a strong and fundamental desire, the fulfillment of which is necessary for the fulfillment of any other desires we might have. Let us call this the desire account.

AV Consider first the desire account as a rival account of the ethics of killing which would provide the basis for rejecting the anti-abortion position. Such an account will have to be stronger than the value of a future-like-ours account of the wrongness of abortion if it is to do the job expected of it. To entail the wrongness of abortion, the value of a future-like-ours account has only to provide a **sufficient**, but not a necessary, **condition** for the wrongness of killing. The desire account, on the other hand, must provide us also with a necessary condition for the wrongness of killing in order to generate a pro-choice conclusion on abortion. The reason for this is that presumably the argument from the desire account moves from the claim that what makes killing wrong is interference with a very strong desire to the claim that abortion is not wrong because the fetus lacks a strong desire to live. Obviously, this inference fails if someone's having the desire to live is not a necessary condition of its being wrong to kill that individual.

One problem with the desire account is that we do regard it as seriously wrong to kill persons who have little desire to live or who have no desire to live or, indeed, have a desire not to live. We believe it is seriously wrong to kill the unconscious, the sleeping, those who are tired of life, and those who are suicidal. The value-of-a-human-future account renders standard morality intelligible in these cases; these cases appear to be incompatible with the desire account.

The desire account is subject to a deeper difficulty. We desire life because we value the goods of this life. The goodness of life is not secondary to our desire for it. If this were not so, the pain of one's own premature death could be done away with merely by an appropriate alteration in the configuration of one's desires. This is absurd. Hence, it would seem that it is the loss of the goods of one's future, not the interference with the fulfillment of a strong desire to live, which accounts ultimately for the wrongness of killing.

It is worth noting that, if the desire account is modified so that it does not provide a necessary, but only a sufficient, condition for the wrongness of killing, the desire account is compatible with the value of a future-like-ours account. The combined accounts will yield an anti-abortion ethic. This suggests that one can retain what is intuitively plausible about the desire account without a challenge to the basic argument of this paper.

It is also worth noting that, if future desires have moral force in a modified desire account of the wrongness of killing, one can find support for an anti-abortion ethic even in the absence of a value of a future-like-ours account. If one decides that a morally relevant property, the possession of which is sufficient to make it wrong to kill some individual, is the desire at some future time to live—one might decide to justify one's refusal to kill suicidal teenagers on these grounds, for example—then, since typical fetuses will have the desire in the future to live, it is wrong to kill typical fetuses. Accordingly, it does not seem that a desire account of the wrongness of killing can provide a justification of a pro-choice ethic of abortion which is nearly as adequate as the value of a human-future justification of an anti-abortion ethic.

~AV The discontinuation account looks more promising as an account of the wrongness of killing. It seems just as intelligible as the value of a future-like-ours account, but it does not justify an anti-abortion position. Obviously, if it is the continuation of one's activities, experiences, and projects, the loss of which makes killing wrong, then it is not wrong to kill fetuses for that reason, for fetuses do not have experiences, activities, and projects to be continued or discontinued. Accordingly, the discontinuation account does not have the anti-abortion consequences that the value of a future-like-ours account has. Yet, it seems as intelligible as the value of a future-like-ours account, for when we think of what would be wrong with our being killed, it does seem as if it is the discontinuation of what makes our lives worthwhile which makes killing us wrong.

AV Is the discontinuation account just as good an account as the value of a future-like-ours account? The discontinuation account will not be adequate at all, if it does not refer to the *value* of the experience that may be discontinued. One does not want the discontinuation account to make it wrong to kill a patient who begs for death and who is in severe pain that cannot be relieved short of killing. (I leave open the question of whether it is wrong for other reasons.) Accordingly, the discontinuation account must be more than a bare discontinuation account. It must make some reference to the positive value of the patient's experiences. But, by the same token, the value of a future-like-ours account cannot be a bare future account either. Just having a future surely does not itself rule out killing the above patient. This account must make some reference to the value of the patient's future experiences and projects also. Hence, both accounts involve the value of experiences, projects, and activities. So far we still have symmetry between the accounts.

The symmetry fades, however, when we focus on the time period of the value of the experiences, etc., which has moral consequences. Although both accounts leave open the possibility that the patient in our example may be killed, this possibility is left open only in virtue of the utterly bleak future for the patient. It makes no difference whether the patient's immediate past contains intolerable pain, or consists in being in a coma (which we can imagine is a situation of indifference), or consists in a life of value. If the patient's future is a future of value, we want our account to make it wrong to kill the patient. If the patient's future is intolerable, whatever his or her immediate past, we want our account to allow killing the patient. Obviously, then, it is the value of that patient's future which is doing the work in rendering the morality of killing the patient intelligible.

This being the case, it seems clear that whether one has immediate past experiences or not does no work in the explanation of what makes killing wrong. The addition the discontinuation account makes to the value of a human future account is otiose [worthless]. Its addition to the value-of-a-future account plays no role at all in rendering intelligible the wrongness of killing. Therefore, it can be discarded with the discontinuation account of which it is a part.

[Objections to the Value of a Future-like-Ours]

The analysis of the previous section suggests that alternative general accounts of the wrongness of killing are either inadequate or unsuccessful in getting around the anti-abortion consequences of the value of a future-like-ours argument. ~AV A different strategy for avoiding these anti-abortion consequences involves limiting the scope of the value of a future argument. More precisely, the strategy involves arguing that fetuses lack a property that is essential for the value-of-a-future argument (or for any anti-abortion argument) to apply to them.

One move of this sort is based upon the claim that a necessary condition of one's future being valuable is that one values it. Value implies a valuer. Given this one might argue that, since fetuses cannot value their futures, their futures are not valuable to them. Hence, it does not seriously wrong them deliberately to end their lives.

AV This move fails, however, because of some ambiguities. Let us assume that something cannot be of value unless it is valued by someone. This does not entail that my life is of no value unless it is valued by me. I may think, in a period of despair, that my future is of no worth whatsoever, but I may be wrong because others rightly see value—even great value—in it. Furthermore, my future can be valuable to me even if I do not value it. This is the case when a young person attempts suicide, but is rescued and goes on to significant human achievements. Such young people's futures are ultimately valuable to them, even though such futures do not seem to be valuable to them at the moment of attempted suicide. A fetus's future can be valuable to it in the same way. Accordingly, this attempt to limit the anti-abortion argument fails. . . .

. . .

The seeming plausibility of Bassen's view stems from the fact that **paradigmatic** cases of imagining someone as a victim involve empathy, and empathy requires mentation of the victim. The victims of flood, famine, rape, or child abuse are all persons with whom we can empathize. That empathy seems to be part of seeing them as victims.

In spite of the strength of these examples, the attractive intuition that a situation in which there is victimization requires the possibility of empathy is subject to counterexamples. Consider a case that Bassen himself offers: "Posthumous obliteration of an author's work constitutes a misfortune for him only if he had wished his work to endure" (*op cit.*, p. 318). The conditions Bassen wishes to impose upon the possibility of being victimized here seem far too strong. Perhaps this author, due to his unrealistic standards of excellence and his low self-esteem, regarded his work as unworthy of survival, even though it possessed genuine literary merit. Destruction of such work would surely victimize its author. In such a case, empathy with the victim concerning the loss is clearly impossible.

Of course, Bassen does not make the possibility of empathy a necessary condition of victimizability; he requires only mentation. Hence, on Bassen's actual view, this author, as I have described him, can be a victim. The problem is that the basic intuition that renders Bassen's view plausible is missing in the author's case. In order to attempt to avoid counterexamples, Bassen has made his thesis too weak to be supported by the intuitions that suggested it.

Even so, the mentation requirement on victimizability is still subject to counterexamples. Suppose a severe accident renders me totally unconscious for a month, after which I recover. Surely killing me while I am unconscious victimizes me, even though I am incapable of mentation during that time. It follows that Bassen's thesis fails. Apparently, attempts to restrict the value of a future-like-ours argument so that fetuses do not fall within its scope do not succeed. . . .

Note

1. A personhood theory (a) argues that "persons" (individuals, who may or may not be human) have moral status, and (b) suggests criteria for personhood. Both pro-life and pro-choice philosophers use personhood theories, though Marquis implies here that only pro-choice philosophers do. [Editor]

L.W. Sumner
Abortion

AV = author's view; ~AV = not the author's view

Among the assortment of moral problems that have come to be known as biomedical ethics none has received as much attention from philosophers as abortion. . . . Despite both the quantity and the quality of this philosophical work, however, abortion remains one of the most intractable moral issues of our time.

. . . Abortion, in the sense in which it is controversial, is the intentional termination of pregnancy for its own sake—that is, regardless of the consequences for the fetus. Pregnancy, in turn, is a peculiar sort of relationship between a woman and a peculiar sort of being. It is a peculiar sort of relationship because the fetus is temporarily lodged within and physically connected to the body of its mother, on whom it is directly dependent for life support. . . .

The fetus is a peculiar sort of being because it is a human individual during the earliest stage in its life history. Although there are some difficult and puzzling questions to be asked about when the life history of such an individual may properly be said to begin, we will assume for convenience that this occurs at conception. It will also be convenient, though somewhat inaccurate, to use the term "fetus" to refer indiscriminately to all gestational stages from fertilized **ovum** through **blastocyst** and **embryo** to fetus proper. A (human) fetus, then, is a human individual during that period temporally bounded in one direction by conception and in the other (at the latest) by birth. . . .

Abortion is morally perplexing because it terminates this peculiar relationship and causes the death of this peculiar being. It thus occupies an ambiguous position between two other practices—contraception and infanticide—of whose moral status we are more certain. . . . Thus, most of us are likely to believe that, barring special circumstances, infanticide is morally serious and requires some special justification while contraception is morally innocuous and requires no such justification. One way of clarifying the moral status of abortion, therefore, is to locate it on this contraception-infanticide continuum, thus telling us whether it is in relevant respects more like the former or the latter.

. . . Clarifying the moral status of abortion thus requires above all clarifying the **moral status** of the fetus. . . . Let us say that a being has **moral standing** if it merits moral consideration in its own right and not just in virtue of its relations with other beings. To have moral standing is to be more than a mere thing or item of property. What, more precisely, moral standing consists in can be given different interpretations; thus, it might be the possession of some set of basic moral rights, or the requirement that one be **treated as an end and not merely as a means**, or the inclusion of one's interest in a calculus of social welfare. However it is interpreted, whether a being is accorded moral standing must make a great difference in the way in which we take that being into account in our moral thinking. Whether a fetus is accorded moral standing must therefore make a great difference in the way in which we think about abortion. . . .

A complete view of abortion, one that answers the main moral questions posed by the practice of abortion, is an ordered compound of three elements: an account of the moral status of the fetus, which grounds an account of the moral status of abortion, which in turn grounds a defense of an abortion policy. It is not enough, however, that a view of abortion be complete—it must also be well grounded. If we explore what is required to support an account of the moral status of the fetus, we will discover what it means for a view of abortion to be well grounded. The main requirement at this level is a **criterion** of moral standing that will specify the natural characteristics whose possession is both **necessary and sufficient** for the possession of moral standing. A criterion of moral standing will therefore have the following form: **all and only** beings with characteristic C have moral standing. . . . Such a criterion will define the proper scope of our moral concern, telling us for all moral contexts which beings must be accorded moral consideration in their own right. Thus it will determine, among other things, the moral status of inanimate natural objects, artifacts, nonhuman animals, body parts, super-intelligent computers, androids, and extraterrestrials. It will also determine the moral status of human fetuses. An account of the moral status of the fetus is well grounded when it is derivable from an independently plausible criterion of moral standing. The independent plausibility of such a criterion is partly established by following out its implications for moral contexts other than abortion. But a criterion of moral standing can also be given a deeper justification by being grounded in a moral theory. . . . By providing us with a picture of the content and structure of morality, a moral theory will tell us, among other things, which beings merit moral consideration in their own right and what form this consideration should take. It will thereby generate and support a criterion of immoral standing, thus serving as the last line of defence for a view of abortion.

The Established Views

We are seeking a view of abortion that is both complete and well-grounded. . . . Our search will be facilitated if we begin by examining the main contenders. ~AV The abortion debate in most of the Western democracies has been dominated by two positions that are so well entrenched that they may be called the established views. The liberal view supports what is popularly known as the "pro-choice" position on abortion. At its heart is the contention that the fetus at every stage of pregnancy has no moral standing. From this premise it follows that although abortion kills the fetus it does not wrong it, since a being with no moral standing cannot be wronged. . . . The conservative view, however, supports what is popularly known as the "pro-life" position on abortion. At its heart is the contention that the fetus at every stage of pregnancy has full moral standing—the same status as an adult human being. From this premise it follows that because abortion kills the fetus it also wrongs it. . . .

AV Before exploring these views separately, we should note an important feature that they share. . . . [W]hile the established views occupy the opposite extremes along the spectrum of possible positions on this issue, there is a logical space between them.[1] . . . Both of the established views are committed to holding that all of the beings at all stages of this transition have precisely the same moral status. The gestational age of the fetus at the time of abortion is thus morally irrelevant on both views. So also is the reason for the abortion. This is irrelevant on the liberal view because no reason is **necessary** to justify abortion at any stage of pregnancy and equally irrelevant to the conservative view because no reason is **sufficient** to do so. The established views, therefore, despite their differences, agree on two very important matters: the moral relevance of both when and why an abortion is performed.

This agreement places the established views at odds with both common practice and common opinion in most of the Western democracies. A moderate abortion policy regulates abortion either by imposing a time limit or by **stipulating** recognized grounds (or both). The abortion policies of virtually all of the Western democracies (and many other countries as well) now contain one or both of these constraints. But neither of the established views can provide any support for a moderate policy. . . .

The existence of this gap is not in itself a reason for rejecting either of the established views. The majority may simply be mistaken on these issues, and the dominance of moderate policies may reflect nothing more than the fact that they are attractive political compromises when the public debate has been polarized by the established views. Neither political practice nor public opinion can provide a justification for a moderate view of abortion or a moderate abortion policy. But the gap does provide us with a motive for exploring the logical space between the established views a little more carefully.

The Liberal View

~AV Meanwhile, however, it is time for a closer examination of the established views. . . . The liberal view requires some criterion that will deny moral standing to fetuses at all stages of pregnancy. Obviously no characteristic will serve that is acquired sometime during the normal course of fetal development. One characteristic that would certainly suffice is that of having been born. This characteristic cannot (logically) belong to any fetus, and it also serves to distinguish fetuses as a class from all later stages of human beings. Building this characteristic into a criterion of moral standing would thus enable the liberal to distinguish abortion, even late abortion, from infanticide, and thus to condone the former while condemning the latter.

AV But it is pretty clear that no acceptable criterion of moral standing can be constructed in this fashion; it is simply an **ad hoc** device designed to yield a liberal view of abortion while avoiding an equally liberal view of infanticide. Nor does it seem to be supportable by some more plausible criterion. Its effect is to mark birth as a crucial moral **watershed**, separating beings that lack moral standing (**gametes**, fetuses) from beings that possess it (infants, children, adults). But birth is merely the process whereby the fetus ceases to be housed within and physically connected to the body of its mother. It is difficult to see how we could justify denying moral standing to a being simply because it is housed within or physically connected to the body of another. Neither of these characteristics appears to be relevant to the question of whether we must accord the being some degree of moral consideration in its own right. Furthermore, birth is an abrupt discontinuity in the normal course of human reproduction. It seems unlikely on the face of it that moral standing could be acquired so suddenly (i.e., that killing a full-term fetus moments before birth could be morally inconsequential while killing a neonate [newborn] moments after birth could constitute homicide). But if this is so, then birth cannot be a crucial moral watershed, and being born cannot be a necessary condition of having moral standing.

~AV . . . Liberals need a more plausible criterion of moral standing that will nonetheless deny standing to all fetuses. It is apparent that any such criterion will need to set a fairly high standard, one that is beyond the reach of any fetus, however highly developed. Liberals who have sought such a standard have tended to favor such capacities as **self-consciousness** and **rationality**. . . .

AV The best defense of a liberal view of abortion grounds it in either a self-consciousness or a rationality criterion of moral standing. . . . But such a high standard generates its own difficulties. Some of these will arise in contexts other than abortion. Thus, for instance, some mentally handicapped adults may have difficulty meeting this standard and may therefore be denied moral standing by it. But the problem that is more pertinent to our inquiry concerns newborn infants. If a full-term fetus is neither self-conscious nor rational, so also a newborn infant is neither self-conscious nor rational. But then the liberal view of abortion has become also a liberal view of infanticide.

In all morally relevant respects, a full-term fetus and a newborn infant appear to be identical. A liberal will therefore find it difficult or impossible to support the common conviction of the moral seriousness of infanticide. . . . At least some of the reasons for seeking an abortion cannot apply to infanticide: an infant cannot pose a physical threat to the life or health of its mother, and if rearing it would be burdensome, there is the alternative of adoption. Furthermore, when the same reason can apply in both contexts—as in the case of a severe abnormality—it is not obvious that infanticide is morally indefensible. Finally, it is also open to the liberal simply to bite the bullet and challenge the common conviction of the moral seriousness of infanticide as a taboo for which there is no rational justification. Abandoning the taboo would in that case be a small price to pay for an otherwise plausible view of abortion.

However, the liberal's difficulties concerning infanticide are not so easily dealt with. Both self-consciousness and rationality are sophisticated bundles of abilities; they may, for instance, be beyond the reach of all nonhuman animals. They are therefore likely to be lacked not only by newborn infants but also by all infants, and perhaps as well by young children. We would need a much fuller account of these capacities in order to be able to locate the stage in the normal course of human development when they are acquired. . . .

The Conservative View

~AV When we turn to the conservative view, most of the difficulties that we encounter are counterparts of those that confront the liberal. This discovery should not surprise us, since these difficulties are caused by the adoption of a uniform account of the moral status of the fetus, a feature that is common to both established views. The conservative requires a criterion of moral standing that will confer such standing upon fetuses at all stages of pregnancy. Obviously no characteristic will serve that is acquired sometime during the normal course of fetal development. One characteristic that would certainly suffice is that of having been conceived. This characteristic must logically belong to all fetuses, and it also serves to distinguish all temporal stages of human beings from the genetic materials out of which they are formed. . . .

AV But it is fairly clear that no acceptable criterion of moral standing can be constructed in this fashion; it is simply an ad hoc device designed to yield a conservative view of abortion while avoiding an equally conservative view of contraception. Nor does it seem to be supportable by some more plausible criterion. Its effect is to mark conception as a crucial moral watershed, separating beings that lack moral standing (gametes) from beings that possess it (fetuses, infants, children, adults). But conception is merely the process whereby two **haploid** cells unite to form a **diploid** cell. It is difficult to see how we could justify conferring moral standing on a being simply because it possesses a complete set of paired chromosomes. This characteristic does not appear to be relevant to the question of whether we must accord the being some degree of moral consideration in its own right. . . .

~AV . . . However, conservatives might have something slightly different in mind. Let us continue to assume that conception marks the beginning of the life history of a human individual. Then conservatives can confer moral standing on all human fetuses and all infants, children, and adults as well while denying it to all gametes simply by adopting being a human individual or belonging to the human species as their criterion of moral standing. . . .

AV . . . But here we encounter a curiosity, for conservatives have tended to favor a high standard—such as self-consciousness or rationality—since they are not eager to accord moral standing to nonhuman animals. As we have seen, however, a high standard appears to yield the liberal view of abortion, and of infanticide as well. Since both these results are abhorrent to conservatives, there is considerable tension between their favored criterion of moral standing on the one hand and their view of abortion on the other.

~AV At least two strategies are available for resolving this tension. The first of them rests on the notion of a **paradigm** member of a species (or natural kind). The basic idea is that if the paradigm member of a particular species displays the characteristic—self-consciousness or rationality—that entails possession of moral standing, then all members of that species have such standing whether or not they display that characteristic. Assuming that the paradigm member of our species is an adult of normal faculties, and assuming further that such an adult is both self-conscious and rational, then these facts are sufficient to accord all human beings moral standing—including fetuses, infants, children, the severely handicapped, and so on. AV This strategy solves the conservative's problem at one blow, but at the cost of apparent inconsistency. The conservative's reason for favouring a high standard is to deny moral standing to those beings (such as nonhuman animals) who fall below the standard. Yet the paradigm-member strategy ends by according moral standing to large numbers of beings, including fetuses, who fall below that standard. Therefore, the strategy seems rather arbitrary. . . .

~AV The second strategy available to the conservative rests on the notion of potentiality. The basic idea is that any being has moral standing who is either actually or potentially self-conscious or rational. . . . AV Let us assume that a being has the potential for self-consciousness or rationality if that being will in the normal course of its development either come to display these capacities itself or be transformed into a being that displays these capacities. The potentiality strategy will then confer moral standing upon normal but immature members of the species, but not upon sufficiently abnormal ones. It will therefore, like the liberal's criterion, deny moral standing to some handicapped fetuses, infants, children, and adults. . . .

. . . If the potentiality strategy is not arbitrary, it is easy to see how it will generate a conservative view of both abortion and infanticide. The conservative therefore has no problem supporting the common conviction of the moral seriousness of infanticide. But a problem does arise at the other temporal boundary of pregnancy. Conception, as we have seen, is the union of two haploid cells to form a diploid cell. If a newly fertilized ovum contains the potential for a self-conscious or rational being, then it appears that the pair of gametes that united to form it must also have contained that potential (otherwise where did it come from?). If every fertilized ovum has moral standing, then it must also be true that every unfertilized ovum and every spermatozoon—or perhaps every pair consisting of one ovum and one sperm—also has moral standing. Artificial means of contraception prevent gametes from realizing their potential, just as abortion prevents a fetus from realizing its potential. But then the conservative view of abortion has become also a conservative view of contraception.

. . . To be consistent, therefore, they must advocate a restrictive contraception policy as well as a restrictive abortion policy. But the consequences of such a policy for women's sexuality, as well as for the problem of overpopulation, are unthinkable.

A Moderate View

We can now catalogue the defects of the established views. The common source of these defects lies in their uniform accounts of the moral status of the fetus. These accounts yield three different sorts of awkward implications. First, they require that all abortions be accorded the same moral status regardless of the stage of pregnancy at which they are performed. . . . Second, these accounts require that all abortions be accorded the same moral status regardless of the reason for which they are performed. . . . Third, these accounts require that contraception, abortion, and infanticide all be accorded the same moral status. Thus, liberals must hold that all three practices are equally innocuous, while conservatives must hold that they are all equally serious. Neither view is able to support the common conviction that infanticide is more serious than abortion, which is in turn more serious than contraception. Awkward results do not constitute a refutation. . . . However, results as awkward as these do provide a strong motive to seek an alternative to the established views and thus to explore the logical space between them.

. . . It should be obvious by now that the moral issues raised by the peculiar nature of the fetus, and its peculiar relationship with its mother, are not simple. . . . The problem of locating a non-arbitrary threshold is easier to deal with when we recognize that there can be no sharp breakpoint in the course of human development at which moral standing is suddenly acquired. . . . If, as seems likely, an acceptable criterion of moral standing is built around some characteristic that is acquired gradually during the normal course of human development, then moral standing will also be acquired gradually during the normal course of human development. In that case, the boundary between those beings that have moral standing and those that do not will be soft and slow rather than hard and fast. . . . The real challenge to a moderate view therefore is to show that it can be well grounded, and thus that it is not simply a way of splitting the difference between two equally unattractive options.

. . . A moderate view of abortion must therefore be built on a differential account of the moral status of the fetus, awarding moral standing to some fetuses and withholding it from others. The further defects of the established views impose three constraints on the shape of such a differential account. It must explain the moral relevance of the gestational age of the fetus at the time of abortion and thus must correlate moral status with level of fetal development. It must also explain the moral relevance, at least at some stages of pregnancy, of the reason for which an abortion is performed. And finally it must preserve the distinction between the moral innocuousness of contraception and the moral seriousness of infanticide. . . .

A moderate view is well grounded when it is derivable from an independently plausible criterion of moral standing. It is not difficult to construct a criterion that will yield a threshold somewhere during pregnancy. Let us say that a being is **sentient** when it has the capacity to experience pleasure and pain and thus the capacity for enjoyment and suffering. Beings that are self-conscious or rational are generally (though perhaps not necessarily) also sentient, but many sentient beings lack both self-consciousness and rationality. A **sentience** criterion of moral standing thus sets a lower standard than that shared by the established views. Such a criterion will accord moral standing to the mentally handicapped regardless of impairments of their cognitive capacities. It will also accord moral standing to many, perhaps most, nonhuman animals.

. . . The moral point of view is just one among many evaluative points of view. It appears to be distinguished from the others in two respects: its special concern for the interest, **welfare**, or well-being of creatures and its requirement of **impartiality**. Adopting the moral point of view requires in one way or another according equal consideration to the interests of all beings. If this is so, then a being's having an interest to be considered is both necessary and sufficient for its having moral standing. While the notion of interest or welfare is far from transparent, its irreducible core appears to be the capacity for enjoyment and suffering: all and only beings with this capacity have an interest or welfare that the moral point of view requires us to respect. But then it follows easily that sentience is both necessary and sufficient for moral standing.

. . . A sentience criterion can be grounded in any member of a class of theories that share the foregoing conception of the nature of morality. Because of the centrality of interest or welfare to that conception, let us call such theories welfare-based. A sentience criterion of moral standing can be readily grounded in any welfare-based moral theory. . . . The diversity of theoretical resources available to support a sentience criterion is one of its greatest strengths. In addition, a weaker version of such a criterion is also derivable from more eclectic theories that treat the promotion and protection of welfare as one of the basic concerns of morality. Any such theory will yield the result that sentience is sufficient for moral standing, though it may also be necessary, thus providing partial support for a moderate view of abortion. . . .

When we apply a sentience criterion to the course of human development, it yields the result that the threshold of moral standing is the stage during which the capacity to experience pleasure and pain is first required. This capacity is clearly possessed by a newborn infant and a full-term fetus (and is clearly not possessed by a pair of gametes for a newly fertilized ovum). It is therefore acquired during the normal course of gestation. But when? We can . . . venture a provisional answer. It is standard practice to divide the normal course of gestation into three trimesters of thirteen weeks each. It is likely that a fetus is unable to feel pleasure or pain at the beginning of the second trimester and likely that it is able to do so at the end of that trimester. If this is so, then the threshold of sentience, and thus also the threshold of moral standing, occurs sometime during the second trimester.

We can now fill in our earlier sketch of a moderate view of abortion. A fetus acquires moral standing when it acquires sentience, that is to say at some stage in the second trimester of pregnancy. Before that threshold, when the fetus lacks moral standing, the decision to seek an abortion is morally equivalent to the decision to employ contraception; the effect in both cases is to prevent the existence of a being with moral standing. Such decisions are morally innocuous and should be left to the discretion of the parties involved. Thus, the liberal view of abortion, and a permissive abortion policy, is appropriate for early (pre-threshold) abortions. After the threshold, when the fetus has moral standing, the decision to seek an abortion is morally equivalent to the decision to commit infanticide; the effect in both cases is to terminate the existence of a being with moral standing. Such decisions are morally serious and should not be left to the discretion of the parties involved (the fetus is now one of the parties involved). . . .

A moderate abortion policy will therefore contain the following ingredients: a time limit that separates early from late abortions, a permissive policy for early abortions, and a policy for late abortions. . . . The grounds for late abortions must be specified more carefully by determining what is to count as a serious risk to maternal life or health, and what is to count as a serious fetal abnormality. . . .

. . . As we saw earlier, from the moral point of view there can be no question of a sharp breakpoint. Fetal development unfolds gradually and cumulatively, and sentience, like all other capacities, is acquired slowly and by degrees. Thus we have clear cases of pre-sentient fetuses in the first trimester and clear cases of sentient fetuses in the third trimester. But we also have unclear cases, encompassing many (perhaps most) second-trimester fetuses. From the moral point of view, we can say only that in these cases the moral status of the fetus, and thus the moral status of abortion, is indeterminate.

This sort of moral indeterminacy occurs also at later stages of human development, for instance when we are attempting to fix the age of consent or of competence to drink or drive. We do not pretend in these latter cases that the capacity in question is acquired overnight on one's sixteenth or eighteenth birthday, and yet for legal purposes we must draw a sharp and determinate line. . . . A time limit anywhere in the second trimester is therefore defensible, at least until we acquire the kind of information about fetal development that will enable us to narrow the threshold stage and thus to locate the time limit with more accuracy.

Conclusions

. . . A healthy respect for the intricacies of these problems and an equally healthy sense of our own fallibility in thinking through them should inhibit us from embracing any view of abortion unreservedly. . . . But a moderate view does appear to . . . [do] less violence than either of the established views to widely shared convictions about contraception, abortion, and infanticide, and it can be grounded upon a criterion of moral standing that seems to generate acceptable results in other moral contexts and is in turn derivable from a wide range of moral theories sharing a plausible conception of the nature of morality. Those who are dissatisfied with the established views need not therefore fear that in moving to the middle ground they are sacrificing reason for mere expediency.

Note

1. Logical space describes the ways in which statements about the world are organized in relation to one another. For example, to say that "all snow is white" is to distinguish between two ways the world might be, either an all-white-snow world or a not-all-white-snow world. Since snow is either all white or not all white, there is no logical space between these two statements; if one of these statements is true then the other must be false. Sumner argues that the established views about abortion are not like this. It is possible that both views are false, because the correct position may be somewhere between these two extremes. [Editor]

Susan Sherwin

Abortion

(AV) = author's view; (~AV) = not the author's view

Although abortion has long been an important issue in **bioethics**, the distinctive analysis of **feminist** ethics is generally overlooked in the discussion. Authors and readers commonly presume a familiarity with the feminist position and equate it with other **liberal** defenses of women's right to choose abortion; but feminist ethics yields a different analysis of the moral questions surrounding abortion from that usually offered by liberal abortion arguments. Although feminists agree with some of the conclusions of non-feminist arguments on abortion, they often disagree with the way the issues are formulated and with the reasoning that is offered in the mainstream literature.

Feminist reasoning in support of women's right to choose abortion is significantly different from the reasoning used by non-feminist supporters of similar positions. (~AV) For instance, most feminist accounts evaluate abortion policy within a broader framework, according to its place among the social institutions that support the subordination of women. (AV) In contrast, most non-feminist discussions of abortion consider the moral or legal permissibility of abortion in isolation; they ignore (and thereby obscure) relevant connections with other social practices, including the ongoing power struggle within sexist societies over the control of women and their reproduction. Feminist arguments take into account the actual concerns that particular women attend to in their decision-making on abortion, such as the nature of a woman's feelings about her fetus, her relationships with her partner, other children she may have, and her various obligations to herself and others. (~AV) In contrast, most non-feminist discussions evaluate abortion decisions in their most abstract form (for example, questioning what sort of being a fetus is); from this perspective, specific questions of context are deemed irrelevant. In addition, non-feminist arguments in support of choice about abortion are generally grounded in **masculinist** conceptions of freedom (such as privacy, individual choice, and individuals' property rights with respect to their own bodies), which do not meet the needs, interests, and intuitions of many of the women concerned.

(AV) Feminists also differ from non-feminists in their conception of what is morally at issue with abortion. Non-feminists focus exclusively on the morality and legality of performing abortions, whereas feminists insist that other issues, including the accessibility and delivery of abortion services, must also be addressed. Disputes about abortion arise even at the stage of defining the issue and setting the moral parameters for discussion. Although many non-feminist bioethicists agree with feminists about which abortion policies should be supported, they tend to accept the proposals of the antifeminists as to what is morally at issue in developing that policy.

. . .

Women and Abortion

The most obvious difference between feminist and non-feminist approaches to abortion lies in the relative attention each gives in its analysis to the interests and experiences of women. Feminist analysis regards the effects of unwanted pregnancies on the lives of women individually and collectively as the central element in the moral examination of abortion; it is considered self-evident that the pregnant woman is the subject of **principal** concern in abortion decisions. ~AV In many non-feminist accounts, however, not only is the pregnant woman not perceived as central, she is often rendered virtually invisible. Non-feminist theorists, whether they support or oppose women's right to choose abortion, generally focus almost all their attention on the **moral status** of the fetus.

AV In pursuing a distinctively feminist ethics, it is appropriate to begin with a look at the role of abortion in women's lives. The need for abortion can be very intense; no matter how appalling and dangerous the conditions, women from widely diverse cultures and historical periods have pursued abortions. No one denies that if abortion is not made legal, safe, and accessible in our society, women will seek out illegal and life-threatening abortions to terminate pregnancies they cannot accept. . . .

~AV Anti-abortion campaigners imagine that women often make frivolous and irresponsible decisions about abortion, AV but feminists recognize that women have abortions for a wide variety of compelling reasons. Some women, for instance, find themselves seriously ill and incapacitated throughout pregnancy; they cannot continue in their jobs and may face insurmountable difficulties in fulfilling their responsibilities at home. Many employers and schools will not tolerate pregnancy in their employees or students, and not every woman is able to put her job, career, or studies on hold. Women of limited means may be unable to take adequate care of children they have already borne, and they may know that another mouth to feed will reduce their ability to provide for their existing children. Women who suffer from chronic disease, who believe themselves too young or too old to have children, or who are unable to maintain lasting relationships may recognize that they will not be able to care properly for a child when they face the decision. Some who are homeless, addicted to drugs, or diagnosed as . . . [HIV positive] may be unwilling to allow a child to enter the world with the handicaps that would result from the mother's condition. If the fetus is a result of rape or incest, then the psychological pain of carrying it may be unbearable, and the woman may recognize that her attitude to the child after birth will be tinged with bitterness. . . .

Finally, a woman may simply believe that bearing a child is incompatible with her life plans at the time. Continuing a pregnancy may have devastating repercussions throughout a woman's life. If the woman is young, then a pregnancy will likely reduce her chances of pursuing an education and hence limit her career and life opportunities. . . . In many circumstances, having a child will exacerbate the social and economic forces already stacked against a woman by virtue of her sex (and her race, class, age, sexual orientation, disabilities, and so forth). Access to abortion is necessary for many women if they are to escape the oppressive conditions of poverty.

Whatever the specific reasons are for abortion, most feminists believe that the women concerned are in the best position to judge whether abortion is the appropriate response to a pregnancy. Because usually only the woman choosing abortion is properly situated to weigh all the relevant factors, most feminists resist attempts to offer general, abstract rules for determining when abortion is morally justified. Women's personal deliberations about abortion involve contextually defined considerations that reflect their commitments to the needs and interests of everyone concerned, including themselves, the fetuses they carry, other members of their household, and so forth. Because no single formula is available for balancing these complex factors through all possible cases, it is vital that feminists insist on protecting each woman's right to come to her own conclusions and resist the attempts of other philosophers and moralists to set the agenda for these considerations. Feminists stress that women must be acknowledged as full **moral agents**, responsible for making moral decisions about their own pregnancies. . . . [N]o one else can be assumed to have the authority to evaluate and overrule their judgments.

. . .

In contrast to most non-feminist accounts, feminist analyses of abortion direct attention to how women get pregnant. ~AV Those who reject abortion seem to believe that women can avoid unwanted pregnancies "simply" by avoiding sexual intercourse. AV These views show little appreciation for the power of **sexual politics** in a culture that oppresses women. Existing patterns of sexual dominance mean that women often have little control over their sexual lives. They may be subject to rape. . . . Often . . . sexual coercion is not even recognized as such by the participants but is the price of continued "good will"—popularity, economic survival, peace, or simple acceptance. Many women have found themselves in circumstances where they do not feel free to refuse a man's demands for intercourse, either because he is holding a gun to her head or because he threatens to be emotionally hurt if she refuses (or both). Women are socialized to be compliant and accommodating, sensitive to the feelings of others, and frightened of physical power; men are socialized to take advantage of every opportunity to engage in sexual intercourse and to use sex to express dominance and power. Under such circumstances, it is difficult to argue that women could simply "choose" to avoid heterosexual activity if they wish to avoid pregnancy. Catharine MacKinnon neatly sums it up: "The logic by which women are supposed to consent to sex [is]: preclude the alternatives, then call the remaining option 'her choice.'"[1]

Furthermore, women cannot rely on birth control to avoid pregnancy. No form of contraception that is fully safe and reliable is available, other than sterilization; because women may wish only to avoid pregnancy temporarily, not permanently, sterilization is not always an acceptable choice. . . .

The safest form of birth control involves the use of barrier methods (condoms or diaphragms) in combination with spermicidal foams or jelly. But these methods also pose difficulties for women. They are sometimes socially awkward to use. Young women are discouraged from preparing for sexual activity that might never happen and are offered instead romantic models of spontaneous passion; few films or novels interrupt scenes of seduction for a partner to fetch contraceptives. Many women find their male partners unwilling to use barrier methods of contraception, and they often find themselves in no position to insist. Further, cost is a limiting factor for many women. Condoms and spermicides are expensive and are not covered under most health care plans. Only one contraceptive option offers women safe and fully effective birth control: barrier methods with the back-up option of abortion.

From a feminist perspective, the central moral feature of pregnancy is that it takes place in women's bodies and has profound effects on women's lives. Gender-neutral accounts of pregnancy are not available; pregnancy is explicitly a condition associated with the female body. Because only women experience a need for abortion, policies about abortion affect women uniquely. Therefore, it is important to consider how proposed policies on abortion fit into general patterns of oppression for women. Unlike non-feminist accounts, feminist ethics demands that the effects of abortion policies on the oppression of women be of principal consideration in our ethical evaluations.

The Fetus

~AV In contrast to feminist ethics, most non-feminist analysts believe that the moral acceptability of abortion turns entirely on the question of the moral status of the fetus. Even those who support women's right to choose abortion tend to accept the premise of the antiabortion proponents that abortion can be tolerated only if we can first prove that the fetus lacks full **personhood**. Opponents of abortion demand that we define the status of the fetus either as a being that is valued in the same way as other humans and hence is entitled not to be killed or as a being that lacks in all value. Rather than challenging the logic of this formulation, many defenders of abortion have concentrated on showing that the fetus is indeed without significant value. . . . In both cases, however, the nature of the fetus as an independent being is said to determine the moral status of abortion.

AV The woman on whom the fetus depends for survival is considered as secondary (if she is considered at all) in these debates. The actual experiences and responsibilities of real women are not perceived as morally relevant to the debate, unless these women too, can be proved innocent by establishing that their pregnancies are a result of rape or incest. In some contexts, women's role in gestation is literally reduced to that of "fetal containers"; the individual women disappear or are perceived simply as mechanical life-support systems.

. . .

~AV In the non-feminist literature, both defenders and opponents of women's right to choose abortion agree that the difference between a late-term fetus and a newborn infant is "merely geographical" and cannot be considered morally significant. . . . AV Arguments that focus on the similarities between infants and fetuses, however, generally fail to acknowledge that a fetus inhabits a woman's body and is wholly dependent on her unique contribution to its maintenance, whereas a newborn is physically independent, although still in need of a lot of care. One can only view the distinction between being in or out of a woman's womb as morally irrelevant if one discounts the perspective of the pregnant woman; feminists seem to be alone in recognizing the woman's perspective as morally important to the distinction.

. . .

~AV Perhaps even more distressing than the tendency to ignore the woman's **agency** altogether and view her as a passive participant in the medically controlled events of pregnancy and childbirth is the growing practice of viewing women as genuine threats to the well-being of the fetus. . . . Concern for the well-being of the fetus is taken as license for doctors to intervene to ensure that women comply with medical "advice." . . . Some [US] states have begun to imprison women for endangering their fetuses through drug abuse and other socially unacceptable behaviors. . . .

In other words, some physicians have joined anti-abortion campaigners in fostering a cultural acceptance of the view that fetuses are distinct individuals who are physically, **ontologically**, and socially separate from the women whose bodies they inhabit and that they have their own distinct interests. . . . Focus on the fetus as an independent entity has led to presumptions that deny pregnant women their roles as active, independent, moral agents with a primary interest in what becomes of the fetuses they carry. The moral question of the fetus's status is quickly translated into a license to interfere with women's reproductive freedom.

A Feminist View of the Fetus

AV Because the public debate has been set up as a competition between the rights of women and those of fetuses, feminists have often felt pushed to reject claims of fetal value, in order to protect women's needs. As Kathryn Addelson has argued, however, viewing abortion in this way "rips it out of the context of women's lives."[2] Other accounts of fetal value are more plausible and less oppressive to women.

On a feminist account fetal development is examined in the context in which it occurs, within women's bodies, rather than in the isolation of imagined abstraction. Fetuses develop in specific pregnancies that occur in the lives of particular women. They are not individuals housed in generic female wombs or full persons at risk only because they are small and subject to the whims of women. Their very existence is relationally defined, reflecting their development within particular women's bodies; that relationship gives those women reason to be concerned about them. Many feminists argue against a perspective that regards the fetus as an independent being and suggest that a more accurate and valuable understanding of pregnancy would involve regarding the pregnant woman "as a biological and social unit."[3]

On this view, fetuses are morally significant, but their status is relational rather than absolute.[4] Unlike other human beings, fetuses do not have any independent existence; their existence is uniquely tied to the support of a specific other. ~AV Most non-feminist accounts have ignored the relational dimension of fetal development and have presumed that the moral status of fetuses could be resolved solely in terms of abstract, **metaphysical** criteria of personhood as applied to the fetus alone. Throughout much of the non-feminist literature, commentators argue that some set of properties (such as genetic heritage, moral agency, **self-consciousness**, language use, or **self-determination**) will entitle all who possess it to be granted the moral status of persons. They seek some feature by which we can neatly divide the world into moral persons (who are to be valued and protected) and others (who are not entitled to the same group privileges).

AV This vision, however, misinterprets what is involved in personhood and what is especially valued about persons. Personhood is a social category, not an isolated state. Persons are members of a community, and they should be valued in their concrete, discrete, and different states as specific individuals, not merely as conceptually undifferentiated entities.[5] To be a morally significant category, personhood must involve personality as well as biological integrity.[6] It is not sufficient to consider persons simply as Kantian atoms of **rationality**,[7] because persons are embodied, conscious beings with particular social histories. Annette Baier . . . explain[s] the sort of social dimension that seems fundamental to any moral notion of personhood:

> A person, perhaps, is best seen as one who was long enough dependent upon other persons to acquire the essential arts of personhood. . . . The fact that a person has a life *history*, and that a people collectively have a history depends upon the humbler fact that each person has a childhood in which a cultural heritage is transmitted, ready for adolescent rejection and adult discriminating selection and contribution. Persons come after and before other persons.[8]

Persons, in other words, are members of a social community that shapes and values them, and personhood is a relational concept that must be defined in terms of interactions and relationships with others.

. . .

A fetus is a unique sort of human entity, then, for it cannot form relationships freely with others, and others cannot readily form relationships with it. A fetus has a primary and particularly intimate sort of "relationship" with the woman in whose womb it develops; connections with any other persons are necessarily indirect and must be mediated through the pregnant woman. The relationship that exists between a woman and her fetus is clearly asymmetrical, because she is the only party to it who is capable of even considering whether the interaction should continue; further, the fetus is wholly dependent on the woman who sustains it, whereas she is quite capable of surviving without it.

. . . Fetuses have a unique physical status—within and dependent on particular women. That gives them also a unique social status. However much some might prefer it to be otherwise, no one other than the pregnant woman in question can do anything to support or harm a fetus without doing something to the woman who nurtures it. Because of this inexorable biological reality, the responsibility and privilege of determining a fetus's specific social status and value must rest with the woman carrying it.

. . .

The Politics of Abortion

Feminist accounts explore the connections between particular social policies and the general patterns of power relationships in our society. . . .

~AV Anti-abortion activists appeal to arguments about the unconditional value of human life. AV When we examine their rhetoric more closely, however, we find other ways of interpreting their agenda. In addition to their campaign to criminalize abortion, most abortion opponents condemn all forms of sexual relations outside of heterosexual marriage, and they tend to support **patriarchal** patterns of dominance within such marriages. Many are distressed that liberal abortion policies support permissive sexuality by allowing women to "get away with" sex outside of marriage. They perceive that ready access to abortion supports women's independence from men.

. . .

When we place abortion in the larger political context, we see that most of the groups active in the struggle to prohibit abortion also support other conservative measures to maintain the forms of dominance that characterize **patriarchy** (and often class and racial oppression as well). The movement against abortion is led by the Catholic Church and other conservative religious institutions, which explicitly endorse not only fetal rights but also male dominance in the home and the church. Most opponents of abortion also oppose virtually all forms of birth control and all forms of sexuality other than monogamous, reproductive sex; usually, they also resist having women assume positions of authority in the dominant public institutions. Typically, anti-abortion activists support conservative economic measures that protect the interests of the privileged classes of society and ignore the needs of the oppressed and disadvantaged. Although they stress their commitment to preserving life, many systematically work to dismantle key social programs that provide life necessities to the [poor]. . . .

~AV In the eyes of its principal opponents, then, abortion is not an isolated practice; their opposition to abortion is central to a set of social values that runs counter to **feminism**'s objectives. Hence anti-abortion activists generally do not offer alternatives to abortion that support feminist interests in overturning the patterns of oppression that confront women. Most deny that there are any legitimate grounds for abortion, short of the need to save a woman's life—and some are not even persuaded by this **criterion**. They believe that any pregnancy can and should be endured. If the mother is unable or unwilling to care for the child after birth, then they assume that adoption can be easily arranged.

AV It is doubtful, however, that adoptions are possible for every child whose mother cannot care for it. The world **abounds with** homeless orphans; even in the industrialized West, where there is a waiting list for adoption of healthy (white) babies, suitable homes cannot always be found for troubled adolescents, inner-city, [HIV-positive] babies, or many of the multiply handicapped children whose parents may have tried to care for them but whose marriages broke under the strain.

Furthermore, even if an infant were born healthy and could be readily adopted, we must recognize that surrendering one's child for adoption is an extremely difficult act for most women. The bond that commonly forms between women and their fetuses over the full term of pregnancy is intimate and often intense; many women find that it is not easily broken after birth. Psychologically, for many women adoption is a far more difficult response to unwanted pregnancies than abortion. Therefore, it is misleading to describe pregnancy as merely a nine-month commitment; for most women, seeing a pregnancy through to term involves a lifetime of responsibility and involvement with the resulting child and, in the overwhelming majority of cases, disproportionate burden on the woman through the child-rearing years. An ethics that cares about women would recognize that abortion is often the only acceptable recourse for them.

Expanding the Agenda

The injunction of feminist ethics to consider abortion in the context of other issues of power and oppression means that we need to look beyond the standard questions of its moral and legal acceptability. This implies, for instance, that we need to explore the moral imperatives of ensuring that abortion services are actually available to all women who seek them. Although medically approved abortions are technically recognized as legal (at least for the moment) in both Canada and the United States, many women who need abortions cannot obtain them; accessibility is still associated with wealth and privilege in many regions. In Canada vast geographical areas offer no abortion services at all, so unless the women of those regions can afford to travel to urban clinics, they have no meaningful right to abortion. In the United States, where there is no universal health insurance, federal legislation (under the Hyde amendment) explicitly denies the use of public money for abortions. Full ethical discussion of abortion reveals the necessity of removing the economic, age, and racial barriers that currently restrict access to medically acceptable abortion services.

The moral issues extend yet further. Feminism demands respect for women's choices; even if the legal and financial barriers could be surpassed, this condition may remain unmet. The focus of many political campaigns for abortion rights has been to make abortion a matter of medical, not personal, choice, suggesting that doctors (but not necessarily women) can be trusted to choose responsibly. Feminists must insist on respect for women's moral agency. Therefore, feminism requires that abortion services be provided in an atmosphere that is supportive of the choices that women make. This could be achieved by offering abortions in centers that deal with all matters of reproductive health in an open, patient-centered manner, where respectful counseling on all aspects of reproductive health is available.

Furthermore, the moral issues surrounding abortion include questions of how women are treated when they seek abortions. All too frequently hospital-based abortions are provided by practitioners who are uneasy about their role and treat the women involved with hostility and resentment. Health care workers involved in providing abortions must recognize that abortion is a legitimate option that should be carried out with respect and concern for the physical, psychological, and emotional well-being of the patient. In addition, we need to turn our moral attention to the effects of anti-abortion protests on women. Increasingly, many anti-abortion activists have personalized their attacks and focused their energies on harassing the women who enter and leave abortion clinics, thereby requiring them to pass a gauntlet of hostile protesters to obtain abortions. Such arrangements are not conducive to positive health care, so these protests, too, must be subject to moral criticism within the ethics of health care.

Feminist ethics promotes the value of reproductive freedom, which is defined as the condition under which women are able to make truly voluntary choices about their reproductive lives. Women must have control over their reproduction if patriarchal dominance over women is to be brought to an end. In addition to reliable and caring abortion services, then, women also need access to safe and effective birth control, which would provide them with other means of avoiding pregnancy.

Moreover, we must raise questions about the politics of sexual domination in this context. Many men support women's right to abortion because they perceive that if women believe that they can engage in intercourse without having to accept an unwanted pregnancy, they will become more sexually available. Some of the women who oppose abortion resist it for this very reason; they do not want to support a practice that increases women's sexual vulnerability. Feminists need to develop an analysis of reproductive freedom that includes sexual freedom as it is defined by women, not men. Such an analysis would, for example, include women's right to refuse sex. Because this right can only be assured if women have power equal to men's and are not subject to domination because of their sex, women's freedom from oppression is itself an element of reproductive freedom.

Finally, it is important to stress that feminist accounts do not deny that fetuses have value. They ask that fetuses be recognized as existing within women's pregnancies and not as separate, isolated entities. Feminists positively value fetuses that are wanted by the women who carry them; they vigorously oppose practices that force women to have abortions they do not want. No women should be subjected to coerced abortion or sterilization. Women must be assured of adequate financial and support services for the care of their children, so that they are not forced to abort fetuses that they would otherwise choose to carry. . . .

Feminists perceive that far more could be done to protect and care for fetuses if the **state** directed its resources toward supporting women who choose to continue their pregnancies, rather than draining those resources to police the women who try to terminate undesired pregnancies. Unlike their conservative counterparts, feminists recognize that caring for the women who maintain the lives of fetuses is not only a more legitimate policy than is regulating them but also probably more effective at ensuring the health and well-being of more fetuses and, ultimately, of more infants.

In sum, then, feminist ethics demands that moral discussions of abortion reflect a broader agenda than is usually found in the arguments put forth by bioethicists. Only by reflecting on the meaning of ethical pronouncements on actual women's lives and the connections that exist between judgments on abortion and the conditions of domination and subordination can we come to an adequate understanding of the moral status of abortion in a particular society.

Notes

1. Catharine MacKinnon, *Toward a Feminist Theory of the State* (Cambridge, MA: Harvard University Press, 1989), p. 192.
2. Kathryn Pyne Addelson, "Moral Passages," in Eva Feder Kittay and Diana T. Meyers, eds., *Women and Moral Theory* (Totowa, NJ: Rowman and Littlefield, 1987). [Sherwin doesn't give a page number for the quote, just the reference.]
3. Barbara Katz Rothman, "Commentary: When a Pregnant Woman Endangers Her Fetus," *Hastings Center Report* 16, 1 (1986), p. 25.
4. "their status is relational rather than absolute": Something with relational status is valued because of its relation to something else. Something with absolute status is valued independently of anything else. [Editor]
5. "conceptually undifferentiated entities": Many philosophers discuss humans in the abstract, ignoring characteristics that distinguish them. According to this view, we are all the same ("conceptually undifferentiated"). Sherwin says this method ignores **morally relevant** features of humans. [Editor]
6. "biological integrity": Biological wholeness, including separate existence. [Editor]
7. "Kantian atoms of rationality": According to Kant and many subsequent philosophers, the defining feature of humans is rationality; they often neglect the existence of the body and of human interdependence. Sherwin disputes this. [Editor]
8. Annette C. Baier, *Postures of the Mind: Essays on Mind and Morals* (Minneapolis: University of Minnesota Press, 1985) pp. 84–5.

Discussion Questions

1. Thomson assumes that the fetus has a right to life from the moment of conception. Why does she make this assumption?
2. What is the point of the unconscious violinist example in Thomson's "A Defence of Abortion"?
3. What does Marquis mean by a "future-like-ours"? How does it support his argument that abortion is immoral?
4. Sumner says both the liberal (pro-choice) and conservative (pro-life) views have the same problem. What is this problem? How does his moderate view avoid this problem?
5. Sherwin says fetuses' moral status is "relational rather than absolute." What does she mean by this? Do you agree with her?
6. Sherwin says that adoption is not really a live option for many women. Why does she say this?

Suggested Readings and Websites

🍁 = Canadian source or author

🍁 Abortion Rights Coalition of Canada. www.arcc-cdac.ca/home.html. [A pro-choice political group]

🍁 Campaign Life Coalition. www.campaignlifecoalition.com/. [A pro-life political group.]

Haldane, John. "Recognising Humanity." *Journal of Applied Philosophy* 25, 4 (2008): 301–13. [An argument for recognizing humanity "all the way to its points of origin and of cessation."]

Johnson, Harriet McBryde. "Unspeakable Conversations." *New York Times Magazine* (16 February 2003), www.nytimes.com/2003/02/16/magazine/unspeakable-conversations.html?pagewanted=all&src=pm. [An American lawyer and disability rights activist discusses her encounters with philosopher Peter Singer, who defends abortion and infanticide in cases of disability.]

Kaczor, Christopher Robert. *The Ethics of Abortion: Women's Rights, Human Life, and the Question of Justice*. New York: Routledge, 2011. [A pro-life view by a philosopher.]

🍁 Kukla, Rebecca. *Mass Hysteria: Medicine, Culture, and Mothers' Bodies*. Lanham, MD: Rowman and Littlefield, 2005. [A feminist examination of pregnancy and motherhood by a philosopher.]

🍁 Richer, Karine. "Abortion in Canada: Twenty Years after *R. v. Morgentaler*." Parliamentary Information and Research Service PRB 08-22E. Ottawa: Parliamentary Information and Research Service, Library of Canada, 24 September 2008, www.parl.gc.ca/content/LOP/ResearchPublications/prb0822-e.pdf. [Non-partisan; surveys the arguments and legal history of abortion in Canada since *Morgentaler*.]

🍁 Sumner, L.W. *Abortion and Moral Theory*. Princeton: Princeton University Press, 1981. [A pro-choice view by a philosopher; cited in *R. v. Morgentaler*.]

Chapter 6

Animal Rights[1]

A Brief History of Animal Welfare and Animal Rights

Animals rights as a philosophy can be traced to ancient India around the ninth century BCE (before the common [Christian] era), when the Jain religion arose. A central tenet in Jain beliefs is *Ahimsa*, the principle of non-violence to all living things. Jains are pacifist vegetarians who try not to harm any living thing, including plants. For example, they do not eat root vegetables because harvesting them requires killing the plant, whereas leafy and fruiting vegetables can be harvested while leaving the mother plant relatively intact. While Jainism is a relatively small religion, its beliefs have been very influential on Hindu and Buddhist attitudes towards animals in India. As a result, India has the largest percentage of vegetarians in the world.

In the West, by contrast, people believed that animals existed for human use. The Greek philosopher Aristotle (384-322 BCE) said living things have three different sorts of "souls" or life forces: plants have a vegetative soul that allows for reproduction and growth, animals have a vegetative as well as an appetitive (appetite-like) soul, which allows for motion and sensation, and humans have vegetative, appetitive, and rational souls, which allow us to think and reflect on our thoughts. In Aristotle's view, humans are more perfect than animals, which in turn are more perfect than plants. Less perfect things may be used by more perfect ones, so animals may be used by humans, and plants may be used by both humans and animals. In the Hebrew bible, God gives Adam **dominion** (the right to rule) over the animals in Genesis. Other parts of the Hebrew bible tell people to treat animals humanely, but it goes without question that humans have the right to use animals. These ideas formed the basis of Western views about animals.

In the thirteenth century St Thomas Aquinas (c. 1225–74) argued that, although animals did not have immortal souls, cruelty to animals was wrong because it would harden people and make them more likely to be cruel to humans. Notice that Aquinas's argument turns on the potential wrong to humans, though, not on actual wrongs to animals—that is, if there were no such moral spillover, cruelty to animals would be morally neutral, no worse than smashing rocks. Nevertheless, Aquinas's view was the strongest Western argument against cruelty to animals for centuries.

The modern animal welfare movement got its start in England in the early nineteenth century. This was a time of religious fervour and social reform. The reformers believed that cruelty was a sin that violated the Christian duties of love and mercy and undermined the Christian virtues of compassion and good will. These nineteenth-century reformers opposed cruelty in many forms: they advocated for prison reform, women's rights, protecting children, and improving conditions in mental asylums and workhouses for the poor, and against capital punishment, the slave trade and slavery, and cruelty to animals. And their efforts bore fruit. Britain abolished the slave trade in 1807, and it abolished slavery in Britain and all its colonies in 1833. Conditions improved in prisons, mental asylums, and workhouses. Many European and North American countries reduced the number of crimes punishable by death from several hundred in 1800 to a handful at the end of the century. Women's legal rights increased. And many countries passed laws protecting animals.

In 1822, the British Parliament banned cruelty to horses, donkeys, sheep, and cows. It later amended the law to include bulls, bears, and dogs; to outlaw bear and bull baiting, cockfighting, and dog fighting; and to limit and license experimentation on animals. In 1824, two years after the passage of the first anti-cruelty act, the first Society for the Prevention of Cruelty to Animals was founded in Britain. Similar laws and societies appeared in other countries. An 1850 French law made it illegal to mistreat domestic animals—though after its passage there was a long-running debate about whether bulls were "domestic animals" and thus whether bull fighting was prohibited.[2] In 1866 the American Society for the Prevention of Cruelty to Animals was founded in New York, and in 1869 the Canadian Society for the Prevention of Cruelty to Animals was founded in Montreal. Other animal protection societies sprang up in cities across North America. Interestingly, some early humane societies protected more than just animals. For example, the Toronto Humane Society, founded in 1887, protected children as well as animals, and the original name of the Winnipeg Humane Society, founded in 1894, was the "Society for the Prevention of Cruelty to Women, Children, and Animals."[3]

The 1960s ushered in another wave of social reform, this time for rights and equality (civil rights, women's liberation, anti-colonialism, anti-racism, etc.), and interest in animal rights and welfare was renewed. In 1964 Ruth Harrison published *Animal Machines: The New Factory Farming Industry*, an exposé of the mass production of veal calves, chickens, and pigs. Other activists began to expose cruelty to animals in experiments. In 1975 Peter Singer's *Animal Liberation* was published, the first modern philosophical defence of animal rights. Animals rights is now a worldwide movement, ranging from groups that promote improvements in animal **welfare** (well-being), to groups that protect wild and/or endangered species, to animal **abolitionists** who argue that humans should become **vegans** (vegetarians who use no animal products) and stop using animals altogether.

In terms of legislation, the animal rights movement has had its largest impact in Europe. In 2009, the European Union passed a law requiring anyone who kills animals to "take the necessary measures to avoid pain and minimize the distress and suffering of animals during the slaughtering or killing process."[4] Several European countries have banned battery cages (in which a hen spends her entire life in a space the size of a sheet of paper); these cages were completely phased out in the EU by 2012. In the US, several states have banned veal and pig crates that do not allow the calves or pigs to turn around or move freely. Canada has no such laws. While animal cruelty has been forbidden since Confederation, the penalties are minor—usually only a fine—and they are rarely enforced.

Philosophical Arguments Against Animal Rights

Some philosophers argue that animals have no **moral status**, that is, that they are not the sorts of beings that must figure in our moral deliberations. Alternatively, some philosophers argue that if animals have moral status, it is only relative to humans—they have no independent moral status. The argument for these claims—or for their contradictories, that animals do possess independent moral status—requires an account of what characteristics something must possess to have moral status, dependent or independent. We must be able to point to a **morally relevant** difference between humans and non-human animals, something that distinguishes us (those who have moral status) from them (those who—or that—do not).

For most of Western history, it has been taken as given that animals are worth less than humans—if, indeed, they are worth anything at all. The Bible says God created humans in his image, and that he gave humans dominion over animals; they are for our use. We are separate from and superior to everything else in the world. Furthermore, humans have eternal souls while non-human animals do not. Hence we are morally superior to animals.

However, in a **secular** world (one not dominated by religion), arguments must be given that do not depend on the acceptance of a particular—or any—religion. Most theorists who argue that only humans have moral status base their claims on properties such as rationality, **autonomy** (self-rule, the ability to run one's own life), **consciousness** (awareness of one's own existence), or **self-consciousness** (the ability to reflect on one's thoughts, desires, hopes, fears, etc.).[5] Something must possess one or more of these properties to have moral status, these theorists claim, and only humans possess these properties. Aristotle argued that rationality is necessary for moral status. Other philosophers have argued that rationality is **necessary** but not **sufficient**;[6] the German philosopher Immanuel Kant (1724–1804), for example, thought autonomy and rationality were jointly **necessary and sufficient**.

Some philosophers base their arguments not on capacities but on a contractarian model of morality. According to this view, we should think of morality as a hypothetical contract between individuals for mutual benefit, and ask ourselves what it would be reasonable to agree to under conditions of non-domination (that is, where no individual or group is strong enough to make itself dictator). We assume individuals prefer their own interests, whatever they are, and so to seek an agreement that allows the maximum scope for their interests. Since animals cannot participate in the moral contract, they have no moral status.

Opponents of animal rights are aware that the capacities or models they suggest apply only to competent adults and not to infants, people with advanced dementia, people with severe or profound intellectual disabilities, and others who are mentally incompetent. Some argue that these humans are not excluded by their view, because the morally relevant capacity is a feature of the species as a whole and does not apply to individual members. It is a human capacity, and it applies to all humans. Others point out that we distinguish between **moral agents**, who are capable of making moral decisions and acting morally, and who can be held morally responsible, and **moral patients**, who are not (fully) capable of acting morally and who cannot be held morally responsible, but who are still objects of moral concern and behaviour (see the Introduction, A Short Primer). Only humans can be moral patients, they say. Non-human animals cannot be moral patients because they are not members of the moral community. We form communities with other humans, and we care about them more than we do about animals; that is as it should be. These theorists may assert that, as a matter of fact, we value humans over animals, using something like a philosopher's "burning building" case to get others to see that they already agree with them: You are standing in front of a burning building. To the left you hear an infant's wail, to the right you hear a dog's howl. You can only save one—which do you save? Opponents of animal rights say it is obvious that you must save the infant, and this tells us something important about the relative moral status of humans and non-humans. If non-human animals have any moral status at all, it is always overridden by the moral claims of humans.

Philosophical Arguments in Favour of Animal Rights

The readings in this chapter survey views in favour of animal rights. Why are there no arguments against animal rights? you might wonder. The answer is that, while some philosophers oppose animal rights for the sake of argument (or notoriety), almost no one really believes that animals have no moral status whatsoever. In fact, we think there is something wrong with anyone who treats animals as if they were the moral equivalent of rocks or firewood. Consider the following case: In 2001, three Toronto art students filmed themselves torturing and killing a cat as part of an art project. When the media learned of the video the public was outraged, and the students were charged. They pled guilty to animal cruelty and mischief, and were sentenced to ninety days. They appealed the sentence, but the Ontario Court of Appeal unanimously rejected their appeal, saying that the video was "torture for torture's sake."[7] We may disagree about what, if anything, ought to be done to people in cases such as this one, but there is little disagreement across the political spectrum that torturing non-human animals "for torture's sake" is wrong. What's more, we think the wrong is to the animal, not to its owner. We would be no less appalled if the students had tortured a porcupine or a **feral** (wild) cat rather than a cat with a name.

We know that at least all vertebrates feel pain, and we think it is wrong to inflict pain unnecessarily. We can argue at length about what, if anything, counts as "necessary" pain—using animals for medical research? Killing them for sport or food? Using them in rodeos? Keeping them in zoos? Spaying and neutering them? But there is widespread agreement in Canada that some animal pain is unnecessary and therefore wrong. Examples of unjustified animal pain include dog-fighting, cosmetic testing on animals, surgery without anaesthesia, or torturing an animal for an art video.

We can distinguish two general views in favour of animal rights. Animal welfare advocates believe we should aim to prevent the grossest abuses against animals, perhaps through animal cruelty laws, or by banning battery cages or veal and pig crates. But they think it is permissible to own, kill, and eat animals, as long as we do not cause them unnecessary suffering (leaving aside the difficulties in defining "unnecessary"). Most animal welfarists are not vegetarians, but they do not oppose laws that prevent the worst suffering experienced by animals raised for food, even though these laws would raise the cost of meat and dairy products. They may choose to buy only free-range eggs and humanely raised meat, despite their increased cost. However, they believe animal suffering that might benefit humans, such as testing human medicines on animals before they are given to people, is justified. Animal welfarists think animals matter, but not nearly as much as humans do.

Animal rights advocates or animal liberationists, by contrast, think most of what we do to animals today is morally unacceptable because it ignores animals' welfare or violates their rights. Animal rights advocates oppose things like **factory farming** (the mass production of animals for food, frequently involving crowding, confinement, discomfort, and pain to the animals), cosmetic testing on animals, and experimentation on animals for human benefit. They have had some success in their campaigns against cosmetic testing and animal experimentation. Most animal rights advocates are vegetarians (they eat no meat but may eat eggs or dairy products) or vegans (they eat no animal products).

The Readings

In the first reading, Tom Regan argues that animals have a right to life. He examines the view that only humans have **intrinsic worth**—that is, they matter morally for their own sake, and not for the sake of someone or something else. Every ground for attributing intrinsic worth to humans is also a ground for attributing intrinsic worth to animals, Regan argues. He advocates vegetarianism, because eating animals violates their rights to life.

Steven Davis accepts Regan's argument that animals have intrinsic worth and therefore a right to life. But he questions Regan's conclusion that this means we should be vegetarians or vegans. Davis adopts Regan's principle that, when faced with options that all cause harm, we should choose the one that causes the least harm. But he says large-scale farming of food crops kills hundreds of millions of field animals a year. He argues that using farmland for pasture-ruminant animals like cows or sheep and then eating them would result in a significant decrease in overall harm to animals.

David Fraser studies animal welfare, the scientific study of animal well-being. He begins with a dilemma: two groups of animal welfare scientists used the same set of data and drew opposing conclusions. He argues that the difference here lies in opposing conceptions of value, not science. Animal welfare science inherently includes both scientific and **normative** values. Animal welfare scientists should become more explicit about the values behind their science, he says, and they should learn to communicate better with those with whom they disagree.

In the last article, Sue Donaldson and Will Kymlicka extend traditional animal rights views such as Regan's from moral to political theory. They suggest using citizenship theory to distinguish different ways that humans and non-humans live together and co-exist. They argue that domestic animals, from cats and dogs to cows and chickens, should be considered co-citizens with the same rights as human citizens; wild animals should be considered **sovereign** over their own territory; and animals like raccoons, hummingbirds, and bees that live among but not with humans should be considered **liminal denizens** (borderline residents).

The Moral and Political Preferences Indicator

Most Canadians of any political stripe are animal welfarists who believe that animal suffering should be lessened, but otherwise the status quo with respect to animals is acceptable.

Animal rights advocates—**utilitarian**, rights-based, or abolitionist—fall strongly on the egalitarian side of the liberal spectrum; virtually everyone who supports animal rights as a political movement is a social democrat. Notice that views on animal rights are the mirror opposite of views on abortion. Almost everyone who supports greater rights for animals is strongly egalitarian. By contrast, almost everyone who supports the right to life for fetuses/unborn children is strongly conservative.

Notes

1. In general I use "rights" as a shorthand for "**moral status**" (moral position or standing). To say that something has rights or moral status is to say that we ought to consider it in our moral deliberations—that its rights, interests, utilities, welfare, etc. matter morally, that the virtues ought to be directed to it, or that it is a member of our moral community.
2. Apparently they are not domestic animals, because bullfighting is still practised in France and advertised on tourism sites, e.g., www.tourisme.ville-arles.fr/us/a7/a7a.htm.
3. www.torontohumanesociety.com/history.htm and www.winnipeghumanesociety.ca/history-of-the-winnipeg-humane-society.
4. Council Regulation (EC) No 1099/2009 of 24 September 2009 on the protection of animals at the time of killing, http://ec.europa.eu/food/animal/welfare/slaughter/regulation_1099_2009_en.pdf.
5. "Consciousness" and "self-consciousness" are technical terms in philosophy. "Consciousness" means awareness and "self-consciousness" means self-awareness, that is, the ability to reflect on and evaluate one's thoughts, emotions, desires, and so on.
6. "Necessary" and "sufficient" are also technical terms in philosophy. Something is necessary if, without it, something else cannot be the case. Being a citizen is necessary for voting in Canada; someone who is not a citizen cannot vote. Something is sufficient if its existence guarantees that something else is the case: being a Supreme Court justice is sufficient for voting in Canada. Something is necessary but not sufficient if it is only part of a requirement; for example, being a citizen is necessary but not sufficient for voting because citizens under eighteen may not vote. And something can be sufficient but not necessary, such as being a Supreme Court justice, because many people besides Supreme Court justices may vote.
7. Christie Blatchford, "Cat torture was not art: judges," *National Post* 14 June 2003, http://forum.dvdtalk.com/archive/t-299453.html. (Warning: the article contains a partial description of the video, which was extremely cruel and violent.)

Tom Regan

Do Animals Have a Right to Life?

(AV) = author's view; (~AV) = not the author's view

My argument . . . turns on considerations about the natural "right to life" that we humans are sometimes said uniquely to possess, and to possess to an equal degree. . . . What I will try to show is that arguments that might be used in defense of the claim that all human beings have this **natural right**, to an equal extent, would also show that animals are possessors of it, whereas arguments that might be used to show that animals do not have this right would also show that not all human beings do either. . . . [H]owever, . . . a disclaimer to completeness is in order. I have not been able to consider all the arguments that might be advanced in this context; all that I have been able to do is consider what I think are the most important ones.

[An Equal Natural Right to Life]

Let us begin, then, with the idea that all humans possess an equal natural right to life. And let us notice, once again, that it is an *equal natural* right that we are speaking of, one that we cannot acquire or have granted to us, and one that we all are supposed to have just because we are human beings. On what basis, then, might it be alleged that all and only human beings possess this right to an equal extent? Well, a number of familiar possibilities come immediately to mind. ~AV It might be argued that all and only human beings have an equal right to life because either (a) all and only human beings have the capacity to reason, or (b) all and only human beings have the capacity to make free choices, or (c) all and only human beings have a concept of "self," or (d) all and only human beings have all or some combination of the previously mentioned capacities. And it is easy to imagine how someone might argue that, since animals do not have any of these capacities, *they* do not possess a right to life, least of all one that is equal to the one possessed by humans.

. . . AV [There are] difficulties such views must inevitably encounter. Briefly, it is not clear, first, that no nonhuman animals satisfy any one (or all) of these conditions, and, second, it is reasonably clear that not all human beings satisfy them. [People with severe or profound intellectual disabilities], for example, fail to satisfy them. Accordingly, if we want to insist that they have a right to life, then we cannot also maintain that they have it because they satisfy one or another of these conditions. Thus, *if* we want to insist that they have an equal right to life, despite their failure to satisfy these conditions, we cannot consistently maintain that animals, because they fail to satisfy these conditions, therefore lack this right.

~AV Another possible ground is that of sentience, by which I understand the capacity to experience pleasure and pain. AV But this view, too, must encounter a familiar difficulty—namely, that it could not justify restricting the right *only* to human beings.

What clearly is needed, then, if we are to present any plausible argument for the view that all and only human beings have an equal natural right to life, is a basis for this right that is invariant and equal in the case of all human beings and only in their case. ~AV It is against this backdrop, I think, that the following view naturally arises. This is the view that the life of every human being has **intrinsic worth**—that, in Kant's terms, each of us exists as "an **end** in himself"—*and* that this intrinsic worth which belongs *only* to human beings, is shared *equally* by all. "Thus," it might be alleged, "it is because of the equal intrinsic worth of all human beings that we all have an equal right to life."

AV This view, I think, has a degree of plausibility which those previously discussed lack. For by saying that the worth that is supposed to attach to a being just because he or she is human is intrinsic, and that it is because of this that we all have an equal natural right to life, this view rules out the possibility that one human being might give this right to or withhold it from another. It would appear, therefore, that this view could make sense of the alleged *naturalness* of the right in question. Moreover, by resting the equal right to life on the idea of the *equal* intrinsic worth of all human beings, this view may succeed, where the others have failed, in accounting for the alleged *equality* of this right.

Despite these apparent advantages, however, the view under consideration must face certain difficulties. One difficulty lies in specifying just what it is supposed to mean to say that the life of every human being is "intrinsically worthwhile." Now, it cannot mean that "each and every human being has a natural right to life." For the idea that the life of each and every human being has intrinsic worth was introduced in the first place to provide a basis for saying that each and every human being has an equal right to life. Accordingly, if, say, "Jones's life is intrinsically worthwhile" ends up *meaning* "Jones has an equal right to life," then the claim that the life of each and every individual is equally worthwhile, judged intrinsically, cannot be construed as a *basis* for saying that each and every human being has an equal right to life. For the two claims would mean the same thing, and one claim can never be construed as being the basis for another, if they both mean the same.

But a second and, for our purposes, more important difficulty is this: On what grounds is it being alleged that each and every human being, and only human beings, are intrinsically worthwhile? Just what is there, in other words, about being human, and only about being human, that underlies this **ascription** of unique worth? ~AV Well, one possible answer here is that there isn't "anything" that underlies this worth. The worth in question, in short, just belongs to anyone who is human, and only to those who are. It is a worth that we simply recognize or intuit, whenever we carefully examine that complex of ideas we have before our minds when we think of the idea, "human being." AV I find this view unsatisfactory, both because it would seem to commit us to an **ontology** of value that is very difficult to defend, and because I, for one, even after the most scrupulous examination I can manage, fail to intuit the unique worth in question. I do not know how to prove that the view in question is mistaken in a few swift strokes, however. All I can do is point out the historic **precedents** of certain groups of human beings who have claimed to "intuit" a special worth belonging to their group and not to others within the human family, and say that it is good to remember that alluding to a special, intuitive way of "knowing" such things could only serve the purpose of giving an air of intellectual respectability to unreasoned prejudices. And, further, I can only register here my own suspicion that the same is true in this case, though to a much wider extent. For I think that falling into talk about the "intuition of the unique intrinsic worth of being human" would be the last recourse of men who, having found no good reason to believe that human beings have a unique intrinsic worth, would go on believing that they do anyhow.

Short of having recourse to intuition, then, we can expect those who believe that human beings uniquely possess intrinsic worth to tell us what there is about being human, **in virtue of** which this worth is possessed. The difficulty here, however, as can be anticipated, is that some familiar problems are going to raise their tiresome heads. For shall we say that it is the fact that humans can speak, or reason, or make free choices, or form a concept of their own identity that underlies this worth? These suggestions will not work here, any more than they have before. For there are some beings who are human who cannot do these things, and there very well may be some beings who are not human who can. None of these capacities, therefore, could do the job of providing the basis for a kind of worth that all humans and only humans are supposed to possess.

[Intrinsic Worth and Positive Interests]

~AV But suppose we try to unpack this notion of intrinsic worth in a slightly different way. Suppose we say that the reasons we have for saying that all and only human beings exist as ends in themselves are, first, that every human being has various positive **interests**, such as desires, goals, hopes, preferences and the like, the satisfaction or realization of which brings intrinsic value to their lives, in the form of intrinsically valuable experiences; and, second, that the intrinsic value brought to the life of any one man, by the satisfaction of his desires or the realization of his goals, is just as good, judged in itself, as the intrinsic value brought to the life of any other man by the satisfaction or realization of those comparable desires and goals he happens to have. In this sense, then, all men are equal, and it is because of this equality among all men, it might be alleged, that each man has as much right as any other to seek to satisfy his desires and realize his goals, so long, at least, that, in doing so, he does not violate the rights of any other human being. "Now, since," this line of argument continues, "no one can seek to satisfy his desires or realize his goals if he is dead, and in view of the fact that every man has as much right as any other to seek to satisfy his desires and realize his goals, then to take the life of any human being will always be ***prima facie*** to violate a right which he shares equally with all other human beings—namely, his right to life."

AV What shall we make of this argument? I am uncertain whether it can withstand careful scrutiny. Whether it can or not, however, is not a matter I feel compelled to try to decide here. What I do want to point out is, of the arguments considered here, this one has a degree of plausibility the others lack, not only because, as I have already remarked, it addresses itself both to the alleged naturalness and the alleged equality of the right in question, but also because it rests on what I take to be a **necessary condition** of being human—namely, that a being must have interests. For these reasons, then, I do not think I can be accused of "**straw-man**" tactics by choosing this as the most plausible among a cluster of possible arguments that might be urged in support of the contention that all human beings have an equal natural right to life. At the same time, however, as can be anticipated, I believe that, whatever plausibility this argument might have in this connection, it would also have in connection with the claim that animals, too, have an equal natural right to life.

For even if it is true that this argument provides us with adequate grounds for ascribing a natural right to life equally to all human beings, there is nothing in it that could tend to show that this is a right that belongs *only* to those beings who are human. On the contrary, the argument in question would equally well support the claim that any being who has positive interests which, when satisfied, bring about experiences that are just as intrinsically valuable as the satisfaction of the comparable interests of any other individual, would have an equal right to life. In particular, then, it would support the view that animals have an equal right to life, if they meet the conditions in question. And a case can be made for the view that they do. For, once again, it seems clear that animals have positive interests, the satisfaction or realization of which would appear to be just as intrinsically worthwhile, judged in themselves, as the satisfaction or realization of any comparable interest a human being might have. True, the interests animals have may be of a comparatively low grade, when we compare them to, say, the contemplative interests of Aristotle's virtuous man. But the same is true of many human beings: their interests may be largely restricted to food and drink, with occasional bursts of sympathy for a few. Yet we would not say that such a man has less of a right to life than another, assuming that all men have an equal right to life. Neither, then, can we say that animals, because of their "base" interests, have any less of a right to life.

~AV One way to avoid this conclusion . . . is to deny that animals have interests. But on what basis might this denial rest? A by now familiar basis is that animals cannot speak;

they cannot use words to formulate or express anything; thus, they cannot have an interest in anything. AV But this objection obviously assumes that only those beings who are able to use words to formulate or express something can have interests, and this, even ignoring the possibility that at least some animals might be able to do this, seems implausible. For we do not suppose that infants, for example, have to learn to use a language before they can have any interests. Moreover, the behavior of animals certainly seems to attest to the fact that they not only can, but that they actually do have interests. Their behavior presents us with many cases of preferential choice and goal-directed action, in the face of which, and in the absence of any rationally compelling argument to the contrary, it seems both arbitrary and prejudicial to deny the presence of interests in them.

The most plausible argument for the view that humans have an equal natural right to life, therefore, seems to provide an equally plausible justification for the view that animals have this right also. But . . . [this] would not imply that the right in question can never be overridden. For there may arise circumstances in which an individual's right to life could be outweighed by other, more pressing moral demands, and where, therefore, we would be justified in taking the life of the individual in question. But even a moment's reflection will reveal that we would not condone a practice which involved the routine slaughter of human beings simply on the grounds that it brought about this or that amount of pleasure, or this or that amount of intrinsically good experiences for others, no matter how great the amount of good hypothesized. For to take the lives of individuals, for this reason, is manifestly not to recognize that their life is just as worthwhile as anybody else's, or that they have just as much right to life as others do. Nor need any of this involve considerations about the amount of pain that is caused the persons whose lives are taken. Let us suppose that these persons are killed painlessly; that still would not alter the fact that they have been treated wrongly and that the practice in question is immoral. If, then, the argument in the present section is sound; and assuming that no other basis is forthcoming which would support the view that humans do, but animals do not, have an equal right to life; then the same is true of any practice involving the slaughter of animals. . . .

Similarly, to attempt to avoid the force of my argument for conditional vegetarianism by buying meat from farms that do not practice intensive rearing methods or by hunting and killing animals oneself . . . will not meet the total challenge vegetarians can place before their meat-eating friends. For the animals slaughtered on even the most otherwise idyllic farms, as well as those shot in the wild, are just as much killed, and just as much dead, as the animals slaughtered under the most ruthless of conditions.

[Conclusion]

Unless or until, then, we are given a rationally compelling argument that shows that all and only human beings have an equal right to life; and so long as any plausible argument that might be advanced to support the view that all human beings have this right can be shown to support, to the same extent, the view that animals have this right also; and so long as we believe we are rationally justified in ascribing this right to humans and to make reference to it in the course of justifying our judgment that it is wrong to kill a given number of human beings simply for the sake of bringing about this or that amount of good for this or that number of people; given all these conditions, then, I believe we are equally committed to the view that we cannot be justified in killing any one or any number of animals for the intrinsic good their deaths may bring to us. I do not say that there are no possible circumstances in which we would be justified in killing them. What I do say is that we cannot justify doing so in their case, any more than we can in the case of the slaughter of human beings, by arguing that such a practice brings about intrinsically valuable experiences for others.

. . . [T]herefore, the onus of justification lies, not on the shoulders of those who are vegetarians, but on the shoulders of those who are not. If the argument of the present section is sound, it is the non-vegetarian who must show us how he can be justified in eating meat, when he knows that, in order to do so, an animal has had to be killed. It is the non-vegetarian who must show us how his manner of life does not contribute to practices which systematically ignore the right to life which animals possess, if humans are supposed to possess it on the basis of the most plausible argument considered here. And it is the non-vegetarian who must do all this while being fully cognizant of the fact that he cannot defend his way of life merely by summing up the intrinsic goods—the delicious taste of meat, for example—that come into being as a result of the slaughter of animals.

This is not to say that practices that involve taking the lives of animals cannot possibly be justified. In some cases, perhaps, they can be, and the grounds on which we might rest such a justification would, I think, parallel those outlined in the preceding section in connection with the discussion of when we might be morally justified in approving a practice that caused animals nontrivial, undeserved pain. What we would have to show in the present case, I think, in order seriously to consider approving of such a practice, is (1) that such a practice would prevent, reduce, or eliminate a much greater amount of evil, including the evil that attaches to the taking of the life of a being who has as much claim as any other to an equal natural right to life; (2) that, realistically speaking, there is no other way to bring about these consequences; and (3) that we have very good reason to believe that these consequences will, in fact, obtain. Now, perhaps there are some cases in which these conditions are satisfied. For example, perhaps they are satisfied in the case of the Eskimo's killing of animals and in the case of having a restricted hunting season for such animals as deer. But to say that this is (or may be) true of *some* cases is not to say that it is true of all, and it will remain the task of the non-vegetarian to show that what is true in these cases, assuming that it is true, is also true of any practice that involves killing animals which, by his actions, he supports.

Steven L. Davis

The Least Harm Principle May Require That Humans Consume a Diet Containing Large Herbivores, Not a Vegan Diet

AV = author's view; ~AV = not the author's view

Although the debate over **moral vegetarianism** has been going on for millennia there has been a resurgence of interest in this issue in the last part of the twentieth century.

One of the foundational philosophical works on this subject is [Tom Regan's] *A Case for Animal Rights.*[1] This paper will not critique Regan's theory on animal rights. Rather, for the moment, suppose he is right; animals are subjects-of-a-life[2] with interests of their own that matter as much to them as similar interests matter to humans. Therefore, animals have the **right** to live their lives without interference from humans. ~AV His conclusion follows, therefore, that animal agriculture interferes in the lives of millions of animals annually, so humans are morally obligated to consume a **vegan** or vegetarian diet. AV The purpose of this paper is to examine the moral vegan conclusion of Regan's animal rights theory, rather than the rights theory itself. It is also the objective of this paper to examine alternative conclusions. In other words, might there be alternatives to the moral vegetarian conclusion drawn from animal rights theory?

The Concept of Least Harm

As I was thinking about the vegan conclusion, I remembered my childhood on the farm and where our food comes from and how it is produced. Specifically, I remembered riding on farm equipment and seeing mice, gophers, and pheasants in the field that were injured or killed every time we worked the fields. Therefore, I realized that animals of the field are killed in large numbers annually to produce food for humans. Kingsolver describes these killings very effectively. "I've watched enough harvests to know that cutting a wheat field amounts to more decapitated bunnies under the combine than you would believe." "She stopped speaking when her memory lodged on an old vision from childhood: A raccoon she found just after the hay mower ran it over. She could still see the matted grey fur, the gleaming jaw bone and shock of scattered teeth. . . ."[3] Consequently, a vegan diet doesn't necessarily mean a diet that doesn't interfere in the lives of animals. In fact, production of corn, beans, rice, etc. kills many animals, as this paper will document. So, in 1999, I sent an email to Regan, pointing this out to him. Then I asked him, "What is the morally relevant difference between the animals of the field and those of the farm that makes it acceptable to kill some of them (field mice, etc.) so that humans may eat, but not acceptable to kill others (pigs, etc.) so we may eat?" His reply was that we must choose the method of food production that causes the least harm to animals. (I will refer to this concept as the Least Harm Principle or LHP.) In his book, Regan calls this the "minimize harm principle" and he describes it in the following way: "Whenever we find ourselves in a situation where all the options at hand will produce some harm to those who are innocent, we must choose that option that will result in the least total sum of harm."

~AV It seems that Regan is saying that least harm would be done to animals in the production of a plant-based diet, because then at least you wouldn't be killing both the animals of the farm and those of the field, thus supporting the conclusion that humans are morally obligated to consume a vegan diet. AV But is that conclusion the one that best satisfies the LHP? Are there other ways of accomplishing least harm?

I find Regan's vegan conclusion to be problematic because he seems to think that there are no other alternatives. There is an old adage to the effect, "There is more than one way to skin a cat." Do alternative food production systems exist that may cause even less harm to animals?

How Many Animals of the Field Would Die If a Vegan Diet Were Adopted?

Animals living in and around agricultural fields are killed during field activities and the greater the number of field activities, the greater the number of field animals that die. A partial list of animals of the field in the US include opossum, rock dove, house sparrow, European starling, black rat, Norway rat, house mouse, Chukar, gray partridge, ring-necked pheasant, wild turkey, cottontail rabbit, gray-tailed vole, and numerous species of amphibians. In addition . . . "production of most crops requires multiple field operations that may include plowing, disking, harrowing, planting, cultivating, applying herbicides and pesticides as well as harvesting." These practices have negative effects on the populations of the animals living in the fields. For example, just one operation, the "mowing of alfalfa caused a fifty per cent decline in gray-tailed vole population."[4] Although these examples represent crop production systems in the US, the concept is also valid for intensive crop production in any country. Other studies have also examined the effect of agricultural tillage practices on field animal populations.

Although accurate estimates of the total number of animals killed by different [agricultural] practices from plowing to harvesting are not available, some studies show that the numbers are quite large. Kerasote describes it as follows:

> When I inquired about the lives lost on a mechanized farm, I realized what costs we pay at the supermarket. One Oregon farmer told me that half of the cottontail rabbits went into his combine when he cut a wheat field, that virtually all of the small mammals, ground birds, and reptiles were killed when he harvested his crops. Because most of these animals have been seen as expendable, or not seen at all, few scientific studies have been done measuring agriculture's effects on their populations.[5]

In a study that has been done to examine the effect of harvesting grain crops, Tew and Macdonald reported that mouse population density dropped from 25/ha [hectare] preharvest to less than 5/ha post-harvest. This decrease was attributed to both migration out of the field and to mortality. They estimated the mortality rate to be fifty-two per cent.[6] In another study, Nass et al. reported that the mortality rate of Polynesian rats was seventy-seven per cent during the harvest of sugar cane in Hawaii. These are the estimated mortality rates for only a single species, and for only a single operation (i.e., harvesting).[7] Therefore, an estimate somewhere between fifty-two and seventy-seven per cent (say sixty per cent) for animals of all kinds killed during the production year would be reasonable. If we multiply the population density shown in Tew and Macdonald's paper (25/ha) times a sixty per cent mortality rate, that equals a mortality of fifteen animals/ha each year.

If that is true, how many animals would die annually in the production of a vegan diet? There are 120 million ha of cropland harvested in the US each year. If all of that land was used to produce crops to support a vegan diet, and if fifteen animals of the field are killed per ha per year, then 15 × 120 million = 1800 million or 1.8 billion animals would be killed annually to produce a vegan diet for the US.

Would a Pasture/Ruminant Model Kill Fewer Animals?

Production of forages, such as pasture-based forages, would cause less harm to field animals (kill fewer) than intensive crop production systems typically used to produce food for a vegan diet. This is because pasture forage production requires fewer passages through the field with tractors and other farm equipment. The killing of animals of the field would be further reduced if herbivorous animals (ruminants like cattle) were used to harvest the forage and convert it into meat and dairy products. Would such production systems cause less harm to the field animals? Again, accurate numbers aren't available comparing the number of animals of the field that are killed with these different cropping systems, but, "The predominant feeling among wildlife ecologists is that no-till agriculture will have broadly positive effects on mammalian wildlife" populations.[8] Pasture-forage production, with herbivores harvesting the forage, would be the ultimate in "no-till" agriculture. Because of the low numbers of times that equipment would be needed to grow and harvest pasture forages it would be reasonable to estimate that the pasture-forage model may reduce animals deaths. In other words, perhaps only 7.5 animals of the field per ha would die to produce pasture forages, as compared to the intensive cropping system (15/ha) used to produce a vegan diet.

If half of the total harvested land in the US was used to produce plant products for human consumption and half was used for pasture-forage production, how many animals would die annually so that humans may eat?

60 million ha, plant production × 15 animals/ha = 0.9 billion

60 million ha, forage production × 7.5 animals/ha = 0.45 billion

Total: 1.35 billion animals

According to this model then, fewer animals (1.35 billion) would die than in the vegan model (1.8 billion). As a result, if we apply the LHP as Regan did for his vegan conclusion, it would seem that humans are morally obligated to consume a diet of vegetables and ruminant animal products.

But what of the ruminant animals that would need to die to feed people in the pasture-forage model? According to USDA numbers . . . , of the 8.4 billion farm animals killed each year for food in the US, approximately eight billion of those are poultry and only thirty-seven million are ruminants (cows, calves)[;] the remainder includes pigs and other species.[9] Even if the numbers of cows and calves killed for food each year was doubled to seventy-four million to replace the eight billion poultry, the total number of animals that would need to be killed under this alternative method would still be only 1.424 billion, still clearly less than in the vegan model.

Other Alternatives

The pasture/ruminant model would have other advantages. For one, it would provide habitat for many species of animals and insects, helping them to survive. In addition, ruminants are capable of surviving and producing on diets containing only forages, which humans cannot digest. This is beneficial in two ways. First, crops such as corn and soybeans could all be fed to humans instead of to animals. Second, pasture forage can be produced on lands that are too rough to be usable to produce crops for human consumption. Grasses are currently grown and harvested by cows in many countries on lands that are too hilly, and/or rocky, and/or dry to be usable for production of crops like corn and soybeans.

Are there other alternatives that would cause "least harm"? As I have discussed this analysis with others, additional alternatives have been suggested. These include the following:

1. (~AV) Another alternative . . . recommends that if we are going to eat meat, we should kill the largest animals possible, thereby reducing the number of animals that would need to die to feed humans (LHP). In fact, [People for the Ethical Treatment of Animals has] suggested that blue whales, the largest known living animal, would be the ideal choice.[10] (AV) This suggestion strikes me as unsustainable, because it would be impossible to find adequate numbers of adult animals to harvest without totally depleting the population.
2. (~AV) A third alternative . . . would be to eliminate intensive agriculture altogether and have everyone produce their own vegan diet on small plots of land using no-till production systems to reduce killing/harm to animals of the field. (AV) I believe that this system would also be unpractical and not viable. The human populations are too large, land is concentrated in the hands of the few rather than many, and social systems would need to revert to those of primitive cultures.
3. (~AV) But if herbivores are used, wouldn't it cause least harm if we used the fewest possible, therefore, the largest herbivores? Elephants might be used, (AV) but in practical terms, I believe that the majority of people would object to eating elephants. (~AV) Large draft horse breeds[,] developed previously as working horses, may be up to twice the size of a cow. Perhaps they could be used to harvest or convert forages into meat and dairy products. (AV) Again, I don't believe many humans would support this option; otherwise there would already be more people willing to consume horsemeat.
4. (~AV) Kerasote proposed that least harm would be done if humans were to hunt locally, particularly large animals like elk for their own food. (AV) But his least harm concept appears to be related as much to least harm to the environment (less fossil fuel consumption) as least harm to animals. Furthermore, this doesn't seem to be a practical idea, because there are too few animals and there would be too many hunters. As Taylor said, one "issue that arises from Kerasote's argument is whether hunting for one's food is practical on a large scale."[11]

Intended vs. Unintended Deaths

Taylor says that another issue arises from Kerasote's argument, and that is the matter of intentional infliction of harm versus harm that is the unintentional, but a foreseeable side effect of one's actions. The animals of the field die not intentionally, but incidentally as a consequence of producing food for humans. On the other hand, farm animals (chickens, pigs, cows, and sheep) are killed intentionally to provide food for humans. Perhaps I don't fully understand the nuances or moral significance of this difference, but it seems to me that the harm done to the animal is the same—dead is dead. Furthermore, many farmers do intentionally kill some animals of the field because their presence causes reduced yields. Taylor says about the questions of intent, "A utilitarian is likely to see no moral difference between the two, since utilitarianism holds that it is consequences that count and not intentions."

Conclusion

1. Vegan diets are not bloodless diets. Millions of animals of the field die every year to provide products used in vegan diets.
2. Several alternative food production models exist that may kill fewer animals than the vegan model.
3. More research is needed to obtain accurate estimations of the number of field animals killed in different crop production systems.
4. Humans may be morally obligated to consume a diet from plant based plus pasture-forage-ruminant systems.

Notes

1. Tom Regan, *A Case for Animal Rights* (Berkeley: University of California Press, 1983), pp. 266–329.
2. According to Regan, a subject-of-a-life is any animal that has interests, and that will experience pain or frustration if its interests are thwarted. This includes but is not limited to humans. [Editor]
3. Barbara Kingsolver, *Prodigal Summer* (New York: Harper Collins, 2001), pp. 322–3.
4. W.D. Edge, "Wildlife of Agriculture, Pastures, and Mixed Environs," in D. H. Johnson and T. A. O'Neill, eds., *Wildlife-Habitat Relationships in Oregon and Washington* (Corvallis, OR: Oregon State University Press, 2000), pp. 342–60.
5. T. Kerasote, *Bloodties: Nature, Culture, and the Hunt* (New York: Random House, 1993), pp. 232–3, 254–5.
6. T.E. Tew and D.W. Macdonald, "The Effects of Harvest on Arable Wood Mice," *Biological Conservation* 65 (1993): 279–83.
7. R.D. Nass, G.A. Hood, and G.D. Lindsey, "Fate of Polynesian Rats in Hawaiian Sugar Cane Fields During Harvest," *Journal of Wildlife Management* 35 (1971): 353–6.
8. J.B. Wooley, Jr., L.B. Best, and W.R. Clark, "Impacts of No-Till Row Cropping on Upland Wildlife," *Transactions of the North American Wildlife and Natural Resources Conference* 50 (1984): 157–68.
9. Gary L. Francione, *Introduction to Animal Rights: Your Child or the Dog?* (Philadelphia: Temple University Press, 2000), p. xx.
10. "Eat the Whales" was a tongue-in-cheek campaign by People for the Ethical Treatment of Animals to get people to think about the morality of eating meat. It asked people to think about the **morally relevant difference** between eating whales and consuming equivalent amounts of chicken, beef, pork, and so on. Davis takes the campaign seriously, but PETA was obviously being sarcastic. [Editor]
11. Angus Taylor, *Magpies, Monkeys, and Morals: What Philosophers Say about Animal Liberation* (Peterborough: Broadview Press, 1999), p. 87.

David Fraser

Understanding Animal Welfare

A Dilemma

To understand animal **welfare** and its scientific assessment, let us begin with a dilemma that threatened to throw animal welfare science into disarray.

In 1997 a scientific committee of the European Union reviewed the literature on the welfare of intensively kept pigs. The committee asked, among other questions, whether welfare problems are caused by housing sows in "gestation stalls" where the animals are unable to walk, socialize, or perform most other natural behaviour during the majority of pregnancy. The review concluded that, "Some serious welfare problems for sows persist even in the best stall-housing system,"[1] and with this review in hand the European Union passed a directive to ban the gestation stall as of 2013.

Not long after, a group of Australian scientists reviewed much the same literature and asked much the same question, but came up with essentially the opposite conclusion. They concluded that, "Both individual (i.e. stalls) and group housing can meet the welfare requirements of pigs." They also cautioned "public perceptions may result in difficulties with the concept of confinement housing" but that "the issue of public perception should not be confused with welfare."[2] The swine industry in the United States has used that review, plus a similar one, to argue that there is no scientific basis for eliminating the gestation stall.

Very accomplished and capable scientists did both of these reviews with great thoroughness, and both groups likely felt that they had done the best and most objective job possible. What, then, went wrong? How could two groups of scientists review the same scientific literature and come up with opposite conclusions? If we can solve this dilemma, the solution will take us a long way toward understanding animal welfare and its scientific assessment.

Different Views of Animal Welfare

To solve this problem, we need to go back to the debate that arose several decades ago when concerns were first expressed about the welfare of animals in the then-new confinement systems of animal production.

~AV The first major criticism of confinement systems came in the book *Animal Machines*, by the English animal advocate Ruth Harrison.[3] She described cages for laying hens and crates for veal calves, and she claimed that these systems are so unnatural that they cause animals to lead miserable and unhealthy lives. She went on to ask, "How far have we the right to take our domination of the animal world? Have we the right to rob them of all pleasure in life simply to make more money more quickly out of their carcasses?" A decade later, in *Animal Liberation*, Australian philosopher Peter Singer[4] based his criticism of confinement production on the principle that actions should be judged right or wrong on the basis of the pain or pleasure that they cause. He claimed, "There can be no moral justification for regarding the pain (or pleasure) that animals feel as less important than the same amount of pain (or pleasure) felt by humans."

AV In these and other quotations a key concern centred on words like "pleasure," "pain," "suffering," and "happiness." There is no simple English word to capture this class of concepts. They are sometimes called "feelings," but that term seems too insubstantial for states like pain and suffering. They are sometimes called "emotions," but emotions do not include states like hunger and thirst. Perhaps the most accurate, if rather technical, term is "affective states," a term that refers to emotions and other feelings that are experienced as pleasant or unpleasant rather than . . . neutral.

~AV In discussing confinement systems, however, some people put the emphasis elsewhere. A British committee that was formed to evaluate the welfare of farm animals concluded, "In principle we disapprove of a degree of confinement of an animal which necessarily frustrates most of the major activities which make up its natural behaviour."[5] . . . And American philosopher Bernard Rollin insisted that we need "a much increased concept of welfare. Not only will welfare mean control of pain and suffering, it will also entail nurturing and fulfilment of the animals' natures."[6]

AV In these quotations, although affective states were often involved implicitly or explicitly, the central concern was for a degree of "naturalness" in the lives of animals: that animals should be able to perform their natural behaviour, that there should be natural elements in their environment, and that we should respect the "nature" of the animals themselves. All of the above quotations reflected the views of social critics and philosophers, but when farmers and veterinarians engaged in the debate, they brought a different focus. ~AV For example, one veterinarian defended confinement systems this way:

> My experience has been that . . . by-and-large the standard of welfare among animals kept in the so-called "intensive" systems is higher. On balance I feel that the animal is better cared for; it is certainly much freer from disease and attack by its mates; it receives much better attention from the attendants, is sure of shelter and bedding and a reasonable amount of good food and water.[7]

Or as the veterinary educator David Sainsbury put it, "Good health is the birthright of every animal that we rear, whether intensively or otherwise. If it becomes diseased we have failed in our duty to the animal and subjected it to a degree of suffering that cannot be readily estimated."[8] AV Here the primary emphasis is on the fairly traditional concerns of veterinarians and animal producers that animals should have freedom from disease and injury, plus food, water, shelter and other necessities of life—concerns that we might sum up as the basic health and functioning of the animals.

In these various quotations, then, we see a variety of concerns that can be grouped roughly under three broad headings: one centres on the affective states of animals, one on the ability of animals to lead reasonably natural lives, and one emphasizes basic health and functioning. These are not, of course, completely separate or mutually exclusive; in fact, they often go hand in hand. Harrison . . . clearly believed that allowing animals to live a more natural life would make them more happy and healthy; Sainsbury clearly believed that unhealthy animals would suffer.

. . .

A Debate about Values

The different views of animal welfare do not necessarily involve disagreements about facts. An intensive animal producer might conclude that welfare is good in a high-health confinement system because the animals are healthy and growing well; a critic might draw the opposite conclusion because the animals are crowded together in barren pens and develop abnormal behaviour. The two parties may agree on factual issues such as the amount of space per animal and the incidence of disease. Their disagreement is about values—specifically about what they consider more important or less important for animals to have good lives.

Why should people hold such different views about what constitutes a good life for animals? To understand this disagreement, it helps to review a debate that erupted over the welfare of humans. During the Industrial Revolution, the so-called "factory system" became the predominant way of producing textiles and other goods throughout much of Europe. Thousands of factories were erected, and they proved so efficient that traditional, hand production disappeared almost completely. Workers moved from villages and rural areas into cities; and instead of working at hand looms in their homes, people operated machinery in the factories. It was a profound social change, and it touched off an intense debate over whether the new industrial system was good or bad for the quality of human life.

~AV On one side of the debate were critics who insisted that the factory system caused people to lead miserable and unwholesome lives. Critics claimed that the cities created cramped, unhealthy living conditions for the workers, and deprived people of contact with nature. The machines themselves caused many injuries, and (critics claimed) they often led to physical deformities because they placed an unnatural strain on the body. Perhaps worst of all, it was claimed that repetitive work with machines made the workers themselves like machines and led to an erosion of their human nature and moral character.

But the factory system also had staunch defenders. Instead of imposing unnatural strains, automation (the defenders claimed) relieved workers of much of the drudgery that manual handicrafts required. Far from being unnatural, the factory system represented a step in the natural progression from a time of human labour to a time when automation would make labour unnecessary. Moreover, the wise factory owner would take care to have healthy, happy workers because maximum productivity would not otherwise be achieved. In fact, the productivity of the system was seen as proof that the factories were actually well suited to human workers.

AV Because the effects of industrialization were so profound, the debate engaged some of the leading intellectuals of the day, and from their writing we can build up a picture of the very different values and worldviews that lay behind their arguments.

The worldview of the anti-industrial critics might roughly be called Romantic/Agrarian. ... This worldview values a simple, natural life. It sees nature as an ideal state that we should strive to emulate. It values emotional experience and the freedom of the individual. And it looks back to a Golden Age in the past when people lived in harmony with nature.

The worldview of the pro-industrialists was more a product of the Enlightenment when people looked to reason and science to replace superstition and ignorance. This worldview involved two concepts that were relatively new to Western thought.

One of these was productivity. Adam Smith opened his book *The Wealth of Nations* by claiming that the quality of life in a nation depends on the goods that are available to supply the citizens with what they need and want. Increasing the productivity of the work force, and thus increasing the supply of goods, should therefore improve the lives of a nation's people. Hence the factory system, whereby automation and specialization lead to greater productivity, would ultimately make life better.[9]

The second idea was progress—the idea that human history moves irreversibly in the direction of improvement. As historian Sydney Pollard points out, belief in progress began with science, because in science each generation was seen as building on the work of earlier generations so that knowledge constantly improves. But during the 1700s the idea of progress took wing, and by 1800, in the words of Pollard, "firm convictions had been expressed about the inevitability of progress in wealth, in civilization, in social organization, in art and literature, even in human nature and biological make-up."[10] And a belief that change represents progress, and that we cannot "stand in the way of progress," has remained a common theme in Western thought ever since.

Thus, the Rational/Industrial worldview was very different from the Romantic/Agrarian worldview. Instead of valuing a simple, natural life, it valued a life improved through science and technology. It viewed nature not as an ideal state that we should emulate, but as an imperfect state that we should control and improve. It valued rationality rather than irrational emotion, and the productivity of the well-organized enterprise more than the freedom of the individual. And instead of looking back to a Golden Age of harmony with nature, it looked forward to a Golden Age in the future when progress through science and technology would lead to a better life.

The debate over human welfare during the Industrial Revolution has obvious parallels with the debate over animal welfare during the intensification of animal agriculture. In fact, much of the disagreement over animal welfare can be traced to the continued influence of the contrasting worldviews.

~AV People who lean more toward a Romantic/Agrarian worldview will see a good life for animals as (primarily) a natural life, to be achieved by emulating nature through such means as free-range systems and access to the outdoors. They will emphasize the emotions of animals (are they suffering? are they happy?), and attach importance to their freedom. For these various reasons, people who favour a Romantic/Agrarian worldview are likely to see confinement systems as inherently incompatible with a high level of welfare, and they may look back to traditional, non-confinement systems as an ideal that we should try to return to.

In contrast, those who lean more toward a Rational/Industrial worldview will tend to see a good life for animals as (primarily) a healthy life, to be achieved by preventing disease and avoiding other vicissitudes of nature. They will value the rationality and scientific basis of the system more than the freedom of the individual animals, and they will see a high level of productivity as evidence that the animals are doing well. Thus, such people are likely to see confinement systems as a form of progress that improves both animal and human welfare, and they may look upon older, non-confinement systems as outmoded models that need to be improved upon.

Animal Welfare and Science

AV When these value-based disagreements began to emerge in the debate about confinement production systems, many people thought that science would provide the way to decide among the different views of animal welfare and tell us which is right and which is wrong. However, scientists themselves are influenced by the different worldviews that are present in our culture. In fact, when we examine the wide range of scientific methods used to study animal welfare, we can see that the different criteria of animal welfare provided the rationale for some of the different scientific approaches.

Some scientists have used the basic health and functioning of animals as a basis for assessing and improving animal welfare. As one classic example Ragnar Tauson and co-workers improved the welfare of laying hens by studying the basic health of birds in cages of different types and then developing cage designs that would prevent the various health problems they observed. The scientists found that the birds developed foot lesions if the floor was too steeply sloped, and neck lesions if the feed trough was too deep and installed too high for comfortable access. There was often feather damage that could be reduced by using solid side partitions, and overgrown claws that could be prevented by installing abrasive strips. Thus, just by focusing on injuries it was possible to make large improvements in animal welfare, and these results formed the basis of regulations on cage design in Sweden and later in the European Union.

Other scientists have tried to improve animal welfare by focusing on natural behaviour and natural living conditions for animals. For example, as a basis for designing better housing for pigs, Alex Stolba and David Wood-Gush began by observing pigs that they had released in a hilly, wooded area. They found that the pigs showed certain characteristic types of behaviour: they rooted in the soil, exercised their neck muscles by levering against fallen logs, built nests in secluded areas before giving birth, and used dunging areas well removed from their resting areas. Stolba and Wood-Gush then designed a complex commercial pen that allowed the animals to behave in these ways. It included an area with peat moss for rooting, logs for levering, and an activity area with a rubbing post, a separate dunging area, and secluded areas at the back where a sow could be enclosed to farrow. The authors claimed that the complex pen significantly improved the animals' welfare. However, because some aspects of basic health (especially neonatal survival) were not as good in this system as in well-run confinement systems, some people disagreed with that conclusion.

In less radical approaches, scientists have incorporated simple elements of natural behaviour into existing rearing systems. On many commercial dairy farms, calves are separated from their mothers within the first day after birth, and are fed milk from a bucket, usually twice per day. With such infrequent meals the total intake has to be limited so that the calf does not receive too much milk at one time. Under natural conditions, cows stay fairly close to the calves for the first two weeks, and the calf will feed many times per day in smaller meals. Although it is normally not feasible to leave calves with the cow on a dairy farm, feeding systems can still be made to correspond more closely to the animals' natural behaviour. If the calves are fed more frequently (as they are by the cow), then they can drink more milk per day without developing digestive problems; and if the calves suck from an artificial teat rather than drinking from a pail, the action of sucking leads to a greater release of certain digestive hormones. As might be expected, therefore, calves fed frequently by teat gain substantially more weight than calves fed twice daily by bucket.

In other cases, scientists have based animal welfare research on the affective states of animals. Dairy calves are commonly dehorned by a variety of methods including surgical removal of the horn bud or the use of a hot iron to burn through the nerves and blood vessels that allow the horn to develop. In many countries these procedures are done without any form of pain management. A research group in New Zealand used plasma cortisol levels as an indicator of the pain caused by dehorning. They found that dehorning is followed immediately by a large increase in cortisol, but that the reaction is blocked if a local anaesthetic is used to freeze the area. In the treated calves, however, cortisol levels showed a marked increase several hours after the dehorning, probably because the injury remained inflamed and painful when the anaesthetic had worn off. If the calves also received an analgesic, the second peak in cortisol could also be eliminated. Thus the research showed that management of the pain of dehorning requires both a local anaesthetic and an analgesic.

All of the approaches described above have been useful for identifying and solving animal welfare problems. However, instead of the science providing a way to determine that one conception of animal welfare is correct and others are not, we see that the different scientists actually adopted the different value-based views of animal welfare—basic health and functioning, natural living, and affective states—as the rationale for different scientific approaches to assessing and improving animal welfare.

In summary, animal welfare is clearly a concept that can be studied scientifically, but our understanding of animal welfare, and even the science that we do to assess and improve animal welfare, is influenced by value-based ideas about what is important or desirable for animals to have a good life. Thus, we have a concept that is both science-based and values-based.

This situation may come as a surprise to scientists who have been taught to think of science as "value-free." During the 1800s, there was active debate about the boundaries of science and how science relates to matters of ethics and policy. Scientists like Max Weber rightly pointed out that science has a fact-finding role that helps to inform policy, but that research itself does not answer ethical or policy questions. Such thinking obviously has merit, but in its crudest form it gave rise to the idea that values play no role in science. However, if a concept like animal welfare can be both science-based and values-based, then clearly we need a more nuanced understanding of the place of values in science.

The term "mandated science" refers to science that has been commissioned or undertaken in order to guide actions, decisions and policy. In this sense mandated science differs from science done simply to understand the natural world. Mandated science includes research on topics such as health, food safety, agricultural sustainability and animal welfare. In all these cases, the science is done to address concepts (health, safety, sustainability, welfare) that incorporate notions of merit or worth. To say that health or safety or sustainability or welfare has increased implies not merely a change but a change for the better. Hence, these concepts, while fully amenable to scientific research, are also rooted in value-based ideas about what people believe to be more or less desirable.

In the case of animal welfare, then, decisions can be based on a sound, scientific understanding of animals and how they are affected by housing, management procedures, and health care measures. However, the data that we choose to collect and consider when making decisions about animal welfare are determined by value-based ideas about what elements are important for animals to have a good life.

Conclusion

Let us return to the dilemma that was created when two scientific reviews arrived at opposite conclusions about the welfare of sows in gestation stalls. If we look carefully at the reviews, we see that they were based on different conceptions of animal welfare.

The Australian reviewers based their analysis almost exclusively on the basic health and functioning of the animals, and they relied especially on what they called "widely accepted criteria of poor welfare such as health, immunology, injuries, growth rate, and nitrogen balance." They did not deny that affective states are involved in animal welfare, but they took the view that all significant risks to welfare would have effects on health and functioning variables. Thus, by presenting evidence that sows in stalls are generally no worse than sows in other types of housing in survival, weight gain, litter size, disease incidence and such variables, they concluded that, "Both individual and group housing can meet the welfare requirements of pigs."

The European reviewers used a conception of welfare that included affective states and natural living as well as basic health and functioning. Thus they included evidence of fear and frustration in their analysis of animal welfare, whether or not the basic health of the animals was affected. They also considered that the opportunity for "exploration of a complex environment, rooting in a soft substratum and manipulation of materials such as straw" is relevant to animal welfare because of its link to natural behaviour. Using such criteria they conclude: "Some serious welfare problems for sows persist even in the best stall-housing system."

In this example, what appeared to be a scientific disagreement—the sort of disagreement that might be resolved by better experiments—was actually due to a difference in values, specifically about what is important for animals to have good welfare.

Given that there are different conceptions of animal welfare that are not resolved by scientific research, and that these are based on values and worldviews that have deep roots in our culture, how should we proceed in creating practical programs and policies to ensure high standards of animal welfare? I think the simplest message is that actions designed to improve animal welfare are not likely to achieve widespread support unless they take account of the different conceptions of animal welfare to at least some degree. Animal producers are not likely to convince their critics that high-health confinement systems are good for animal welfare if these systems cause frustration and prevent animals from carrying out most of their natural behaviour. Free-range producers are not likely to convince their critics that seemingly natural systems are good for animal welfare if the animals suffer from harsh weather, parasites and have poor neonatal survival. For actions to be widely accepted as achieving high animal welfare, in addition to being based on good animal welfare science, they will need to make a reasonable fit to the major value positions about what constitutes a good life for animals.

Notes

1. Scientific Veterinary Committee, *The Welfare of Intensively Kept Pigs: Report of the Scientific Veterinary Committee* (Brussels: European Union, 1997).
2. J.L. Barnett, P.H. Hemsworth, G.M. Cronin, E.C. Jongman, G.D. Hutson, "A review of the welfare issues for sows and piglets in relation to housing," *Australian Journal of Agricultural Research* 51 (2001): 1–28.
3. R. Harrison, *Animal Machines* (London: Vincent Stuart Ltd., 1964).
4. P. Singer, *Animal Liberation*, 2nd edition (New York: Avon Books, 1990).
5. F.W.R. Brambell (chairman), *Report of the Technical Committee to Enquire into the Welfare of Animals Kept under Intensive Livestock Husbandry Systems* (London: Her Majesty's Stationery Office, 1965).
6. B.E. Rollin, "Animal Welfare, Science, and Value," *Journal of Agricultural and Environmental Ethics* 6, Supplement 2 (1993): 44–50.

7. G.B. Taylor, "One Man's Philosophy of Welfare," *Veterinary Record* 91 (1972): 426–8.
8. D. Sainsbury, *Farm Animal Welfare: Cattle, Pigs and Poultry* (London: Collins, 1986).
9. A. Smith, *The Wealth of Nations*, Book 1, Chapter 5 (London: Dent and Sons, 1904).
10. S. Pollard, *The Idea of Progress: History and Society* (Harmondsworth, UK: Penguin Books, 1968).

Sue Donaldson and Will Kymlicka

From Polis to Zoopolis: A Political Theory of Animal Rights

AV = author's view; ~AV = not the author's view

Introduction

In our book, *Zoopolis*, we propose a new and distinctively political approach to the **rights** of non-human animals in an effort to bypass some of the increasingly stale debates that have dominated the field of animal ethics. To oversimplify, much of the debate to date has revolved around the question of the intrinsic **moral status** of animals. Many animal rights theorists have claimed that because animals possess **sentience** or **consciousness** and therefore have a subjective good, they have the sort of **moral standing** that justifies certain **inviolable** rights—to life and liberty, and in particular the right not to be used as a means to human well-being.

~AV In response critics have argued that to be a possessor of such inviolable rights requires something more than sentience or a subjective good. It requires some alleged higher capacity, typically a cognitive capacity such as **rationality** or **autonomy** or moral reasoning. And therefore only humans can be the bearers of such rights and, moreover, by virtue of possessing these higher capacities, humans have the right to use other beings who lack these capacities. AV Animal rights theorists (hereafter AR theorists) in turn have responded that restricting inviolable rights to those with a certain degree of cognitive complexity is both theoretically arbitrary and at odds with our actual practices. Indeed the evolution of the theory and practice of **human rights** in the last sixty years has been to repudiate any limitation based on the rationality or autonomy of the beings involved. Inviolable rights are first and foremost for the protection of the weak and vulnerable, not some sort of prize awarded to the most rational or cognitively complex.

In our view, the claim of AR theorists is indeed correct: any being with a subjective good, any being who experiences life from the inside, should have basic inviolable rights. Indeed, they must have these rights precisely to protect themselves from the judgement (and actions) of those who would assess their lives as less valuable, less complex, or less meaningful. However, we have little new in our book to say on that topic. Rather, our aim is to emphasize how little that debate actually tells us about the rights of animals or more generally about what justice requires in relations between humans and animals. . . .

We can see this by comparison with the human case. To be sure, one step in developing a theory of the rights that human beings possess, or a theory of justice amongst humans, is to ask what we owe each other simply **in virtue of** our intrinsic moral standing. And this might give us something like a universal theory of basic human rights, as reflected in the UDHR [Universal Declaration of Human Rights]. However, most political theory is not about the question of what all human beings owe all other human beings in virtue of their intrinsic moral standing, but rather about the specific rights and responsibilities we have towards particular others in virtue of a range of morally significant relationships, including relationships of cooperation, of collective **self-government** and of histories of interaction and injustice.

To illustrate this, imagine that we come across a crowd of human beings getting off a plane at an airport somewhere in our country. Without knowing anything about our more specific relationships with particular individuals in the crowd, we already know that we have certain universal obligations to all of them, simply because they are sentient beings with a subjective good. These are the universal rights we owe to all persons as such. (For example, we cannot torture them.)

But as the crowd proceeds to passport control, it quickly becomes apparent that these individuals have quite different legal and political rights. Some of them are our co-citizens, and as such, they have the unqualified right to enter and reside in the country, and once inside, they have the right to be considered full and equal members of the political community. That is to say, they are co-guardians or co-creators of the country, with the right that their interests and concerns count equally with others in determining the direction of the country. As citizens, they are members of "the **people**" in whose name the government acts, they have the right to share in the exercise of **popular sovereignty**, and society has a duty to create mechanisms of representation or consultation by which their interests will be counted equally in determining the **public good** or the national interest.

By contrast, other passengers on the plane are tourists, foreign students, refugee **claimants**, business visitors or temporary workers, who are not citizens. As such, they do not have an unqualified right to enter the country—they may need to have secured permission beforehand (e.g., through a visa). And even if they have permission to enter, they may not have the right to settle permanently, or to work, in the country. Perhaps their visa only allows them to stay for a short period of time before having to leave. As such, they are not included in the people in whose name the government acts, they do not participate in the exercise of popular sovereignty, and there is no duty to create mechanisms of representation to ensure that their interests are counted in determining the public good.

Of course, to repeat, these non-citizens are still human beings, and as such have certain universal inviolable human rights. It would be impermissible to kill or enslave them, or to engage in other acts that deny their **essential personhood** and dignity. But there is no obligation to restructure our public spaces to make them more enjoyable for, or accommodating of, such non-citizens, or to restructure our political **institutions** to make them more accessible to such non-citizens. . . . [T]here is no obligation on citizens to make their cities more welcoming to visitors, and it is the citizens, not the visitors, who make this collective decision about the shape of their society and its public space. . . .

In short, we typically distinguish between universal human rights, which are not dependent on one's relationship to a particular political community, and citizenship rights, which are dependent on membership in a particular political community. As they embark from the plane, all passengers possess the former, but only some possess the latter. . . .

Now this is an oversimplification because, as we will see, there are various "in-between" categories of people who are more than mere visitors but not (or not yet) citizens, and whose interests need to be considered in a way that is more complicated than this simple dichotomy allows. For example, immigrants who gain long-term residency acquire a certain legal and political standing that differs from that of temporary visitors, even if they do not have citizenship. There may also be groups who are affiliated to the state through some form of historic political association other than standard citizenship. For example, the Amish have historically opted-out of many citizenship practices to accommodate the demands of their conscience. . . . [T]he existence of such in-between groups with partial or overlapping citizenship statuses simply confirms the underlying point: namely, that the fact of being a "person" with universal human rights **underdetermines** one's legal rights and political status.

In *Zoopolis* we argue that the same general principle applies in the case of animals. Here too, the intrinsic moral standing of animals underdetermines the rights that animals are owed, which will vary with the types of political relationships they have with human communities. Indeed we think the same general categories often apply in the animal case as in the human case. That is to say, some animals are best seen as co-citizens of our political community, some are best seen as citizens of their own separate sovereign communities, and some fall into a range of intermediate categories, each of which generates distinctive claims of justice.

Domestic Citizens

Domesticated animals are those who have been selectively bred to serve human **ends** for food, protection, companionship, and so on. Such animals, by definition, have been brought into our community and over a long period of time have become dependent on their relationship to human beings. Our actions have thereby deprived them of any alternative existence (at least in the short term). The process of domestication historically has been full of injustices—forced captivity, forced breeding, forced labour, usually ending in premature death. . . .

We believe, however, that a just relationship is possible, if domesticated animals are **accorded** the status of co-citizens of a shared political community with us. To say that some animals are co-citizens of our community is to make a number of inter-related claims. In addition to respecting their basic inviolable rights, it means that domesticated animals have the right to reside here in our community: this is their home—they belong here. It also means that they have the right to be considered members of the self-governing community. As members of "the people" in whose name the state acts, their interests must be taken into account in determining the public good. And, insofar as they are able, domesticated animals have the right to be co-creators of the shared polis.

. . .

What **concretely** would co-citizenship mean? It would have radical implications across a wide range of issues. For example, if domesticated animals are co-citizens, then they are entitled to the equal protection of the law (and hence criminalization of harms to them), and to other forms of public protection (e.g., emergency services should be trained and equipped to rescue domesticated animals in case of fire, flood, and other perils). Similarly, they are entitled to benefit from public spending (e.g., health care, retirement schemes), and to have their interests weighed in the design of public space and institutions. Any community that denied such claims could not possibly be said to be treating its domesticated animals as co-citizens.

We cannot address all of these implications here, but in order to illustrate the approach, we will briefly consider two issues in more detail—socialization and work. . . .

Consider socialization. Membership in any community involves a process of socialization. Existing members must pass on the basic skills and knowledge that children or newcomers will need to fit in. Learning the niceties of social interaction—the duties of **civility**—is essential both for children to flourish and also to ensure that they do not impose unreasonable or unfair burdens on others. In the human case, failure to socialize a child is a form of abuse, like failing to feed, protect, or nurture. This is true of domesticated animals as well. Like human infants, animals arrive in the world ready to learn, to explore, to figure out the rules, to find their place. If this readiness isn't channelled appropriately, they are harmed. Socialization in this sense is a right of membership in the community, but which community? The citizenship model says that the relevant community is a mixed community. Dogs, horses, and other domesticated animals need to be socialized not just into their own species community, but into the community they share with humans and other animals. This will undoubtedly involve regulating certain **natural** inclinations or behaviours—jumping, biting, defecating—that might be regulated differently if animals lived only amongst their own species. But for both humans and animals, socialization into the rules of membership in a mixed community is needed to sustain the cooperative relations that make the rights of citizenship possible.

. . .

. . . [M]any domesticated animals undergo training of a more specific sort, usually in order to provide services to humans (e.g., guide dogs). This raises the issue of animal work. Today, this sort of training is almost always exploitative, ~AV and some AR theorists argue that any sort of animal work constitutes exploitation, because it involves treating animals as means not ends.

AV We would argue, however, that citizenship does not preclude all uses of animal labour or animal products. Indeed, a refusal to "use" others—effectively to prevent them from contributing to the general social good—can itself be a form of denying them full citizenship. Consider cases such as excluding Jews from certain professions, or prohibitions on Arab Israelis from serving in the army. Citizenship is a cooperative social project, one in which all are recognized as equals, all benefit from the goods of social life, and all, according to their ability and inclination, contribute to the general good.

From a citizenship perspective, what matters is that the terms of use uphold the equal membership of all, rather than turning some into a subordinated caste group that exists to serve others. For example, many societies admit immigrants in the hope and expectation of benefitting from them, but in some countries, these immigrants are permanently relegated to the status of exploited outsiders who lack basic control over their labour, while in other countries immigrants gain full membership, including the right to control their lives and labour. The former is a case of illegitimate exploitation, the latter is legitimate "use," or opportunity to participate.

. . .

Consider some examples. **Benign** use might include collecting manure from animals to fertilize our gardens, or encouraging sheep to graze in a field of solar panels to keep the grass in check, or simply enjoying their company as companions. At the exploitation end of the spectrum, consider the case of guide dogs or other kinds of assistance dogs. Tractable animals are identified early and intensively moulded to their future "roles." Training, often lengthy and arduous, can involve considerable **coercion** and deprivation. Many working animals are denied any real downtime in which they run free, or socialize with others, or simply explore and experience their world. Their agency isn't enabled, but suppressed in order to turn them into effective tools for humans. Somewhere in-between might be the case of a dog or donkey used to protect a flock of sheep, whose natural guard instincts do not require intensive training. Providing the animal has appropriate labour rights (limited hours, breaks, safe working conditions, a rich life outside of work, retirement scheme, etc.), this would seem to be an activity from which they can derive genuine satisfaction.

. . .

Wild Animal Sovereigns

Let us now turn to the case of wild animals—those whose evolutionary trajectory has not been deliberately shaped by humans, and who remain independent of humans to meet their basic needs for food, shelter, etc. Within the broad category of non-domesticated animals we find many different kinds of human-animal relations. We will begin by considering the case of "truly wild" animals, i.e. those animals who avoid humans and human settlement, maintaining a separate and independent existence (insofar as they are able to) in their own shrinking habitats. In this case the model of co-citizenship in a mixed human-animal community which we've just outlined for domesticated animals is neither feasible nor desirable.

Nonetheless wild animals are still vulnerable to a wide range of injustices at the hands of human beings and any comprehensive theory of animal rights must address these. One threat, of course, is the violation of the basic inviolable rights that all animals have in virtue of being conscious individuals. Such violations include hunting and trapping, or the capturing of wild animals for zoos or medical experimentation. . . .

. . . [T]here are many other threats and injustices to wild animals beyond the deliberate violation of such basic rights. These include the rapid loss of wild animal habitat by **encroaching** human settlement or development, the harmful side-effects of human activity (like pollution and climate change), and a wide range of inadvertent harms from contact with human activities and infrastructure (e.g. highways, tall buildings, shipping lanes). Traditional AR theory has had little to say about these harms.

. . .

In our view, these problems can't be resolved from within a traditional AR theory perspective that focuses solely on the intrinsic moral standing of animals. As we've seen, that question underdetermines our moral obligations to particular animals (or humans), which vary with the nature of our relationship to them. And so the first question we need to ask concerns the appropriate relationship between human and wild animal communities. If that relationship is not one of co-citizenship, as with domesticated animals, what is it?

Our suggestion is that the relationship is best captured by ideas of sovereignty—that is, we should view wild animals as forming organized communities, **competent** in general to address the challenges they face and to look after their own needs and interests, who typically neither need nor want their lives to be managed or governed by humans. As with sovereign human communities, respect for **norms** of sovereignty does not preclude various forms of aid and assistance, or even in extreme circumstances, intervention. We will discuss some cases below. However, respect for sovereignty entails that intervention be constrained by recognition of the inclination and competence of wild animals to live apart from human control in their own self-regulating societies, and a commitment to supporting that capacity.

Extending the idea of sovereignty to wild animal communities may seem like a strained analogy, but there are important comparisons between the injustices wild animals suffer and those suffered by various human communities whose self-government and sovereign control of territory have historically been denied. Throughout human history, stronger **nations** have engaged in acts of colonization or conquest over weaker nations, and have justified this on the grounds that the subordinated people were incompetent to govern themselves, or were being wrongfully denied the fruits of civilization, or on the grounds that the subordinated people did not even exist (for example, European colonizers defining Australia as "*terra nullius*" [unowned land]). The colonized or conquered are then subjected to processes of displacement, often pushing them onto other poorer lands (which in turn generate resource and cultural conflicts with the pre-existing population on those lands).

We see similar dynamics at work in relation to wild animals. (Recall that for the moment we are considering "truly wild" animals, i.e. those who avoid and flee humans and our efforts to regulate their lives.) Human development is seen as transforming "empty land," ignoring the organized communities of wild animals that already exist on that land, either killing them or displacing them onto other lands that are already occupied by other animal communities. The obvious remedy for this chain of injustices, as in the human case, is to establish norms of respect for the sovereignty of existing communities, prohibiting acts of aggression, colonization, and displacement. Recognizing the sovereignty of a territorial-based community means recognizing that the "people" inhabiting the territory have a right to be there and to determine the shape of their communal life; and that they have the ability to do so.

. . .

It is worth emphasizing here that our defence of a sovereignty model is not based on the idea that natural processes are somehow benign or sacred. The suffering involved in predation and food cycles is morally significant, and it is always appropriate to ask what can be done to alleviate suffering. But a sovereignty approach requires that we situate our concern for suffering within a larger framework which recognizes that wild animals form independent, self-regulating communities, and that they have an interest in autonomy and freedom from human management of their communal lives.

. . .

Liminal Animal Denizens

So far we have discussed domesticated animal citizens and sovereign communities of truly wild animals, i.e. those who live independently of humans and tend to avoid contact with them. But there are many kinds of non-domesticated animal who live in and amongst humans. They are all around us—sparrows and mallard ducks, squirrels and mice, badgers and rabbits, and countless others. They don't live "out there" in the wilderness, but gravitate towards, and often thrive in, human settlement. So we can't divide the animal kingdom into a simple dichotomy of domesticated animals whom humans have brought into our communities, and wild animals whom we've left alone. This ignores the role of animal agency in human-animal relations. Countless animals have chosen us, and adapted to the environmental niches we create. They are not co-citizens whom we socialize into our community, but nor can they be simply left largely alone, as sovereign communities on their own habitat.

We call such animals "**liminal**" animals, since they are neither fully members of our community, nor fully external to it. In this case we need yet another model. Indeed, more than one model, since the liminal category incorporates many different subtypes, each reflecting different histories of interaction, and different patterns of agency and dependency. Consider some examples. One subtype of liminal animal is "opportunistic" animals. These are the highly adaptive species like raccoons and sparrows and others who gravitate to the opportunities of urban life. Another group is "agricultural symbiotics." These are the animals who have evolved in tandem with traditional agricultural and other human practices. Consider a traditional English farm with hedgerows, the abundant species who thrive there, and the complex role they play in a sustainable agricultural system—eating pests, pollinating, aerating soil, and so on. A further subtype is "exotic species"—those animals who have been introduced by humans, whether intentionally or inadvertently, into new environments and have become ecologically viable in the liminal zone. And we mustn't forget "feral" animals—escaped domesticated animals who exist on the edges of human settlement.

Some of these liminal animals we tolerate or even entice to our communities—consider backyard bird feeders. Some are typically considered pests who we try to keep away—e.g. rodents who take up residence in our homes, or geese who foul parkland. Many other liminal animals are simply ignored.

There is no single model that can encompass all of these different forms of liminality. But it is worth noting that we see similar forms of liminality in the human case too. There are many groups of people who reside in the community but are not citizens of it. We've already mentioned some of these in our airplane example—visitors, refugees, temporary workers, members of indigenous nations and opt-out communities. Some of these cases are called "denizenship" to reflect their liminal status. Here again, we can see a complex web of relationships. As with liminal animals, some of these groups of human **denizens** are welcomed, some tolerated, some stigmatized, some ignored and essentially invisible, and others actively barred.

. . .

Consider now the case of migrant denizenship. All contemporary states assert the right to control migration into their territory, and to control access to citizenship. Most political theorists accept that there is indeed such a right, with various caveats especially in a world of gross injustice between states. But in general we recognize a right of sovereign states to regulate who can enter, settle permanently, and become a full citizen of the political community. It is permissible to accept non-citizens as visitors or workers on a temporary basis, and to insist that they then return home. And it is permissible to exclude them entirely, at least if they have a safe place to return to (the **refoulement** principle). Of course, some of these excluded would-be migrants may try to enter the country anyway, without legal authorization. And so one of the challenges facing **liberal democracies** is how to deal with potential illegal immigration.

Faced with this challenge, we see two principles at work. First, states have a legitimate right to try to prevent unauthorized entry. The state cannot of course shoot illegal immigrants, but it can erect border controls and barriers to prevent entry, and undertake policing efforts to identify and remove illegal migrants who do enter. It can also change the social conditions which act as an inducement for illegal entry in the first place. For example, it can punish companies that employ illegal migrants, or can deny illegal immigrants access to, say, driving licenses, so as to make life as an illegal immigrant less attractive.

However, if illegal immigrants have been able to escape detection and deportation for a certain period of time, then a second principle kicks in. Sooner or later they acquire the right to stay, akin to squatter's rights. They may have entered a community illegally, but over time as they become enmeshed in that community, the costs of uprooting them become too high. This is often formalized in **amnesty** programs for illegal migrants. And once their presence is regularized, then justice requires that their distinctive needs and interests be taken into account—e.g. through the provision of language and other support services. In short, states can use barriers and disincentives to keep migrants out, but once they are in, the **calculus** starts to change over time, requiring accommodation of the new facts on the ground.

We think a similar story applies to the case of many opportunistic liminal animals. We can legitimately try to keep them out by making our environment less hospitable to them. (In this respect, they stand in a stark contrast with domesticated animals, whose right to belong and to be accommodated flows from their status as co-citizens). However, if we are unable to keep them out, then at some point we need to regularize their status, and to accept and accommodate to their presence.

In the case of human migrants, this regularization will typically (though not always) take the form of access to citizenship. But in the case of liminal animals, their accommodation is almost certainly going to take the more attenuated form of denizenship, akin to the case of opt-out denizens. Liminal animals live in our midst, but their forms of life are radically different from our own, and incompatible with the demands of full citizenship. Unlike domesticated animals, liminal animals are not typically suited to close and cooperative relations with humans. Fostering closer relations with liminal animals—from coyotes to deer to raccoons—often leads to conflict, and puts these animals in peril. We could of course try to breed and socialize liminal animals so that they become more capable of the sort of trust, communication and physically proximate relations that are required for citizenship—that is to say, we could in effect try to domesticate them. But this could only be done through massive forms of coercion and confinement, and violation of their basic rights (as indeed was required for the initial domestication of currently domesticated species). So we need to accept that liminal animals are neither capable of participating, nor seek to participate, in our cooperative scheme. Like the Amish, they have no desire to be press-ganged into our modern practices of citizenship.

The denizenship model suggests that in living amidst us, but apart, a fair accommodation will involve reduction both in what we can expect from liminal animals (by way of cooperation and self-regulation) and also what we owe to them (e.g. equal access to medical care and other communal resources). They are permanent residents of our community, and their vital interests must count in how we organize our community (e.g. by constructing green corridors, redesigning infrastructure to reduce animal injuries, etc.), but this falls short of the kinds of positive benefits of support which we owe to co-citizens.

Conclusion

To recap, we have tried to make two broad arguments:

First, many of the most important issues in human-animal relations cannot be addressed solely in terms of a theory of the rights owed to animals based on their intrinsic moral standing and capacities, but rather require identifying a range of morally significant political relationships between humans and animals, each with their own distinctive rights and responsibilities. The result of any such theory will be a more differentiated theory of animal rights.

Second, certain concepts from human political theory—particularly, citizenship, sovereignty and denizenship—are helpful in identifying these relationships. . . . There are real moral puzzles in our relations with domesticated animals—e.g., puzzles about limits of permissible use of animal labour and products—and we believe that we gain insight into these dilemmas by asking which uses are consistent with viewing animals as co-citizens, as opposed to those uses which condemn animals to a second-class status. Similarly, there are deep moral puzzles about whether or how to intervene in the lives of wild animals when they are threatened by, say, starvation or natural catastrophes—and we gain insight into these dilemmas by asking which forms are consistent with viewing wild animals as sovereign communities.

Needless to say, these concepts do not provide a magic formula to resolve these dilemmas—as in the human case, what is required by respect for co-citizenship or for sovereignty will be contested. But thinking in these terms does clarify the goals and safeguards that should guide our judgements. Or so we have argued.

Discussion Questions

1. Regan says that animals have intrinsic worth, as humans do, and as a result they have rights to life, as humans do. What are his reasons for this claim? Do you agree? Why or why not?
2. Do you think Regan would accept Davis's claim that we should eat large animals like cows rather than be vegetarians? Do you agree with Davis? Why or why not?
3. Fraser says animal welfare scientists define "welfare" in at least three ways: as basic health and functioning, as the ability to engage in species-typical behaviour, and as positive affective states. How do these definitions of welfare map onto his distinction between the Romantic/Agrarian and Rational/Industrial worldviews?
4. Animal rights theory traditionally has not distinguished between companion animals, farm animals, wild animals, and animals that live among but not with humans. Do you agree with Donaldson's and Kymlicka's claim that we should distinguish between animals based on our relationships with them? Why or why not?

5. Donaldson and Kymlicka say that "for both humans and animals, socialization into the rules of membership in a mixed community is needed to sustain the cooperative relations that make the rights of citizenship possible." What do they mean by this? Do you agree with them? Why or why not?
6. Would Regan agree with one or more of Fraser's definitions of animal welfare? Would Davis? Donaldson and Kymlicka? Why or why not?

Suggested Readings and Websites

♣ = Canadian source or author

This is not a topic on which Canadians have made major contributions, so the Canadian content of this list is less than in most chapters.

♣ Canadian Coalition for Farm Animals. www.humanefood.ca/. [Advocates improving conditions of animals raised for food, particularly banning battery cages and sow stalls, and improving conditions of animal transport; under "Resources > Humane Choices" (www.humanefood.ca/humane.html) there is a list of stores in each province that sell humanely raised animals.]

DeGrazia, David. *Taking Animals Seriously: Mental Life and Moral Status*. Cambridge: Cambridge University Press, 1996. [A philosophical discussion of animals' minds, grounded in empirical research.]

Deutsche Referenzzentrum für Ethik in den Biowissenschaften (German Centre for Ethics in the Life Sciences): Animal Experiments in Research (in English). www.drze.de/in-focus/animal-experiments-in-research [A defence of scientific experimentation on animals.]

♣ Duncan, Ian J.H. "The Changing Concept of Animal Sentience." *Applied Animal Behaviour Science* 100 (2006): 11–9. [A prominent animal welfare scientist, who studies animal welfare from a scientific rather than a philosophical perspective, discusses philosophical and scientific reasons for thinking that animals have feelings, and some scientific ways to measure animals' preferences and pains.]

Francione, Gary L. "Personhood, Property and Legal Competence." In *The Great Ape Project*. Edited by Paola Calavieri and Peter Singer. New York: St Martin's Griffin, 1993, 248–57. [Argues that the law should abolish legal ownership of all animals.]

♣ Narveson, Jan. "Animal Rights." *Canadian Journal of Philosophy* 7, 1 (1977): 161–78. [An argument against animal rights, based on egoism (rational self-interest).]

People for the Ethical Treatment of Animals, www.peta.org/. [PETA describes itself as "The largest animals rights organization in the world."]

Regan, Tom. *The Case for Animal Rights*. Updated edition. Berkeley and Los Angeles: University of California Press, 2004. [The leading rights theorist on animal rights.]

Singer, Peter. *Animal Liberation*. New York: Random House, 1975. [The first modern philosophical defence of animal rights.]

Sunstein, Cass R., and Martha C. Nussbaum, eds. *Animal Rights: Current Debates and New Directions*. Oxford: Oxford University Press, 2004. [An important, more recent collection of essays.]

Part III

What Do We Owe Each Other?

Introduction

In Part I we asked who we are as Canadians, focussing on our history, immigration, and our multicultural make-up. In Part III we ask the same question, this time focussing on Canadian answers to traditional issues in political philosophy. What should the (federal, provincial, territorial, and municipal) governments do, and what should they stay out of? What is society for? What guarantees we should provide for each other?

Canada is a **liberal welfare state** with a **market economy**. As a liberal state, we guarantee rights and liberties to citizens. So, for example, section 2 of the *Charter* guarantees basic liberal freedoms like freedom of belief and expression, freedom of religion, freedom of the press and other media, and freedom of association. Other sections guarantee the right to vote, the right to "life, liberty, and security of the person," the right against "unreasonable search or seizure," and the right to move where we want in Canada. Section 15 says each of us is "equal before and under the law and has the right to the equal protection and equal benefit of the law without discrimination." (Many conservatives dislike section 15. They claim the equal protection and benefit of the law create **positive rights**, rights *to* specific things rather than just *against* government interference. Governments should protect us from interference and no more, they argue. See the reading by Kheiriddin and Daifallah in Chapter 7, The Role of Government.) Canada has taken a fairly egalitarian path in its interpretation of rights and liberties. This is clear not only in section 15 of the *Charter*, but also in some Supreme Court decisions. For example, the Court has upheld the law forbidding hate propaganda, required provincial health care programs to provide sign language interpretation to deaf patients, and ruled that discrimination may exist even in the absence of intent to discriminate.[1]

Welfare states aim to guarantee that everyone has a certain minimum level of welfare, and that no one falls below that minimum. This means, for example, that

- everyone should get enough education to earn their own keep;
- everyone should get at least basic medical care;
- all citizens who live long enough should be able to retire at some point and live the remainder of their lives with some **dignity**;
- people who are unemployed should be retrained or should receive benefits until they do find work again;
- people with a disability who are unable to work should receive benefits so they can live with some dignity; and
- no one who accepts help should starve or freeze to death.

Welfare states insure their citizens against misfortune, the vagaries of the market, bad luck, and even bad choices. In a welfare state citizens promise each other no one's welfare will fall below a certain level.

If people want more than the minimum, however, they must work for it. Most Canadians believe the market is the best way to distribute many but not all social goods. We allow the market to distribute not only luxuries but also many necessities, such as housing and heat. But we do not have a free market. Some things, like health care, education, and roads, are largely taken out of the free market. They may be supplied by independent operators—most doctors are in private practice, for example—but the costs are set by the government and the services are paid for through taxes, not on a fee-for-service basis. And businesses that offer goods and services at market prices operate under many restrictions, including laws banning child labour, minimum wage laws, workplace and product safety regulations, fair hiring practices, and **progressive taxation** (people with higher incomes pay a greater proportion of their incomes in taxes). We have a market economy, then, but it is not a free market economy.

In sum, we are a country that values and promotes individual rights, that insures its citizens against extreme hardship, and that supports a regulated market. The chapters in this part deal with Canadian rights, social guarantees, and markets. Chapter 7, The Role of Government, examines conservative, centrist, and egalitarian views about what governments should do in a liberal society, focusing largely on the relationship between governments and markets. Chapter 8, Health and Health Care, examines universal health care as a guarantee to all Canadians and public health's focus on the social causes of illness. And chapter 9, Euthanasia and Assisted Suicide, discusses whether people who are dying should have the right to choose the method and time of their deaths, or whether allowing this right puts the lives of people who are already vulnerable in even greater danger.

Notes

1. For more than ten years James Keegstra, a high school teacher in rural Alberta, taught his students that Jews are plotting to destroy Christianity and that the Holocaust did not occur. When a parent complained, Keegstra was fired and, eventually, charged with promoting hatred against an identifiable group. He was convicted. He appealed the conviction, arguing that the law against hate propaganda violated his *Charter* right to freedom of expression. The case went to the Supreme Court, which upheld both Keegstra's conviction and the law (*R. v. Keegstra*).

   Robin Eldridge and John and Linda Warren are deaf British Columbians who communicate via sign language. They argued that the absence of sign language interpreters in the BC health care system hindered their access to medical services, which was a violation of their equality rights under the *Charter*. In 1997, the Supreme Court ruled in their favour (*Eldridge v. British Columbia*).

   In the 1990s, the BC Ministry of Forests developed a fitness test for firefighters. Though it was meant to be equally fair to men and women, twice as many men as women passed it. A firefighter, Tawney Meiorin, challenged the fairness of the fitness test. The Supreme Court ruled that, although the Ministry of Forests did not intend to discriminate against women, nevertheless the test adversely affected them and was discriminatory. Discrimination is determined by its effects, the Court said, not by the intent of the discriminator (*British Columbia (PSERC) v. BCGSEU*).

Chapter 7

The Role of Government

Canada is a **liberal democracy**, a **state** in which free and equal citizens collectively rule themselves through elected representatives. What form of government would such individuals choose? (I use "government" and "state" interchangeably.)

As we saw in the Introduction, "A Short Primer," there are three main forms of **liberalism** in Canada: **conservative**, **egalitarian**, and centrist. **Conservative liberals** believe the primary value in liberalism is freedom—freedom to choose, believe, and live our lives as we want, as long as we do not harm others—and the **free market** is the primary forum for freedom. Equality plays a secondary role in conservative liberalism. Citizens are politically and legally equal: each citizen has a single vote, and the law applies to all citizens equally. Beyond that, however, most conservative liberals consider equality irrelevant, and many oppose equality when it interferes with individual freedom. **Egalitarian liberals** define freedom as access to meaningful choices. Equal freedom means citizens have roughly the same number of meaningful choices available to them, and roughly the same likelihood of succeeding. Social inequalities—group-based inequalities in status and income, such as sexism, racism, and large economic inequalities—undermine freedom by giving some people fewer good choices, or less likelihood of succeeding, than others. Liberal freedom requires social equality, egalitarians say. **Centrist liberals** give a higher priority to liberty than **social democrats** do but less than conservatives, and they support more equality than conservatives do but less than social democrats.

Add to these differences conservatives' pessimism about human nature and egalitarians' optimism, and the stage is set for very different views about the role of government.

But first, a brief word on theory, practice, and philosophy. Most people's political views are **pragmatic**, based on their experiences and what they believe will fix problems in their society, not on philosophy. Governments too are pragmatic; they want policies that will work and get them re-elected. But philosophers always demand justifications. If a view is right or wrong, we want to know why. In this introduction I discuss philosophical justifications of conservative, egalitarian, and centrist views on the role of government. These are not how people who hold these views actually do justify them, because their views are likely to be more pragmatic than philosophical. The authors of the readings in this chapter mix philosophical and pragmatic views.

Conservative Views of Government

Conservatives believe freedom is the most important—perhaps the only—political value. (I use "freedom" and "liberty" interchangeably.) Of course individuals have other values, such as love, family, music, or service to humanity. But their values and interests are protected best when they have the most freedom that is consistent with similar freedom for others. That is, people should be able to do whatever they want, as long as they do not harm others or limit their liberty. ("Harm" includes physical harm, **coercion**, fraud, and breaking contracts. It does not include emotional or psychological harm, or harm to oneself.) Liberty for conservatives is **formal liberty**: people may pursue non-harmful values and interests, whatever those values and interests are, without interference from others.

Conservatives believe private property and the free market are central components of freedom. Private property allows people to do what they want with things they own, as long as they do not harm others—that is, it increases freedom. If you own a bicycle, you can ride it, sell it, throw your clothes on it, or torch it. You do not need to consult others beforehand, as you would if the bike were shared. Conservatives say both private property and liberty are protected best by the free market. It provides people with the most options for using their property and exercising their freedom. Any limits on the free market, such as business regulations or redistributive taxation, are limits on liberty.

Libertarian Views

Libertarians believe the state's role is to protect and uphold the liberty rights of citizens, to protect citizens from force and fraud, and to honour their contracts. The state must have a monopoly on the legitimate use of force—that is, only the state may rightfully use force against anyone. State force is justifiable solely to maintain an environment in which all can pursue their own values without interference from others, however. The state enforces contracts, punishes wrongdoers, and defends its citizens—it maintains courts, police forces, and military defence. That's it. And it may tax only to protect and enforce liberty rights. Any more is a misuse of state power and an unjust violation of individuals' liberty.

According to libertarians, individuals deserve whatever and however much—or little—they get by fair means. Wise individuals plan for their futures, including retirement, and insure themselves against illness and disability. Forcing people to pay into government services like employment insurance or the Canada Pension Plan is unjustified **paternalism**—it treats them like children who are unable to make their own decisions. If people do not save money or buy insurance and they become sick, injured, or disabled, that is their problem; no one else owes them aid, and they cannot expect government handouts. Individuals may choose to give to charities that help sick children, people with disabilities, battered women, or whatever. But taxing people for anything except protecting and upholding liberty rights is unjust, libertarians say.

The free market's rule is *caveat emptor*, "let the buyer beware." This means individuals and not the state must protect themselves from unsafe products or unqualified practitioners, such as infant pacifiers laced with lead, cancer-causing food additives, and unsafe cars, bridges, and drugs. In a libertarian state there are no tax-funded fire departments, education, health care, roads, or sewers. These are provided by private individuals or firms in the free market, and only to those people who buy their services. There are no workplace or product safety regulations, or laws forbidding discrimination or child labour, because they restrict the free market and interfere with people's free choices. Most Canadians, including most conservatives, find these consequences unacceptable; there are very few libertarians in Canada. One Canadian libertarian wrote, "generally when I ask who agrees with me, I find that we can continue our meeting in a telephone booth."[1]

Neo-conservative Views

Neo-conservatives believe the state's *primary* role is to protect liberty and ensure the free market runs smoothly, but they justify a slightly larger state than libertarians. The Conservative Party of Canada is largely neo-conservative. The party explicitly supports public health care (anything else would be political suicide in Canada), and it does not challenge public school funding, workplace safety laws, or laws against child labour, as libertarians would. However, neo-conservatives generally do oppose

- human rights commissions and section 15 of the *Charter* (the equality section), because they impair individuals' freedom and overstep the bounds of what governments should do;
- minimum wage laws, unions, most business regulations, and most environmental protection laws, because they interfere with individuals' freedom and businesses' profits;
- welfare, employment insurance, support for people with disabilities, pensions, and other publicly funded programs that redistribute wealth, because they interfere with the free market and individuals' freedom to spend their money as they choose; and
- most taxes, because individuals and businesses should decide for themselves how to spend their money.

Neo-conservatives believe governments should focus on liberty, the free market, and providing just enough social programs to allow people to enter and compete in the market. (Hence their support for public education and health care.) But Canadian governments—federal, provincial, and municipal—are too large, intrusive, and expensive. Most government services ought to be privatized, they say, ranging from public corporations such as the Canadian Broadcasting Corporation (the CBC), the Canada Deposit Insurance Corporation, and Atomic Energy of Canada Limited, to entire industries such as municipal water services, television and radio broadcasting, and airports, harbours, and roads.[2] The private sector provides better services at a lower cost than governments do. Once services have been privatized, governments should return money to citizens and businesses in the form of tax cuts.

Social Conservative Views

Tradition and family hold pride of place in **social conservatives'** political views, and governments should not interfere with either. Social conservatives oppose making society more **secular** and relegating religion to the private sphere. They believe women's and **lesbian/gay/bisexual/transgendered/queer** (l/g/b/t/q) rights undermine the traditional family. The state should recognize only the traditional family composed of a husband, a wife, and their children. They also believe **moral status** begins at conception, so they oppose abortion.

Conservatives, social and otherwise, focus on traditional values and oppose most social change. Most social conservatives also support the free market, but some are centrists on issues not involving tradition and the family. Liberty, equality, and the market generally concern social conservatives much less than social policy does.

Egalitarian Views of Government

Egalitarian liberals—social democrats—believe liberty and equality are equally important. They define these principles differently than conservatives do, however. Liberty is much more than private property and freedom from interference, the **formal liberty** that conservatives endorse. Free people should be able to be agents in their own lives and choose among equally good or bad alternatives, as the case may be; they should have **substantive liberty**. And equality is much more than equality before the law and one person, one vote. Equal citizens should have fair and **equitable** shares of social benefits and burdens; they should have **substantive equality**. Citizens exercise their liberties in social circumstances, and they are equal when social benefits and burdens are distributed fairly. When members of some groups have fewer meaningful choices accessible to them than members of other groups, or when those in some groups enjoy benefits or suffer burdens that others do not, their society is less free and less equal than it should be. To that extent, it is unjust.

Egalitarians deny that the free market contributes to freedom; it does not support a range of meaningful choices for all citizens. Members of some groups have fewer opportunities available to them than others in their society, not because they deserve or have earned less, but because of where and to whom they were born. For example, given a fairly short list of socially relevant characteristics—in Canada, these include but are not limited to sex, race, first language, religion, ethnicity, geographical region, and parents' income and education[3]—we can predict the statistical life chances of newborns with a fair degree of accuracy. Some will be much more likely to thrive than others. But newborns cannot deserve characteristics they were born with, much less their parents' characteristics. The free market only amplifies the unfairness of people's starting points. These are social problems that need social solutions.

Substantive freedom and equality require active maintenance by governments. Egalitarians believe governments should promote citizens' well-being and ensure that all have opportunities to lead fulfilling lives and to play active roles in their communities and the larger society. If it turns out that some people have fewer opportunities through no fault of their own, governments should intervene by, for example, providing retraining, compensation, or accommodation, and sometimes by making anti-discrimination laws and educating citizens about liberty-restricting practices. Governments also must ensure that social benefits and burdens remain at least roughly equal. This means egalitarians support laws against discrimination, section 15 of the *Charter*, human rights codes and commissions, and government programs that promote greater equality—most or all of which give conservatives fits and conservative centrists qualms. Without active maintenance, freedom and equality are shams.

Egalitarians believe substantive liberty and equality require community and social justice, not private property and the market, for their realization. This requires activist governments that foster conditions in which communities and social justice, and thus individuals, flourish. Fostering community means governments should provide support for community-building organizations, such as neighbourhood groups, immigrant centres, Native Friendship centres, parks and athletic facilities, public libraries, and music and arts festivals. They should help immigrants integrate into our multicultural society. Governments should help members of groups that traditionally have been **disenfranchised**—such as Aboriginal people, poor people, and people with disabilities—feel like they are valuable members of their communities and the larger society, and governments should encourage others also to see members of traditionally disenfranchised groups as valuable. Governments should help people re-integrate into their communities, such as people who are homeless and women who have been abused. In communities where many people's livelihoods have collapsed, such as fishing on the east coast and manufacturing in Ontario, governments should help people develop alternative means of support without destroying or impoverishing their communities. This may involve helping them develop new industries or businesses and the skills to operate them successfully, as well as temporary financial support to get them started.

Egalitarians believe governments must actively maintain social justice in society. They do not think there is an "invisible hand" in the market; if there were such a thing, it would be better described as an iron fist. Without government oversight, opportunities become restricted, inequalities undermine citizens' dignity and self-worth, and the society becomes unjust. Government's role is to ensure that there is a level playing field in the society, that all citizens have equitable shares of benefits and burdens, rights and responsibilities, and liberties and opportunities. Shares are equitable if members of one group would be willing, in principle, to trade their shares with members of another group. Shares are not equitable in Canada today, egalitarians say. Aboriginal people, people of colour, women, immigrants, and people with disabilities earn less and occupy fewer positions of power and prestige than non-Aboriginal people, white people, men, Canadian-born citizens, and (temporarily) able-bodied people. Egalitarians believe those who have more owe something back to their society for fostering conditions in which they can flourish. Thus, taxes should be more progressive than they are now, and profitable businesses should pay a greater share of taxes than they do now.

Centrist Views of Government

Centrists' views of liberty and equality are neither fully formal nor fully substantive, but something in-between. Centrists support private property and the free market, but they also believe we owe things to our fellow citizens that require limits on the market and more than minimal taxation. They support more equality than conservatives do, but less than egalitarians. Governments should focus on jobs and the economy, but they also should maintain a social safety net for those who truly need it.

Conservative Centrist Views

Conservative centrists believe the market is usually the best method of distribution—people get what they want and can afford. But the market is not always fair. A few goods and services, such as education, workplace safety regulations, food and drug testing, and health care, are so complex and/or expensive that many people cannot afford them, yet they are necessary for people to be able to compete fairly in the market. Governments should ensure that all citizens have access to these goods and services, either by providing these things themselves or by funding private not-for-profit or for-profit providers. People should be kept out of such severe poverty that they cannot find or keep jobs, so governments ought to provide some welfare and disability payments. Governments also should make sure people are able to retire at some point and not live their final years in poverty. But conservative centrists do not support much more than this. In general they distrust big government, and they think taxes should be kept as low as possible. They believe governments ought to be economically conservative, partly to protect these social programs, and partly because they think most things are better done by non-governmental organizations, whether in the market or the voluntary sector.

Egalitarian Centrist Views

Egalitarian centrists support more substantive freedom and equality than conservatives do, but less than egalitarians. So they support everything that conservative centrists support—education, health and safety regulations, universal health care—and more, but not the substantive liberty-enhancing policies of egalitarians. Governments must intervene in society and the economy, because large economic and social inequalities lead to social injustice. They must promote equality for all citizens by, for example, legislating, educating, authorizing employment and educational equity laws, and ensuring that all stakeholders have a say in policy decisions affecting them. But given a fair start in an equal society, individuals should make their own choices, for better or for worse. This requires more limits on the market, and more taxes, than conservatives or conservative centrists allow. But egalitarian centrists believe the market is the best way to distribute most social goods. Some people will be wealthier or more powerful than others. Some people will be unlucky or foolish, and they will be worse off than others. But the differences between individuals should never become so great that some citizens cannot participate meaningfully in Canadian society.

The Readings

In the first reading, Karen Wendling argues against four myths about government that hinder good thinking about the role of government: all government is **coercive**, all taxes are bad, all bureaucracies are bad, and governments ought to be run like businesses. Each is partly true but false overall, she claims. Governments coerce but they also create liberties. Taxes fund services we want, and if we want the services, the taxes cannot all be bad. Bureaucracies create fairness and consistency, not just headaches. And governments should be run in the public interest, not the private interests that businesses serve.

Tasha Kheiriddin and Adam Daifallah argue in the second reading that Canadian conservatives need to develop a vision—what they are for, rather than simply what they oppose—if they are to succeed politically. The vision should not be focussed on equality, which they say has been enforced by the Liberals and New Democratic Party (NDP), but rather freedom, particularly "freedom of speech, choice, and opportunity; freedom to enjoy one's property and the fruits of one's labours; and freedom from oppression and authoritarianism." They call their vision "Opportunity Conservatism" because the focus is on providing opportunities to all Canadians and allowing them to do what they choose with their opportunities.

John Roberts, author of the third reading, is an egalitarian centrist. He describes liberalism as "pragmatic but not ideological." Like conservative liberals, he believes the market is the best way to distribute many social goods, but like egalitarians, he thinks an unfettered market generates inequalities that undermine democracy. He examines reasons for the rise of neo-conservatism over the last thirty to forty years—globalization, the belief that governments are inefficient and sometimes corrupt, and the belief that the market does almost everything better than governments do. But neo-conservative doctrines undermine human dignity and equality, he says. It is time to return to the values of egalitarian centrism.

Ed Broadbent, a former leader of the NDP and a social democrat, disagrees with Kheiriddin and Daifallah that freedom is central to Canadian liberal democracy. Rather, he says, our core value is equality. He cites evidence that in more egalitarian societies the rich and the poor are "better off in almost every way"—health, life expectancies, crime, and so on. Canadian society is going in the wrong direction, because inequality is increasing rather than decreasing. But show Canadians that greater equality will create a fairer and more caring society *and* make everyone better off, and they will support it, he says.

Notes

1. Karen Selick, "The Moral Myths of Medicare," www.karenselick.com/Moral_Myths_of_Medicare.html.
2. Conservatism.ca, Privatization, www.conservatism.ca/privatize/. (Note: This is not the Conservative Party of Canada's site.)
3. Sex: Statistics Canada, "Women in Canada: A Gender-based Statistical Report," 5th edition (2006), www.statcan.gc.ca/pub/89-503-x/89-503-x2005001-eng.pdf; race: Feng Hou and Simon Coulombe, "Earnings Gaps for Canadian-Born Visible Minorities in the Public and Private Sectors," Canadian Public Policy 36, 1 (2010), pp. 29 -43; parents' education and income: Jo Blanden, "Love and Money: Intergenerational Mobility and Marital Matching on Parental Income," Statistics Canada (2005), http://dsp-psd.pwgsc.gc.ca/Collection/Statcan/11F0019MIE/11F0019MIE2005272.pdf; place of birth: Statistics Canada, "Median Total Income, by Family Type, by Province and Territory," www40.statcan.ca/l01/cst01/famil108a-eng.htm.

Karen Wendling

Four Myths about Government

AV = author's view; ~AV = not the author's view

Discussions in Canada about what we want governments to do and not do often are derailed by slogans, bad thinking, and mistaken beliefs. There are at least four common myths about the nature and purpose of government that get in the way of good thinking: that all government is coercive, that all taxes are bad, that all bureaucracies are bad, and that governments ought to be run like businesses. The first claim is common among political philosophers and social scientists, whereas the other three are common in the general population. All four claims commit the **fallacy** (mistake in reasoning) of **hasty generalization**—they overgeneralize from unrepresentative samples. No useful discussion about what governments ought to do can occur if these myths cloud our judgment.

The myths that all government is coercive and that all taxes are bad involve complex claims; unpacking them and showing why they are wrong takes the bulk of this reading. I dispense with the myths that all bureaucracies are bad and that governments should be run like businesses fairly quickly at the end.

Myth #1: All Government Is Coercive

~AV The claim that all government is coercive is common among political philosophers and social scientists; it can be found in everything from introductory textbooks to the works of some of the most famous political philosophers of the past century. The claim means that all government action is, ultimately, backed up by coercive threats: "Do this (or do not do that), or else we will put you in jail, take your property, make you do community service, take away your passport, or . . ." Governments require that we obey the law, fight in wars, pay taxes, attend school until we reach a certain age, and support our children, and they forbid us to violate contracts, work under the table, operate vehicles without licences, and ignore speed limits. Their rules are backed up by punishment or the threat of punishment, most often in the form of jail and fines. Some political philosophers and theorists argue that a logical consequence of this claim is that the **private sphere** (the family and/or the economy) is characterized by liberty, where people may do as they wish, and the **public sphere** (government) is characterized coercion, where people are forced to do things whether they want to or not.

AV However, both claims—that all government is coercive and that the private sphere involves liberty while the public sphere involves coercion—are problematic for at least three reasons. First, the distinction between public and private is fluid, not fixed, so it is unlikely that liberty resides in one and coercion in the other. Second, the private sphere involves coercion as well as liberty. And third, governments not only coerce, they also create liberty.

The Fluid Public-Private Distinction

The distinction between the public and private sphere is often employed as if it were natural, when it is anything but. What is considered public in one time or place may be considered private in another, and vice versa. Even in a particular time and place, the boundary between public and private is fluid: something can be private with respect to one thing and public with respect to something else. The economy is private with respect to the government (private property, private enterprise), but public with respect to the family (the family is considered a haven from the impersonal and competitive market, as well as from government). It is no defence against murder or assault to say that it occurred at home, in private—a crime committed in a private home makes the home public until the investigation is complete. Businesses can make certain rules about who they will serve, such as "No shirt, no shoes, no service," but they cannot make others, such as "Whites only." Private businesses must follow public rules about providing service to the public, and these permit the first rule but not the second.

The public-private distinction is politically drawn; it is not a natural distinction. Given the fluidity and the political nature of the boundary between private and public, it makes no sense to link liberty with one and coercion with the other.

Private Coercion

The private sphere involves coercion as well as liberty, whether by "private" we mean the family or the economy. Individual, familial, and social pressure can sometimes be very coercive. This may be good—peer pressure sometimes makes people behave better than they otherwise would have—or it may be bad—bullying, prejudice. Either way, however, it is coercive. Social disapproval, and disapproval by those who matter to an individual, can be powerful forms of coercion. Think of the social stigma still associated with homosexuality, long after the laws against it were repealed and discrimination on the basis of sexual orientation was banned; many people still fear their families' and their peers' disapproval. And domestic abuse—not only physical but also psychological and emotional abuse—is very coercive to its victims; they may be harmed, belittled, kept prisoner, starved, tortured, and even killed.

Coercion also occurs in the economic sphere. When jobs are scarce, employers can exert enormous coercive power over employees. Salaried employees may be expected to work seventy or eighty hours a week. People may put up with abusive employers because they have no other options. They may work in unsafe conditions, not because they want to, but because they have no other choice if they want to eat. People who are sexually or racially harassed at work are coerced into doing things against their wills, whether they stand up for themselves, give in to the abuser, or find another job. Scientists may be ordered to suppress data that indicate a product is unsafe. Whistleblowers are often fired for reporting wrongdoing. Medical residents (trainee doctors) regularly work twenty-four-hour or longer shifts in Canada, despite empirical evidence that not sleeping for twenty-four hours impairs performance as much as being legally intoxicated does.

The private sphere is not only a site of liberty. It also can be a place of coercion from which we may desire state protection.

Public Liberty

Governments do much more than coerce; by helping citizens attain the benefits of cooperating with others, governments increase citizens' liberties. Public education ensures that everyone gets enough education to become a productive citizen. Pensions ensure that people will be able to retire at some point, and Old Age Security and the Guaranteed Income Supplement keep most seniors out of poverty. Universal, publicly funded health care allows citizens to know that the health care costs of an unforeseen illness or accident will not bankrupt them. Deposit insurance guarantees that our money will not disappear if the market collapses or the bank closes. Zoning laws allow people who buy houses to be confident that a toxic waste dump will not open up next door. Public roads, railways, airports, and harbours make travel within and between provinces and countries easy. Safety regulations—e.g., workplace safety, building codes, manufacturing standards, standards for roads, bridges, tunnels, railways, airports, and harbours—increase liberty by making our lives safer. In these and many other ways, governments increase citizens' liberties and allow them to live their lives in relative freedom and safety.

In any large-scale society, private liberty depends on public rules and, as a last resort, public enforcement of those rules. Sometimes people interfere with others' liberty. In those cases the state steps in and stops the offenders. While this does involve coercing offenders, notice that the state also preserves victims' and potential victims' liberty. A fair and effective state allows individuals to live their lives free of most interference, knowing they are protected by the law if their liberty is violated. The state also protects economic liberty. The **market** depends on a great deal of trust—confidence that others will honour their contracts, do what they promise to do to an acceptable standard, fix their mistakes, pay for goods and services, advertise honestly, compete fairly, and so on. If that trust is violated, or if there are disagreements between businesses or between individuals and businesses, people rely on state-run courts for enforcement or mediation of disputes.

(~AV) Someone might argue that this proves government is coercive—it uses its coercive power to preserve liberty. (AV) But governments also create and maintain liberties. Governments maintain the market, not only by creating courts that settle disputes and enforce contracts when necessary, but also by making uniform rules and generally ensuring that economic behaviour is predictable. Governments also limit some of the worst excesses of a completely free market. This enhances employees' and consumers' freedom, because effective freedom requires background safety. Workplace safety laws protect employees from unsafe working conditions. (In China there are illegal mines; imagine the safety conditions there.) Regulations restricting the number of hours bus drivers and airline pilots may work without a break protect not only the drivers and pilots, but also their passengers and the public. Truth in advertising laws protect consumers from unscrupulous businesses that make false claims about their products. Product testing protects consumers from unsafe manufactured goods. Ingredients labels on food products allow people to know what they are eating and avoid things they do not want to eat. Pharmaceutical testing protects people from dangerous medications. Laws regulating the professions set minimum standards of competence and protect consumers from fraudsters. Laws prohibiting discrimination in hiring increase the number of positions available to most people. While all such laws and regulations restrict the market, most people consider them to be justified because they increase the liberty of employees, consumers, and the public. These restrictions coerce one group—unscrupulous or careless people and businesses—in order to increase the freedom of a much larger group—those who do not become their victims.

((~AV) Some people argue that laws against discrimination are unnecessary. Discrimination is economically irrational, they claim, because it limits the pool of qualified applicants: businesses that discriminate will do less well than businesses that do not, so discrimination will not occur. (AV) Clearly this is empirically false. Many businesses thrived with discriminatory hiring practices—with workforces that were overwhelmingly white and/or male—before human rights codes came into effect in Canada in the 1960s and 70s. This claim is also based on the assumption that qualified applicants are a scarce resource. Most of the time there are many more qualified applicants than there are good jobs, and in those cases discrimination *is* economically rational. Assume that all groups contain relatively equal numbers of qualified applicants. Eliminating one or more groups from consideration, whether on the basis of sex, race, or shoe size, narrows the applicant pool and makes hiring decisions easier.)

The criminal law coerces some people, both those who are convicted of crimes and those who would commit crimes if not for the law. In doing so, however, it creates greater freedom for those who were or would have been the criminals' victims. In stable, relatively fair and uncorrupt societies, police and the courts protect citizens' rights and enforce the rules fairly, thus making most citizens' lives safer. Where they do not, as happened in Robert Pickton's murders of dozens of women in Vancouver, the problem is that the rules and police resources were not applied fairly. Better police and court protection would have increased those women's liberties, and possibly spared some of their lives.

Only **libertarians** and other **anarchists** truly believe that all government is coercive. Other political philosophers and theorists who say this have unthinkingly adopted libertarians' views on this issue; they have not thought well about how governments enhance and do not only limit liberty.

Myth #2: All Taxes Are Bad

Many Canadians have a deep-seated belief that all taxes are bad and therefore tax cuts are always good. This view involves at least six different but interconnected and mistaken beliefs: first, that all politicians and governments are corrupt; second, that we get nothing for our tax dollars; third, that tax money is *our* money, not the governments'; fourth, that governments spend money on things we do not agree with, and so should not have to support; fifth, that government is wasteful and the private sector could supply the same services for less money; and sixth, that our taxes are too high. I will deal with each of these views in turn.

Are All Politicians and Governments Corrupt?

~AV Some people who believe all taxes are bad are cynics who think all politicians are the same—they're just in it for themselves—and all governments are corrupt. They point to news stories of political scandals such as the sponsorship scandal or spending on the G-8 Summit in 2010.[1] AV Certainly we want our tax dollars to be spent responsibly. That is why we have auditors who examine government spending to see if there has been waste or fraud, news media that examine public corruption, and citizen-run groups that expose public corruption. And, of course, sometimes they find it, as the federal Auditor General did in the sponsorship and G-8 Summit spending scandals. But notice that in both cases government officials broke *already-existing* rules for approving and spending government money. These rules require that the approval processes be transparent and fair, that no one on the government's side has personal or financial interest in the projects or the companies carrying them out, that accurate records of all meetings be kept, and so on. Claiming that all politicians and governments are corrupt, based on a few well-publicized scandals, no more proves the cynic's case than the Bre-X gold scandal[2] proves that all corporations defraud investors, or Robert Pickton's crimes prove that all men are serial killers. These claims are hasty generalizations based on a few bad cases, not representative samples.

What Do We Get for Our Tax Dollars?

~AV Many people seem to believe that governments are little more than giant toilets down which we flush our hard-earned dollars. AV However, those people almost certainly expect governments to help if there is a disaster and they have nowhere to go, if they are injured at work and require medical care, or if they cannot find work and cannot feed their children. In fact, the vast majority of Canadians expect government to do much more than this. Most Canadians want at least:

- Universal health care: This is the most popular social program in Canada. Eighty per cent of Canadians support universal health care without qualification, and another ten per cent somewhat support it. Unqualified support for health care is strongest among people between eighteen and twenty-nine years old, who are least likely to need it now.[3]
- Public education: We think all children should have access to at least a basic education, regardless of their parents' ability to pay for it, so they have opportunities to live good and productive lives.
- Universities and colleges: Given that it is no longer possible for most people to get middle-class jobs with only a high school education, we want affordable higher education.
- Pensions and Old Age Security: We want to be able to retire in at least relative comfort. We think people who are not independently wealthy should not have to work until they die, and they should not spend their retirement years in poverty.
- A social safety net: We think at least children, people with disabilities, and senior citizens should not go hungry or be homeless. We want employment insurance to tide us over if we lose our jobs and cannot find another one for a while.
- Child protective services: We want neglected and abused children to be protected.
- Roads, harbours, railways, airports, bridges, etc.: We want to be able to travel.
- Regulations and regulatory bodies to ensure the safety of roads, harbours, railways, airports, bridges, etc.: We want to travel safely.
- Police, courts, military defence, firefighters: We want to live safely.
- Waste disposal: We want waste disposed of safely. We want toxic waste cleaned up.
- Elected representatives and civil servants: We need lawmakers and civil servants to establish, interpret, and enforce regulations, and to deliver services to the public.
- Laws regulating businesses: We want pharmaceutical testing, food labelling, truth in advertising laws, and at least some environmental protection laws. We do not think businesses should be able to put up "Whites Only" signs.
- Laws regulating labour: We do not want child labour. We do not want to be required to work seventy to eighty hours a week and we do not want to work in unsafe conditions. We want workers compensation if we are injured at work.
- Deposit insurance: We want to know that our life savings will not be wiped out by market or bank failures.
- Zoning laws: We want to be sure that our houses are not built on toxic waste sites, and that noisy factories will not be built next door to us. On the other

side, legitimate businesses want to be able to operate without dealing with residents' complaints.
- Immigration policies: We want immigration policies that are fair and reasonable.

We can disagree about whether we should have more or less of some things on the list, or whether the criteria for access to services and benefits should be more or less inclusive. But there is little disagreement that we want these things, and that we want governments to provide or at the very least regulate them. They all cost money, though—in some cases, such as health care and education, a great deal of money.

We also want government services to be fair. Fairness is expensive, however. Take criminal justice. A fair criminal justice system requires police, Crown attorneys, judges, and other court officials who are well trained, who understand the communities they work in, who have enough money to do thorough investigations, who treat victims, witnesses, families, and accused people fairly, who are paid well enough to prevent most corruption, and so on. Our criminal justice system assumes people are innocent until proven guilty, so there must be safeguards for accused people, including

- court-appointed lawyers for people who cannot afford them,
- rules about how the police and Crown to may obtain evidence and confessions,
- judges who decide if search warrants have **reasonable cause**, if evidence should be admitted, and if lines of questioning should be allowed,
- appeals procedures in case the system erred, and
- Parliament and the Supreme Court to examine the fairness of the laws and their application.

A fair system also requires prisons that punish but do not dehumanize. An *un*fair criminal justice system may come cheaply, but a fair one is very expensive.

Now, apply similar criteria to all the other things we expect of government—civil courts, education, health care, roads, child protective services, and so on. Good government costs a lot of money. People who think all taxes are bad but also expect government to provide services to them either think badly, or they are **free riders** who want others to pay but not them.

Is Tax Money "Our" Money?

~AV Some people believe that governments take *their* money. AV However, most of what we earn comes to us from living in a society, so the claim that our money is "ours" alone is problematic. Our jobs depend on others, whether we are self-employed or employed by someone else: businesses need customers, doctors need patients, teachers need students, lawyers need clients, and so on. Those of us with middle-class jobs earn enough to live comfortably because the skills we have developed are valued in Canadian society—and because, in Canada in the twenty-first century, we *can* develop our skills. Fifty or sixty years ago, the majority of students reading this book would have had difficulty getting into college or university or getting any decent-paying job, because of their sex, race, and/or ethnicity. Employers were permitted to—and did—discriminate on all those bases, and doing so had been upheld by the Supreme Court.[4] (Discrimination on the basis of race and religion—sex and other grounds were added later—was banned only when human rights codes and commissions were adopted in the 1960s and 70s.)

How plausible is the claim that tax money is "ours," and governments unjustly take it from us? Let's look at two fairly typical Canadians.

- Robert lives in the suburbs and commutes to a job in the downtown core. He went to publicly funded grade, middle, and high schools, and he got training for his job at a publicly funded university. His house was built according to the specifications of the building code. Robert makes his morning oatmeal with municipally tested water, and pours milk on it that has passed provincial safety standards. He drives a car that meets safety standards set by the federal government. He drives on city and provincial roads to get to his workplace. He and the other drivers are licensed by the province, which ensures they have at least some knowledge of the rules of the road and excludes the worst offenders. Last night twelve centimetres of snow fell; the suburb's roads were plowed by contractors paid by the municipality, while city roads were plowed by city employees. Robert picks up his lunch from a restaurant that meets health and safety requirements, and eats it in a public park. On his way home from work he stops at a grocery store, where he buys food that meets federal and provincial health standards, with nutrition labels mandated by the government. That night he puts out his garbage and recycling, which will be collected by the municipality. His brother calls, saying he will be flying in for a visit—on a plane inspected by Transport Canada, flown by a pilot and co-pilot who have been licensed by Transport Canada, and taking off from and landing at federally owned and locally managed airports that meet federal safety standards.
- Seema is on maternity leave from her job. Her income comes from EI, and her job is protected by law while she is on maternity leave. Her daughter Alia was born in the local publicly funded hospital. Like some infants, Alia has had a series of earaches, which have required many trips to the doctor. The doctor is paid by the provincial health plan; she attended a publicly funded medical school in Canada, and is licensed by the province to practice medicine. Alia's toys and her crib meet government-set safety standards for infants and her pyjamas are fire-resistant, also a government standard. Seema drives a car and puts Alia in a child safety seat that meet safety standards set by the government, and she drives on city, county, and provincial roads. Seema and Alia go to a mothers-and-toddlers group at a local publicly funded community health centre, and later they go swimming at the publicly funded rec centre. On her way home, Seema picks up a prescription for Alia; the medicine was tested and approved by Health Canada and is dispensed by a pharmacist who passed provincial and federal exams before he got his license to practice.

Every day everyone uses many publicly funded goods and services, ranging from municipal water for our morning showers and coffee, to roads, schools, health care, recycling and waste disposal, products whose safety we can trust, and street lights that make the streets safer at night. We also benefit from laws that aim to ensure all Canadians have opportunities to live good lives. These goods, services, and protections are funded by taxes. "Taxes are the price we pay for civilized society," US Supreme Court Justice Oliver Wendell Holmes, Jr. said in 1904—and for a safer and more fair society, we might add today. Tax money is no more "our" money than the cost of food or gas is "ours." We pay businesses individually for their goods and services. We prepay governments' goods and services, however, through taxes set by representatives that we elect. That way the services are available to everyone when they—or we—need them.

What If We Oppose What Governments Fund?

~AV Some people oppose taxes that fund things they oppose, whether this is abortion (conservatives) or tax breaks for big businesses (egalitarians). AV People who say taxes are bad for these reasons misunderstand the nature of democracy, though. Canada is a representative democracy, which means we elect representatives who make decisions on our behalf. We do not get to cherry-pick, to decide that we will support these programs or services but not those. If we disagree with government policies we can write our elected officials, lobby, protest, try to vote representatives out of office, or run for political office ourselves—but we still must pay our taxes and governments will decide how they will be allocated. That is the nature of representative democracies.

Are Privatized Services Better than Public Services?

~AV Many people believe most services provided by the government should be privatized. Governments privatize services for several reasons. They may shed money-losing or debt-ridden industries or services to save tax dollars. They may sell money-making services because they need short term cash. They may have a political commitment to smaller governments and private ownership. The arguments in favour of privatization are that private businesses are more profitable and efficient than public services, they lower costs for consumers, privatization raises money for governments, and it reduces taxes. AV The arguments against privatization are that privatized companies replace well-paying jobs with fewer, lower-wage jobs, costs to consumers sometimes skyrocket after privatization, private businesses do not provide universal coverage, private businesses may provide inferior service, and privatizing sometimes costs governments more money rather than lowering their costs.

These are empirical claims, which means we can examine the evidence for and against them. Privatized services often do make more money and are more efficient—that is, they produce the same amount of goods or services at lower costs—than public services. And privatization does make short term money for governments. If the government sells a money-losing enterprise it may save money, and this may result in lower taxes. If it sells a money-making enterprise, however, it trades short term gains for long term losses, as people do if they sell their houses and rent instead. Furthermore, this may result in higher taxes to replace the money the public enterprise used to bring in.

On the other side, privatized businesses' profits and efficiency result largely from the fact that they employ fewer people—sometimes twenty-five or more per cent fewer[5]—and pay lower wages. And the profits of these privatized businesses now go to shareholders, not taxpayers. On cost to consumers, the evidence is mixed. In Canada airline deregulation led to lower costs, but air*port* deregulation led to dramatically increased costs, doubling in the first year after privatization and continuing to rise since then. Telephone deregulation initially led to overall price decreases, but that trend has reversed in recent years. In Ontario electricity costs doubled, on average, in the year after privatization. In response to public outrage, the government lowered and froze retail prices, and ordered companies not to cut off customers who could not afford to pay their bills. In Alberta wholesale prices of electricity tripled after privatization, so the government issued rebates of forty dollars per month to consumers and built more power plants.[6]

Do private businesses provide better services than governments? In health care, the evidence indicates that they do not. Publicly funded health care "does a better job of controlling costs and it facilitates **equitable** access," Roy Romanow, head of the Royal Commission on the Future of Health Care in Canada, wrote. Public health care has lower administrative costs than private insurance companies "because of the large infrastructure required to assess risk, set premiums, design complex benefit packages, review claims, and pay (or deny) individual claims."[7] And public health care is more equitable because it covers everyone, regardless of income or health status. Private insurers charge people who are less healthy higher rates, refuse to insure some people, and do not cover "pre-existing conditions" (that is, health care costs arising, even in part, from any condition the person had before becoming insured). Moreover, privately funded health care is often inferior to publicly funded care. In the US, the risk of death is greater in for-profit than in not-for-profit hospitals—partly, perhaps, because they hire fewer and less-skilled staff than not-for-profit hospitals.[8] A recent Canadian study indicates that for-profit long term care for seniors is "likely to produce inferior outcomes" compared to not-for-profit or public long term care.[9] For example, nurses in for-profit facilities are generally responsible for more patients, and the incidence of bed sores is higher in for-profit than not-for-profit or public facilities. "The evidence suggests that the greater the profit, the worse the outcomes," the study's lead author writes.[10]

Comparing private corporations and government services may be like comparing apples and oranges, though. Many government services, such as health care, education, and pensions, are universal and affordable, whereas private services are not necessarily either. Private health care and education, for example, can cherry-pick patients and students, taking only the ones who will cost the service the least money, or charging higher fees for those with greater needs. Private companies often charge more to provide goods and services to people who live in northern, rural, or remote areas than they do to people in the south and cities. By contrast, public programs serve everyone, regardless of where they live or how much they cost the system.

Finally, does privatizing save governments money? If a government sells a money-making enterprise, it trades short term gain for longer term losses. If it sells a money-losing enterprise it seems it should save money, but that is not always the case. Privatizing electricity in Ontario and Alberta continues to cost both provincial governments money. Romanow says there is no evidence that privatizing health care would save money. Even the author of the entry on privatization in the *Encyclopedia of Business* says, "While there is no large body of empirical evidence supporting or refuting the idea that privatization saves money, the literature is replete with anecdotal evidence that it does in fact save tax dollars."[11] Now, as any introductory statistics student knows, the claim that there is anecdotal but no empirical evidence means that either that the evidence does not support the claim, or that adequate studies have not been done. The claim that privatization saves governments—and therefore citizens—money appears to be based on faith or **ideology**, not facts.

Are Taxes Too High in Canada?

~AV Many Canadians believe taxes are far too high. AV By now we can dismiss the claim that *any* level of taxation is too high, but still, we might be paying too much. Here we need to ask how much "too much" is. According to the Organization for Economic Co-operation and Development, which represents thirty-four of the richest countries in the world, in 2009 Canada was seventeenth—right in the middle—in terms of its total tax-to-**GDP** ratio (the ratio of all taxes paid, at every level, to the gross domestic product). These ratios are not tied to financial stability—Germany, which is very financially stable, has the thirteenth-highest ratio, while Italy and Greece, which have severe financial crises, come in third and twenty-fourth, respectively.[12] Nor is the tax ratio a measure of standard of living. The United Nations' Human Development Index, which measures health, education, and per-capita income for countries worldwide, ranked Canada sixth in the world in 2011. Of the five countries ahead of us, two (Norway and the Netherlands) have higher total tax-to-GDP ratios, two (Australia and the US) have lower tax ratios, and one (New Zealand) has the same.[13]

The questions to ask about taxes are (1) What do we think governments ought to provide their citizens? and (2) Do governments provide good value for their citizens' money? Only then can we decide if our taxes are too high. Since most Canadians expect governments to do a lot, we should expect to pay our fair share for those services.

Myth #3: All Bureaucracies Are Bad

Most of us have been frustrated by apparently meaningless rules and regulations, endless waits for service, phone menus that do not provide the options we need, and bureaucratic indifference to our requests. ~AV What's the problem here? Bureaucracies! we say. AV This is a hasty generalization that overlooks the good that bureaucracies can and should, and often do, provide. Bureaucracies ensure that governments' laws, policies, and projects are carried out, services are provided, and laws, regulations, policies, and services apply uniformly and fairly between individuals or groups and across jurisdictions. People in Yellowknife should get their passports in roughly the same length of time, and at the same price, as people in Halifax. A doctor who graduates from the University of Manitoba should be as qualified to practise medicine as a doctor who graduates from Dalhousie. Food bought in Saskatchewan should be as safe as food bought in PEI. Education in rural areas should be as good as education in cities. An abused child in northern Ontario should receive the same protection as an abused child in downtown Toronto. All this is impossible without ministries, departments, and civil servants to provide services, set appropriate standards, ensure the standards are applied fairly and consistently, and ensure compliance with the standards—that is, they are impossible without bureaucracies.

Of course some bureaucracies appear to exist for the sake of bureaucrats rather than citizens, and bureaucracies' rules sometimes seem pointless or even perverse. Those are serious problems with bureaucracies, and public authorities, the news media, and citizens point out and work to correct many of these problems. But bureaucracies' problems are far less serious than their absence would be. Without bureaucracies, citizens would not be able to expect consistent treatment or service across the country, or even across town. Government officials could interpret laws and policies on a case-by-case basis, according to local practice, or based on whim or prejudice. Government offices in each jurisdiction could make up their own rules and procedures, if they had any at all. People would get their tax refunds or student loans . . . eventually. Slipping a government official a bribe might speed up the process, or it might just make you a dupe.

Despite their many problems, no large-scale society whose governments aim to be fair and open could survive without bureaucracies. Winston Churchill once famously said, "Democracy is the worst form of government, except for all those other forms that have been tried from time to time." We could make a similar claim about bureaucracies. They can be frustrating, irritating, maddening, and infuriating, but they are still better than their alternatives. (By the way, governments are not the only organizations with frustrating bureaucracies. Dispute a charge on your phone or credit card bill and you will see corporate bureaucracies in action—or inaction.)

The claim that all bureaucracies are bad is a hasty generalization; it concentrates only on the problems and ignores the benefits of bureaucracies.

Myth #4: Governments Should Be Run like Businesses

~AV We often hear the claim that governments should be run like businesses. People who believe this usually mean that businesses pay attention to the bottom line (and so should governments), that businesses do not spend beyond their means (nor should governments), and that businesses are efficient (and governments should be also). AV However, these generalizations about business are false. For example:

- The US-based energy giant Enron falsely inflated its assets and kept its debts off the books for years; when its accounting practices became public, the company went bankrupt. Enron's shareholders lost eleven billion dollars, and several of its officers were prosecuted criminally. A bad way to pay attention to the bottom line.
- According to a US Senate report on the financial meltdown in 2008, the crisis in the US was "the result of high risk, complex financial products; undisclosed conflicts of interest; and the failure of regulators, the credit rating agencies, and the market itself to rein in the excesses of Wall Street."[14] Hardly an example of businesses keeping within their means.
- Multinational corporations often give very large bonuses to CEOs even when the company has lost money. This rewards *in*efficiency rather than efficiency.

Certainly we do not want our governments to be run in any of those ways. Another hasty generalization.

But the real problem with this claim is that it is false—governments are not businesses and should not try to be like them. The purpose of a business is to make a profit, or at least a decent living, for its owners or shareholders. The purpose of a government, however, is to protect its citizens and help them lead good lives—whether we believe that governments do this best by ensuring the smooth operation of the free market, by ensuring that everyone is on a level playing field, by ensuring that everyone has at least a minimally decent life, by some combination of these, or something else. The myth that governments ought to be run like businesses is another hasty generalization. It latches onto superficial similarities, such as that both have budgets, while ignoring deeper dissimilarities.

Conclusion

These myths about government are common among both academics and the general public. Those who believe them have not thought well enough about their beliefs, however. Governments do coerce, but they also create liberties. Taxes are necessary to fund services we want; we should be concerned that they are spent wisely, but it is hypocritical both to expect governments to help us or others and to be unwilling to pay for these services through taxes. Bureaucracies not all bad; they create fairness and consistency, which is good. And governments should not be run like businesses—or like families, religious organizations, clubs, and so on. They should be run in the public interest, however we define that interest.

Notes

1. The sponsorship scandal: After the 1995 Quebec referendum on separation, the Liberal government set up a fund to promote **federalism**. Some years later the Auditor General issued a scathing report, saying that the money went to Liberal supporters, not to improving the image of Canada in Quebec. The scandal cost the Liberals the 2004 election.

   G8 Summit spending: The 2010 G-8 Summit was held in Huntsville, Ontario, in Minister of Industry Tony Clement's riding. Fifty million dollars that had been approved for border security went to projects in Clement's riding, which contains no borders. The Auditor General criticized the Conservative government because, among other things, there are no records of how the $50 million was spent in Clement's riding.
2. In 1995 the Canadian company Bre-X announced they had found one of the richest gold deposits in the world, sending their stock soaring. However, the gold samples from the deposit had been salted—that is, gold dust had been added to the samples. When this came to light in 1997, the company went bankrupt, and investors lost billions of dollars.
3. Nanos Poll, "90% of Canadians support public health care," www.medicare.ca/wp-content/uploads/2009/11/nanos-poll.pdf.
4. *Christie v. York* [1940] S.C.R. 139.
5. John Nellis, "The International Experience with Privatization: Its Rapid Rise, Partial Fall and Uncertain Future," *SPP [School of Public Policy] Research Papers* (University of Calgary) 5, 3 (January 2012): 17.
6. Edward Iacobucci, Michael Trebilcock, and Ralph Winter, "The Political Economy of Deregulation," Phelps Centre for the Study of Government and Business Working Paper 2006—05: 22–3, 12, 5, and 9, http://csgb.ubc.ca/working_papers.html.
7. Roy Romanow, *Building on Values: The Future of Health Care in Canada – Final Report*, Commission on the Future of Health Care in Canada, November 2002: 60–1.
8. Romanow, 7.

9. Margaret J. McGregor and Lisa A. Ronald, "Residential Long-Term Care for Canadian Seniors: Nonprofit, For-Profit or Does It Matter?," *IRPP [Institute for Research on Public Policy] Study* 14 (January 2011): 1, www.irpp.org/pubs/IRPPstudy/2011/IRPP_Study_no1.pdf.
10. Margaret McGregor, "For-profit care hurts quality in long run," *Edmonton Journal*, 25 February 2012, www.edmontonjournal.com/health/profit+care+hurts+quality+long/6208871/story.html.
11. Michael Knes, "Privatization," Encyclopedia of Business, www.referenceforbusiness.com/encyclopedia/Per-Pro/Privatization.html.
12. OECD, "Total tax revenue as percentage of GDP, 2009," *Revenue Statistics 1965–2010: 2011 Edition*, www.oecd.org/ctp/revenuestats.
13. UN Human Development Reports, http://hdr.undp.org/en/statistics/.
14. United States Senate Permanent Subcommittee on Investigations, Committee on Homeland Security and Governmental Affairs, Carl Levin, Chairman, and Tom Coburn, Ranking Minority Member, *Wall Street and the Financial Crisis: Anatomy of a Financial Collapse* (13 April 2011): 1, www.hsgac.senate.gov//imo/media/doc/Financial_Crisis/FinancialCrisisReport.pdf?attempt=2.

Tasha Kheiriddin and Adam Daifallah

Vision Wanted: Tax Cuts Aren't Enough

"Where there is no vision, the people perish."

—Proverb inscribed on the Peace Tower

Building a conservative infrastructure is the long-term plan for rescuing Canada's right. Conservatives must invest in ideas, build a conservative culture in media, law, and academia, bring young people, New Canadians and Quebecers into the conservative family and "train the troops" to be the leaders of tomorrow.

But a political movement also requires something beyond the bricks and mortar of leadership schools, media monitoring centres, and think-tanks. Something intangible, that will inspire people to come together and work for a better tomorrow, that will make Canadians actually care about politics and the conservative point of view.

That something is vision.

Here, we are speaking not just to small-c conservatives, but to the big-c's as well. Going into the next election, and the one after that, big-c Conservatives will have to offer Canadians something better than "we're not the other guys." While small-c conservatives are building the infrastructure to sustain the movement, big-c politicians will still be on the front lines fighting for votes and promoting the Conservative brand to Canadians.

But as it stands now, they suffer from the same problem as former US president George HW Bush: a lack of what he called "the vision thing." Big-c Conservatives rarely speak of conservative principles: the morality of the marketplace, the value of freedom or the importance of opportunity. Talk too much about those sorts of ideas, and the lefties will accuse you of overdosing on Ayn Rand.[1] Talk too little about them, and you end up where the federal Tories are today [2005]: a party without a true political foundation.

This isn't about defining conservatism by how much you cut taxes, or by how many civil servants you fire in a given mandate. It is about developing a vision based on the core principle of freedom: freedom of speech, choice, and opportunity; freedom to enjoy one's property and the fruits of one's labours; and freedom from oppression and authoritarianism. It is about recognizing how free markets in particular are fundamental to our democratic way of life, and that respecting and encouraging the efficient operation of those markets is in everybody's interests. . . .

Conservatives by definition respect tradition. In building on this link between markets, freedom and opportunity, Canadian conservatives would be drawing on ideas that have been present since Confederation. . . .

The origins of Canada are not statist. Our nation was built by capitalists trading in furs, lumber, gold and other natural resources. The great expanses of our country were opened up by entrepreneurs and adventurers, not bureaucrats and civil servants. And contrary to accepted conventional wisdom, from Confederation until the Trudeau era, "Canadians enjoyed smaller governments and a greater degree of economic liberty" than our neighbours to the south.[2]

In fact, the Americans brought in income tax, gas tax, and sales tax before Canada did. America created a national bank first. Canada brought in family allowances, unemployment insurance, and the Canada Pension Plan years after the United States implemented similar programs. And until the 1950s, the size of the public sector in both countries was similar—around 25 per cent of GDP.

In other words, from a "progressive" point of view, Canada lagged behind the United States in many areas. Yet the political chattering classes claim our country defines itself by social programs, setting us apart from our Darwinian neighbours. Canadians are said to be kinder and more caring than Americans—assuming that you define state dependency as a symbol of kindness.

Throughout the 1960s and 1970s, . . . the federal government actively promoted the image of Canada as a "caring and sharing" nation more inclined to collectivism. It used millions of tax-payer dollars to fund programs, think-tanks, and interest groups that reinforced this state-centred vision of Canada. And it did so under a banner that is, on its face value, impossible to oppose: that of "equality."

How the Liberals Enforced Equality

The notion of "state-enforced equality," to borrow a term used by the economist Frederic Bastiat, was carefully cultivated by Trudeau Liberals. It formed the cornerstone of Trudeau's "Just Society" and was enshrined in section 15 of the *Charter of Rights and Freedoms*, which reads:

> (1) Every individual is equal before and under the law and has the right to the equal protection and equal benefit of the law without discrimination and, in particular, without discrimination based on race, national or ethnic origin, colour, religion, sex, age, or mental or physical disability.
>
> (2) Subsection (1) does not preclude any law, program or activity that has as its object the amelioration of conditions of disadvantaged individuals or groups

> including those that are disadvantaged because of race, national or ethnic origin, colour, religion, sex, age, or mental or physical disability.

... [S]ection 15 set Canada up for a massive increase in state intervention by mandating government to correct every inequity—real or perceived—under the sun. Perversely, it has become an advantage to be disadvantaged. Groups that are not named in the *Charter*, such as gays and lesbians, have pursued "disadvantaged" status through the courts to oblige the state act on their behalf. The unintended consequence has been a surge in rights-based litigation and the growth of an entire enforced equality industry: human rights commissions, pay equity legislation and all sorts of special-interest lobby groups. . . .

The goal of these groups isn't to solve their problems by market means; rather, it is to attain special legal status to get the government to intervene and protect their interests. The government inevitably becomes more and more interventionist as it attempts to erase every new inequality that arises.

The result is to further embed the state in Canadians' daily lives. As Alan Cairns presciently pointed out twenty years ago, when *Charter* litigation was in its infancy, all of this has had unintended consequences for Canada's political and social unity: "By singling out particular groups or categories for individualized treatment, [the state] simultaneously attracts those particular groups or categories to it as patron to client, accords political **salience** to some and not to others, and fractures the possibilities of a common citizenship focusing on more abstract and more general concerns. . . ."[3]

This notion of enforced equality—and the Conservatives' failure to repudiate it—has led our country to the mess we are in today. The result is a government that works around the clock to entrench statism in the national fabric.

. . .

As in George Orwell's *Animal Farm,* all Canadian animals are equal—but some are more equal than others. This isn't just true of interest groups; it is also true of entire regions of the country. In Canada, we redistribute income through federal transfer payments, in areas from health to corporate handouts. The goal is to "level the playing field" and equalize standards of living; the unintended consequences are to penalize wealth-generating provinces and to make it an advantage for poorer provinces to remain poor, or risk losing their benefits. Not to mention giving people an incentive to stay in economically depressed areas and discouraging them from moving to places where jobs can be found.

Witness what happened when Newfoundland and Nova Scotia struck a deal with Ottawa over oil royalties. The offshore revenues threatened to make them wealthier, thus resulting in a reduction in transfer payments. When Martin threatened to renege on his election promise to remove oil and gas revenues from the equalization equation, Newfoundland Premier Danny Williams became enraged, skipped out on a First Ministers' meeting, and yanked Canadian flags from provincial government buildings. Eventually, the Martin government capitulated. The Atlantic Accord was included as part of the 2005 budget, and Ontario and Alberta taxpayers will continue to send their eastern neighbours equalization cheques for years to come.

Canadians' obsession with enforced equality is not ill-intentioned. Most **socialists**, liberals,[4] and even **Red Tories** genuinely believe they are helping people by having the government solve their problems for them. But their policies produce the **antithesis** of a society based on opportunity. They stifle social mobility and expand the role of the state, resulting in a rigid, classist society. In the name of equality, these policies generate a new type of inequality—namely, that people who work harder, are smarter, more talented, or just more tenacious than others should not be allowed to achieve a better outcome than those who are less hard-working, less intelligent, less, talented, or less determined.

This is not to say that small-c conservatives do not believe in equality. But they define it as equality of opportunity, not of result. This critical distinction is not made enough in the public discourse, but it is the one that truly sets the Left apart from the Right. Where you stand on equality determines how you define the state's role in society. If you believe that the state should ensure the same outcome for all, regardless of ability or effort, you are an advocate of enforced equality, and by extension, a statist. If you believe the state should ensure the same opportunity for all, and leave the outcome to the individual, then you advocate less government intervention and are what we call an "Opportunity Conservative."

Introducing Opportunity Conservatism

Opportunity Conservatives frame the role of the state, and every policy it implements, through the lens of creating opportunity. The true "just society" is not about levelling, it is about lifting. It is about allowing maximum freedom and empowering Canadians to raise themselves up. It is not about redistributing the same pie into smaller and smaller slices. Former Tory Belinda Stronach got one thing right when she remarked in the 2004 Conservative Party leadership race that Canada must bake a bigger economic pie. The trick is to find the right recipe.

The Opportunity Conservative vision we prescribe combines free-market ideas and common-sense concepts in a blueprint for a better Canada. These include the following:

- reducing taxes, for businesses and individuals, to stimulate the economy and job growth;
- increasing free-market competition, and eliminating state monopolies in all sectors, including health care;
- ending subsidies to business, cutting regulation, and red tape;
- strengthening the family through fiscal policies that encourage choice in childcare and the formation of legally recognized family units;
- strengthening community by encouraging voluntarism as opposed to state intervention to alleviate poverty and social problems;
- preserving our environment through market-based environmental policies;
- reforming **federalism** by decentralizing power and encouraging freedom of action by the provinces; and
- maintaining a positive and patriotic outlook that focuses on what conservatives stand for, not what they are against.

Opportunity Conservatism is a vision based on merit. It values and rewards—rather than punishes—excellence and achievement. As a nation, we must abandon the loser-worship that threatens to cripple us. . . . We are a country of winners—if only we can shake the shackles of statism that are holding us back.

. . .

Opportunity Conservatism challenges a number of concepts. It rejects *noblesse oblige*, where the rich redistribute money to the poor to keep them quiet and "in their place." It does not believe that the state should dictate personal morality. And it runs counter to the prevailing Liberal view, which is that who you know matters more than what you know when it comes to getting ahead.

But it is in sync with what many ordinary Canadians want and believe, including those who don't even define themselves as conservative. Polling done in April 2005 commissioned by the Fraser Institute and the Montreal Economic Institute found that:

- 52 per cent of respondents said they think the Canadian economy would perform better if government allowed more freedom, vs. 37 per cent who said it would do better with more regulation;
- 68 per cent of those surveyed believed their standard of living would improve if their taxes were reduced; only 25 per cent thought they would be better off if taxes increased;
- 70 per cent of Canadians polled said they should be able to buy health care services from any provider they choose; only 26 per cent disagreed; and
- 51 per cent said they are prepared to take more personal responsibility for their retirement, vs. 41 per cent who said retirement should remain the government's responsibility.

Clearly, a smaller government approach resonates with many Canadians. Yet neither the Liberals nor the Conservatives have come up with a policy platform that speaks to this view.

Adopting an Opportunity Conservative perspective would set big-c Conservatives apart from Liberals. Today's Liberal Party isn't pro-opportunity at all. It is *pro-opportunist.* Liberals excel at giving your money to their friends. As Naresh Raghubeer, executive director of the Canadian Coalition for Democracies, quipped, "Canada has become the Guyana of the North." He would know: he was born and raised in Guyana! If you're pals with people in government, you benefit. . . . Today's Liberal Party is about power, not empowerment. And to quote Lord Acton, as seems to be a must for any political book taking the Liberals to task, absolute power corrupts absolutely.

Opportunity Conservatives would open the door to success, on the understanding that Canadians take the initiative and walk through it themselves. The Liberals and the NDP don't grasp this. The Liberals give free handouts to people they know and free passes to others who qualify because they belong to a special interest group. The NDP, in their obsession with enforced equality, would level society to such an extent that opportunity would simply cease to exist (for a case in point, time-travel to the former Soviet Union). The Liberal Party sees government programs as a way to buy votes, while the NDP sees them as a way of punishing achievement and making "the rich" pay for their success. Either path reduces opportunity while encouraging dependence on the state. Each approach strengthens the state to the detriment of the individual.

Accentuating the Positive

Of course, the crucial challenge will be selling this concept to Canadians. Conservatives, big and small-c, certainly won't have any help from the media or the country's self-appointed elites. But we would argue that this vision can be sold.

First, it is a vision—an actual alternative view of . . . how the country should look—not just the usual mishmash of policies the Conservative Party has espoused for decades. It gives conservatives something to stand for. Conservatives do well when they have a vision and can champion bold ideas.

Secondly, it is inherently positive in nature. A big part of the problem with the current state of the Conservative Party and conservatism in general is that it is unrelentingly negative. Conservatives are seen as always opposing things instead of proposing. Ask the average Joe what he knows of the Conservative Party's policy today and he will say, "They're *against* gay marriage."

Worse, they are sometimes seen as unpatriotic or even as hating Canada. As just one example, MP Monte Solberg wrote on his Internet weblog just after the gay marriage vote in Parliament on June 28, 2005: "Gay marriage is now on the fast track to becoming the law in Canada. The new Canada. You can have it. . . ." Solberg's frustration in losing the same-sex marriage vote is understandable, but bashing the country is not.

. . .

Frustration with today's Canada is reasonable, but this is not the way to express it. Conservatives must stop the ultimatum talk. It makes them look mean-spirited and no better than the lefty Hollywood celebrities who threaten to move to France every time a Republican wins the US presidency.

. . .

In an exclusive interview in August 2005 with the *Western Standard,* Harper commented, "The real issue is whether the country as we know it will survive. . . . I think people are willing to make a change. I think if they are not willing to make a change, the long-term consequences for the country are devastating. . . . I don't think it will survive this government. . . ."[5] Translation: Vote for me or the country is finished. Not exactly the most uplifting message.

Conservatives must give people hope for a better life. They have to explain why conservatism is good for Joe Sixpack, Jane Lunchbox and their kids. The message of conservatism cannot just be about reducing the size of government and cutting taxes. Though these things are important, conservatives must offer more. They must show how their ideas will empower people and above all, improve their lives.

. . .

Notes

1. Ayn Rand was a Russian-born novelist and philosopher who was famous for advocating a kind of **libertarian** philosophy which she labeled "Objectivism." She continues to be a significant influence on American conservative and libertarian thought. [Editor]
2. Chris Leithner, "What on Earth Has Happened to Canada?" *Le Québécois Libre,* October 25, 2003. www.quebecoislibre.org/031025-6.htm.

3. Alan Cairns, "The Embedded State: State-Society Relations in Canada," in Keith Banting, ed., *State and Society: Canada in Comparative Perspective* (Toronto: University of Toronto Press, 1986), p. 67.
4. By "liberals" Kheiriddin and Daifallah mean centrists. They do not mean people who accept liberalism as a political philosophy, because they themselves are that sort of liberal. [Editor]
5. Bruce Cheadle and Sue Bailey, "Stephen Harper to Spend Summer Bolstering Image, Showing Sunny Disposition," *Canadian Press*, June 14, 2005.

John Roberts

Liberalism: The Return of the Perennial Philosophy

AV = author's view; ~AV = not the author's view

Liberal Values

. . . [**Liberalism** is] **pragmatic** rather than **ideological**. . . . Political decisions . . . require perspective and proportion, and a practical consideration of the facts of the moment. Free speech does not extend to libel; tolerance does not extend to the promotion of racial hatred; during a time of terrorism some **rights** may be temporarily suspended; the pursuit of **social justice** should not be so dominant that it prevents the market from being an engine of economic growth; rights of property do not extend to activities, like pollution, contrary to a clear **public good**. One size does not fit all occasions.

Liberals' . . . concerns are with the law, revenue, expenditure, and administration, not the **extirpation** of personal sin. Pragmatism rather than righteousness should decide the public agenda. For while there may be many people who would be pleased to have their moral viewpoint imposed on others by government, there are very few who wish to have the moral views of others imposed upon themselves. Moral rectitude is not the purpose of government but practical action to enhance the opportunity for individuals to be self-realizing. As President Kennedy[1] remarked, the questions for a governmental leader to ask are "Will it pass?"; "Will it work?"; "Will it help?" (to which we might add, "And then what?").

This does not mean that governmental decisions are necessarily valueless. To ask whether a proposed governmental action will help raises the questions of who is to be helped, and at what cost to others, and to do what. And these ultimately do involve value judgments. They may be immediate practical responses to questions that events have suddenly made important. They may be the incremental response to long-standing issues that require continuing management. They may be undertaken with regard to their practical consequences, not because they fit some preconceived vision of what is intellectually or morally right. But pragmatic decisions are not simply questions of technique or administration. They inevitably reflect the standards and political values of those that make them. For liberal decision-makers their overall effect will likely be the re-enforcement of liberal values.

. . . [L]iberals historically . . . have considered that it is their task to make [life] fairer. This implies a belief in our ability through experience, knowledge, and intellectual imagination to conceive a future other than that which the unimpeded processes of society, free from action by government, would bring—not through **Utopian** blueprints, or visionary grand plans, but incrementally by programs that enable individuals to fulfil their purposes by expanding their means to do so through specific interventions. . . . Twentieth century liberalism has recognized that a person deprived of economic opportunity can be as cut off from the possibility of fulfilment as one who is deprived of political freedom.

All the subsidiary principles of the liberal philosophy flow from a basic belief in the value of freedom of individual choice, and the conviction that respect for the primacy of the **interests** of the individual citizens is the **foundation** of political processes and purposes. . . . [C]ontemporary liberalism includes, primarily, the following precepts:

- the equality of all members of society rather than class, religious, ethnic, or sexual distinction as the order in principle of government;
- the recognition of individual rights, the **rule of law**, and **democratic** structures as a means to the equal protection of the citizens' interests;
- insistence on a **secular** rather than a spiritual or ideological role for government;
- a belief in freedom of thought and expression, and in tolerance and the promotion of diversity as a means both to individual fulfilment and the generation of progress;
- an attachment to property rights and the structure of a free and competitive **market economy** as the best generator of economic growth and prosperity, and the need for government to provide the legal framework to maintain the free and fair working of that economy;
- an obligation on government to ensure that the pursuit of private sector purposes does not generate extraneous adverse social consequences and thus damage the common good;
- that government should not only ensure security and stability in society but also play an active role in expanding opportunity for individuals by programs such as infrastructure development, education, research, and the provision of essential public services at affordable rather than unregulated costs;
- a commitment to ensuring that the benefits of living collectively in a liberal society are used to help achieve the conditions of social justice by narrowing the disparity of opportunity between those who are disadvantaged and those who are fortunate; and
- pragmatism in pursuing, and balancing, these goals one with another.

These **salient** characteristics of liberalism are especially appropriate to the social and political conditions of Canada; its size, diversity, **federal system [of government]**, ***Charter*** of rights, rule of law, democratic **institutions**, **multiculturalism**, historically active role for government in economic development, government provision of essential services, and concern for government as a means to social justice, are rooted in its geography, history, and cultural traditions.

. . .

What Has Happened?

But . . . how can one account for the disillusion with liberalism (and Liberalism) that has occurred from the mid-1980s until the present day?. . . [L]iberal political policies [have been] contested on all sides. ~AV In the world's **democracies** we have seen the emergence of a multitude of new movements—**neo-liberal**s, [**neo**-]**conservatives**, ecological and environmental parties, **libertarians**, **communitarianism**, institutionalized anti-globalization, and a whole range of religious and spiritual cults. Liberalism no longer seems to be the automatic path we should follow to the future. It is attacked on practical grounds—it does not "work"—and on ideological grounds—its values, or professed values, are empty, or a distortion of reality.

It would be tempting—and perhaps to some extent correct—to argue simply that liberalism has become doubted because it has worked. Liberalism seeks to provide opportunity for those who do not have it. To the extent that it succeeds in giving that opportunity—in creating prosperity—it produces a society where more people are better off. It therefore, to some extent, may plant the seeds for its own rejection. As the weight of society shifts to those who are no longer disadvantaged but have advantages they wish to conserve and protect, the impulse for liberal policies of redistribution may be weakened. And a society that prizes novelty, and suffers from the discontent generated by advertising and a media devoted to commercial objectives, may lapse into a frustration of expectations rather than the general mood of optimism and vitality that liberal thinkers had expected.

Cracks within Liberalism

~AV It is not, however, only the advantaged who have come to suspect liberalism. The disadvantaged see that the North American belief in an **egalitarian** society conflicts with the real distribution of ownership, wealth, and power in our political and economic life. They are frustrated in their aspiration to have more of the community's resources devoted to giving them the opportunities and comforts of those who are well off. It is difficult for them to understand how the promises of technology and progress to provide us with a better life have led to longer working hours for them, wealth for the established, a growing gap between the rich and the poor, and insecurity in their working and family lives. They are discontented with political processes of compromise and brokerage, and electoral financing which seems to ignore their interests, or provides them with too little too late.

The middle classes also have expectations—that they are entitled to enjoy the material rewards of the good life, and that their traditional position in society will be respected. But they bear a heavy tax burden, and they have become more and more suspicious that their tax burden is supporting inefficient and wasteful government programs devoted to others.

AV So liberalism is not simply a victim of its past successes. Its problems are rooted in the changing nature of our society—in particular the transforming impact upon us of the substance and pace of change.

For two centuries change has been regarded as the ally of liberal reform. Liberals reflected the confident faith that change—properly directed by the wisdom of liberal reformers, of course—could ultimately cure the wretched condition of mankind. Change was seen as a particular remedy for faults in society. It was not viewed as the dominating characteristic of society itself. ~AV Now, however, change presents us with pervasive transformation of our social and economic environment. No part of the world is untouched by it; no economic sector is left unaffected.

We live within global networks of production, distribution, exchange and consumption; sometimes these seem to work with dazzling but unfeeling efficiency, at other times they seem not to work well at all. Governments have often seemed powerless to manage these systems and protect individuals from their unintended consequences. In this age of specialization and complication it has become difficult for individuals to identify with the processes of government or the main institutions of society. Government, instead of being seen as a guardian of individual interests, is regarded as an integral part of that incomprehensible system of industrial structures, world markets, military establishments, transportation, communication and information systems, and culture and energy conglomerates that make up the confusing superstructure of our society. Social and political institutions are seen as things which act for citizens, not as things through which citizens act.

And so the conventional wisdom that had supported liberalism and its policies began to change. The characteristic of conventional wisdom is not that it is necessarily wise but that it is convenient. Conventional wisdom is accepted because it comfortably fits the implicit **self-interest** of those who thus have no incentive to challenge it. By the mid-1980s the precepts of liberalism in action no longer seemed convenient—that is, they no longer seemed to be successful. The old liberal approaches, which had fostered prosperity through the post-war years, seemed not to work in the new world of the 1980s. Keynesian economics[2] failed to manage the problems of stagflation.[3] . . . Governments, while happy to apply Keynesian tax reductions to stimulate lagging economies, proved reluctant to apply tax hikes to restrain buoyant demand during good times. Moreover the time lags between the implementation of Keynes's principles and their impact on the economy made them suspect as tools for economic management. Fine tuning the economy through macro-economic management proved a difficult task.

The Rise of Neo-conservatism

In this context of social frustration and economic confusion, it is hardly surprising that the vacuum was filled by the policies of [neo-]conservatism which, with a proud disdain for the public realm, and the attractive notion that the new problems of political and economic management were too complicated for governments to manage, assured us that the simple techniques of market fundamentalism[4] would set all problems to right. One had only to dismantle the role of government to let the "invisible hand"[5] of unfettered markets reward the able and allocate the resources of society in what would ultimately through social Darwinism,[6] be for the collective good.

The political face of neo-conservatism was presented by Margaret Thatcher[7] and Ronald Reagan,[8] but an intellectual establishment gave it respectability. Milton Friedman,[9] preeminently, as an economist justified the rejection of Keynesian economics in favour of monetarist theory. Political theorists like Robert Nozick[10] argued, on the basis of the primacy of rights, for minimal government and against any role for the **state** in redistribution, indeed against any role for the state other than the provision of security. . . . The precepts of neo-conservatism were strongly reinforced by the establishment of right-wing think tanks, especially in the United States, in a calculated attempt to provide intellectual and academic respectability for the positions of the privileged.

. . .

AV Three dominating assumptions [had] characterized Canada's post-war Liberal governments. One was that economic management could, through economic fine-tuning, sustain continuing growth. Another was that government could be good at administration, at running things. The third was that large-scale expenditure programs could meet the needs of social security, diminish poverty, and reduce the gap in opportunity between rich and poor.

~AV By the 1980s these three beliefs had lost much of their credibility. It was difficult to apply overall macro-economic direction to an economy as open as that of Canada, dependent on foreign markets and hostage to the economic management of other countries, especially the United States. A decade dominated by low productivity, high inflation, and high unemployment hardly seemed a good argument for the cyclical economic management that Liberals had acclaimed.

Nor . . . did the government appear to be an efficient manager. . . . Government was poor . . . at managing for a variety of reasons—the political processes of government militate against flexibility, decentralization, and the delegation of responsibility; personnel management, an essential instrument of management, remains largely outside the hands of political direction; government does not have profit as a bottom-line objective and therefore finds it difficult to apply as a means of bureaucratic control; [and] the objectives of government are as mixed and as varied and as contradictory as the aspiration of the members of society. These amorphous purposes, the lack of precision in purposes, make public management cumbersome rather than streamlined. The public generally assumes that it is simply wasteful.

. . . [T]he public became sceptical of the massive expenditure programs which form the essential network of social security in Canada. Our economy seemed unlikely to expand at a rate that, given the requirements of fiscal stability, would generate automatically the revenues needed to sustain these programs. Hard choices, it seemed, would have to be made.

It is hardly surprising, therefore, that Canada swung towards the Conservatives . . . AV But the neo-conservative argument is not impressive. It suffers from historical myopia—it neglects our past and forgets how the market place, left unchecked and unbalanced, can undermine human **dignity**. The painful lessons running through the industrial revolution to the great depression and on to the corporate excess of today—of how markets can ignore human needs when government does not, or cannot, protect the general interest, and how they may give sanction for individuals who pursue only greed and seek prosperity at the expense of their fellows—go unremembered. Nor has neo-conservatism been impressive in action. In both the United States and Canada, in spite of its **rhetoric**, it saddled governments with extraordinary debt loads; in both countries it led to a growing gap between the rich and the poor; in both countries it has undermined democratic politics by creating a dependence on corporate financing.

The Return of Liberalism

The criticisms of liberalism over the past . . . decades, many of them justified, are not substantially effective criticism[s] of the structure of liberal beliefs and purposes but, rather, criticisms of technique. The underlying principles of action remain **sound**, the specific applications at times faulty. That is an argument not for the rejection of liberal principles but for a shrewder use of methods to achieve liberalism's goals.

As Benjamin Barber has . . . written, the myth of market fundamentalism is as foolish and wrong-headed as the **socialist** myth of omnipotent states. It tricks people, he says, "into believing that their own common power represents some bureaucrat's **hegemony** over them, and that buying power is the same as voting power. But consumers are not citizens, and markets cannot exercise democratic **sovereignty**. The ascendant market **ideology** claims to free us, but it actually robs us of the **civic** freedom by which we control the social consequences of private choices."[11] But we are now moving . . . away from a time when selfish purpose was regarded as the dominant value to one in which social responsibility and concern for others, and how we can work through government to pursue common goals effectively, have returned to the front lines of political thought and **discourse**.

There is, therefore, once again, an openness to liberal approaches. We do not need a grand new political idea—today's big new idea often becomes tomorrow's bust. We do not need a new overarching intellectual structure for we already have one that has served us well and still corresponds to the values of most Canadians. Nor do we need novelty simply for fashion's sake. That does not mean we do not need new ideas. On the contrary it is vitally important to use our intellectual imagination to come forward with pragmatic approaches to the inevitably difficult problems we will face in this new century. Those new approaches, I believe, will be found within the framework of historical liberalism. . . .

Notes

1. John F. Kennedy was President of the United States from 1961 until his assassination in 1963. He is famous for promoting **civil rights**, escalating the Vietnam War, and numerous conspiracy theories surrounding his assassination. [Editor]
2. Keynesian economics is an economic theory elaborated by John Maynard Keynes in his 1936 book *The General Theory of Employment, Interest, and Money*. The theory claims that the quantity of goods and services produced by a country in a given time period is strongly influenced by the total demand at that time. According to one interpretation of Keynesian economic theory, in order to stop the cycle of strong economic growth followed by severe recession, governments ought to increase taxes and reduce government spending during economic "booms," and decrease taxes and increase government spending during economic "busts." [Editor]
3. Stagflation describes a period in which the inflation rate is high, unemployment is high, and economic growth is slow. This situation is particularly difficult to address from a Keynesian theoretical standpoint because government actions used to increase inflation are supposed to decrease unemployment. If Keynesian economic theory is correct, the cost of ending stagflation is considerable. [Editor]
4. Market fundamentalism is the belief that the market can solve virtually all social and economic problems. It is a term used only by opponents of this view. People who believe the market has this power call themselves free market theorists or libertarians. [Editor]
5. The "invisible hand" is a metaphor describing the idea that if people are left to their own devices in a free market, their economic transactions will lead to the greater common good, as if an invisible hand were guiding the market. [Editor]
6. Social Darwinism was a late nineteenth and early twentieth century theory that claimed individual humans and groups of humans—classes, races, nations, and so on—were subject to the same Darwinian laws of natural selection that plants and animals are. It was a very conservative theory that justified imperialism and colonialism, classism, and the racial superiority of Northern Europeans,

and discouraged attempts to improve the social conditions of poor people, colonized people, and people of colour. [Editor]

7. Margaret Thatcher was Prime Minister of the United Kingdom from 1979 to 1990. Her economic policies included privatizing government-run industries such as coal mines, gas, and electricity, curbing labour union powers, and deregulating England's financial sector. [Editor]
8. Ronald Reagan was President of the United States from 1981 to 1989. His economic policies included reducing federal income tax rates, cutbacks to various government programs such as federal education programs and the US Environmental Protection Agency, and promoting what critics labelled "trickle-down economics," the belief that making the rich richer inevitably benefits the poor as well. [Editor]
9. Milton Friedman was a Nobel prize–winning economist who challenged Keynesian economic theory. He argued that managing demand would do little to reduce the severity of economic recessions, and said governments should intervene much less in the economy. His theories and proposals influenced the policies of Margaret Thatcher and Ronald Reagan. [Editor]
10. Robert Nozick was a philosopher who argued for a libertarian political theory in his book *Anarchy, State, and Utopia* (New York: Basic Books, 1974). He argued the only legitimate role of the state is to provide protection and law enforcement (military, police, and law courts), leaving all other institutions and public goods to private enterprise and market forces. [Editor]
11. Benjamin Barber, "A Failure of Democracy, Not Capitalism," *New York Times* 29 July 2002, www.nytimes.com/2002/07/29/opinion/29BARB.html?src=pm&pagewanted=1.

Ed Broadbent

Equality Is the Core Value of Democracy

There has never been a better time in recent history when the core democratic value of equality can be seen as both an ethical and practical option. Governments in advanced democracies around the world have been forced by the current prolonged economic crisis to openly acknowledge that the dominant political and economic **ideology** has been a failure. Its system of values, with the minimal role assigned to government, has been proven by experience to be disastrously wrong, both in terms of stability and social justice.

Even governments and economists openly on the right of the political spectrum have been compelled by history to acknowledge they were at least partially mistaken. So, if ever there was a time for discussing the relevance of alternative values to practical politics and to the daily lives of Canadians, it's now.

In the 1930s, when Canadians faced dire economic circumstances supported by a dysfunctional ideology, they made important changes in both. I hope we can do the same.

I graduated from university half a century ago. For the first half of the period since then, we Canadians were busy creating one of the most productive and **equitable** societies in the world. We ensured that high economic growth rates were accompanied by a wide-ranging set of social entitlements. Under prodding by **social democratic** parties, and in continental Europe also by Christian Democrats, it came to be understood that, left to its own devices, capitalism would be inherently unstable and produce a distribution of goods and services that was profoundly unfair. If citizens in the North Atlantic democracies were to have half a chance at a life of **dignity**, governments believed they had to act.

Here in Canada, we were part of this widespread political and economic change. While pushed by the CCF and the NDP, the other federal parties in varying degrees came to share in this shift in ideology and practice. For both ethical reasons and the functional need for stability, an expanding role for government and increasing equality became national practice. Left behind was the belief that individuals and the economy should be left to fend for themselves. In its place was the model of democracy best expressed by Abraham Lincoln: government not only by and of the people, but also for the people.

What emerged from this thinking was a Canada characterized by a wide range of new social and economic rights: government pensions, universal health care, trade union rights, comprehensive unemployment insurance, the expectation that every boy and girl with ability could go to university—and all were paid for by adequate levels of **progressive taxation**. Achieving more equality in our everyday lives, we became a nation of greater social cohesion, and started to describe ourselves as "sharing and caring."

This higher level of social and economic equality, symbolized by our signing on to the International Covenant on Economic, Social and Cultural Rights[1] in the mid-1970s, also produced greater tolerance and a reaching out to provide new freedoms—to women, to First Nations, to gays, to ethnic minorities, and to the artistic community. These freedoms were best illustrated by the civil society activism and political leadership that led to the provisions of our new ***Charter of Rights and Freedoms***.

Whether put in place by political parties self-described as social democratic or by other political formations, this post-war combination of political, civil, social, and economic rights aimed at citizens' equality came to be known by social policy experts and the general intellectual community as the social democratic alternative to the pre-war minimal-state market-based system.

However, long before the 2008 crash in the global economy, Canada and many other Western countries had undergone an **ideological** and material reversal. Writing last year in the *New Yorker* magazine, David Frum, the Canadian-born **ideologue** of the American right, asserted that the conservative (small "c") revolution launched by Margaret Thatcher and Ronald Reagan in the 1980s had as its purpose the rolling back of the "social democratic" model I have just described.

In Canada, the reversal first took place in open ideological form in Ontario when the Harris government turned its back on the **red Toryism** of Bill Davis. It came to be joined at the federal level not only by the Reform Party and the Conservatives, but also by the market-driven Liberal party of the 1990s. This became apparent in the middle of that decade, after the deficit had been overcome and surpluses restored.

Federal programs were not fixed; they were abolished. Budgets were not simply reduced; they were slashed. Artists and the CBC [Canadian Broadcasting Corporation] were cut loose and encouraged to rely more on the market. Income taxes needed for the restoration of social programs were not only cut, but also made less progressive. During that decade, the number of poor children in Canada increased almost every year, while the rich continued to get richer.

In marked contrast to continental Europe, environmental reform never got established; national housing programs disappeared, and post-secondary education spending was slashed.

Reflecting the ideological shift at the time, the Minister of Finance, Paul Martin, actually boasted that government spending as a proportion of GDP had been reduced to the level of 1951. During the 1990s and continuing since, virtually all the real growth in market-based income has gone to the top ten per cent of Canadians. Instead of increasing taxes on the rich to compensate for this—as Bill Clinton did in the US—the Liberal government severely reduced capital gains taxes and carved nine percentage points off income taxes for the wealthiest.

The scale of the increase in inequality, beginning in the last decade of the twentieth century, is immense. Remember that was the best decade of economic growth in forty years, a period during which the trickle-down soothsayers said everyone would benefit from it. Between 1998 and 2007, the average wage of full-time workers went up from $33,000 to $40,000, but that was less than the rate of inflation. In contrast, during the same period, the top one per cent of Canadians increased their share of total income by one hundred per cent, and the compensation of the top one hundred CEOs went from an annual average of $3.5 million to $10.4 million—up three hundred per cent.

The vast majority of Canadians have actually seen a downward shift in their share of the national income that they worked to create. Seventy per cent of Canadian households have a smaller share now than they had at the end of the 1990s. Apart from the elderly, the bottom fifty per cent of Canadians actually have lower after-tax incomes than their equivalents in the 1980s.

The present federal government has simply continued its predecessors' onslaught on equality. As a consequence of the continuing underfunding of social spending and irresponsible and unfair tax cuts, it came as no surprise when we were criticized by the United Nations for failing to live up to our obligations under the Covenant on Economic, Social and Cultural Rights. This was followed by an OECD [Organization for Economic Cooperation and Development] report showing that the level of inequality in Canada is now among the worst in the OECD. This in turn was confirmed recently by the Conference Board of Canada.

In continental western Europe, where increases in inequality in general have been less severe, in April of 2008 (six months before the crash) finance ministers at the European Union meeting in Brussels, with the exception of the British Chancellor, committed themselves to taking action to deal with inequality. It was the same group of continental Europeans who took the lead at the last G-20 meeting to curb the outrageous salaries and bonuses of the super-rich.

This, then, was the legacy of recent federal governments leading into the economic crisis that befell us in the fall of 2008. While we Canadians can congratulate ourselves on the relatively healthy structure of our financial institutions, we must not allow this to obscure the other, deeper democratic problem—the alarming increase in inequality that is now being openly debated in Western Europe.

In fostering this inequality in Canada, what our recent federal governments have done is not only to reject the political legacy of the CCF and the NDP, but also that of Lester Pearson, John Diefenbaker, Pierre Trudeau, and Bob Stanfield[2]—all of whom came to see the importance of social programs and the use of government as a stabilizing and equalizing force in the economy.

Under the leadership of my parents' generation, we Canadians began to transform ourselves in the 20th century—a transformation that was reflected to some extent in all of our political parties. Under various political labels, as a nation we had embarked on the social democratic journey which combines a regulated and efficient market-based economy with strong social and fiscal policies aimed at overcoming poverty and achieving greater equality. In the process, we Canadians also became more tolerant and more cohesive. Sharing and caring was not only a slogan; it was characteristic Canadian Behaviour.

It is this journey that has been dangerously undermined—not by inherent forces in the economy, but by willful decisions made by politicians.

The progressive politics of my generation were driven by an equality agenda because of ethical considerations, and also concern for macro-economic stability. However, we now have recent and clear evidence that more than stability and ethical concerns about equality is at stake. More equal societies are not simply more stable and just; they are also healthier in virtually every respect for everyone in them.

Bringing together data from a large number of international studies (UN, World Bank, US Census, Statistics Canada), two leading British epidemiologists, Richard Wilkinson and Kate Pickett, in their book, *The Spirit Level*,[3] published [in 2009] . . ., show the society-wide positive social consequences of more equality.

As a result of their comprehensive analysis of data from dozens of countries, we now know that ethics and practical benefits come together: that equality works.

Their research has shown that more equal nations like Sweden, Norway, and Denmark are better off in almost every way. Their citizens are healthier, live longer, have fewer teenage pregnancies, are more law-abiding, participate more in civic projects, and are more trusting of their neighbours. Contrary to those who claim freedom is sacrificed with more equality, the opposite is true. With more equality comes a greater flourishing of the kind of responsible individualism and citizenship favoured by the great liberal John Stuart Mill.[4]

Transcending any differences in religion, language, and culture, it is the higher degree of equality that makes those nations so much better off than the US or the UK, which are now among the most unequal. I repeat and emphasize that, once a certain minimum level of wealth is reached in a country, the evidence shows it is not more growth, but more equality, that leads to a better quality of life for everyone.

Wilkinson and Pickett's work demonstrates that unequal societies are not only unfair; they are also dysfunctional. The status-related insecurity and anxiety produced by unequal societies promotes more isolation, social estrangement, and negative health outcomes than in societies that are more equal. Not just the poor, but everyone is worse off. Rich and highly educated British and Americans do worse than their equivalents in more equal societies. Furthermore, the evidence also indicates that more inequality leads to higher levels of consumerism, which further depletes the planet's resources.

As a country, Canada is somewhere in the middle of the pack, but, as the OECD and Conference Board reports have shown, we're going backwards. We're becoming more unequal more rapidly than most of the countries studied. The implications are clear. Once we are firmly out of the current crisis, if we continue promoting only more growth and not more equality, we will continue to foster only more negatives in health and social behaviour.

Such a policy could hardly be more dysfunctional. Low wages, low social benefits, low spending on health care and education are not only ethically unfair for the poor whose market-based incomes are the lowest and whose human potential to flourish they deny. But, because such policies maintain or increase inequality and exacerbate social tensions and anxiety in general, they are also bad for everyone else. In contrast, more equality benefits all classes: lower, middle, and upper.

Child poverty in Toronto or in Montreal or Vancouver is little different from what it was twenty years ago, when Parliament said it should be abolished within a decade.[5] Every day, thousands of unemployed men and women are being denied EI [Employment Insurance] benefits; all across Canada, middle-income families are re-mortgaging their homes so their kids can go to university; and in every community seniors are being forced back to work because their pensions have been wiped out since our OAS [Old Age Security] and CPP [Canada Pension Plan] are now inadequate. Based on recent evidence, the policy implications are clear: More growth alone won't fix Canada, but sharing our money and resources, as other democracies have shown, can make a huge difference.

I have long believed that the best kind of democratic politics is that which combines both idealism and practicality. People like to be inspired, but, before they vote, they need to be persuaded. Only when the ideal is seen to be real does idealism work in the real world of politics. In the 1960s, Canadians liked the idea that health care should be a right and not a privilege. But they were persuaded to vote for a party promising a public universal system only after they were convinced it was a practical answer to their medical problems. Democratic citizens will support even radical change when they are convinced that those promising it can make it work.

We have known for a long time that inequality is bad for those directly affected by it—the unemployed, poor kids, anxious seniors, over-burdened families. But, in thinking beyond the current crisis, we now also know that inequality harms us all. In recent decades, many Canadians who have become members of the middle class in income and expectations have not readily seen themselves as beneficiaries of new social initiatives aimed at equality. Many are afraid that they will pay, but that only others will benefit.

For those of us, however, who believe in equality as the core democratic value, the task is perhaps easier now than it once was. Because of the new evidence, we can show the middle-class majority that equality-building measures do indeed directly benefit them and their children.

In most respects, all will be better off with a more equal Canada: a Canada characterized not only by better health outcomes for everyone, but also by less violence, more citizen engagement, fewer teenage pregnancies, more voluntarism, and less consumerism.

Surely this is the Canada we all desire.

From Periclean Athens[6] to the twenty-first century, liberty and equality have been seen as the essence of democracy. Given that we now know the positive impact more equality can have on the quality of life for all Canadians, and since inequality is getting worse, all democrats should speak out. This trend must be reversed. To say that in recent decades it is only the rich who have virtually enjoyed all the real gains in income is to speak the truth. To say that they should now be paying more of the tax burden is neither class envy nor theft; it is a call for justice. We must get back on the road to building a more equal Canada.

We now need a comprehensive reform of taxation. But let me give you an example of how we might start now. There are approximately 180,000 Canadians who are in the highest income tax category and who make more than $250,000 a year. This group, on average, has a taxable income (including capital gains income) of about $600,000. By increasing their tax rate from twenty-nine per cent to thirty-five per cent, we could generate an extra $3.7 billion a year, which would be more than is needed to double the National Child Benefit Supplement for low-income families. This would bring the total child benefit close to $5000, a sum that the Caledon Institute has said would make a major dent in child poverty.

With just this single move, we would reduce inequality and take the lives of thousands of children out of a state of misery. It is only one example of what can be done to get us back on the path to a more equal Canada.

Our overall task is to restore the dream of social justice. But it isn't just a dream. We know that it's both ideal and possible to create a Canada that is healthier in every respect—a Canada with more involvement by our citizens; a Canada where neighbours are seen as friends, not competitors; a Canada where babies born on the same day in Alberta and New Brunswick will have equal opportunities in life.

Our task is to show and persuade Canadians that, with more equality, this kind of Canada is possible.

Notes

1. The International Covenant on Economic, Social and Cultural Rights (ICESCR) is a UN treaty involving, as of 2013, 160 countries committed to guaranteeing the economic, social, and cultural rights of individual persons. These rights include, but are not limited to, labour rights, rights to health, education, and an adequate standard of living. [Editor]
2. Lester Pearson, former leader of the Liberal Party and the fourteenth Prime Minister of Canada, initiated a number of Royal Commissions concerning inequality in Canada, such as the Royal Commission on the Status of Women and the Royal Commission on Bilingualism and Biculturalism. Pearson's government is also credited with instituting the world's first immigration system free from racial discrimination. John Diefenbaker, former leader of the Progressive Conservative Party and the thirteenth Prime Minister of Canada, is most famous for overseeing the introduction of the *Canadian Bill of Rights* and granting the vote to First Nations and Inuit peoples. Pierre Trudeau's Liberal government established the *Canadian Charter of Rights and Freedoms*. Robert Stanfield, former leader of the Progressive Conservative Party and seventeenth Premier of Nova Scotia, modernized the province's education and health services. [Editor]
3. Richard G. Wilkinson and Kate Pickett, *The Spirit Level: Why More Equal Societies Almost Always Do Better* (London: Allen Lane, 2009).
4. John Stuart Mill was a British politician and philosopher who advocated the active participation of all citizens in the democratic process, both at the local and national level. He was also the first person in the history of the British Parliament to propose extending the right to vote to women. [Editor]
5. In 1989, the Parliament of Canada passed a resolution to eliminate child poverty by the year 2000. Needless to say, this has not been accomplished. The percentage of children living in poverty has not changed significantly since 1989. [Editor]
6. Pericles is considered by many historians to have been the greatest statesman and orator in ancient Athens. He strengthened Greek democracy, supported the arts, began the building projects that resulted in the buildings on the Acropolis, and led Athens in the first two years of the Peloponnesian War. [Editor]

Discussion Questions

1. Probably the most important anti-tax argument is that taxes are *our* money that governments (unjustly) take from us. What is Wendling's argument against this claim?
2. "Where you stand on equality determines how you define the state's role in society," Kheiriddin and Daifallah write. What kind of equality do they support, what kind do they oppose, and why?
3. How does Kheiriddin's and Daifallah's view of freedom differ from Roberts's and Broadbent's? Which view of freedom do you support, and why?
4. Roberts says a central belief of liberalism is "that government should not only ensure security and stability in society but also play an active role in expanding opportunity for individuals by programs such as infrastructure development, education, research, and the provision of essential public services at affordable rather than unregulated costs." How does his view of liberalism differ from a conservative view, such as Kheiriddin's and Daifallah's, and a social democratic view such as Broadbent's?
5. "For two centuries change has been regarded as the ally of liberal reform," Roberts writes. How did change become the ally of neo-conservatism? What does Roberts think egalitarian centrism must do to regain its place in Canadian politics?
6. What are social and economic rights? How, according to Broadbent, do they enhance freedom?
7. What is Broadbent's argument for the claim in his title, that equality is the core value of democracy? Would Kheiriddin and Daifallah agree? Would Roberts? Which view of equality do you prefer, and why?

Suggested Readings and Websites

♣ = Canadian source or author

♣ The Canadian Centre for Policy Alternatives. www.policyalternatives.ca/ [A social democratic think-tank.]

♣ The Conference Board of Canada. www.conferenceboard.ca/ [A centrist think-tank.]

♣ The Conservative Party of Canada's website: www.conservative.ca/home/

♣ The Conservative Party's 2011 federal election platform, "Here for Canada": www.conservative.ca/media/ConservativePlatform2011_ENs.pdf [The Conservative Party laid out five priorities: creating jobs, supporting families, eliminating the deficit, making streets safe, and standing on guard for Canada.]

♣ The Fraser Institute. www.fraserinstitute.org/ [A conservative think-tank, on the **libertarian** end of the spectrum.]

♣ The Green Party of Canada's website: www.greenparty.ca/

♣ The Green Party's 2011 federal election platform, "Smart Economy. Strong Communities. True Democracy.": www.greenparty.ca/platform2011 [The platform is focused on the three priorities in the title.]

- Ignatieff, Michael. "Liberal Values in Tough Times." Isaiah Berlin Lecture. London (July 8, 2009). http://multimedia.thestar.com/acrobat/aa/3f/294d856a4acbaf89a2adcc6ce300.pdf [A lecture given by the former leader of the Liberal Party, a conservative centrist.]
- The Liberal Party of Canada's website: www.liberal.ca/
- The Liberal Party's 2011 federal election platform, "Your Family. Your Future. Your Canada.": http://cdn.liberal.ca/files/2011/04/liberal_platform.pdf [The Liberal Party laid out five priorities: the economy; families, finances, and the future; clean resources, healthy environment, and the economy of tomorrow; bringing Canadians together; and Canada in the world: a global networks strategy.]
- Mackenzie, Hugh, and Richard Shillington, "Canada's Quiet Bargain: The Benefits of Public Spending." Canadian Centre for Policy Alternatives. April 2009. www.policyalternatives.ca/sites/default/files/uploads/publications/National_Office_Pubs/2009/Benefits_From_Public_Spending.pdf [The authors argue that Canadians average $17,000 in benefits from public spending, and say that, for most Canadians, "public services are . . . the best deal they are ever going to get."]
- The New Democratic Party of Canada's website: www.ndp.ca/
- The New Democratic Party's 2011 federal election platform, "Giving Your Family a Break: Practical First Steps": http://xfer.ndp.ca/2011/2011-Platform/NDP-2011-Platform-En.pdf [The NDP laid out seven "practical first steps": giving families a break, rewarding job creators, improving health services, tackling climate change, leadership in Canada, leadership on the world stage, and fixing Ottawa.]
- Watson, William. "Public Goods: How Should They Be Provided?" *The Fraser Forum* (November 2009): 30–1. [Watson argues that military defence is a public good that governments should provide, but not much else. One in a series of "Key Concepts" by the Fraser Institute.]

See also the readings under Conservative, Egalitarian, and Centrist Liberalism in the Introduction.

Chapter 8

Health and Health Care

A Brief History of Health Care in Canada

In Canada's early days health care was an individual responsibility; people paid doctors on their own, and most people never went to hospitals at all. Many people could not afford doctors' fees. Some doctors charged poor people less than they charged wealthier patients, or nothing at all. When poor people needed hospital care the costs might be funded by a charity, but most often they went without hospital care.

In the early twentieth century, Liberals and Conservatives argued that individuals and not the **state** should take responsibility for health care. In 1932 the Cooperative Commonwealth Federation, the precursor to the New Democratic Party, was founded. The CCF argued that health care was a right and provinces should provide it to everyone, as they provided public education. In 1944 Saskatchewan voters elected a CCF government, led by Tommy Douglas, and in 1947 the Douglas government introduced Canada's first provincially funded hospital insurance program.

Residents of other provinces demanded similar programs. Most Canadians agreed that hospital care should be provided for the poorest people, but then views split. According to the CCF, everyone should receive health care based on need, not the ability to pay. Others argued that everyone but the poorest people ought to pay for their own hospital care, either directly or by purchasing private hospital insurance. However, insurance frequently did not cover all the costs of hospitalization, leaving people with hundreds or thousands of dollars of debt in a time when most households earned two to four thousand dollars a year.

Other provinces introduced a variety of plans, often combining private insurance with public coverage for the poorest people, but none was as popular with citizens as Saskatchewan's plan. Eventually, several provinces asked the federal government to develop a national program. In 1957, the Liberal government passed the *Hospital Insurance and Diagnostic Services Act*. The act funded fifty per cent of the cost of certain hospital and diagnostic procedures, provided that the provincial plans met planning, budget, and reporting criteria. By 1961, all provinces and territories had adopted publicly funded hospital insurance programs that met the federal criteria.

The federal money was a windfall to Saskatchewan. It had already been paying for hospital insurance on its own, so in 1962 it increased coverage to include doctors' services outside of hospitals. Despite strong opposition from the Canadian Medical Association and the insurance industry, Canadians in other provinces demanded similar programs. In 1966 the Liberal minority government, with the support of the New Democrats, passed the *Medical Care Act*, which extended health coverage to doctors outside of hospitals and funded fifty per cent of the costs. By 1972, all provinces and territories provided universal health care.

In 1984 Parliament unanimously passed the *Canada Health Act*, which specified five criteria that provincial health insurance programs must meet to qualify for federal funding:

1. Public administration: Health care costs must be paid for with tax dollars.
2. Universality: Everyone gets health care, regardless of income.
3. Comprehensiveness: Health care programs must cover "medically necessary" services.
4. Accessibility: Everyone must have "reasonable access" to health care, without financial or other barriers.
5. Portability: Health care costs must be covered for people who visit other provinces, and for those who move to other provinces until the new province's residency requirements have been met.

If a province violates any one of these criteria, the federal government may withhold part or all of the transfer payment for health care, depending on how serious the violation is.

Comparison with Other Countries

Health care is our most cherished social program. How does it compare with health care in other countries? In 2000 the World Health Organization's report *Health Systems: Improving Performance* examined 191 countries. The report evaluated health care systems according to five criteria: overall population health, health inequalities within the population, how well the system performs, how well the system serves people in all income levels, and how fairly the system distributes costs among the population. The report compared each country's performance on these criteria to the best health care system that country could achieve, given its resources and other political commitments. Canada was thirtieth. The two top-ranking countries were France and Italy; the US was thirty-seventh.[1] We have room for improvement.

In 2010 the Health Council of Canada compared access, affordability, timeliness, and coordination of health care in Canada and ten other rich countries: seven western European countries plus Australia, New Zealand, and the United States. Overall, Canadians are satisfied with the quality of our medical care, and we believe we will receive the most effective medical care if we become seriously ill. However, Canada did not fare so well on other criteria. Of the eleven countries, we had the poorest access to medical care after hours, and as a result, we visited emergency departments more often than people in any of the other countries. Of those Canadians who went to an emergency department and who have a family doctor, nearly half said their condition could have been treated by their family doctor had the doctor been available—again, more than any other country. Canada also ranked last on how long it takes to see a specialist and on timeliness of care (whether someone who is sick can get an appointment the same or the next day), and second-last in how long it takes to get a diagnosis. We are above average on affordability of care, but third-last on affordability of prescriptions; one in ten people said they did not fill a prescription in the previous year because it was too expensive.[2] Given that nine of the ten comparison countries also have universal health care and so face many of the same difficulties that we do, this is further evidence that our health care system can improve.

The Debate about Health Care in Canada

The Debate Leading to Universal Health Care

Both proponents (supporters) and opponents of hospital insurance and universal health care agreed that governments should pay the health care costs of the poorest people. Where they differed was on who should pay the health care costs of the remaining citizens. The CCF's arguments in favour of universal health care were based on **social democratic** and **egalitarian** principles. Social democrats believe that government's role is to ensure that all citizens have the means to live good, worthwhile lives (see Introduction, A Short Primer). Tommy Douglas put it this way when universal health care was introduced in Saskatchewan:

> The measure of abundance and greatness [of Saskatchewan] is not just its farms, uranium mines, oil wells, factories, or its steel mills. These things are a **means to an end** and not an **end in themselves**. In the final analysis the greatness of this province will depend on the extent to which we are able to divert a reasonable share of wealth production . . . to raise the standard of living of our people, and to give them a reasonable security against old age, against sickness and other catastrophes.[3]

Health is a component of a good life: by itself, it does not make our lives good, but without health, our lives are less likely to go well. More than almost any other expense, health care costs can bankrupt even a middle-class family, and often families cannot plan adequately for these costs. Social democrats said health care should be taken out of the market and provided by government; citizens should pool their risks through tax-funded health care insurance. Thus they advocated that health care should be distributed based on need, not ability to pay, and that everyone should receive publicly funded health care insurance.

Opponents of hospital insurance and universal health care agreed that health care can be costly, so they thought the provinces should fund health care for the very poorest people. Everyone else should buy health insurance from either private for-profit insurance companies or private not-for-profit plans. If, despite its availability, people did not purchase health insurance, that was their business; the government had no right to force them to buy it. The opponents also argued that universal health care interfered with the market and private enterprise. It limited the freedom not only of patients and doctors but, ultimately, all citizens—the government would tell citizens how they must spend their money, even if the citizens had other priorities. In 1954 William Anderson, Vice-President of North American Life Insurance Company, said,

> What most people who favour compulsory health insurance fail to realize [is] that it is a **Trojan horse**. They fail to discern that under a superficially attractive exterior it hides the forces which will destroy their freedom of choice and import a full-fledged system of state medicine into their midst. . . . [C]ompulsory health insurance cannot be separated from state medicine and **socialism**.[4]

When universal health care was introduced in Saskatchewan in 1962, the provincial medical association called it "compulsory state medicine" and argued that it led to poorer quality of care and loss of freedom. These were serious charges in the first decades after the Cold War began, when many people in Canada feared the Soviet Union and equated anything that sounded like socialism with dictatorship.

The Debate Today

To understand the debate about health care today, we need to distinguish health care funding—who pays—from health care delivery—who provides. The *Canada Health Act* requires that all "medically necessary" care be publicly funded. Private funders, whether individuals or insurance companies, pay for health care that the provinces do not consider medically necessary. This includes things like semi-private or private rooms in hospitals, prescription medicines, home care, and nursing home care. The Act does not require public *delivery* of medical services, though, including services that are medically necessary. Governments deliver some health services, such as public health. The private sector—individuals, not-for-profits, and businesses—deliver the rest. We can subdivide private services into private not-for profit and private for-profit services, and further subdivide the for-profit services into small for-profit services and corporate for-profit services. Private not-for-profit services include most hospitals and some home care. Small private for-profit services include doctors and dentists (most of whom are small-business operators in private practice), and some pharmacies. Corporate private for-profit services include food and cleaning services in hospitals and laboratory services. (See Table 1, Funding and Delivery of Health Care Services in Canada.)

Most Canadians want to keep health care publicly funded. Many people also think they should be able to pay privately for some services normally provided by provincial health care plans, though, whether diagnostic procedures such as MRIs or surgical procedures such as knee or hip replacements. Wait times for procedures can be long in Canada—the longest in the Health Council of Canada study—which is terrible for someone waiting for diagnosis of a suspected cancer, or in pain and waiting for an operation. People who support a parallel private health care system argue that private payment provides more choices for those who can afford them, and more choices are better than fewer, especially when someone is sick or in pain. In addition, they say, private services free up resources in the public system. People who pay for private medical care do not cost the public system time or money, and thus both are more available to patients still in the public system.

Critics of privatization say that private medical services allow richer people to queue jump. For example, rich people can get faster diagnoses in the private system and then return to the public system for their procedures, ahead of those who could not afford

Table 1
Funding and Delivery of Health Care Services in Canada

		Delivery			
			Private Providers		
				For-Profit Providers	
		Public Providers	*Not-for-Profit Providers*	*Small Providers*	*Corporate Providers*
Funding	Public	• public health • provincial psychiatric institutions	• most hospitals • addiction treatment	• most doctors • emergency dental care provided in hospitals	• hospital food & cleaning services • most laboratory & diagnostic services
	Private	• semi-private rooms in provincial psychiatric institutions	• home care • nursing homes • MRI & CT clinics	• prescriptions • dental care • eye care • nursing homes • MRI & CT clinics	• prescriptions • eye care • home care • nursing homes • MRI & CT clinics

Source: Adapted from Odette Madore and Marlisa Tiedemann, "Private Health Care Funding and Delivery under the *Canada Health Act*," Parliamentary Information and Research Service, Library of Parliament, PRB 05-52E (2005), p. 3.

private diagnoses. In addition, allowing widespread private medical care alongside public care means the system is no longer universal; rather, public health care covers only poor people who cannot afford private health care. And poor people will get poor service, because middle-class voters are all too willing to cut funding for services they do not use themselves. When everyone benefits from government services, though, as Canadians do with health care, voters realize that budget cuts mean cutting their own services, and they are more likely to pay to support the services.[5]

Some people argue that we should extend the scope of health care to cover prescription medicines and/or some medical procedures or services not currently covered under provincial programs. The *Medical Care Act* of 1966 covered hospital care and most care by physicians, but it did not require payment for prescriptions, medical care by other health professionals such as nurses and physiotherapists, or medical care provided at home or in a nursing home. At the time, none of these forms of care was significant. But costs have shifted in health care. While hospitals remain the largest single item in health care budgets, the proportion of funds going to them decreased by a third between 1975 and 2010. During that time the amount spent on drugs and "other services," which includes home care and medical care by other health professionals, increased by a similar amount.[6] The

National Forum on Health has suggested that health care programs fund "the care, not the provider or the site." They say funding should focus on home care, prescription drugs, and primary care (a patient's first contact with the health care system, usually a doctor).[7]

Public Health

The *Canada Health Act* covers medical care provided by doctors and hospitals. The health care system focuses on curing diseases, repairing injuries, and restoring individuals to health. Public health, on the other hand, focuses on preventing disease and injury and promoting healthy communities. While today most people associate it with sexually transmitted infections and pandemics, public health also addresses population health, "the health outcomes of a group of individuals, including the distribution of such outcomes within the group."[8] Population health addresses the social factors that influence health, disease, and injury, such as education and literacy, income and social status, and social support networks. Researchers call these the "social determinants of health," and say they influence population health more than medical care, genes and biology, and health behaviours (e.g., exercising, not smoking) *combined.*[9]

Think of diseases and injuries as fires. The health care system is like the fire department, then—it comes in and puts out the fires. Public health, on the other hand, is like fire prevention programs that aim to prevent fires from starting. It is not as glamorous as the health care system. We only see its successes in the long run, through statistics that show the average lifespan has increased or that the health gap between income or racial groups has narrowed. Public health has no poster children; we cannot point to specific people and say, "He survived infancy because his parents' education was affordable" or "She lived an extra seven years because of her city's excellent seniors' programs." However, everyone knows that not becoming sick or injured is better than getting cured or repaired. Public health aims at preventing illnesses and injuries.

Ethical and Political Issues in Public Health

Public health ethics is a new field, so the basic concepts are still being worked out. Some authors argue the main issues involve **autonomy** and the rights of individuals versus the rights of the group. For example, can we make everyone get vaccinated to prevent a potential epidemic, or do individuals have the right to refuse vaccinations? Feminist ethicists say this **individualistic** view creates a false dichotomy: individuals always live in groups, groups are always composed of individuals, and responsibilities go both ways. Feminist ethicists say we should discuss individuals' responsibilities to groups and not just to themselves, and we also should work to ensure that communities do not trample on individuals' rights.

Public health tends to be quite political, because there is a strong correlation between poverty, unemployment, and underemployment, on the one hand, and poor health, on the other. In the 1960s and again in the 1980s, British researchers studied the health of civil servants, all of whom had secure, full-time jobs with good benefits. Those who were higher on the hierarchy were healthier, on average, than those who were lower down, even when smoking cigarettes and drinking were factored in. And the gap was between not only those at the top and those at the bottom; it was smooth all the way down. So, for example, deputy ministers (the highest rank) had heart disease rates that were less than one-quarter the rates of doctors and lawyers, the next step down in the hierarchy.[10] Epidemiologists Richard Wilkinson and Kate Pickett argue that greater equality benefits everyone in society, rich and poor. For example, the rich in more egalitarian societies are healthier than are the rich in less equal societies.[11]

How should provinces divide the health budget between health care and public health? Prevention is clearly preferable to curing from both an individual and a social perspective; no one wants to become sick or injured, and provinces struggle to contain steeply rising health care costs. Prevention is also a good investment: for example, every dollar spent on addictions and mental health saves seven dollars in future health care costs and thirty dollars in lost productivity and other social costs.[12] The word "future" is the problem, though. Savings from prevention do not show up for years or even decades. Since governments tend to look only as far as the next election, it can be hard to convince them to commit to long term goals. In addition, while prevention programs reduce disease and injury, they do not eliminate them, and those who become sick or injured still need health care. People want assurances that health care will still be there when they need it.

The Readings

The first reading sets the stage for the debate. Odette Madore works for the Parliamentary Information and Research Service, which provides non-partisan research and background material for Members of Parliament, so she explains the various arguments but does not take sides. She gives an overview of federal and provincial responsibilities for health care, why universal health care was adopted, the *Canada Health Act* and why it was adopted, and the criteria and provisions of the *Act*. She discusses the arguments for and against privatization in some detail, and ends with a discussion of whether to change the *Canada Health Act*, keep it as it is, or repeal it.

The second reading comes from the Supreme Court's ruling in *Chaoulli v. Quebec*. Like most provinces, the Quebec government prohibited private payment for medical care covered by the *Canada Health Act*. The Supreme Court argued, by the narrowest of margins—four to three[13]—that the relevant sections of the Quebec *Health Insurance and Hospital Insurance Acts* violated the rights to liberty and security of the person in the *Quebec Charter of Human Rights and Freedoms*. That is the first majority argument in the reading. Three of the judges in the majority argued that the Quebec *Health Insurance* and the *Hospital Insurance Acts* also violated the same rights in the Canadian *Charter*; that is the second majority argument. And three judges disagreed with the majority's view, arguing that the Quebec laws did not violate rights to liberty or security of the person; that is the third—**dissenting** (disagreeing with the majority)—argument. (If you live in one of the provinces that still forbids private payment for medical care, you may wonder how the province can do that, given the Court's decision. This is because the four justices agreed only that the laws violated Quebec's *Charter*. Three justices thought the laws also violated the Canadian *Charter*, but since that was not a majority, the ruling does not apply directly to laws outside Quebec. However, none of the provinces wants to risk the Court saying that a similar law in another province violates the Canadian *Charter*, so all are working to reduce wait times for treatment and surgery.)

In the third reading, Susan Sherwin challenges the traditional split between theory and practice. Too many philosophers focus only on theories and do not think about how they apply to real people in real situations, she says. Even in **bioethics** (the study of ethical issues in medicine), philosophers generally focus more on concepts than on practice. Sherwin says that theory and practice need each other, and neither should be done without the other. She uses the concept of justice in bioethics as an example. Justice in health care involves more than simply who pays for health care; we also should examine injustices in our current health care system. She reconceives "health care" and "justice" from a feminist perspective to show how theory and practice must inform each other.

Finally, Baylis, Kenny, and Sherwin propose a framework for public health ethics that is sensitive to public health's focus on communities rather than individuals. They begin by examining a view of public health ethics that uses standard individualistic ethical concepts. Such views miss many ethical issues unique to public health, Baylis, Kenny, and Sherwin say. Instead, they propose a **relational** account of public health ethics, based on a view of humans as always in relation to other humans. They develop three relational views—of **personhood**, autonomy, and **solidarity**—that they say provide a better basis for public health ethics.

The Moral and Political Preferences Indicator

Universal health care is Canada's most popular social program. While **libertarians** oppose universal health care because they believe all government-funded social programs limit individual freedom, they are a tiny minority in Canada. Most Canadians support continuing public *funding* of most medical care. They do not all agree on delivery, however. In particular, they disagree about (a) what sort of health care should be publicly or privately funded, (b) whether health care should be delivered by for-profit, not-for-profit, or public institutions, and (c) whether doctors who take public patients should be allowed to take private patients as well. In general, **neo-conservatives** and **social conservatives** favour (a) a greater balance of private funding, (b) for-profit over not-for-profit or public delivery, and (c) allowing doctors to take both public and private patients. **Social democrats** favour (a) a greater balance of public funding, (b) public or not-for-profit over for-profit delivery, and (c) continuing to permit doctors to take public or private patients but not both. As usual, **conservative** and **egalitarian centrists** sit somewhere in between on most of these issues, although on health care they generally lean more toward social democratic than conservative views.

Most conservative and centrist liberals—including the Supreme Court—favour an individualistic understanding of ethics. Social democrats lean toward the views of Sherwin and Baylis, Kenny, and Sherwin. While they agree that injustice affects people as members of groups and not simply as individuals, some social democrats reject a relational analysis of injustice.

Notes

1. The World Health Report 2000, *Health Systems: Improving Performance* (Geneva, Switzerland: World Health Organization, 2000), p. 200.
2. Health Council of Canada, "How Do Canadians Rate the Health Care System? Results from the 2010 Commonwealth Fund International Health Policy Survey," *Canadian Health Care Matters*, Bulletin 4 (Toronto: Health Council of Canada, 2010).

3. A.W. Johnson with Rosemary Proctor, *Dream No Little Dreams: A Biography of the Douglas Government of Saskatchewan, 1941–1961* (Toronto: University of Toronto Press, 2004) p. 240, quoted in Canadian Museum of Civilization, Making Medicare: The History of Health Care in Canada, 1914–2007: 1948–1958: Conclusion, www.civilization.ca/cmc/exhibitions/hist/medicare/medic-4h23e.shtml.
4. Malcolm G. Taylor, *Health Insurance and Canadian Public Policy: The Seven Decisions That Created the Canadian Health Insurance System and Their Outcomes*, 2nd ed. (Montreal and Kingston: McGill-Queen's University Press, 1987), 194–5, quoted in Making Medicare: 1948–1958: Conclusion, www.civilization.ca/cmc/exhibitions/hist/medicare/medic-4h23e.shtml.
5. For empirical evidence for these claims, see Madore and Tiedemann, "Private Health Care Funding and Delivery," pp. 8–11, and Odette Madore, "Duplicate Private Health Care Insurance: Potential Implications for Quebec and Canada," Parliamentary Information and Research Service, Library of Parliament, PRB 05-71E (2006), pp. 4–7.
6. Canadian Institute for Health Information, *Health Care in Canada 2010* (Ottawa: CIHI, 2010) p. 99.
7. National Forum on Health, *Canada Health Action: Building on the Legacy, Vol. I, The Final Report* (Government of Canada, 1997), 1.2 Building a More Integrated System, www.hc-sc.gc.ca/hcs-sss/pubs/renewal-renouv/1997-nfoh-fnss-v1/index-eng.php#a1_2.
8. David Kindig and Greg Stoddart, "What Is Population Health?," *American Journal of Public Health* 93, 33 (2003): 380.
9. Alvin R. Tarlov, "Public Policy Frameworks for Improving Population Health," in *Socioeconomic Status and Health in Industrial Nations: Social, Psychological, and Biological Pathways*, vol. 896 of Annals of the New York Academy of Sciences (New York: New York Academy of Sciences, 1999), p. 283.
10. Public Health Agency of Canada, What Makes Canadians Healthy or Unhealthy? www.phac-aspc.gc.ca/ph-sp/determinants/determinants-eng.php.
11. Richard Wilkinson and Kate Pickett, *The Spirit Level: Why Greater Equality Makes Societies Stronger* (NY: Bloomsbury Press, 2009, 2010).
12. Ontario Chronic Disease Prevention Alliance, "Make Ontario the Healthiest Province in Canada: A statement to Ontario Political Party Leaders" (2011), www.rrasp-phirn.ca/index.php?option=com_content&view=article&id=204%3Acampaign-launch-make-ontario-the-healthiest-province-in-canada&catid=6%3Alatest-news&Itemid=17&lang=en.
13. Seven instead of nine justices participated in the ruling because one had retired and another was about to retire.

Odette Madore

The *Canada Health Act*: Overview and Options

Issue Definition

The *Canada Health Act* (hereafter called the *Act*) received Royal Assent on 1 April 1984. Through this *Act*, the federal government ensures that the provinces and territories meet certain requirements, such as free and universal access to publicly insured health care. These requirements, or "national principles," have helped shape provincial health care insurance plans throughout the country.

Since its inception, the *Act* has been subject to debate. This debate focuses on the national principles and is part of a broad picture involving factors that are political (distribution of powers), fiscal (trade-off between health care and other priorities), and economic (greater cost-effectiveness and efficiency). It also addresses fundamental concerns about the public sector's role, including that of the federal government, in health care funding.

This document gives an overview of the *Canada Health Act*. It does not set out to offer a legal interpretation of the *Act*; rather, it seeks to take stock of the evolution of the way it is implemented and examine its future prospects. The first section reviews the justifications for government intervention in the health care sector, while the second describes the respective roles of the federal government and the provinces. The third section traces the historical background of the *Act*, and the fourth presents an overview of the requirements attached to it. In the fifth section, penalties for defaults under the *Act* are described, and the sixth section discusses the imposition of penalties. The seventh section examines the issue of privatization. In the eighth section, some options are set out for maintaining the *Act* or improving it.

Background and Analysis

Justification for Government Intervention in Health Care

In Canada, governments are the main source of funding for health care because they play a key role in the insurance market. The proponents of government intervention in this field generally cite economic and social equity factors, as well as administrative efficiency. First, they explain that government intervention is necessary to correct potential problems for social equity in the operation of the private insurance market. They claim that private insurance companies could refuse to insure high-risk clients or force them to pay a much higher premium to offset the risk. They believe that government insurance can correct the shortcomings in the private market by protecting the broadest possible cross-section of the population and avoiding unreasonable premium hikes which ultimately effect [cause, create] no improvement in the state of health. Second, they maintain that the private insurance market does not have a regard for economic equity. They argue that in a private insurance market, individuals with health problems and a low income would be subject to the same fee structure as high-income individuals; thus, economically disadvantaged individuals would have to assume a relatively higher proportion of health care costs. Government intervention would, then, guarantee increased access to insurance, regardless of the individual's ability to pay. And third, another argument in favour of public health care insurance is that it yields more efficiencies than private insurers, in terms of lower administrative costs and economies of scale. Public insurance eliminates costs associated with the marketing of private health care insurance policies, billing for and collecting premiums, and evaluating insurance risks. This is one of the reasons cited for the relatively higher administration costs of the American system relative to Canada's.

For these reasons, governments in Canada have favoured public health care insurance over private insurance. This approach, which protects all people against risks related to illness, is essentially based on income tax: all citizens contribute in accordance with their income, rather than in accordance with the benefits they expect to derive. Thus, since its introduction, public health care insurance in Canada has stressed the principle of transferring resources from the richer to the poorer and pooling the risks between the healthy and the less healthy.

This does not mean, however, that the private sector is totally absent from this field in Canada. Private health care insurance exists, but its scope is limited. To be more precise, the private market provides additional coverage for health services that are not insured by the public plan or that are only partially insured by it.

The fact that government is present in the field of health care insurance does not mean that it is also involved in the delivery of publicly insured health services. Indeed, the delivery of health care in Canada is largely in the hands of the private sector: most medical practitioners are in private practice (small businesses) and hospitals are to a great extent private, non-profit organizations (however, physician and hospital services and remuneration for these are subject to government regulation). Laboratory and diagnostic services paid for by public health care insurance are delivered by private for-profit facilities in most provinces. Laundry services, meal preparation, and other support or ancillary services that are provided in publicly funded hospitals are often delivered by private for-profit companies.

The Role of Governments in Health Care in Canada

The federal and provincial governments have very different responsibilities in health care. Strictly speaking, the federal government cannot establish and maintain a national health care insurance plan because it cannot regulate the delivery of health care to individuals; under the Canadian Constitution and its interpretation by the courts, health care is a field primarily under provincial jurisdiction. The only explicit references in the Constitution to health care issues give the federal government jurisdiction in matters relating to navy hospitals and quarantine. In addition, the federal government is responsible for delivering health services to groups that fall under its jurisdiction, such as Aboriginal peoples, the Canadian forces, veterans, and inmates in federal penitentiaries. Provincial governments are responsible for administering the public health care insurance plan in their own province. They also have responsibility for health care delivery. This includes, for example: determining how many beds will be available in a province; deciding what categories of staff will be hired; determining how the system will serve the population; approving hospital budgets; and negotiating fee scales with the medical association and other health professional organizations.

The federal government has intervened in the provincial health care field by using its constitutional "spending power," which enables it to make a financial contribution to certain programs under provincial jurisdiction, generally subject to provincial compliance with certain requirements. Pierre Blache, in an article published in 1993 in the *Revue generale de droit*, indicates that in his opinion, it is the constitutional imbalance between powers and responsibilities, together with inter-provincial equity factors, that brought about federal transfers such as those to the health care sector:

> The scale of transfer payments from the federal government to the provincial governments has increased in Canada as a result of the characteristics of the constitution and reality. It is because Canadian provinces have been given the potentially most expensive responsibilities in the modern state, while being limited to direct taxation, and because many of them have found themselves faced with a tax base below the national average, that recourse to the spending power

> has become so important in the practical workings of Canadian federalism. . . . Against such a background, it appeared unfair to leave it to the provinces to fund the social programs demanded by the people, out of their own resources. (p. 38) [translation]

Consequently, the federal government has intervened in an area under provincial jurisdiction, but without changing the division of powers stipulated in the Constitution. Although the federal government is not responsible for health care administration, organization, or delivery, it can exert considerable influence on provincial health care policies by using the political and financial leverage afforded by the spending power. In fact, by setting the requirements for providing federal funding, the *Canada Health Act* has to a large extent shaped provincial health care insurance plans throughout the country.

Historical Background

Public health care insurance as it is known today, in which the federal government's financial contribution is linked to provincial compliance with specific requirements, dates back to the late 1950s. Under the *Hospital Insurance and Diagnostic Services Act* of 1957 and the *Medical Care Act* of 1966, the federal government made an offer to the provinces to fund approximately half the cost of all insured health services. In return for federal contributions, the provinces—as part of their public health care insurance plans—undertook to insure hospital and physician services and to comply with certain requirements, such as universality. These two *Acts* did not prevent provinces from demanding a financial contribution from patients; however, because federal contributions were proportional to provincial government expenditures, the provincial governments had nothing to gain from imposing direct patient charges. In fact, the revenue from such charges would have resulted in a reduction in the federal contribution. This implicit reduction mechanism thus strongly deterred provinces from adopting any form of direct patient charges, such as extra-billing and user charges.[1]

In 1977, this formula of shared costs was replaced by a method of block funding based on cash transfers and tax point transfers as part of Established Programs Financing (EPF). Both federal Acts on hospital services and medical care and the requirements attached to them were retained. However, the implicit mechanism for deducting federal contributions was eliminated with the EPF, because federal funding was no longer linked to provincial government expenditures; this resulted in a proliferation of direct patient charges. For example, Newfoundland, New Brunswick, Quebec, Ontario, Saskatchewan, Alberta, and British Columbia levied user charges; and extra-billing was authorized in most provinces. The federal government saw this situation as posing a threat to the principle of free and universal access to health services throughout the country. It was therefore anxious to reassert its commitment to the principle of universal health care insurance; and it relied heavily on the **criterion** of economic equity to justify its intervention. A document issued by Health and Welfare Canada in 1983 stated:

> The Government of Canada believes that a civilized and wealthy nation, such as ours, should not make the sick bear the financial burden of health care. Everyone benefits from the security and peace of mind that come with having pre-paid

> insurance. The misfortune of illness which at some time touches each one of us is burden enough: the costs of care should be borne by society as a whole. That is why the Government of Canada wishes to re-affirm in a new *Canada Health Act* our commitment to the essential principle of universal health insurance.

This document paved the way for the *Canada Health Act*, which, as stated earlier, was passed on 1 April 1984. The *Act* combined and updated the two federal *Acts* of 1957 and 1966. The national principles were reaffirmed in the *Act*, but extra restrictions were specifically added to deter any form of direct patient charges and to provide citizens of all provinces with access to health care regardless of ability to pay.

On 1 April 1996, the *Canada Health Act* was linked to the Canada Health and Social Transfer (CHST), which merged EPF transfers with Canada Assistance Plan (CAP) transfers. The method of calculation adopted for the CHST was similar to that used for the EPF, and included both cash transfers and tax point transfers. The provinces had to meet all the requirements of the *Act* in order to be eligible for the full CHST cash transfer. Since 1 April 2004, the *Canada Health Act* is linked to the Canada Health Transfer (CHT). The CHT resembles its predecessor; it is made up of both cash and tax point transfers, and its cash component is subject to the requirements of the *Canada Health Act*. In contrast to the CHST, however, the CHT is expressly dedicated to health care.

The Requirements Stipulated in the *Act*

The *Canada Health Act* sets out nine requirements that provincial governments must meet through their public health care insurance plan in order to qualify for the full federal cash contribution under the CHT. These nine requirements include five criteria, two specific provisions, and two conditions. The five criteria, which are often referred to as the "national principles," are public administration, comprehensiveness, universality, portability, and accessibility; they apply to insured health services. The two specific provisions relate to user charges and extra-billing for insured health services. The two conditions pertain to the provision of provincial information and provincial recognition of federal contributions; they apply to both insured health services and extended health care services.

Criteria

Section 8 of the *Act* deals with public administration. Under this section, each provincial health care insurance plan must be administered on a non-profit basis by a public authority, which is accountable to the provincial government for its financial transactions. This arrangement is largely explained by the considerable amount of money devoted to the health care sector and the need for governments to keep some control over the growth of these expenditures. It is also designed to allow information to be consolidated. Perhaps more importantly, the original policy objective of this criterion was to prevent provinces and territories from using federal contributions to subsidize the coverage of provincial and territorial residents by private insurance companies. In Canadian literature, reference is frequently made to the concept of "single payer" to describe the concept of administration of health care insurance by a public authority.

Under the criterion of comprehensiveness stipulated in section 9, the health care insurance plan of a province must insure all services that are "medically necessary." The criterion of comprehensiveness refers in a way to a minimum basket of services, because the *Act* neither mentions the quantity of services to be provided nor gives a detailed list of what services will be insured; provincial governments can define these. Thus, the range of insured services may vary among provinces and from one year to the next.

Under section 10, the criterion of universality demands that all residents in the province have access to public health care insurance and insured services on uniform terms and conditions. Initially, the concept of universality focused on two specific objectives. First, it sought to make insured services available to everyone, everywhere. Second, it sought to pool the risks among those insured; the more people the plan covered, it was said, the more the risk-sharing would be cost-effective.

As stipulated in section 11, the criterion of portability requires provinces to cover insured health services provided to their citizens while they are temporarily absent from their province of residence or from Canada. For insured health services provided in another province, payment is made at the rate negotiated by the governments of the two provinces. For out-of-Canada services, the *Act* states that the amount paid will be at least equivalent to the amount the province of residence would have paid for similar services rendered in that province.

The fifth criterion, accessibility, is set out in section 12: insured persons must have reasonable and uniform access to insured health services, free of financial or other barriers. No one may be discriminated against on the basis of such factors as income, age, and health status.

Provisions

Free access to insured health services is the key factor of the *Canada Health Act*. The two provisions of the *Act* specifically discourage financial contributions by patients, either through user charges or extra-billing, for services covered under provincial health care insurance plans.

Conditions

With respect to the two conditions, provincial governments are required by regulation to provide annual estimates and statements on extra-billing and user charges. They are also required to provide voluntarily an annual statement describing the operation of their plans as they relate to the criteria and conditions of the *Act*. This information serves as a basis for the *Canada Health Act* annual report. In addition, provinces are required to give public recognition of federal transfers.

Insured Health Services and Extended Health Care Services

The *Act* makes a distinction between "insured health services" (i.e., those that have been deemed "medically necessary") and "extended health care services." So-called medically necessary services are defined only in the broad sense of the term in the *Act*. Section 2 states that insured health services—which must be fully insured by provincial health care insurance plans—comprise:

- hospital services that are medically necessary for the purpose of maintaining health, preventing disease or diagnosing or treating an injury, illness

or disability, including accommodation and meals, physician and nursing services, drugs, and all medical and surgical equipment and supplies;
- any medically required services rendered by medical practitioners; and
- any medically or dentally required surgical-dental procedures which can only be properly carried out in a hospital.

Section 2 of the *Act* also stipulates that extended health care services include intermediate care in nursing homes, adult residential care service, home care service, and ambulatory health care services. Because these services are not subject to the two provisions relating to user charges and extra-billing, they can be charged for at either partial or full private rates. Similarly, extended health care services are not subject to the five criteria of the *Act*. As such, they do not have to be publicly administered, universal, comprehensive, accessible, or portable. In addition, provincial health care insurance plans may cover other health services, such as optometric services, dental care, assistive devices[2] and prescription drugs, which are not subject to the *Act*, and for which provinces may demand payment from patients. The range of such additional health benefits that are provided under provincial government plans, the rate of coverage, and the categories of beneficiaries vary greatly from one province to another.

Penalties for Defaults Under the *Act*

Penalties under the *Canada Health Act* are linked to federal transfers to the provinces. More precisely, each provincial health care insurance plan must comply with the requirements of the *Act* before the province receives its total entitlement of cash transfers. If a province fails to comply, the federal government may impose a penalty and withhold part or all of the transfers. Between 1984–1985 and 1990–1991, this financial penalty was applied to that portion of EPF cash transfers earmarked for health care. Between 1991–1992 and 1995–1996, financial penalties were not limited solely to federal cash transfers for health care. In fact, the government expanded the penalties to cover other cash transfers. It had become necessary to extend the financial penalty to transfer payments in other fields because of the federal government's continued restriction on the growth rate of EPF transfers and its specific impact on cash transfers. Studies such as those conducted by the National Council of Welfare in 1991 and Jenness and McCracken in 1993 had predicted that EPF cash transfers to some provinces would be non-existent by the year 2000. These additional withholdings or deductions were not stipulated in the *Canada Health Act*, but were specifically set out in paragraphs 23.2(1), 23.2(2) and 23.2(3) of the *Federal-Provincial Fiscal Arrangements Act*, the legislation that established the EPF and then governed the CHST. These provisions apply as well to the CHT under paragraphs 25.6(1), 25.6(2) and 25.6(3).

By introducing the CHST, the federal government moved to prevent the erosion of its power to enforce compliance with the *Canada Health Act* across the country. Obviously, if a province were to decide to forgo its cash entitlement under the CHST, it would no longer be required to comply with the requirements of the *Canada Health Act*. Although the *Act* is now linked to the new CHT, the penalties still apply to total cash transfers to the provinces for health and social programs, as well as to other federal cash transfers.

The financial penalties stipulated in the *Act* vary depending on whether a default is directly related to extra-billing and user charges or involves failure to satisfy any of the five criteria or the two conditions. Sections 18 to 21 of the *Act*, which describe the provisions relating to penalties for extra-billing and user charges, stipulate that the federal government may withhold one dollar of cash transfer for every dollar collected through direct patient charges. In the case of failure to satisfy the criteria or conditions, section 15(1)(a) of the *Act* stipulates that

> the cash value of the penalty is left to the discretion of the Governor in Council, who sets the amount depending on the "gravity" of the default. As Sheilah L. Martin suggested in a paper published in 1989, the discretionary nature of this penalty does not require the federal government to impose a fine, but leaves it the option of doing so. At one extreme, Cabinet could decide to withhold all CHT cash transfers, and even reduce federal contributions paid as part of other programs. At the other extreme, the federal government could decide not to impose any financial penalty and to confine its action to persuasion and negotiation.

The *Act* also includes a conflict resolution mechanism for cases where a province violates the requirements of the *Act*. It is a long process, however, with the result that federal contributions are not reduced immediately. In the event that Health Canada deems that a provincial plan is failing to satisfy anyone of the five criteria or the two conditions, under section 14(2) it must inform the province of the problem, obtain its explanations, draft a report on its concerns and, if the provincial Health Minister so requests, hold a meeting to discuss the issue. Section 15 states that where the Governor in Council is convinced that a province no longer meets the criteria and conditions of the *Canada Health Act*, the Minister of Health may direct by order that federal contributions be reduced or withheld.

Since April 2002, the conflict resolution mechanism embodied in the *Canada Health Act* is facilitated by a Dispute Avoidance and Resolution (DAR) process. The purpose of the DAR is to formalize and make transparent the process that the federal Minister of Health must follow prior to forming an opinion as to whether a provincial or territorial health care insurance plan has ceased to satisfy any of the *Act's* criteria, provisions, or conditions. As a first step the federal Minister of Health invokes, in a letter to the province(s) or territory(ies) concerned, the DAR process in relation to a potential case of non-compliance with the *Canada Health Act*. Within 60 days of the date of that letter, the governments involved in the dispute will jointly: collect and share all relevant facts; prepare a fact-finding report; negotiate to resolve the issue in dispute; and prepare a report on how the issue was resolved.

If, however, there is no agreement on the facts, or if negotiations fail to resolve the issue, any Minister of Health involved in the dispute may undertake to refer the issue to a third-party panel by writing to his or her counterpart. Within 30 days of the date of that letter, a panel will be struck. The panel will be composed of one provincial (or territorial) appointee and one federal appointee, who, together, will select a chairperson. The panel will assess the issue in dispute in accordance with the provisions of the *Canada Health Act*, will undertake fact-finding and provide advice and recommendations. The panel will then report to the governments involved on the issue within 60 days of appointment.

The final authority to interpret and enforce the *Canada Health Act* remains with the federal Minister of Health. In deciding whether to invoke the penalty provisions of the *Act*, the Minister will take the panel's report into consideration.

Imposition of Penalties

On three occasions, the federal government has resorted to mandatory penalties and reduced its contributions to some provinces that were authorizing extra-billing or imposing user charges. First, it deducted more than $244,732,000 from EPF transfers to all the provinces from 1984–1985 to 1986–1987. However, it also complied with section 20(6) of the *Act*, under which a province was able to recover these funds if it terminated all forms of direct patient charges within three years after the *Act* came in.to force, i.e., before 1 April 1987. Because all provinces complied with the *Act* within this timeframe, the amounts withheld were all reimbursed.

Second, from 1992–1993 to 1995–1996, the federal government withheld some $2,025,000 in EPF cash transfers to British Columbia because approximately 40 medical practitioners in that province had opted out of the province's health care insurance plan in 1993 and resorted to extra-billing. These doctors have since discontinued this practice.

Finally, since 1995–1996, the federal government has imposed penalties on provinces that permit private clinics to demand facility fees from patients for medically required services, having determined that such facility fees constitute user charges. These penalties have applied to five provinces. By the time the deductions from transfers to Alberta ended in July 1996, a total of $3,585,000 had been deducted from that province. Similarly, a total of $284,430 had been deducted from Newfoundland, which started to comply with the *Act* in January 1998. The penalties imposed on Manitoba ($2,355,201 in total) were discontinued as of 1 February 1999. A total of $372,135 was deducted from transfers to Nova Scotia, which was deemed in compliance with the *Act* in November 2003. Between 2002–2003 and 2003–2004, a deduction totaling $173,385 was made to British Columbia's CHST cash transfer in respect of instances of user charges levied in private surgical clinics. Although no other deductions have been made, the issue of imposing user charges at private facilities is still ongoing in British Columbia.

Until now, however, there has been no discretionary penalty for failure to comply with the five criteria stipulated in the *Act*, despite some complaints regarding, for example, portability and comprehensiveness.

There are claims that several provinces are violating the criterion of portability. For example, in 1988, Quebec refused to sign the reciprocity agreement whereby other provinces would be reimbursed according to their own rates for services they provided to Quebeckers outside Quebec. Moreover, Canadians must increasingly resort to private insurance when abroad: New Brunswick, Quebec, Saskatchewan, Alberta, and British Columbia have reduced their coverage for emergency hospital services obtained outside Canada. Some experts, who accuse the federal government of inaction in this area, explain that the scope of the portability criterion is clearly defined in the *Act*, where the terms and conditions for reimbursement of out-of-province services are stipulated. For its part, the Commission on the Future of Health Care in Canada (Romanow Commission) recommended that the criterion of portability be limited to guaranteeing portability of coverage within Canada.

Likewise, some people believe the criterion of comprehensiveness is not being observed in practice, because provinces do not necessarily cover the same basket of insured health services or medically required services. They also believe that cutting government expenditures could compromise this principle even further and that the process of de-insuring begun in recent years could lead to the balkanization of provincial health care insurance plans. Federal legislation defines only the major outline of insured services and leaves each province complete freedom to determine what services its public plan will provide. However, de-insurance emphasizes the gaps between provinces in their coverage of health services; these discrepancies are likely to become increasingly difficult to justify. Moreover, de-insurance with the sole purpose of reducing public health expenditures could ultimately undermine the criterion of free access, inasmuch as it has not been proved which services are or are not medically necessary. This raises the thorny problem of how to determine when a service is medically necessary. It could prove difficult to determine the limits of any list of medically necessary health services. Furthermore, it is hard to know how far the federal government can intervene in defining insured services, without encroaching on provincial jurisdiction.

It is important to note that, although discretionary penalties have never been applied, a number of cases of non-compliance have been resolved through discussion, negotiation, and persuasion. Although this approach may lead to less friction in federal provincial relations, it does not lead to a speedy resolution of violations to the *Act*. In his November 1999 report (Chapter 29), the Auditor General of Canada pointed out that six cases of non-compliance had been resolved through discussion and negotiation; however, four of them took 14 to 48 months to resolve, while the remaining two went on for as long as five years without any penalty. In her September 2002 report (Chapter 3), the Auditor General of Canada identified twelve new possible cases of non-compliance that had arisen since 1999; Health Canada once again attempted to resolve them through means other than penalties. Only two of these cases have been resolved.

The Issue of Privatization

This section attempts to shed some light on the current confusion over the concept of privatization and its implications in terms of the *Canada Health Act*.

Privatization is the process whereby the government transfers some of its activities or responsibilities to the private sector. With respect to health care, privatization of financing is not the same as privatization of delivery.[3] Privatization of financing is achieved by shifting the burden of funding away from public health care insurance plans and towards patients and/or their private insurance companies. Privatizing the delivery of health care implies greater reliance on individuals and institutions outside government for the production and provision of health services. In Canada, difficulties with respect to privatization revolve primarily around the financing of health care, because health care delivery is already largely private in nature. In fact, governments deliver relatively few health services directly. Most health care providers (e.g., physicians, physiotherapists, and pharmacists) are in private practice; they are not government employees. The vast majority of hospitals and long-term care institutions are not-for-profit and are privately owned; although they are funded by government, they are not owned by government.

Privatization of health care financing can be achieved in two ways: either actively, by containing public health care costs; or passively, by shifting the care outside traditional settings. Active privatization is the direct result of the partial or total de-insurance of publicly funded health services. In the 1990s, in an effort to reduce public health care costs and to balance their budgets, most provinces limited the coverage provided under their health care insurance plans. . . . For the most part, medically required hospital and physician services remain covered by provincial health care insurance plans. In fact, public funding accounts for approximately ninety-one per cent of hospital expenditures, while ninety-nine per cent of total physician services are financed by the public sector (according to data from the Canadian Institute for Health Information). Nevertheless, de-insurance has generated disparities in provincial health care coverage. For example, the removal of warts is no longer covered in Nova Scotia, New Brunswick, Ontario, Manitoba, Alberta, Saskatchewan, and British Columbia, but it remains publicly insured in Newfoundland, Quebec, and Prince Edward Island. Although stomach stapling is covered in most provinces, it is not insured in New Brunswick, Nova Scotia, and the Yukon, and patients in these provinces/territories must pay for this procedure. In addition, coverage varies widely across the country in the areas of reproductive services.

Passive privatization mainly refers to the gradual shift towards non-institutional care provided in the home and the community. Less invasive medical techniques and shorter hospital stays have allowed Canadians to receive more medical care in their homes and in the community. As a result, many services that are deemed medically necessary today are not publicly insured because they are not provided in hospitals or by physicians. Consequently, many commentators contend that the realities of health care have shifted considerably since 1984, when the *Canada Health Act,* with its focus on hospitals and physician services, was passed. In other words, the definition of "medically necessary services" has not kept pace with the way services are now delivered. The National Forum on Health subscribed to this view when it stressed that it would be essential to "fund the care, not the institution." Accordingly, it recommended that public health care insurance be expanded to cover a wider range of services and, in the first instance, home care and prescription drugs. It is believed that the scope of the *Canada Health Act* could be broadened without challenging in any way the requirements embodied in that *Act*. The report of the Romanow Commission supported this view and made very similar recommendations.

In the Canadian context of health care, the main concern with respect to privatization is that it can lead to a "two-tier" system—one that allows some patients to pay privately and receive priority access to health care, while the rest of the population who use the publicly funded health services must face longer waiting times. The issue over privatization surfaced in 1995, when the federal government implemented its policy on private clinics.

There are two categories of private clinics: semi-private clinics, and fully private clinics. Semi-private clinics are facilities that receive public funding for medically required services under a provincial health care insurance plan, but also demand payment ("facility fees") from the patient. For the federal government, facility fees present a problem because people who can afford to pay them get faster access to services. In 1995, the federal Minister of Health stated that such semi-private clinics fall under the *Canada Health Act* because: (1) they are included in the definition of "hospitals" set out in the *Act*; (2) they provide medically necessary services; and (3) they receive public funding. Therefore, semi-private clinics contravene the *Canada Health Act* because the facility fees they require from patients constitute a form of user charges.

Fully private clinics are facilities that receive no government funding: the physicians are not reimbursed by the provincial health care insurance plan and their patients must pay the full cost of the services rendered to them. The creation of such clinics does not result in a reduction in provincial transfers, and the provisions relating to extra-billing or user charges do not apply in such cases. It is, however, possible that the federal government might decide to intervene by invoking the *Act*'s criterion of accessibility should it be decided that fully private clinics threaten access to the insured services provided by the public system. This could happen if these clinics were to offer financial incentives to health care providers that might draw them away from the public system.

In practice, few physicians leave the public system because it is hard to attract a sufficient number of patients who want to pay full health care costs when they also have access to the public system. Private insurance for medically necessary services is discouraged, by both federal and provincial legislation. The *Canada Health Act* requires provincial health care insurance plans to be accountable to the provincial government and to be non-profit, thereby effectively preventing private insurance plans from covering medically required services. Moreover, the majority of provinces (British Columbia, Alberta, Saskatchewan, Manitoba, Ontario, Quebec, New Brunswick, and Nova Scotia) prohibit private insurance companies from covering services that are also guaranteed under public health care insurance plans.

Concerns over privatization were raised again in 2000, when the Alberta government enacted legislation (Bill 11) with respect to contracting with the private sector for medically necessary surgical services. This legislation allows Regional Health Authorities (which are publicly funded) to contract with a private provider—either a for-profit or a not-for-profit entity for the provision of surgical services. The patient is not supposed to incur any out-of-pocket expenditures, as the costs related to the surgery will be fully insured by the provincial health care insurance plan. Regional Health Authorities are also responsible for coordinating the delivery of uninsured surgical services requiring an extended stay by the patient. The Alberta government believes that contracting with privately operated facilities for surgical services will reduce waiting lists in the public system, improve access, and enhance efficiency. Private providers will be required to operate within the requirements of the *Canada Health Act*. The Alberta government believes that the *Act* does not prevent a public health care facility from contracting out any of its services to the private sector.

Nonetheless, the then federal Minister of Health expressed concerns over the long term impact of the Alberta legislation. Among other things, he questioned whether private providers would provide faster or more cost-effective services than would existing public hospitals (if these were receiving the additional funding). He also raised the issue of whether the expansion of private for-profit facilities would help sustain the delivery of health care, or would undermine the letter and spirit of the *Canada Health Act*.

In some provinces, the operation of private clinics that offer magnetic resonance imaging (MRI), X-ray, ultrasound, and computed tomography (CT) scanning services also raises concerns over the accessibility criterion of the *Act*. Queue jumping is one of the dangers of these clinics. For example, individuals who can afford to pay may be able to get their diagnostic tests done more quickly. They then return to the publicly funded system for treatment one step ahead of patients awaiting diagnostic tests. In September 2000, the federal Minister of Health wrote to his counterparts in Alberta and Quebec to obtain more information on private diagnostic imaging clinics operating in those provinces. In July 2003, the Minister wrote again to four provinces to outline concerns about private MRI and CT scan clinics. Although consultations with provincial officials followed, these discussions were postponed at the request of the provinces.

Once again in April 2005, the federal Minister of Health wrote to Alberta, British Columbia, Quebec, and Nova Scotia to express concerns over private for-profit diagnostic imaging clinics that operate in those provinces. The concerns relate to medical necessity (comprehensiveness), private payment (user charge provisions), and queue jumping (accessibility) and the potential for non-compliance under the *Canada Health Act*. Should consultations with the four provinces prove inconclusive, the DAR process could be initiated with the view of ensuring that private clinics delivering diagnostic imaging services do so in compliance with the *Canada Health Act*. This process could yield useful information and clarification concerning the role and impact of private for-profit health care delivery.

The Options: Should We Keep the *Act* As It Is, Amend It or Repeal It?

In the current context of structural health care reform, it has often been asked whether the *Canada Health Act* can be maintained or whether it would be wiser to amend it. Some analysts believe the *Act* should be kept as it is. In their view:

- any change in the five criteria on which public health care insurance is based would undermine the greatest achievements of the health care system in Canada;
- the need to contain public health care costs should not be used to justify overhauling the *Act*;
- the five criteria of the *Act* can be maintained while the system is reorganized to improve clinical and economic effectiveness;
- effective allocation of public funds, together with a more judicious use of staff and medical care, would enable the government to reduce overall public health care expenditures and fund a wide (or even wider) range of effective and necessary services; and
- the *status quo* is to some extent preferable, given that most provinces have already reformed their health care delivery system by focusing on greater efficiency.

For a growing number of experts, however, the *status quo* is unacceptable. They say the *Canada Health Act* must be amended. Some suggest clarifying what is meant by "comprehensiveness" or "medically necessary services." Those who believe the criterion of comprehensiveness in the *Act* is vague and imprecise point out that clarification in this area would produce many benefits. First, the services for which the public sector must be responsible would be clearly set out; second, greater uniformity in the range of services throughout the country could be achieved, thus ending the balkanization of provincial health care insurance plans. Clarification could also help define medical necessity, taking into account important factors such as clinical, economic, and ethical considerations.

The *Act* could be clarified in three different ways. First, a definition of the term "medically required" could be added to section 2. Second, also in section 2, definitions relating to physician services, hospital services and extended health care services could be given. Third, the provisions in section 22 could be invoked, under which the federal government may establish by regulation: (1) a definition of extended health care services; and (2) the list of hospital services that would be excluded from all insured services. The *Act* stipulates that such regulations cannot be made unilaterally, without the agreement of each province.

However, there is no general agreement on these three options. Some analysts claim that until now the *Act* has given the provinces the latitude they need to interpret these terms in keeping with their own economic, political and social conditions. They believe that excessively specific definitions might limit the options of provincial governments to address the specific needs and values of their own residents.

Some experts favour the imposition of direct patient charges for services covered by government health care insurance plans. They explain that such action would help limit the abuse of health care by some patients, while reducing public health care expenditures. The effects of user charges on the use of health services and on public expenditures have been the subject of lively debate for some time and will not be discussed here. However, it should be pointed out that many analysts believe user charges are a step backwards, because the *Act* was adopted with the express purpose of discouraging such fees.

Finally, some people believe the *Act* creates inflexibility by limiting the options available to provincial governments in their fight to reform the delivery of health care and increase effectiveness and efficiency in this sector. Their solution, which is undoubtedly the most radical, would be to repeal the *Act*. It is difficult to foresee thc consequences of such an action. For example, it might have no effect: if the vast majority of Canadians remain satisfied with the current system, pressure from voters might in itself be sufficient to force provincial governments to maintain the requirements of public health care insurance across the country. On the other hand, repeal of the *Act* might result in a large number of experimental systems in Canada; provincial health care insurance plans would undoubtedly vary greatly, especially among provinces with very different tax bases.

The federal government has already made its position known. By introducing the Canada Health and Social Transfer and its successor, the Canada Health Transfer, it has taken steps to maintain an adequate level of funding as well as the authority conferred upon it by the *Canada Health Act*. Moreover, the 1995 federal policy on private clinics and the successive letters of concern related to private diagnostic imaging clinics (2000, 2003, 2005) suggest that the federal government is prepared to initiate the DAR process to ensure compliance with *the Canada Health Act*.

Parliamentary Action

In Canada, governments have intervened in health care in order to promote social and economic equity in this area. First, with the adoption of the *Hospital Insurance and Diagnostic Services Act* in 1957, and then with the *Medical Care Act* in 1966, the federal government used its spending power to transfer funds and attach requirements it considered important, but without regulating this sector, which is under provincial jurisdiction. By passing the *Canada Health Act* in 1984, however, Parliament did affect the provincial health care insurance plans in that it imposed nine requirements, including five specific criteria. These criteria guarantee all Canadians access to medically necessary physician and hospital services, free of financial or other barriers, within a system publicly administered on a non-profit basis. They also guarantee reimbursement for insured health care services received anywhere in Canada or abroad.

The five criteria stipulated in the *Canada Health Act* are not new: they were already set out in previous legislation on medical and hospital care. What was new in the 1984 *Act* was the provision of penalties for defaults, i.e., for the failure of provincial governments to comply, as part of their health care insurance plan, with the criteria stipulated in the *Act*. Federal cash transfers made as part of the EPF, CRST or CRT, as well as other transfers to provincial governments, were or are conditional on the province's compliance with these criteria.

In the years since the *Act* was adopted, the provinces have complied to a great extent with the five criteria and other provisions of the *Act*, although the federal government has had to intervene to ensure compliance with respect to extra-billing and user charges. The federal government has not, however, imposed penalties for some of the failures to comply with the five criteria of public health care insurance. It has preferred to limit its action, at least so far, to persuasion and negotiation. Some people have criticized this approach and have referred to the federal government's inaction and inability to enforce the criteria. Given the division of powers between the two levels of government, it can be expected that intervention by the federal government in this area could lead to conflict with the provincial governments and that warnings alone might not be enough to secure the provincial governments' cooperation.

Overall, any proposal for reforming the *Canada Health Act* will inevitably have to consider factors that are constitutional (distribution of powers), political (feasibility and voter approval), and economic (cost effectiveness).

Chronology

- 1 April 1984—The *Canada Health Act* received Royal Assent.
- May 1994—In accordance with the *Act*, the Governor in Council withheld $1,750,000 in EPF transfer payments from British Columbia, because some medical practitioners in that province had withdrawn from the government health care insurance plan and resorted to extra-billing in 1993.
- September 1994—Federal/provincial/territorial meeting of Health Ministers in Halifax, Nova Scotia. All Ministers present, except the Alberta Minister, agreed to "take whatever steps are required to regulate the development of private clinics in Canada, and to maintain a high quality, publicly funded Medicare system."
- January 1995—The federal Health Minister, the Honourable Diane Marleau, sent her provincial counterparts a letter informing them of the federal government's intention to impose financial penalties on provinces whose private clinics demand extra fees from patients in addition to the amount reimbursed by health insurance. The provinces had until 15 October 1995 to comply with this new interpretation of the *Act*.
- June 1995—Bill C-76, under which EPF transfers would be combined with CAP transfers to create a new form of block funding, received Royal Assent.
- Section 6 of the *Canada Health Act* was removed as a consequential amendment to Bill C-76. Despite this repeal, extended health care services continue as part of the *Act* in the same manner they have since 1984. As such, they still

remain subject only to conditions related to the provision of information and recognition of federal transfers, as set out in section 13 of the *Act*.

- November 1995—The federal Health Minister, the Honourable Diane Marleau, stated that the federal government had begun imposing cash penalties on all provinces in which semi-private clinics charged user fees. These provinces were Alberta, Manitoba, Nova Scotia, and Newfoundland.
- April 1996—The new CHST came into force, combining EPF and CAP transfers.
- July 1996—Health Canada lifted the penalties imposed on Alberta when that province began complying with the *Act*.
- January 1998—The penalties imposed on Newfoundland with respect to private clinics were lifted.
- February 1999—Health Canada discontinued the penalties imposed on Manitoba with respect to the federal policy on private clinics.
- September 2000—The federal Health Minister, the Honourable Allan Rock, wrote to his Alberta and Quebec counterparts to obtain more information on private MRI clinics operating in these provinces.
- July 2003—The federal Minister of Health, the Honourable Anne McLellan, wrote to Alberta, British Columbia, Nova Scotia, and Quebec to communicate her objection to the queue jumping that results from private diagnostic imaging clinics.
- April 2005—The federal Minister of Health, the Honourable Ujjal Dosanjh, wrote to the same four provinces to express concerns about private MRI and CT scan clinics.

Notes

The original version of this Current Issue Review was published in January 1995; the paper has been updated regularly since that time.

1. Extra billing is a fee charged by a doctor that is over and above what the provincial health care plan pays for the service. User charges are fees charged over and above what the provincial health care plan pays for any other insured health service, such as diagnostic testing, hospital care, and so on. Both are considered barriers to health care for patients, especially those with limited incomes. [Editor]
2. Assistive devices are aids and devices that help people with disabilities in their everyday activities. They include wheelchairs, hearing aids, prosthetic limbs, ventilators, and so on. [Editor]
3. See the Introduction to this chapter. [Editor]

Supreme Court of Canada

Chaoulli v. Quebec[1]

. . . Present: McLachlin C.J. [Chief Justice] and Major, Bastarache, Binnie, LeBel, Deschamps, and Fish JJ. [Justices] . . .

Over the years, Z [George Zeliotis] experienced a number of health problems that prompted him to speak out against waiting times in Quebec's public health care system. C [Jacques Chaoulli] is a physician who has tried unsuccessfully to have his home-delivered medical activities recognized and to obtain a licence to operate an independent private hospital. . . . [T]he **appellants**, Z and C, contested the validity of the prohibition on private health insurance provided for in s. 15 of the *Health Insurance Act* ("*HEIA*") and s. 11 of the *Hospital Insurance Act* ("*HOIA*"). They contended that the prohibition deprives them of access to health care services . . . [due to] the waiting times inherent in the public system. They claimed, **inter alia** [among other things], that s. 15 *HEIA* and s. 11 *HOIA* violate their rights under s. 7 of the *Canadian Charter of Rights and Freedoms* and s. 1 of the Quebec *Charter of Human Rights and Freedoms*. . . .

Held [by the majority] . . . : The appeal should be allowed.[2] Section 15 *HEIA* and s. 11 *HOIA* are inconsistent with the *Quebec Charter*. . . .

[The Majority Decision by Justice Deschamps]

[Three of Justice Deschamps' sentences are very complex. The gist of those sentence is indicated by an underscore.—Editor]

In the case of a challenge to a Quebec statute, it is appropriate to look first to the rules that apply specifically in Quebec before turning to the *Canadian Charter*, especially where the provisions of the two **charters** produce cumulative effects, but where the rules are not identical. Given the absence in s. 1 of the *Quebec Charter* of the reference to the principles of fundamental justice found in s. 7 of the *Canadian Charter*,[3] the scope of the Quebec Charter is potentially broader than that of the *Canadian Charter*, and this characteristic should not be disregarded. What is more, it is clear that the protection of s. 1 of *the Quebec Charter* is not limited to situations involving the administration of justice.

In the instant [current] case, the trial judge's [lower court's] conclusion that s. 11 *HOIA* and s. 15 *HEIA* constitute a deprivation of the rights to life and security of the person [which are] protected by s. 7 of the *Canadian Charter* applies in full to the rights to life and to personal inviolability [which are] protected by s. 1 of the Quebec Charter. The evidence shows that, in the case of certain surgical procedures, the delays that are the necessary result of waiting lists increase the patient's risk of mortality or the risk that his or her injuries will become irreparable. The evidence also shows that many patients on non-urgent waiting lists are in pain and cannot fully enjoy any real quality of life. The right to life and to personal inviolability is therefore affected by the waiting times.

The infringement of the rights protected by s. 1 is not justified under s. 9.1 of the *Quebec Charter*.[4] The general objective of the *HOIA* and the *HEIA* is to promote health care of the highest possible quality for all Quebeckers regardless of their ability to pay. The purpose of the prohibition on private insurance in s. 11 *HOIA* and s. 15 *HEIA* is to preserve the integrity of the public health care system. Preservation of the public plan is a pressing and substantial objective, but there is no proportionality between the measure adopted to attain the objective and the objective itself. While an absolute prohibition on private insurance does have a rational connection with the objective of preserving the public plan, the Attorney General of Quebec has not demonstrated that this measure meets the minimal impairment test. It cannot be concluded from the evidence concerning the Quebec plan or the plans of the other provinces of Canada, or from the evolution of the systems of various OECD[5] countries[,] that an absolute prohibition on private insurance is necessary to protect the integrity of the public plan. There are a wide range of measures that are less drastic and also less intrusive in relation to the protected rights.

This is not a case in which the Court must show deference to the government's choice of measure. The courts have a duty to rise above political debate. When, as in the case at bar [before the court], the courts are given the tools they need to make a decision, they should not hesitate to assume their responsibilities. Deference cannot lead the **judicial** branch to abdicate its role in favour of the **legislative** branch or the **executive** branch. While the government has the power to decide what measures to adopt, it cannot choose to do nothing in the face of a violation of Quebeckers' right to security. Inertia cannot be used as an argument to justify deference. . . .

[Additional Arguments by Chief Justice McLachlin and Justices Major and Bastarache, Agreeing with the Majority Decision]

The conclusion of [Justice] Deschamps that the prohibition on private health insurance violates s. 1 of the *Quebec Charter* and is not justifiable under s. 9.1 is agreed with. The prohibition also violates s. 7 of the *Canadian Charter* and is not justifiable under s. 1.

While the decision about the type of health care system Quebec should adopt falls to the legislature of that province, the resulting legislation, like all laws, must comply with the *Canadian Charter*. Here, it is common ground [the appellants and the respondents agree] that the effect of the prohibition on private health insurance set out in s. 11 *HOIA* and s. 15 *HEIA* is to allow only the very rich, who can afford private health care without need of insurance, to secure private care in order to avoid any delays in the public system. Given the prohibition, most Quebeckers have no choice but to accept any delays in the public health regime and the consequences this entails.

The evidence in this case shows that delays in the public health care system are widespread, and that, in some serious cases, patients die as a result of waiting lists for public health care. The evidence also demonstrates that the prohibition against private health insurance and its consequence of denying people vital health care result in physical and psychological suffering that meets a threshold test of seriousness.

Where lack of timely health care can result in death, the s. 7 protection of life is engaged; where it can result in serious psychological and physical suffering, the s. 7 protection of security of the person is triggered. In this case, the government has prohibited private health insurance that would permit ordinary Quebeckers to access private health care while failing to deliver health care in a reasonable manner, thereby increasing the risk of complications and death. In so doing, it has interfered with the interests protected by s. 7 of the *Canadian Charter*.

Section 11 *HOIA* and s. 15 *HEIA* are arbitrary, and the consequent deprivation of the interests protected by s. 7 is therefore not in accordance with the principles of fundamental justice. In order not to be arbitrary, a limit on life, liberty or security of the person requires not only a theoretical connection between the limit and the legislative goal, but a real connection on the facts. The task of the courts, on s. 7 issues as on others, is to evaluate the issue in the light, not just of common sense or theory, but of the evidence. Here, the evidence on the experience of other western democracies with public health care systems that permit access to private health care refutes the government's theory that a prohibition on private health insurance is connected to maintaining quality public health care. It does not appear that private participation leads to the eventual demise of public health care.

The breach of s. 7 is not justified under s. 1 of the *Canadian Charter*. The government undeniably has an interest in protecting the public health regime but, given that the evidence falls short of demonstrating that the prohibition on private health insurance protects the public health care system, a rational connection between the prohibition on private health insurance and the legislative objective is not [has not been] made out. In addition, on the evidence, the prohibition goes further than would be necessary to protect the public system and is thus not minimally impairing. Finally, the benefits of the prohibition do not outweigh its deleterious effects. The physical and psychological suffering and risk of death that may result from the prohibition on private health insurance outweigh whatever benefit—and none has been demonstrated here—there may be to the system as a whole. . . .

[The Dissenting Arguments of Justices Binnie, LeBel, and Fish]

The question in this appeal is whether the province of Quebec not only has the **constitutional** authority to establish a comprehensive single-tier health plan, but to discourage a second (private) tier health sector by prohibiting the purchase and sale of private health insurance. This issue has been the subject of protracted debate in Quebec and across Canada through several provincial and federal elections. The debate cannot be resolved as a matter of constitutional law by judges.

Canadian Charter interests under s. 7 are enumerated as life, liberty and security of the person. The trial judge found that the current state of the Quebec health system, linked to the prohibition against health insurance for insured services, is capable, at least in the cases of some individuals on some occasions, of putting at risk their life or security of the person. The courts can use s. 7 of the *Canadian Charter* to pre-empt the ongoing public debate only if the current health plan violates an established "principle of fundamental justice." That is not the case here.

The public policy objective of "health care of a reasonable standard within a reasonable time" is not a legal principle of fundamental justice. There is no "societal consensus" about what this non-legal standard means or how to achieve it. It will be very difficult for those designing and implementing a health plan to predict when judges will think its provisions cross the line from what is "reasonable" into the forbidden territory of what is "unreasonable."

A deprivation of a right will be arbitrary, and will thus infringe s. 7, if it bears no relation to, or is inconsistent with, the state interest that lies behind the legislation. Quebec's legislative objective is to provide high-quality health care, at a reasonable cost, for as many people as possible in a manner that is consistent with principles of efficiency, **equity**, and fiscal responsibility. An overbuilt health system is no more in the larger public interest than a system that on occasion falls short.

The Quebec health plan shares the policy objectives of the *Canada Health Act*, and the means adopted by Quebec to implement these objectives are not arbitrary. In principle, Quebec wants a health system where access is governed by need rather than wealth or status. To accomplish this objective, Quebec seeks to discourage the growth of private sector delivery of "insured" services based on wealth and insurability. The prohibition is thus rationally connected to Quebec's objective and is not inconsistent with it. In practical terms, Quebec bases the prohibition on the view that private insurance, and a consequent major expansion of private health services, would have a harmful effect on the public system.

The view of the evidence taken by the trial judge supports that belief. She found that the expansion of private health care would undoubtedly have a negative impact on the public health system. The evidence indicates that a parallel private system will not reduce, and may worsen, the public waiting lists and will likely result in a decrease in government funding for the public system. In light of these findings, it cannot be said that the prohibition against private health insurance "bears no relation to, or is inconsistent with" the preservation of a health system predominantly based on need rather than wealth or status. Prohibition of private insurance is not "inconsistent" with the State interest; still less is it "unrelated" to it. People are free to dispute Quebec's strategy, but it cannot be said that the province's version of a single-tier health system, and the prohibition on private health insurance designed to protect that system, is a legislative choice that has been adopted "arbitrarily" by the Quebec National Assembly as that term has been understood to date in the *Canadian Charter* jurisprudence.

The limits on legislative action fixed by the *Quebec Charter* are no more favourable to the appellants' case than are those fixed by the *Canadian Charter*. Section 1 of the *Quebec Charter*, in essence, covers about the same ground as s. 7 of the *Canadian Charter*, but it does not mention the principles of fundamental justice. Here, the prohibition against private insurance is justifiable under s. 9.1 of the *Quebec Charter*, which requires rights to be exercised with "proper regard" to "**democratic** values, public order and the general well-being of the citizens of Quebec." On the evidence, the exercise by the appellants of their claimed *Quebec Charter* rights to defeat the prohibition against private insurance would not have proper regard for "democratic values" or "public order," as [because] the future of a publicly supported and financed single-tier health plan should be in the hands of elected representatives. Nor would it have proper regard for the "general well-being of the citizens of Quebec," who are the designated beneficiaries of the health plan, and in particular for the well-being of the less advantaged Quebeckers. The evidence amply supports the validity of the prohibition of private insurance under the *Quebec Charter*: the objectives are compelling; a rational connection between the measure and the objective has been demonstrated, and the choice made by the National Assembly is within the range of options that are justifiable under s. 9.1. In respect of questions of social and economic policy, the minimal impairment test leaves a substantial margin of appreciation to the Quebec legislature. Designing, financing, and operating the public health system of a modern democratic society remains a challenging task and calls for difficult choices. Shifting the design of the health system to the courts is not a wise outcome.

The safety valve (however imperfectly administered) of allowing Quebec residents to obtain essential health care outside the province when they are unable to receive the care in question at home in a timely manner is of importance. If, as the appellants claim, this safety valve is opened too sparingly, the courts are available to supervise enforcement of the rights of those patients who are directly affected by the decision on a case-by-case basis. . . .

Notes

1. *Chaoulli v. Quebec (Attorney General)*, [2005] 1 S.C.R. 791, 2005 SCC 35.
2. Zeliotis and Chaoulli were appealing the decisions of two lower courts, the Quebec Superior Court and the Quebec Court of Appeal. Those courts had ruled that neither s. 1 of the *Quebec Charter* nor s. 7 of the *Canadian Charter* had been violated. The Supreme Court overturned their rulings. [Editor]
3. Section 7 states, "Everyone has the right to life, liberty and security of the person and the right not to be deprived thereof except in accordance with the principles of fundamental justice." Principles of fundamental justice are legal principles that are central to Canadian conceptions of justice, and capable of being stated with some precision. They include rights such as the right against self-incrimination and the right that laws be clear and consistently applied. [Editor]
4. In a previous case, the Supreme Court had ruled that s. 9.1 of the *Quebec Charter* "is of the same nature as s. 1 of the Canadian *Charter*" (*Ford v. Quebec (Attorney General)*, [1988] 2 SCR 712, quoted in *Chaoulli*, para. 47). Here the Court analyzes the purpose of s. 11 HOIA and s. 15 *HEIA* using the criteria of a s. 1 analysis in the Canadian *Charter* (see "Canada's Legal System—The *Charter*" in the Introduction: A Short Primer). [Editor]
5. The Organization for Economic Cooperation and Development. [Editor]

Susan Sherwin

Theory versus Practice in Ethics: A Feminist Perspective on Justice in Health Care

AV = author's view; ~AV = not the author's view

A Methodological Proposal

My main concern in this essay is to dismantle the widely accepted distinction between conceptual and practical questions in **ethics** and **bioethics**. ~AV In the usual organization of ethical activity, conceptual and practical activities are treated as distinct and separate tasks. The conceptual category includes matters such as the pursuit of questions aimed at developing systems for investigating moral claims and also efforts to clarify the nature of the terms, principles, and arguments that are used in moral discussions. The practical category is thought to encompass the explorations of questions that arise out of the human experience of trying to live as a **moral agent**, including efforts to propose, critique, and defend solutions to identified moral problems. While most theorists assume that there are connections between these two tasks, the precise nature and strength of those connections tend to be unexamined.

Within this familiar model for organizing ethical thought, it is generally agreed that, of the two broad types of concerns, the conceptual questions are the more truly philosophical.

Indeed, conceptual questions are usually addressed as **paradigmatically** philosophical, best approached as purely abstract, theoretical problems that demand a relatively high level of philosophic inclination and experience. In contrast, practical problems are thought to represent questions that confront all moral agents when they discover contradictions or ambiguities among their personal beliefs about moral behaviour. Since identifying and exploring practical questions is an activity demanded of all moral agents, and since philosophers do not seem to be especially good at actually living morally, it is not at all clear that practical ethics even requires any special philosophical acumen. Indeed, there are debates in the philosophical literature about whether the study of actual moral problems is appropriately addressed within philosophy at all.

. . .

AV I want to dispute this common assumption, however, and I shall argue that the two sorts of ethics tasks are inextricably linked. In support of this thesis, I shall explore the concept of justice and show how important it is to attend to the intimate interrelationship of conceptual and practical concerns when we invoke this central concept in health care discussions. I shall argue that the connections between theoretical and practical concerns run both ways; that is, both [1] that the conceptual discussions of the terms of the debates about justice in health care cannot be adequately addressed in **abstraction** from the practical questions at issue and also [2] that the practical proposals we might make about justice in health care must involve important theoretical decisions. Neither task should be pursued in isolation of the other. . . .

. . .

I am convinced that we need a more explicit expression of the importance of doing theory and practice together, and, in the course of arguing for a more self-conscious connection between these two domains, I shall spell out some of the particular ways in which those links are to be made. I shall look at the central question of justice in health care as a specific example of how these issues must be investigated in tandem. By spelling out the outlines of a particular interpretation of the concept of justice in the context of health care discussions and contrasting it with other approaches that are less committed to doing both levels of analysis together, I hope to demonstrate why theoretical and practical concerns must be explored in concert with one another.

. . .

Feminist Reflective Equilibrium

Because this proposal is, in many respects, similar to the idea of reflective equilibrium proposed by John Rawls, it is useful to spell out both the similarities and the differences between our approaches. Like Rawls, I am recommending a **dialectical** type of process for ethics in which we are to explore theoretical questions by simultaneously examining the practical effect of the theoretical proposals we entertain and by searching for theoretical expressions of our initial moral values. In his conception, ethical theory is to be developed by engaging in an ongoing practice of shifting our focus back and forth between the level of abstract, theoretical concepts and principles, and that of our considered moral judgments. Each level is envisioned as correcting and informing the other until our intuitions at both levels can be brought into line with one another. Since neither is sufficient in itself or logically prior to the other, both levels of reflection are necessary to the construction of adequate moral views. In order to ensure an adequate scope to these reflections, Rawls recommends that we look at a wide range of moral alternatives and weigh competing moral ideals before settling on any particular one; this can best be achieved by taking into account the considered moral views of others as well as our own.

. . .

. . . I propose that we . . . include practical concerns and observations of real life in this process. In my view, we should strive to ensure that any ethical proposals we come up with address the specific concerns that are generated by attention to our actual world. We ought to evaluate the adequacy of any theoretical proposals by considering very carefully what effect they have on actual moral problems within existing circumstances and arrangements. . . .

. . .

. . . [I]n a world in which powerful systems of oppression and domination have a significant and unjustifiable impact on the relative **privilege** or disadvantage of members of different social groups, such systemic forces must be seen to be morally objectionable. Because systemic oppression [see **systemic discrimination**], such as sexism and racism, has devastating consequences on many human lives, and because it is manifestly unjust, it is a matter of moral urgency that we identify, condemn, and find ways to eliminate these sorts of forces from our society. . . .

In the light of the centrality that concerns about oppression play in **feminist** moral thought, I use the term "feminist ethics" to identify those approaches to ethics that direct us to include attention to these sorts of features of social and political life in our moral deliberations. My methodological proposal, then, is that ethics and bioethics proceed by a practice that might be called "feminist reflective equilibrium," in which we make a conscious effort to consider questions of domination and power as morally relevant concerns when we explore the conceptual and practical dimensions of issues in bioethics.

. . .

. . . [M]y proposal of feminist reflective equilibrium works from the assumption that everyone has a stake of some sort or other in existing patterns of oppression and that adequate moral analysis requires that we acknowledge this social fact and find ways of ensuring that moral concerns are not obscured by the **self-interested** ignorance of any particular group. Thus, whereas Rawls envisioned a process of reflective equilibrium that seems to be aimed at producing timeless, static, universal rules for ethics, the feminist version I am proposing promotes a process that is collaborative, situated in time and place, dynamic, and sensitive to the ways in which one's own experience may limit one's moral vision.

. . . To illustrate my position, I shall sketch out some proposals about how feminist ethics suggests that we understand the concept of justice in health care contexts, and I shall contrast my interpretation with some familiar, non-feminist alternatives. I shall pay particular attention to the fact that the alternative (non-feminist) conceptions in the literature purport to be apolitical and **disinterested** with respect to questions of oppression and domination. As such, they represent themselves as evolving within a philosophical framework in which the theoretical work of concept formation is done in isolation from the particular circumstances in which that concept will be invoked. I shall argue that these alternative conceptions are not as apolitical and abstract as they claim to be, but, because of their proponents' unwillingness to acknowledge their practical and political roots explicitly, these conceptions are insensitive to important moral dimensions of the very contexts they are meant to address. . . .

The Traditional Approaches to Justice in Health Care

Let us begin, then, with the most familiar bioethical formulations of the ethical issues associated with questions of justice in health care. Typically, arguments about justice in health care are defined as being about accessibility to health care services and about the associated question of who should pay for those services. There is a vast literature addressing this topic and most of it focuses on two basic questions: (1) What should be the basis for access to health services? (2) How are particular resources to be allocated when the demand exceeds the supply? . . . I shall limit my remarks to the first question, since it is the more fundamental of the two.

The issue of access to health services is often formulated in terms of the question: Who is to pay for these services? In either version, the discussion is typically cast in the language of **rights**. In most cases, those who argue in favour of socialized medical services [universal healthcare] . . . argue that universal access to needed health care must be assured in response to a universal **positive right** to health care—a right that is ultimately grounded in a particular theory of justice. In contrast, those who place greatest value on individual liberty rights . . . define **coercive** taxation for the purpose of paying for the health care of others as a violation of individual liberty, and so they oppose the conditions required to fund any form of socialized medicine program. Hence, the traditional debate tends to be about the nature of rights and the primacy to be placed on positive and **negative rights**.

. . .

Note that this debate, although ultimately of enormous practical and political significance, is carried out as if it were an abstract contest about the concepts of justice and rights, where each side constructs the issue and the central concepts differently. Both sides approach the issue as one of determining the proper meaning of these general moral terms; both assume that those meanings can then be invoked in a purely deductive argument in favour of their own preferred social policies, although that is not how their own reasoning usually proceeds. Rather, proponents on both sides of this issue tend to be well aware of the policy implications of their conceptual commitments before they make them. Hence, there is, at best, something disingenuous about the implied suggestion that the conceptual work is being done in abstraction from any political concerns.

. . .

Feminist ethics has been quite explicit about acknowledging the relevance of the political consequences of moral decisions in its ethical deliberations. Although that explicitness exposes feminist ethicists to criticism from traditionalists who believe ethics can and should be done in the absence of political calculations, their [feminists'] self-conscious focus on questions of power and privilege actually ensures that they are more aware of and hence better able to address the kinds of considerations that I believe most theorists actually engage in when evaluating issues in bioethics. Feminist reflective equilibrium makes visible the kinds of political values that I believe do—and should—enter into all discussions of justice in health care, and that fact makes it easier to weigh the hidden assumptions that may be biasing thought at both the conceptual and the practical level of analysis.

...

Expanding the Agenda

Feminist approaches to justice in health care have other benefits as well. For instance, they generally extend the range of concern far beyond the established boundaries of the traditional debate, where discussion is often limited to deciding who is to pay for health services. They recognize the necessity of identifying and addressing many other complex issues that fall under the rubric of justice in the context of health care. By virtue of their explicit concern about matters of oppression and privilege, feminist approaches make clear that even though our highly valued, universal (though increasingly precarious), socialized health care system in Canada would seem to resolve the questions of the traditional debate—that is, who is to pay and who is to have access to health services—many problems of justice remain. For instance, though its coverage is far more extensive than that of the United States, it still leaves many gaps: health care costs tend to be narrowly defined in terms of doctors' and hospital fees, and this arrangement excludes provision for many other important health needs (e.g., prescription drugs, special diets, home nursing). Also, poor women often have to contend with potentially insurmountable problems in pursuit of health services, such as arranging for transportation to the clinic and finding child care while they are being treated.

In addition, because feminism is highly sensitive to the disproportionate number of women and children living in poverty and to the continuing economic disparity between women and men, it directs our attention to the moral significance of the strong correlation that exists between economic status and health. Despite several decades of widespread feminist activism and now nearly universal rhetoric in support of equality of opportunity and pay equity, it is still the case that women in North America face significant economic disadvantages relative to men of the same race, class, and ethnic background: on average, women earn only two-thirds of what men do and they are much more likely than men to be living in poverty. The fact that people with low incomes are much less likely than others to have access to adequate nutrition, proper exercise, home and work environments free of toxins, and needed stress management programs, surely falls into the category of justice in health care, but it is often overlooked in discussions of this topic.

We also ought to reflect on the fact that women are likely to find themselves responsible for seeking health care services far more often than men do, even though they usually have fewer resources with which to work. Their reproductive needs are more frequent and more complex than are those of men and their dependence on health professionals for reproductive health care is exacerbated by the fact that all aspects of their relatively complex reproductive lives (menstruation, contraception, pregnancy, childbirth, lactation, menopause) have been subject to medical surveillance and control. As well, the existing sexual division of labour means that women are generally the primary caregivers at home, so they are the ones usually assigned the role of monitoring and maintaining the health of other family members. They are expected to recognize illness in children, elderly or disabled relatives, and sometimes in husbands, and it is usually women's responsibility to obtain medical care when a problem is identified. In health care, as in other spheres, questions of justice regarding the sexual division of labour in society have repercussions in the uneven demands put on women to negotiate their way through an expensive, complex, and often intimidating health care system. Here, as elsewhere, injustice in the **public sphere** is inseparable from injustice in the **private sphere**: each is replicated and reinforced in the other domain. Bioethical discussions should reflect the fact that ongoing injustice in the domestic and economic spheres produces unjust restrictions on many different levels with respect to access *to* and responsiveness of health care services.

Moreover, many other questions beyond the matter of funding must be raised about how health care services are distributed. There seems to be a marked discrepancy in the effectiveness of medical treatments made available to women and men. . . . [W]omen are significantly less likely than men to receive the diagnostic and therapeutic interventions considered to be medically appropriate for their conditions (e.g., women are only 10 per cent as likely to be referred for cardiac catheterization[1] as are men with the same symptoms). In cases where the proposed therapy is especially controversial, however, women may receive more than their share (e.g. psychosurgery[2] is performed twice as often on women as on men).

There are significant and disproportionate gaps in medical knowledge about treatments for women. The overwhelming majority of medical research to date has been done on men; often the data simply are not collected to determine how best to treat women for the same diseases. Studies of heart disease, for example, are almost universally conducted on men, even though heart disease is as big a killer of older women as it is of men. The record is even worse on certain diseases that particularly affect women. For example, although it is now estimated that breast cancer will affect one in nine women in North America, until very recently breast cancer research received only a very small proportion of cancer research funding.

. . .

It is a mistake, then, for the traditional debate to presume or suggest that payment for actual medical services provided and the allocation of scarce medical resources are the only major issues of justice that arise in health care contexts. There are many different ways in which women in general, and some groups of women in particular, get less than their fair share of needed health care services. While the many types of failure to provide for the health needs of oppressed groups have been widely documented, to date only feminists and other political reformers have been inclined to investigate these non-monetary dimensions of the justice in health care question.

. . .

Feminist Approaches to "Justice" and "Health Care"

Yet even if we expand the scope of our investigation of differential benefits and burdens associated with the health care system to deal with these sorts of concerns, it will still not be sufficient to capture all the forms of injustice that feminist critics have revealed as inherent in our health care system. To capture these further dimensions, we need to rethink the central concepts of the discussion and extend the meanings of the terms of this debate beyond the traditional measures of justice as fairness in the distribution of defined health services. The terms of the debate—both "justice" and "health care"—must be made subject to feminist re-visioning. In revising these concepts we change the scope of the questions to be explored under the rubric of justice in health care. By making these changes we shall be able to see more clearly how conceptual decisions have significant practical import in this sphere of bioethical study and to understand why the social realities we inhabit need to be reflected in the concepts we use in our ethical deliberations about the world.

Beginning with "health care," then, we should first observe that this term usually is reserved for the services that happen to be offered within existing health care systems. . . . [T]he services that are at issue in most discussions of justice in health care are largely those that health care professionals, especially the most powerful among them (doctors), perform. In fact, however, while this conception may seem to fit the health care needs of a certain advantaged portion of the population, it is inadequate for capturing the actual health needs of many members of society. A more effective, and arguably more efficient and fair, health care system would allow patients access to forms of treatment outside the domain of **allopathic medicine** if they have been proved effective in some types of cases, for example, herbal remedies, special diets, acupuncture, and massage therapy, even if most physicians lack expertise in their practice.

Moreover, as is well known but often forgotten, most of the dramatic improvements in the morbidity and mortality [sickness and death] rates of western nations are attributable not to expensive, technological medical services, but rather to progressive improvements in such ordinary human requirements as basic hygiene and nutrition.[3] Conversely, many of the continuing health care problems in western societies can be explained by the fact that large segments of the population still suffer from inadequate access to the necessities of life and health: proper nutrition, clean water, adequate housing, prenatal care, safety from physical violence, protection against toxic chemicals in the environment, and a strong sense of self-esteem.

Thus, rather than simply arguing for more universal provision of health care services as they are now defined, we should rethink the foundation of the arguments put forward in defence of a positive right to health care. Arguments for universal health care typically are based on a recognition of the importance of good health to individuals' sense of well-being and to their opportunity to participate fully in their communities. These arguments should be reformulated to include not only medical services but all of the controllable conditions that contribute to good health. We ought not to restrict our attention to the artificial boundary that is implicit when we limit our focus to the concerns and activities of physicians. A more foundational analysis of the standard of justice in the domain of health would begin with a much broader conception of health care that includes all measures that contribute to opportunities for improved health, for example, protection against avoidable threats such as environmental poisons, physical assault, and psychological abuse.

. . .

By revising our initial conception of health care we shall be able to place a higher priority on preventative and protective health measures and to empower individuals to assert a right to health that is more fundamental than their derivative right to medical care. While political and economic realities may make it impractical at this time to provide everyone with everything that is required to ensure the good health of each, there is a meaningful sense of a right to health in which the ideal we should be striving for is to assure everyone an equal chance at good health at least in so far as this is a condition amenable to social, economic, or political adjustments. Such a right would include, at least, efforts to provide a safe environment, an adequate diet, clean water, health education, and an opportunity to develop self-esteem. Obviously such an ideal would organize political and social priorities quite differently than the current system does.

Moreover, all of these factors should be seen as public responsibilities, since they are inaccessible to most individuals acting independently. This fact is clearest in the case of ensuring access to clean water and a non-toxic environment, for these conditions of health are beyond the scope of most individuals' power and initiative and can be achieved only through public efforts. More sustained political argument will be necessary to achieve agreement on the importance of insisting on public responsibility for ensuring the other goods identified as requirements for individual health. In support of that argument, we shall need to show that women, children, blacks, native people, gays, and lesbians (among others) all are at risk of being subjected to systemic (and systematic) violence in their daily lives and that, as individuals, they often are unable to protect themselves from such violence. In the face of existing levels of sexism, racism, homophobia, anti-Semitism, and classist prejudice in our communities and the documented evidence of well-organized campaigns of hatred and anger directed against certain groups, it is probable that only the state has the **institutional** power and authority to protect most victims of discrimination from assault. . . .

These broader concerns for health lead us into the case for re-evaluating the other concept that is central to this discussion. Feminists have reason also to challenge traditional understandings of the term "justice." Discussions of justice are usually taken to be concerned with establishing a fair distribution of benefits and burdens among members of a society. When the issue is health care, the presumption is generally that we need to determine a fair mechanism for providing and allocating a certain level of health care services (however they may be defined). But as Iris Marion Young has argued, the distributive **paradigm** that is assumed by most justice theorists is inadequate; it does not capture all the relevant considerations that should be addressed under the concept of justice.[4] Young argues that justice cannot be reduced simply to questions of distribution of some limited set of resources, because such reductions avoid important questions of social structure and organization. Moreover, the distributive paradigm focuses attention on a particularly **atomistic** conception of persons in society that fails to recognize that persons are socially interconnected, not independent, beings. In particular, it avoids examination of the social relations that control the application of distributive policies.

. . .

Of course, distributive questions are still important within feminist ethics. The demand is not to abandon such investigations but to recognize that they are only part of the much broader moral question of justice. Young's concept of social justice recognizes that the elimination of institutionalized oppression and domination is an important aspect of justice. In contrast to the more familiar distributive paradigm where persons are regarded simply as possessors or consumers of goods, this feminist theory of social justice allows us to see people as responsible moral agents who create the social institutions that determine social, political, and economic privileges and constraints; it encourages us to evaluate those institutions in terms of a wider range of criteria. Moreover, by directing attention to the social context in which goods or opportunities are distributed, her conception of justice has the further advantage of providing a better basis for considering even the familiar questions of distribution. Most distributive accounts focus on questions of comparison of narrowly construed outcomes. Young's account expands this focus and provides us with a larger set of relevant information for evaluating patterns of distribution. Thus, it actually offers greater promise of ultimately achieving truly just distribution patterns in matters of health and other goods. . . .

Conclusion

This sketch of a feminist perspective on justice in health care does not, of course, constitute an exhaustive theory of justice. If I am right about what such a theory involves, it will turn out that a comprehensive and empirically adequate theory of justice in health care cannot be produced by a single theorist working in the abstract. A full theory of justice in health care will require a much more detailed investigation of the workings of oppression and the role of health care within those forces. It will also require a much wider conversation, where the views of other members of society, especially those who are differently oppressed, are sought and considered. The demands of feminist reflective equilibrium cannot be satisfied by a single researcher but require a collaborative process of dialogue and reflection. This paper is meant to provide support for the project of engaging in such conversations and to offer some methodological direction to questions that will need to be addressed.

I have sought to show that traditional (non-feminist) formulations of the question of justice in health care ethics tend to restrict inappropriately the focus of our ethical attention and discussion. To the degree that theorists have attempted to settle on the formulations of the key concepts of justice and health care in advance of exploring their role in setting health care policies, they have produced concepts that do not capture all relevant dimensions of the concerns they represent. Similarly, so long as those involved in the formation of health care policies accept existing theoretical formulations uncritically, they fail to include relevant aspects of existing injustice in their proposals. Both approaches have the effect of narrowing our conceptions of what constitutes the important ethical questions to be raised and also our sense of what sorts of answers we should pursue in response. I draw on feminist work to spell out a richer set of concepts that reflect the ways in which bioethical work needs to engage with both theoretical and practical issues simultaneously if it is to develop a reliable understanding of justice in health care.

. . .

Notes

1. Cardiac catheterization is a medical procedure in which a doctor inserts a small tube in a patient's arm, groin, or neck and guides it to the patient's heart. It is used to diagnose and treat certain heart conditions. [Editor]
2. Psychosurgery is surgical treatment for mental illnesses that have not responded to any other form of treatment. It involves cutting or burning an area of the brain believed to regulate emotions. In North America it is used primarily for the treatment of major depression and obsessive-compulsive disorder. [Editor]
3. Sherwin is referring to the literature on the **social determinants of health** (see chapter introduction). See, for example, Richard G. Wilkinson and Kate Pickett, *The Spirit Level: Why More Equal*

Societies Almost Always Do Better (London: Allen Lane, 2009) and Robert William Fogel, *The Escape from Hunger and Premature Death, 1700–2100: Europe, America, and the Third World* (Cambridge: Cambridge University Press, 2004). [Editor]

4. Iris Marion Young, *Justice and the Politics of Difference* (Princeton: Princeton University Press, 1991).

Françoise Baylis, Nuala P. Kenny, and Susan Sherwin

A Relational Account of Public Health Ethics

AV = author's view; ~AV = not the author's view

Introduction

In the wake of the 2003 SARS [severe acute respiratory syndrome] near-pandemic, **public health** has gained importance in policy circles, as **nation-states** and international organizations hasten to develop and implement regulatory policies and programs to address emerging threats to public health. The most visible results of this renewed interest in public health are the pandemic plans developed by at least thirty-seven countries . . . and the World Health Organization. . . .

To those involved in developing public health responses to the legal, technical, and scientific issues of an impending global pandemic, it is clear that ethics is of central importance. In our view, however, many of the ethical tools at hand for pandemic planning are inadequate to the task and fail to effectively address key challenges. On the brighter side, interest in pandemic planning provides those of us who work in bioethics with a window of opportunity to help decision makers develop and implement policies and programs within a sound ethics framework for public health—an ethics framework that is firmly grounded in our common interest in preventing illness, building physically and socially healthy communities and eliminating health inequities.

. . .

In this paper, we propose a public health ethics that reaches beyond pandemic planning to embrace the full spectrum of public health responsibilities from poverty, to sanitation, to pollution, to infectious disease, to epidemics and pandemic threats, to global warming, to bioterrorism. In this proposal we insist on a public health ethics with a very broad scope and an orientation that is thoroughly relational (rather than **individualistic**). . . .

. . .

Ethical Frameworks and Pandemic Planning

~AV Much of the recent discussion of public health ethics among policy makers has occurred in the context of pandemic planning. This focus is not surprising given the urgent, uncertain, risky, and fear-generating conditions of pandemic[s]. What is surprising, however, is the primary focus in pandemic planning on the values and priorities of individuals. Many pandemic plans appear to **privilege** the values of liberty, **dignity**, and privacy, and to highlight the **rights** and interests of individuals with particular attention given to such issues as restrictions on individual liberty and freedom, potential social stigma and isolation, and access to antivirals, vaccines, and other potentially scarce resources. AV From the perspective of pandemic planning and public health, this is an odd and limited list of ethical concerns—a list that likely would not have been generated but for the fact that the analysis remains steeped in an individual rights **discourse** inherited from clinical ethics and research ethics, and consonant with the dominant moral and political culture.

In 2006, the Canadian government updated its pandemic planning materials and published the *Canadian Pandemic Influenza Plan for the Health Sector*. This report explicitly recognized that "clinical ethics is focused on the health and interests of an individual . . . [while] public health ethics is focused on the health and interests of a population."[1] According to the authors of this report,

> In an effective health system, these interests are in a dynamic balance. . . . The importance given to individual and collective interests will shift according to the nature of the health risk being addressed. When a health risk primarily affects an individual, clinical ethics will predominate and a high value will be placed on individual interests. When a health risk affects a population, however, public health ethics will predominate and a high value will be placed on collective interests.[2]

~AV And yet, with the exception of the principle "to protect and promote the public's health," and some vague commitment to distributive justice, the focus remains on the personal (i.e., the inherent dignity of all persons; individual freedom; personal **autonomy**; and risk/benefit analysis). This focus is pervasive despite the development of a pandemic plan specific to on-reserve First Nations communities. . . . This individualistic orientation is perhaps best explained by the fact that "respect for the individual" is identified as one of only two seminal values for public health ethics (the other seminal value being justice).

. . .

AV The problem with focusing on the rights and interests of individuals, as Wendy Rogers astutely notes, is that it "allows researchers and politicians alike to ignore the social and political context, leading to increased risks of ill health."[3] Public health, unlike clinical medicine, must be concerned with the well-being of the public—i.e., its concern must extend beyond individuals to communities and to populations. Further, public health ethics, like clinical ethics and research ethics, must become more relational and less individualistic. In this context, issues of trust, neighborliness, reciprocity and solidarity must be made central. As Jaro Kotalik . . . argues convincingly, pandemic plans should be ". . . instruments for building mutual trust and solidarity at such time that will likely present a major challenge to our societies."[4] And, as the Bellagio Group attests in the *Bellagio Statement of Principles*, the need for trust extends beyond the privileged: ". . . public health efforts are more likely to succeed in an atmosphere of social solidarity and trust, including the trust of disadvantaged people." From this it follows that in addition to "equal protection and quality of services," and "additional support in the event of quarantine," a third ethical priority for pandemic planning could be "responding to the unique needs of various at-risk populations."[5] This might include, for example, the elderly who are shut-in and who have limited access to health care, or it might include persons with a long history of discrimination who may not trust public health officials and for this reason, in a pandemic, may resist public health and infection control measures.

. . .

Ethics and Public Health

We believe that the ethics framing pandemic plans should be an ethics of public health, not a slightly modified version of clinical or research ethics. Further, an appropriate ethic for public health should be grounded first and foremost in the nature of public health, which is generally understood to refer to what society does collectively to assure the conditions for people to be healthy. Such an ethics must be differentiated from the theoretical tools that frequently emerge from autonomy-driven mainstream bioethics.

~AV Throughout its brief history, the field of bioethics has been dominated by issues of clinical care and research and in both of these contexts most theorists have adopted conceptions of ethics that are rooted in **liberal individualism**, notably principle-based reasoning with its identification of the principles of respect for autonomy, **beneficence**, **nonmaleficence** and justice. . . . Many theorists (notably those working from feminist and **communitarian** perspectives) have sought to convert these principles to a "social rather than individual starting point for ethical analysis."[6] Nonetheless, orientations where individual autonomy is given highest priority remain the dominant approach.

AV In our view, it is a mistake to simply import the familiar bioethical perspectives and concerns that were designed to address conflicts between individuals in a clinical or research context into a discourse that really calls for a much richer framework—a framework that is attentive to the communal aspects and values of public health ethics. A public health ethics must begin with a recognition of the values at the core of public health, not a modification of values used to guide other kinds of health care interactions.

. . .

A Relational Account of Public Health Ethics

The nature and scope of public health require an approach to ethics that is itself "public" rather than individualistic, i.e., one that understands the social nature of public health work. It must do more than simply identify the tensions between individual benefit and community benefit, individual freedom and public safety, resource allocation to known affected individuals and to the community as a whole. It must make clear the complex ways in which individuals are inseparable from communities and build on the fact that the interests of both are interrelated. Hence, we now propose a positive vision of the core values of public health ethics that draws on theoretical work on **relational personhood** (including **relational autonomy** and social justice) and relational solidarity.

Relational Personhood

~AV In much bioethical discussion, the core unit of analysis is the individual person (e.g., patient or research participant), just as it is in medical practice and Western political theory.

The concept of the person is treated, for the most part, as unproblematic except insofar as questions arise regarding the personhood status of humans at the boundaries (specifically, human embryos and patients in **persistent vegetative state**). The concept of personhood that is assumed in most bioethical discussions is the liberal ideal of an independent, rational, **self-interested** deliberator whose values are transparent to himself/herself. Persons are conceived of as discrete and circumscribed, separate from one another, each with his or her own private interests that must be respected and accommodated as far as possible. This picture has been widely deployed to discuss ethical issues that arise in the context of clinical medicine or research where interventions are targeted at specific patients or research participants; in these circumstances, the larger social contexts that patients and research participants inhabit tend to be treated as either irrelevant or as obstacles to their autonomy.

The difficulty with this familiar picture is that individuals are not really independent, purely rational, separate, and self-interested. We are all social through and through. Humans develop within historical, social and political contexts and only become persons through engagement and interaction with other persons. When called upon to make important decisions we often do not arrive with a clear, well-ordered set of values that can be rationally applied, but rather feel our way to a decision in conversation with others who help us to determine who we are and what we stand for. In medicine, patients are not self-contained units in terms of their health needs, for their health status is inevitably affected by their particular historical, social and economic position. Hence, even in ordinary medical interactions the traditional individualistic model of persons is limited. Several feminist theorists have identified this difficulty and proposed a relational conception of personhood as a more adequate conception for clinical and research ethics.

Relational personhood does more than acknowledge the social nature of humans, however. As feminists have developed the concept, it also allows us to see how questions of social justice are central to many aspects of personhood. In particular, it allows us to recognize the ways in which membership in particular social groups helps to constitute identity by shaping the ways in which others see and respond to each person. In societies that treat gender, race, class, age, disability, and ethnicity as socially **salient** characteristics, people will find themselves on either the privileged or the disadvantaged side of the divides generated by these descriptors. If they belong to one or more groups that are systematically disadvantaged by virtue of these sorts of characteristics, they will find that many social structures systematically reinforce their disadvantage. They will have fewer opportunities in life than their more privileged cohorts and they will be more likely to face discrimination and stereotyping. Their sense of self-worth may be diminished as a result (just as those who belong to privileged groups may have an inflated sense of their self-worth). Hence, relational personhood not only makes evident that all persons are (at least partially) **socially constructed**, it also reminds us that we are not all constructed as equals.

Problematic as the traditional individualistic conception of personhood is for an ethics focused on clinical interactions with specific patients, or research interventions with research participants, it is even more objectionable as the basis of a public health ethics. Public health deals with the health needs of communities and populations through actions that are taken at a social or political level. As such, it requires a conception of persons that recognizes and responds to their fundamental social and politically and economically situated nature. Persons are constituted by their relationships, and the communities they inhabit are complex layers of different sorts of social connections. Their interests cannot easily be divided into discrete units that operate independently of the interests of others since the interactions among persons are constitutive of persons to the point that we cannot fully make sense of individual interests apart from those of her/his community. . . .

When we adopt a relational conception of persons, we need also to reinterpret other core bioethical concepts, especially autonomy and justice, in order to acknowledge this important shift in understanding of our fundamental unit of analysis. Fortunately, we are able to draw on a growing body of feminist work concerning relational autonomy and social justice as a guide to how we should think about our obligations with respect to these important values in public health. . . .

Relational Autonomy

Even within a relational framework, autonomy remains an important value as it is in virtually all contemporary ethics frameworks in Western societies. While it looms especially large in clinical and research ethics where the primary target of intervention is a specific—and vulnerable—patient and/or research participant, it is also a value that must be present in public health initiatives. Indeed, because public health involves actions and programs aimed at the common good, where the focus is often on the health of entire populations (or sub-populations), it is easy to lose track of the rights and interests of specific individuals. Public health measures may involve explicit violations of individual autonomy, and when they do, there is a **burden of proof** to establish that these violations are necessary. Thus, as the various pandemic planning documents observe, it is essential to demonstrate that the interests of the group truly do outweigh the values of the individual whenever policy seems to require violations of individual autonomy. If there is a way of achieving the desired outcome without sacrificing autonomy interests, public health policy makers need to investigate these options.

We differ from most other accounts in insisting that the notion of autonomy to be used in such discussions be understood relationally rather than in its traditional individualistic formulation. Relational autonomy embraces (rather than ignores) the fact that persons are inherently social and politically and economically situated beings, raised in social settings, who learn to develop their interests and values in conversation with other social and politically and economically situated beings. Rather than pretending that individuals can make decisions "free" of outside influences, relational autonomy encourages us to pay close attention to the types of forces that may shape an individual's decisions. . . .

No matter what their social position, the choices individual persons can make depend fundamentally on the options available to them. These options are often determined by policy decisions in their societies. Consider a simple example: the ability of individuals to choose to do their part in preventing the spread of infectious viruses and bacteria will be largely determined by the availability of clean water and disinfecting soap. While hospitals and restaurants may direct workers to wash their hands frequently and well, we can expect compliance only in workplaces that have readily available and safe water supplies. By a similar argument, the ability of individuals to avoid the mutation of antibiotic resistant bacteria by limiting antibiotic use is constrained if they have no access to affordable antibiotic-free food supplies. In such ways, the autonomous choices of individuals can be severely limited by the options yielded by prevailing practices and policies.

Relational theory helps us to appreciate how things get even more complicated as we attend to features of social justice and take seriously the fact that we are not all equally situated with respect to the opportunities we encounter to develop our autonomy skills and pursue our preferences. Membership in disadvantaged social groups interferes with people's ability and occasions to exercise autonomy. . . . For instance, it is well known that poverty leads to cramped living conditions in which infections can be difficult to contain, such that poor people often have particularly limited options in avoiding the spread of disease within households; when poverty leads to homelessness, the range of options over which an agent can exercise autonomy may disappear entirely. . . .

. . . [A] relational approach to autonomy directs us to attend to the many and varied ways in which competing policy options affect the opportunities available to members of different social groups (for example, quarantine may have a very different impact on persons with significant disabilities than on persons who can look after their own bodily needs), and to make visible the ways in which the autonomy of some may come at the expense of the justice demands of others. It also directs us to attend to the ways in which policy decisions limit or expand the range of options available to individuals who will be called upon to make responsible decisions. . . .

Social Justice

We need also to rethink our understanding of the concept of justice through a relational lens. . . . There are two principal concepts of justice at work in public health ethics: **distributive justice** and **social justice**. In most of the existing discussions of public health ethics that are focused on pandemic planning, the primary conception at work is that of distributive justice (the fair distribution of quantifiable benefits and burdens among discrete individuals). This is an important consideration as regards the allocation and possible diversion of public funds (available through taxation or global aid) and scarce resources (e.g., vaccines or hospital beds). As well, appreciation of the role of **social** and economic **determinants of health** makes clear the importance of many questions of just distribution not only of health care, but also of income and the conditions of social stability.

Social justice takes us even farther into matters that contribute to health and adds complexity to health policy deliberations. . . . Where distributive justice is occupied with the distribution of finite, quantifiable goods to individuals, . . . social justice is concerned with fair access to social goods such as rights, opportunities, power, and self-respect.

Social justice directs us to explore the context in which certain political and social structures are created and maintained, and in which certain policy decisions are made and implemented. It asks us to look beyond effects on individuals and to see how members of different social groups may be collectively affected by private and public practices that create inequalities in access and opportunity. In this way, social justice reflects our relational understanding of persons as socially constituted and situated. Social justice further enjoins us to correct patterns of systemic injustice among different groups, seeking to correct rather than worsen systematic disadvantages in society.

. . .

Powers and Faden offer their own definition of social justice. . . . They take as given that "social justice is concerned with human well-being."[7] They then spell out six distinct dimensions of human well-being to stand as criteria for evaluating the requirements of social justice in the context of public health: health, personal security, reasoning, respect, attachment, and **self-determination**. While these dimensions can be overlapping and often affect one another, each is a separate lens through which existing patterns of social organization—political structures, social practices, and institutions—must be evaluated. These dimensions of well-being, according to Powers and Faden . . . are "an account of those things characteristically present within a decent life, whatever a person's particular life plans and personal commitments"; . . . they "are of special moral urgency because they matter centrally to everyone."[8] Social justice requires policy makers to seek, so far as possible, to secure a sufficient level of each dimension for each individual.

. . . [Powers and Faden argue that] "inequalities of one kind beget and reinforce other inequalities, and their cumulative effect on human well-being will depend on their causal interaction."[9] Hence, although they claim to be ultimately "interested in the well-being, flourishing, and rights of individuals," they understand that "in the real, historically situated world, how individuals fare is generally a function of the status, standing, and position within densely woven patterns of systematic disadvantage of the groups of which they are a part."[10] It follows for public health ethics that particular attention must be paid to identifying and unraveling complex webs of privilege and disadvantage.

Relational Solidarity

Many in bioethics have proposed that we include the value of solidarity in public health ethics. . . . ~AV We find, however, that references to solidarity are generally problematic in various ways, not the least of which is the common failure to clearly define the concept and the tendency to ground this value in self-interest and self-protection rather than communal welfare. AV Thus, we find it necessary to theorize the concept of solidarity. And, just as we need to rethink our understanding of the concepts of personhood, autonomy and justice through a relational lens, so, too, we need to rethink our understanding of the concept of solidarity in a relational way. Indeed, it is imperative that we develop a relational understanding of solidarity if appeals to this concept are to have more than rhetorical value. In the face of increasing individualism, privatization and consumerism and **moral pluralism**, what does solidarity require/demand of us, especially as we are enjoined to look beyond our familiar circles of belonging and engagement? . . .

. . .

A relational understanding of solidarity would not have us ignore important differences between people. A commitment to social justice requires us to recognize the special disadvantages that face members of social groups who are subject to systematic discrimination and reduced power. As regards matters of public health, it is important to remember . . . that health risks are generally higher for those with lowest social status and power, and these risks are compounded by the multiple dimensions of hardship that affects members of the most vulnerable groups. Hence, when we attend to relational solidarity, we need to be attentive to the increased and quite particular risks faced by members of some social groups as compared with others. While this sort of attentiveness should not deteriorate into an "us" versus "them" mentality, it does require us to be more specific in our attitudes of solidarity and to eschew a vague concern for all of humanity and replace it with one that is **cognizant** of, and responsive to, the particular types of needs experienced by those who are socially and economically disadvantaged.

. . .

A relational concept of solidarity, built on a relational understanding of personhood, . . . eschews all manners of exclusion and aims to expand the category of "us" to "us all." Relational solidarity values interconnections without being steeped in assumptions about commonality or collective identity. What matters is a shared interest in survival, safety and security—an interest that can be effectively pursued through the pursuit of public goods and through ongoing efforts to identify and unravel the complex webs of privilege and disadvantage that sustain and foster an "us" versus "them" divide.

Following Ronald Labonté and Ted Schrecker we understand a **public good** to be a good "that is non-excludable . . . and, in pure form, is non-rivalrous."[11] We further recognize that there are few pure public goods and that health per se is not among them. Importantly, from the perspective of public health ethics, however, there are numerous public goods for health. These public goods include: scientific knowledge, communicable disease control (including vaccination), and control of antibiotic resistance.[12] Indeed, it is in this function of public health—to promote public goods—that we can best appreciate the role of solidarity at work. It is precisely because we all need such programs that we must commit ourselves to the solidarity necessary for helping them to go forward as collective enterprises.

To be successful in public health, we must acknowledge our mutual vulnerability. In addition, we need to recognize that the pursuit of public goods for health, for the benefit of us all requires trust, collective responsibility, and accountability. As such, concrete expressions of relational solidarity in the context of public health ethics are to be found in our accepting of responsibility for ourselves and our actions, in our willingness to be held accountable for others (especially the weakest and most disadvantaged in society), and in our awareness of mutual vulnerability and interdependence.

The deepest challenge to solidarity arises when we appreciate that pursuing the public goods of public health is no easy task. A relational understanding of solidarity requires us to include explicit attention to social justice in our reflections on solidarity. That is, we must be mindful of the particular needs of members of the most vulnerable social groups in our efforts to pursue the public goods of public health. This is necessary for both pragmatic and moral reasons. First, many of the illnesses that are the focus of public health (because of the threat they represent to the general population) begin among the most disadvantaged. For example, avian influenza, and possibly severe acute respiratory syndrome, arose in the live-animal markets in China where the poor living conditions for humans and animals make this a ripe area for **zoonotic** infection. . . . Second, . . . social justice constitutes the moral foundation for public health. Public health programs have generally recognized this and have been organized to anticipate and respond to many of the health risks facing members of disadvantaged social groups. It is essential that this moral commitment be made explicit in development of any new types of public health programs (e.g., pandemic planning).

If we recognize the commitment to relational solidarity at the heart of the very project of public health and infuse it with concerns for social justice and relational autonomy, we see that the moral task is very challenging. . . .

. . .

Conclusions

Public health ethics is in need of a theoretical basis that is built on the aims of the enterprise and the moral values inherent in its practices. That requires an ethical framework that will help us to make visible the role of public health in promoting important public goods and help us to understand the importance of attending to relations among humans, rather than focusing on humans as isolated rights holders. Such an ethics must begin in a different place than clinical or research ethics for its target is populations, not individual patients or research participants. We propose a theory that is relational in its understandings, i.e., one that appreciates the social nature of persons and recognizes the moral significance of social patterns of discrimination and privilege as they affect different groups. We have argued that autonomy, social justice, and solidarity are the core values of public ethics and have proposed relational ways of interpreting each of these values. We suggest that public health provides an important context for understanding the richness of relational interpretations of these concepts. If public health ethics proceeds with the proposed relational understandings of these core values as its guide, it will be well-positioned to address the complex and diverse roles of public health activities. In particular, it will yield a more adequate ethical framework to guide pandemic planning than is present when policy makers begin with the fears and anxiety of an impending pandemic and rely on the limited tools of clinical bioethics. . . .

Notes

1. Public Health Agency of Canada. (2006). *The Canadian Pandemic Influenza Plan for the Health Sector. Section Two: Background*: 14. www. phac-aspc.gc.ca/cpip-pclcpi /pdf-e /CPIP-2006 e.pdf (accessed 16 February 2008). (PHAC)
2. PHAC, 14.
3. W, Rogers, "Feminism and Public Health Ethics," *Journal of Medical Ethics* 32 (2006): 353.
4. J, Kotalik, "Preparing for an Influenza Pandemic: Ethical Issues," *Bioethics* 19 (2005): 431.
5. Bellagio Group, *Bellagio Statement of Principles* (2007). www.hopkinsmedicine.org/bioethics/bellagio/statement.html (accessed 16 February 2008).
6. D, Callahan, "Individual Good and Common Good: A Communitarian Approach to Bioethics," *Perspectives in Biology and Medicine* 46 (2003): 506.
7. M, Powers and R, Faden, *Social Justice: The Moral Foundations of Public Health and Health Policy* (New York: Oxford University Press, 2006), p. 15.
8. Powers and Faden, p. 15.
9. Powers and Faden, p. 31.
10. Powers and Faden, p. 61.
11. Labonté, R., and Schrecker, T. (2007). "Globalization and Social Determinants of Health: Promoting Health Equity in Global Governance" (Part 3 of 3). *Globalization and Health*, 3: 4, www.globalizationandhealth.com/content/3/1/7. Public goods, as defined by economists, have two characteristics. First, they are non-excludable, which means it is impossible to prevent anyone from consuming or benefitting from the good. Streetlights and oceans are examples of non-excludable goods. Second, they are non-rivalrous, which means use or consumption of the good by one person does not reduce the amount available for anyone else. Air and television signals are examples of non-rivalrous goods. Of the examples given here, only streetlights and air are public goods–they are both non-excludable and non-rivalrous. Oceans are rivalrous (their contents can be used up), and some television signals are excludable. [Editor]
12. Labonté and Schrecker, p. 4.

Discussion Questions

1. Madore writes, "In the Canadian context of health care, the main concern with respect to privatization is that it can lead to a 'two-tier' system." Do you think this is a problem? Why or why not?
2. The three justices who wrote the second majority opinion in *Chaoulli* argued that prohibiting private funding of medical services covered by the *Canada Health Act* violates the Canadian *Charter*. What were their reasons? Do you agree with them? Why or why not?
3. Madore distinguishes between active privatization and passive privatization. Which form of privatization does the Supreme Court's ruling in *Chaoulli* fit? Why?
4. Sherwin argues that a feminist perspective on justice in health care would pay more attention to what are now called the social determinants of health. What is her argument for this claim? Do you agree with her? Why or why not?
5. Baylis, Kenny, and Sherwin say that "an appropriate ethic for public health should be grounded first and foremost in the nature of public health." What is the nature of public health? How does it differ from non-public health?
6. How, according to Baylis, Kenny, and Sherwin, can autonomy be relational? Do you agree with their analysis? Why or why not?

Suggested Readings and Websites

♣ = Canadian source or author

♣ Canadian Institute for Health Information. www.cihi.ca/CIHI-ext-portal/internet/EN/Home/home/cihi000001 [A wealth of information on healthcare in Canada, including "Quick Stats" and many downloadable reports.]

♣ Canadian Museum of Civilization. Making Medicare: The History of Health Care in Canada, 1914–2007. www.civilization.ca/cmc/exhibitions/hist/medicare/medic01e.shtml [A lively history of universal healthcare in Canada, focused on the federal government's contribution.]

♣ Narveson, Jan. "Insurance Arguments and the Welfare State." Chapter 18 of *The Libertarian Idea*. Peterborough: Broadview Press, 2001. [Narveson, a well-known Canadian libertarian philosopher, outlines libertarian arguments against the welfare state, including universal health care.]

♣ Norris, Sonya. "The Wait Times Issue and the Patient Wait Times Guarantee." Parliamentary Information and Research Service, Library of Parliament, PRB 05-82E (2009). [A **non-partisan** discussion of the wait times issue since the *Chaoulli* decision.]

♣ Public Health Agency of Canada. What Determines Health? www.phac-aspc.gc.ca/ph-sp/determinants/index-eng.php [Plain-language discussion of the determinants of health and population health, including evidence for each determinant.]

♣ Rachlis, Michael. *Prescription for Excellence: How Innovation Is Saving Canada's Health Care System*. Toronto: HarperCollins, 2004. [Rachlis, a health policy analyst and specialist in community medicine, discusses ways to improve Canada's health care system.]

- Selick, Karen. "The Moral Case for Private Health Care." www.karenselick.com/NP001122.html and "The Moral Myths of Medicare." www.karenselick.com/Moral_Myths_of_Medicare.html. [Selick, a libertarian lawyer, argues against universal health care.]
- Sherwin, Susan. "Whither Bioethics? How Feminism Can Help Reorient Bioethics." *International Journal of Feminist Approaches to Bioethics* 1, 1 (2008): 7–27 [Sherwin proposes a new approach to bioethics, public ethics, which she argues can handle ethical situations ranging from individuals to global organizations.]
- Tiedemann, Marlisa. "Health Care at the Supreme Court of Canada II: *Chaoulli v. Quebec (Attorney General)*." Parliamentary Information and Research Service, Library of Parliament, PRB 05-31E (2005) [A non-partisan analysis of the background, court decisions, and political responses to *Chaoulli v. Quebec*.]
- Your heart's on the left: musings on health and politics. http://yourheartsontheleft.blogspot.ca/; posts on healthcare, http://yourheartsontheleft.blogspot.ca/search/label/healthcare. [A blog by a social democratic physician.]

Chapter 9

Euthanasia and Assisted Suicide

Some people who are alive today would have died had they lived a hundred or even fifty years ago, before the development of more effective medical treatments. Most of those people are thankful for their extended lives. In some cases, however, medicine has saved people who regret having been saved, or it keeps people alive when they no longer wish to live. How should we respond to their wishes to die, while at the same time protecting the lives of those who wish to live or who have expressed no wishes either way?

First we must define our terms so we can be clear about what is proposed or opposed. This is how the terms are most commonly used in the debate:

- **Competent** people understand and appreciate relevant information concerning their situations and the consequences of any actions or decisions that will be made.
- **Voluntary** means in accordance with a competent person's wishes.
- **Non-voluntary** means without knowing the person's wishes, either because she/he has not expressed them or because she/he is **incompetent**.
- **Involuntary** means against the person's wishes.
- **Palliative care** is care given to patients with terminal illnesses that focuses on making the patients comfortable and respected as they near death, and maximizing the patient's, family's, and other loved ones' quality of life. It does not aim to cure the illness.
- **Refusal of treatment** means either not starting potentially life-preserving treatment, such as not performing CPR on a person having a heart attack, or stopping life-preserving treatment, such as unplugging a ventilator.
- **Terminal sedation** means sedating a patient to the point of unconsciousness, with the intent of relieving suffering before the patient dies. Often no fluids or nutrition are given to the patient.

- **Euthanasia** is deliberately causing a patient's death by an act or omission, in order to relive that person's suffering. It is sometimes called **assisted death**.
- **Voluntary euthanasia** is causing a competent patient's death in order to relieve the patient's suffering. The person who requests voluntary euthanasia must be competent, and the request must be voluntary.
- **Assisted suicide** is the suicide of a competent patient with the assistance of another who provides knowledge or the means of suicide. The person who requests assisted suicide must be competent, and the request must be voluntary.

Assisted suicide and voluntary euthanasia differ according to who directly causes the death. In assisted suicide, the people who die kill themselves with someone else's help. For example, A provides the lethal medication or hooks B up to a "suicide machine" that will give B a lethal injection. But B herself takes the pills or presses the button to deliver the lethal dose—that is, she commits suicide with someone else's help; she causes her own death. In voluntary euthanasia, A causes directly B's death at B's request. For example, at B's request, A gives B a lethal injection.

The Current Legal Situation

Refusal of Treatment

Legal. In the **common law**, competent people have the right to refuse any and all treatment. However, many doctors worry that the *Criminal Code* forbids refusal of treatment, even at the request of a competent person. Sections 215–218 of the *Criminal Code* cover "Duties Tending to Preservation of Life." Section 215 establishes a duty to provide the necessities of life to anyone under one's care, and section 217 requires that anyone who begins an act must continue it if ceasing "is or may be dangerous to life." Courts had ruled that both sections apply to the medical profession. In a series of decisions in the 1990s, though, the Supreme Court ruled that competent people have the right to refuse life-saving treatment, even if the treatment would extend their lives by decades, and that doctors must respect advance directives that indicate what patients want if they are unable to decide on their own. More controversially, courts have ruled that substitute decision-makers may refuse life-saving treatment on behalf of incompetent patients even where there are no advance directives, if doing so is in the best interests of the incompetent patient.

Terminal Sedation and Other Life-shortening Treatments

Legal or voluntary. Some hospitals and regional health services have developed explicit guidelines for providing terminal sedation. The Catholic Church, which is adamantly opposed to assisted suicide, allows terminal sedation under strictly defined criteria that do not include withdrawing fluids and nutrition. The authors of one such policy write, "It should be emphasized that the intention of this practice is exclusively to relieve the refractory symptoms"—that is, symptoms that cause "severe suffering," especially delirium, difficulty breathing, and extreme pain, and that have not responded to any form of treatment.[1]

Doctors sometimes give large doses of morphine and other immune-suppressing pain medications to terminal patients who are in a lot of pain, knowing that this will shorten the patients' lives. Do terminal sedation and other life-shortening treatments constitute "causing death by criminal negligence" (section 220 of the *Criminal Code*) or "counselling or aiding suicide" (section 241)? It appears the Supreme Court thinks they do not. In *Rodriguez v. British Columbia*, Justice Sopinka, writing for the majority, distinguished palliative care from assisted suicide based on intent: "in the case of palliative care the intention is to ease pain, which has the effect of hastening death, while in the case of assisted suicide, the intention is undeniably to cause death. . . . While factually the distinction may, at times, be difficult to draw, legally it is clear."[2]

Assisted Suicide

Illegal. Parliament decriminalized suicide in 1972, but "counselling or aiding suicide" remains a crime. The Supreme Court ruled by a 5–4 margin in *Rodriguez* that the law against aiding suicide does not violate the *Charter*. (See the excerpt from the decision in this chapter.)

Euthanasia

Illegal. The law considers all forms of euthanasia to be murder, which is punishable by life in prison with no possibility of parole for ten years for second-degree murder or twenty-five years for first-degree murder.

International Comparisons

These issues are largely irrelevant in poor countries that lack the technology to keep people alive even if they wish to die, so my discussion focuses on richer countries. Refusing treatment is permitted in most Western countries. Terminal sedation and other life-shortening treatments subsist in a grey zone, as they do in Canada, not clearly permitted or forbidden. Assisted suicide and, occasionally, euthanasia are permitted in a few countries. The Netherlands is the best-known place where euthanasia is permitted. (The Dutch do not distinguish between assisted suicide and euthanasia.) While euthanasia has been legal only since 2002, it has been practised openly for over thirty years, and a large body of case law developed to regulate it. It is permissible only under the following conditions:

- The patient must repeatedly and explicitly express the desire to die.
- The patient's decision must be well informed, free, and enduring.
- The patient must be suffering from severe physical or mental pain with no prospect of relief, but need not be terminally ill.
- All other options for care must have been exhausted, so that euthanasia is a last resort, or the patient must have refused other available options.
- The euthanasia must be carried out by a qualified physician.
- The physician must consult at least one other physician (and may also consult other health care professionals).
- The physician must inform the local coroner that the euthanasia has been carried out.[3]

In addition, the physician must discuss different options with the patient, and must be sure the patient's request is voluntary and well thought out.

In Belgium, assisted suicide is not a criminal offence, and euthanasia is permitted under certain conditions. Luxembourg permits both assisted suicide and euthanasia under certain conditions. Switzerland permits assisted suicide as long as the person assisting has "unselfish reasons," but it forbids euthanasia. In the UK assisted suicide is technically illegal, but the person assisting will not be prosecuted if certain conditions are met; euthanasia is illegal. In the US, assisted suicide is legal in Oregon and Washington state if certain conditions are met. In Montana, a doctor charged with assisted suicide may use a defence of consent. (The claim that someone consented to her/his own death normally is not a valid defence against murder.) Euthanasia is illegal in all fifty states. In Colombia, a doctor cannot be prosecuted for euthanasia if the patient had a terminal illness and consented to her/his death. It is not clear if this applies to assisted suicide as well.[4]

Arguments against Euthanasia and Assisted Suicide

The main arguments against euthanasia and assisted suicide are:

- euthanasia and assisted suicide violate the sanctity of life;
- the possibility of abuse is too great;
- euthanasia and assisted suicide undermine the purpose of medicine, which is to save lives;
- euthanasia and assisted suicide are unnecessary if there is good palliative care and adequate pain relief; and
- euthanasia and assisted suicide are "deadly forms of discrimination against old, ill and disabled people."[5]

I will deal with the first four arguments briefly, because they are better known. I will deal with the fifth argument at some length.

The first three arguments, about the sanctity of life, the possibility of abuse, and the purpose of medicine, are **slippery slope** arguments. They claim that allowing euthanasia or assisted suicide puts us on a slippery slope that ends in people being killed against their wills, as in Nazi Germany. The sanctity of life refers to the general presumption in the law that life is an ultimate value and can be taken only under extraordinary circumstances. We undermine life's sacredness if we make exceptions. We will start permitting euthanasia in more and more cases—people who do not have terminal illnesses, people who are depressed, children, people with disabilities, and so on. The possibility of abuse argument states that any law permitting euthanasia or assisted suicide opens the door to abuses in which people are pressured into requesting euthanasia or assisted suicide, or even killed against their wills. For example, younger family members might imply that elderly relatives are burdens, or a person with a disability who has never requested euthanasia or assisted suicide might be killed "for her/his own good." (See the discussion of Tracy Latimer, below.) The purpose of medicine argument states that medicine aims to save lives, and euthanasia and assisted suicide undermine this. Doctors who perform euthanasia and assisted suicide will become callous and less interested in saving patients' lives, thus putting us all at risk.

Palliative care treats patients with incurable conditions who are near death and who accept their impending deaths. It assumes that medicine cannot and should not always fight death, and it aims to relieve dying patients' distress rather than to cure them. It focuses on caring rather than curing, and its main form of treatment is symptom control. Good palliative care combines medical and non-medical therapies to achieve adequate symptom relief in dying patients. Opponents of euthanasia and assisted suicide argue that good palliative care can relieve almost all pain and suffering. If we focus on improving dying patients' lives we can forestall or eliminate demands for euthanasia and assisted suicide.

The Views of Disability Rights Activists

Most philosophers who write about euthanasia and assisted suicide, whether in support or opposition, give no more than passing attention to the strong objections of many disability rights activists to euthanasia and assisted suicide. If philosophers address these objections at all, they usually lump them in with right to life objections.[6] However, disability rights activists ground their objections to euthanasia and assisted suicide in claims about equality, discrimination, and social justice, not the sanctity of life.

In Canada, disability rights activists particularly object to the media's and most Canadians' reactions to the murder of Tracy Latimer by her father. Tracy was a twelve-year-old Saskatchewan girl with cerebral palsy and an intellectual disability. On 24 October 1993, while the rest of the family was at church, Tracy's father put her in his truck, ran a hose into the cab, turned on the engine, and poisoned her with carbon monoxide. When he was sure she was dead, he carried her back to her bed and tried to make it appear that she had died of natural causes. However, a toxicology report showed Tracy had died of carbon monoxide poisoning, and her father was charged with first-degree murder. He confessed to killing her but denied it was wrong. Rather, he claimed that he wanted to end her pain. After two jury trials and many appeals, Latimer was convicted of second-degree murder and sentenced to life imprisonment with no possibility of parole for ten years, the minimum sentence for second-degree murder. Despite enormous public support for him, the Supreme Court upheld both his conviction and the sentence. Latimer spent seven years in prison and two and a half years on day parole. He has never expressed any remorse; in fact, he sees himself as the victim in this case. After his first conviction he told the court, "I still feel I did what was right. I don't think you people are being human."

Many Canadians agree that Latimer was the real victim in this case. They view his actions as mercy killing rather than murder because they think Tracy's life was intolerable. For example, the *New York Times* reported in 1994 that Marilynne Seguin, executive director of the Toronto group Dying with Dignity, "said that the Latimers had already lived under a sentence during the 12 years that Tracy was alive and that to add the 10-year punishment 'is quite unconscionable.'" Eike Kluge, a professor of bioethics at the University of Victoria, told the same reporter that "[t]he case could lead to decriminalization of euthanasia under 'carefully controlled conditions.'"[7]

Latimer's defence team presented much evidence about Tracy's pain, but none that Tracy found her pain intolerable and wished to die. In fact, there is plenty of evidence that people with similar disabilities who can communicate find their lives worth living.[8] The fact that so many people think Tracy Latimer's death was a mercy killing fuels disability rights activists' belief that legalizing euthanasia and assisted suicide will further endanger their lives.

If you still believe Tracy Latimer's death was a mercy killing, try a thought experiment. Consider Tracy alongside two other twelve-year-old girls, who we can call Catherine and

Sarah. Catherine has severe cerebral palsy but no intellectual disability; she communicates using a tablet. She is in chronic pain, treated with painkillers. Sarah has an intellectual disability but no physical disabilities; she is in no pain. Would you consider it a "mercy killing" if Catherine's or Sarah's father killed her? If not, then you have no reason to think that Tracy Latimer's death was anything other than murder. The fact that she could not express her wishes in a way her parents could understand does not justify her death or make it "merciful." Someone might respond that the chronic pain or the intellectual disability alone did not justify Tracy Latimer's father, but rather the combination of the two. That person would have to explain how an intellectual disability makes chronic pain bad enough to justify non-voluntary euthanasia, or how chronic pain makes an intellectual disability bad enough to justify non-voluntary euthanasia.

The issue is not what we think we would want in that situation, much less what is best for the parents of a child like Tracy, but rather what is best for that person. Was Tracy Latimer's life not worth living to *her*, rather than to her parents? Tracy's parents found her care to be a burden, but that is irrelevant. We don't allow parents to kill their children because caring for them is difficult, or many teenagers' lives would be in danger. We offer them support. Tracy's parents received lots of support, including respite care, where Tracy was sent to a care facility for a while to give her parents a break. If parents still find a child's care overwhelming they can put the child into care, but they may not kill them.

Disability rights activists argue that justice and equality require us to oppose any legal changes that weaken the prohibition—such as it is—on killing people with disabilities. Instead of fighting for euthanasia and assisted suicide, we should be fighting to improve the lives of people with illnesses and disabilities and to convince non-disabled people that living with disabilities is as worthwhile a life as any other. Disabilities on their own are neutral; social prejudices are what make living with a disability difficult. If social prejudices lessened, so would the demand for euthanasia and assisted suicide, they say.

Arguments in Favour of Assisted Suicide

Most proponents of euthanasia in Canada today argue only in favour of assisted suicide, not euthanasia in general. Their main arguments are:

- assisted suicide is justified by the liberal right to **autonomy**, individuals' right to live or die as they choose, without interference, as long as they do not harm others;
- there is no **morally relevant** distinction between refusing treatment and assisted suicide, and since competent patients can refuse life-saving treatment, they also should be able to request assisted suicide;
- palliative care cannot eliminate all the pain and suffering associated with dying, particularly "existential pain";
- assisted suicide does not undermine the purpose of medicine;
- the possibility of abuse can be minimized by permitting only competent people to consent to assisted suicide; and
- disability rights activists' other objections to assisted suicide are overridden by the principle of autonomy.

Downie and the **dissenting** justices in *Rodriguez* discuss all but disability rights activists' objections. In this section I will discuss the response that proponents of assisted suicide can make to the possibility of abuse and the other objections of disability rights activists.

We can avoid the problem of abuse by limiting assisted suicide to competent people who request it, proponents say. Granted there has been some abuse in jurisdictions that have decriminalized or legalized assisted suicide. But there is abuse of any law. The relevant question to ask is not whether there is abuse, but whether people who do not want to die are safer when assisted suicide is illegal than when it is legal. Certainly people with disabilities believe they are safer when assisted suicide is illegal. However, that is an empirical question and we do not have the relevant data. Jocelyn Downie (in this chapter) cites evidence that euthanasia and assisted suicide are occurring even where they are illegal. People with disabilities might be better protected by laws that restrict assisted suicide to competent people who request it. Under such a system, it is clearer that Tracy Latimer's death was murder, because it met neither the competency or nor the voluntariness criterion.

Proponents of assisted suicide also might argue that people with disabilities are better protected by addressing the many forms of discrimination, abuse, and social injustice they face than by opposing assisted suicide. In a society in which people with disabilities were viewed as equals, as valuable participants with lives worth living, the problem of people "helping" others die against their wills would be no more serious for people with disabilities than anyone else. Opposing assisted suicide is not the best way to end discrimination and injustice toward people with disabilities.

Disability rights advocates want to change the world so people who are old, sick, and increasingly dependent on others do not find their lives so intolerable that they prefer death to their changed circumstances. Proponents of assisted suicide ought to agree with them, because such changes would increase people's autonomy. But even with more opportunities and less prejudice, some people, particularly those who are dying, still might find their changed circumstances intolerable. Perhaps they will not have time to adapt to the changes. Perhaps the combination of physical pain and psychological or cognitive changes is too much for them to bear. Perhaps they are too stuck in their ways to adapt. It does not really matter. If we take the principle of autonomy seriously, then we ought to let those individuals make their own choices about assisted suicide. We might find the choices unfathomable, as we would if (pick your favourite example) a woman chose to subordinate herself to her husband, a young man chose to be celibate and become a priest, a transgendered person chose a gender that does not match her/his chromosomal sex, or someone chose to give up a job with status and a high salary to teach children in a poor neighbourhood. One or more of these choices might not make sense to us, but that is irrelevant. Autonomous people do not have to explain themselves to us. Once we have assured ourselves that they are competent and their decisions are voluntary, they have a right to make their own choices without interference from others.

The Readings

The first reading comes from the Supreme Court's ruling in *Rodriguez*. Sue Rodriguez was a forty-two-year-old single mother who contracted amyotrophic lateral sclerosis (ALS, or Lou Gehrig's disease). She challenged section 241(b) of the *Criminal Code*, which forbids aiding suicide. She knew there would come a time when she no longer wanted to live but would be unable to commit suicide on her own. In a 5–4 decision, the Court upheld the law. The majority argued that it upholds the sanctity of life, which is fundamental to at least Western legal systems. They also worried about the possibility of abuse. And they argued that while the law does infringe section 15 (the equality section) of the *Charter*, the infringement could be justified by section 1.[9] There are three dissenting opinions. In the first, Justices L'Heureux-Dubé and McLachlin find that section 241(b) violates Rodriguez's section 7 *Charter* right to security of the person, and that the violation cannot be justified by section 1. Chief Justice Lamer argues in the second that section 241(b) infringes section 15 of the *Charter*, and that this could not be saved by section 1. Justice Cory argues in the third that there is no relevant difference between refusing treatment and assisted suicide. A person who was dying who did not have a physical disability would be able to commit suicide, and the law should not deny the same right to people who need assistance in doing the same thing.

Catherine Frazee, a former Chief Commissioner of the Ontario Human Rights Commission, was asked by the Attorney General of Canada to present the views of people with disabilities on assisted suicide in a Quebec court case. She discusses the difficulties that people with disabilities have in getting medical treatment because so many people think they would be better off dead, the principle of autonomy as it is used in the assisted suicide debate, and the direct and indirect harms that people with disabilities will suffer if assisted suicide is permitted.

Finally, Jocelyn Downie takes on the objections to assisted suicide and voluntary euthanasia in the third reading. She argues that opponents of assisted suicide and voluntary euthanasia make distinctions that do not stand up to scrutiny, such as the distinction between acts and omissions or between causing death and "letting nature take its course." She argues against opponents' use of sanctity of life arguments and against the claim that there is a morally relevant difference between killing and letting die. Finally, she takes on claims that allowing assisted suicide and voluntary euthanasia will lead to serious abuses.

The Moral and Political Preferences Indicator

Between two-thirds and three-quarters of Canadians believe assisted suicide should be legal. When there is such a large majority on one side of an issue, usually the people in the minority occupy a small part of the political spectrum and the people in the majority span the rest. This is generally true of the assisted suicide debate. Most people who oppose euthanasia and assisted suicide are social conservatives. Like abortion, this is a social conservative make-or-break issue. On the other side, people who support assisted suicide range from egalitarians to libertarians. (While libertarians are very conservative, on this issue their strong support for liberty usually places them in the "proponent" camp.)

When it comes to the views of disability rights activists, though, these distinctions fall apart. Disability rights is a social justice movement, and social justice movements fall squarely on the egalitarian side of the spectrum. Thus we have social conservatives and egalitarian disability rights activists opposing euthanasia and assisted suicide for very different reasons, the majority of people who support assisted suicide spanning the political spectrum, and a few uncomfortable egalitarians who are not sure which side to support.

Notes

1. Covenant Health Palliative Sedation Guideline, Regional Palliative Care Program (Edmonton), Alberta Health Services (September 2006), 2, www.palliative.org/NewPC/_pdfs/management/3A6%20Palliative%20Sedation%20and%20Addendum.pdf.
2. *Rodriguez v. British Columbia (Attorney General)*, [1993] 3 S.C.R. 519, 103.
3. Marlisa Tiedemann, Julie Nicol, and Dominique Valiquet, "Euthanasia and Assisted Suicide: International Experiences," Parliamentary Information and Research Services, Library of Parliament, 2011-67-E (2011), 6, 7–8.
4. Tiedemann, Nicol, and Valiquet, i.
5. Not Dead Yet, www.notdeadyet.org/.
6. See, for example, Wayne Sumner, "The Morgentaler Effect: What the champion of reproductive rights has to teach the right-to-die movement," *The Walrus* (January 2011), http://walrusmagazine.com/articles/2011.01-society-the-morgentaler-effect.
7. Clyde H. Farnsworth, "Mercy Killing in Canada Stirs Calls for Changes in Law," *The New York Times*, 22 November 1994, www.nytimes.com/1994/11/22/world/mercy-killing-in-canada-stirs-calls-for-changes-in-law.html.
8. Ruth Enns, *A Voice Unheard: The Latimer Case and People with Disabilities* (Halifax: Fernwood Publishing, 1999) pp. 30–9, 100–24.
9. Section 1 states: "The *Canadian Charter of Rights and Freedoms* guarantees the rights and freedoms set out in it subject only to such reasonable limits prescribed by law as can be demonstrably justified in a free and democratic society."

Rodriguez v. British Columbia (Attorney General)[1]

The **appellant**, a 42-year-old mother, suffers from amyotrophic lateral sclerosis. Her condition is rapidly deteriorating and she will soon lose the ability to swallow, speak, walk, and move her body without assistance. Thereafter she will lose the capacity to breathe without a respirator, to eat without a gastrotomy [incision in the stomach] and will eventually become confined to a bed. Her life expectancy is between 2 and 14 months. The appellant does not wish to die so long as she still has the capacity to enjoy life, but wishes that a qualified physician be allowed to set up technological means by which she might, when she is no longer able to enjoy life, by her own hand, at the time of her choosing, end her life. The appellant applied to the Supreme Court of British Columbia for an order that s. [section] 241(*b*) of the *Criminal Code*, which prohibits the giving of assistance to commit suicide,[2] be declared invalid on the ground that it violates her rights under ss. [sections] 7, 12, and 15(1) of the *Charter*, and is therefore, to the extent it precludes a terminally ill person from committing "physician-assisted" suicide, of no force and effect by virtue of s. 52(1) of the *Constitution Act, 1982*. The court dismissed the appellant's application and the majority of the Court of Appeal affirmed the judgment.

Held [by the majority] . . . : The appeal should be dismissed. Section 241(*b*) of the *Code* is constitutional.

[The Majority Opinion, by Justices La Forest, Sopinka, Gonthier, Iacobucci, and Major]

The appellant's claim under s. 7 of the *Charter*[3] is based on an alleged violation of her liberty and security of the person interests. These interests cannot be divorced from the sanctity of life, which is the third value protected by s. 7. Even when death appears imminent, seeking to control the manner and timing of one's death constitutes a conscious choice of death over life. It follows that life as a value is also engaged in the present case. Appellant's security of the person interest must be considered in light of the other values mentioned in s. 7.

Security of the person in s. 7 encompasses notions of personal **autonomy** (at least with respect to the right to make choices concerning one's own body), control over one's physical and psychological integrity which is free from state interference, and basic human dignity. The prohibition in s. 241(*b*), which is a sufficient interaction with the justice system to engage the provisions of s. 7, deprives the appellant of autonomy over her person and causes her physical pain and psychological stress in a manner which impinges on the security of her person. Any resulting deprivation, however, is not contrary to the principles of fundamental justice. The same conclusion is applicable with respect to any liberty interest which may be involved.

The expression "principles of fundamental justice" in s. 7 of the *Charter* implies that there is some consensus that these principles are vital or fundamental to our societal notion of justice. They must be capable of being identified with some precision and applied to situations in a manner which yields an understandable result. They must also be legal principles. To discern the principles of fundamental justice governing a particular case, it is helpful to review the common law and the legislative history of the offence in question and, in particular, the rationale behind the practice itself (here, the continued criminalization of assisted suicide) and the principles which underlie it. It is also appropriate to consider the state interest. Fundamental justice requires that a fair balance be struck between the interests of the state and those of the individual. The respect for human dignity, while one of the underlying principles upon which our society is based, is not a principle of fundamental justice within the meaning of s. 7.

Assisted suicide, outlawed under the common law, has been prohibited by Parliament since the adoption of Canada's first *Criminal Code*. The long-standing blanket prohibition in s. 241(*b*), which fulfils the government's objective of protecting the vulnerable, is grounded in the state interest in protecting life and reflects the policy of the state that human life should not be depreciated by allowing life to be taken. This state policy is part of our fundamental conception of the sanctity of life. A blanket prohibition on assisted suicide similar to that in s. 241(*b*) also seems to be the norm among Western democracies, and such a prohibition has never been adjudged to be unconstitutional or contrary to fundamental human rights. These societies, including Canada, recognize and generally apply the principle of the sanctity of life subject to narrow exceptions where notions of personal autonomy and dignity must prevail. Distinctions between passive and active forms of intervention in the dying process continue to be drawn and assisted suicide in situations such as the appellant's is prohibited with few exceptions. No consensus can be found in favour of the decriminalization of assisted suicide. To the extent that there is a consensus, it is that human life must be respected. This consensus finds legal expression in our legal system which prohibits capital punishment. The prohibition against assisted suicide serves a similar purpose. Parliament's repeal of the offence of attempted suicide from the *Criminal Code* was not a recognition that suicide was to be accepted within Canadian society. Rather, this action merely reflected the recognition that the criminal law was an ineffectual and inappropriate tool for dealing with suicide attempts. Given the concerns about abuse and the great difficulty in creating appropriate safeguards, the blanket prohibition on assisted suicide is not arbitrary or unfair. The prohibition relates to the state's interest in protecting the vulnerable and is reflective of fundamental values at play in our society. Section 241(*b*) therefore does not infringe s. 7 of the *Charter*.

As well, s. 241(*b*) of the *Code* does not infringe s. 12 of the *Charter*.[4] The appellant is not subjected by the state to any form of cruel and unusual treatment or punishment. Even assuming that "treatment" within the meaning of s. 12 may include that imposed by the state in contexts other than penal or quasi-penal, a mere prohibition by the state on certain action cannot constitute "treatment" under s. 12. There must be some more active state process in operation, involving an exercise of state control over the individual, whether it be positive action, inaction or prohibition. To hold that the criminal prohibition in s. 241(*b*), without the appellant being in any way subject to the state administrative or justice system, falls within the bounds of s. 12 would stretch the ordinary meaning of being "subjected to . . . treatment" by the state.

It is preferable in this case not to decide the difficult and important issues raised by the application of s. 15 of the *Charter*,[5] but rather to assume that the prohibition on assisted suicide in s. 241(*b*) of the *Code* infringes s. 15, since any infringement of s. 15 by s. 241(*b*) is clearly justified under s. 1 of the *Charter*.[6] Section 241(*b*) has a pressing and substantial legislative objective and meets the proportionality test. A prohibition on giving assistance to commit suicide is rationally connected to the purpose of s. 241(*b*), which is to protect and maintain respect for human life. This protection is grounded on a substantial consensus among western countries, medical organizations and our own Law Reform Commission that in order to protect life and those who are vulnerable in society effectively, a prohibition without exception on the giving of assistance to commit suicide is the best approach. Attempts to modify this approach by creating exceptions or formulating safeguards to prevent excesses have been unsatisfactory. Section 241(*b*) is thus not overbroad since there is no halfway measure that could be relied upon to achieve the legislation's purpose fully. In dealing with this contentious, complex and morally laden issue, Parliament must be accorded some flexibility. In light of the significant support for s. 241(*b*) or for this type of legislation, the government had a reasonable basis for concluding that it had complied with the requirement of minimum impairment. Finally, the balance between the restriction and the government objective is also met.

[The First Dissenting Opinion, by Justices L'Heureux-Dubé, and McLachlin]

Section 241(*b*) of the *Code* infringes the right to security of the person included in s. 7 of the *Charter*. This right has an element of personal autonomy, which protects the dignity and privacy of individuals with respect to decisions concerning their own body. A legislative scheme which limits the right of a person to deal with her body as she chooses may violate the principles of fundamental justice under s. 7 if the limit is arbitrary. A particular limit will be arbitrary if it bears no relation to, or is inconsistent with, the objective that lies behind the legislation. When one is considering whether a law breaches the principles of fundamental justice under s. 7 by reason of arbitrariness, the focus is on whether a legislative scheme infringes a particular person's protected interests in a way that cannot be justified having regard to the objective of this scheme. The principles of fundamental justice require that each person, considered individually, be treated fairly by the law. The fear that abuse may arise if an individual is permitted that which she is wrongly denied plays no part at the s. 7 stage. Any balancing of societal interests against the interests of the individual should take place within the confines of s. 1 of the *Charter*. Here, Parliament has put into force a legislative scheme which makes suicide lawful but assisted suicide unlawful. The effect of this distinction is to deny to some people the choice of ending their lives solely because they are physically unable to do so, preventing them from exercising the autonomy over their bodies available to other people. The denial of the ability to end their life is arbitrary and hence amounts to a limit on the right to security of the person which does not comport with the principles of fundamental justice.

Section 241(*b*) of the *Code* is not justified under s. 1 of the *Charter*. The practical objective of s. 241(*b*) is to eliminate the fear of lawful assisted suicide's being abused and resulting in the killing of persons not truly and willingly consenting to death. However, neither the fear that unless assisted suicide is prohibited, it will be used for murder, nor the fear that consent to death may not in fact be given voluntarily, is sufficient to override appellant's entitlement under s. 7 to end her life in the manner and at the time of her choosing. The safeguards in the existing provisions of the *Criminal Code* largely meet the concerns about consent. The *Code* provisions, supplemented, by way of remedy, by a stipulation requiring a court order to permit the assistance of suicide in a particular case only when the judge is satisfied that the consent is freely given, will ensure that only those who truly desire to bring their lives to an end obtain assistance.

Section 15 of the *Charter* has no application in this case. This is not a case about discrimination and to treat it as such may deflect the equality jurisprudence from the true focus of s. 15.

Although some of the conditions stated by Lamer C.J. seem unnecessary in this case, the remedy proposed is generally agreed with. What is required will vary from case to case. The essential in all cases is that the judge be satisfied that if and when the assisted suicide takes place, it will be with the full and free consent of the applicant.

[The Second Dissenting Opinion, by Chief Justice Lamer]

Section 241(*b*) of the *Code* infringes the right to equality contained in s. 15(1) of the *Charter*. While, at first sight, s. 241(*b*) is apparently neutral in its application, its effect creates an inequality since it prevents persons physically unable to end their lives unassisted from choosing suicide when that option is in principle available to other members of the public without contravening the law. This inequality—the deprivation of the right to choose suicide—may be characterized as a burden or disadvantage, since it limits the ability of those who are subject to this inequality to take and act upon fundamental decisions regarding their lives and persons. For them, the principles of self-determination and individual autonomy, which are of fundamental importance in our legal system, have been limited. This inequality is imposed on persons unable to end their lives unassisted solely because of a physical disability, a personal characteristic which is among the grounds of discrimination listed in s. 15(1).

Section 241(*b*) of the *Code* is not justifiable under s. 1 of the *Charter*. While the objective of protecting vulnerable persons from being pressured or coerced into committing suicide is sufficiently important to **warrant** overriding a constitutional right, s. 241(*b*) fails to meet the proportionality test. The prohibition of assisted suicide is rationally connected to the legislative objective, but the means chosen to carry out the objective do not impair the appellant's equality rights as little as reasonably possible. The vulnerable are effectively protected under s. 241(*b*) but the section is over-inclusive. Those who are not vulnerable or do not wish the state's protection are also brought within the operation of s. 241(*b*) solely as a result of a physical disability. An **absolute** prohibition that is indifferent to the individual or the circumstances cannot satisfy the constitutional duty on the government to impair the rights of persons with physical disabilities as little as reasonably possible. The fear that the decriminalization of assisted suicide will increase the risk of persons with physical disabilities being manipulated by others does not justify the over-inclusive reach of s. 241(*b*).

In view of the findings under s. 15(1), there is no need to address the constitutionality of the legislation under ss. 7 or 12 of the *Charter*.

Pursuant to s. 52(1) of the *Constitution Act, 1982*, s. 241(*b*) is declared to be of no force or effect, on the condition that the effect of this declaration be suspended for one year from the date of this judgment to give Parliament adequate time to decide what, if any, legislation should replace s. 241(*b*). While a personal remedy under s. 24(1) of the *Charter* is rarely available in conjuncture with action under s. 52(1), it is appropriate in this case to grant the appellant, subject to compliance with certain stated conditions, a constitutional exemption from the operation of s. 241(*b*) during the period of suspension. A constitutional exemption may only be granted during the period of a suspended declaration of invalidity. During that one-year suspension period, this exemption will also be available to all persons who are or will become physically unable to commit unassisted suicide and whose equality rights are infringed by s. 241(*b*), and it may be granted by a superior court upon application if the stated conditions, or similar conditions tailored to meet the circumstances of particular cases, are met.

[The Third Dissenting Opinion, by Justice Cory]

Substantially for the reasons given by [Chief Justice] Lamer and [Justice] McLachlin, s. 241(*b*) of the *Code* infringes ss. 7 and 15(1) of the *Charter* and is not justifiable under s. 1 of the *Charter*.

Section 7 of the *Charter*, which grants Canadians a constitutional right to life, liberty, and the security of the person, is a provision which emphasizes the innate dignity of human existence. Dying is an integral part of living and, as a part of life, is entitled to the protection of s. 7. It follows that the right to die with dignity should be as well protected as is any other aspect of the right to life. State prohibitions that would force a dreadful, painful death on a rational but incapacitated terminally ill patient are an affront to human dignity.

There is no difference between permitting a patient of sound mind to choose death with dignity by refusing treatment and permitting a patient of sound mind who is terminally ill to choose death with dignity by terminating life preserving treatment, even if, because of incapacity, that step has to be physically taken by another on her instructions. Nor is there any reason for failing to extend that same permission so that a terminally ill patient facing death may put an end to her life through the intermediary of another. Since the right to choose death is open to patients who are not physically handicapped, there is no reason for denying that choice to those that are. This choice for a terminally ill patient would be subject to conditions. With those conditions in place, s. 7 of the *Charter* can be applied to enable a court to grant the relief proposed by Lamer C.J.

Section 15(1) of the *Charter* can also be applied to grant the same relief at least to handicapped terminally ill patients. . . .

Notes

1. [1993] 3 S.C.R. 519
2. S. 241 of the *Criminal Code* states:

   241. Everyone who

   (*a*) counsels a person to commit suicide, or

   (*b*) aids or abets a person to commit suicide,

   whether suicide ensues or not, is guilty of an indictable offence and liable to imprisonment for a term not exceeding fourteen years. [Editor]
3. Section 7 states, "Everyone has the right to life, liberty, and security of the person and the right not to be deprived thereof except in accordance with the principles of fundamental justice." Principles of fundamental justice are legal principles that are central to Canadian conceptions of justice, and capable of being stated with some precision. They include rights such as the right against self-incrimination and the right that laws be clear and consistently applied. [Editor]
4. Section 12 states: "Everyone has the right not to be subjected to any cruel and unusual treatment or punishment." [Editor]
5. Section 15(1) states: "Every individual is equal before and under the law and has the right to the equal protection and equal benefit of the law without discrimination and, in particular, without discrimination based on race, national or ethnic origin, colour, religion, sex, age or mental or physical disability." [Editor]
6. Section 1 states: "The *Canadian Charter of Rights and Freedoms* guarantees the rights and freedoms set out in it subject only to such reasonable limits prescribed by law as can be demonstrably justified in a free and democratic society." See the discussion of the Oakes test (the s. 1 analysis) in the Introduction, under "The *Charter*." [Editor]

Catherine Frazee

Affidavit of Catherine Frazee, Intervener, *Ginette Leblanc v. Attorney General of Canada*[1]

. . .

Qualification and Expertise

. . . I currently hold the position of Professor Emerita at Ryerson University, School of Disability Studies. Prior to my retirement in 2010, I was a Professor of Distinction in the School of Disability Studies and Co-Director of the Ryerson-RBC Institute for Disability Studies Research and Education.

From 1989 to 1992, I served as Chief Commissioner of the Ontario Human Rights Commission, a full-time position of senior executive responsibility for the enforcement and promotion of the Ontario Human Rights Code. . . .

. . .

I have spinal muscular atrophy, a neurological condition that is progressive and irreversible. My physical impairments as a result of this condition are significant. I rely upon extensive technological support to function in the world: a highly customized motorized wheelchair, a ventilator, suction machine, patient lifting device, and voice recognition software for computer access. I am dependent upon 24-hour personal assistance for the most intimate details of my self-care: bathing, toileting, dressing, body positioning, and feeding.

Mandate

The Attorney General of Canada has asked me to address the following issues:

- the experience of people with disabilities in Canadian society broadly and in the medical system in particular;
- the principle of **autonomy** in relation to the disability experience; and
- the potential impacts of **assisted suicide** on people with disabilities.

. . .

Analysis

The Experience of People with Disabilities in Canada, Particularly in the Medical System

Relevant Research and Policy

. . .

Between 1999 and 2002, I was part of a team of three researchers investigating the legal and policy frameworks affecting the health and well-being of disabled women in Canada. . . . The project's final report underscored the extent to which a lack of regard for the **rights** and **dignity** of people with disabilities has been evident in clinical encounters within the health care system. . . . [It] highlighted policies and clinical decisions that "have harmed and disadvantaged people with disabilities. Treatment has been denied or not offered, either because it was not physically accessible, or because the person concerned was judged "unable to benefit" or the circumstances of his or her life were considered to be such that they did not warrant aggressive intervention."

In 2007/2008, I joined a team of investigators engaged in a study of end-of-life care for people who experience **socially-constructed** vulnerability. . . . [T]he Vulnerable Persons and End-Of-Life New Emerging Team (VP-NET) brought an interdisciplinary perspective to policy and practice issues related to disability and end-of-life. . . . Of paramount concern for the VP-NET team was the negotiation of deep and long-standing tensions between persons with disabilities and health care professionals . . . .

> The belief that disability and illness inevitably lead to a lower quality of life is widespread both among people working in the health care system and people in the general population. This belief often leads to a lack of health care options because the idea of trying to prolong a life that is assumed to be unpleasant seems futile. However, this belief is not based on the experiences of people with disabilities, whose perspectives are rarely incorporated into health care systems or decision making.
>
> . . .
>
> . . . Public and media discussion is dominated by the concept of "the right to die with dignity" which reinforces the belief that "some forms of living are too burdensome, too hopeless, or too unaesthetic to merit support."[2] This is further supported by an increasing intolerance for human limitation and glorification of the perfect body throughout the media. . . .

For nearly two decades, I have been associated with the Council of Canadians with Disabilities (CCD), Canada's national, cross-disability human rights organization, working for an accessible and inclusive Canada. Similarly, I have been associated as a Director and Task Force chair for the Canadian Association for Community Living (CACL) for over 10 years. CACL is a national federation of associations assisting people with intellectual disabilities and their families working to advance inclusion in Canadian society.

In these roles, I have acquired direct knowledge of how disabled Canadians and members of the Community Living movement[3] have engaged in serious reflection, research, and debate in formulating policy positions with respect to the legalization of assisted suicide.

In November 1994, the CACL strongly urged the Senate Committee on **Euthanasia** not to legalize euthanasia or **physician-assisted suicide**. . . . CACL reasoned that "in a society which legitimizes the practice of euthanasia or assisted suicide, people who are perceived to be less valuable and their families will face increasing pressure and reinforcing messages regarding their value to society. The result will be that many will "choose" assisted suicide based on their devalued sense of themselves." The submission went on to identify broader social impacts from a permissive approach to physician-assisted dying: ". . . selected **active euthanasia** will be seen as a social alternative to the provision of supports, services and the recognition of human rights."

In 2010, representatives of CACL appeared before the House of Commons Committee on **Palliative** and Compassionate Care. In their submission, . . . they detailed the Association's deep concern about the extent to which "quality-of-life" assessments distort the advice of medical professionals and place the lives of people with intellectual disabilities in "immediate peril." They reported that families " . . . are told by medical professionals and experts that their family member's life is in immediate peril, that efforts to support him or her are futile, that the family should leave their loved one be and let him or her die with dignity. . . ."

. . .

In 1996, the CCD went on record as opposing "any government action to decriminalize assisted suicide because of the serious potential for abuse and the negative image of people with disabilities that would be produced if people with disabilities are killed with state **sanction**." . . . In 2003, with support of the Canadian Bar Association, CCD commissioned a detailed review of the "issues involved in the legalization of physician-assisted death." . . . The 80-page report concluded:

> . . . there are serious risks to persons with disabilities in societies where **assisted death** is regarded as a solution to the suffering and anxiety that many experience as they near the end of their lives. For most people in that circumstance, assisted death may be regarded as "merciful" because it relieves them of the physical and mental ordeal they would otherwise have to endure. For people with disabilities, however, the "mercy" is often seen in terms of ending a life that is perceived by others to be devoid of value because of the individual's disability, rather than being intolerable for the individual because of pain and suffering. . . . Until it can be convincingly demonstrated that all Canadians enjoy full equality and security of the person, regardless of disability, as guaranteed by the ***Charter of Rights and Freedoms***, then any steps toward legalized assistance in dying should be resisted.
>
> . . .

In that **brief** . . . , CCD concluded that legalizing assisted suicide "would violate our principles supporting equal, dignified, and **self-determining** lives for people with disabilities."

. . . Rhonda Wiebe, Chair of CCD's Ending of Life Ethics Committee, spoke of "the insidious stereotypes that bring harm to people with disabilities." She recounted the experience of a now-deceased colleague who had gone to hospital to be treated for pneumonia: "[Mike] expected treatment to cure his illness. However, his doctors offered to make him comfortable while nature took its course. Members of the disability community had to advocate on his behalf to get him the treatment he needed." In my thirty-odd years of research, study and human rights work, I have encountered many, many such narratives that underscore the precarious hold that disabled citizens have upon life itself, when those with gate-keeping authority in medical and other professions permit their own subjective assessments of the value of life with significant impairment to shape judgment and advice. Although to my knowledge there are no definitive studies that offer statistical tracking of such incidents, I have no doubt about the frequency of their occurrence and the authenticity of their reporting. It is my opinion that narrative accounts such as these chronicle a recurring pattern of socially constructed vulnerability to death-hastening policies or practices.

The following account . . . offers a vivid recounting of the extraordinary strength that must be mustered to resist the influence of those whose framings of suffering, quality of life, and compassion conform to prevailing presuppositions about disability.

Mr. Justice Sam Filer, first diagnosed with ALS[4] in 1987, went into respiratory failure while in hospital in January, 1989. His wife Toni Silberman describes what followed:

The doctors would not allow me into his bedroom because they, in their mercy, didn't want me to watch him die. I thank them for that. What I don't thank them for is their reluctance to proffer [offer], except under extreme duress, alternatives to his death.

Six attending physicians encircled me, offering assurance that it would be inhumane to not let him die with dignity; that his care would become financially ruinous; that I had an infant at home to whom I owed my devotion; that there is, not could be but is, no quality of life once ventilated; and that I had ten minutes in which to make my decision. [Sam and I] had discussed ventilation as an option—but those discussions were academic and distant at the time. The reality was far more ominous and frightening.

Being well trained as a psychologist, I thanked the doctors for sharing their feelings with me, and suggested that their expressed concerns were our responsibility, and keeping Sam alive was theirs. In retrospect, I recognize that the doctors, based on their experiences, were making medically and socially approved assumptions. But those assumptions were, in our case, the wrong ones. Only two of the six doctors, to their credit, had the courtesy to say that although they disagreed with the decision, they would do everything possible to ensure that the procedure would be a successful one. They did, and it was. Sam's new life began when he left the ICU.

Justice Filer continued to work as an Ontario Superior Court Judge until his retirement in 2004. Defying all prognostications [predictions], he lived until 2007.

Summary and Opinion with Respect to the Social Position of Disabled People And, in Particular, Their Relations with Institutions of Contemporary Medicine

. . .

Disabled people have a distinct experience. We are perceived as less fortunate than non-disabled people and assigned a diminished status in everyday life—these perceptions and status shape our experience, both when we are lively and **autonomous** and when we are fragile and vulnerable.

Disability rights advocates have for decades fought against negative stereotypes, discriminatory barriers, and persistent cultural devaluation in the effort to achieve equality. Discrimination on the basis of disability—both direct and **systemic**—is pervasive and persistent. As acknowledged by the Supreme Court of Canada in the *Eldridge*[5] decision, "It is an unfortunate truth that the history of disabled persons in Canada is largely one of exclusion and marginalization. Persons with disabilities have too often been excluded from the labour force, denied access to opportunities for social interaction and advancement, subjected to **invidious** stereotyping and relegated to institutions. . . ."

Judgments about the particular conditions of disabled people's lives are overwhelmingly dominated by anxiety, prejudice, and stigma. Disabled people's functional limitations and reliance upon human and technological supports are both pitied and feared. Conditions that become routine aspects of life for disabled people—such as reliance upon ventilators or feeding tubes, or the need for human assistance with intimate personal care, or bodily difficulties such as drooling or incontinence or the inability to communicate through conventional means—give rise to deep and persistent unease among people immersed in the values of an **ableist** culture. For this reason, the lives of disabled people are widely held to be tragic. As noted by Orville Endicott . . . , "Society in general attributes negative characteristics to persons with disabilities. Their lives are regarded as having less value, both to themselves and to the society around them, than the lives of individuals who do not have disabilities." . . . [D]isabled people have had an ambivalent and troubled relationship with institutions of health care and medicine. Many health care professionals tend, like others in positions of economic and social power and authority, to regard the quality of life of disabled people as unacceptably poor when compared with their own.

A consistent thread running through narratives of disabled peoples' encounters with medical professionals suggests that disabled patients have a qualitatively different experience from the acutely ill—but otherwise non-disabled—patient. Recurring accounts from Canadians with disabilities and their family members report situations of denial or withdrawal of life-saving treatment, presumptive steering toward Do Not Resuscitate orders and/or premature surrender to "comfort care." At the heart of these accounts are fundamental assumptions about quality of life. As noted by Orville Endicott . . . , "Do Not Resuscitate orders are often entered in patient charts, not because an attempt to resuscitate the person would be futile, but because the individual's life is negatively valued because of disability." Research studies . . . indicate that physicians in particular, and medical professionals in general, consistently and dramatically underestimate quality of life for their disabled patients, as compared to the assessments which those same individuals make of their own lives.

Aside from quality-of-life assumptions, there are other significant challenges that people with disabilities face within the medical system. Many examination and treatment facilities are not accessible to people with various impairments . . . [and] few health care professionals have had any exposure to a disability perspective on fundamental questions of ethics and practice.

The Principle of Autonomy in Relation to the Disability Experience

. . . [L]anguage is a powerful tool in the ordering of human relations. Words such as dignity, autonomy and choice, like vulnerability and compassion, can be distorted, and their meanings effectively reversed. In the language used to support demands for physician-assisted suicide, we have many examples of this kind of inversion.

The concepts of dignity, autonomy, and choice have been **clarion** calls of the disability rights movement in Canada and around the world. These concepts have served the movement well, as respect for the autonomy of disabled people is universally recognized as a precondition for any claim to **substantive equality**. . . .

Proponents of suicide assistance argue that the decision to choose the precise time and method of one's own death is the ultimate exercise of personal autonomy. However, organizations mandated to advance the equality rights of citizens with disabilities in Canada and the US, including CCD and CACL, overwhelmingly reject this argument, standing together in opposition to any decriminalization of suicide assistance. . . .

At first glance, there may appear to be a problematic inconsistency in the positions taken by CCD and CACL in relation to the principle of autonomy. On the one hand, respect for autonomy and **self-determination** are cornerstone principles of the disability rights movement, and embraced as such in the core principles of both of these organizations. On the other hand, both organizations firmly oppose any framing of a request for assistance in committing suicide as an exercise of personal autonomy.

On closer examination, however, what may appear at first as a selective disregard for the principle of autonomy, is, in my opinion, quite the opposite. The accounts and positions developed by Canada's leading disability rights organizations in fact reflect an unqualified commitment to a robust and nuanced account of autonomy that is entirely consistent with fundamental principles of equality.

In this section of the report, I shall attempt to delineate the principal features of this account of autonomy. . . . My observations will be organized under the following headings:

- Autonomy must not be compromised;
- Autonomy must not be confused with **sovereignty**;
- Autonomy must not be invoked in support of wrongly construed rights;
- Autonomy must not be invoked ***simpliciter*** in ways that undermine, rather than protect, human dignity and equality.

Autonomy Must Not Be Compromised

It is, for all practical purposes, impossible to isolate a request for assistance to end one's life from the context within which such a request is made. For this reason, within a social order that widely perceives disabled people's lives and lifestyles to be of diminished value, the availability of medical assistance to terminate life upon demand places some people at risk of making a "choice" that does not reflect their true, autonomous desires.

This is of course not to say that disabled people are incapable of or universally precluded from exercising true autonomy, or that there are no circumstances under which a competent adult could choose autonomously to be assisted to die, rather than to permit a terminal, disabling condition to run its course. It is, however, an argument that affirms the inevitability that some persons will be vulnerable to internalizing pervasive messages of social fear and shame, and find themselves effectively backed into a request for suicide assistance as their only "reasonable" or "honourable" option.

Such requests . . . would decidedly *not* be autonomous in nature. . . .

Autonomous choices cannot be assured in the context of the social and material deprivations of disabled person's lives, and the immense social and cultural pressures that erode disabled people's sense of belonging and equal human worth.

As long as people with disabilities are **disenfranchised** and made to feel that they are burdens to their society and to those who support them in their community, there can be no assurance that assisted suicide is pursued as a free choice. There can be no assurance that such requests are indeed expressions of true personal autonomy as long as people with disabilities are overwhelmingly denied adequate health care, housing, transportation, personal support services, assistive technology, education, employment, and community access.

Disability turns many social relations upside down. Whereas non-disabled people conceive of assisted suicide as a method of preserving autonomy in the face of debilitating illness and decline, many disabled people will experience the possibility of an assisted death as one that undermines autonomy, depending upon their place in social hierarchies of power.

Moreover, protocols aimed at safeguarding vulnerable populations from the hostile influence of socially embedded disability prejudice are, at best, naïve in their confidence that autonomy can be protected and assured. It is impossible to conceive of any procedural intervention so astute as to detect, unfailingly, the influence of stigma, shame, guilt, or prejudice in an end-of-life decision making process. Such influences by their very nature are subtle, insidious, and pervasive. Their effects are felt over the course of a lifetime, long before the triggering moment of a request for suicide assistance. And they are enacted in the most informal and seemingly inconsequential everyday encounters, well beyond the reach of even the most rigorous screening procedure.

Autonomy Must Not Be Confused with Sovereignty

Disability rights organizations in Canada have given critical attention to the unexamined proposition that deciding to end one's own life is the ultimate expression of autonomy. Increasingly, their policy discussions on the subject of assisted suicide reject the suggestion that suicide is an expression of autonomy, freedom or liberty.

Instead, suicide is, by its nature, a matter of an individual's sovereignty over their body—a matter of each person's sovereignty over their existence, quite distinct from a freedom, liberty or expression of autonomy that is accorded the protection of law.

Suicide is not so much an expression of autonomy, as it is a place that the law cannot touch. Suicide can be seen as an act that is an expression of "sovereignty"—a purely private act, outside of the domain of rights and freedoms as these concepts are understood in the context of the assisted suicide debate.

Autonomy Must Not Be Invoked in Support of Wrongly Construed Rights

Similarly, disability rights organizations have challenged the notion that suicide is a "right" enjoyed by people who are physically capable of ending their own lives. They assert that no specific entitlement to commit suicide can be gleaned from its removal from the *Criminal Code* in 1972. The decriminalization of suicide does not amount to the establishment of a so-called "right to die."

Suicide cannot be construed as a right to which a claim for equality can be made. Death is not a right. Neither is dementia, necrosis, myopia, infection, or any other pathology or biological process.

...

Invoking the principle of autonomy to claim a "right" to a particular method of suicide gravely distorts the meaning of autonomy for persons with disabilities and trivializes hard-fought-for rights secured under the *Charter*'s guarantee of equality. Autonomy is inherently a life-affirming value, a vital thread running through myriad acts of self-creation. Suicide stands apart from this tapestry as a single act of self-destruction.

Philosophically, there is support for this position in the argument that autonomy cannot justify actions which remove or terminate the future exercise of autonomy. Since the publication of John Stuart Mill's essay *On Liberty* in 1869,[6] there is a well-established line of ethical thought that such actions as committing suicide or selling oneself into slavery should be prevented in order to avoid precluding the further exercise of freedom. More recently, Charles Taylor's articulation of the notion of "radical re-evaluation" gives rise to affirmations that autonomy can be infringed to preserve the possibility that our views may radically change in the future.[7] To the extent that assisted suicide forecloses the possibility for radical re-evaluation of one's threshold for life worth living, its prohibition can be ethically justified.

Autonomy must Not Be Invoked *Simpliciter*, in Ways That Undermine, Rather than Protect, Human Dignity and Equality

Disability prejudice and stereotype are embedded in the discourse around physician-assisted suicide. Loss of control of bodily fluids is repeatedly and emphatically represented as an assault of suffering and indignity, such as to render life no longer worth living. Loss of mobility and diminished capacity for independent self-care are consistently described as a stripping away of dignity. Despair and surrender are uncritically accepted as the only possible response to a hopeless predicament—a predicament invariably associated with social shame. Yet the link between dignity and independent physical self-care is not absolute.

The reasons most frequently given for people wanting to avail themselves of assisted suicide are related not to pain or physical suffering, but to anxieties about loss of independence—in particular, loss of independent capacity to bathe, dress, and go to the bathroom. Such anxieties are serious and worthy of responses that are sensitive and attuned to the circumstances of each individual, but they do not constitute a social imperative sufficiently compelling to warrant a legal measure that could imperil the life of another.

When we accept uncritically that reliance upon assistance with bodily functions diminishes dignity to such an extent that life is no longer worth living, we trivialize the true meaning of human dignity and denigrate the lives of people who rely upon others for intimate physical support in their daily lives. Only the most simplistic and superficial formulation of autonomy can seriously posit death as a proportionate response to anxieties surrounding bodily functions.

The Potential Impacts of Assisted Suicide on People with Disabilities

Disability rights organizations such as the CCD and the National Council of Disability in the US have struggled with the policy implications of physician-assisted suicide for decades. The issue poses an excruciatingly difficult question, because the effect of leaving intact existing criminal prohibitions against assisted suicide is to frustrate the deep desire of some individuals with disabilities, such as the petitioner [Ginette Leblanc] in this case. This position is not taken lightly or without considerable regard for Ms. Leblanc and others in similar circumstances.

However, the availability of physician-assisted suicide would put many disabled people at risk. In this final section of my report, I shall elaborate upon the nature of that risk, detailing two distinct categories of harm that are not only likely but in my opinion inevitable, should paragraph 241(b) of the *Criminal Code* be struck down.

> Direct and immediate harm: Some people with disabilities will be unjustly denied the opportunity to live life to its natural end; and
>
> Systemic and symbolic harm: Socially and culturally embedded patterns of disability disadvantage, prejudice, and exclusion will be perpetuated and reinforced.

Direct and Immediate Harm

As reported by Orville Endicott . . . :

> There is a considerable body of public opinion in Canada and elsewhere that ending the life of a person with a disability is much less blameworthy than killing a person who does not have a disability. Often the killing of a person with a disability is characterized as "mercy killing" regardless of whether the individual was experiencing severe pain. . . . If the movement to legalize physician-assisted death gains momentum, there is every reason to expect that a disproportionate number of those who will be "assisted." . . . will be persons with disabilities.

Although early studies in jurisdictions which permit physician-assisted suicide have not pointed to a disproportionate number of people with disabilities receiving such "assistance," it is entirely possible that longer term experience will reveal otherwise. Whether or not this kind of empirical data ultimately supports Endicott's assertion, there are equally significant, though far less easily measurable ways in which people with disabilities may have pursued assisted suicide for reasons that are rooted in social disadvantage rather than free and autonomous choice. In other words, it is possible that people with disabilities have been and will continue to be disproportionately influenced by discriminatory factors in their end-of-life decision making.

The direct and immediate harm therefore occasioned by the availability of suicide assistance is perhaps not that too many people with disabilities will choose to die, but that too many of those who do make this choice will do so because of injustice, rather than autonomy.

I know of no way accurately to measure the extent to which a lifetime of exclusion, marginalization, and material and social deprivation erodes the will to live. Nor can I point to studies that document how exposure to distorted representations of disability determines the intensity of one's refusal to embrace disablement at life's end. I cannot precisely quantify how an absence of regard in homes, places of work, and communities undermines our authority and confidence when we are thrust into the turbulent waters of end-of-life decision making. It is decidedly my opinion, however, that such factors have cumulative effect, and that such effect will at times diminish one's resilience to pain, adversity, and misfortune, dampen one's creativity, and incline one toward hasty surrender.

Many who have contemplated suicide, myself included, experience a change of circumstances or heart, in time growing through a personal but radical rethinking of the value of life in the particular form it has taken. The availability of physician-assisted suicide may cause direct and immediate harm to those who are enabled to act on their first impulse, and thereby denied this opportunity for fundamental rethinking.

Most people who express suicidal wishes are strongly supported to resist self-destructive impulses. Regardless of protocols put in place to protect the vulnerable, there can be no certainty that persons whose quality of life has been judged as unacceptable will receive the full benefit of such intervention. Hence, another potential for direct and immediate harm, occurring well "below the radar" of procedural safeguards and monitoring mechanisms.

. . .

Moreover, there already exists an ambivalent relationship between the medical professions and people with disabilities. These relationships would not be made less difficult, less ambivalent, or less troubled if the professionals entrusted with our care could legally terminate our lives, even upon our own direction. Disabled people might become less, rather than more, likely to be forthright with their physicians about their fears and desires.

Perhaps most worrisome, in the context of a more permissive approach to death hastening for people with impairments, it is conceivable that some physicians and family members may feel less inhibited from covert (and unlawful) practices of involuntary euthanasia—an area where procedural safeguards are of no effect.

. . . In my view, given that real risks of discriminatory influence do exist, and that regulatory protocols put in place to minimize such risks cannot be stripped of all human subjectivity, and that anxieties about disability take hold well below the level of liberal consciousness, there is at least a reasonable possibility of harm to vulnerable persons.

I would emphasize that this reasoning does not rely upon the spectre of an all-out genocide or **eugenic** slippery slope. Such a catastrophic outcome may or may not be the ultimate endpoint that begins with socially sanctioned suicide assistance, but for the purpose of the present discussion, it is not necessary to settle that debate.

Instead, in my opinion, if even one person dies prematurely for reasons that accord with a compromised autonomy, then limiting the privilege to choose the precise time and manner of one's death is justified.

Systemic and Symbolic Harm

Notwithstanding the seriousness of the potential for direct and immediate harm where suicide assistance is pursued in the absence of true autonomy, the striking down of section 241(b) of the *Criminal Code* would have other more far-reaching and profound effects.

As acknowledged by Chief Justice Dickson in *R. v. Keegstra*,[8] "A person's sense of human dignity and belonging to the community at large is closely linked to the concern and respect accorded the groups to which he or she belongs." The removal of long-standing *Criminal Code* protections contained in section 241(b) would constitute a highly visible and authoritative endorsement of a particular set of ideas and values. In my opinion, . . . those ideas and values demonstrate a clear lack of respect for the life experience of disabled persons.

The ideas and values that find expression in support for physician-assisted suicide cluster around a basic acceptance that loss of control over one's body at end-of-life constitutes a catastrophic and irreversible violation of human dignity, serious enough to warrant taking direct measures to end one's own life. Mobility, speech, physical independence, and control of bodily functions are highly prized capacities, considered by many to be requisite conditions for the enjoyment of privacy, autonomy, and well-being.

Yet across this country and around the world, people with disabilities negotiate physical dependence and functional limitation as routine dimensions of everyday life. Those with access to adequate and appropriate supports live with their dignity intact and their privacy, autonomy, and well-being undiminished. Most do not perceive themselves to be "suffering" by virtue of their impairments. The ideas and values that find expression in their lives cluster more around a perennial quest for recognition, respect, and equality, rather than avoidance, pity, and shame.

I would emphasize here that there is nothing inherently harmful or destructive about assigning a high value to physical fitness and capacity. Nor is it problematic to recognize and honour the grief that flows from serious losses in this domain. What is harmful, and ultimately destructive of efforts to nurture a just and pluralistic society, is to denigrate bodily incapacity to such an extent that it becomes a **sufficient condition** for assisted suicide.

Typically, petitions for assistance in dying rely upon a logic that equates bodily incapacity with indignity. While such assertions are deeply personal and no doubt subjectively authentic at the point in time when they are uttered, they cannot be teased apart from the milieu of negative ideas and values about disability in which they took root. To craft a legal right to die in response to a petition of this nature is to elevate its flawed core assertion to the status of social policy. It is impossible to grant a request for suicide assistance while rejecting the underpinning logic that bodily incapacity is shameful and undignified.

In other words, when the state sanctions measures to hasten death in response to a claim that certain levels of physical impairment are so undignified and degrading as to render life intolerable, long-standing patterns of disabled people's devaluation are affirmed and reproduced. Others will become more—rather than less—inclined to take up and embrace cultural taboos about disability. In this way, a diffuse yet pervasive social harm is inflicted.

This harm is complex and multifaceted. It is carried not only in the logic of petitions and legal arguments, but in the language with which the debate is framed. For example, descriptions of petitioners' circumstances frequently draw from an ableist vocabulary that frames adaptive technologies such as wheelchairs, voice synthesizers, ventilators, and feeding tubes not as marvels of modern invention, but rather as symbols of degradation and confinement. Similarly, acts of caregiving and personal support are described in language that strips both the care provider and the care recipient of their humanity, and erases any recognition of the delicate relational chemistry of such arrangements. Assertions such as Ms. Leblanc's painful claim that "I will become a prisoner of my own body and lose all autonomy" or Gloria [Taylor]'s[9] assertion that "What I fear is a death that negates, as opposed to concludes, my life" become sound-bites in the court of public opinion where prejudice and fears about disability abound.

The offer of suicide assistance as a disability-related accommodation is a paltry gesture when the promise of equality in every other social domain remains unfulfilled. There is cold comfort in the offer of death as a response to suffering and indignity within a society that overwhelmingly considers disabled lives to be, ***de facto***, lives dominated by suffering and indignity.

For these reasons, I am of the opinion that the recognition of a legal right to suicide assistance would deliver devastating social and cultural impacts for a group already severely disadvantaged by prejudice and stigma. To move in this direction would not **ameliorate** disadvantage but rather entrench it, in a manner utterly inconsistent with the values expressed in the equality guarantees of the *Charter*.

Turning to the particular context of this case, the **plaintiff**, in paragraph 10 of her affidavit, bases her request for suicide assistance upon "the loss of dignity and privacy *that inevitably comes* with amyotrophic lateral sclerosis" [emphasis added]. The notion of what constitutes dignity, and what conditions of life make its loss inevitable, is therefore pivotal in the determination of her claim.

. . . [H]owever, bodily incapacity must not be presumed to compromise human dignity. Such a presumption negates the experience of many people with severe impairments, including people with amyotrophic lateral sclerosis, who do live with their dignity intact. To conclude that human dignity is inevitably lost when one is no longer capable of self-care, is to declare as diminished and undignified, the lives of people like myself who rely each day upon intimate human and technological support. Such a position serves to undermine the precarious claim that people with disabilities have to equality, by authenticating the devaluation of particular bodily experiences.

Loss of physical capacity and the concomitant need for intimate personal care do not by definition constitute "indignity." To accept uncritically that these states violate or diminish human dignity, is to affirm deep and long-standing patterns of thought that have relegated disabled people to the margins of social acceptance. Any measure such as assisted suicide that so squarely aligns with the fears and antipathies of a socially **privileged** group (people who do not require assistance with intimate personal care), must take into careful account the perspective of persons who are disadvantaged by those fears and antipathies (people who do require assistance with intimate personal care).

There are far-reaching implications when one person's "indignity" is another person's daily routine of life. The threshold of human dignity is far too variable to be an appropriate condition for the termination of life.

To conclude that a request to end one's life is justified by the presumed indignity of bodily incapacity, would greatly undermine dignity as a cornerstone principle of disabled people's claim to equal status and regard within the living human family.

Conclusion

If the promise of equality for disabled Canadians is to be honoured, any consideration of legalizing physician-assisted suicide must take into careful account the context of disabled peoples' history and social reality. The social context for any claim of a "right" to suicide assistance in a context that can be traced back in just two generations to the atrocities of a global eugenic frenzy,[10] and in one generation to freewheeling practices of institutional confinement, involuntary sterilization,[11] and medical experimentation. It is a context that situates contemporary disabled Canadians in a social order which authorizes pandemic **triage** exclusion, selective genetic elimination, and the withdrawal of life-supporting technologies on the basis of disability status. Disabled people constitute a group whose profound social disadvantage manifests in acts of compassion-cloaked homicide, coercion, and abandonment. Violence, and social ambivalence in the face of violence, are writ large in the context and social history of disability.

In such a context, suicide assistance for people with disabilities cannot be considered an enabling—or neutral—accommodation. . . .

Notes

1. Province of Québec District of Trois-rivières, No: 400-17-002642-110 Superior Court (Civil Division). Ms. Leblanc died before the case was heard in court. [Editor]
2. Carol J. Gill, "Disability, Constructed Vulnerability, and Socially Conscious Palliative Care," *Journal of Palliative Care* 22, 3 (2006): 186.

3. The community living movement argues that people with intellectual disabilities are citizens with the same rights as non-disabled citizens. Its proponents argue that most people with intellectual disabilities can, with the right supports, live on their own and participate in their communities like anyone else. [Editor]
4. Amyotrophic lateral sclerosis (ALS, also known as Lou Gehrig's disease) is a disease of the neurons that control muscle movement. It is usually fatal within three to five years. [Editor]
5. In *Eldridge v. British Columbia (Attorney General)*, [1997] 2 SCR 624, the Supreme Court ruled that not providing sign language interpreters to deaf people in the health care system was a violation of their s. 15 equality rights. [Editor]
6. In *On Liberty*, John Stuart Mill argued for liberty of thought and expression. His arguments were so convincing that today we take most of them for granted. [Editor]
7. Charles Taylor, "What Is Human Agency?" in *Human Agency and Language: Philosophical Papers 1* (Cambridge: Cambridge University Press, 1985), pp. 15–44. [Editor]
8. In *R. v. Keegstra*, [1990] 3 SCR 697, the Supreme Court upheld both the conviction of high school teacher James Keegstra for spreading hate propaganda (he taught that the Holocaust was a fiction and that Jews were conspiring to take over the world) and the constitutionality of the law forbidding hate propaganda. [Editor]
9. Gloria Taylor was a plaintiff with ALS in *Carter v. Canada (Attorney General)*, 2012 BCSC 886, which challenged the law against assisted suicide. A BC Supreme Court justice ruled in 2012 that the law violated the *Charter*. The government appealed, and in 2013 the BC Court of Appeals ruled that the law does not violate the *Charter*. Taylor died in 2012 from a severe infection. [Editor]
10. In the late nineteenth and early twentieth centuries, eugenics (the practice of trying to improve humans genetically) was widely supported around the world. Its practices included marriage restrictions, forced sterilization of "undesirable" people, euthanasia, and even genocide. "Undesirable" people included people with intellectual or physical disabilities, poor people, promiscuous women, drug addicts, the Roma, members of non-European races, and homosexuals. Eugenics lost most of its appeal after news of the Holocaust hit the world at the end of World War II. [Editor]
11. Most forced sterilizations in Canada occurred in the west, particularly in Alberta. Alberta ended forced sterilization of people with intellectual disabilities only in 1972. [Editor]

Jocelyn Downie

Dying Justice

AV = author's view; ~AV = not the author's view

Unsustainable Distinctions

Nature of Conduct (Act vs. Omission)

~AV The acts/omissions distinction argument generally takes the following form: (1) to omit to save a life is acceptable whereas to act to end life is unacceptable; (2) the withholding and withdrawal of potentially life-sustaining treatment are omissions, but **assisted suicide** and **euthanasia** are acts; therefore, (3) the withholding and withdrawal of potentially life-sustaining treatment are acceptable but assisted suicide and voluntary euthanasia are not.

AV There are at least two [arguments against this claim]. . . . First, the withdrawal of potentially life-sustaining treatment is as much an act as assisted suicide and euthanasia are acts. Second, there is no moral significance to the distinction between acts and omissions.

. . . In the context of **assisted death**, something is an act when you *do* something knowing that, but for your action, the person would not die. Something is an omission when you *do not do* something knowing that, but for your omission, the person would not die. When you withhold a necessary blood transfusion you are *not doing* something knowing that, but for your inaction, the person would not die. Therefore, withholding treatment is an omission. When you withdraw a respirator you are *doing* something knowing that, but for your act, the person would not die. Therefore, withdrawing treatment is an act. When you give a person a lethal injection you are doing something knowing that but for your act the person would not die. Therefore, euthanasia is an act. Therefore, it cannot be concluded that the withholding and withdrawal of potentially life-sustaining treatment are acceptable because they are omissions, and assisted suicide and euthanasia are unacceptable because they are acts. Withholding is an omission, while withdrawal, assisted suicide, and euthanasia are acts.

. . .

Second, consider my claim that there is no significance to the distinction between acts and omissions. James Rachels makes this argument through the following well-known, oft-repeated, and hotly contested illustration:

1. Smith stands to gain a large inheritance if anything should happen to his six-year-old cousin. One evening while the child is taking his bath, Smith sneaks into the bathroom and drowns the child, and then arranges things so that it will look like an accident.
2. Jones also stands to gain if anything should happen to his six-year-old cousin. Like Smith, Jones sneaks in planning to drown the child in his bath. However, just as he enters the bathroom Jones sees the child slip, hit his head, and fall face down in the water. Jones is delighted; he stands by, ready to push the child's head back under if it is necessary, but it is not necessary. With only a little thrashing about, the child drowns all by himself, "accidentally," as Jones watches and does nothing.[1]

To give a related example, suppose that we have the same Smith and Jones as above. The cousin is in hospital following a car accident. He is on a respirator but is expected to recover fully. In the first scenario, Smith enters the hospital room surreptitiously and disconnects the respirator. In the second scenario, Jones visits his cousin and watches as he has a violent seizure and accidentally disconnects the power supply to the respirator. In both scenarios, the young cousin dies. Although Smith acts and Jones omits to act, both the act and the omission are reprehensible but the distinction between acts and omissions plays no role in Smith's and Jones's culpability.

A number of arguments have been made in response to the conclusion that there is no morally significant distinction between acts and omissions. These arguments all share a fatal flaw: they all end up relying upon a feature *in addition to* the acts and omissions feature. . . . The addition of a feature means that something other than the distinction between acts and omissions itself is critical. . . . The distinction between acts and omissions alone does not do the work desired of it. An additional element is required. . . .

~AV The distinction between acts and omissions has been widely relied upon to justify distinguishing between the withholding and withdrawal of potentially life-sustaining treatment and assisted suicide and voluntary euthanasia. AV However, . . . it has been fairly described as "backed by tradition but not by reason"[2] and as "both morally and intellectually misshapen."[3] I too conclude that the distinction between acts and omissions must not be permitted to shape the legal **regime** dealing with assisted death.

Cause of Death (Disease/"Natural" vs. Action/"Unnatural")

~AV The argument frequently made with respect to cause of death is that when a health care provider withholds or withdraws treatment, the disease kills the patient, whereas when a health care provider performs euthanasia, a drug kills the patient. Framed another way, in the former, death results from "natural causes," whereas in the latter, it results from "unnatural causes." So, for example, Yale Kamisar argues, "in letting die, the cause of death is seen as the underlying disease process or trauma. In assisted suicide/euthanasia, the cause of death is seen as the inherently lethal action itself."[4] However, this distinction does not map at all onto the line between the withholding and withdrawal of potentially life-sustaining treatment, on the one side, and assisted suicide and voluntary euthanasia, on the other.

AV As with assisted suicide and euthanasia, an "unnatural cause" (the removal of a respirator) rather than a "natural cause" (the underlying disease) can cause death in a case involving withdrawal of potentially life-sustaining treatment. An example should help to illustrate this point. Consider someone who had polio as a child and requires a respirator for daily living. If a thief removed the respirator from that person, few would say that the polio killed the person or that the person died of "natural causes." Most, if not all, would say that the removal of the respirator killed the person and the person died of "unnatural causes." Consider also a person with a pacemaker. Someone intentionally releases a strong electromagnetic pulse when she enters a room, the pulse causes her pacemaker to stop working, and she dies. Did she die of natural causes? Was the agent of her death the underlying heart disease that required that she have a pacemaker or was it the electromagnetic pulse? Most, if not all, would say that the pulse killed the woman and that she died of "unnatural causes," and yet, this is ultimately an example of withdrawal of treatment.

~AV One could respond to these examples by denying the intuition that the person who took the respirator or released the electromagnetic pulse caused the death. One could claim that the person did not cause the death but was nonetheless **culpable** [legally responsible] in the death. AV However, this manoeuvre will not rescue this distinction for the purposes of sustaining differential treatment of withholding and withdrawing life-sustaining treatment, on the one hand, and assisted suicide and euthanasia, on the other, because on this manoeuvre a person who withdraws treatment is culpable. Both culpable and **non-culpable** conduct will be found on both sides of the line drawn by causation. Thus, even by denying the causal intuition, the distinction fails to do the work required of it. Again, something else is required to sustain the differential treatment.

. . .

Intention (To End Life vs. to Alleviate Suffering)

~AV Intention is frequently cited in an attempt to draw a distinction between the withholding and withdrawal of potentially life-sustaining treatment, on the one hand, and euthanasia, on the other. Some argue that the intention of withholding and withdrawal of potentially life-sustaining treatment is to alleviate suffering while the intention of assisted suicide and euthanasia is to end life. Hastening death with the intention of alleviating suffering is considered acceptable and hastening death with the intention of ending life is considered unacceptable. Therefore, they conclude, the withholding and withdrawal of potentially life-sustaining treatment are acceptable and assisted suicide and euthanasia are not.

AV One must, however, distinguish between two senses of intention: subjective foresight, and motive or goal. . . . First, consider the issue of foresight. Just as when a health care provider injects a lethal dose of potassium chloride, when a health care provider withdraws artificial hydration and nutrition, he or she knows that a consequence of that action will be death. The subjective foresight test can be met by categories of assisted death on either side of the line between withholding and withdrawal of potentially life-sustaining treatment and assisted suicide and euthanasia.

Second, consider the issue of motive or goal. When a health care provider withdraws artificial hydration and nutrition, his or her motive is to alleviate suffering. When a health care provider injects a lethal dose of potassium chloride, his or her motive is to alleviate suffering. Again, the motive test can be met by categories of assisted death on either side of the line.

It is here that the principle of **double effect** must be considered. On this principle, "it is sometimes permissible to bring about by oblique intention what one may not directly intend."[5] However, this principle cannot ground a distinction between the categories of assisted death because it, too, captures some events on both sides of the line. Just as when a health care provider injects a lethal dose of potassium chloride, when he or she withdraws artificial hydration and nutrition at the request of a patient, no primary effect excuses the secondary effect. No effect of alleviating suffering exists apart from the effect of ending life. The intention to end life is direct rather than "oblique," and hence, on the principle of double effect, impermissible. And yet, . . . the withdrawal of artificial hydration and nutrition from a patient is legally permissible. Therefore, the principle of double effect cannot be used to ground the distinction between the withholding and withdrawal of potentially life-sustaining treatment, on the one hand, and assisted suicide and voluntary euthanasia, on the other.

Nature of the Effect of the Prohibition (Violation of Bodily Integrity vs. No Violation)

~AV It might be argued that, in its effort to preserve individuals' lives, the state is willing to override autonomy unless that would require violating the patients' bodily integrity. . . . [B]y allowing third parties to treat patients against their wishes, the state would allow third parties to violate the patients' bodily integrity (evoking images of strapping an unwilling patient to an operating table). Whereas, . . . by not permitting third parties to provide patients with assisted suicide or euthanasia, the state is merely preventing third parties from doing something to the patients and is not allowing any violation of bodily integrity. Thus, it might be claimed, a bright line is drawn between the withholding and withdrawal of potentially life-sustaining treatment, on the one side, and euthanasia and assisted suicide, on the other.

AV This distinction does not, however, do the work required of it. Suicide and attempted suicide are legal and the state could prevent them without violating bodily integrity (e.g., by confining suicidal individuals). Potentially life-shortening palliative treatment is legal and the deaths caused by it could be prevented without violations of bodily integrity (by simply not allowing the provision of potentially life-shortening palliative treatment). These are two examples of situations in which the state could preserve individuals' lives without violating the individuals' bodily integrity—yet chooses not to.

Therefore, it can be concluded that the distinction based on violation of bodily integrity does not support permitting the provision of potentially life-shortening palliative treatment and the withholding and withdrawal of potentially life-sustaining treatment, on the one hand, and prohibiting assisted suicide and euthanasia, on the other.

Other Areas of Law

. . . AV [T]hese . . . distinctions are not uniformly applied in other areas of law to distinguish between culpable and non-culpable conduct. Acts that cause death are sometimes regarded as non-culpable conduct (e.g., shooting a person in self-defence or war) and omissions that cause death are sometimes regarded as culpable conduct (e.g., a lifeguard leaving a child to drown in a pool). Naturally caused death sometimes generates **ascriptions** [assignments] of culpability (e.g., not taking a child with pneumonia to a physician for treatment) and unnaturally caused death sometimes fails to generate ascriptions of culpability (e.g., shooting a home invader who is trying to kill your child). Causing a certain death is sometimes regarded as non-culpable conduct (e.g., shooting a person who is threatening you with a gun). Causing an uncertain death is sometimes regarded as culpable conduct (shooting someone in the abdomen such that it is possible but not certain that he will die). Intending to end life (on both senses of intention) is not always culpable (e.g., shooting a person in self-defence). Ending life unintentionally is sometimes culpable (e.g., manslaughter). Violating bodily integrity is sometimes non-culpable (e.g., shooting in self-defence or war). Not violating bodily integrity is sometimes culpable (e.g., a lifeguard not saving a drowning swimmer or a parent not taking his child with pneumonia to a doctor). Clearly, these distinctions are not used on their own in the law to distinguish between culpable and non-culpable conduct. Something more is needed.

Inconsistencies across Categories of Assisted Death

Freedom

~AV The concern most frequently expressed with respect to freedom and assisted death is that individuals may not always be acting voluntarily when they make requests for assisted death. Some argue that many individuals will see themselves as a burden on their loved ones or on society in general and they may feel pressured into choosing an earlier death Others may be vulnerable to financial or other sorts of pressures that virtually coerce them into consenting to assisted death. Such circumstances, some conclude, suggest that these requests for assisted death are not fully free.

AV At least three sorts of limits on freedom can be identified. First, pressure to seek assisted death might come from within the individual because that individual has internalized societal attitudes against being a burden on others. Second, explicit external pressures might come from others telling the individual not to be a burden. Third, implicit external pressures might come from society having made assisted death available; individuals might feel compelled to seek out assisted death because society has made it available.

Although concerns about voluntariness in the context of assisted death are legitimate, they are not being raised consistently. . . . It is indeed true that some competent individuals may see themselves as a burden on their loved ones or society and refuse potentially life-sustaining treatment. However, that has not led to calls for prohibiting respect for requests to withhold treatment. Assisted suicide and voluntary euthanasia should not be treated differently.

The freedom argument applies as much to individuals consenting to the withholding or withdrawal of life-sustaining treatment as it does to assisted suicide and voluntary euthanasia. As long as it does not block accepting the former, it cannot block accepting the latter.

. . . I accept that freedom is a matter for serious concern in the context of assisted death. Indeed, an assessment of the voluntariness of a decision is a central feature of my alternative approach. . . . However, I am saying that concerns about freedom cannot serve as the basis to keep assisted suicide and voluntary euthanasia illegal in a regime that permits the withholding and withdrawal of potentially life-sustaining treatment. Voluntariness is a matter for serious concern but it is a matter for concern across all of the categories of assisted death. It cannot ground a distinction between the categories.

. . .

Inequality

~AV In 1994, the New York State Task Force on Life and the Law expressed concern about the dangers of a permissive regime for the most vulnerable in society: "It must be recognized that assisted suicide and euthanasia will be practised through the prism of social inequality and prejudice that characterizes the delivery of services in all segments of society, including health care. Those who will be most vulnerable to abuse, error or indifference are the poor, minorities, and those who are least educated and least empowered."[6]

. . .

. . . AV [C]oncerns about implications for the vulnerable of a permissive regime with respect to assisted suicide and voluntary euthanasia must be taken seriously. However, again, they apply as much to the withholding and withdrawal of potentially life-sustaining treatment as to assisted suicide and voluntary euthanasia.

. . .

Concerns about the vulnerable must be taken into account when building protections into the permissive regime to regulate all forms of assisted death. However, the concerns do not provide grounds for distinguishing between categories of assisted death and permitting some while prohibiting others.

Invalid Arguments

Sanctity of Life

~AV Sanctity of life arguments can be divided into two categories: religious and secular. . . . The secular arguments tend to be based on deontological arguments positing a rule: Do not kill. This rule can be derived from a moral theory such as that of Immanuel Kant.[7] The secular arguments are also frequently grounded in the following argument: the principle that "killing is wrong" is widely recognized as a foundational principle in our society; euthanasia and assisted suicide violate this principle; therefore they ought not to be permitted.

. . .

AV With respect to the [argument] . . . that "killing is wrong" is a foundational principle in our society the following responses can be made. First, . . . "killing is wrong" is not an absolute principle in our society For example, self-defence is an **absolute defence** to a charge of murder. Killing is permitted (indeed ordered) by the state in times of war. Suicide is legal. Therefore, it will take more than a simple recitation of the principle "killing is wrong" to ground a prohibition of assisted suicide and voluntary euthanasia.

A further response to the secular sanctity of life argument is available. One consequence of [the previous arguments] is that it is impossible to construct a definition of "killing" such that:

- Withdrawal of potentially life-sustaining treatment is not killing while euthanasia and assisted suicide are killing, and
- Killing is morally wrong.

In other words, a definition of "killing" with moral plausibility does not map onto the desired distinction. Therefore, the principle "killing is wrong" does not effectively distinguish between the withdrawal of potentially life-sustaining treatment, on the one hand, and euthanasia and assisted suicide, on the other.

. . .

Lack of Necessity

~AV Two related arguments should be considered under the heading "lack of necessity": first, the argument that the decriminalization of assisted suicide and voluntary euthanasia would not be necessary if adequate pain control were made available to everyone; and second, the argument that the decriminalization of assisted suicide and voluntary euthanasia would not be necessary if adequate palliative care were made available to everyone.

AV These related arguments are grounded in false premises. First, they assume that people seek assisted suicide or euthanasia because of uncontrolled pain or lack of access to palliative care. However, a close review of the empirical data on the factors that lead to requests for assisted suicide and euthanasia reveals that uncontrolled pain or lack of access to palliative care is not the only, or even the most common, reason people seek assisted suicide or euthanasia. Access to adequate pain control and palliative care will reduce—but not eliminate—the number of requests for assisted suicide or euthanasia.

. . .

[Second], not all physical pain can be controlled. Some of the leading physicians in Canada testified before the Senate Committee on Euthanasia and Assisted Suicide that, even with the best palliative care, some physical pain cannot be controlled.[8] Assisted suicide and voluntary euthanasia will not be rendered completely unnecessary by making pain control and palliative care more widely available.

[Third], the alleviation of physical pain is not necessarily congruent with the alleviation of suffering. For example, individuals whose physical pain is controlled by morphine may suffer from incessant vomiting and other forms of serious physical discomfort. Consider the following example from palliative care physician Marcel Boisvert: "Shortness of breath is the best example [of suffering that is not physical pain]. In the palliative care field it is very often the paradigm of a difficult death—running after and catching each breath, forty, fifty times per minute. We can administer drugs that will relieve this. We can very often relieve one hundred per cent of the pain, but rarely can we relieve one hundred per cent of severe shortness of breath except by severe sedation."[9]

Individuals may also suffer from mental anguish such as grief and fear. Such non-physical suffering cannot always be controlled by pain control or palliative care. Thus, proper pain control and palliative care will reduce—but not eliminate—the number of requests for euthanasia and assisted suicide.

. . .

[Fourth], the argument could just as easily be applied to the withholding and withdrawal of potentially life-sustaining treatment as to assisted suicide and euthanasia. If adequate pain control and palliative care were made available to all, refusals of treatment would drop. Therefore, until pain control and palliative care are available to all, refusals of treatment should not be respected. However, so long as this argument is not used to restrict respect for refusals of treatment, it cannot be used to restrict access to assisted suicide and euthanasia.

Before leaving this discussion of palliative care, I should note that nothing I have said goes against vigorous expansion of access to better pain control and symptom management for all Canadians. Indeed, such expansion is critical for appropriate care of patients as it increases the options available to patients and thereby contributes to respect for autonomy and dignity Nonetheless, palliative care and other forms of pain control and symptom management must remain options to be chosen or rejected by patients. The availability or unavailability of these options must not be used to deny the selection of other options, such as assisted death.

Slippery Slope Arguments

~AV The slippery slope argument is commonly expressed in the following terms. If society allows assisted suicide and voluntary euthanasia, then there will be a slide towards the bottom of a slippery slope and many clearly unacceptable practices will become prevalent. For example, it is feared that we will soon find ourselves unable to prevent involuntary euthanasia of the elderly, the disabled, and other vulnerable individuals. Once it is accepted that one particular life is not worth living and can be deliberately terminated, then there will be no good (or persuasive) reason to claim that the lives of the disabled, the elderly, and other vulnerable people are worth living. To prevent such an undesirable result, all lives must be valued and assisted suicide and voluntary euthanasia must not be permitted.

AV There are two forms of slippery slopes: logical and empirical. In the interest of analytical clarity, I examine each type independently.

The Logical Slippery Slope

AV The logical slippery slope argument takes the following form: if we allow assisted suicide and voluntary euthanasia, we will not be able to draw any logical distinction between acceptable and unacceptable killings, and, hence, we will slide towards the bottom of the slope (i.e., towards allowing involuntary euthanasia and thus the killing of demented, mentally handicapped, and indigent persons as well as any other group deemed "unfit" for continued existence).

However, if a logically sustainable distinction can be drawn between the evaluation of life at the top of the slope and the evaluation of life at the bottom of the slope, then we have sufficient materials to erect a barrier on the slope. . . . So long as we retain a firm criterion of free and informed consent, the logical slide to involuntary assisted death will not be a problem.

The Empirical Slippery Slope

The empirical slippery slope argument is not so easily addressed. ~AV The argument here is that "once certain practices are accepted, people shall in fact go on to accept other practices as well. This is simply a claim about what people will do, and not a claim about what they are logically committed to."[10] Clearly, this version of the slippery slope argument is more difficult for advocates of assisted suicide and voluntary euthanasia.

AV Obviously, we have no direct empirical data on whether people in Canada would in fact over the next five, ten, or twenty years move from accepting assisted suicide and voluntary euthanasia to accepting involuntary euthanasia. Indeed, it is doubtful that any study could be designed to gather that data without tracking practice in a trial period of regulated but decriminalized assisted suicide and voluntary euthanasia. In the absence of such specific data, many turn to history and to other countries in search of evidence as to whether slippage would in fact follow decriminalization. . . .

. . .

The Comparative International Slippery Slope

~AV The slippery slope argument is also grounded in the assumption that the incidence of non-voluntary euthanasia is higher in [the countries where it is permitted] than in those countries where it is illegal. . . . AV [T]here are now data to suggest that the assumption is false. The authors of a recent Australian study summarized their results as follows: ". . . In thirty per cent of all Australian deaths, a medical end-of-life decision was made with the explicit intention of ending the patient's life, of which four per cent were in response to a direct request from the patient. Overall, Australia had a higher rate of intentional ending of life without the patient's request than the Netherlands."[11]

The authors concluded that "Australian law has not prevented doctors from practising euthanasia or making medical end-of-life decisions explicitly intended to hasten the patient's death without the patient's request."[12] J. Griffiths et al. also provide the following as support for their dismissal of the comparative international slippery slope argument: "Recent research in the United States gives rates of assistance with suicide roughly comparable to the Dutch figure for euthanasia. . . . "Physician-negotiated death" is estimated at about seventy per cent of all deaths in the United States. . . ."[13] These facts cast even more doubt on the use of [the jurisdictions that allow assisted suicide] in the empirical slippery slope argument against decriminalization of assisted death.

Finally, . . . that there is evidence of societies decriminalizing assisted suicide and/or voluntary euthanasia and not sliding down the slippery slope to involuntary euthanasia.

Indeed, examples point in the opposite direction. . . . Assisted suicide has not been illegal in Switzerland for many years without a slide.[14] Oregon decriminalized assisted suicide in 1997 and has not witnessed any precipitous slide down the slippery slope.[15] The comparative international empirical data are thus, for the proponents of the slippery slope argument, at best mixed and, at worst, counter to their argument.

The Current Canadian Location on the Slope

. . .

. . . (AV) [A]ssisted suicide and euthanasia are already occurring in North America. For obvious reasons, it is difficult to gain accurate and complete data on the incidence of assisted suicide and euthanasia; they are illegal acts and health care providers are likely to under-report criminal activity. Nonetheless, studies provide some indication of the incidence of assisted suicide and euthanasia. Russel Ogden, a criminologist, testified before the Senate Committee: "I discovered that here in British Columbia, euthanasia in the AIDS population occurs both with and without the assistance of physicians. Between 1980 and 1993, I learned of thirty-four cases of assisted suicide and euthanasia amongst the AIDS population. I also learned of other deaths outside of the AIDS population, but did not include those in my data. I have learned of many more deaths amongst patients with ALS, cancer, and AIDS since the publication of these findings."[16]

In a study of Manitoba physicians released in 1995, seventy-two per cent of those who responded to the survey said that they believe that euthanasia is performed by some physicians and fifteen per cent said that they had participated in an assisted suicide or euthanasia.[17]. . .

Studies in the United States yield similar results. A "National Survey of Physician-Assisted Suicide and Euthanasia in the United States" was published in the *New England Journal of Medicine* in April 1998. The authors concluded that "a substantial proportion of physicians in the United States in the specialties surveyed report that they receive requests for physician-assisted suicide and euthanasia, and about six per cent have complied with such requests at least once."[18]

Clearly, assisted suicide and euthanasia are occurring in North America. How often, why, and under what conditions they are occurring remains unclear.

Slippery Slope Risks/Harms of the Status Quo

(~AV) While there may be harms associated with decriminalizing assisted suicide and voluntary euthanasia (e.g., potential for slippage down the slope), (AV) there are also harms associated with maintaining the status quo. Arn Shilder of the British Columbia Persons with AIDS Society described the *status quo* as follows:

> What is the status quo? From my vantage point, the status quo is my friends dying from botched back-street euthanasias. Heroin from Hastings Street for lethal injections and plastic bags for suffocation are the order of the day. Guns and razor blades have also been used by those who do not have access to drugs . . .
>
> The status quo regarding euthanasia in Canada is about people being denied a sense of control over decisions regarding their final days. It is about people who care for each other being forced to lie and disregard the rule of the law.[19]

If we retain the *status quo*, we may see individuals refuse clearly life-sustaining treatment in order to ensure that they never end up in a situation in which they wish to die but are unable to commit suicide and have no access to an assisted suicide or voluntary euthanasia. We may see individuals attempt to commit suicide without the assistance of trained professionals, fail, and end up suffering even more. We may see an erosion of the criminal justice response to assisted death. Juries might refuse to convict because of the mandatory minimum life sentence attached to murder even if they disapprove of the accused person's conduct. Others may take this refusal to convict as decreasing the risk of penalty for non-voluntary euthanasia and we may see an increase in euthanasia of the vulnerable. As appears to be happening in Australia, we may see an incidence of non-voluntary euthanasia (and non-voluntary withholding and withdrawal of potentially life-sustaining treatment) that is greater than that in [places that allow assisted suicide]. There are clearly real slippery slope risks to the vulnerable in the status quo.

. . .

Consistency

AV The consistency argument . . . can be made again here. If slippage from voluntary euthanasia to non-voluntary or involuntary euthanasia is possible, then slippage is also possible down the slope from voluntary to non-voluntary and involuntary withholding and withdrawal of potentially life-sustaining treatment. So long as the danger of the slippery slope does not preclude these latter sorts of assisted death practices, it cannot preclude assisted suicide and voluntary euthanasia.

The empirical slippery slope is a matter for serious concern. However, the solution to the concern must be the same for assisted suicide and voluntary euthanasia as for the withholding and withdrawal of potentially life-sustaining treatment. The solution is not to prohibit any particular form(s) of assisted death but rather to be vigilant with respect to the satisfaction of the necessary conditions for permissible assisted death.

Notes

1. James Rachels, "Euthanasia, Killing, and Letting Die," in J. Ladd, ed., *Ethical Issues Relating to Life and Death* (New York: Oxford University Press, 1979) p. 154.
2. Rachels, p. 153.
3. *Airedale NHS Trust v. Bland*, [1993] Appeal Cases 789 at 887 per Lord Mustill.
4. Yale Kamisar, "Euthanasia Legislation: Some Nonreligious Objections," in T. Beauchamp and S. Perlin, eds., *Ethical Issues in Death and Dying* (New York: Oxford University Press, 1978) p. 220.
5. P. Foot, "The Problem of Abortion and the Doctrine of Double Effect," in B. Steinbock and A. Norcross, eds., *Killing and Letting Die*, 2nd ed. (New York: Fordham University Press, 1994) p. 266.
6. The New York State Task Force on Life and the Law, *When Death Is Sought: Assisted Suicide and Euthanasia in the Medical Context* 102 (1994).
7. I. Kant, *Foundations of the Metaphysics of Morals*, L.W. Beck, translator (Indianapolis: Bobbs-Merrill Educational Publishing, 1980).
8. See testimony before the Senate Special Committee on Euthanasia and Assisted Suicide of Brian Mishara, Elizabeth Latimer, and Balfour Mount. *Senate Special Committee*, No. 2 (20 April 1994) at 26, No. 4 (4 May 1994) at 16, and No. 5 (11 May 1994) at 30, respectively. See also N. MacDonald et al., "A Quebec Survey of Issues in Cancer Pain Management" *Journal of Pain and Symptom Management* 23(1) (2002): 39.

9. *Senate Special Committee*, No. 6 (18 May 1994) at 35.
10. J. Rachels, [no title given], in S. Spicker and T. Engelhardt, eds., *Philosophical Medical Ethics: Its Nature and Significance* (Boston: Reidel, 1977) p. 65.
11. H. Kuhse, P. Singer, P. Baume, M. Clark, and M. Rickard, "End-of-Life Decisions in Australian Medical Practice" *Medical Journal of Australia* 166 (1997): 191.
12. Kuhse et al., p. 191.
13. J. Griffiths, A. Bood, and H. Weyers, *Euthanasia and Law in the Netherlands* (Amsterdam: Amsterdam University Press, 1998), p. 127.
14. G. Bosshard et al., "Open Regulation and Practice in Assisted Dying: How Switzerland Compares with the Netherlands and Oregon" (2002) 132 *Swiss Medical Weekly* 527.
15. "Oregon's Death with Dignity Act: Three Years of Legalized Physician-Assisted Suicide," Portland, OR: Oregon Health Division, 22 Feb. 2001.
16. Special Senate Committee on Euthanasia and Assisted Suicide, *Of Life and Death: Report of the Special Senate Committee on Euthanasia and Assisted Suicide* (June 1995) p. 54.
17. N. Searles, "Silence Doesn't Obliterate the Truth: A Manitoba Survey on Physician Assisted Suicide and Euthanasia" (1996) 4 *Health L. Rev.* 9.
18. D.E. Meier, C.-A. Emmons, S. Wallenstein, T. Quill, R.S. Morrison, and C. Cassel, "A National Survey of Physician-Assisted Suicide and Euthanasia in the United States" *New England Journal of Medicine* 228 (1998): 1193–201.
19. *Senate Special Committee*, No. 16 (28 Sept. 1994), p. 24.

Discussion Questions

1. How, according to the majority opinion in *Rodriguez*, does the law against aiding suicide uphold the sanctity of life? Do you agree with them? Why or why not?
2. What reasons do Justices L'Heureux-Dubé and McLachlin give for arguing that the law against aiding suicide violated Sue Rodriguez's section 7 right to security of the person? Do you agree with them? Why or why not?
3. Frazee distinguishes between autonomy and sovereignty. What does she mean by "autonomy"? What does she mean by "sovereignty"? Do you agree with her distinction? Why or why not?
4. Frazee writes, "The direct and immediate harm . . . occasioned by the availability of suicide assistance is perhaps not that too many people with disabilities will choose to die, but that too many of those who do make this choice will do so because of injustice, rather than autonomy." Why does she say this? Do you agree with her? Why or why not?
5. What is Downie's criticism of the distinction between acts and omissions? What are its implications for her discussion of assisted suicide and voluntary euthanasia? Do you agree with her? Why or why not?
6. How, if at all, does Downie's argument that there is no relevant difference between causing death and "letting nature take its course" differ from Justice Cory's view in *Rodriguez* that there is no relevant difference between refusing treatment and aiding suicide? Do you think one has better arguments? If so, which one and why?

Suggested Readings and Websites

♣ = Canadian source or author

♣ Council of Canadians with Disabilities. "Tracy Latimer, the Victim; Robert Latimer, the Murderer." www.ccdonline.ca/en/humanrights/endoflife/latimer/victim-murderer. [An analysis of the Tracy Latimer case from a disability rights perspective.]

♣ Council of Canadians with Disabilities. "We Are Not Dead Yet." www.ccdonline.ca/en/humanrights/endoflife/euthanasia/Canadians-with-disabilities-we-are-not-dead-yet. [A disability rights argument against assisted suicide.]

♣ Dying with Dignity. www.dyingwithdignity.ca/. [Supports advance planning and assisted suicide.]

♣ Euthanasia Prevention Coalition. www.epcc.ca/. [Opposes euthanasia and assisted suicide.]

Gill, Carol J. "No, We Don't Think Our Doctors Are out to Get Us: Responding to the Straw Man Distortions of Disability Rights Arguments Against Assisted Suicide." *Disability and Health Journal* 3 (2010): 31–8. [A disability rights activist responds to criticisms.]

Johnson, Harriet McBryde. "Unspeakable Conversations." *New York Times Magazine* (16 February 2003), www.nytimes.com/2003/02/16/magazine/unspeakable-conversations.html?pagewanted=all&src=pm. [An American lawyer and disability rights activist discusses her encounters with philosopher Peter Singer, who defends abortion and infanticide in cases of disability.]

♣ Schuklenk, Udo, Johannes J,M, van Delden, Jocelyn Downie, Sheila McLean, Ross Upshur, and Daniel Weinstock. *End-of-Life Decision Making*. Report of the Royal Society of Canada Expert Panel. Royal Society of Canada, November 2011. [Examines the range of end-of-life decisions, from palliative care to assisted suicide; supports patient autonomy and choice.]

♣ Somerville, Margaret. *Death Talk: The Case Against Euthanasia and Physician-Assisted Suicide*. Montreal: McGill–Queen's University Press, 2001. [A philosopher opposed to euthanasia and assisted suicide presents arguments based on sanctity of life.]

♣ Sumner, L.W. *Assisted Death: A Study in Ethics and Law*. Oxford and New York: Oxford University Press, 2011. [Argues in favour of voluntary euthanasia and assisted suicide.]

Suggested Readings and Websites

[illegible]

Part IV
Living in a Global World

Introduction

What kind of global citizens are we? What kind do we want to be? Do we have obligations to people in other countries? Do we have obligations to those in poor countries? Or do our obligations end at our borders? These are the sorts of questions that Part IV will address.

The average person today knows more about other countries than people have known at any previous time in history. We watch television shows, movies, and videos about people in other countries. We listen to music from other countries, follow fads that began in South Korea or Australia, browse small-town supermarkets for food that was available only in ethnic stores in big cities ten years ago, and get up-to-the-minute news about international conflicts or live scores from the World Cup on our smartphones. We hear about wars, famines, and natural disasters almost as soon as they occur, and relief efforts can be quickly coordinated to send aid where it is most needed.

But globalization has its downside too. Greenhouse gases caused by the oil sands in Alberta and coal-fired plants in Ontario contribute to climate change in Indonesia, Mauritania, and the Arctic. Overfishing is causing fish stocks to dwindle and collapse, not only on our east and west coasts but around the world. We can decide a product is hazardous and ban it, but the manufacturer can continue to sell it to other countries with fewer regulations, harming people and the environment elsewhere. Many Canadian corporations decided it was cheaper to pay people in poor countries to manufacture products or provide services for the Canadian market—including, ironically, souvenirs of Canada. With improved communication, skirmishes can become all-out wars in hours. Genocides can be planned and executed. Anyone can go on the Internet and learn to make a bomb. Add in 24-hour news stations, and mass murderers and terrorists have a ready-made audience for their acts.

Canadians are proud of their contribution to World Wars I and II and to peacekeeping (though the torture and murder of Somali teenager Shidane Arone in 1993 did a great deal of damage to our international reputation[1]). How involved in the United Nations do we want to be? How involved in peacekeeping? Traditionally, we have been a big supporter of the UN, as are many middle-sized rich nations. We also used to be one of the biggest contributors to peacekeeping missions, but that has not been true for some time. Since the 1990s, the Canadian Forces have concentrated on NATO-led initiatives, such as the bombing of Serbian troops in Kosovo in 1999[2] and the invasion of Afghanistan in 2001 following the 9/11 bombings. How should we decide which conflicts to participate in and which to avoid? And what should our role be after a war has ended? Here again, Canadians have had tremendous influence. Former Supreme Court Justice Louise Arbour was the chief prosecutor for the International Criminal Tribunals for Rwanda and the former Yugoslavia from 1996 to 1999.[3] Canada actively supported the creation of the International Criminal Court, and the court's first president was Philippe Kirsch, a Canadian diplomat. Is our pride justified? Should we be doing more? If so, where?

Since 9/11, fear of terrorism has gripped many Canadians. It frightens us even when others tell us that far more people have died from the flu than in terrorist attacks. In this way, it is like many people's fear of flying: it is useless to tell them that many more people die in car accidents than in plane crashes, not just in raw numbers but also per miles travelled. The difference is that, from the perspective of a citizen or passenger, both terrorism and plane crashes are beyond our control; there is virtually nothing we can do to prevent them. This is not true of the flu or car accidents. Furthermore, our chances of walking away unscathed from the flu or a car accident are reasonably good, but our chances even of surviving a terrorist attack or a plane crash are poor. So what should Canada's role be in preventing terrorism? How should citizens respond to the threat of terrorism? How vigilant should we—or must we—be? How should we balance **civil liberties** against public safety? The courts have answered some of these questions, but ultimately they must be answered by citizens.

In 1987, almost everyone who had heard of climate change was a climate scientist. In 1988 two UN organizations set up the Intergovernmental Panel on Climate Change. When the IPCC submitted its first assessment report in 1990, climate change came onto the public agenda. There has been much sound and fury about climate change in the intervening years. But with each successive report, the evidence mounts that the global climate is changing owing to human activity. The real question concerns what we should do: reduce greenhouse gas production? (Who? How much?) Look for alternative sources of energy that do not produce greenhouse gases? (Still pretty far in the future.) Look for ways to dispose of greenhouse gases? (Not always feasible.) Try technological fixes such as spraying particles in the atmosphere to block the sun? (Pretty risky.) Something else? Not doing anything is not an option—or rather, it is, but it is probably the worst one.

What kind of global citizens should we be? The chapters in Part IV should help you decide what you think.

Notes

1. The Canadian Airborne Regiment was sent to Somalia in December 1992 to assist in peacekeeping and famine relief. In March 1993, Shidane Arone, a sixteen-year-old Somali, was apprehended in the toilet stall of an abandoned US base. He was brutally tortured for forty-eight hours, and died from the resulting injuries. Four people were subsequently convicted of various criminal charges, and the Canadian Airborne Regiment was disbanded.
2. The Kosovo War was a civil war in the former Yugoslavia fought between the Yugoslav (Serbian) government and Albanian separatist forces. Armed conflict began in February 1996, with Canada and NATO becoming directly involved in 1998, supporting the Albanian separatists both politically and militarily. The war ended with Serbian forces pulling out of Kosovo in June 1999, after eleven weeks of strategic bombings by NATO.
3. The Rwandan Genocide was the mass murder of approximately 800,000 people that occurred in 1994. Similarly, human rights violations were reported in the Bosnian wars as well as the Kosovo war that occurred in the former Yugoslavia, including the killing of civilians, rape, torture, and ethnic cleansing. In her capacity as Chief Prosecutor, Louise Arbour prosecuted several people involved in both conflicts for their involvement in human rights violations.

Chapter 10

War, Peacekeeping, and Transitional Justice

War is sustained, widespread armed conflict between two or more **states**, or between a state and a sub-state group wishing to take over or break away from the larger state. The fifty-year civil war in Colombia is an example of a state and a sub-state group vying for power within a state. The American Civil War was an example of a sub-state group that fought to break away from the larger state.

Philosophical Evaluations of War

War is a terrible thing, but many people think at least some wars have been justified. Most people think stopping Hitler justified World War II. Most people today think humanitarian reasons justify some wars, for example if a government wages war on its own people. The most commonly cited example of justified humanitarian intervention is India's support of the Mukti Bahini (liberation army) in East Pakistan in 1971, which led to East Pakistan **seceding** from Pakistan and becoming Bangladesh.

What conditions, if any, justify war? Philosophers give three main answers: **Political realists** argue that a country may do whatever it considers necessary to protect itself and its **interests. Just war theorists** argue that just wars must meet certain conditions. **Pacifists** argue that war is never, or almost never, justified.

Political Realism

Political realists describe countries as rational, self-interested actors that seek to further their own security and survival. They say only **anarchy** and the continual threat of war guide countries' behaviour internationally. Ethics has no place in the international arena because morality applies only when it can be enforced. However, no international body with the power to enforce morality does or can exist. The United Nations and other international organizations have no teeth, political realists believe; no country can or should rely on them. In such a world, war is inevitable. This does not mean political realists favour war, though. They say a country should wage war only if doing so advances its interests better than the alternatives. Many times, perhaps most of the time, war will harm rather than promote a country's interests, so most of the time it should not wage war. But if war will advance its interests better than the alternatives, and if the country is likely to win, then it ought to go to war. During the war, the country should do whatever is necessary to win. Probably it should not commit war crimes—or if it does, it should not get caught. These "shoulds" are purely **pragmatic**, though; political realism is an **amoral** view. Most of its proponents are political scientists and politicians. Very few philosophers support it.

Just War Theory

Just war theorists believe ethics does apply on the international scene, and that some but not all wars are morally justified. Just war theory has three parts. *Jus ad bellum* conditions address reasons for resorting to war, *jus in bello* conditions address how to fight wars, and *jus post bellum* conditions concern how to end wars and restore peace.

Jus ad bellum conditions specify when going to war is permitted. The most important condition is a just cause—a country must have a very good reason for resorting to war. "Good reasons" include defending itself from attack and defending another country from attack, especially if the other country is an ally. A country also must go to war for the right reasons; it must fight because of the just cause. It cannot, for example, claim it is fighting to save an oppressed people from a brutal dictator when in fact it only wants access to the other country's resources, land, industries, etc. A country contemplating war must pursue all peaceful alternatives before it can declare war. It must declare war publicly, according to its proper authorities. (This rules out undeclared or so-called "dirty" wars.) And finally, the war must be proportional: waging the war must be likely to create more overall good than evil to both the war-fighting country and the innocent civilians of the other country. (Thomas Hurka addresses proportionality in this chapter.)

Jus in bello conditions specify how to fight a just war. A country may not use weapons prohibited by international treaties, such as chemical and biological weapons. It may not use tactics that are "evil in themselves," such as mass rape, genocide, or making prisoners fight against their own countries. Its force must be proportionate: it may use no more force than is necessary to achieve its goals. This rules out nuclear weapons and other weapons of mass destruction; they are so destructive that almost nothing can justify them. The war-fighting country may target soldiers, military bases, and strategic war-promoting industries on the other side, but it may not deliberately target civilians.[1] A country must treat prisoners of war decently; it may not torture, starve, or work them to death. And finally, even if one side breaks these rules, the other side must still fight fairly. According to just war theorists, even in war two wrongs do not make a right.

A just war must fulfill every item in both sets of conditions, those for going to war as well as fighting in war. Clearly, many wars, possibly even most wars, have not met these criteria. But some wars have. Most people today think stopping Hitler met the just war conditions for going to war, although probably the Allies did not satisfy all the conditions for fighting the war. According to most just war theorists, India's intervention in the war that created Bangladesh met both sets of conditions.

Jus post bellum, or the conditions of ending a war justly, has been discussed much less by political theorists and philosophers, so there are no principles that all theorists accept.

However, the idea is that wars must be ended in ways that make lasting peace more likely. Many historians believe the punitive conditions put on Germany after World War I created widespread resentment among the German people that contributed to Hitler's rise and World War II. In contrast, the conditions imposed on Germany and Japan after World War II aimed to turn them into allies rather than resentful conquered people, and have resulted in peace and stability. (Brian Orend discusses *jus post bellum* in this chapter.)

Pacifism

Pacifists reject war because they reject killing. The argument is simple: killing is wrong; war involves killing; therefore war is wrong. Pacifists come in many kinds. Absolute pacifists reject all forms of killing and violence—war, harsh punishment, and the death penalty, perhaps factory farming and meat-eating, perhaps abortion, and perhaps even self-defence. Most absolute pacifists criticize war on **deontological** (principle-based) grounds. They say it treats people as **means rather than ends** or it violates their **rights** to life. Contingent pacifists reject the mass violence and killing of wars, but not necessarily killing in self-defence. Here the argument is: almost all killing is wrong; war kills people wrongly; therefore almost all war is wrong. Contingent pacifists might, under very restrictive circumstances, support a just war. Albert Einstein and the philosopher Bertrand Russell both considered themselves pacifists, but they thought fighting Nazi aggression in World War II was both justified and necessary. Some pacifists believe that, since killing is wrong for everyone, everyone should be a pacifist. Others believe pacifism's demands go beyond the requirements of ordinary morality, and so while pacifism is good, everyone does not have to be a pacifist. And some pacifists go beyond opposing war and aim to create positive peace—societies that promote the well-being and rights of everyone, where war is only a historical memory.[2]

Peacekeeping

According to the United Nations, peacekeepers provide security and the political and peacebuilding support to help countries make the difficult, early transition from conflict to peace. UN peacekeeping is guided by three basic principles:

- consent of the parties;
- impartiality; and
- non-use of force except in self-defence and defence of the mandate.[3]

"Consent of the parties" means that UN peacekeeping operations enter a country or region only when all parties to the conflict agree to their presence. "Impartiality" means UN peacekeeping forces do not take sides in conflicts. "Non-use of force except in self-defence and defence of the mandate" means UN peacekeepers use the minimum force necessary to promote and restore peace.

Modern peacekeeping arose during the Suez Crisis in 1956. Egypt (backed by other Arab countries) nationalized the Suez Canal, and Israel (backed by Britain and France) threatened to go to war to keep the Canal international. The possibility of a third world war loomed. Lester Pearson, Canada's Minister for External Affairs, proposed a UN-backed multinational military force in the Suez to maintain the ceasefire agreement between Israel and Egypt. This was the first UN mission in which UN peacekeepers possessed the force to maintain ceasefires and peace. Previous UN peacekeeping missions had involved a few unarmed or lightly armed observers and advisors, not troops. Pearson got the Nobel Peace Prize in 1957 for developing the idea of a UN-led international military force that maintains and restores peace in conflict-ridden zones, for convincing the UN to authorize peacekeeping forces, and for showing the world "that moral force can be a bulwark against aggression and that it is possible to make aggressive forces yield without resorting to power."[4]

Canada's military forces did not fight in a war for nearly fifty years, from the end of the Korean War in 1953 until the war in Afghanistan in 2001, but they participated in many peacekeeping missions. Many Canadians proudly considered themselves "a nation of peacekeepers." But two nearly opposite events rocked our self-image in the 1990s: first, the torture-murder of sixteen-year-old Shidane Arone by several members of the Canadian Airborne Regiment in Somalia in 1993, and second, the utter failure of the UN Security Council, France, the US, and the world community to aid the tiny UN peacekeeping force in Rwanda and prevent genocide in 1994. (See the readings by Dallaire in this chapter.) Today, our presence in UN peacekeeping missions has dwindled; in the last twenty years, Canadian Forces have supported NATO more than the UN.

UN peacekeepers' image has been tarnished by other problems as well. Some peacekeepers have been accused of rape, sexual exploitation and abuse, gun smuggling and trading, extortion, theft, and murder. "[P]eacekeeping operations unfortunately seem to be doing the same thing that other militaries do. Even the guardians have to be guarded," said Gita Saghal, head of Amnesty International's Gender Unit.[5]

Many commentators have argued that peacekeeping requires soldiers to do work that conflicts with their training. Soldiers are trained as warriors who fight, shoot to kill, take prisoners, and perhaps end wars, but not keep peace. Police officers receive training and learn skills more appropriate to peacekeeping, but they usually operate in places where basic security and the **rule of law** can be taken for granted, not where they are pipe dreams. Some peacekeepers wish they had more training in cultural sensitivity, local history and practices, and practical ethics, so they could improve situations rather than unwittingly fan the flames of smoldering resentments. In 2000 the United Nations commissioned an international panel to review its peacekeeping operations, in an attempt to correct some of the mistakes that had led to disasters in Somalia, Rwanda, and elsewhere. As a result, peacekeepers now receive cultural and gender sensitivity training.

War and Crimes against Women

Women generally suffer more than men during war. They are not only killed but raped, gang-raped, and prostituted. In World War II Japan forced approximately 200,000 women, mostly from China and Korea, to provide sexual services to its soldiers. More than three-quarters of them died. In the former Yugoslavia over 50,000 women, most of them Muslim, were raped, mostly by Serbs. Many Muslim and Croatian women were kept in "rape camps," where Serbian men deliberately impregnated them and forced them to give birth to Serbian children. (Children in these cultures take their fathers' ethnicities.) In the Rwanda genocide, between 250,000 and 500,000 women were raped. Almost every woman who was killed was raped first, and most of the female survivors were raped or sexually violated.[6] When war ends, frequently raped women's own communities often reject them as "tainted," as if their rapes were their own faults.

Until the nineteenth century, rape was considered one of the benefits of war to soldiers. Gradually, through various international treaties, rape began to be viewed as a war crime. The Nuremberg and Tokyo Tribunals after World War II made prosecution of rape during war possible but not actual. Feminists in the 1960s and 1970s made rape a political issue. They began to argue that violence against women was a human rights violation, and that rape in war is a war crime. It was first prosecuted as a war crime in the International Criminal Tribunal for Yugoslavia. (See the reading by Louise Arbour in this chapter.)

Transitional Justice

What happens when wars end? Usually victors impose treaties on the vanquished, often involving reparations for the vanquished's aggression. But the horrors of the Nazi death camps during World War II changed that. For the first time, the victors put the vanquished on trial for war crimes, crimes against humanity, in the Nuremberg and Tokyo Tribunals. Some legal scholars and philosophers of law challenged the legitimacy of such tribunals, mostly on two grounds. First, they argued that the tribunals had no **jurisdiction**. The military officers and government officials on trial had not broken the laws of their own countries, and there was no international legal system under which they could be tried. Second, the Nuremberg and Tokyo Tribunals imposed laws retroactively, but almost every legal system forbids retroactive laws. Most people consider it wrong to punish people for acts that were not crimes when they committed them. However, the prosecutors argued that the Nazi atrocities and crimes against humanity were so abominable that anyone would know they were wrong. The Nuremberg and Tokyo Tribunals paved the ground for the International Criminal Tribunals for Yugoslavia and Rwanda, which in turn paved the way for the creation of the International Criminal Court in 2002.

Some people argue that war crimes trials may not be the best way to move on after an extended conflict. Rather than **retributive justice**, based on punishment, they favour truth commissions or other forms of **restorative justice**. Several countries have established truth commissions as an alternative to public trials. The most famous was the South African Truth and Reconciliation Commission, set up in 1995 after the fall of **apartheid**. Supporters of truth commissions say that war crimes trials focus on wrongdoers. Because of the adversarial nature of trials, the defence challenges victims' credibility, further victimizing them. Truth commissions, on the other hand, focus on victims and give them a forum for telling their stories in a non-adversarial setting. They also aim to rebuild the relationship between victims and their abusers so they can live together in peace.

The Readings

The first two readings are by the most prominent Canadian philosophers writing about war. Thomas Hurka discusses the concepts of proportionality and necessity in just war theory. Proportionality appears in two places in the theory: first, as a requirement that the anticipated benefits of going to war be proportionate to the costs both to the country contemplating war and to the innocent civilians on the other side, and second, that the harm of any particular military act, including to non-combatants on the other side, be proportionate to its benefits. The necessity condition forbids unnecessary harm, such as deliberately targeting non-combatants. Hurka says these three conditions require assessing consequences, which makes them partly **consequentialist**, but the benefits and burdens are balanced in a deontological way.

Brian Orend discusses a relatively new part of just war theory, *jus post bellum* or justice after war. In addition to ending the aggression and taking back any unjust gains from the aggressor, the victor should ensure that victims of the war receive compensation, set up war crimes trials, and rehabilitate the aggressor politically. Compensation should not bankrupt the aggressor because "to beggar thy neighbor is to pick future fights." War crimes trials should punish top-level aggressors on the other side, and they should also punish soldiers and officers on both sides who committed or permitted war crimes. Punishing only the aggressor's war crimes applies a double standard and undercuts the moral authority of the victor. Rehabilitation should aim to turn the aggressor into a peaceful neighbour or even an ally.

The last three readings are by Canada's most prominent practitioners of peacekeeping and justice after war today. In the third and fourth readings, former Lieutenant General Roméo Dallaire reflects on the genocide in Rwanda. He discusses his attempts to alert the international community of the growing danger of genocide, to get more troops, the Western powers' refusal to allow casualties among their own soldiers, and the failed "responsibility to protect." He says soldiers need additional skills in the modern world, especially in peacekeeping, intellectual skills "built on the ability to proactively function in ambiguity." And he asks his audiences why Western countries were so willing to commit troops to the former Yugoslavia but not to Rwanda.

The final reading is by Louise Arbour, Chief Prosecutor for the International Criminal Tribunals for Yugoslavia and Rwanda, former Supreme Court justice, former UN High Commissioner for Human Rights, and current president and CEO of the International Crisis Group. Arbour discusses the creation of the International Criminal Tribunals, their groundbreaking prosecutions of rape as war crimes, their tactical discussions of who to prosecute and how, ending with the creation of the International Criminal Court.

The Moral and Political Preferences Indicator

All political realists are conservative, but all conservatives are not political realists; political realists tend to cluster at the most conservative end of the liberal spectrum. Most Canadians who know anything about the philosophy of war subscribe to some version of just war theory rather than political realism or pacifism. As a result, just war theorists span the political spectrum. Conservatives tend to have more permissive definitions of what counts as a just war, while egalitarians tend to interpret the criteria more strictly. Pacifists range from egalitarians to egalitarian centrists, with a smattering of conservative centrists whose views are grounded in their religious faith. Many egalitarian and egalitarian centrist pacifists ground their views in religion as well.

There is little political disagreement about the value of peacekeeping, though much disagreement on whether peacekeeping or traditional war-fighting is appropriate in a particular context. Unsurprisingly, conservatives tend to favour war more often and egalitarians tend to favour peacekeeping or other non-aggressive solutions. The New Democrats were the only political party to oppose Canadian participation in the war in Afghanistan. The Bloc Québécois initially supported the war, but they opposed extending its original mandate.

On transitional justice, conservatives tend to favour conservative interpretations of war crimes and war crimes trials over truth commissions. While initially they opposed extending war crimes to include rape, today most conservatives consider rape a war crime. Egalitarians tended to support rape's inclusion as a war crime much earlier, especially of course the feminists who pushed for it in the first place. Egalitarians are also more likely to support truth commissions and restorative justice than conservatives.

Notes

1. While all contemporary international conventions concerning war contain this condition, almost every war fought in the last century has caused more civilian than military deaths, often many times more.
2. This section owes much to Andrew Fiala, "Pacifism," *Stanford Encyclopedia of Philosophy* (2010), http://plato.stanford.edu/entries/pacifism/.
3. United Nations Peacekeeping, "What Is Peacekeeping?," www.un.org/en/peacekeeping/operations/peacekeeping.shtml.
4. Gunnar Jahn, Presentation Speech awarding Lester Pearson the Nobel Peace Prize, www.nobelprize.org/nobel_prizes/peace/laureates/1957/press.html.
5. Michael J Jordan, "Sex charges haunt UN forces," *Christian Science Monitor*, 26 November 2004, www.csmonitor.com/2004/1126/p06s02-wogi.html.
6. Anne-Marie LM de Brouwer, *Supranational Criminal Prosecution of Sexual Violence* (Cambridge, UK and Hove, Belgium: Intersentia, 2005), pp. 4–11.

Thomas Hurka

Proportionality and Necessity

AV = author's view; ~AV = not the author's view

Consequence Conditions

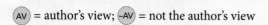

Just war theory, the traditional theory of the morality of war, is not a **consequentialist** theory, since it does not say a war or act in war is permissible whenever it has the best consequences. On the contrary, its *jus ad bellum* component, which concerns the morality of resorting to war, says a war with the best overall outcome can be wrong if it lacks a just cause, that is, will not produce a good of one of the few types, such as resisting aggression or preventing genocide, that alone can justify war. It can likewise forbid a war that is not declared by a competent authority or fought with a right intention. Similarly, the theory's *jus in bello* component, which concerns the morality of waging war, contains a discrimination condition that can forbid military tactics with the best outcome if they target civilians rather than only soldiers. In all these ways the theory is **deontological** rather than consequentialist.

But just war theory does not ignore the consequences of war and would not be credible if it did: a morally crucial fact about war is that it causes death and destruction. The theory therefore contains several conditions that forbid choices concerning war if their consequences are in some way unacceptable. The *jus ad bellum* insists that a war must have a *reasonable hope of success* in achieving its just cause and other relevant benefits; if it does not, its destructiveness is to no purpose and the war is wrong. A further, *proportionality* condition says that even if a war does achieve relevant benefits, it is wrong if the destruction it causes is excessive, or out of proportion to, those benefits. And a *last resort* condition forbids war if its benefits, though significant, could have been achieved by less destructive means such as diplomacy. The *jus in bello* contains conditions parallel to these last two. An *in bello proportionality* condition says an act in war is wrong if the harm it causes, especially to civilians, is out of proportion to its military benefits, while a *necessity* condition forbids acts that cause unnecessary harm, because the same benefits could have been achieved by less harmful means.

These *consequence conditions*, as I will call them, have been central to recent moral debates about particular wars. Before the 1991 Gulf War,[1] some critics said it would be disproportionate because it would result in a wider Middle East conflagration. Many objected that the Iraq War of 2003[2] was not a last resort because any weapons of mass destruction Saddam Hussein had could just as well be eliminated by UN inspections. And a common critique of Israel's anti-terrorist operations in the Palestinian territories[3] is that they have caused disproportionate harm to Palestinian civilians.

~AV Just war theory could interpret these conditions in a consequentialist way, so that, for example, a war is proportionate if the total of all its benefits, of whatever type and however caused, is even slightly greater than its total harms, and a last resort if its net benefits minus harms are even slightly better than any alternative's. And indeed some of the theory's proponents have interpreted it this way. Then the theory, while not as a whole consequentialist, because it contains just cause, discrimination, and other non-consequentialist conditions, mimics **consequentialism** in how it assesses a war's results.

AV But this interpretation is neither most intuitive nor truest to how the conditions have usually been understood. A more attractive reading departs from consequentialism, first, by distinguishing among types of benefit and harm, saying only some are relevant to the assessment of a war or act in war while others are not. Second, it distinguishes among causal processes, saying benefits and harms with one kind of causal history can count toward the assessment of a war or act while the same benefits or harms with another history cannot. Finally, it does not always weigh benefits and harms equally but gives more weight to harms an act directly causes than to any benefits it produces. In all three respects the resulting theory assesses consequences in a deontological way.

. . .

. . . Imagine that a war to remove a brutal dictator will cause 10,000 deaths among his country's civilians, but that if he remained in power he would kill 100,000 civilians. The relevant fact about the war is not that it will kill 10,000; it is that it will result in a net saving of 90,000. But what is the baseline situation with which this comparison is made?

~AV The simplest view is that the baseline is whatever a nation would have done had it not fought the war or, better, if the just cause for the war had not arisen. AV But this view is problematic at at least two points. Imagine that a nation is contemplating a war that has a trivial just cause and will be immensely destructive, but that if it does not fight this war it will fight another even more destructive war with no just cause. The fact that the second war will have an even worse result surely cannot make the first war proportionate, and to exclude this implication we must consider only alternatives that do not involve the nation's doing something morally wrong. Now imagine that two nations are contemplating the same war, with the same just cause and same level of destruction. If the first nation does not fight the war, it will spend the money the war would cost on welfare programs that will significantly benefit its poor. If the second does not fight, it will spend the money on tax breaks for the rich, which while not strictly forbidden will be much less beneficial. If the proportionality assessment considers just what a nation would otherwise do, the first nation's war will be less likely to be proportionate. That seems wrong: why should a nation's doing more good in its activities outside war make its resorting to war less permissible? To avoid this implication, we should compare the net effect of war with that of the least beneficial alternative that is morally permitted: then the two nations in our example will have their option of war compared with the same baseline, which is now not purely factual but at two points moralized.

Relevant Benefits

Given this baseline, the first step in assessing the proportionality and then the necessity of a war or act in war is identifying its relevant benefits. Consequentialism counts benefits of all types, but just war theory seems not to, holding that some types of good are as types irrelevant. . . .

Which types of benefit are relevant, then? They clearly include those in a war's just causes. If the war will prevent aggression or major rights-violations by a government, the goods thereby achieved count uncontroversially against the harm the war will cause. ~AV And some very restrictive versions of just war theory say they are the only goods that count. In determining whether a war is proportionate and a last resort, we weigh the harm it will cause against only those benefits involved in its initial just causes.

AV But most versions of the theory are less restrictive, because they recognize what have been called "conditional" just causes. Unlike "independent" just causes such as resisting aggression, merely conditional ones cannot on their own supply a just cause; if one has only conditional just causes, one is not permitted to fight. But once some other, independent just cause is present, conditional causes become legitimate goals of war and can contribute to its justification, in particular by helping to make it proportionate and a last resort. Three main such causes have been recognized: forcibly disarming an aggressor, deterring future aggression, and preventing humanitarian wrongs that, though serious, do not mount to the level of an independent just cause.

On most versions of just war theory, the mere fact that a nation has weapons it may or even is likely to use aggressively at some time in the future is no justification for war against it now; ***pace*** [with all due respect to] the Bush Doctrine,[4] merely preventive war is wrong. But once a nation has committed aggression, forcibly disarming it to prevent it from doing so again becomes on most views a legitimate goal of war and can even justify continuing the war after its initial goals have been achieved. . . .

A similar point applies to deterrence. The mere fact that war against a nation will deter future aggressors cannot justify war, but once there is another, independent just cause, deterrence becomes a relevant benefit of war and can play a vital role in its justification. . . .

The final type of conditional just cause is illustrated by the 2001 Afghanistan War.[5] While the Taliban government's oppression of the Afghan people, and especially of Afghan women, was serious, I think most would deny that it constituted an independent just cause; a war fought only to liberate Afghan women would have been wrong. But once the Taliban provided an independent just cause by harbouring terrorists, the fact that war against them would end their oppression became for many an additional relevant benefit that counted toward its proportionality.

A less restrictive view, then, counts as relevant benefits the goods in both a war's independent and its conditional just causes. What weighs against the war's destructiveness is not just its initial justifying goal but also its potential to prevent future wars by disarming and deterring would-be aggressors and to correct lesser humanitarian wrongs. And there may be further relevant benefits. Imagine that in 1990 Saddam Hussein conquered Saudi Arabia as well as Kuwait and used the resulting control of their oil supplies to drive up the world oil price, causing significant harm to the world economy. I think many will say that preventing that economic harm would then have been a relevant benefit, making the case for war against Saddam stronger than if his aggression had not affected the oil price. But how can that be if preventing an economic recession is not a relevant benefit? How can economic goods count in the one case but not the other? The answer may lie in how the goods are produced.

When war lifts an economy out of recession, the benefit results from a means to the war's just cause: in order to reverse an aggression, say, we invest money in military production, and the resulting increase in industrial activity boosts our economy. But in the Saddam example the benefit results from the achievement of the war's just cause itself: it is the ending of Saddam's occupations of Kuwait and Saudi Arabia that prevents the increase in the world oil price. So it may be that economic goods count when they are causally downstream from a war's just cause, but not when they result only from a means to that cause. . . .

. . . Not all goods allow this treatment, however. If a nation's citizens get pleasure from its military victory, that seems irrelevant to the war's justification even if the pleasure results from the nation's achieving a just cause. But if it holds for even some goods, the just war conditions depart even further from consequentialism: not only do they exclude some types of good as types, they count others only when they result from one causal process rather than another.

The restrictions on relevant goods we have identified also bear on the last resort condition. Any time a nation fights a war, it could have spent the money the war cost in some other way, which could have had better consequences. For example, rather than fight the Gulf War the United States could have spent the billions of dollars it cost on development aid to Africa, which might well have produced greater benefits. For consequentialism this makes the war morally wrong, but it does not do so for just war theory. The reason is that the benefits of development aid, no matter how great, are of the wrong type to be relevant to assessing the Gulf War. They are not involved in the war's just causes, either independent or conditional, nor are they causally downstream from those causes, and they therefore cannot make development aid a morally mandatory alternative to war. For last resort purposes, the relevant alternatives to a war are only alternative ways of achieving the war's benefits, not policies that produce benefits of some totally different type.

These issues about relevant benefits also bear on the *in bello* proportionality condition. . . . [I]f an act in war is justified it surely can only be because it contributes to the war's relevant benefits, which means those in the war's independent and conditional just causes, and perhaps others causally downstream from them. But then any other benefits are irrelevant to *in bello* proportionality: an otherwise disproportionate tactic cannot become proportionate because it will please soldiers or have economic benefits, for example by testing a technology with civilian applications. Just as these benefits cannot count in assessing a war as a whole, so they cannot count in assessing acts within it.

It also follows that what counts as a proportionate tactic varies with the magnitude of a war's benefits, and in particular with the moral significance of its just causes. A level of harm to civilians that would be permissible in war against a genocidal enemy such as Nazi Germany would not be permissible in the Falklands[6] or Kosovo War[7]. . . .

Relevant Harms

Having identified relevant benefits, the next task in assessing proportionality or necessity is to identify relevant harms. Here again some types may be excluded as types. For example, if an aggressor nation's citizens will be saddened by its defeat, that does not count at all against a war to reverse its aggression. But there seem to be many fewer such exclusions than in the case of benefits. If a war will cause pain to soldiers who do not want to fight, prevent the creation of great art, or harm the world's economy, these evils seem all to count fully against the war's benefits, and to do so whether they result from the war's just cause or not. While many types of benefit are irrelevant to the justification of war, most types of harm are relevant.

The more important exclusions of harms concern their causal histories, and in particular the role of other agents' choices in those histories. Consider first the deaths of enemy soldiers. The *jus in bello* seems to give these deaths very little weight. Its necessity condition forbids killing enemy soldiers wantonly or to no purpose, and this is not a trivial restriction. It can, for example, justify the ban on explosive bullets: once a soldier has been hit by gunfire he is effectively disabled, making any further harm to him unnecessary. But if killing an enemy soldier will produce even a small benefit, it seems to be permitted. . . .

This discounting of soldiers' deaths again distinguishes just war theory from consequentialism, which ignores the causal histories of harms. It is also connected to the discrimination condition in the *jus in bello*, which permits soldiers on each side to target enemy soldiers but not civilians. Different justifications have been proposed for this permission, but the one I find most plausible is most clearly available given volunteer militaries on the two sides. Then we can say that by voluntarily entering military service, soldiers on each side freely took on the status of soldiers and thereby freely accepted that they may permissibly be killed in the course of war. More specifically, by volunteering they gave up their right not to be killed by particular people in particular circumstances, namely enemy soldiers in a declared war, and so made their killing in those circumstances not unjust. Their situation is like that of boxers who, in agreeing to a bout, permit each other to do in the ring what would be forbidden as assault outside it. This explains not only why targeting them in war is not wrong, but also why their deaths count less in assessing a war or act for proportionality or necessity: by making their deaths not unjust they themselves gave them less weight. . . .

This justification applies most clearly when soldiers are full volunteers, but often they are not. They may be conscripts, or have enlisted only because of lies told to them by their government or because they had no acceptable career alternatives. Are their deaths still discounted, or discounted as much? ~AV A hardline view says they are. Even though not fully voluntary, their enlistment was voluntary to some degree: the conscripts could have fled the country or gone to jail. And its being voluntary to that degree is sufficient to give them the same **moral status** as full volunteers. They are likewise legitimate targets during war, and their deaths likewise have minimal weight against our soldiers' deaths. AV But a softline view adjusts soldiers' **moral standing** by the degree of voluntariness of their enlistment. If they are conscripts they may be legitimate targets while actively fighting, but not when sleeping in barracks far behind the front lines, and their deaths have more weight against the benefits of war than the deaths of full volunteers. . . .

On the view just described, the moral weight of soldiers' deaths is diminished by choices they made in the past, and the same can be true of non-soldiers. Imagine that some enemy civilians install themselves as voluntary shields around a military target, hoping to deter attacks on it. Their deaths still have some moral weight. If we can attack either this target or another of equal military value that lacks shields, we should attack the one without shields. But if the civilians placed themselves near the target, that surely discounts their deaths to some extent, so attacking it may be proportionate where it would not be if their proximity were not their choice. Or imagine that if we win a war with a just cause some terrorists on the other side will launch suicide attacks on our civilians. Setting aside the civilians' deaths for a moment, can it count against the war's proportionality that it will result in the suicide bombers' deaths? The answer is surely no, and the obvious explanation is that by themselves choosing their deaths the bombers took the responsibility for them on themselves and removed it from us.

In all these cases harm to a person is discounted because of his own wrongful choices, but can it also be discounted because of others' choices? Imagine that, losing on the battlefield, enemy troops retreat into a city where our pursuing them will inevitably cause civilian deaths. In assessing that pursuit for *in bello* proportionality, do we count the resulting civilian deaths fully against our act or can we discount them partly as the enemy's responsibility for bringing the civilians into the line of fire? International law seems to say we cannot. It forbids using civilians as involuntary shields, which the enemy troops in effect are doing. But it also says that one side's violating its legal obligations does not release the other side from its obligations, which suggests that our proportionality assessment should remain unchanged. . . .

. . .

Weighing Benefits Against Harms

Having identified relevant benefits and harms, just war theory must weigh the two against each other. ~AV Consequentialism does so by giving them equal moral weight, so an act can be right even though its benefits are only slightly greater than its harms. AV But deontological moralities are much more restrictive. If they do not contain **absolute** prohibitions against acts of direct harming such as killing the innocent, they allow these acts only in extreme cases, where their benefits are not just somewhat but vastly greater. Thus they allow killing an innocent person not to save just two other innocents, as consequentialism would, but only to save a hundred or a thousand, and in so doing they weigh harms much more heavily than benefits. As an instance of **deontology**, just war theory follows this line, but in two different ways at two different points.

When deontological views forbid acts of direct harming, they understand the directness at issue using either or both of two distinctions. The first says it is morally worse to cause harm by what one actively does than merely to allow harm to happen by not acting to prevent it; thus it is worse to kill than merely to allow to die. The second says it is worse to cause harm intending it as one's end or as a means to one's end than to do so merely foreseeing that the harm will result; thus aiming at harm is worse. These two distinctions are independent of each other. One can actively cause harm while not intending but only foreseeing it, and one can allow a harm because one wants it as an end or means, for example, allow someone to die because one wants to inherit her wealth.

Of these two distinctions, the second, between intending and merely foreseeing harm, is the more important in just war theory. When the discrimination condition forbids targeting civilians, it on most readings forbids acts that intend serious harm to civilians as an end or a means, while not in the same way forbidding acts that merely foresee civilian harm, as when bombing a legitimate military target unavoidably kills civilians living nearby. . . .

The theory gives rather less weight to the other distinction, between doing and allowing, since it often allows active doings that cause significant harm to civilians. But it still seems to make some use of this distinction, and to count the harms a doing causes somewhat more than its benefits. This is, however, not always easy to see.

Consider a trade-off between different civilian lives, as when a war to prevent our civilians from being killed in terrorist attacks will inevitably kill some civilians in an enemy country; this was the case in the Afghanistan War. ~AV The simplest versions of consequentialism weigh all lives equally and will forbid this war if it takes just one more life than it saves. AV But most adherents of just war theory start from a different position. They say a nation is permitted and even required to weigh its own citizens' interests more heavily than non-citizens'. When deciding trade, immigration, and other policies, it should look primarily to the effects on its own people. Does this view transfer to the case of war, so there too a nation may care more about its own citizens' good? I think it does, but only in a significantly weakened form. Whereas a nation may be permitted to save its own citizens from a natural disaster rather than save up to *n* times as many foreign citizens, it may not be permitted to save its citizens from terrorism if that will involve its killing *n* times as many foreigners. Even if some national preference is allowed in the second case, the degree allowed is less. But then the doing/allowing distinction is doing some work, making harms that result from a doing count more against its benefits than they would if the harms were merely allowed.

. . .

. . . Consider the commonly accepted just cause of resisting aggression. An aggressor may, if successful, kill or imprison citizens of the victim nation; if so, preventing those wrongs is one justification for military self-defence. But sometimes the aggressor has no such aim. If not resisted, it will merely absorb the victim nation's territory and replace its government, with no further rights-violations to follow. In this case all that is threatened is the political self-determination of the nation's citizens. How much harm is permitted to protect that?

~AV Some philosophers argue that none is, and that war against merely political aggression is always disproportionate and wrong: though political rights are important, they are not nearly as important as the right to life and may not be protected by taking life. This is a radical argument, and would make many widely accepted wars wrong. AV But there are several responses to it. First, by threatening to kill the victim nation's citizens if they resist, the aggressor brings their right to life into play and so increases the level of force they may use in self-defence. Second, a defensive war will kill mostly soldiers, and if they freely entered military service that greatly reduces the weight their deaths have in a proportionality assessment. Third, even if the war will kill some of the aggressor's civilians, it will presumably do so without intent, which again reduces those deaths' weights. And even if one person's right of political self-determination does not count much against a death, aggression threatens millions of people's self-determination, and their rights added together may justify substantially more resistance. Finally, aggression threatens not just a political right, but the right to remain secure in a cultural and political home, one to which citizens normally feel deeply attached. In the morality of self-defence an attack inside one's home has special moral status, raising the level of defensive force one may use; and international aggression too invades a home.

These responses show, I think, that war against merely political aggression can be morally permitted, but they do not give a precise algorithm for determining when that is so. More generally, proportionality and necessity judgments can never be made with complete precision. There are, first, daunting empirical demands on these judgments. To know in advance whether a proposed war or tactic will be proportional or necessary, we need to know what consequences it will have, which before the fact we can only estimate roughly. Even after the fact, when its consequences are known, we have to compare them with various hypothetical scenarios: with the baseline situation of acting as we could otherwise permissibly have done, for the proportionality conditions, and with the results of relevant alternatives, for the necessity conditions. As merely hypothetical, these scenarios can again only be roughly estimated. And beyond these empirical challenges is the moral challenge of comparing different types of value. To reach a decisive conclusion about proportionality or necessity we must know how to weigh our soldiers' lives against those of enemy civilians, political self-determination against the lives of soldiers, economic costs against deterrence, and much more. These weightings are very difficult, and different people may make them differently, leading to different moral assessments of particular wars or actions even given an agreed-on set of facts.

. . .

Conclusion

As it must to be credible, just war theory evaluates wars and acts in war partly in light of their consequences. It does not do so, however, in a consequentialist fashion. It does not include all consequences in its assessments, holding that some types of harm and especially benefit are irrelevant as types, so they cannot count morally for or against a war or military tactic. Nor does it include consequences regardless of how they came about. It may deem certain benefits relevant if they result in one way from a war but not if they result in another, and may discount harms if their causal history includes certain choices, for example by soldiers to enter military service or by an enemy to bring civilians into the line of fire. Nor, finally, does it weigh benefits and harms equally. If certain harms will result from what we actively do, then even if we do not intend them they count more heavily against our act than if we merely allowed them to happen. The resulting morality of war is sometimes more restrictive than consequentialism, for example when acts that will save our soldiers will kill enemy civilians. And it is sometimes more permissive, as when the same acts will kill only enemy soldiers. But it takes a distinctively deontological approach to assessing the consequences of war, as befits its overall character as a version of deontology.

Notes

1. The (Persian) Gulf War was a UN-**sanctioned** war led by the United States in response to Iraq's invasion and occupation of Kuwait. In August 1990 Iraqi troops invaded Kuwait. The invasion was the result of both a dispute over rights to petroleum deposits and President Hussein's desire for a commercial seaport (Iraq is almost entirely landlocked, whereas Kuwait is banked on one side by the Persian Gulf). A coalition of thirty-four UN nation members began attacks on Iraq in January 1991, with a ceasefire and peace settlements commencing in February 1991. The political independence of Kuwait was reinstated, and by March 1991 over 500,000 UN coalition troops, the vast majority of which were American, began to move out of the Persian Gulf. Saddam Hussein remained President of Iraq. [Editor]
2. The Iraq war was an invasion led by the United States beginning March 2003 and ending December 2011. Prior to the invasion, both the US and United Kingdom claimed that Iraq possessed weapons of mass destruction (WMDs), in spite of 2002 UN weapon inspectors concluding that Iraq possessed no WMDs. The US also claimed that the Iraqi government was harbouring and supporting al Qaeda terrorists. In December 2003, Saddam Hussein was captured, and on December 2006, he was executed by hanging. US troops remained in Iraq to assist with the political stabilization of the region. No evidence for either WMDs or al Qaeda support was ever substantiated. [Editor]
3. A number of criticisms from the international community have been lodged against Israeli anti-terrorist policies and practices, particularly in their dealings with the Palestinian people, notably accusations of **human rights** violations such as unlawful assassination, inhumane imprisonment, torture, the destruction of civilian property, and **illiberal** restrictions on economic and political freedoms. [Editor]
4. The "Bush Doctrine" is a term used to describe the unofficial principles apparently underlying the foreign policy decisions of former US President George W Bush. These include **unilateral** decision making (minimal consultation with other nations, including allies), attacking countries alleged to harbour terrorists, preventive attacks, and forced **democratic regime** changes. [Editor]
5. The Afghanistan War began in October 2001 and continues to this day, conducted by NATO allies and led by the US. Following the September 2001 attacks on US soil, the US identified the terrorist group al Qaeda as the perpetrators of the attacks. At that time, al Qaeda was based in Afghanistan and allied

with the Taliban, the government of Afghanistan. Although al Qaeda leader Osama bin Laden did not assume responsibility for the attacks until 2004, US military operations against Afghanistan began in October 2001. Osama bin Laden was killed by US Special Forces in Pakistan in May 2011. As of 2013, an exit strategy has been endorsed by the NATO countries involved, which proposes to withdraw most of the 130,000 NATO troops from Afghanistan by the end of December 2014. [Editor]

6. The Falklands War was a conflict between Argentina and the United Kingdom, resulting from disputes over the **sovereignty** of the Falkland, South Georgia, and South Sandwich Islands. The War began in April 1982 when Argentine forces invaded the Falkland and South Georgia Islands. Conflict ended in June 1982, with the Argentine surrender and return of the islands to British rule. [Editor]
7. The Kosovo War was a civil war in the former Yugoslavia fought between the Yugoslav government and Albanian separatist forces. Armed conflict began in February 1996, with the US and NATO becoming directly involved in 1998, supporting the Albanian separatists both politically and militarily. The war ended in June 1999 with the pull-out of Yugoslav armed forces, the occupation of Kosovo by NATO forces, and the return of over 800,000 Albanian refugees to the region. Kosovo remains politically administered by the UN to this day. [Editor]

Brian Orend

Justice after War

Sadly, there are few restraints on the endings of wars. There has never been an international treaty to regulate war's final phase, and there are sharp disagreements regarding the nature of a just peace treaty. There are, by contrast, restraints aplenty on starting wars, and on conduct during war. These restraints include: political pressure from allies and enemies; the logistics of raising and deploying force; the United Nations, its Charter and Security Council;[1] and international laws like the Hague and Geneva Conventions.[2] Indeed, in just war theory—which frames moral principles to regulate wartime actions—there is a robust set of rules for resorting to war (*jus ad bellum*) and for conduct during war (*jus in bello*) but not for the termination phase of war. Recent events in Afghanistan, and the "war against terrorism," vividly underline the relevance of reflecting on this omission, and the complex issues related to it.

The international community should remedy this glaring gap in our ongoing struggle to restrain warfare. The following facts bear this out:

- Recent armed conflicts—in the Persian Gulf,[3] Bosnia,[4] Rwanda,[5] and Kosovo[6]—demonstrate the difficulty, and illustrate the importance, of ending wars in a full and fair fashion. We know that when wars are wrapped up badly, they sow the seeds for future bloodshed.
- To allow unconstrained war termination is to allow the winner to enjoy the spoils of war. This is dangerously permissive, as winners have been known to exact peace terms that are draconian and vengeful. The Treaty of Versailles,[7] terminating World War I, is often mentioned in this connection.
- Failure to regulate war termination may prolong fighting on the ground. Since they have few assurances regarding the nature of the settlement,

belligerents will be sorely tempted to keep using force to jockey for position. Many observers felt that this reality plagued the Bosnian civil war, which saw many failed negotiations and a three-year "slow burn" of continuous violence as the very negotiations took place.

- Allowing war termination to be determined without **normative** restraints leads to inconsistency and confusion. First, how can we try to regulate the first two phases of war—the beginning and middle—yet not the end? Second, the lack of established **norms** to guide the construction of peace treaties leads to patchwork "solutions," mere **ad hoc** arrangements that may not meet well-considered standards of prudence and justice.

Peace treaties should still, of course, remain tightly tailored to the historical realities of the particular conflict in question. But admitting this is not to concede that the search for general guidelines, or universal standards, is futile or naïve. There is no inconsistency, or mystery, in holding particular actors in complex local conflicts up to more general, even universal standards of conduct. Judges and juries do that daily, evaluating the factual complexities of a given case in light of general principles. We should do the same regarding war termination.

This article will consider what participants should do as they move to wrap up a war. It will do so while drawing on the resources contained within the just war tradition, particularly its reworking offered by Michael Walzer.[8] Since just war theory has played a constructive role thus far in its influence on political and legal discourse concerning launching and carrying out war, there is reason to believe it has light to shed on war termination. My goal is to construct a general set of plausible principles to guide communities seeking to resolve their armed conflicts fairly.

The Ends of a Just War

The first step is to answer the question: What may a participant rightly aim for with regard to a just war? What are the goals to be achieved by the settlement of the conflict? We need some starting assumptions to focus our thoughts on these issues. . . .

. . . [A] just and lawful war is defined by just war theorists as one that was begun for the right reasons, and that has been fought appropriately. The resort to war was just (*jus ad bellum*), and only the right methods were used during the war (*jus in bello*). A war begun for the right reasons is a war fought in response to aggression, defined by Walzer as "any use of force or imminent threat of force by one state against the political **sovereignty** or territorial integrity of another" (62). Such state **rights** are themselves founded, ultimately, upon individual **human rights** to life and liberty. The most obvious example of an act of international aggression would be an armed invasion by one state bent on taking over another, much as Iraq did to Kuwait in August 1990. But this requirement of just cause, in terms of resisting aggression, is not the only rule just war theorists insist on prior to beginning war. They also **stipulate** that the war in question be launched as a last resort, be publicly declared by a proper authority, have some probability of success, be animated by the right intention of resisting aggression, and also be expected to produce at least a proportionality of benefits to costs. These general norms have worked their way into various pieces of international law.

A war begun justly must also be fought appropriately. For just war theorists, this means that a state's armed forces obey at least three rules of right conduct: they must discriminate between combatant (military) and non-combatant (civilian) targets and direct their armed force only at the former; they may attack legitimate military targets only with proportionate force; and they are not to employ methods which, in Walzer's words, "shock the moral conscience of mankind." Examples of such heinous methods include the deployment of weapons of mass destruction, and the use of mass rape campaigns as instruments of war. These principles of *jus in bello*, alongside those of *jus ad bellum*, offer a coherent set of plausible values to draw on while developing an account of just war settlement.

It is often contended that the just goal of a just war is the proverbial *status quo ante bellum* [the situation before the war]: the victorious regime ought simply to reestablish the state of affairs that obtained before the war broke out. Restore the equilibrium disturbed by the aggressor, traditionalists advise. As Walzer points out, however, this assertion makes little sense: one ought not to aim for the literal restoration of the *status quo ante bellum* because that situation was precisely what led to war in the first place. Also, given the sheer destructiveness of war, any such literal restoration is **empirically** impossible. War simply changes too much. So the just goal of a just war, once won, must be a more secure and more just state of affairs than existed prior to the war. This condition Walzer refers to as one of "restoration plus" (xx, 119). What might such a condition be?

The general answer is a more secure possession of our rights, both individual and collective. The aim of a just and lawful war is the resistance of aggression and the vindication of the fundamental rights of political communities, ultimately on behalf of the human rights of their individual citizens. The overall aim is, in Walzer's words, "to reaffirm our own deepest values" with regard to justice, both domestic and international. It is not implausible to [say] that, in our era, no deeper, or more basic, political values exist than those human rights that justify a reasonable set of social **institutions** and ultimately enable a satisfying political existence.

From this general principle, that the proper aim of a just war is the vindication of those rights whose violation grounded the resort to war in the first place, more detailed commentary needs to be offered. For what does such "vindication" of rights amount to: what does it include; what does it permit; and what does it forbid? The last aspect of the question seems the easiest to answer, at least in abstract terms: The principle of rights vindication forbids the continuation of the war after the relevant rights have, in fact, been vindicated. To go beyond that limit would itself become aggression: men and women would die for no just cause. This bedrock limit to the justified continuance of a just war seems required in order to prevent the war from spilling over into something like a crusade, which demands the utter destruction of the demonized enemy. The very essence of justice of, in, and after war is about there being firm limits, and constraints, upon its aims and conduct. Unconstrained fighting, with its fearful prospect of degenerating into barbarity, is the worst-case scenario—regardless of the values for which the war is being fought.

. . .

What does the just aim of a just war—namely, rights vindication, constrained by a proportionate policy on surrender—precisely include or mandate? The following seems to be a plausible list of propositions regarding what would be at least permissible with regard to a just settlement of a just war:

- The aggression needs, where possible and proportional, to be rolled back, which is to say that the unjust gains from aggression must be eliminated. If, to take a simple example, the aggression has involved invading and taking over a country, then justice requires that the invader be driven out of the country and secure borders reestablished. The equally crucial **corollary** to this principle is that the victim of the aggression is to be reestablished as an independent political community, enjoying political sovereignty and territorial integrity.
- The commission of aggression, as a serious international crime, requires punishment in two forms: compensation to the victim for at least some of the costs incurred during the fight for its rights; and war crimes trials for the initiators of aggression. I will later argue that these are not the only war crimes trials required by justice in war's aftermath.
- The aggressor state might also require some demilitarization and political rehabilitation, depending on the nature and severity of the aggression it committed and the threat it would continue to pose in the absence of such measures. "One can," Walzer avers, "legitimately aim not merely at a successful resistance but also at some reasonable security against future attack" (118). The question of forcible, forward-looking rehabilitation is one of the most controversial and interesting surrounding the justice of settlements.

. . .

Sufficient comment has already been offered on what the first proposition requires and why: aggression, as a crime that justifies war, needs to be rolled back and have its gains eliminated as far as is possible and proportional; and the victim of aggression needs to have the objects of its rights restored. This principle seems quite straightforward, one of justice as rectification. But what about compensation, "political rehabilitation," and war crimes trials?

Compensation and Discrimination

Since aggression is a crime that violates important rights and causes much damage, it is reasonable to contend that, in a classical context of interstate war, the aggressor nation, "Aggressor," owes some duty of compensation to the victim of the aggression, "Victim." This is the case because, in the absence of aggression, Victim would not have to reconstruct itself following the war, nor would it have had to fight for its rights in the first place, with all the death and destruction that implies. Walzer says that the deepest nature of the wrong an aggressor commits is to make people fight for their rights, that is, make them resort to violence to secure those things to which they have an elemental entitlement, and which they should enjoy as a matter of course. To put the issue bluntly, Aggressor has cost Victim a considerable amount, and so at least some restitution is due. The critical questions are how much compensation, and by whom in Aggressor is the compensation to be paid out?

The "how much" question, clearly, will be relative to the nature and severity of the act of aggression itself, alongside considerations of what Aggressor can reasonably be expected to pay. Care needs to be taken not to bankrupt Aggressor's resources, if only for the reason that the civilians of Aggressor still, as always, retain their claims to human rights fulfillment, and the objects of such rights require that resources be devoted to them.

There needs, in short, to be an application of the principle of proportionality here. The compensation required may not be draconian in nature. We have some indication, from the financial terms imposed on Germany at the Treaty of Versailles, that to beggar thy neighbour is to pick future fights.

. . .

Rehabilitation

The notion under this heading is that, in the postwar environment, Aggressor may be required to demilitarize, at least to the extent that it will not pose a serious threat to Victim—and other members of the international community—for the foreseeable future. The appropriate elements of such demilitarization will clearly vary with the nature and severity of the act of aggression, along with the extent of Aggressor's residual military capabilities following its defeat. But they may, and often do, involve: the creation of a demilitarized "buffer zone" between Aggressor and Victim (and any Vindicator), whether it be on land, sea or air; the capping of certain aspects of Aggressor's military capability; and especially the destruction of Aggressor's weapons of mass destruction. Once more, proportionality must be brought to bear upon this general principle: The regime in Aggressor may not be so demilitarized as to jeopardize its ability to fulfill its function of maintaining law and order within its own borders, and of protecting its people from other countries who might be tempted to invade if they perceive serious weakness in Aggressor. Another way this requirement could be met would be for the victors to provide reliable security guarantees to the people of Aggressor.

The imposition of some substantial requirement of political rehabilitation seems the most serious and invasive measure permitted a just regime, following its justified victory over Aggressor. As Walzer asserts, the "outer limit" of any surrender by Aggressor to Victim, and any Vindicator, is the construction and maintenance of a new kind of domestic political regime within Aggressor, one more peaceable, orderly, and pro-human rights in nature. It is probably correct to agree with him, however, when he cautions that, as a matter of proportionality, such measures are in order only in the most extreme cases, such as Nazi Germany at the close of World War II (113, 119, 267–68).

If the actions of Aggressor during the war were truly atrocious, or if the nature of the regime in Aggressor at the end of the war is still so heinous that its continued existence poses a serious threat to international justice and human rights, then—and only then—may such a regime be forcibly dismantled and a new, more defensible regime established in its stead. But we should be quick to note, and emphasize, that such construction necessitates an additional commitment on the part of Victim and any Vindicators to assist the new regime in Aggressor with this enormous task of political restructuring. This assistance would be composed of seeing such "political therapy" through to a reasonably successful conclusion—which is to say, until the new regime can stand on its own, as it were, and fulfill its core functions of providing domestic law and order, human rights fulfillment, and adherence to the basic norms of international law, notably those banning aggression. The rehabilitations of the governing structures of both West Germany and Japan following World War II, largely by the United States, seem quite stellar and instructive examples in this regard. They also illustrate the profound and costly commitments that must be borne by any Victim or Vindicator seeking to impose such far-reaching and consequential terms on the relevant Aggressor following defeat.

. . .

. . . I suggest that there should be a presumption in favour of permitting rehabilitative measures in the domestic political structure of a defeated aggressor. But such rehabilitation does need to be proportional to the degree of depravity inherent in the political structure itself. This way, complete dismantling and **constitutional** reconstruction—like the sea change from totalitarian fascism to **liberal democracy**—will probably be reserved for exceptional cases. . . . But comparatively minor renovations—like human rights education programs, police and military retraining programs, reform of the **judiciary** and bureaucracy into accountable institutions, external verification of subsequent election results, and the like—are permitted in any defeated aggressor, subject to need and proportionality. . . .

. . .

We should also expect, to return to rehabilitation in general, a formal apology by Aggressor to Victim and any Vindicator for its aggression. . . . [E]ven though formal apologies cannot of themselves restore territory, revive casualties, or rebuild infrastructure, they do mean something real to us. If not, why do formal apologies, and victims' campaigns to secure such apologies, generate considerable political and media attention? If not, why do informed people know that Germany has apologized profusely for its role in World War II whereas Japan has hardly apologized at all? . . . We feel that victims of wrongdoing are owed that kind of respect and that aggressors must at least show recognition of the moral principles they violated. Apologies are a nontrivial aspect of a complete peace treaty.

. . .

War Crimes Trials

This leaves the vexed topic of war crimes trials, perhaps the one issue of justice after war that has already received searching attention. The normative need for such trials follows from Walzer's dictum: "There can be no justice in war if there are not, ultimately, responsible men and women" (228). Individuals who play a prominent role during wartime must be held accountable for their actions and what they bring about. There are, of course, two broad categories of war crimes: those that violate *jus ad bellum* and those that violate *jus in bello.*

Jus ad bellum war crimes have to do with "planning, preparing, initiating, and waging" aggressive war. Responsibility for the commission of any such crime falls on the shoulders of the political leader(s) of the aggressor regime. Such crimes, in the language of the Nuremberg prosecutors, are "crimes against peace." What this principle entails is that, subject to proportionality, the leaders of Aggressor are to be brought to trial before a public and fair international tribunal and accorded full due process rights in their defence. Why subject this principle of punishment to proportionality constraints? Why concur with Walzer when he says that "it isn't always true that their leaders ought to be punished for their crimes" (123)? The answer is that sometimes such leaders, in spite of their moral decrepitude, retain considerable popular legitimacy, and thus bringing them to trial could seriously destabilize the polity within Aggressor. . . . Care needs to be taken, as always, that appeal to proportionality does not amount to rewarding aggressors, or to letting them run free and unscathed despite their grievous crimes. Yet this care does not **vitiate** the need to consider the destruction and suffering that might result from adhering totally to what the requirements of justice as retribution demand.

Should political leaders on trial for *jus ad bellum* violations be found guilty, through a public and fair proceeding, then the court is at liberty to determine a reasonable punishment, which will obviously depend upon the details of the relevant case. . . . It is not possible, ***a priori***, to stipulate what exactly is required with regard to such personal punishments. The point here is simply that the principle itself, of calling those most responsible for the aggression to task for their crimes, must be respected as an essential aspect of justice after war. It is relevant to add that the actual enforcement of this principle might constitute a nontrivial deterrent to future acts of aggression on the part of ambitious heads of state. If such figures have good reason to believe that they will themselves, personally, pay a price for the aggression they instigate and order, then perhaps they will be less likely to undertake such misadventures in the first place.

. . .

Jus ad bellum war crimes trials are not the only ones mandated by international law and just war theory: attention must also, in the aftermath of conflict, be paid to trying those accused of *jus in bello* war crimes. Such crimes include: deliberately using indiscriminate or disproportionate force; failing to take due care to protect civilian populations from lethal violence; using weapons that are themselves intrinsically indiscriminate and/or disproportionate, such as those of mass destruction; employing intrinsically heinous means, like rape campaigns; and treating surrendered prisoners of war in an inhumane fashion, for example, torturing them. Primary responsibility for these war crimes must fall on the shoulders of those soldiers, officers, and military commanders who were most actively involved in their commission. Officers and commanders carry considerable moral burdens of their own during wartime. They are duty-bound not to issue orders that violate any aspect of the laws of war. Furthermore, they must plan military campaigns so that foreseeable civilian casualties are minimized, and must teach and train their soldiers not only about combat but also about the rules of just war theory and the laws of armed conflict.

Something of note here is that, unlike *jus ad bellum* war crimes, *jus in bello* war crimes can be, and usually are, committed by all sides in the conflict. So, care needs to be taken that Victim and any Vindicator avoid the very tempting position of punishing only *jus ad bellum* war crimes. In order to avoid charges of applying a double standard and exacting revenge, the justified side must—despite the justice of its cause in fighting—also be willing to submit members of its military for the commission of *jus in bello* war crimes to an impartially constructed international tribunal. . . .

Publicity

Do the terms of the settlement, as thus far discussed, need to be public? . . . People who have suffered through a war deserve to know what the substance of the settlement is.

This does not mean that the people must explicitly and immediately endorse the proposed settlement, for instance through a **plebiscite**. Nor does it mean that the settlement must be drafted up in a formal treaty. Both things are clearly permissible, and perhaps desirable as well: a show of popular support for a settlement might bolster its endurance; and writing out the peace terms can enhance the clarity of everyone's understandings and expectations. But it seems needlessly stringent to insist that both phenomena must be there for the settlement to be legitimate. We can imagine numerous practical difficulties with running a plebiscite in the immediate postwar period, and we can imagine communities that come to an understanding on the settlement—even going so far as to adhere to it—without nailing down every possible contingency in a detailed legal document.

Summary of the Set

Perhaps it would be helpful to list the proffered set of settlement principles. A just state, seeking to terminate its just war successfully, ought to be guided by all of the following norms:

Proportionality and Publicity. The peace settlement should be both measured and reasonable, as well as publicly proclaimed. To make a settlement serve as an instrument of revenge is to make a volatile bed one may be forced to sleep in later. In general, this rules out insistence on unconditional surrender.

Rights Vindication. The settlement should secure those basic rights whose violation triggered the justified war. The relevant rights include human rights to life and liberty, and community entitlements to territory and sovereignty. This is the main substantive goal of any decent settlement. Respect for rights is a foundation of civilization, whether national or international. Vindicated rights, not vindictive revenge, is the order of the day.

Discrimination. Distinction needs to be made between the leaders, the soldiers, and the civilians in the country one is negotiating with. Civilians are entitled to reasonable immunity from punitive postwar measures. This rules out sweeping socioeconomic sanctions as part of postwar punishment.

Punishment #1. When the defeated country has been a blatant, rights-violating aggressor, proportionate punishment must be meted out. The leaders of the regime, in particular, should face fair and public international trials for war crimes.

Punishment #2. Soldiers also commit war crimes. Justice after war requires that such soldiers, from all sides of the conflict, likewise be held accountable at trial.

Compensation. Financial restitution may be mandated, subject to both proportionality and discrimination. A postwar poll tax on civilians is impermissible,[9] and enough resources need to be left so that the defeated country can begin its reconstruction. To beggar thy neighbour is to pick future fights.

Rehabilitation. The postwar environment provides a promising opportunity to reform decrepit institutions in an aggressor regime. Such reforms are permissible but they must be proportional to the degree of depravity in the regime. They may involve: demilitarization and disarmament; police and judicial retraining; human rights education; and even deep structural transformation toward a peaceable liberal democratic society.

Any serious defection, by any participant, from these principles of just war settlement should be seen as a violation of the rules of just war termination, and so should be punished. At the least, violation of such principles mandates a new round of diplomatic negotiations—even binding international arbitration—between the relevant parties to the dispute. At the very most, such violation may give the aggrieved party a just cause—but no more than a just cause—for resuming hostilities. Full recourse to the resumption of hostilities may be made only if all the other traditional criteria of *jus ad bellum* are satisfied in addition to just cause.

Conclusion: An Ethical "Exit Strategy"

The topic of justice after war, or *jus post bellum*, has been somewhat neglected, yet has recently become prominent, even pressing, in international relations. This article offers one plausible set of just war settlement norms, which communities seeking to conclude their just wars properly ought to obey. The terms of a just peace should satisfy the requirements listed above in the summary. There needs to be an ethical "exit strategy" from war, and it deserves at least as much thought and effort as the purely military exit strategy so much on the minds of policy planners and commanding officers.

One final aspect merits consideration: To what extent can these principles of just war settlement, developed mainly in a conventional interstate context, be applied to non-traditional intrastate conflicts? . . . [W]ith modifications, the principles developed here no doubt serve as a compelling moral blueprint for application to these other cases. . . . The principles offered here deal with the core controversies involved in any use of mass political violence, and they capture precisely those values and concepts we all employ to reflect on, and speak intelligently about, the ethics of war and peace.

Notes

1. The Charter of the United Nations was drafted in June 1945, following the end of World War II, and came into force in October 1945. The Charter establishes the purpose of the United Nations, its formal structure, and the enforcement of its powers. One of the **principal** substructures of the United Nations is the Security Council, which is charged with the maintenance of international peace and security. The powers of the Security Council, as outlined in the UN Charter, include powers to investigate and mediate political disputes, to authorize economic, diplomatic and military sanctions, and to use military force to resolve political disputes. [Editor]
2. The Hague Conventions were among the first international treaties negotiated to formalize just rules of war. These conferences occurred at The Hague in the Netherlands, the first in 1899, the second in 1907. These treaties established wartime rights for prisoners, the rights and obligations of neutral countries, and banned certain technologies such as air bombings, chemical weapons, and hollow point bullets.

   The Geneva Conventions are a series of four treaties signed between 1864 and 1949, and amendment protocols signed between 1977 and 2005. Like the Hague Conventions, the Geneva Conventions deal with rules of war, but expand the sphere of consideration to include the authority of the United Nations, as well as the responsibility of nations to protect civilians and victims of international armed conflicts. [Editor]
3. The (Persian) Gulf War was a UN-**sanctioned** war led by the United States in response to Iraq's invasion and occupation of Kuwait. The war began in January 1991, with a ceasefire and peace settlements commencing in February 1991. Following the war, the UN continued to impose economic sanctions on Iraq, which contributed to a lowered standard of living for its citizens. The US bombing of military targets renewed in June 2002, before a second declared war in 2003. [Editor]
4. The Bosnian War was an international armed conflict that took place in Bosnia and Herzegovina between March 1992 and December 1995. The war arose from the political breakup of Yugoslavia and was enflamed by ethnic and regional aspirations for political dominance. Ethnic cleansing, ranging from forced expulsion to mass rape to mass murder, was perpetrated by both Serbian and Croatian forces involved in the conflict. [Editor]
5. The Rwandan Genocide was the mass murder of approximately 800,000 people that occurred in 1994 in Rwanda. The genocide was led by powerful Hutu elites, who occupied top positions in government offices, the military, and mass media outlets. Hutu elites alleged that the Tutsi ethnic minority

intended to enslave the Hutu ethnic majority. Despite the presence of UN peacekeepers in Rwanda prior to and during the genocide, the UN failed to intervene. [Editor]

6. Many human rights violations had been reportedly perpetrated by Serbian, Albanian, and Yugoslav combatants during the Kosovo War, including killing civilians, rape, torture, and the destruction of civilian property. Following the June 1999 ceasefire, Kosovo has been marked by a sharp increase in the trafficking of women, human organ theft, and organized crime directly linked to political elites. As of 2008, Kosovo has declared political independence from the **dominion** of post-Yugoslav Serbia, but continues to be administered by the UN. [Editor]
7. The Treaty of Versailles was a peace treaty between German and Allied forces following the end of World War I. Harsh legal and political restrictions, the annexation of German lands by neighbouring countries, and the burdensome sums required of Germany in reparation, may have contributed to the German resentment leading up to the armed conflict of World War II. [Editor]
8. Michael Walzer, *Just and Unjust Wars*, 3rd ed. (New York: Basic Books, 2000). All references in this reading are to this book. [Editor]
9. A poll tax is a flat tax (everyone pays the same amount, regardless of income) levied per adult. Sometimes it is a requirement to vote. Poll taxes have become unpopular because their burden falls disproportionately on the poor. For example, a tax of $20 might seem minor to someone making $60,000 a year, but could be a serious burden to someone making $10,000 a year. [Editor]

Lieutenant-General (Retired) Roméo A. Dallaire

Force Commander, UNAMIR (United Nations Assistance Mission in Rwanda)

Speech at Carnegie Council for Ethics in International Affairs

AV = author's view; ~AV = not the author's view

Introduction

Ambassador Heinbecker: . . . General Dallaire is a Canadian hero. He served in the Canadian Army for thirty years. . . . He has commanded an artillery regiment, a brigade group, the Collège Militaire Royal[1] itself, the First Canadian Division.[2] . . . He has won the Meritorious Service Cross, the Vimy Award, and the Legion of Merit from the United States.[3]

In January 1994, General Dallaire sent out the alarm with credible information of an impending catastrophe. The United Nations and the membership of the Security Council failed General Dallaire, it failed the people of Rwanda, and it failed humanity. "Never again" was what we had all said. General Dallaire told us that "never again" was happening again, and the Security Council played word games with the Genocide Treaty.[4] It was one of the darker moments of history. . . . General Dallaire is here to talk to you today about his experiences and about "never again." . . .

Remarks

Gen. Dallaire: . . . Rwanda is a paradise of hills and of valleys, of the eternal spring, but also the memories of a very dark cloud, of a smog of death, that enveloped that country now nearly ten years ago.

I would like to speak of that, but also try to move it to another plateau—the whole arena of conflict, of ethical and moral decisions, of humanity, the arena in which one could sit back and ponder the following question: are all humans human, or are some more human than others?

When one looks back at Rwanda or now at the Congo[5]—still on and still the terrible pestilence and destruction of human life—our enormous concentration on Iraq, we want to ponder that question: are all humans human, or are some more human than others?

In January 1994, warnings were sent out with the information that we wanted to take offensive action against the extremists who had weapons that ultimately we were sure were to be used against us, or against the Rwandans if the situation fell into catastrophic failure.

Nine years ago in January, I was sending the third message in that regard, saying: We have an insight into the extremist organization. We are capable of milking this individual since he can help us wrest the initiative from the extremists and permit the moderates to move forward—and move with the moderates, not in a subversive fashion, but at least in an assistance fashion—with **demobilization**, reintegration of the different forces, and the bureaucracies to build a **nation** in a peaceful fashion.

That third cable got a similar response to the previous cables, but it had a particularly sad connotation to it. The informant, now having fed us significant information at enormous risks—and we were able to confirm that information, because I had a couple of my Franco-African officers in civvies go into some of the sites and find the weapons and who owned the buildings—told us that he was running out of capability, that is, he was ready to give us everything we wanted, or as much as he could, but he would have to leave. His concern for his family was enormous. He had three children, a wife. He wanted a guarantee that he could escape once he fed us this information, and probably continue to feed information from outside the country. All he wanted was five thousand dollars, a couple of tickets, and a country somewhere to take him in.

No one took him in. The United Nations and the processes that we were involved with, Department of Peacekeeping Operations [DPKO] did not have the authority to move a person out of a country and provide him exile protection.

France, the UK, the US, Belgium, Germany were directly requested. I went personally to try with the ambassadors to find a few dollars and a willingness to move this person, even temporarily, into their countries so that we could get the essence of the structure of the extremists to throw them off kilter, to take the initiative, and move, not necessarily the political process that had stagnated by then, but the military process through the Joint Military Committee and with the moderates undermine the extremists' power base. It didn't happen.

Two more messages were sent, and ultimately he disappeared. We never knew or will never know what happened to Jean-Pierre.

That is one example of a number of quandaries, ambiguities, and certainly a number of ethical and moral decisions that were taken not just during the genocide but up to the genocide. The bulk of [my book *Shake Hands with the Devil*] leads you to the genocide and all the peregrinations, the different interactions between . . . all the different players, all the different opportunities which were lost by process, lost by mandated complexity, lost by inflexibility of decision-making and interpretation, but, worst of all, lost by the apathy of the same international community that makes up the UN.

There was no lack of information. All the major players had ambassadors, military attachés. They knew, intelligence-wise, very well certainly most of the dimensions of what was about to happen. There was no transfer of information whatsoever, none. Nothing was transferred to the UN before, during, and certainly after, to my military force or to the mission in order to assist us in preventing genocide—or even during the genocide, being able to adjust whatever force I had at the time to help those who were in danger, help the humanitarian effort that was going on throughout the country.

One country was prepared to sell me satellite photographs so that I could find out where the bulk of the displaced people were—fifty thousand people are fairly easy to find—where they camped so we could move the humanitarian aid to help them. It wasn't in the budget. I couldn't find the money to buy those satellite photographs, even as I saw electronic warfare aircraft from Western powers, NATO powers, flying overhead.

The ethical dilemmas in which we find ourselves in conflict resolution go far beyond where we found ourselves in classic warfare during the Second World War, even in Korea, or Vietnam. Since the fall of the [Berlin] Wall[6] and the end of the Cold War,[7] we have entered an era that is revolutionary, where classic warfare, with known enemies, with all the instruments, all the sophistication, is passé. . . .

[W]e [have] continued to move in an era of imploding nations, of complexity, of mandates, and of **ad hoc**'ery, even on-the-job training by many of us, in attempting not to solve the crises, but to try to get ahead of them, to prevent them, and once in them bring innovative solutions. And I speak not only military—I speak diplomatic, I speak humanitarian. I speak of methodologies that we developed during the Cold War that we have been trying to adapt to respond to these very complex situations in which simple solutions simply won't meet the requirement.

It is the new era of conflict resolution that brings about not only complex solutions but also long-term commitment. We're into conflict resolution in these countries for ten, twenty, thirty, forty years, not two years. . . . But [we're] in it in a new way. Gone should be the era of a military, humanitarian, diplomatic, political, or nation-building plan. . . . We're in conflict resolution. We are not in war. We're into a whole new dimension of flexibility of instruments, but we also need a new dimension or arena of skills.

We don't even know the real verbs to be able to operate in these new conflict arenas. It became easy, in the Cold War. NATO had its lexicon. And militaries operate with action verbs—defend, attack, withdraw. Everybody knew what it meant.

What does "establish an atmosphere of security" mean, which was my mission? Does it mean that I defend Rwanda while they're demobilizing from an opportunistic neighbour? Does it mean I watch? How far do I go? How much force do I use? What are my rules of engagement? How much can I defend the process? How much can I protect civilians under a [UN peacekeeping] mandate?

We are in an era where it's no more simple action verbs. It's an era where you need more intellectual rigueur, more depth. . . . The era of isolation between us is no more. How do we integrate those capabilities and how do we bring them about?

The skill sets of this era are intellectual. They're not tactical, they're not **doctrinal**, they're not process. They're based on anthropology, sociology, philosophy, and on trying to understand the nuances that are in play—and try not to simply witness, as we had to, to fall back, because we couldn't use force—but they're built on the ability to proactively function in ambiguity.

Now, imagine the military operating in that context. It is a revolution. It is a whole new set of skill sets in order not to use the force, but in fact keep that in an over-watch, but be instruments integrated with the political, diplomatic and humanitarian in order to advance in the long term a change—not a revolution, a change.

Change takes time. Change means that you will work at all levels, including grassroots levels. It means that yes, you're going to demobilize child soldiers, but you're going to educate them, give them an opportunity. . . .

Currently we're involved with this new dimension of conflict, which is the use of children. . . . Children are replacing adults because the weapons are so light and easy to operate. Children are expendable. And children create enormous quandaries in those who face them.

There is a young sergeant with a dozen or so soldiers who was able to move into a village after negotiating through various roadblocks. The village had been wiped out. There were people who had hidden in the surrounding banana plantations. When they saw the soldiers arrive, they came out and congregated around one of the few churches that had not become a slaughterhouse. . . .

The sergeant is there with a couple of hundred people congregating. . . . Suddenly, from one side of the village comes a group of young boys, twelve, thirteen, fourteen, and they're shooting at him and the people he is defending. And from the other side there is a group of girls coming, and behind them are boys shooting at the sergeant, at his troops, but, most importantly, at the people they're supposed to be protecting.

What does the sergeant do? Do you kill children? This is one example of the moral and ethical dilemmas in which we find ourselves in many of these conflicts. They're not high-tech, but they require a depth of intellectual rigueur, they require values and people who know to go beyond themselves and potentially sacrifice themselves—not because the order or mandate is there, but because morally and ethically that's the right thing to do.

The sergeant opened up fire and took casualties. He killed children. Is that the solution? Is that how conflict is going to be resolved? Do we move to another level of inhumanity, create a higher plain of **human rights**, a higher plain of the respect of the individual, a higher plain of humanity?

Ladies and gentlemen, we're very concerned about Iraq. How many people have been talking about the slaughter in the Congo?

. . .

Question & Answer

[. . .]

Question: I wonder if the **rhetorical** question that you posed just now isn't the point. Some human beings are different from others because they have the misfortune to live in countries which do not attract the same degree of international attention, and it is a fact of life that results from the inability to match resources to the demands that you're posing. Neither the international community nor the leading members of the United Nations have unlimited financial, military, or moral resources to tackle every single problem.

That means, therefore, that in **realpolitik** there are only some countries that are prepared to make the effort. If you have a disaster in the South Pacific, we all look to the Aussies to go and sort it out. If you have a disaster in Francophone Africa, there's nobody else but the French who are prepared to put their money where their mouth is and go and sort it out.

With great respect, there is no British self-interest whatsoever in Sierra Leone, but we felt a moral compunction to go and help sort it out.

The problems with Rwanda were precisely that, that there were only two countries in the world that took Rwanda seriously, the Belgians and the French. You talked about the lack of intelligence. We, the British, . . . had no mission in Kigali [Rwanda] or Bujumbura [Burundi]. The only intelligence we had on what was going on in Rwanda came via the French, who were constantly nagging us to do something about the RPF [Rwandan Patriotic Forces], most certainly. But we had no intelligence, nor did we have any national interest whatsoever in the lead-up to the genocide.

You must recognize, therefore, that some humans are different from others because they have the misfortune to live in countries, like the Congo, which, regrettably, simply do not attract the same degree of emotional or national interest of those who can do something about it.

Gen. Dallaire: Yes, I totally agree. You argue very well the situation of realpolitik. That's why 800,000 can be slaughtered in one hundred days in Rwanda and nobody gives a damn, in fact pull out, and we're pouring billions and still have over 10,000 troops in Yugoslavia. There were more people killed, injured, displaced internally, and made refugees in one hundred days in Rwanda than the whole of the Yugoslavian campaign. But the Yugoslavs are white, they're European, they're friends, they were allies during the Second World War—they count.

Eight hundred thousand Rwandans don't count. The question is: why don't they count? Why do we continue with that sort of premise that they don't count as much? . . .

[I]t makes no sense to humanity that eighty per cent of it will stay in the mud, eighty per cent of it will still eat the handouts of the twenty per cent. We are like many countries. The residual of any of our budgets, if there is a residual, will go to aid. It is not a primary focus. It's not a mainstream activity. . . .

To me, humanity is one hundred per cent. The aim is to move towards that. The aim is to move from the self-interest level to the humanity level. . . .

In this era of conflict, in many of the zones, we could send in middle powers, we can send in nations that have achieved a certain level of development in human rights and the ability to conduct operations under the premise of the Charter [of the UN], and have the larger nations in over-watch, keep the political will behind the effort of the middle powers. If we find ourselves into catastrophic failure, then the world power, with its might, can come in and re-establish the situation.

The way of the future in many of these conflicts is the ability of middle powers to take on more of the responsibility in many of the conflict zones under the UN auspices.

. . .

Question: . . . [Y]ou talked about the orphaned parts of the world where the major powers have no interest. I wonder if part of the problem is that we present these cases as humanitarian problems, where both sides are called crazy and they have comic book names [*sic*] like Hutu and Tutsi. But there is never any talk about them being political problems, which is how we described Afghanistan and also Bosnia, where we have something at stake. Would it be more effective to describe these situations as political problems? Does this humanitarianism approach undermine itself?

Gen. Dallaire: In Rwanda, for nine months, there was a massive political exercise with moderates, extremists, rebels, and others to bring about a political solution. But no one was interested; diplomats simply reported the news to their superiors. There was also no real intellectual effort the other way to understand the situation and bring about peaceful compromise. The military was there purely as an instrument to stop the warring factions. The political effort never came. The humanitarian effort, in fact, was more involved with the Burundians, who had just had a **coup d'état**. Over three hundred thousand Burundians were on the southern border, and the humanitarian aid was going there, but the Rwandans, who were dying because of a drought and were not being fed, were killing the Burundians to get the food that the Burundians had been given by the international community because they had refugee status. So a lot of that nuancing could have happened if the political will and resources were there. It would have also been more cost effective.

. . .

The Americans got a bloody nose in Somalia.[8] Yet there are 1.6 million people in uniform in the United States military. The Americans still packed it in, leaving the Pakistanis and the Canadians and others to handle the situation. I feel terrible about the September 11 terrorist attacks—it was absolutely grotesque—but you mobilized the world. No one was mobilized when eight hundred thousand were killed in Rwanda, and they are just as human.

Question: We had a discussion here not long ago with a realpolitik-er who answered no to my question about whether the US had any self-interest in the Rwandan problem in 1994. What would you say to American political leaders back then who said we had no interest in Rwanda? What do you say about the realistic interests?

Gen. Dallaire: . . . [T]he real question is: is the Western world prepared to spill blood for advancing human rights in far-off lands that mean nothing, except for one small fact: they are exactly the same as us. People are not different; the circumstances are different.

Question: I used to think Rwanda was an aberration, but I soon learned that what happened in Rwanda was the result of a structural problem. You basically have a tension between what is in our hearts—to help the downtrodden and oppressed and others—and the international system, which is based entirely on national interest. You can come to the Carnegie Council on Ethics and International Affairs and discuss these issues, but if you go to the Security Council [of the UN], ethics and international affairs is an oxymoron. Is it kinder to make the eighty per cent of humanity that needs help to believe in the illusion that there is a world that will help them, or is it kinder for us to tell them there is no international safety net, that the UN system focuses purely on the short-term national interest?

Gen. Dallaire: Well, the first thing I want to say is that it's not a time factor. If time was a factor for me, I'd be a pessimist. The optimism comes with the fact that humanity continues. We constantly fiddle and manoeuver, and every now and again, we realize humanity isn't just us. I believe the UN is critical to avoiding crises and managing crises. Whether we can move that eighty per cent depends on our ability over the years.

I was a soldier in the 1960s. If somebody mentioned human rights back then, we'd call him a commie pinko. Today, we teach it. Today, we educate soldiers about human rights and provide medical support and other services to prisoners. So that is one reason why I am optimistic.

Fifty years from now, what should historians be writing about the United States, or Canada, where I am from? What is our vision? Our self-interest and the advancement of our nations? Yes. But there should also be a strategic focus on that higher plane called humanity. I don't think we're allowed to abdicate that responsibility.

. . .

Notes

1. Dallaire was commandant (officer-in-charge) of Collège Militaire Royal de Saint-Jean, a military college in Quebec. [Editor]
2. The First Canadian Division was raised in August 1914 in order to serve with British forces in World War I. The division was involved in several famous battles, including the Battle of Vimy Ridge. [Editor]
3. The Meritorious Service Cross is presented by the Queen of Canada to award actions of considerable benefit to the Canadian forces. The Vimy Award is presented to persons who make significant and outstanding contributions to the defence and security of Canada and **democratic** values. The Legion of Merit is presented by the United States Department of Defense for exceptional conduct in the performance of outstanding service. [Editor]
4. The Convention on the Prevention and Punishment of the Crime of Genocide is a UN treaty that came into force in January 1951. The convention defines genocide and what sorts of actions are punishable under the convention, such as attempting and conspiring to commit, and complicity in, genocide. Both the Rwandan genocide and the Kosovo War involved many breaches of the convention. [Editor]
5. The Second Congo War (also known as the Great War of Africa) began in August 1998, and although it officially ended in 2003, hostilities continue to this day. As of 2008, the war and its aftermath have killed over five million people, and over a million people have been displaced. The war involved twenty-five armed groups and eight African nations, and concerned disputes over rights to land and the deposits of high-value minerals in it. [Editor]
6. At the end of World War II, Germany was divided between Allied and Soviet forces who occupied the western and eastern portions respectively. To prevent German political ascendency immediately following disarmament, Berlin, the German capital, was split between the western and eastern occupations. The Berlin Wall was built in 1961 by Soviet-occupied East Germany in order to contain Allied-occupied West Germany, and to prevent East Berliners from defecting to the West. The wall was fortified with watch towers, anti-vehicle trenches, and armed guards. Free passage from East to West Germany unofficially began in November 1989, when citizens began to literally chip away parts of the wall without East German guards intervening. [Editor]
7. The Cold War was a sustained period of political and military tension between Western liberal nations, led by the United States and NATO forces, and Eastern socialist nations, led by the Soviet Union. It lasted from 1947 until 1991. The war was "cold" because neither Western nor Eastern forces engaged in direct armed conflict, although wars were frequently waged by satellite poor nations aligned with either Western or Eastern powers. [Editor]

8. The Somali Civil War is an ongoing civil war that began in 1991. In December 1992, The United Nations Security Council approved a coalition of United Nations peacekeepers led by the United States, whose mandate was to use all necessary means to ensure the delivery of humanitarian aid to civilians. Somali militias, threatened by the UN presence, engaged in armed combat with UN troops until their total withdrawal from Somali in March 1995. [Editor]

Lieutenant-General (Retired) Roméo A. Dallaire

Force Commander, UNAMIR (United Nations Assistance Mission in Rwanda)

The Lessons of Rwanda

. . .

Since the end of the Cold War[1] a central issue has been how to advance the cause of humanity—of all human beings in the world. One of the main questions has been: does the international community, in particular the powers to be, recognize that all humans have to be seen in the same light, that there should be no pecking order that would favour one group over another? When providing support and assistance to victims of internal conflicts should Africans receive less protection than victims on other continents?

One of the lessons of Rwanda, where 800,000 Africans were slaughtered [in 1994], is that the international community has failed and continues to fail to pay sufficient attention to the plight of victims in distant lands. . . . [We must raise] awareness of the nature of the threats and of the common responsibility we have to protect humans regardless of geographic or ethnic or political considerations.

The Responsibility to Protect

. . . [A] recent, important study . . . was prepared under the title *The Responsibility to Protect.* This study is an outstanding contribution to the debate about the responsibility of the international community in dealing with major humanitarian crises. It raises the important question: "Who has the ultimate responsibility and authority to protect the **dignity** and even the survival of humans, of innocent individuals?" In the first place it is their governments in place, but if the government does not exist, or it is itself a perpetrator, it has to be an internationally recognized agency like the United Nations if it is not the UN itself.

The Limits of Sovereignty

However, what I have found in the debate about the responsibility to protect is that we have often concentrated too much on the legal analysis and on the issue of **sovereignty**. The concept of sovereignty has too often been misused . . . to allow governments to ignore their responsibility to protect their own citizens, and also too often it has allowed the international community to remain passive even when faced with massive violations of **human rights**.

I believe that if we want to advance the cause of humanity and the universal protection of human beings, sovereignty is not the main issue to be considered. . . . [It] has been too often used as an excuse for abuses and for inaction.

Focusing on the issue of sovereignty has often prevented us from going to the fundamentals of the needs of human security and of individual protection. Sovereignty . . . must not be allowed to be an impediment to action when obvious crimes against humanity are being committed against the population by their own government.

The Fear of Casualties and Its Consequences

With regards to security, one of the most tragic dimensions is the security of those outsiders who can intervene, or at least participate in the efforts of advancing security in the **nation states** that are imploding and that are facing humanitarian catastrophes.

One of the most damaging or negative aspects has been the fear of casualties. The fear of casualties is very high both in the NGO [non-governmental organization] community and in the UN organizations. The risk assessments influenced by this fear lead to decisions of rapid extraction from the field of those who, in fact, are part of the potential solution during the conflict as well as part of its aftermath.

An even more disquieting phenomenon can be observed where outside forces are required and made available to provide security. . . . [M]any **nations** consider the lives of soldiers—who are professionals and committed to their missions—to be more important than the lives of those whom they are supposed to be protecting.

. . .

In Rwanda . . . [t]he Belgian troops took ten casualties. . . . This was not an insignificant happening at a time when nations are not at war. . . .

However, to withdraw because of these casualties, raises the question: "What was the depth of commitment to the mission in the first place?" Was there a commitment only when there was no human cost, and you pull out abandoning those that you were there to help? . . .

And so, the dimension of security and self-defence, particularly in the case of the use of force, has moved to a plateau that I consider almost perverse. I do not speak irresponsibly of the terrible cost of casualties. But when responsible decisions are taken, does the security of the individual soldiers committed to the mission dominate the actual mission that they are being asked to accomplish? This self-serving approach has created a terrible dilemma for commanders on the ground. What was the risk assessment in the first place? Do we want to accomplish these missions to the best of our ability or . . . are we to be constantly looking over our shoulders to determine the reaction at home with regards to possible losses and holding back our troops in order to meet a primary aim of self-security? Does this become the principal yardstick to measure mission success?

The Absence of the Middle Powers

Over the years, through my own experience and research pondering the issue of peacekeeping, of protecting citizens of other nations, I have discovered, as probably others have also, that the "middle powers" have been relatively absent from these tasks or UN mandates.

We expect the larger powers to get involved (and we readily criticize them if they do not) because they have the military capability, and more importantly they also have the strategic capability of moving and sustaining troops around the world.

In many crisis situations, as in Africa during the Rwanda affair, there were a number of African countries that were prepared to send troops to reinforce my mission. The simple fact is that they could not transport them there. Worse yet, those countries that had the strategic lift capability simply did not want to provide it.

What I contend to be a major obstacle to conflict resolution is the absence of the "middle powers" as full participants in making the UN more effective and more responsive to the emergencies occurring around the world.

I am concerned about our current inability to provide options other than **unilateral** action, to discover other nuances, or skills. . . .

. . .

In this era of complex missions what is absolutely required are skill sets and backgrounds that permit troops at all levels to commune with the **indigenous** people in order to build confidence, to facilitate reconciliation and to build from the grassroots up the ability of these nations to move on. To be "value-added" to the resolution of conflicts which are steeped in ambiguity. The big powers do not generally have the subtlety that is required. The warrior **ethic** must be complemented by a more intellectually based competency founded on the humanities where knowledge of the arena is far deeper than overt peace and security measures.

Because of that I do not think the Americans should be the world police—they, in fact, should be or remain the backbone of the world army for global peace.

Thus, when the middle powers like Canada and others go into the Rwandas and the Congos[2] of the world, always under the auspices of the UN, they should be able to rely on the fact that if the situation threatens to explode beyond their control, the American, French, or British Rapid Reaction formations will be deployed within 48 hours. In Rwanda, when the war started, I was not screaming for the 82nd Airborne to come in automatically. I was screaming originally for the quite qualified troops of middle powers to come in, as I needed reinforcements. If that was not going to meet the requirements then and only then bring in the forces of the big powers under earnest, vigorous, and determined mandates and leadership. To stabilize the situation and then hand the task back to the middle powers to pursue the aim of conflict resolution in a calmer and manageable atmosphere.

Thus, I would argue that a key reason for the current weakness of the United Nations to meet the complex challenges to peace and human rights is its inherent inability to be more flexible, and adaptive, more timely and more integrated in its responses to easing the tensions and getting the big powers involved too soon with often drastic results for all. This profound weakness in the only impartial and transparent world body is the result of the **abdication** of the middle powers to take on, to the fullest possible extent, their leadership responsibilities in conflict resolution and crisis management.

New Skills and Responsibilities for the Middle Powers

. . .

We are in an era when war-fighting skills are not enough for middle powers. Their officers and non-commissioned officer corps must acquire the skills of conflict resolution.

These skills may be considered "soft skills"—including knowledge in such subjects as anthropology, philosophy, and sociology. The question we have to ask of our soldiers standing there with a rifle is not just whether they can shoot or not, but what they can bring to the resolution of the conflict at their levels.

These troops of the middle powers must maintain their warrior ethic and competency so that if required they can ultimately fight effectively. The key is in the balance of these seemingly conflicting skill sets.

. . .

The middle powers can risk ambiguity because of the "overwatch" provided by the big powers. They can inculcate the relevant skills in their militaries and diplomats more readily. However, they have been far too absent in trying to deal with the situations we are talking about.

Humanitarian Action

Integrated Missions

What is now required is an integration of several disciplines (politics, security, etc.) into a single plan. No longer can we have missions/mandates based on three or four separate plans that might be coordinated, but rarely integrated, that rely on the good will of field leaders. The future missions must be based on mission statement marriages, in which, at times more humanitarian, security or other resources will be required but fundamentally all separate plans of the past are wholly integrated.

Thus, I am arguing that the separate disciplines as we have known them in the past cannot continue to operate in near isolation of each other—and hope for personalities to make them work.

Taking the humanitarian dimension as an example, the emergency may have come from a humanitarian crisis that has led to a security problem, or in other cases, like Rwanda, it was the security problem that created the humanitarian crisis; the humanitarians and the security forces cannot operate in isolation. Thus, the old theory that NGOs must get involved because people are hurting regardless of the situation on the ground is simply not an acceptable approach anymore.

It is the same with the much respected concept of neutrality. The idea that non-government organizations must stay neutral—meaning that they can function independently of the political and military dimensions of a crisis, arguing that helping people will stabilize the situation and will help bring about reconciliation— . . . is passé, because it is ineffective. The NGOs have to be integrated in the search of solutions—they have to be aware of the whole situation and they have to be involved in the process of stabilization, of bringing serenity and comfort, and by that permitting the political process to be able to function. So the NGOs are part of, not separate from the process. And any NGO that tries to operate in absolute isolation is in fact creating rather than solving problems. (I can illustrate this point with an example of a small NGO in Rwanda that had set up a very small hospital that obviously could not handle the hundreds of Rwandans bleeding and dying in front of its tents. However, when the military doctors from countries that had provided large field hospitals dedicated for these refugees and internally displaced, with Red Crosses on their uniforms, offered their hospitals, their ambulances, and their help in the **triage** of the wounded, they were rebuffed by the NGO in the name of neutrality. The person knew full well that the difficulties he raised in working with the military medical teams would lead to the death of hundreds of victims.)

Furthermore, I believe that the practice in areas of conflict whereby aid agencies and NGOs accept, although under duress, to pay a tax to warlords and belligerents from the resources destined for the victims, should be stopped and condemned as unethical.

. . .

So what can be done in such situations? We know that these resources, precious as they are, are being prevented by force from getting through to the people who need them. NGOs must operate within the mission context in order to guarantee that one hundred per cent of the resources will get to those in desperate need. This requires *integrating their effort with the other disciplines of the mission*. This means a marriage of security capabilities and negotiating capabilities on the political side. And if the resources are not getting through this way—then we have overt crimes against humanity and with that the whole circumstance changes.

. . .

Every Human Being Is a Human

Bluntly, until the developed nations of the world decide that the eighty per cent of humanity living in poverty and disease is just as human as the twenty per cent of the "haves" and move to the support and development and protection of the eighty per cent instead of simply considering them a residual concern and cost, we will continue to see millions of people die and suffer and our security put at risk as never before. The rage welling up in the eighty per cent has started to express itself through terrorism and will get more audacious and destructive.

One cannot consider eighty per cent of humanity as purely residual. This must be a mainstream concern and activity in the developed world. It has to be on par with health, welfare, infrastructure, national defence, and other key concerns of **sovereign** nations. Until that eighty per cent of humanity has regained dignity, hope, serenity, and the ability to see future generations advance, the developed world cannot claim that it is advancing and it will never be secure. When the fundamental rights of all humans are established and guaranteed, only then will we be able to speak of a real advancement of humanity in the peace and serenity we all aspire to achieve.

The unassailable essence of humanity is that every human is equal, that every human being is as human as the other. No more, no less must dominate our future considerations for mankind.

. . .

The Military and Humanitarian Action

. . .

. . . In the arena where we find ourselves, the military have discovered that they have to find new intellectual skills to operate in ambiguity and growing complexity.

If there is anything obvious and fundamental about military structure, it is to build operating procedures, drills, and acquire equipment according to stated doctrines that will eliminate ambiguity. The mission must be clear. That the mission is met by clear deductive reasoning and detailed option analysis to ultimately articulate the aim and achieve it successfully must be the result.

Yet, we are now in areas of ambiguity. The military searches for ways to comprehend what this means. The political structures are finding that to meet what might be the perceived threats is not any more as clear as giving, or not, money to a narrowly defined defence effort.

So the military and the political structures are moving to this still ill-defined line. At this line both sides have to comprehend that they are in one of the most complex eras in history: an era where there are so many factors at work that cannot be understood and dealt with through the classic nation-state framework of government, military and the people. There is a new total amalgam of factors, and the military is one component of this amalgam.

The Challenge of the New Missions

In 1993 the mission I was given in Rwanda was "to establish an atmosphere of security." The diplomats and politicians did not exactly know what this meant or more specifically, what ultimately was the responsibility to protect. Was it the limits of the use of force? They were going after a "state of being" and not a definitive and clinically definable objective. In such a vacuity of direction the modern military commander cannot commit troops and risk lives using passé concepts, doctrines, training, and procedures.

In this instance did it mean that if during **demobilization** of the ex-belligerent armies, if a third party attacked, I was responsible for the defence of the nation? Or does it mean that we simply watch them demobilize? Does it mean that I provide them with the training for their future needs? What does it mean to establish an atmosphere of security?

In fact, we are now in a new, very transitional period in which the old methods are ineffective but the new methods are not as yet articulated. So we are extemporizing. We are crisis managing. We are on-the-job training. What is certain is that we must get away from the segregated disciplines of conflict resolution and quite literally move to multi-disciplined persons who have depth in all of these areas. The Generals of today and the future may have to be politically knowledgeable and savvy, versed in the nuances of diplomacy, capable of functioning inside the humanitarian world and understanding how they function. We need Generals who can be part of the nation building, who understand how to integrate capabilities to build nations.

We are in an era that is screaming for a renaissance of those extraordinary people of the Renaissance that can master so many disciplines and what we are getting are more and more specialists.

Notes

1. The Cold War was a sustained period of political and military tension between Western liberal nations, led by the United States and NATO forces, and Eastern socialist nations, led by the Soviet Union. It lasted from 1947 until 1991. The war was "cold" because neither Western nor Eastern forces engaged in direct armed conflict, although wars were frequently waged by satellite, poor nations aligned with either Western or Eastern powers. [Editor]
2. The Second Congo War (also known as the Great War of Africa) began in August 1998, and although it officially ended in 2003, hostilities continue to this day. As of 2008, the war and its aftermath have killed over five million people, and over a million people have been displaced. The war involved twenty-five armed groups and eight African nations, and concerned disputes over rights to land and the deposits of high value minerals therein. [Editor]

The Honourable Madam Justice Louise Arbour

Crimes against Women under International Law

. . .

. . . [I]in September of 1998, Jean-Paul Akayesu, the *quarter-meister* of the Taba community of Rwanda was convicted of several counts of genocide and crimes against humanity, and violations of common Article 3 to the Geneva Convention,[1] and Article 4 to the Condition of Protocol 2, amongst other things, for crimes that are called outrages upon personal **dignity**, including rape, degrading and humiliating treatment, and indecent assault.

In December of 1998, Anto Furundžija was convicted of torture, inhuman treatment, and rape. His conviction has subsequently been upheld on appeal. And then, in December of 2001, three men from Foca, in an indictment that is usually referred to as the Foca indictment—Foca is a town in Bosnia and Herzegovina—were convicted of rape and torture as crimes against humanity, and as violations of the laws and customs of war. They were also convicted, again, in relation to the sexual exploitation of girls and women, and of enslavement as a crime against humanity. There are many, many similar charges pending before the International **Tribunal**.

. . . The incidents that gave rise to these convictions could have gone largely unnoticed. Without the creation of the International Criminal Tribunal for the former Yugoslavia, and the International Criminal Tribunal for Rwanda, the world would have long ago closed the book on these events. . . .

I'm not persuaded that members of the Security Council thought very seriously that there would ever be a trial and convictions for anyone who would fall in the jurisdiction of the tribunals. Even on the assumption that they thought there would be some accounting, I can't imagine that there was much of a sense in that institution that launching these tribunals under Chapter 7 of the UN Charter as a tool to restore international peace and security, would mean that sexual violence had to be denounced and prosecuted. Basically, there are three broad issues that I would like to discuss with you: How did we get there? What have we learned? And where do we go from here?

First, how did we get there? I'm not sure to what extent you know the history of the creation of these tribunals. I won't spend much time on that because much of that information is readily available in the literature that has been produced since the tribunals were created. I think history will show that these tribunals had, in a sense, an accidental birth—completely unexpected. After the Nuremberg and Tokyo trials, the general consensus was that if there was to be that kind of personal criminal liability or enforcement of international humanitarian law, and if that was to take place before an international institution, it would have to be done by a consensus in the international community.

The Security Council Chapter 7 powers are very broad. They are the most coercive forms of power that can be exercised on the international scene. When the Security Council imposes duties, they bind all states. It is sometimes in the form of sanctions—economic sanctions, political denunciation, any ultimately military intervention—but the creation of the criminal judicial organ, a subsidiary organ emanating from the Security Council, had never really been contemplated. I think that it had been born, it's fair to say, out of the utter despair of the international community as to how to manage these unmanageable conflicts in the Balkans. Hundreds of Security Council resolutions have been issued in the conflict in the Balkans, and the creation of the tribunal was one of them.

Second, how did we get there, and what are these resolutions? When I was involved with these two tribunals, I spent a lot of time defending against the accusation that, like Nuremberg and Tokyo, these tribunals were just another form of victor's justice. I claimed that, technically, this was not the case. The tribunals at Nuremberg and Tokyo were not simply international, they were multi-national; they were created by the victorious Allies, essentially to try their defeated enemies. I would make the argument that these two *ad hoc* tribunals were created by the United Nations, by the Security Council, whose budget is governed by the General Assembly. But, in a sense, I've withdrawn from this technical defense of these institutions after reading a wonderful book by Gary Bass, called *Seta and the Vengeance: The Politics of War Crimes Tribunals*, which was published at the end of the year 2000. Gary Bass says if in fact these tribunals are victor's justice, they can't be otherwise. It makes a difference who the victors are. They can't be otherwise, because only advanced **liberal democracies** could have created these kinds of institutions. So, in a sense, they are a product of the developed, advanced democracies that are fully engaged in a culture of **rights**, and the impetus for creating this kind of institution could have only come from there.

. . . I believe that the prosecution of sexual violence on the international scene could not have happened without the immense progress that had been made throughout the Western World. Certainly in North America and in Europe, in the preceding twenty or thirty years, we have enhanced our understanding of sexual violence. In developing and modernizing our rules of substantive law and evidence, we have developed a new method for denouncing sexual violence, prosecuting it and punishing it appropriately. I don't think that it's a coincidence that sexual violence was not prosecuted at Nuremberg, but is now at the forefront of the international prosecutorial agenda. It reflects very much what is happening throughout the liberal democracies that have been the champions of the protection of rights in the court system.

. . . [B]ecause of the progress that had been made domestically in countries that were attentive to what was happening internationally, it would have been unthinkable for the international tribunal, in particular the international prosecutor, not to be fully engaged in the prosecution and denunciation of sexual violence. It could not have happened without the work that happened domestically, and, because of that, it could not have happened internationally.

. . .

What have we learned? . . . In the prosecution of sexual offenses before these international tribunals, the very first thing you have to do is look at the broad policy choices. One of the debates that we had constantly in the office of the prosecutor was: should we "normalize" the prosecution of sexual violence, or should we keep nurturing it as a separate issue? The debate was whether we should just announce that a sexual offence was like any other offence that all investigators must be attentive to and must prosecute as part of any investigation.

When you investigate crimes against humanity or crimes of genocide, violations of **human rights**, murder or extermination, you look for torture and rape. The question is how sexual offenses should be investigated. Should we investigate them as we would any other crime, or, alternatively, because of the difficulty of investigating sexual offenses, should we continue to use a team that is particularly trained and sensitive to the special needs of this kind of an investigation, one that will ensure that these investigations are not neglected? We have these policy debates all the time.

Another debate that was a constant source of tension in the office of the prosecutor was the exercise of prosecutorial discretion. The offenses in the former Yugoslavia and Rwanda that fell within our jurisdiction were so numerous and deserving of prosecution that we had to be very strict about how we prioritized cases. In general terms, we determined that we had to concentrate on the most serious offenses that could bring us to the highest possible echelons of command. . . .

Part of the debate concerned whether prosecuting the direct perpetrators of sexual offenses was an equally appropriate prosecutorial strategy. We discussed whether there was more to be gained by prosecuting actual perpetrators, the Mr. Nobodies who actually committed the crimes, rather than deciding that the goal of prosecution was to move up the chain of command. Punishment would, in the case of sexual violence, be particularly difficult to visit on the commanders under the doctrine of **command responsibility**. It would require proving that the commanders either participated in the offenses, or knew that the offenses were being committed but failed to punish those responsible.

The use of the doctrine of command responsibility in sexual violence was also a source of constant debate: should we create a special team for these kinds of offenses and actually focus on the actual perpetrators? If so, would we be trivializing these crimes by not normalizing them and putting them in the fold of our general prosecution? We had enormous operational difficulties. Our contacts were obviously extremely traumatized witnesses and victims. In addition, all of our conversations took place through interpreters. It was very difficult work for the interpreters, who got the first shock wave of stories they were being told. All of the difficulties of investigation in a domestic setting were amplified.

We also had tremendous difficulties with respect to protecting victims. This is endemic in the work of these international institutions, and is particularly keen in sexual violence cases. In that field more than any other, it was obvious how difficult it was to offer a criminal justice system without the rest of the infrastructure that we take for granted in our own national systems. There was no Children's Aid Society, no social services and no health care of any sort to work in partnership with criminal law enforcement. This was particularly acute in Rwanda, where we had a lot of interaction particularly with local NGOs, who worked with women in the country. This interaction, which was certainly helpful to us in performing our work, was also creating completely unrealistic expectations as to what this international institution could deliver.

By the time we went to trial, the difficulties were even more enormous. There may be some of you here who have looked at these issues. The cases can be found on the website of the tribunals. Real progress has been made in the development of, for instance, providing a definition of rape in an international environment. It's amazing that, in so little time, writing of such quality was produced. The judgments were not without controversy, however, and there are parts of them that I found rather timid in their approach. But the judgments made progress. If you look at the definitions of sexual offenses that were provided in the *Akayesu*, *Kovač*, *Furundžija* and *Foča* cases,[2] you can see that they were forming a definition of **actus reus** [a crime] and **mens rea** [criminal intent], bringing the international forum to the cutting edge of what is being done in most domestic departments.

Lawyers also bring cutting-edge issues and litigation techniques to these international tribunals. Any lawyer in good standing from any jurisdiction can appear before these international institutions. This country [the US], this state [California], produces very good lawyers. Some of them appear in the defense of accused war criminals before international institutions. These lawyers bring with them the latest issues in the litigation of sexual violence from their own country to an environment where it is just beginning.

I'll give you one example, which is documented in one of the cases. In *Furundžija*, after the case was closed for both parties I received a phone call at my office. The phone message was the following: a trial opinion in another case had come to the disturbing discovery that we had not disclosed to the defense the records of therapy of the main complainant. This woman had received psychotherapy after extremely brutal sexual violence which she'd been subjected to at the hands of, not the accused personally, but his associate. There were records of therapy in existence and we had, of course, a disclosure obligation that would be familiar to those of you taking criminal law and criminal procedure: the prosecution must turn over to the defense essentially its case, and any **exculpatory** evidence that may be relevant to the presentation of the defense. The issue of the disclosure of therapy records of the plaintiffs was an issue that in Canada we had just finished struggling with. The Supreme Court of Canada had pronounced on the relevance of, and the level of access that a defendant in criminal proceedings should be afforded to therapy materials, a matter that goes to the very heart of the right to privacy of the complainant.

In my view, we had to disclose the records. We had to disclose them and then argue vigorously that they were weak, irrelevant and not admissible, but we could not undertake the responsibility to make that decision without telling the court and the defence. Eventually, we did disclose the records and took a huge penalty for having disclosed late. The only reason that I bring this point to your attention is that, in domestic **jurisdictions**, it took us one hundred years to get to that level of sophistication with respect to the relevance of certain materials in the prosecution and the defense of sexual violence. And, yet, in these international institutions where we were only starting, where the environment was so challenging and the witnesses were so vulnerable, defendants were presenting aggressive, modern defenses. And that is probably how it should have been. In the end, it's probably a good thing that these international institutions are catching on to the cutting-edge litigation that is taking place in our own systems.

Where do we go from here? I'll have to preface my next remark by saying, in Canada, there is a great feeling of optimism towards the future of these international criminal tribunals. You may know that, in the summer of 1998 in Rome, 120 countries signed the Rome Treaty creating the International Criminal Court. The expectations were that it would take years to collect the sixty ratifications necessary to bring the court into existence. We speculated that it would take about six, eight or even ten years. But now, there are fifty-two ratifications at last count. Conventional wisdom is that there will be sixty by the summer for sure.[3] It is happening. It's an amazing development. It's a development that holds promise. It's also an environment in which there will be enormous difficulties. I won't spend a lot of time discussing it, but I'll just put forth, for the true international lawyers among you, a few questions that really trouble me.

With the advent of the ICC we have also seen, in a parallel movement, the growth of universal jurisdiction in domestic states. The two are sort of competing for prominence. Again, I'll use the example of Canada. In the statute that Canada enacted in order to ratify the International Criminal Court, Canada, by the same act, broadened its universal jurisdiction, giving itself jurisdiction over genocide, crimes against humanity, and war crimes. The act did not limit jurisdiction to crimes committed in Canada.

Other countries went even further. Belgium, for instance, equipped itself with a form of universal jurisdiction that created a severe headache for its government when a magistrate interpreted that jurisdiction literally, and with a vengeance. Belgium gave itself jurisdiction over crimes committed against humanity, regardless of whether committed by or against a Belgian national. Essentially, it declared jurisdiction over all crimes against humanity committed anywhere by anyone. That decision led, as you may know, to a recent decision of the International Court of Justice which ratified an arrest warrant against a foreign minister of the Democratic Republic of the Congo, which had been issued by a Belgian magistrate.

With respect to the International Criminal Court, the one question that is on everybody's mind is whether we can do this without the United States.[4] The answer seems to be, "We have no choice but to do so." It will happen. And it will, unfortunately, with or without the United States. Speaking for myself, it seems that, in view of this growth of universal jurisdiction, the ICC, the International Criminal Court, is bound to become the least unattractive alternative for the United States. I cannot imagine a nation facing potential exposure to prosecution in a multiplicity of national forums without mastering exactly how they will operate. It seems to me that, if that growth continues, this is the one forum where you can be a player, where you can have your own people influencing the thinking of the court and staffing the office of the prosecutor, as unattractive as that might be. It might just become considerably more attractive than what the world is going to look like with this checkered view of universal jurisdiction.

. . .

The question that I ask myself on all of these issues is, "What is it that we are afraid of; is it people or is it institutions?" Someone said, and I very much regret that I cannot attribute that quote to anybody, but it stayed with me when I heard it said by somebody else: "Nothing happens without people, but nothing lasts without institutions." I think that the prosecution of sexual violence could not have happened without the impetus that was generated in many national jurisdictions by people, very many in the legal profession, who made it a lifetime project to tackle this issue. From there, it could not have happened on the international scene without institutions like the International Tribunal. I think people deserve immense credit in the years to come, not only for the prosecution of genocide, crimes against humanity and war crimes generally, but, more particularly, for having been at the forefront of the policy and the prosecution of sexual violence. Thank you very much.

I'm very happy to answer your questions.

. . .

Question: [How does the ICC determine whether it has jurisdiction over a criminal defendant?]

Answer: First of all, it would depend on what crimes it is alleged these people committed. The ICC only has jurisdiction over war crimes and crimes against humanity, genocide, and the breaching of the Geneva Convention. You first have to determine what it is that these people are to be charged with, whether it falls under the jurisdiction of the ICC, and whether there is a competent national jurisdiction that is asserting its primacy. And, if so, that's the end of the case.

Question: I wanted you to articulate a little further why you think the ICC [will be a better alternative even for nations, like the United States, that oppose it].

Answer: I think I was trying to develop an argument that, from the point of view of those who are reluctant to embrace the idea of an ICC, they don't have much choice with respect to universal jurisdiction. Given that lack of choice, I believe the ICC would be a better forum. Why? Because it's an international institution, and, if the United States were to become a signatory, it could . . . have judges, it could have prosecutors.

You know, when you work within an institution, you give it a culture. The International Criminal Tribunal for the former Yugoslavia was originally staffed by twenty-five US attorneys who donated their time for a couple of years. Many European countries were outraged by the large number of Americans and felt that the United States had basically hijacked the institution culturally. And it had, to a large extent. It was a common-law jurisdiction, and the way of doing business was very North American because the Americans were there from day one. It's easier to fight something from within, if you're not comfortable with it, than it is to fight this growth of universal jurisdiction. I can't imagine that the universal jurisdiction of the laws of Belgium did not create a problem for the United States.

. . .

Question: If we consider briefly the record of allegedly Western enlightened democracies, the US has No [Gun] Ri in Korea;[5] Japan has the Rape of Nanking,[6] for which they have not apologized and which is not discussed in Japanese history books; France has Algeria,[7] where someone who actually acknowledged the events is in trouble with French law right now; and the UK [has similar events in its history, as well]. If these nations are not willing to apologize and prosecute those responsible for such acts, how likely is it that renegade countries would?

Answer: I think the gamble we have to take is that we could actually invest a huge amount of effort into **redressing** history. In some cases, it's important because there are issues that were such an affront to all of mankind that we can never turn our backs and say, "It's too late. It's too far in the past." There are very few of those.

You have to be sort of forward-looking and say, "It starts now." From now on, there will be accountability, there will be a forum. Maybe you can do both. And maybe the impetus to go forward will also revive an interest in revisiting some events of the past. The range of remedies then becomes very difficult. There is no longer anyone to apply criminal sanctions to, but you can use various forms of compensation, and expose the truth. But I would like to think that for the most part the gamble is in making a better future. If there's only so much energy going to be applied, it should be applied to the future.

. . .

Question: Just to shift away from the ICC a bit, I'm really interested in the victims in all this, and I'm wondering if you had time to get a sense of how an institutional litigation solution to these atrocities felt for the victim. There's a debate about whether truth commissions are better; should we prosecute these people; and how does that work for them? Did you get any sense of the women how they felt?

Answer: Frankly, I can't speak for all of them. At times, you despair because, now, for instance, you hear from the press in the Balkans that people see Milošević on trial[8] and say, "Well, I don't care about him, he's not the one who killed my brother or burned my house." And that's so true. The same thing is true in Rwanda: there are 130,000 people in jail inside Rwanda awaiting trial on genocide-related charges. For a lot of the victims, they're the ones who could identify who had done it. But that's not the mandate that was given to this kind of partnership. So there are times that we feel very disconnected from the people who were actually victimized by the conflict.

This is going to be my final war story. At the height of the NATO air strikes in Kosovo[9]—in February or March of 1999—there was an exodus of people leaving Kosovo, and there were camps set up in Albania and Macedonia. A journalist came to the Hague to interview me. He had just come back from the camp of Kukes in Albania, which was full of Kosovar Albanian refugees, and he said to me, "I'll tell you a story. I'd like to have your reaction." He said that he met a woman in this camp. She had just crossed the border. She had just arrived in total despair, extremely traumatized by the conflict. I've forgotten all of the details—her son was missing, her husband had been killed, her entire village burned, and she was there, completely desperate. At this point, there was zero hope. Her papers had been seized and burned at the border, and this journalist told me he asked her, "If you can ever go back to Kosovo, what are your hopes, what do you want to do?" And she said, "When I go back, if I can, I will kill all the Serbs, but if I can't do that, I want to talk to that woman judge."

He said, "What do you think about that?" I said, "If we had not been there, I know what she would have said. She would have said, when I go back to Kosovo, I will kill all the Serbs, and if I cannot do that I will tell my friends to kill all the Serbs, and I will tell all of my children and grandchildren to kill all the Serbs and I will work on that program until it's accomplished. There is no other alternative." What she articulated for the first time, however, was the **rule of law** as an alternative. Now, let's be very clear which alternative she preferred. But I felt very strongly that it was up to us to give her that choice. We have introduced the alternative, the rule of law alternative. The big step is to promote it as the better alternative, and that is a long road ahead of us.

Notes

1. The Geneva Conventions were among the first international treaties negotiated for the purpose of formalizing just rules of war. They are a series of four treaties signed between 1864 and 1949, and amendment protocols signed between 1977 and 2005. [Editor]
2. Jean-Paul Akayesu was mayor of the Taba commune in Rwanda. He ordered house-to-house searches for local Tutsis and supervised many of their murders. In October 1998 he was tried by the

International Criminal Tribunal for Rwanda (ICTR), found guilty of nine counts of genocide and crimes against humanity and sentenced to life in prison.

Radomir Kovač was a former Serbian paramilitary leader. He kept four Muslim girls in his apartment, repeatedly raped them, and eventually sold three of them as sex slaves. He was tried and convicted by the International Criminal Tribunal for former Yugoslavia (ICTY). Kovač was just one of many perpetrators involved in a series of events referred to by Arbour, the Foča Massacres, which comprised of mass killings and rapes committed by Serbian military and police in the Foča region of Bosnia and Herzegovina.

Anto Furundžija was charged and convicted by the ICTY for his involvement in the Lašva Valley ethnic cleansing, which was perpetrated by Croatians against Bosnian Muslims.

3. The International Criminal Court came into being in June 2002, the very summer referred to by Arbour. [Editor]
4. The United States, having signed the Rome Statute, has both abstained from ratifying (accepting as legally binding) it, and has informed the UN Secretary General that the US government assumes no legal obligation toward the International Criminal Court. [Editor]
5. In July 1950, during the Korean War, three hundred to five hundred South Korean refugees were killed by US troops near the village of No Gun Ri. Orders were given to kill the refugees out of fear of possible North Korean infiltration. [Editor]
6. The Nanking Massacre, also known as the Rape of Nanking, was a mass murder and war rape conducted by Japanese soldiers that began in December 1937 and lasted until February 1938. Approximately two hundred thousand Chinese civilians were killed. [Editor]
7. Algeria was invaded and colonized by France in 1830. As the result of violence and disease the indigenous Algerian population declined by one-third from 1830 to 1872. Algeria regained its independence in 1962, following a revolutionary war conducted by Algerian separatists. During the revolutionary war, torture was used extensively by French officials to interrogate captured Algerian separatists. [Editor]
8. Slobodan Milošević was the President of Serbia from 1989 to 1997 and the President of the Federal Republic of Yugoslavia from 1997 to 2000. Milošević was accused of war crimes and was tried from 2002 until 2005. He died of a heart attack while in custody before a verdict was reached. [Editor]
9. The NATO bombing campaign was conducted in the hopes of quickly drawing Serbian troops out of Kosovo to fortify vulnerable points in their defence. Instead the Serbians remained, and increased the rate at which they deported Albanian Kosovars. The bombing campaign lasted from March to June 1999, with the eventual withdrawal of Serbian forces. [Editor]

Discussion Questions

1. Hurka says the apparently consequentialist proportionality and necessity criteria are interpreted deontologically. What are his reasons for this claim? Do you agree with him? Why or why not?
2. Is political rehabilitation compatible with holding war crimes trials? Why or why not?
3. Do you think Hurka would agree with Orend's views about war crimes trials? Why or why not?
4. Dallaire writes in "The Lessons of Rwanda," "The warrior ethic must be complemented by a more intellectually based competency founded on the humanities where knowledge of the arena is far deeper than overt peace and security measures." Why does he say this? Do you agree with him? Why or why not?

5. What does Dallaire mean by "that eighty per cent of humanity"? What does he think the relationship should be between the eighty per cent and the other twenty per cent?
6. Arbour discusses the decision to prosecute rape as a war crime. What were the reasons for this decision?

Suggested Readings and Websites

🍁 = Canadian source or author

🍁 Arbour, Louise. "Self-Determination & Conflict Resolution: From Kosovo to Sudan." Carnegie Council for Ethics in International Affairs. 23 September 2010. www.carnegiecouncil.org/studio/multimedia/20100923/index.html#section-20553.

🍁 Arbour, Louise. *War Crimes and the Culture of Peace*. Toronto: University of Toronto Press, 2002. [More about the aftermath of war from the former Chief Prosecutor for the International Criminal Tribunals for Yugoslavia and Rwanda and UN High Commissioner for Human Rights.]

🍁 Dallaire, Roméo. *Shake Hands with the Devil*. Toronto: Random House Canada, 2003. [Dallaire's account of the genocide in Rwanda and the Western powers' failure either to prevent or to stop it.]

The Elders. "Independent global leaders working together for peace and human rights." www.theelders.org/home. [A group of eminent elder leaders founded by Nelson Mandela, which includes former US President Jimmy Carter and Ela Bhatt, founder of the Self-Employed Women's Association and the first women's bank in India.]

🍁 Ignatieff, Michael. "Getting Iraq Wrong." *The New York Times*, 5 August 2007. [The former leader of the Liberal Party, originally a supporter of the US-led war in Iraq, has second thoughts.]

International Crisis Group. www.crisisgroup.org/en.aspx. [The world's leading independent, non-partisan, source of analysis and advice to governments, and intergovernmental bodies like the United Nations, European Union, and World Bank, on the prevention and resolution of deadly conflict.]

🍁 Orend, Brian. "War." *Stanford Encyclopedia of Philosophy* (2009). http://plato.stanford.edu/archives/spr2009/entries/war/. [A more thorough discussion of political realism, just war theory, and pacifism.]

Sharp, Gene. *From Dictatorship to Democracy*, 4th edition. East Boston, MA: Albert Einstein Institution, 2010. [A prominent American peace activist discusses "the most effective ways in which dictatorships could be successfully disintegrated with the least possible cost in suffering and lives."]

TFF, the Transnational Foundation for Peace and Future Research. www.transnational.org/. [An international group that describes itself as "an experiment in applied peace research and global networking."]

Walzer, Michael. *Just and Unjust Wars: A Moral Argument with Historical Illustrations*, 3rd edition. New York: Basic Books, 2000. [The best-known book on just war theory by its best-known proponent.]

Chapter 11

Real and Suspected Terrorism

Terrorism in Canada

When most Canadians hear the word "terrorism" today, they think of Muslim extremists. They forget that the two major acts of terrorism in Canadian history—the 1970 October Crisis in Quebec and the 1985 Air India bombing—had nothing at all to do with Islam. They were committed by extremists, but not Muslim ones.

The October Crisis

On 5 October 1970, members of the Front de Libération du Québec (FLQ) kidnapped James Cross, the British trade commissioner in Montreal. They demanded that the government free over two dozen FLQ members in custody and broadcast the FLQ's manifesto. On 10 October the FLQ kidnapped Pierre Laporte, the Quebec minister of labour and immigration. Five days later the Quebec government requested help from the Canadian Forces in apprehending the kidnappers. On 16 October the federal government invoked the *War Measures Act*, a 1914 statute that allowed the government to suspend **civil liberties** in case of "war, invasion or insurrection, real or apprehended." The military and the police arrested nearly five hundred people and held them without charges or bail. Few were even suspected of being FLQ members; they just supported Quebec nationalism. Most were eventually released without charges.

On 17 October, the day after the federal government proclaimed the *War Measures Act*, Laporte was found dead in the trunk of a car. The crisis dragged on. Finally, after eight weeks of captivity, the police discovered where Cross was being held and negotiated his release in exchange for his captors' safe conduct to Cuba. Two men were sentenced to life in prison for Laporte's murder, and two more were convicted of kidnapping him.

The Air India Bombing

On 23 June 1985, a bomb killed two baggage handlers in Tokyo who were transferring bags from a Canadian Pacific to an Air India flight. Less than an hour later, a bomb exploded in mid-flight in Air India Flight 182, which had originated in Vancouver, killing all 329 passengers and crew members. Both bombs were planted by the same group of Sikh extremists, which advocated a separate Sikh homeland in India. The investigation and trials were the most expensive in Canadian history. There have been three criminal trials. One man was convicted of manslaughter in the first two trials for his involvement in the conspiracy that led to the bombing. In 2005—twenty years after the bombing—two other men were acquitted of all charges against them. In 2006, the federal government appointed former Supreme Court Justice John Major to head a Royal Commission on the bombing. The report, released in 2010, strongly criticized Canadian Security Intelligence Service (CSIS), the Royal Canadian Mounted Police (RCMP), the federal government, Transport Canada, and practically every agency involved in counter-terrorism, aviation safety, and the investigation. Major said the attack was "the result of a cascading series of errors" and could have been prevented at several points.[1]

Major Post-9/11 Cases

There have been two high-profile cases in Canada involving men who were suspected—one falsely and the others possibly falsely—of being Muslim extremists. In a third case, eleven men were convicted of participating in a terrorist group and planning terrorist actions.

The first case involved a Canadian citizen, Maher Arar, who came to Canada from Syria in 1987, at the age of seventeen. In 2002 he was returning from a holiday in Tunisia when US officials detained him on a stopover. They suspected he had ties to al Qaeda, partly based on information from the RCMP that was later shown to be wrong. The US **rendered** Arar to Syria, despite his Canadian passport and the fact that Syria is well known for its use of torture. After eleven months of torture and solitary confinement, Arar was released; the Syrian government said there was no evidence that he had links to al Qaeda. When he returned to Canada, Arar fought to clear his name and to be compensated for his ordeal. A 2006 Royal Commission report exonerated him, saying "there is no evidence to indicate that Mr. Arar has committed any offence or that his activities constitute a threat to the security of Canada."[2] In 2007 Prime Minister Harper officially apologized to Arar, and the federal government awarded him $10.5 million in damages.

The second case involved five men originally from Middle Eastern countries who were held under **security certificates**. These are legal tools for detaining and possibly deporting foreign nationals or permanent residents who the federal government considers a danger to national security. Neither the people held under security certificates nor their lawyers may see the evidence against them; they see only a summary provided by a judge. In 2007 the Supreme Court heard a case brought by three of the men, arguing that security certificates violate the *Charter*. The Court ruled unanimously in their favour. (See *Charkaoui v Canada* in this chapter.) The federal government re-wrote the security certificate law. Since then, Charkaoui and one of the other men have been released. The third, Mohamed Harkat, challenged the new security certificate law and its application in his case. In 2014, the Supreme Court said the law is constitutional and was properly applied. The federal government has ordered Harkat's deportation. He is fighting it, saying he will be tortured and killed if he is returned to Algeria.

In the third case, Canadian authorities aborted a terrorist plot in 2006 when police charged fifteen men and youths under the *Anti-terrorism Act*. Two more men were already in prison for trying to smuggle weapons into Canada, and an eighteenth was arrested two months later. All were conservative, disaffected Muslims who believed the West was waging war against Islam. Police said the group, dubbed the "Toronto 18" by the media, planned to bomb two buildings in Toronto and one at a nearby military base. They bought three tonnes of fertilizer to make the bombs, and one of the men built remote-controlled detonators. Their goal was to force the Canadian government to withdraw its troops from Afghanistan. Charges were stayed against four of the men and three youths. Seven men pleaded guilty to belonging to a terrorist group and planning terrorist acts. The remaining four opted for trials and were convicted. The eleven men's sentences ranged from two and a half years to life in prison.

Philosophical Issues

What Is Terrorism?

Most philosophers and political commentators agree that terrorism includes three elements: violence, terror, and political aims. Beyond that, though, there is much disagreement. Some authors define terrorism broadly. These definitions include *all* cases of terrorism, but critics claim they also include some "false positives" that differ from terrorism. Other authors define terrorism narrowly. These definitions include *only* cases of terrorism, but critics say they also exclude cases that most people think are terrorism. Compare the following definitions:

- Igor Primoratz: Terrorism is "[t]he deliberate use of violence, or threat of its use, against innocent people, with the aim of intimidating some other people into a course of action they otherwise would not take." People are innocent if they "have not lost their immunity against lethal or other extreme violence by being directly involved in, or highly responsible for, (what terrorists consider) insufferable injustice or oppression. . . . [I]n a violent conflict that falls short of war, these are common citizens."[3]
- David Claridge: "Terrorism is the systematic threat or use of violence, whether for, or in opposition to, established authority, with the intention of communicating a political message to a group larger than the victim group by generating fear and so altering the behaviour of the larger group. Either the victim or the perpetrator, or both, will be operating outside a military context; both will never be operating within a military context."[4]

Primoratz's definition is both too broad and too narrow. It is too broad because the "aim of intimidating some other people into a course of action they otherwise would not take" can include not only terrorist acts but also threats by kidnappers and members of organized crime, as well as almost everything done in war. Primoratz has left terrorism's political aims out of his definition. Primoratz's definition is also too narrow because it excludes acts that harm or kill government officials, police officers, and soldiers. By this definition, the planes that hit the World Trade Center on 9/11 were acts of terrorism but the plane that hit the Pentagon on the same day was not, because those who work for the military are not "innocent." Primoratz might reply that flying a plane into the Pentagon was a terrorist attack because the passengers and crew on the plane were innocent. But this will not work. Had the 9/11 terrorists expelled the passengers and crew from the all planes before they crashed them into the World Trade Center and the Pentagon, Primoratz would have to say that the attack on the World Trade Center was terrorism but the attack on the Pentagon was not. This is odd; all still would have been part of a single, coordinated attack. Terrorists may believe all employees of a government or the military contribute to the oppression of those whom terrorists claim to defend and so are not innocent, but that is no reason for philosophers to adopt their view of innocence and culpability. Finally, Primoratz's use of the word "innocent" loads his definition morally. This weakens his argument that terrorism is wrong or almost always wrong, because it goes without saying that killing innocent people is almost always wrong. Is it wrong for terrorists to target people who are partially responsible for, or who benefit from, injustice? Primoratz's definition **begs the question**.

Claridge's definition is more plausible. It is not too broad; it distinguishes terrorism from both criminal activity (the political message) and war (victims, perpetrators, or both are non-military). Nor is it too narrow; it acknowledges that the victims of terrorism may be government officials and military personnel as well as civilians. This fits with most people's beliefs that both the FLQ kidnappings, which targeted government ministers, and the plane that hit the Pentagon on 9/11 were terrorist acts. Claridge's view also does not prejudge the question of whether terrorism can ever be justified; that requires further argument. (See "Evaluating Terrorism," below.)

What Terrorists Hate

People often say that terrorists hate freedom, what the West stands for, "our way of life," a particular country such as the US, or a people such as English Canadians. Certainly terrorists hate something, or they would not do what they do. But the belief that terrorists hate everything that is right or good in their larger targets is simplistic at best. The FLQ did not hate freedom—they wanted a free Quebec. And they didn't so much hate English Canadians as they hated how English Canadians had treated the Quebecois. Today many Quebecois and some English Canadians agree with the FLQ's goals but not their methods. The Toronto 18 and the Sikh men who planted bombs in two airplanes in 1985 hated Western governments and the Indian government, respectively, but that does not mean they hated freedom, all Westerners, or all Indians. This claim is a comfortable self-deception that allows us to feel righteous.

Sometimes, of course, terrorists do hate what we value—but so do many non-terrorists. The Toronto 18 considered Western **secular** society decadent. Many conservative Christians, Jews, Hindus, and other conservative Muslims agree, but they are not terrorists. The Toronto 18 wanted to live in a society that operated according to strict Islamic principles. But this desire is not unique to Muslim terrorists; many fundamentalists of all stripes want to live in societies run according to the principles of their faith. Christian fundamentalists in the US and Hindu fundamentalists in India want their governments to follow strict interpretations of Christianity and Hinduism, respectively. Their views are intolerant and extreme—both societies are multi-faith and multicultural—but that does not make them terrorists. Nor are fundamentalist religions the only religions with political as well as spiritual aims and practices. Canadian religious leaders regularly weigh in on political issues such as abortion, poverty, international aid, and war.

It is also bad thinking to believe that, because we were unjustly targeted by terrorists, we are beyond reproach. Of course the FLQ was wrong to kidnap Cross, and to kidnap and murder Laporte. But that does not alter the facts that anglophones had tried to wipe out the French language in Quebec and the rest of Canada, and that they had discriminated against the francophone majority in Quebec. Being the real or possible victim of a terrorist attack does not make us morally innocent of all the wrongs the terrorists seek to right. Victims may have dirty hands.

Evaluating Terrorism

Is terrorism ever justified? Some people say that one person's terrorist is another's freedom fighter. This claim is at least plausible. For example:

- The British considered the Irish Republican Army and its offshoots to be terrorist groups, while the Americans did not.
- Before the end of apartheid (the system of racial separation, white dominance, and black **disenfranchisement** in South Africa from 1948 to 1994), the government of South Africa considered the African National Congress a terrorist group. Much of the world considered it a group of freedom fighters who were the legitimate representative of the black South African majority.
- The Animal Liberation Front (ALF) frees animals from laboratories and then vandalizes or destroys the laboratories so they cannot continue operating. They have a strict policy of never physically harming people or animals, and there are no reports that anyone has been physically harmed by their actions. The US government considers the ALF "one of the most serious terrorism threats to the nation,"[5] and the British government defines them as "domestic extremists"[6] (people who engage in criminal behaviour for political purposes). However, some animal rights activists consider them heroes.
- The Army of God is a pro-life, anti-gay, anti-government group in the US whose members have bombed abortion clinics and a lesbian bar, set off a bomb during the 1996 Atlanta Olympics (killing two people and injuring 111 others), and killed abortion providers. Most pro-choice and pro-life supporters consider the AOG a terrorist group. However, some pro-life supporters believe the AOG's acts are justified because they prevent the slaughter of unborn children.

The actions of all four groups fit the definition of terrorism, but at least some people think each group's actions are justified. So when, if ever, is terrorism justified?

Terrorists believe ends can justify means. Sometimes they do; some people really do thank their parents for forcing them to take music lessons or play hockey. Not every end can justify every means, though. Terrorists believe the justice of their cause turns death, mayhem, and terror into collateral damage. Since those are some of the worst possible means, though, terrorists need some of the best possible ends to justify them. In addition, many people deny that ends can justify means—just ends require just means, they say. That's part of what Ghandi meant when he said, "Be the change you wish to see in the world."

Some terrorists claim they take an eye for an eye. The larger group at which their act aims has committed great wrongs against the terrorists' group, and the terrorists want to make members of the larger group pay. This argument employs a simplistic form of **retributive justice** that would quickly descend into violence, vendettas, and feuds. As Canadian MP George Perry Graham said during a debate on capital punishment in the House of Commons in 1914, "If in this present age we were to go back to the old time of 'an eye for an eye and a tooth for a tooth,' there would be very few Honourable Gentlemen in this House who would not, metaphorically speaking, be blind and toothless."[7]

Both war and terrorism aim to cause political change. Fear is usually a part of war, as it is of terrorism. War's violence kills many more people and causes much more damage than terrorism does, but philosophers have argued it is sometimes justified. According to just war theorists (see Chapter 10, War, Peacekeeping, and Transitional Justice), we can inflict widespread death, mayhem, and destruction on other people only if

1. we have a just cause,
2. we have just intentions,
3. we have pursued all peaceful alternatives,
4. doing so will cause more overall good than evil to people on both sides,
5. we do not use chemical or biological weapons,
6. we do not commit **crimes against humanity**,
7. we use the least force necessary to achieve our aims,
8. we do not target civilians,
9. we treat prisoners decently, and
10. we fight fairly, that is, we do not violate the criteria simply because the other side did.

Most terrorism does not come close to meeting these criteria, but then again, neither do most wars. If we think of the criteria for a just war as ideals to be aimed for, then we can say some wars are better, or at least less bad, than others. If we use a similar set of criteria for terrorism, perhaps we can say that some terrorist acts are better or less bad than others.

Almost no terrorist acts that physically harm or kill people will be justified, though, because there are always, or nearly always, non-violent alternatives. Gandhi led a non-violent revolution for Indian independence. The civil rights movement in the US was non-violent. In 1963, Vietnamese Buddhist monk Thich Quang Duc self-immolated (burned himself to death) on a busy Saigon street to protest religious persecution. His death sparked protests that led to the downfall of the government. In 2010 Mohamed Bouazizi, a street vendor in Tunisia, self-immolated after his wares were confiscated and he was roughed up by police for the umpteenth time. His death became a symbol of the Tunisian revolution and the Arab Spring. Both Quang Duc's and Bouazizi's acts had an enormous political impact, but they harmed no one except themselves.

The Readings

In the first reading, Thomas Homer-Dixon discusses "complex terrorism," terrorism that uses sophisticated technology to target complex economic and technological systems rather than people. He calls these "weapons of mass disruption." Taking down the power grid in a major city, disrupting banks' or governments' computer systems, causing a massive oil or chemical spill, or poisoning the water or food supply could create an exponential series of effects that would devastate us. Homer-Dixon says we must decentralize complex systems and "loosen couplings" so problems do not multiply so quickly.

At the time Louise Arbour wrote the second reading, she was the United Nations High Commissioner for Human Rights. Previously she had been a Canadian Supreme Court Justice and Chief Prosecutor of the International Tribunals for Rwanda and the former Yugoslavia. Arbour begins with what she call the "old normal," where courts declared coercive questioning and arrests without **due process** of law illegal. She contrasts this with the "new normal," where states' fears of terrorism are quickly eroding basic civil rights and the rule of law. The "new normal" involves "a complete repudiation of the law and of the justice system" that we must resist, she says.

Louis Delvoie had a distinguished career as a Canadian diplomat and as an Assistant Deputy Minister in the Department of Defence. He acknowledges that the threat of terrorism is real, but says it has been blown out of proportion; it is "a limited and manageable threat." The total number of people killed by terrorists pales in comparison to, say, the numbers that are dying because of wars and AIDS in Africa. Our "terrorism fixation" has worsened the already tense relationship between the West and Islamic societies, and it has allowed some governments to engage in human rights violations under the cover of fighting terrorism.

The fourth reading comes from the Supreme Court's unanimous decision in *Charkaoui v. Canada*. Adil Charkaoui and two other men who had been held indefinitely on security certificates challenged their constitutionality. The men argued security certificates violated s. 7 of the *Charter*, which forbids depriving someone of life, liberty, or security of their person "except in accordance with the principles of fundamental justice"; s. 9, which forbids arbitrary detention; s. 12, which forbids cruel and unusual treatment, and s. 6 (mobility rights) because security certificates treat citizens and non-citizens unequally. (The Court had ruled previously that the *Charter* applies to everyone in Canada, regardless of citizenship status.) In addition, they argued that security certificates violated the rule of law. The Court agreed that security certificates violated ss. 7, 9, and 12, but not s. 6 or the rule of law. They declared the security certificate procedure unconstitutional, but gave the government a year to bring it back in line with the *Charter*.

In the final reading Trudy Govier and Wilhelm Verwoerd, a philosopher and a former staff researcher for the South African Truth and Reconciliation Commission, argue that we must move beyond the **false dichotomy** of "victims" and "perpetrators." Perpetrators are usually supported by many people who contributed to their crimes in numerous ways—financially, strategically, by storing supplies, and by supporting their cause. If we hope to re-integrate perpetrators and their supporters after a conflict has ended, we must realize that both perpetrators and their victims are more complex than we usually think, the authors say.

The Moral and Political Preferences Indicator

Most people agree that most terrorism is wrong. Among that small set of terrorist acts that might be justifiable, people tend to focus on the justice of causes more than on the justice of acts. Conservatives might sympathize with terrorism that targets repressive left-wing regimes, while egalitarians might sympathize with terrorism that targets repressive right-wing regimes. Egalitarians also might sympathize with terrorism in defence of sub-state nations and racial or ethnic minorities, because they are more likely to accept the legitimacy of these groups' claims. Because conservatives are more likely to accept the legitimacy of states' and majorities' claims, they are more likely to criticize terrorism in defence of sub-state nations and other minorities. (See the introductions to Chapter 1, Aboriginal Peoples, and Chapter 2, Quebec Nationalism.) When it comes to terrorism in the Middle East, conservatives tend to sympathize with Israel while egalitarians tend to sympathize with Palestinians and the Islamic states.

Conservatives and egalitarians also differ on how best to respond to terrorist threats. Conservatives usually focus on security. So, for example, they are more likely to believe in coercive interrogation and in the justice and necessity of security certificates. Egalitarians usually focus on preserving civil liberties and the rule of law, so they are more likely to reject coercive interrogation and security certificates.

Notes

1. *Air India Flight 182: A Canadian Tragedy*, report of the Commission of Inquiry into the Investigation of the Bombing of Air India Flight 182, vol. 1 (Ottawa: Public Works and Government Services Canada, 2010), p. 21.
2. *Report of the Events Relating to Maher Arar: Analysis and Recommendations*, report of the Commission of Inquiry into the Actions of Canadian Officials in Relation to Maher Arar (Ottawa: Public Works and Government Services Canada, 2006), p. 9.
3. Igor Primoratz, "Terrorism," *Stanford Encyclopedia of Philosophy* (2011) http://plato.stanford.edu/entries/terrorism/.
4. David Claridge, "State Terrorism? Applying a Definitional Model," *Terrorism and Political Violence* 8, 3 (1996): 50.
5. Terry Frieden, "FBI, ATF address domestic terrorism," CNN.com (19 May 2005), www.cnn.com/2005/US/05/19/domestic.terrorism/.
6. Association of Chief Police Officers, "NCDE National Co-ordinator Domestic Extremism," www.acpo.police.uk/NationalPolicing/NCDENationalCoordinatorDomesticExtremism/Defa.ult.aspx.
7. Official Report of the Debates of the House of Commons of the Dominion of Canada: Third Session, Twelfth Parliament, Mr. Graham speaking, Volume CXIII (5 February 1914), 496. The quote "an eye for an eye will make the whole world blind" is often attributed to Gandhi, but there is no evidence that he said or wrote it. Graham's quote is the earliest the Quote Investigator could find. See Garson O'Toole, "An Eye for an Eye Will Make the Whole World Blind," Quote Investigator (27 December 2010), http://quoteinvestigator.com/2010/12/27/eye-for-eye-blind/.

Thomas Homer-Dixon

The Rise of Complex Terrorism

It's four a.m. on a sweltering summer night in July 2003. Across much of the United States, power plants are working full tilt to generate electricity for millions of air conditioners that are keeping a ferocious heat wave at bay. The electricity grid in California has repeatedly buckled under the strain, with rotating blackouts from San Diego to Santa Rosa.

In different parts of the state, half a dozen small groups of men and women gather. Each travels in a rented minivan to its prearranged destination—for some, a location outside one of the hundreds of electrical substations dotting the state; for others, a spot upwind from key, high-voltage transmission lines. The groups unload their equipment from the vans. Those outside the substations put together simple mortars made from materials bought at local hardware stores, while those near the transmission lines use helium to inflate weather balloons with long silvery tails. At a precisely coordinated moment, the homemade mortars are fired, sending showers of aluminum chaff over the substations. The balloons are released and drift into the transmission lines.

Simultaneously, other groups are doing the same thing along the Eastern Seaboard and in the South and Southwest. A national electrical system already under immense strain is massively short-circuited, causing a cascade of power failures across the country. Traffic lights shut off. Water and sewage systems are disabled. Communications systems break down. The financial system and national economy come screeching to a halt.

Sound far-fetched? Perhaps it would have before September 11, 2001, but certainly not now. We've realized, belatedly, that our societies are wide-open targets for terrorists. We're easy prey because of two key trends: First, the growing technological capacity of small groups and individuals to destroy things and people; and, second, the increasing vulnerability of our economic and technological systems to carefully aimed attacks. While commentators have devoted considerable ink and airtime to the first of these trends, they've paid far less attention to the second, and they've virtually ignored their combined effect. Together, these two trends facilitate a new and sinister kind of mass violence—a "complex terrorism" that threatens modern, high-tech societies in the world's most developed nations.

Our fevered, Hollywood-conditioned imaginations encourage us to focus on the sensational possibility of nuclear or biological attacks—attacks that might kill tens of thousands of people in a single strike. These threats certainly deserve attention, but not to the neglect of the likelier and ultimately deadlier disruptions that could result from the clever exploitation by terrorists of our societies' new and growing complexities.

Weapons of Mass Disruption

The steady increase in the destructive capacity of small groups and individuals is driven largely by three technological advances: more powerful weapons, the dramatic progress in communications and information processing, and more abundant opportunities to divert non-weapon technologies to destructive ends.

Consider first the advances in weapons technology. Over the last century, progress in materials engineering, the chemistry of explosives, and miniaturization of electronics has brought steady improvement in all key weapons characteristics, including accuracy, destructive power, range, portability, ruggedness, ease-of-use, and affordability. Improvements in light weapons are particularly relevant to trends in terrorism and violence by small groups, where the devices of choice include rocket-propelled grenade launchers, machine guns, light mortars, land mines, and cheap assault rifles such as the famed AK-47. The effects of improvements in these weapons are particularly noticeable in developing countries. A few decades ago, a small band of terrorists or insurgents attacking a rural village might have used bolt-action rifles, which take precious time to reload.

Today, cheap assault rifles multiply the possible casualties resulting from such an attack. As technological change makes it easier to kill, societies are more likely to become locked into perpetual cycles of attack and counterattack that render any normal trajectory of political and economic development impossible.

Meanwhile, new communications technologies—from satellite phones to the Internet—allow violent groups to marshal resources and coordinate activities around the planet. **Transnational** terrorist organizations can use the Internet to share information on weapons and recruiting tactics, arrange surreptitious fund transfers across borders, and plan attacks. These new technologies can also dramatically enhance the reach and power of age-old procedures. Take the ancient hawala system of moving money between countries, widely used in Middle Eastern and Asian societies. The system, which relies on brokers linked together by clan-based networks of trust, has become faster and more effective through the use of the Internet.

Information-processing technologies have also boosted the power of terrorists by allowing them to hide or encrypt their messages. The power of a modern laptop computer today is comparable to the computational power available in the entire US Defense Department in the mid-1960s. Terrorists can use this power to run widely available state-of-the-art encryption software. Sometimes less advanced computer technologies are just as effective. For instance, individuals can use a method called steganography ("hidden writing") to embed messages into digital photographs or music clips. Posted on publicly available Web sites, the photos or clips are downloaded by collaborators as necessary. (This technique was reportedly used by recently arrested terrorists when they planned to blow up the US Embassy in Paris.[1]) At latest count, 140 easy-to-use steganography tools were available on the Internet. Many other off-the-shelf technologies—such as "spread-spectrum" radios that randomly switch their broadcasting and receiving signals—allow terrorists to obscure their messages and make themselves invisible.

The Web also provides access to critical information. The September 11 terrorists could have found there all the details they needed about the floor plans and design characteristics of the World Trade Center and about how demolition experts use progressive collapse to destroy large buildings. The Web also makes available sets of instructions—or "technical ingenuity"—needed to combine readily available materials in destructive ways. Practically anything an extremist wants to know about kidnapping, bomb making, and assassination is now available online. One somewhat facetious example: It's possible to convert everyday materials into potentially destructive devices like the "potato cannon." With a barrel and combustion chamber fashioned from common plastic pipe, and with propane as an explosive propellant, a well-made cannon can hurl a homely spud hundreds of meters—or throw chaff onto electrical substations. A quick search of the Web reveals dozens of sites giving instructions on how to make one.

Finally, modern, high-tech societies are filled with supercharged devices packed with energy, combustibles, and poisons, giving terrorists ample opportunities to divert such non-weapon technologies to destructive ends. To cause horrendous damage, all terrorists must do is figure out how to release this power and let it run wild. . . .

High-Tech Hubris

The vulnerability of advanced nations stems not only from the greater destructive capacities of terrorists, but also from the increased vulnerability of the West's economic and technological systems. This additional vulnerability is the product of two key social and technological developments: first, the growing complexity and interconnectedness of our modern societies; and second, the increasing geographic concentration of wealth, human capital, knowledge, and communication links.

Consider the first of these developments. All human societies encompass a multitude of economic and technological systems. We can think of these systems as networks—that is, as sets of nodes and links among those nodes. The US economy consists of numerous nodes, including corporations, factories, and urban centers; it also consists of links among these nodes, such as highways, rail lines, electrical grids, and fiber-optic cables. As societies modernize and become richer, their networks become more complex and interconnected. The number of nodes increases, as does the density of links among the nodes and the speed at which materials, energy, and information are pushed along these links. Moreover, the nodes themselves become more complex as the people who create, operate, and manage them strive for better performance. (For instance, a manufacturing company might improve efficiency by adopting more intricate inventory control methods.)

Complex and interconnected networks sometimes have features that make their behavior unstable and unpredictable. In particular, they can have feedback loops that produce vicious cycles. A good example is a stock market crash, in which selling drives down prices, which begets more selling. Networks can also be tightly coupled, which means that links among the nodes are short, therefore making it more likely that problems with one node will spread to others. When drivers tailgate at high speeds on freeways, they create a tightly coupled system: A mistake by one driver, or a sudden shock coming from outside the system, such as a deer running across the road, can cause a chain reaction of cars piling onto each other. We've seen such knock-on effects in the US electrical, telephone, and air traffic systems, when a failure in one part of the network has sometimes produced a cascade of failures across the country. Finally, in part because of feedbacks and tight coupling, networks often exhibit nonlinear behavior, meaning that a small shock or perturbation to the network produces a disproportionately large disruption.

. . .

Terrorists must be clever to exploit these weaknesses. They must attack the right nodes in the right networks. If they don't, the damage will remain isolated and the overall network will be resilient. Much depends upon the network's level of redundancy—that is, on the degree to which the damaged node's functions can be offloaded to undamaged nodes. As terrorists come to recognize the importance of redundancy, their ability to disable complex networks will improve. Langdon Winner, a theorist of politics and technology, provides the first rule of modern terrorism: "Find the critical but non-redundant parts of the system and sabotage . . . them according to your purposes." . . .

The range of possible terrorist attacks has expanded due to a second source of organizational vulnerability in modern economies—the rising concentration of high-value assets in geographically small locations. Advanced societies concentrate valuable things and people in order to achieve economies of scale. Companies in capital-intensive industries can usually reduce the per-unit cost of their goods by building larger production facilities. Moreover, placing expensive equipment and highly skilled people in a single location provides easier access, more efficiencies, and synergies that constitute an important source of wealth. That is why we build places like the World Trade Center.

In so doing, however, we also create extraordinarily attractive targets for terrorists, who realize they can cause a huge amount of damage in a single strike. On September 11, a building complex that took seven years to construct collapsed in ninety minutes, obliterating ten million square feet of office space and exacting at least thirty billion dollars in direct costs. A major telephone switching office was destroyed, another heavily damaged, and important cellular antennas on top of the towers were lost. Key transit lines through southern Manhattan were buried under rubble. Ironically, even a secret office of the US Central Intelligence Agency was destroyed in the attack, temporarily disrupting normal intelligence operations.

Yet despite the horrific damage to the area's infrastructure and New York City's economy, the attack did not cause catastrophic failures in US financial, economic, or communications networks. As it turned out, the World Trade Center was not a critical, non-redundant node. At least it wasn't critical in the way most people (including, probably, the terrorists) would have thought. Many of the financial firms in the destroyed buildings had made contingency plans for disaster by setting up alternate facilities for data, information, and computer equipment in remote locations. Though the NASDAQ[2] headquarters was demolished, for instance, the exchange's data centers in Connecticut and Maryland remained linked to trading companies through two separate connections that passed through twenty switching centers. NASDAQ officials later claimed that their system was so robust that they could have restarted trading only a few hours after the attack. . . .

But when we look back years from now, we may recognize that the attacks had a critical effect on another kind of network that we've created among ourselves: a tightly coupled, very unstable, and highly nonlinear psychological network. We're all nodes in this particular network, and the links among us consist of Internet connections, satellite signals, fiber-optic cables, talk radio, and twenty-four-hour television news. In the minutes following the attack, coverage of the story flashed across this network. People then stayed in front of their televisions for hours on end; they viewed and reviewed the awful video clips on the CNN Web site; they plugged phone lines checking on friends and relatives; and they sent each other millions upon millions of e-mail messages—so many, in fact, that the Internet was noticeably slower for days afterwards.

Along these links, from TV and radio stations to their audiences, and especially from person to person through the Internet, flowed raw emotion: grief, anger, horror, disbelief, fear, and hatred. It was as if we'd all been wired into one immense, convulsing, and reverberating neural network. Indeed, the biggest impact of the September 11 attacks wasn't the direct disruption of financial, economic, communications, or transportation networks—physical stuff, all. Rather, by working through the network we've created within and among our heads, the attacks had their biggest impact on our collective psychology and our subjective feelings of security and safety. This network acts like a huge megaphone, vastly amplifying the emotional impact of terrorism.

To maximize this impact, the perpetrators of complex terrorism will carry out their attacks in audacious, unexpected, and even bizarre manners—using methods that are, ideally, unimaginably cruel. By so doing, they will create the impression that anything is possible, which further magnifies fear. From this perspective, the World Trade Center represented an ideal target, because the Twin Towers were an icon of the magnificence and boldness of American capitalism. When they collapsed like a house of cards, in about fifteen seconds each, it suggested that American capitalism was a house of cards, too. How could anything so solid and powerful and so much a part of American identity vanish so quickly? And the use of passenger airplanes made matters worse by exploiting our worst fears of flying.

Unfortunately, this emotional response has had huge, real-world consequences. Scared, insecure, grief-stricken people aren't ebullient consumers. They behave cautiously and save more. Consumer demand drops, corporate investment falls, and economic growth slows. In the end, via the multiplier effect of our technology-amplified emotional response, the September 11 terrorists may have achieved an economic impact far greater than they ever dreamed possible. The total cost of lost economic growth and decreased equity value around the world could exceed a trillion dollars. Since the cost of carrying out the attack itself was probably only a few hundred thousand dollars, we're looking at an economic multiplier of over a million-fold.

The Weakest Links

Complex terrorism operates like jujitsu—it redirects the energies of our intricate societies against us. Once the basic logic of complex terrorism is understood (and the events of September 11 prove that terrorists are beginning to understand it), we can quickly identify dozens of relatively simple ways to bring modern, high-tech societies to their knees.

... [T]he critical complex networks upon which modern societies depend ... include networks for producing and distributing energy, information, water, and food; the highways, railways, and airports that make up our transportation grid; and our health care system. Of these, the vulnerability of the food system is particularly alarming. However, terrorism experts have paid the most attention to the energy and information networks, mainly because they so clearly underpin the vitality of modern economies.

The energy system—which comprises everything from the national network of gas pipelines to the electricity grid—is replete with high-value nodes like oil refineries, tank farms, and electrical substations. At times of peak energy demand, this network (and in particular, the electricity grid) is very tightly coupled. The loss of one link in the grid means that the electricity it carries must be offloaded to other links. If other links are already operating near capacity, the additional load can cause them to fail, too, thus displacing their energy to yet other links. We saw this kind of breakdown in August 1996, when the failure of the Big Eddy transmission line in northern Oregon caused overloading on a string of transmission lines down the West Coast of the United States, triggering blackouts that affected four million people in nine states.

Substations are clear targets because they represent key nodes linked to many other parts of the electrical network. Substations and high-voltage transmission lines are also "soft" targets, since they can be fairly easily disabled or destroyed. Tens of thousands of miles of transmission lines are strung across North America, often in locations so remote that the lines are almost impossible to protect, but they are nonetheless accessible by four-wheel drive. Transmission towers can be brought down with well-placed explosive charges. Imagine a carefully planned sequence of attacks on these lines, with emergency crews and investigators dashing from one remote attack site to another, constantly off-balance and unable to regain control. Detailed maps of locations of substations and transmission lines for much of North America are easily available on the Web. Not even all the police and military personnel in the United States would suffice to provide even rudimentary protection to this immense network.

The energy system also provides countless opportunities for turning supposedly benign technology to destructive ends. For instance, large gas pipelines, many of which run near or even through urban areas, have huge explosive potential; attacks on them could have the twin effect of producing great local damage and wider disruptions in energy supply. And the radioactive waste pools associated with most nuclear reactors are perhaps the most lethal targets in the national energy-supply system. If the waste in these facilities were dispersed into the environment, the results could be catastrophic. Fortunately, such attacks would be technically difficult.

Even beyond energy networks, opportunities to release the destructive power of benign technologies abound. Chemical plants are especially tempting targets, because they are packed with toxins and flammable, even explosive, materials. Security at such facilities is often lax: An April 1999 study of chemical plants in Nevada and West Virginia by the US Agency for Toxic Substances and Disease Registry concluded that security ranged from "fair to very poor" and that oversights were linked to "complacency and lack of awareness of the threat." And every day, trains carrying tens of thousands of tons of toxic material course along transport corridors throughout the United States. All a terrorist needs is inside knowledge that a chemical-laden train is traveling through an urban area at a specific time, and a well-placed object (like a piece of rail) on the track could cause a wreck, a chemical release, and a mass evacuation. . . .

Modern communications networks also are susceptible to terrorist attacks. Although the Internet was originally designed to keep working even if large chunks of the network were lost (as might happen in a nuclear war, for instance), today's Internet displays some striking vulnerabilities. One of the most significant is the system of computers—called "routers" and "root servers"—that directs traffic around the Net. Routers represent critical nodes in the network and depend on each other for details on where to send packets of information. A software error in one router, or its malicious reprogramming by a hacker, can lead to errors throughout the Internet. Hackers could also exploit new peer-to-peer software (such as the information-transfer tool Gnutella) to distribute throughout the Internet millions of "sleeper" viruses programmed to attack specific machines or the network itself at a predetermined date.

. . .

Preparing for the Unknown

Shortly following the September 11 attacks, the US Army enlisted the help of some of Hollywood's top action screenwriters and directors—including the writers of *Die Hard* and *McGyver*—to conjure up possible scenarios for future terrorist attacks. Yet no one can possibly imagine in advance all the novel opportunities for terrorism provided by our technological and economic systems. We've made these critical systems so complex that they are replete with vulnerabilities that are very hard to anticipate, because we don't even know how to ask the right questions. . . . Terrorists can make connections between components of complex systems—such as between passenger airliners and skyscrapers—that few, if any, people have anticipated. Complex terrorism is particularly effective if its goal is not a specific strategic or political end, but simply the creation of widespread fear, panic, and economic disruption. This more general objective grants terrorists much more latitude in their choice of targets. More likely than not, the next major attack will come in a form as unexpected as we witnessed on September 11.

What should we do to lessen the risk of complex terrorism, beyond the conventional counterterrorism strategies already being implemented by the United States and other nations? First, we must acknowledge our own limitations. Little can be done, for instance, about terrorists' inexorably rising capacity for violence. This trend results from deep technological forces that can't be stopped without producing major disruptions elsewhere in our economies and societies. However, we can take steps to reduce the vulnerabilities related to our complex economies and technologies. We can do so by loosening the couplings in our economic and technological networks, building into these networks various buffering capacities, introducing "circuit breakers" that interrupt dangerous feedbacks, and dispersing high-value assets so that they are less concentrated and thus less inviting targets.

These **prescriptions** will mean different things for different networks. In the energy sector, loosening coupling might mean greater use of decentralized, local energy production and alternative energy sources (like small-scale solar power) that make individual users more independent of the electricity grid. Similarly, in food production, loosening coupling could entail increased **autonomy** of local and regional food-production networks so that when one network is attacked the damage doesn't cascade into others. In many industries, increasing buffering would involve moving away from just-in-time production processes. Firms would need to increase inventories of feedstocks and parts so production can continue even when the supply of these essential inputs is interrupted. Clearly this policy would reduce economic efficiency, but the extra security of more stable and resilient production networks could far outweigh this cost.

Circuit breakers would prove particularly useful in situations where crowd behavior and panic can get out of control. They have already been implemented on the New York Stock Exchange: Trading halts if the market plunges more than a certain percentage in a particular period of time. In the case of terrorism, one of the factors heightening public anxiety is the incessant barrage of sensational reporting and commentary by twenty-four-hour news TV. As is true for the stock exchange, there might be a role for an independent, industry-based monitoring body here, a body that could intervene with broadcasters at critical moments, or at least provide vital counsel, to manage the flow and content of information. In an emergency, for instance, all broadcasters might present exactly the same information (vetted by the monitoring body and stated deliberately and calmly) so that competition among broadcasters doesn't encourage sensationalized treatment. If the monitoring body were under the strict authority of the broadcasters themselves, the broadcasters would—collectively—retain complete control over the content of the message, and the procedure would not involve government encroachment on freedom of speech.

If terrorist attacks continue, economic forces alone will likely encourage the dispersal of high-value assets. Insurance costs could become unsupportable for businesses and industries located in vulnerable zones. In twenty to thirty years, we may be astonished at the folly of housing so much value in the exquisitely fragile buildings of the World Trade Center. Again, dispersal may entail substantial economic costs, because we'll lose economies of scale and opportunities for synergy.

Yet we have to recognize that we face new circumstances. Past policies are inadequate. The advantage in this war has shifted toward terrorists. Our increased vulnerability—and our newfound recognition of that vulnerability—makes us more risk-averse, while terrorists have become more powerful and more tolerant of risk. (The September 11 attackers, for instance, had an extremely high tolerance for risk, because they were ready and willing to die.) As a result, terrorists have significant leverage to hurt us. Their capacity to exploit this leverage depends on their ability to understand the complex systems that we depend on so critically. Our capacity to defend ourselves depends on that same understanding.

Sidebar: Feeding Frenzies

Shorting out electrical grids or causing train derailments would be small-scale sabotage compared with terrorist attacks that intentionally exploit psychological vulnerabilities. One key vulnerability is our fear for our health—an attack that exploits this fear would foster widespread panic. Probably the easiest way to strike at the health of an industrialized nation is through its food-supply system.

Modern food-supply systems display many key features that a prospective terrorist would seek in a complex network and are thus highly vulnerable to attack. Such systems are tightly coupled, and they have many nodes—including huge factory farms and food-processing plants—with multiple connections to other nodes.

The recent foot-and-mouth disease crisis in the United Kingdom [in 2001] provided dramatic evidence of these characteristics. By the time veterinarians found the disease, it had already spread throughout Great Britain. As in the United States, the drive for economic efficiencies in the British farming sector has produced a highly integrated system in which foods move briskly from farm to table. It has also led to economic concentration, with a few immense abattoirs [slaughterhouses] scattered across the land replacing the country's many small slaughterhouses. Foot-and-mouth disease spread rapidly in large part because infected animals were shipped from farms to these distant abattoirs.

Given these characteristics, foot-and-mouth disease seems a useful vector for a terrorist attack. The virus is endemic in much of the world and thus easy to obtain. Terrorists could contaminate twenty or thirty large livestock farms or ranches across the United States, allowing the disease to spread through the network, as it did in Great Britain. Such an attack would probably bring the US cattle, sheep, and pig industries to a halt in a matter of weeks, costing the economy tens of billions of dollars.

Despite the potential economic impact of such an attack, however, it wouldn't have the huge psychological effect that terrorists value, because foot-and-mouth disease rarely affects humans. Far more dramatic would be the poisoning of our food supply. Here the possibilities are legion. For instance, grain storage and transportation networks in the United States are easily accessible; unprotected grain silos dot the countryside and railway cars filled with grain often sit for long periods on railway sidings. Attackers could break into these silos and grain cars to deposit small amounts of contaminants, which would then diffuse through the food system.

Polychlorinated biphenyls (PCB)—easily found in the oil in old electrical transformers—are a particularly potent group of contaminants, in part because they contain trace amounts of dioxins. These chemicals are both carcinogenic and neurotoxic; they also disrupt the human endocrine system. Children in particular are vulnerable. Imagine the public hysteria if, several weeks after grain silos and railway cars had been laced with PCBs and the poison had spread throughout the food network, terrorists publicly suggested that health authorities test food products for PCB contamination. (US federal food inspectors might detect the PCBs on their own, but the inspection system is stretched very thin and contamination could easily be missed.) At that point, millions of people could have already eaten the products.

Such a contamination scenario is not in the realm of science fiction or conspiracy theories. In January 1999, five hundred tons of animal feed in Belgium were accidentally contaminated with approximately fifty kilograms of PCBs from transformer oil. Some ten million people in Belgium, the Netherlands, France, and Germany subsequently ate the contaminated food products. This single incident may in time cause up to eight thousand cases of cancer.

Notes

1. The Paris Embassy attack plot was uncovered around the time of the September 11 attacks that destroyed the World Trade Center. [Editor]
2. The NASDAQ (National Association of Securities Dealers Automated Quotations) stock market is the second-largest stock exchange in the world. [Editor]

The Honourable Madam Justice Louise Arbour

In Our Name and On Our Behalf

All law enforcement systems operating under the **rule of law** rely on a few fundamental assumptions. One of them is that there are limits to the power of governments to investigate, apprehend, prosecute, and convict persons suspected of crimes. Rules govern the legality of arrest, detention, interrogation, and of investigative methods such as wiretapping, DNA testing, etc. These rules, amongst many others, are a bar to the absolute efficiency of a system that, if absolutely efficient, would be absolutely tyrannical. Transposed into the international realm where true tyrants (war criminals, terrorists) are targeted for prosecution, the national **norms** of restraint may sometimes appear less necessary, less appropriate, less attractive.

... [R]ules that have served us well even in the most challenging times in the past may need to be adapted to a different environment. I would therefore like to examine briefly the environment described by some as "the new normal" to explore whether indeed we have entered a different legal landscape. But first a quick word about the "old normal."

The Old Normal

Ibrahim, a natural-born subject of the Ameer [ruler] of Afghanistan, was enlisted in an Indian native Regiment of the British army and was posted to Canton. On 14 September 1912, he was charged with the murder of a native officer in his regiment, tried before the Supreme Court of Hong Kong, convicted and sentenced to death.

His appeal to the Judicial Committee of the Privy Council gave rise to the pronouncement of what became known as the rule in the *Ibrahim* case, a celebrated rule upon which refinements but no departures were ever expressed throughout most of the **common law** world. I expect that most students of criminal law to this day could recite it by heart:

> It has long been established as a positive rule of English criminal law, that no statement by an accused is admissible in evidence against him unless it is shown by the prosecution to have been a voluntary statement, in the sense that it has not been obtained from him either by fear of prejudice or hope of advantage exercised or held out by a person in authority.[1]

The rule is one of policy. The Privy Council continues:

> A confession forced from the mind by the flattery of hope or by the torture of fear comes in so questionable a shape, when it is to be considered as evidence of guilt, that no credit ought to be given to it. It is not that the law presumes such statements to be untrue, but from the danger of receiving such evidence judges have thought it better to reject it for the due **administration of justice**.[2]

This left no ambiguity about the desirability of avoiding the use of oppression and inducement—let alone of torture, inhumane or degrading treatment—in the official interrogation of suspects. As long as confessions were sought to obtain convictions, torture was therefore, if nothing else, inefficient.

In the old normal, there was, however, considerably more ambiguity in the law regarding the legality of arrests and the consequences of illegal arrest. Where a person was brought into the **jurisdiction** of a trial court as a result of an international abduction or some **state** sponsored act of deception, the traditional approach for most common law countries was to follow the ***male captus bene detentus*** [wrongly captured, rightly detained] rule, which in essence provides that the illegality of an arrest does not affect a court's jurisdiction over the accused. However, the rule was gradually eroded by decisions throughout the **Commonwealth**, beginning in the 1970s, with the first major departure coming from the New Zealand Court of Appeal in *R v. Hartley*. The Court of Appeal held that a fugitive who had been arrested in Australia and forcibly placed on a flight back to New Zealand, without regard to the formal **extradition** process, was the victim of an illegal arrest which, as an **abuse of process**, gave the court the discretion to order a **stay of proceedings**. Hartley was subsequently approved and applied, in varied degrees, by courts in Australia, South Africa, Canada, and the United Kingdom.

The position developing in the Commonwealth remained in stark contrast to the American approach which, to this day, largely recognizes the *male captus bene detentus* doctrine as good law. The US Supreme Court has repeatedly and consistently held that a forcible, extra-territorial abduction constituting an illegal arrest will not injure a court's jurisdiction to prosecute. . . . It should be noted that US courts, however, have been more reluctant to accept jurisdiction where **extrajudicial** transfers were accompanied by torture by, or with the acquiescence of, the United States.

Nevertheless, despite its strong foothold in American courts, global erosion of the *male captus bene detentus* rule continues throughout the Commonwealth. In England, departure from the old rule started in the 1980s, but was most notably affirmed by the House of Lords in the celebrated Bennett decision, which explicitly rejected the US . . . approach, and ruled that a circumvention of formal extradition procedures could constitute an abuse of process such that a court could enter a stay of proceedings. . . .

Reasonable people may disagree about the appropriate framework that should govern the apprehension and transfer to trial of an international terrorist suspect, war criminal or torturer. Eichmann was illegally kidnapped from Argentina, brought to Israel, tried, convicted and executed.[3] Pinochet was legally transferred from the UK to Chile where he is unlikely ever to have to serve any sentence for the charges against him despite the continuation of judicial proceedings in that country.[4]

But what all these cases have in common, *Ibrahim*, *Eichmann*, *Pinochet*, and many others, is that they were ultimately aimed at bringing alleged criminals to justice.

The New Normal

We now enter the "new normal." I would like to examine some of the features of this era as I search not so much for answers but, rather, for an appropriate basis upon which to phrase the relevant questions.

The responses of governments to terrorist activity, particularly democratic governments bound by law, raise a very wide range of human rights issues. I have already mentioned the constraints that regulate arrests and interrogations. Other issues include the role of national courts in supervising counter-terrorism measures, including fair trial rights and the use of special and military courts; the definition of terrorism and related offences in national legislation, including the question of criminalizing the legitimate exercise of rights and freedoms; the principle of non-discrimination, including the issue of the techniques used to screen terrorist suspects; the protection of vulnerable groups, including human rights defenders, non-citizens and journalists; the determination of a state of emergency and/or of the existence of an armed conflict; the deprivation of liberty, including judicial and administrative detention, incommunicado detention and secret detention; the right to privacy, including the questions of methods of investigation, and information collection and sharing; the right to property, including compiling lists and freezing assets of persons suspected of terrorism, etc.

... [I will focus] on two of such issues that have led to considerable debate. . . . The first is the alleged use of secret detention centres and of irregular transfers of persons suspected of engagement in terrorist activities, which would allow governments to detain these persons without any legal process and presumably obtain information from them using interrogation methods that would be impermissible under national or international law. The second and related issue is the use of **diplomatic assurances** to justify the return and transfer of suspects to countries where they face a risk of torture.

These features of the "new normal" are characterized by the fact that it would appear that terrorist suspects are being arrested, detained and interrogated with no apparent intention of bringing them to trial. I say "it would appear" because the unprecedented level of secrecy that surrounds what democratic governments are doing in our name and on our behalf severely curtails examination and debate.

And I say "with no apparent intention of bringing them to trial" because the circumstance of their arrest, detention and interrogation—take only the length of their detention—would in any credible jurisdiction amount to such an abuse of process that trial jurisdiction, if it ever existed, could never be exercised.

Secret Transfers and Secret Detentions

The issue of clandestine prisons is receiving a lot of attention recently. The Committee on Legal Affairs and Human Rights of the Council of Europe recently issued an information memorandum on "Alleged Secret Detentions in Council of Europe Member States" and concluded that though it had not found, at this stage of the investigations, any formal, irrefutable evidence of the existence of secret detention centres in Europe, there were nevertheless many indications from various reliable sources that justified the continuation of the investigation in this regard. Troubling also is the conclusion that "there is a great deal of coherent, convergent evidence pointing to the existence of a system of "relocation" or "outsourcing" of torture. Acts of torture, or severe violations of detainees' dignity through the administration of inhuman or degrading treatment, are carried out outside national territory and beyond the authority of the national intelligence services." The report refers to various cases of "abduction" of persons subsequently transferred to detention centres abroad. Judicial investigations have begun in some Member States.[5]

. . .

It is indeed difficult to engage in an examination of this issue where the factual basis for a public democratic debate is largely withheld.

On the existence of secret detention centres, I believe the electorate is entitled, indeed is required, to ask of its government at least the following questions: are you operating or assisting in the operation of secret (undisclosed) places of detention either at home or abroad? If so, how many people are detained in these centres, and under what general circumstances? Are they detained incommunicado? Does the ICRC [the Red Cross[6]] have access to all of them? How long have they been detained? Have charges been brought against them? Will there be? Why are they detained and what is planned for them?

Absent forthcoming answers to these and similar questions by those who know, one can only turn to the efforts of others who are attempting to expose the factual foundation for the important debate that we must have about the methods of repression used by our governments.

. . .

We know that countries are using various laws at their disposal—asylum, immigration, extradition, and so on—to remove persons alleged to constitute national security threats from their territories. In particular one sees an attempt to avoid the heavy **due process** requirements of the criminal system by turning instead to the **administrative law** framework. . . . Administrative measures are used to effect the detention of an individual much earlier in an investigation than would be required under criminal law principles such as the **presumption of innocence**. In my view, the onus should be squarely on governments to establish that the procedures used in "standard" criminal investigations—surveillance use of informers, searches, forensic expertise, etc.—which allow the arrest to be made close to the charge, are unsuitable to their counter-terrorism efforts.

Any extradition, expulsion, deportation, or other transfer of foreigners suspected of terrorism to their country of origin or to other countries where they face a real risk of torture or ill-treatment violates the principle of **non-refoulement**, which prohibits absolutely that a person be surrendered to a country where he or she faces a real risk of torture. The Committee against Torture (CAT) has often confirmed this principle contained in Article 9 of the Convention Against Torture and also indicated that: "The nature of the activities in which the person concerned engaged cannot be a material consideration when making a determination under Article 9 of the Convention." Regional human rights bodies have expressed similar views concerning the prohibition of torture in the context of expulsions in their case law and/or reports. This principle is absolute [exceptionless], **non-derogable** [cannot be limited or suspended], even in times of emergency.

The obligation of non-refoulement encompasses all types of transfers. Formal processes of extradition, expulsion or deportation, as well as administrative schemes and "extra-legal transfers," are equally bound to comply with this absolute prohibition.

Some governments claim that the threat of international terrorism requires a change in the rules and that exceptions should be applied to the principle of non-refoulement. As the law stands, threats to national security, including the challenge posed by international or domestic terrorism, cannot affect the absolute nature of the principle of non-refoulement. The CAT reaffirmed this principle recently in *Agiza v. Sweden* in which it stated that "the Convention's protections are absolute, even in the context of national security concerns. . . ."[7] Of course I see no objection for governments to argue, in good faith, that the constraints imposed upon them by the law should be relaxed. What they cannot do is blatantly disregard them. Whether any law should be changed gives rise to an appropriate debate at the legislative level and to judicial oversight. This is as it should be. On the merits, no case has been made for recourse to the use of torture. Indeed, few credible voices have argued for the necessity of removing the total bar on the use of torture and no justification has been advanced for relaxing the required vigilance in ensuring protection against torture and related mistreatments.

As I referred to earlier, whereas transfers of individuals outside any legal process have been used for years by States, it would appear that their main purpose was to obtain a suspect's presence so that he may stand trial. The tendency has apparently shifted in the context of the "war on terror" as both suspects as well as sources are apparently transferred to secret detention facilities or to places where it is known or should be known that the person may be tortured. If my working hypothesis is correct that persons transferred to secret detention facilities are not intended to be brought to trial, then only two reasons could indeed explain their plight. They must be detained either for interrogation, or for warehousing, or both.

. . .

The entire system of abductions, extra-legal transfers and secret detentions is thus a complete repudiation of the law and of the justice system. No State resting its very identity on the rule of law should have recourse or even be a passive accomplice to such practices.

It is helpful to recall that applicable human rights protections require that any deprivation of liberty be based upon grounds and procedures established by law, that detainees be informed of the reasons for the detention and promptly notified of the charges against them, and that they be provided with access to legal counsel. In addition, prompt and effective oversight of detention by a judicial officer must be ensured to verify the legality of the detention and to protect other fundamental rights of the detainee. Even in states of emergency, minimum access to legal counsel and **prescribed** reasonable limits upon the length of preventative detention remain mandatory. The HRC [Human Rights Committee] has held that denying individuals contact with family and friends violates the States' obligation under the ICCPR [International Covenant on Civil and Political Rights] to treat prisoners with humanity.[8] It has also stressed the importance of provisions requiring that detainees should be held in places that are publicly recognized and that there must be proper registration of the names of detainees and places of detention. The prohibition against unacknowledged detention, taking of hostages or abductions is absolute.

In addition, transfers into secret detention centres contravene the protection against disappearances or "enforced disappearances." Various international legal instruments condemn the act of disappearance as a serious violation of human rights and, when committed as part of a widespread or systematic attack directed against any civilian population, with knowledge of the attack, it constitutes a **crime against humanity**.

According to international human rights tribunals and other bodies, "disappearance" not only creates the conditions for torture, but amounts itself to torture or ill-treatment of the "disappeared" person, as well as ill-treatment of their family members—deliberately deprived of any information and desperate for news. A Draft International Convention for the protection of all persons from enforced disappearances was also adopted recently. . . . The creation of a new human rights convention is a sign of the importance the international community affords to the issue. Disappearances have often been used by ruthless regimes as an unlawful but convenient way of dealing with those seen as "undesirable." "Disappearing" alleged terrorists, regardless of how dangerous they may be presumed to be, amounts to officials taking the law into their own hands, asserting themselves at once as secret accusers, **adjudicators**, and, in the worst cases, torturers, accountable to no one. In these circumstances, is there anything left of the rule of law?

To my knowledge, no argument has been advanced to justify the need to act outside the law. It must be acknowledged that the investigation of terrorist offences undoubtedly presents the authorities with acute challenges. But they also present commensurate risks, including the risk of mistreating the innocent. As Justice O'Connor stated in her **plurality opinion** in the *Hamdi* case, "as critical as the Government's interest may be in detaining those who actually pose an immediate threat to the national security of the United States during ongoing international conflict, history and common sense teach us that an unchecked system of detention carries the potential to become a means for oppression and abuse of others who do not present that sort of threat."[9]

Legal processes can be adapted, but not eliminated altogether. "Unconventional methods" cannot displace the fundamental guarantees enacted for our own protection under the rule of law. Those certainly include the prohibition of torture and the protection against disappearances and incommunicado detentions.

Let me now turn to the emerging practice of seeking diplomatic assurances that transferred detainees will not be subjected to torture.

Diplomatic Assurances

Fully aware of their obligation of non-refoulement, some States have sought to obtain diplomatic assurances that torture and cruel, degrading or inhuman treatment will not be inflicted by the proposed receiving State [the state to which the prisoner is sent]. Assurances by no means nullify the obligation of non-refoulement, nor, in my view, based on the information available to us, do they provide adequate protection against torture and ill-treatment. . . .

. . .

Some have postulated that diplomatic assurances could work if effective post-return monitoring mechanisms were put in place [in the country the person is deported to]. Based on the long experience of international monitoring bodies and experts, it is unlikely that a post-return monitoring mechanism set up explicitly to prevent torture and ill-treatment in a specific case would have the desired effect. These practices often occur in secret, with the perpetrators skilled at keeping such abuses from detection. The victims, fearing reprisal, are often reluctant to speak about their suffering, or are not believed if they do.

Although efforts could be made to improve on the practice of seeking these assurances, in my view it is fundamentally flawed in several ways. First, we must acknowledge that diplomatic assurances would presumably only be sought after an assessment has been made that there is a risk of torture in the receiving State. Otherwise the **démarche** would be both useless and insulting.

Secondly, in most cases, assurances are concluded between States who are already parties to binding international and regional treaties which prohibit torture and cruel, inhuman or degrading treatment or punishment and refoulement to such practices. This system was devised by the community of States and they agreed to be bound by it. **Ad hoc** arrangements, such as assurances concluded outside the system, threaten to weaken its foundations and retard the progress that has been achieved over more than half a century to extend its ambit and protection to all.

Of course, while receiving States are under binding legal obligations to respect and protect human rights, including the prohibition of torture, they often are far from fully implementing their obligations, resulting in wide-spread violations. It is difficult to make a case that if a Government does not comply with binding law it will respect legally non-binding bilateral agreements that are concluded on the basis of trust only, without enforcement or sanctions if violated.

Thirdly, even though all persons are entitled to the equal protection of existing treaties, assurances basically create a two-class system amongst those transferred, attempting to provide special bilateral protection and monitoring for a selected few while ignoring the plight of many others in detention. By seeking assurances for a chosen few, sending Governments could in fact be seen as condoning torture and cruel, inhuman or degrading treatment by acknowledging that these practices exist in the receiving State but conveniently ignoring their systemic nature.

In the end we are back to the same fundamental question: why are these people sent to countries where they face the risk of torture? They may be sent to face trial, or simply to be held in custody, possibly indefinitely, or to be interrogated with the hope that that the interrogation abroad will yield more information than the methods that could be used at home.

The last two scenarios involve, at best, legal avoidance: suspects will be transferred because what will be done to them abroad could not legally be done at home. I fail to see any justification for any State to be a party to such practice.

If they are transferred to face trial, prudence would dictate that their transfer should not be tainted with illegality since in many countries this could lead to the courts declining to exercise jurisdiction.

If they are transferred to countries where very few due process requirements are likely to stand in the way of prolonged detention, illegal interrogations or unfair trials, then we should be clear about our endorsement of such double standards: we are not willing, or not able, to dilute our domestic legal protections in the name of counter-terrorism, but we will happily resort to the methods used by others that we otherwise overtly denounce and deplore.

Conclusion

What then is the most striking difference between the old and the new normal? I suggest that it is both the magnitude of the perceived threat posed by international terrorism and the response that some governments appear to be employing to address it, a response tainted by secrecy and a tendency to avoid judicial scrutiny.

In looking at this issue overall, we must never lose sight of the legitimate expectations of the victims of terrorism: to compensation, to justice, and to protection from further assault. The roll call of terrorist victims is a heavy one. . . .

The seriousness of the challenge posed by the need to combat terrorism must not be underestimated. In fact, its most unique aspect is that it calls for what traditional criminal law is [most poorly] equipped to address, that is the prevention of specific criminal activity. Nor should be underestimated the critical obligation of governments to provide for the safety and security of all those who fall under their authority.

But in discharging that obligation, governments must show a heightened awareness and concern for the fundamental values of the society they are seeking to protect. To undermine that would be to serve, in effect, as the **Trojan Horse** of the terrorists.

In this regard, of paramount importance is the obligation on governments that they not bypass the judicial process, as some often appear determined to do. In reality, they will not be able to avoid judicial scrutiny for a very long time. The courts will be called to play their role one way or the other, sooner rather than later. Abusive legislation will be challenged in courts, some individuals released after prolonged or illegal detention, or who have been tortured, abroad or at home, will sue governments, and soon short-term advantages will yield to appropriate exposure and liability.

. . .

As a branch of governance, the judiciary has a critical role to play in ensuring that all are secure under the law. . . . There are always heightened risks of abuse and misjudgment, even in democracies, when emergency powers are exceptionally concentrated in the executive branch. The independent supervisory power of the civilian judiciary is then even more critical.

. . .

Judges are well aware of the danger of erosion of the rule of law and the importance of upholding the fundamental principles upon which our societies are built. Major recent decisions by the highest courts in many countries have also reaffirmed the critical role of the judiciary in reviewing counter-terrorism measures.

In the *Hamdi* case, the US Supreme Court held that a citizen-detainee seeking to challenge his classification as an enemy combatant must receive notice of the factual basis for his classification, and a fair opportunity to rebut the Government's assertions before a neutral decision-maker. As the Court resoundingly declared, "state of war is not a blank check for the President when it comes to the rights of the Nation's citizens. . . ."

In another important US decision known as *Rasul*, the Supreme Court took the view that detainees must be given access to the courts, despite the fact that their place of detention was situated outside of the United States and that the petitioners were non-citizens.

. . . [I]n December 2004, the [British] House of Lords ruled that though there is a terrorist threat to the UK, indefinite detention of foreign terrorist suspects is disproportionate and discriminatory. The ruling confirms that even in exceptional circumstances and even if supervised by courts, it is not acceptable to hold anyone in open-ended detention without trial. In a follow-up judgment . . . , the House of Lords declared unambiguously that evidence obtained by torture was not admissible in a court of law. The Supreme Court of Canada has accepted to hear the case of Mr Charkaoui concerning his detention on the basis of a **security certificate**, a detention policy about which the United Nations Working Group on Arbitrary Detention expressed grave concern. Courts the world over are rightly asked to exercise their duty of oversight of the very difficult decisions Governments have to make in the face of the serious threat caused by terrorism.

. . .

The strength of our rule of law and human rights norms can only be measured by whether they can resist the temptations to surrender to fear in times of crisis. . . . With the continuing threat of terrorism, and indeed with persistent armed conflicts and the ever more perverse effects of extreme poverty, as we experience this prolonged exposure to real and perceived threats to our security, we are also faced with an extraordinary opportunity to forge a worldwide **jurisprudence** capable of protecting fundamental human rights when it matters most.

Notes

1. *Ibrahim v. The King*, Privy Council Appeal No 112 of 1913 (6 Mar 1914) (from the Supreme Court of Hong Kong), para. 18.
2. *Ibrahim*, para. 20.
3. Eichmann was a high-ranking German Nazi. During World War II he coordinated the mass deportation of Jews to ghettos and concentration camps. After the war, he fled to Argentina and lived under a false identity. In 1960 he was captured in Argentina by Israeli agents and covertly transferred to Israel, where he was tried for **crimes against humanity** and war crimes. He was found guilty and executed in 1962. [Editor]

4. Pinochet was an army general and dictator of Chile from 1973 to 1990. Numerous human rights violations are attributed to his regime, including murdering and torturing political opponents and their families. In 1998, Pinochet travelled to England for medical treatment. While there, he was indicted for human rights violations by a Spanish magistrate. A legal battle ensued over the legality of extraditing Pinochet to Spanish authorities. Eventually he was surrendered to Chilean authorities, who gave him immunity from prosecution. His immunity was revoked in 2004. Pinochet died in 2006 while under house arrest, with more than three hundred criminal charges pending. [Editor]
5. In September 2006, President George W. Bush publicly admitted to the existence of secret prisons and the extrajudicial transfer of people outside the United States by the CIA. No locations were disclosed except for the Guantanamo Bay detention camp in Cuba. [Editor]
6. The International Committee of the Red Cross (ICRC) is a humanitarian organization based in Geneva, Switzerland. Signatory states to the Geneva Conventions have given the ICRC a mandate to protect victims of national and international armed conflicts. [Editor]
7. CAT *Agiza v. Sweden*, 2005.
8. The United Nations Human Rights Committee (HRC) is a group of experts the compliance of UN member states with the International **Covenant** on Civil and Political Rights. This covenant requires all signatory states to protect and uphold individuals' civil and political rights, including freedom of speech, freedom of religion, and freedom of assembly. [Editor]
9. *Hamdi v. Rumsfeld*, 542 US 507 (2004) 124 S Ct 2633, 2655 (2004).

Louis A. Delvoie

Terrorism: Global Insecurity or Global Hyperbole?

Over the [few] years, the words "terrorism" and "9/11" have come to occupy in our lexicon a place once reserved for terms such as "the red menace"[1] or "the yellow peril."[2] They are intended to convey the idea of something essentially menacing and frightening on a very grand scale, if not a **metaphysical** or **existential** scale. They are used to refer equally to the real and the potential, the known and the unknown. And they are everywhere—the front pages of newspapers, the shelves of bookstores, the pronouncements of politicians and experts. In the discourse of the responsible, they are meant to counsel prudence and vigilance, but given the atmosphere that has been created around them, they tend to engender fear, if not paranoia.

The threat of terrorism is, of course, real. It demands that governments act to protect the safety of their citizens and their realms. As Canada's deputy prime minister, Anne McLellan, said in a speech in 2004: "We must always be vigilant about new threats, and we must always be looking for ways to improve and coordinate our intelligence, our prevention strategies and our emergency response capabilities. We must continuously review our plans, update our systems and test our people." This all makes perfect sense, and for a government to do anything less would be downright irresponsible in terms of protecting Canadians and of ensuring Canada's continued access to the all-important US market. This is, however, a very far cry from the **jeremiads** of pundits of all professions and persuasions, who daily proclaim that, because of international terrorism, we are now living in a world of unprecedented danger and that combating terrorism should be or should become the first and overarching priority of all Western governments. Such pronouncements, in fact, betray a wilful or woeful ignorance of history, and of contemporary realities.

A sense of proportion is essential in all things, including the assessment of threats. What is al Qaeda and its associated networks? It is a loose grouping of perhaps a few hundred or a few thousand more-or-less well-educated and more-or-less well-organized individuals spread out across Northern Africa and the Eurasian landmass. In recent years, it has proved itself capable of mounting a few localized but spectacular operations in New York, Washington, Bali, Casablanca, Mombasa, and Madrid. These operations resulted in the deaths of some five thousand people and the destruction of a dozen buildings. All eminently regrettable, but hardly the Third World War.

But, the argument goes, al Qaeda or one of its offshoots could acquire nuclear weapons and/or intercontinental ballistic missiles (ICMBs), and thus become far more dangerous to the West. True, it could. And the Queen could undergo a sex change operation and become King. Both eventualities are, however, somewhat remote. The acquisition, storage, transport, and detonation of nuclear weapons are all full of complexities that far exceed the competencies required to highjack and pilot civilian aircraft. As for ICBMs, the technological, industrial and military capabilities required to produce, deploy and launch them are ones that are totally beyond the reach of non-**state actors**. And even if al Qaeda could, by stealth, acquire one or two small nuclear devices (the so-called "suitcase bombs" of Cold War era folklore) the damage they could inflict would be essentially limited to one location, and would certainly pose no generalized threat to the West as a whole.

The simple fact is that the people of the Western world have not, in living memory, enjoyed a more **benign** international security environment than the one they enjoy today. The first half of the twentieth century was dominated by two world wars, in which it is estimated that nearly one hundred million people died. The second half of the century was dominated by the Cold War, in the course of which the superpowers arrayed against each other arsenals comprising thousands of nuclear weapons and delivery systems capable of killing hundreds of millions of people, and of taking much of the planet back to the Stone Age. And, of course, the Cold War played itself out in numerous bloody proxy conflicts in Vietnam, Cambodia, Afghanistan, Angola, Mozambique, Nicaragua, and so on. No comparable threat exists today. When stacked up against the armed might of Nazi Germany, Imperial Japan and Soviet Russia, the ragtag bands of al Qaeda cut a pretty pathetic figure.

This is not to suggest that major security issues and threats do not exist in the contemporary world. Africa is still the scene of horrendous civil wars. In the Congo alone more than three million people have died in five years of **internecine** conflict, and fighting continues in Sudan, Somalia, the Ivory Coast, and Uganda. For the peoples of Southern Africa, the ravages of HIV/AIDS may lead to the collapse of entire societies. At a more conventional level of inter-state rivalries, the highly complex set of relationships that link Pakistan, India, China, and Japan could lead to conflict in the longer term, and they merit sustained attention. But these are not threats directed at the West, and they certainly do not emanate from terrorism.

The question may well be asked whether all of the hyperbole about international terrorism really matters. The answer is a resounding "yes," on several fronts. In countries such as Canada, the United States, and Great Britain, it has led to the adoption of emergency legislation that calls into question a host of traditional **civil rights** and that are amenable to widespread abuse. It has also led to hasty and ill-thought-out governmental reorganizations, most notably in the United States where the . . . Department of Homeland Security has been described by one American commentator, Michael Crowley in the *New Republic*, as "a bureaucratic Frankenstein, with clumsily-stitched-together limbs and an inadequate, misfiring brain." Finally, it has resulted in the diversion of vast budgetary resources to anti-terrorism programs, some of which at least could have been devoted more usefully to health care, higher education, or conventional defence capabilities.

The terrorism fixation also has perverse consequences internationally. In the discourse of political and religious **ideologues**, and in that of ignoramuses of all persuasions who do not even understand the simple distinction between Islamic and **Islamist**, it is used to demonize and convict one billion Muslims for the sins of a few hundred. In so doing, it creates heightened levels of animosity and suspicion on both sides in relations between Western and Muslim societies. The fixation has also been systematically exploited by the leaders of countries such as Russia, India and Israel, to cover up the excesses and wide-spread **human rights** violations committed by their security forces in Chechnya, Kashmir, and Palestine. By portraying these complex political, ethnic, and territorial conflicts as little more than theatres in the war on terrorism, they have managed to escape the scrutiny and censure to which they would otherwise have been subjected on the part of Western countries. That too does not go unnoticed in the Muslim world.

In short, international terrorism of the al Qaeda variety is a real threat that should not be taken lightly. What is more, it is unlikely to disappear soon, for it goes to the heart of deep divisions within the Muslim world itself, just as much as it represents a campaign against Western interests and policies. That said, it is not an existential threat, and there is not a bearded terrorist under every bed in the Western world. It is a limited and manage-able threat. It can be managed and minimized through effective action by, and cooperation among, intelligence and security services worldwide. The sooner politicians and others perceive and portray it in its true proportions, the better off we shall all be.

Notes

1. The "red menace" refers to the surges of fear in the United States following the end of World War I and again after World War II, directed at real and perceived threats of terrorism and Soviet espionage. The First Red Scare involved deportations of immigrants, labour union leaders, and people allegedly associated with radical **leftists** and **anarchists**. The Second Red Scare involved arrests of political leaders, and blacklists preventing people from working in certain businesses and industries. [Editor]
2. The "yellow peril" refers to American fears of East Asian cultural dominance, first arising in the late nineteenth century due to large inflows of East Asian immigrants, and again in the mid-twentieth century in response to Japanese military expansion. People of East Asian ancestry were denied citizenship, and American women who married men of East Asian ancestry had their citizenship revoked. [Editor]

Charkaoui v. Canada[1]

[Unanimous decision, written by Chief Justice McLachlin]

The *Immigration and Refugee Protection Act* ("*IRPA*") allows the Minister of Citizenship and Immigration and the Minister of Public Safety and Emergency Preparedness to issue a certificate declaring that a foreign national or permanent resident is inadmissible to Canada on grounds of security, among others (s. 77), and leading to the detention of the person named in the certificate. The certificate and the detention are both subject to review by a judge of the **Federal Court**, in a process that may deprive the person of some or all of the information on the basis of which the certificate was issued or the detention ordered (s. 78). Once a certificate is issued, a permanent resident may be detained, and the detention must be reviewed within 48 hours; in the case of a foreign national, the detention is automatic and that person cannot apply for review until 120 days after a judge determines the certificate to be reasonable (ss. 82–84). The judge's determination on the reasonableness of the certificate cannot be appealed or judicially reviewed (s. 80(3)). If the judge finds the certificate to be reasonable, it becomes a removal order, which cannot be appealed and which may be immediately enforced (s. 81).

Certificates of inadmissibility have been issued by the Ministers against the **appellants** C [Adil Charkaoui], H [Mohamed Harkat] and A [Hassan Almrei]. While C is a permanent resident, H and A are foreign nationals who had been recognized as Convention refugees. All were living in Canada when they were arrested and detained on the basis of allegations that they constituted a threat to the security of Canada by reason of involvement in terrorist activities. C and H were released on conditions in 2005 and 2006 respectively, but A remains in detention. Both the Federal Court and the Federal Court of Appeal upheld the **constitutional** validity of the *IRPA*'s certificate scheme.

Held: The appeals [challenging the constitutionality of the *IRPA*] should be allowed.

(1) Procedure for Determining Reasonableness of Certificate and for Review of Detention

The procedure under the *IRPA* for determining whether a certificate is reasonable and the detention review procedures infringe s. 7 of the *Charter*.[2] While the deportation of a non-citizen in the immigration context may not in itself engage s. 7, features associated with deportation may do so. Here, s. 7 is clearly engaged because the person named in a certificate faces detention pending the outcome of the proceedings and because the process may lead to the person's removal to a place where his or her life or freedom would be threatened. Further, the *IRPA*'s impairment of the named person's **right** to life, liberty, and security is not in accordance with the principles of fundamental justice. The procedure for determining whether a certificate is reasonable and the detention review procedure fail to assure the fair hearing that s. 7 requires before the **state** deprives a person of this right.

The right to a fair hearing comprises the right to a hearing before an independent and **impartial** magistrate who must decide on the facts and the law, the right to know the case put against one, and the right to answer that case. While the *IRPA* procedures properly reflect the **exigencies** of the security context, security concerns cannot be used, at the s. 7 stage of the analysis, to excuse procedures that do not conform to fundamental justice. Here, the *IRPA* scheme includes a hearing and meets the requirement of independence and impartiality, but the secrecy required by the scheme denies the person named in a certificate the opportunity to know the case put against him or her, and hence to challenge the government's case. This, in turn, undermines the judge's ability to come to a decision based on all the relevant facts and law. The judges of the Federal Court, who are required under the *IRPA* to conduct a searching examination of the reasonableness of the certificate, in an independent and judicial fashion and on the material placed before them, do not possess the full and independent powers to gather evidence that exist in an inquisitorial process.[3] At the same time, the person named in a certificate is not given the disclosure and the right to participate in the proceedings that characterize the **adversarial** process. The result is a concern that the judge, despite his or her best efforts to get all the relevant evidence, may be obliged, perhaps unknowingly, to make the required decision based on only part of the relevant evidence. Similar concerns arise with respect to the requirement that the decision be based on the law. Without knowledge of the information put against him or her, the person named in a certificate may not be in a position to raise legal objections relating to the evidence, or to develop legal arguments based on the evidence. If s. 7 is to be satisfied, either the person must be given the necessary information, or a substantial substitute for that information must be found. The *IRPA* provides neither.

The infringement of s. 7 is not saved by s. 1 of the *Charter*.[4] While the protection of Canada's national security and related intelligence sources constitutes a pressing and substantial objective, and the non-disclosure of evidence at certificate hearings is rationally connected to this objective, the *IRPA* does not minimally impair the rights of persons named in certificates. Less intrusive alternatives developed in Canada and abroad, notably the use of special counsel to act on behalf of the named persons, illustrate that the government can do more to protect the individual while keeping critical information confidential than it has done in the *IRPA*.

(2) Detention of Foreign Nationals

The detention of foreign nationals without warrant does not infringe the guarantee against arbitrary detention in s. 9 of the *Charter*.[5] The triggering event for the detention of a foreign national is the signing under s. 77 of the *IRPA* of a certificate stating that the foreign national is inadmissible on grounds of security, violation of human or international rights, serious criminality or organized criminality. The security ground is based on the danger posed by the named person, and therefore provides a rational foundation for the detention. However, the lack of review of the detention of foreign nationals until 120 days after the reasonableness of the certificate has been judicially confirmed (s. 84(2)) infringes the guarantee against arbitrary detention in s. 9 of the *Charter*, which encompasses the right to prompt review of detention under s. 10(*c*) of the *Charter*.[6] While there may be a need for some flexibility regarding the period for which a suspected terrorist may be detained, this cannot justify the complete denial of a timely detention review.

The infringement of ss. 9 and 10(*c*) is not justified under s. 1 of the *Charter*. The *IRPA* provides permanent residents who pose a danger to national security with a mandatory detention review within 48 hours. It follows that denial of review for foreign nationals for 120 days after the certificate is confirmed does not minimally impair the rights guaranteed by ss. 9 and 10(*c*).

(3) Extended Periods of Detention

While the s. 12[7] guarantee against cruel and unusual treatment cannot be used as a mechanism to challenge the overall fairness of a particular legislative **regime**, indefinite detention without hope of release or recourse to a legal process to procure release may cause psychological stress and therefore constitute cruel and unusual treatment. The *IRPA* in principle imposes detention only pending deportation, but it may in fact permit lengthy and indeterminate detention, or lengthy periods of detention subject to onerous release conditions. The principles of fundamental justice and the guarantee of freedom from cruel and unusual treatment require that, where a person is detained or is subject to onerous conditions of release for an extended period under immigration law, the detention or the conditions must be accompanied by a meaningful process of ongoing review that takes into account the context and circumstances of the individual case. The person must be accorded meaningful opportunities to challenge his or her continued detention or the conditions of his or her release.

Extended periods of detention pending deportation under the certificate provisions of the *IRPA* do not violate ss. 7 and 12 of the *Charter* if accompanied by a process that provides regular opportunities for review of detention, taking into account all of the relevant factors, including the reasons for detention, the length of the detention, the reasons for the delay in deportation, the anticipated future length of detention, if applicable, and the availability of alternatives to detention. However, this does not preclude the possibility of a judge concluding at a certain point that a particular detention constitutes cruel and unusual treatment or is inconsistent with the principles of fundamental justice.

(4) Differential Treatment of Citizens and Non-citizens

Since s. 6 of the *Charter*[8] specifically provides for differential treatment of citizens and non-citizens in deportation matters, a deportation scheme that applies to non-citizens, but not to citizens, does not for that reason alone infringe s. 15 of the *Charter*.[9] Even though the detention of some of the appellants has been long, the record does not establish that the detentions at issue have become unhinged from the state's purpose of deportation.

(5) Rule of Law

The **rule of law** is not infringed by (1) the unavailability of an appeal of the designated judge's review of the reasonableness of the certificate; or (2) the provision for the issuance of an arrest warrant by the executive in the case of a permanent resident, or for mandatory arrest without a warrant following an executive decision in the case of a foreign national. First, there is no constitutional right to an appeal, nor can such a right be said to flow from the rule of law in the present context. Second, the rule of law does not categorically prohibit automatic detention, or detention on the basis of an executive decision, and the constitutional protections surrounding arrest and detention are set out in the *Charter*.

(6) Remedy

The *IRPA*'s procedure for the judicial approval of certificates is inconsistent with the *Charter*, and hence of no force or effect. This declaration is suspended for one year from the date of this judgment. If the government chooses to have the reasonableness of C's certificate determined during the one-year suspension period, the existing process under the *IRPA* will apply. After that period, H and A's certificates will lose their "reasonable" status and it will be open to them to apply to have the certificates quashed. Likewise, any certificates or detention reviews occurring after the one-year delay will be subject to the new process devised by Parliament. Further, s. 84(2), which denies a prompt hearing to foreign nationals by imposing a 120-day **embargo**, after confirmation of the certificate, on applications for release, is struck, and s. 83 is modified so as to allow for review of the detention of a foreign national both before and after the certificate has been deemed reasonable.[10]

Notes

1. *Charkaoui v. Canada* (Citizenship and Immigration), [2007] 1 S.C.R. 350, 2007 SCC 9.
2. Section 7 states, "Everyone has the right to life, liberty and security of the person and the right not to be deprived thereof except in accordance with the principles of fundamental justice." Principles of fundamental justice are legal principles that are central to Canadian conceptions of justice, and capable of being stated with some precision. They include rights such as the right against self-incrimination and the right that laws be clear and consistently applied. [Editor]
3. In an inquisitorial process, criminal evidence is overseen by an independent prosecutor or magistrate who gathers all the evidence, interviews complainants, witnesses, and suspects, and prepares a dossier outlining the case. At trial, the judge plays an active role, deciding which witnesses will be heard and in what order, and questioning the witnesses. [Editor]
4. Section 1 states: "The *Canadian Charter of Rights and Freedoms* guarantees the rights and freedoms set out in it subject only to such reasonable limits prescribed by law as can be demonstrably justified in a free and democratic society." [Editor]
5. Section 9 states, "Everyone has the right not to be arbitrarily detained or imprisoned." [Editor]
6. Section 10 of the *Charter* states, "Everyone has the right on arrest or detention . . . (c) to have the validity of the detention determined by way of *habeas corpus* and to be released if the detention is not lawful." *Habeas corpus* (Latin for "You have the body") requires a government to justify in court the reasons for a prisoner's detention. [Editor]
7. Section 12 states, "Everyone has the right not to be subjected to any cruel and unusual treatment or punishment." [Editor]
8. Section 6 lays out the mobility rights of citizens and permanent residents. [Editor]
9. Section 15(1) states: "Every individual is equal before and under the law and has the right to the equal protection and equal benefit of the law without discrimination and, in particular, without discrimination based on race, national or ethnic origin, colour, religion, sex, age or mental or physical disability." [Editor]
10. In September 2009 the Crown, admitting insufficient evidence to uphold the security certificate against Charkaoui, lifted all restrictions imposed by the security certificate. [Editor]

Trudy Govier and Wilhelm Verwoerd

How Not to Polarize "Victims" and "Perpetrators"

(AV) = author's view; (~AV) = not the author's view

In contexts of political reconciliation, it is common to speak of "victims" and "perpetrators." While many have suspected that such terminology is polarizing and counter-productive, there seems little alternative to it. Here we explore this topic from four perspectives: those of logic, ethics, prudence, and social psychology. As we'll see, the distinction between "victims" and "perpetrators," as it is often used, is logically simplistic, ethically unfair, psychologically misleading, and **prudentially** undermining.

False Dichotomies

From the point of view of language, the labelling of a person as either a "victim" or a "perpetrator" is often an over-simplification. One phase of a person's experience or action is treated as overwhelmingly significant, providing a label to characterize the whole person. Clearly, a person who has been harmed is never only that; he or she may also be a parent, gardener, musician, and so on. While serious injuries may endure and affect one's life in profoundly significant ways, those harmed by violent conflict are never merely victims; they are persons with many qualities and capacities. The "victim" label is objectionable if it is interpreted as implying that the person harmed is nothing but a passive party in an act in which she or he was hurt by another. This aspect of the "victim" terminology has led many harmed persons to insist on the term "survivor" instead of "victim."

Labels such as "offender," "perpetrator," "terrorist," "murderer," "combatant," and even "ex-combatant" or "ex-prisoner" pose similar problems. At the time a person commits an act of political violence, he or she is an agent who harms another and may be termed an "offender," "perpetrator," "combatant," or "militant." But even during the period when an agent commits such an act, that agent is not only the person who commits that act. He or she is a person, a human being, with many other qualities and capacities. In the aftermath of political conflict, such agents are likely to have changed in many respects and thus it is even more misleading to label them as perpetrators, solely and simply. This point was underlined by a direct participant in the Northern Ireland "Troubles"[1] who served many years in prison for a politically motivated killing. Introducing himself at a meeting in Belfast, he said, "Hi, I am John. I am a Loyalist ex-prisoner . . . but I am also an ex-baby, an ex-shipyard worker, an ex-football player, and an ex-husband."

Such labels as "victim," "offender," "perpetrator," and "combatant" encourage polarized thinking or—as it is known in textbooks—the **fallacy** of false dichotomy. To appreciate the problem, consider the contrast between ugliness and beauty. These are contrary notions—"opposites," we colloquially say—and people often assume that a person must be characterized by one or by the other and cannot be characterized by both. On reflection, we can see the mistake. To think that one must be ugly because one is not beautiful amounts to an error in logic, since there are many intermediate possibilities—moderate attractiveness being an obvious example. In this case as in many others ("friend/enemy," "winner/loser" . . .) there are many possibilities, falling on a spectrum. People often tend to focus on the contrastive ends of that spectrum, neglecting the middle zone. They lapse into false dichotomies, seeking to divide reality into two distinct chunks, thinking that an opposition exhausts the possibilities when it does not. Such distorted thinking causes problems well beyond the realm of logic itself. Falsely dichotomous thinking limits the imagination and opportunities and can be harmful to mental health.

False dichotomies can also fail to be exclusive: both "opposites" may apply. (For instance, a person might be a success in some respects and a failure in others, or beautiful in some respects though ugly in others.) The same can be said of the polarized opposition between "victims" and "perpetrators." These roles are opposite and opposed. And yet the dichotomy between "victims" and "perpetrators" is neither exhaustive nor exclusive. It is not exhaustive because many persons are neither victims nor perpetrators. And it is not exclusive because some persons are both victims and perpetrators. A person may be the relative of someone killed in political violence, and in that respect a "victim," while also supporting the use of physical force against "the other side" and in that respect a "perpetrator."

The notion of a victim who is purely innocent and good is unrealistic, and functions to encourage moral arrogance and discourage moral humility. Persons identifying as "victims" may have been able to remain "pure" for circumstantial reasons: they may have profited from "**moral luck**." Often, persons who are harmed in the course of a conflict have also been involved in some way to support agents of physical force and for that reason share responsibility for the actions of some combatants.

In much talk, the roles of "victim" and "perpetrator" function as polarized opposites. These opposites construct a polarized framework that is simplistic and counter-productive. "One person acts; the other is acted upon. One harms; the other is harmed. One is evil; the other is good. One bears responsibility; the other none." Such starkly oppositional thinking is both inaccurate and unhelpful. Many are neither "victims" nor "perpetrators" and some are both.

Ethical Unfairness

From an ethical perspective, it is commonly recognized that people may suffer harm during political violence on several levels. Besides the person directly injured, the primary victim, there are secondary victims, those family members and close friends of the primary victim hurt by the latter's injury or death. Furthermore, there is the broader community, which may be harmed in various ways. We need a deeper theory of militant agency ("perpetration") or participation in violent political conflict as a counterpart to this broader understanding of victims. Such an account can begin with the direct or primary participants. Two sorts of persons fall into this category: agents on the ground and those who direct them—followers and leaders. Agents on the ground are those who engage physically in acts of force or violence. They may commit assaults, pull the trigger on guns, place bombs under a bus, and so on. Behind them are leaders, planners, and financers who urge and organize such actions. These persons have a crucial causal role and should be regarded as having primary responsibility—as they would in legal proceedings.

At a secondary level are persons close to action but neither immediate agents nor instigators. In legal language, these persons would be said to "aid and abet." They might drive getaway cars, shelter attackers, or store guns or explosives. While not primary agents, their contribution to the acts is clear. Such persons can be called secondary participants. Behind primary and secondary participants are others who take sides in the conflict and support it without being closely involved in actions on the ground. Such people contribute through their participation in a broader community, supporting the political struggle. They can be regarded as tertiary [third-level] participants. While explicit discussion of primary, secondary, and tertiary "perpetration" or participation in violent political conflict is rare, the idea that responsibility for acts on the ground is shared has been acknowledged in some contexts.

In South Africa, under **apartheid**, policemen who brutally interrogated and in some cases killed black activists did so using state resources and with the support of an ideology insisting that black activists endangered the survival of the community and state. This was recognized in the final report of the South African Truth and Reconciliation Commission (TRC).[2]

Tertiary participants should not be identified with beneficiaries, because the beneficiaries of policies and actions are often alive only after the damaging actions have occurred and played no role in causing them. Nor should persons who are purely bystanders be regarded as tertiary participants—although persons who appear to be merely bystanders but who in effect supported actions by their failure to intervene can be regarded as tertiary participants.

A primary level of participation can only exist because there are secondary and tertiary levels. Thus it is a serious inaccuracy, and an injustice, if the agents on the ground—a subset of the primary agents—and they alone, are held responsible for harmful actions. To criminalize and stigmatize these people, and only them, amounts to scapegoating.

(-AV) Sometimes, when conflicts wind down—such as in Northern Ireland—primary participants from **paramilitary** backgrounds are labelled as perpetrators or ex-criminals and in effect scapegoated. They're socially shunned, have criminal records, and are barred from many occupations and opportunities. At the same time, many who share causal responsibility as secondary and tertiary participants suffer no such after-effects. Leaders who were primary participants may have been needed to reach a political settlement. As a result, they may assume a political role that restores them to respectability. Some of these leaders can sit in parliament and appear on television as respected commentators, while many they helped to recruit are burdened by criminal records and restricted opportunities after hard years spent in jail. (AV) Such differential treatment is clearly unfair.

When such scapegoating is conjoined with labelling and polarization, the result undermines the human dignity of many ex-combatants. These people are human beings and in many cases they made considerable personal sacrifices to defend their community. (-AV) Yet it is not uncommon to hear middle class people (many of whom share responsibility as tertiary participants) speak condescendingly about them, even to the point of alluding to "criminals" or "terrorists loose on the streets." (AV) Such dismissal treats participants in a political conflict as common criminals—or worse. To think of primary participants in this way is to dismiss their humanity and is ethically objectionable. It seriously violates their fundamental moral rights.

The Complexity of Motives

Social psychological research supports these arguments. For example, the central message of a chapter on the "Causes, Motives and Perspectives of Perpetrators" in the South African TRC Report is that the most plausible explanations for why people become directly involved in political violence are not to be found in the realm of individual psychology. Instead, they are provided by the complex interplay of political frameworks, social identities, and specific situations.

It is unlikely that the search to understand the security policeman's or soldier's often brutal use of lethal force against fellow black South Africans will be very productive if it focuses mainly on the man's individual personality traits. To merely ascribe his actions to his being some kind of sadist or psychopath or having an authoritarian personality type would be simplistic. Nor will inner psychological states, such as rage, frustration, or revenge, throw enough light on his dark political actions.

Instead, one must start by locating his specific actions within the broad political frameworks of, say, the Cold War,[3] **decolonization** in Africa, and the legacy of the Anglo-Boer War.[4] These historical trends effectively framed the political violence by Afrikaners,[5] who saw themselves as fighting under the banner of the "defence of an Afrikaner homeland against Communist inspired black terrorists." To understand the actions of a typical white security force member in apartheid South Africa, one must unravel his intertwined social identities. These would include a racial (and racist) identity as a white South African under the apartheid system; an ethnic identity as an Afrikaner; the powerful influence of the Dutch Reformed Church on his religious identity; and growing up in a **patriarchal** culture, with its macho values further deepened by the militarism and patriotism.

According to the South African TRC Report, these political frameworks and social identities functioned as "preconditions" for the violence carried out by many security force members in apartheid South Africa. The report also states that, "if there is a single dominant message emerging from psychological research over the past fifty years, it is a tale that emphasizes the persuasive power of the immediate situation." Certain situations provide "triggers of violence." If a white, Afrikaner, Christian, militarized, security policeman were faced with a black person held in detention for demonstrating against the apartheid state, he would deem himself authorized to use force against a person who has been dehumanized as a "terrorist" or "Communist" enemy.

During the Troubles in Northern Ireland, many people became immersed in centuries of Irish-British conflict and developed strong Republican or Loyalist social identities, often deepened by membership in military or paramilitary organizations. Many did not resist the "persuasive power" of immediate situations where extreme force was an option against a dehumanized enemy. These "boys" or "lads" would probably not have become engaged in political violence if it were not for the Troubles.

This plea for a deeper understanding does not mean suspending judgments about choices and moral responsibility. In this regard, Christopher Browning, in his book *Ordinary Men*, emphasized the choices available for many agents involved in Nazi killings, indicating that "Explaining is not excusing; understanding is not forgiving."[6]

Once one acknowledges the vital roles of political frameworks and social identities in political violence, it becomes more difficult to disown primary participants. The scapegoating of primary participants is deeply objectionable from the standpoint of social psychology because there are many who, directly and indirectly, share in the formation of the person who committed the acts. The point was eloquently put to the South African TRC by the United Democratic Front—an internal resistance movement affiliated with the African National Congress.[7] "For us to disown these people would mean that we don't understand the history of these people . . . we own them, they are part of us, and they are part of our history."

Understanding the vulnerability of ordinary people to the "persuasive power" of certain situations argues against rigid distinctions between innocent "victims" and tainted "perpetrators." Given the pull of situations, it becomes more difficult to point arrogant moral fingers at those with blood on their hands. The humbling point is: "If I were placed in the same situation, with the same set of social identities, it could have been me."

The perspectives of social psychology are vital in order to develop effective measures to prevent further or future political violence. If certain contextual factors make political violence likely, one needs to understand them so as to avoid perpetuating them. A better understanding of political contexts, multiple social identities, and the special situations in which political violence occurs should encourage us to expend less energy on scapegoating individuals and more energy on prospects for political transformation and institutional change. To undermine the preconditions for political violence we must nurture a culture of **human rights**, and a society that promotes transparency, especially in the use of state power. Reducing the persuasive power of situations in which "crimes of obedience" flourish requires a culture of dialogue, debate, and sensitivity to various forms of dehumanization.

Prudential Concerns

Because efforts toward reconciliation after political violence seek a sustainable peace, the victim/perpetrator dichotomy must be seen from a **pragmatic** perspective. Minimally, a sustainable peace will require an ongoing and secure cease-fire. If the political conflict continues, it will be waged by non-violent political means.

Persons who have been primary participants in a conflict have often built their lives and sense of self around their struggle. Engaging in a militant struggle deemed indispensable for the survival of one's community is likely to provide an especially rich and deep sense of identity and purpose. When such a struggle ends, these ex-combatants risk being left disoriented, with no firm sense of identity or role. If they are not reabsorbed into society, they may resume activities harmful to others, resorting either to renewed political violence or to criminal acts. Thus, responding to the situation and needs of ex-combatants is a crucially pragmatic matter within reconciliation processes.

In Northern Ireland, both Republican and Loyalist groupings include many ex-combatants who are also ex-prisoners. Those who have criminal records have been restricted in their opportunities by those records. They were primary agents in a political conflict now diminishing in intensity; they no longer occupy those roles. Some have organized for mutual support and to do community work, sometimes aimed at preventing youth from falling into patterns of petty crime and violence. Many, perhaps most, do not commit crimes or acts of violence. But all will know of other ex-prisoners who do so and for whom the resumption of political or criminal violence is an ongoing and serious temptation.

A man who might have bombed a bus or committed an execution at the height of the Troubles can gain professional training and commit himself to community leadership, accomplishing many valuable things in the aftermath. **Reductionism**, objectionable already from a logical and ethical point of view, is refuted by the facts of some striking and inspiring cases. There are powerful examples of ex-prisoners from Northern Ireland who have gained considerable skills in mediation and conflict resolution and have travelled to Bosnia, Kosovo, Macedonia, Moldova,[8] and elsewhere to work with youth. If an ex-combatant is to accomplish such things, he must be able to engage with people who receive him as a human being with creative abilities and not as permanently and merely a "perpetrator" or "terrorist."

If labelling, polarization, and stigmatization persist, these attitudes will be perceived by primary participants. It is a virtual certainty that they will be resented and will contribute further to alienation and discontent.

Conclusion

~AV Despite all the reasoning offered here, victims may insist that their role is entirely different from that of perpetrators and that their needs and interests should take priority. Victims are likely to see themselves as innocents who have suffered, while seeing ex-combatants as agents guilty of harmful acts. Ex-combatants are, by definition, capable of using lethal force so as to threaten the physical security of others. AV This is a serious matter. If primary agents are not reabsorbed into society, they will likely re-engage in political violence or resort to criminal acts. Those acts would also have their victims. Failure to reintegrate ex-combatants will create more victims and could even re-victimize some of the same persons harmed in the original conflict. Thus a concern for the interests of victims should lead directly to a concern for the proper understanding and social reintegration of ex-combatants.

~AV From the nature of their acts, some may wish to infer that ex-combatants are morally irredeemable. AV Yet even when an act is gravely wrong, the logical distinction between that "act" and the "agent" who performed it remains valid. A commitment to norms of human dignity and rights carries with it a commitment to the possibility of moral change in any human being. To regard ex-combatants as irredeemably evil is to disregard their humanity—and to ignore the reality that some have gone on to make profound contributions in their community and internationally.

~AV A simplistic focus on individual perpetrators is encouraged by the individualistic workings of the criminal justice system, the sensationalism of many media reports, and the all-too-human tendency to deny shared responsibility. AV We must work against such temptations and avoid the pernicious "privatization" of responsibility. One does not have to condone violent acts to appreciate the importance of reintegrating persons who have been primary participants in a political struggle. If we endorse a simplistic polarization of "victims" and "perpetrators," we will be handicapped in our ability to understand and to prevent political violence.

Notes

1. The "Troubles" refers to the violent conflict in Northern Ireland from the late 1960s until 1998. Most **Republicans** (Catholics) in Northern Ireland wanted to be more closely allied with Ireland, while most Loyalists (Protestants) wanted to be more closely aligned with Great Britain. While the sides split on religious lines, the conflict was primarily political, not religious. [Editor]
2. The South African Truth and Reconciliation Commission was a court-like body formed in 1995 by the first post-**apartheid** government in South, based on **restorative justice** rather than **retributive justice**. It focused on "investigating human rights abuses committed from 1960 to 1994, including the circumstances, factors, and context of such violations; allowing victims the opportunity to tell their story; granting amnesty; constructing an impartial historical record of the past; and drafting a reparations policy" (Archbishop Desmond Tutu, head of the TRC, "Truth and Reconciliation Commission, South Africa (TRC)," *Encyclopaedia Britannica*, www.britannica.com/EBchecked/topic/607421/Truth-and-Reconciliation-Commission-South-Africa-TRC. [Editor]
3. The Cold War was a state of political and military tension between the US and its allies in NATO (the North Atlantic Treaty Organization), on the one side, and the USSR (Union of Soviet Socialist Republics) and its allies, on the other side. It lasted from the end of World War II until the dissolution of the USSR in 1991. [Editor]

4. The Anglo-Boer War (1899–1902), also known as the Boer War, was fought between Great Britain and the Boers (the descendants of Dutch settlers in South Africa). Britain won the war and annexed the Boer colonies. They became part of the Union of South Africa in 1910. [Editor]
5. Afrikaners are the descendants of Dutch settlers in South Africa. This is the modern name for Boers. [Editor]
6. Christopher Browning, *Ordinary Men: Reserve Police Battalion 101 and the Final Solution in Poland* (New York: HarperCollins 1992), p. xx. [Editor]
7. The African National Congress, formed in 1912, fought for voting and other rights for Coloured (mixed race) and black South Africans. It has been the ruling party in South Africa since apartheid ended in 1994. [Editor]
8. Countries in Eastern Europe that have experienced civil war or violent ethnic conflict. [Editor]

Discussion Questions

1. What does Homer-Dixon mean by "complex terrorism"? Does complex terrorism fit the definition of terrorism discussed in the chapter introduction? That is, does it contain all three of the basic elements of terrorism, violence, terror, and political aims?
2. What does Arbour mean by the "new normal"? What are her criticisms of it? Do you agree with her? Why or why not?
3. Delvoie believes the threat of terrorism is real, but our response to it is out of proportion to it. Do you agree with him? Why or why not?
4. Both Delvoie and Lomborg (Chapter 12, Responding to Climate Change) argue that terrorism and climate change are real, but they should not be considered the most important problems facing the world today. Do you agree with them? Why or why not?
5. In response to the Supreme Court's ruling in *Charkaoui*, the federal government created a special advocate for people subject to security certificates. The special advocate's role is to protect the interests of the person held under a security certificate during the closed hearing where the secret evidence is produced. Do you think that adds enough protection to withstand another *Charter* challenge? Why or why not?
6. What do you think Arbour, a former justice on the Supreme Court of Canada, would say about security certificates? Do you think the government should be able to use security certificates to detain people suspected of terrorism? Why or why not?
7. Why do Govier and Verwoerd say we cannot simply view those who commit terrorist acts as evil? Do you think Arbour would agree with them? Would Delvoie? How do you think we should view terrorists, and why?

Suggested Readings and Websites

🍁 = Canadian source or author

🍁 *Air India Flight 182: A Canadian Tragedy*. Report of the Commission of Inquiry into the Investigation of the Bombing of Air India Flight 182. Volume 1: *The Overview*. Ottawa: Public Works and Government Services Canada, 2010, www.publications.gc.ca/pub?id=371132&sl=0. [This hard-hitting report said the Air India bombing was "the result of a cascading series of errors" and that, after the crash, government officials misled families of the victims, the public, and a previous government review.]

♣ Barnett, Laura. "Extraordinary Rendition: International Law and the Prohibition of Torture." Parliamentary Information and Research Service PRB 07-48E. Ottawa: Library of Parliament, 2008. [A non-partisan discussion of extraordinary rendition and torture. The author says that a variety of international law and conventions prohibit both extraordinary rendition and torture, even to prevent terrorism.]

♣ "Building Resilience Against Terrorism: Canada's Anti-terrorism Strategy." Ottawa: Government of Canada. 2011. www.publicsafety.gc.ca/prg/ns/_fl/2012-cts-eng.pdf. [Outlines the Canadian government's approach to dealing with terrorist threats: prevent, detect, deny (means and opportunities), and respond.]

♣ Commission of Inquiry into Actions of Canadian Officials in Relation to Maher Arar. *Report of the Events Relating to Maher Arar: Analysis and Recommendations*. Ottawa: Public Works and Services Canada, 2006, http://publications.gc.ca/pub?id=298241&sl=0. [This report said there is no evidence Arar was ever a threat to Canada, strongly criticized the RCMP for its actions both before Arar's detention and after his return, and recommended the government apologize to and compensate Arar.]

♣ Ignatieff, Michael. "Lesser Evils." *New York Times Magazine*, May 2004. www.nytimes.com/2004/05/02/magazine/lesser-evils.html. [Michael Ignatieff, former head of the Liberal Party of Canada, says, "To defeat evil, we may have to traffic in evils," by doing things like detaining suspected terrorists indefinitely and interrogating them coercively. Citizens, politicians, and the courts must oversee policies concerning terrorism; publicity will ensure that the lesser evil does not become the greater, he says.]

♣ Roach, Kent. "Must We Trade Rights for Security? The Choice between Smart, Harsh, or Proportionate Security Strategies in Canada and Britain." *Cardozo Law Review* 27, 5 (2006): 2151–222. [Argues against the view that we must favour either rights or security in preventing terrorism—says some of the best anti-terrorist strategies do not violate rights, and some of the most right-violating strategies do not prevent terrorism.]

♣ Tetonio, Isabel. "Toronto 18." *Toronto Star*, 2010. www3.thestar.com/static/toronto18/index.html. [An in-depth series on the Toronto 18—the plot, investigation, arrests, trials and pleas, and aftermath of the case; includes many photos and videos.]

Townshend, Charles. *Terrorism: A Very Short Introduction*. Oxford: Oxford University Press, 2002. [History, philosophical and political analysis, and an analysis of the media's role.]

♣ Van Harten, Gus. "*Charkaoui* and Secret Evidence." *Supreme Court Law Review* 42, 2 (2008): 251–79. [Argues that the Supreme Court did not go far enough in its decision in *Charkaoui*, and that courts need their own investigators and experts in order to provide adequate oversight of the executive by the judiciary.]

Chapter 12

Responding to Climate Change

Environment Canada defines climate change as "Changes in long-term weather patterns caused by natural phenomena and human activities that alter the chemical composition of the atmosphere through the build-up of **greenhouse gases** which trap heat and reflect it back to the earth's surface."[1] In this chapter, we will discuss human-caused climate change. Most scientists today believe human-caused climate change began with the industrial revolution, and has sped up significantly since the twentieth century. They believe human-produced greenhouse gases—particularly carbon dioxide and methane, which are by-products of burning fossil fuels (coal and oil), deforestation, cattle, and garbage, among other things—have disrupted weather patterns worldwide, by raising temperatures, causing droughts, and causing more severe storms. And because the atmosphere is continuous, greenhouse gases emitted in Canada affect not just us, but also people living Indonesia, Sierra Leone, Italy, and Brazil. By nature, climate change is a global phenomenon.

The Evidence for Climate Change

In 1988 the United Nations set up the Intergovernmental Panel on Climate Change (IPCC) to provide scientific information about climate change and its potential environmental and social effects, and options for lessening or adapting to the effects. The IPCC has released four reports, in 1990, 1995, 2001, and 2007. Each has been more strongly worded than the last. The 2007 report stated there is a ninety to ninety-nine per cent chance that human activity has caused the increase in temperatures worldwide since the middle of the twentieth century, and predicted world temperatures will increase in the twenty-first century by 1.1 to 6.4 degrees Celsius (1.1 degrees Celsius if most countries drastically reduce their greenhouse gas emissions now, and as much as 6.4 degrees Celsius under "business as usual").

Almost all climate scientists agree that climate change is human-caused and potentially disastrous. Isn't there controversy over this data, though? Here we need to stop for a minute and think about science, knowledge, and certainty. We know many things because we have experienced them ourselves—we know that snow is cold, that getting from here to there takes *x* minutes, and so on. But we know most things because we read or heard them somewhere—for example, that Newfoundland joined Confederation in 1949 or that water consists of two hydrogen and one oxygen molecules. Why do we believe these things? Certainly not because we were there or we did the experiments ourselves. We believe them because we learned them from credible authorities—in these cases, probably textbooks. But how do we know which authorities are credible? In science, experts in each branch of science establish the standards in their branches. Scientists become credible authorities in their fields when they publish papers in peer-reviewed journals (that is, journals in which papers are reviewed by other experts), and when other scientists cite their papers in their research. So the statement "Almost all climate scientists agree that climate change is human-caused and potentially disastrous" means the experts in climate science—those with enough scientific training to contribute to and evaluate knowledge in their discipline—believe the scientific evidence supports the conclusions that climate change is real and that it is a very serious threat.

What about the scientists who dispute climate change? Here we have to ask *which* scientists dispute climate change. If some chemists say viruses don't cause the flu, we have no reason to believe them. Why? Because chemists are not experts in viruses or medicine. Scientists are experts only in their own fields, not in all branches of science. Almost all climate scientists—more than ninety-seven per cent—agree that climate change is occurring faster than at any previous time in human history, and that human activity is the accelerant.[2] On the other hand, almost none of the scientists who dispute climate change are climate scientists.[3] Their criticisms are no more relevant than a chemist's skepticism about viruses would be. While scientists are more comfortable reading scientific material outside their specialties than most non-scientists, that does not make them experts in those other areas.

The overwhelming consensus among climate scientists, who are the experts on the evidence for or against climate change, is that it is real and is accelerating. There is room for reasonable disagreement about what we ought to do about climate change, but not about the fact that it is occurring.

The Precautionary Principle

How bad will climate change be? Scientists cannot say with certainty whether it will be pretty bad, completely disastrous, or something in-between. We must decide based on uncertain outcomes. Philosophers call this "decision under uncertainty." It is not unusual; everyone makes decisions under uncertainty all the time, such as choosing a major in an uncertain economy. But it is philosophically interesting, particularly when some or all of the outcomes are bad. How do we decide in such cases? Some theorists say we should follow the precautionary principle in such situations, which says we have an ethical duty to prevent harm to others. The strength of this duty increases as the amount or likelihood of harm increases, and it decreases as the amount or likelihood of harm decreases. So, for instance, the precautionary principle justifies laws against dangerous and impaired driving. Someone can be convicted of one of these offences even if no one is harmed, because no one has the right to subject others to the likelihood of harm.

But the precautionary principle does not require us to avoid the possibility of all harm, because that would paralyze us. All motor vehicles create risks, both to safety and the environment, but that does not mean everyone should stop riding in or driving them. (Although Vandana Shiva, in this chapter, might believe they should.) Almost all methods of heating cause greenhouse gases, but no one thinks we should not heat our houses and other buildings. So when does a risk of bad consequences become unacceptable? The 1992 *Rio Declaration on Environment and Development* put it this way:

> In order to protect the environment, the precautionary approach shall be widely applied by States according to their capabilities. Where there are threats of serious or irreversible damage, lack of full scientific certainty shall not be used as a reason for postponing cost-effective measures to prevent environmental degradation.[4]

If an environmental threat is "serious or irreversible," we must use "cost-effective measures" to avoid it. That still leaves a lot of room for interpretation; like all such documents, the *Rio Declaration* was a compromise. When is a threat to the environment "serious or irreversible"? What are "cost-effective measures"? The *Rio Declaration* does not tell us. But it does say that no state should wait for "full scientific certainty" before it takes action on climate change.

To Whom Do We Owe Duties?

Climate change brings several standard issues in political philosophy into sharp focus. What do we owe our fellow citizens? What do we owe people in other nations? Future generations? Members of other species? (See Chapter 6, Animal Rights.) Do we owe anything to species or the environment themselves? Many political philosophers have discussed obligations to future generations, but until recently, only a few considered whether we have duties to people in other countries. While most commentators agree that we have duties not to harm people in other countries, climate change presents particular difficulties because it involves diffuse harms from many sources. (Thomas Hurka addresses these issues in this chapter.)

What Should We Do?

Climate scientists can tell us that temperatures will likely rise between 1.1 to 6.4 degrees Celsius over the next century, and they can predict how certain policies will affect the climate. That ends their expertise, though. They can tell us what they think we ought to do, but on policy questions they have no more expertise than anyone else. In a **democracy**, we must decide as citizens, as a nation, how to respond to climate change. Good science must inform our decisions, but the final choices involve deciding what we value, how we want to live, and what kinds of global citizens we want to be. These choices are moral and political, not scientific. (See the reading by Thomas Homer-Dixon in this chapter.) Our choices fall into two general categories:

- We can adapt to climate change. If sea levels rise, we dredge harbours and either build better seawalls or move people and businesses further inland. If temperatures rise, we heat less and cool more. If storms become more severe, we improve building codes and strengthen hydro lines. If droughts worsen, we grow different crops and landscape with different plants. And so on.

- We can mitigate (lessen) the effects of climate change by reducing our greenhouse gas emissions. We can require that cars and trucks become more fuel efficient, and that industries reduce their emissions. We can encourage or require businesses and individuals to conserve energy and reduce waste. We can subsidize energy that does not produce greenhouse gases, such as solar and wind power. And so on.

Adaptation

The first option, adaptation, would be relatively easy for us. While rising sea levels threaten most of eastern Canada and parts of Quebec and British Columbia, we can afford either to build seawalls or to move people and businesses. Rising temperatures might actually be a boon for us—they will extend growing seasons for farmers and gardeners, lessen the need for heating and snow and ice removal, and make more of Canada inhabitable. Of course adaptation has drawbacks. Rising sea levels will destroy homes, businesses, and harbours. Rising temperatures means new pests will invade Canada. Many plant and animal species will suffer because their habitats will change faster than they can adapt. Many regions will experience increased drought. While sea levels will rise, freshwater lake levels, including in the Great Lakes, will drop. Forest fires will increase. Skiers, snowboarders, and ski resorts will have to move northward. Rising temperatures in the Arctic mean less sea ice, which will disrupt the Inuit way of life and may cause polar bears to become extinct.

We are a rich country, and probably we can adapt to these changes. But poor countries will suffer disproportionately from climate change. Rising sea levels and temperatures will turn millions of people into climate refugees and increase the spread of diseases. Waterfront resorts, a large part of many poor countries' income, will be swamped. Increasingly severe storms will kill tens or hundreds of thousands of people and make millions homeless and destitute. Drought will become more common and more severe. Climate disruption will cause political unrest as well. Elsewhere, Thomas Homer-Dixon writes,

> By weakening rural economies, increasing unemployment and disrupting livelihoods, global warming will increase the frustrations and anger of hundreds of millions of people in vulnerable countries. . . . [It] will undermine already frail governments—and make challenges from violent groups more likely—by reducing revenues, overwhelming bureaucracies, and revealing how incapable these governments are of helping their citizens.[5]

Those who can least afford it, and who have contributed least to climate change, will suffer greatly if we do nothing, while those who have contributed most will suffer relatively little.

Adaptation has its proponents, including the first US President Bush, who said at the Earth Summit in Rio de Janeiro in 1992, "The American way of life is not negotiable." Bjørn Lomborg, in this chapter, presents a more nuanced argument for adaptation.

Mitigation

The Kyoto Protocol

The second option, mitigation, involves reducing greenhouse gas emissions. In 1997 Canada signed the Kyoto Protocol, an international agreement in which thirty-seven industrialized countries and the European Union committed to reduce greenhouse gas emissions by an average of five per cent below 1990 levels by 2012. The US refused to sign the accord because it did not include limits for large-emitting poor countries like China. The Canadian government did nothing to put the accord into force, and by 2010 Canada's greenhouse gas emissions had increased more than seventeen per cent over 1990 levels (more than twenty-four per cent over our Kyoto targets).[6] In December 2011 Canada became the first and only country to withdraw from the Kyoto Protocol. The Minister of the Environment, Peter Kent, said the agreement was pointless because we would not meet our targets, and even trying to meet them would cost billions of dollars.[7]

Equal Per-capita Emissions

So what is a fair way to divide up greenhouse gas emissions? Many philosophers, political scientists, and other commentators say the fairest scheme would give countries permits for equal per-capita (per person) emissions and allow high emitters to buy excess emissions permits from another country that will be under its limit. The intuitive idea here is that everyone in the world has an equal right to the atmosphere, and no one has a right to make it worse for everyone else. In practice, this means that Canada, with thirty-five million people, and Uganda, with thirty-four million people, will receive roughly the same number of emissions permits. On a per-capita basis, we produce far more greenhouse gases than Uganda (twenty-three times as many in 2005).[8] We would have to buy extra permits—a lot, in fact—and Uganda might be one country from whom we would buy them. The cost of the permits would give us a strong incentive to reduce our emissions. And Uganda would have plenty of room to industrialize, probably with permits to spare that it could sell in the emissions market.

Equal per-capita emissions has much to recommend it. It is simple and easy to understand. Given that the atmosphere is continuous and cannot be divided, allocating emissions **rights** on a per-person basis seems the fairest way to distribute them. This way a country that produces more greenhouse gases than its permits allow will have to compensate other, presumably poorer, countries by buying their unused permits. While of course no single rich country will compensate every poor country for its excess emissions, most poor countries will benefit by selling their excess emissions permits. For example China, which currently produces more greenhouse gases than any other country, produces less than a quarter per capita of what Canada produces, while India produces about a thirteenth per capita of what we produce.[9] Probably both countries would be able to continue industrializing and still have spare emissions permits to sell on the market. And if a rich country decided it did not want to alter its high-emissions practices, it would have to pay the price in the open market.

Equal per-capita emissions also has problems, though. First, it assumes that all countries will be benefited or harmed equally by climate change. But we know that climate change is likely to harm some countries more than others. India and most countries in

Africa will be hit hard, the US and China less so, and Canada and Russia might even benefit from climate change.[10] India and the African countries will need more money to adapt to climate change than countries like Canada and Russia, but they will be allotted the same number of emissions permits per capita. This seems unfair, particularly since India and the African countries have contributed so little to climate change.

Second, this scheme assigns emissions permits to nations. Many poor countries are run by small, rich elites, or they have corrupt governments. In these countries, money from unused emissions permits is unlikely to reach the people who most need it. Once again, equal per-capita emissions might not distribute the harms of climate change fairly.

Finally, we have no effective way to enforce equal per-capita emissions—or any climate agreement, for that matter. World government is still in its infancy. International bodies like the International Criminal Court and the World Trade Organization can enforce decisions against countries that have signed the treaties establishing them, but they have no authority against countries that have not signed the treaties. If a country considered equal per-capita emissions too expensive it could simply refuse to sign the agreement, as the US did with the Kyoto Protocol, or it could "unsign" it, as Canada did. But even if a country did sign an emissions reduction treaty, no international body has the power to enforce it. In some cases international pressure makes a difference, but not necessarily; it did not stop Canada from withdrawing from Kyoto. Trade **sanctions** would be a deterrent to many countries, but they are hard to enforce. Furthermore, they make little difference to large countries like the US and China. They are enormous markets, and trade with them is so important to almost every country in the world that many—perhaps most—would ignore trade sanctions if they were imposed.[11]

The Readings

In the first reading, Thomas Hurka says that, while everyone in the world does not agree what is the best ethical theory, most people agree that consequences and rights matter. He uses these principles to examine adaptation and mitigation (which he calls "avoidance") as responses to climate change. He also asks to whom our principles apply, beginning with what he calls "humans here and now," the view that ethical principles apply only to our current fellow citizens. Then he considers whether we have obligations to future generations, distant people, and the environment. He considers who should pay for climate change, and discusses rights as constraints on policies and rights to compensation. He concludes that avoidance (mitigation) is the best policy overall.

Bjørn Lomborg acknowledges that climate change is real, but argues its consequences are often enormously exaggerated. He examines several predicted consequences of climate change—heat deaths, rising sea levels, more severe storms, and the spread of malaria—and argues either that the consequences have been exaggerated or that we can avoid them with smarter policies. Putting money into alternative technologies such as solar power, to improve them and bring their costs down, would be not only cheaper but also more effective than the Kyoto Protocol. What's more, there are many important global problems, such as HIV/AIDS and malnutrition, that would give us a much greater bang for our buck than reducing greenhouse gases would.

Thomas Homer-Dixon says we need to make **cognitive**, economic, political, and **normative** transformations to deal with climate change. The cognitive transformation involves realizing that climates are inherently complex. The economic transformation involves abandoning economists' faith that economic growth is necessary for a society to function, and replacing it with resilience, which involves decentralizing economic, energy, and other systems. (Compare what he says here to his arguments in Chapter 11, Real and Suspected Terrorism.) The political transformation requires reinvigorating democracy, particularly by not letting experts hijack policy debates. The normative transformation is the deepest: we need to expand who we mean by "we." (For different ways of expanding who "we" are, see Part II, Who Are "We"?)

Finally, Vandana Shiva argues we need to abandon destructive free-market **ideologies** and reject the mantras of industrialization and development that have caused our climate and environmental crises. We should replace this deadly **paradigm** with Earth Democracy, which is "based on equal rights of all beings to ecological space, including atmospheric space." On this paradigm biodiversity, not technology, industrialization, or markets, is the way to end climate change and save the planet for all its inhabitants. Notice that Shiva's proposed changes extend beyond humans to include the entire world, spiritual as well as physical. (By the way, Shiva has Canadian philosophical connections: she has an MA in philosophy from the University of Guelph and a PhD in philosophy from the University of Western Ontario.)

The Moral and Political Preferences Indicator

Virtually everyone in Canada who denies the reality of climate change is very conservative. Probably they believe that economic liberty is more important than the environment. Many conservatives and virtually all centrists and egalitarians in Canada believe that climate change is real and we ought to do something about it. They may disagree strongly about what we ought to do, however. Views here range from adaptation and voluntary greenhouse gas reductions to deep, enforced reductions. By and large, those on the more conservative end tend to favour voluntary reductions and market solutions, consistent with their belief that liberty trumps other political values and the market is the best distribution system. People on the egalitarian end of the spectrum tend to favour enforced reductions, consistent with their beliefs that the equal right to a decent life and our responsibilities to distant and future people trump the bottom lines of large corporations.

Notes

1. Environment Canada, Climate Change > Canada's GHG Inventory > Definitions and Glossary, www.ec.gc.ca/ges-ghg/default.asp?lang=En&n=B710AE51-1#section3.
2. William R. L. Anderegg, James W. Prall, Jacob Harold, and Stephen H. Schneider, "Expert Credibility in Climate Change," *Proceedings of the National Academy of Sciences* 107, 27 (2010): 12107–9; PT Doran & MK Zimmerman, "Examining the Scientific Consensus on Climate Change," *Eos Transactions American Geophysical Union* 90, 3 (2009): 22; N Oreskes, "Beyond the Ivory Tower: The Scientific Consensus on Climate Change," *Science* 306, 5702 (3 December 2004): 1686.
3. See Naomi Oreskes and Erik M. Conway, *Merchants of Doubt: How a Handful of Scientists Obscured the Truth on Issues from Tobacco Smoke to Global Warming* (NY: Bloomsbury, 2010).

4. United Nations Environment Program, *Rio Declaration on Environment and Development* (1972), Principle 15, www.unep.org/documents.multilingual/default.asp?documentid=78&articleid=1163.
5. Thomas Homer-Dixon, "Terror in the Weather Forecast," *The New York Times* (24 April 2007), www.nytimes.com/2007/04/24/opinion/24homer-dixon.html?_r=0.
6. Environment Canada, Environmental Indicators > Air and Climate Indicators > Data and Methods, www.ec.gc.ca/indicateurs-indicators/default.asp?lang=en&n=BFB1B398-1#ghg1.
7. Bill Curry and Shawn McCarthy, "Canada formally abandons Kyoto Protocol on climate change," *The Globe and Mail* (12 December 2011), www.theglobeandmail.com/news/politics/canada-formally-abandons-kyoto-protocol-on-climate-change/article4180809/. Canada's emissions are small compared to total emissions, but very large on a per-capita basis. Canada ranks third among seventeen rich countries in emissions per capita, behind Australia and the US. See the Conference Board of Canada, How Canada Performs > Details and Analysis > Environment > GHG Emissions Per Capita (July 2011), www.conferenceboard.ca/hcp/Details/Environment/greenhouse-gas-emissions.aspx.
8. Google Public Data Explorer, Global Greenhouse Gas Emissions by Country, Economic Sector, and Gas (data from World Resources Institute, 9 November 2012), www.google.com/publicdata/explore?ds=cjsdgb406s3np_#!strail=false&bcs=d&nselm=h&rdim=country&idim=country:31:181&ifdim=country&hl=en_US&dl=en_US&ind=false.
9. Google Public Data Explorer, Global Greenhouse Gas Emissions by Country, Economic Sector, and Gas.
10. Eric A Posner and Cass R Sunstein, "Justice and Climate Change," The Harvard Project on International Climate Agreements Discussion Paper 08-04 (2008), p. 8.
11. The same would be true if the European Union violated its agreements. However, the EU requires that member countries meet or come close to meeting their Kyoto reductions. Here the market's importance works in favour of reducing greenhouse gases: membership in the EU is so important that countries are willing to make sacrifices to remain in it. If the EU threatened trade sanctions against Canada for withdrawing from Kyoto, our government might re-think its withdrawal. Threatening trade sanctions would be unlikely to change the behaviour of China or the US, however, even in the unlikely case that the EU risked its economic interests to impose them.

Thomas Hurka

Ethical Principles

. . . [T]he challenge of global climate change raises **ethical** issues. What response to this challenge, whether by an individual, corporation, or government, would be ethically right? Resolving these issues is crucial to making responsible decisions about the climate. An ethical judgement about a climate policy is not just one judgment among many, to be weighed against economic, political, and other judgments in deciding how, all things considered, to act. It is itself an all-things-considered judgment, which takes account of economic and other factors. If a climate policy is ethically right, it is simply right; if it is ethically wrong, it is wrong, period.

To resolve these ethical issues we need to combine **empirical** facts about the threat of global climate change . . . with general ethical principles that say what is right and wrong in all policy areas. Combining these general principles with the specific facts about climatic change will lead to specific policy recommendations.

There is dispute, however, about what the correct ethical principles are, both between cultures and within Western culture; and this can lead to conflicting judgments about policies. Even if there were no uncertainty about the facts concerning climatic change—even if there were universal agreement about the consequences of different policies—the use of different principles could lead to different ethical conclusions.

The situation is not, however, entirely bleak. Some proposed ethical principles are relatively uncontroversial and widely accepted: it is hard to deny them, and few writers on ethics do. Other principles are more radical. There is, in fact, a continuum of possible principles, from ones that are well grounded and widely held to ones that are more speculative and contentious. This fact can be exploited in discussing a particular issue such as climatic change. If one can show that a climate policy is justified using only uncontentious principles, one can justify it to most people, whatever their disagreements about more radical principles. In fact, this is a useful general response to ethical disagreement: on any issue, try to establish ethical conclusions using the least contentious principles possible, to maximize the chances of agreement.

I will organize this survey of ethical principles so as to allow this kind of response. For each of the two main considerations relevant to the ethical evaluation of acts or policies, I will move from less controversial principles to ones that are more radical. . . .

Consequences: Humans Here and Now

An important class of ethical principles consider[s] consequences. If an act or policy has good consequences, these principles say, this counts ethically in its favour; if it has bad or, especially, disastrous consequences, this counts ethically against it. A concern for consequences is especially relevant to the choice between the broad climate policies of adaptation and avoidance.

. . . [C]hoosing adaptation means continuing our present practices such as burning fossil fuels, letting global temperatures rise, and then making whatever further changes this requires: building sea walls, moving populations from environmentally damaged areas, and so on. Avoidance means changing our practices to prevent any warming from occurring. Mixed policies combine elements of adaptation and avoidance: they include some measures to reduce the rate of climatic change and some to adapt to the warming that does occur. The first ethical issue concerning climate policy is what mix of adaptation and avoidance is ethically preferable: to what extent should we allow global climate change to occur, and to what extent should we prevent it? In trying to resolve this issue we will surely be concerned with the two policies' consequences. First, however, we require a more precise statement of what our ethical concern for consequences involves.

One issue is the form of this ethical concern. A simple principle, popular among philosophers, says that each **agent** has the duty always to bring about the best consequences, or the most good, possible. This maximizing principle is central, for example, to the ethical theory of **utilitarianism**. . . . But there are other possible principles about consequences. **Egalitarian** principles care not only about the total good an act produces but also about its distribution: they may prefer a smaller quantity of good that is equally distributed to a larger total of which some have a disproportionate share. . . . What have been called satisficing principles (from the idea of "making satisfactory") are less demanding than maximizing. They give each agent the duty only to bring about consequences that are reasonably good, either because those consequences are above an **absolute** threshold of satisfactoriness or because they represent a reasonable proportion of the most good the agent can produce. . . . Finally, any principle about consequences can be limited by a permission allowing agents to give some more weight to their own interests than to others'. They may still have a duty to sacrifice their interests for the sake of large benefits to others, but need not accept very great losses to secure just a small increase in the aggregate good. . . .

Whatever their exact form, these various principles are relatively easy to apply when we know with certainty what the consequences of different acts will be. . . . [H]owever, this is not our situation with respect to climate policy: there is great uncertainty about, for example, both the magnitude and the rate of the threatened rise in temperature. But it does not follow that principles about consequences cannot be applied. If an act or policy involves some risk of bad consequences this is a reason to avoid it, and this reason is weightier the worse the consequences are and the higher the risk. If the consequences are extremely bad, even a small risk of producing them is a reason to avoid the act and to accept some costs in doing so. . . . If the result of allowing climatic change would be disastrous, it is prudent to avoid this result even if we are not certain that it would come about.

Once the form of a principle about consequences is settled we must specify its content, or the kind of consequences it cares about. If an act's consequences are good or bad, it is because they affect beings that matter ethically, or have ethical "standing,"[1] in ethically significant ways. These matters too need to be spelled out.

A relatively uncontentious ethical principle says that we have a duty to consider the effects of our actions on other humans living in our own country at the present time. (I assume that the view that each of us should care only about his or her own interests does not count as ethical.) Since humans in our country now have ethical standing, this principle says, it counts in favour of an act if it benefits them and against the act if it harms them. But what do benefits and harms consist in? On no plausible view can they consist ultimately in effects on people's wealth or income. Money is a means to the good life, but it is only a means, and we must know what deeper values it serves. There are two main theories about this. According to welfarism, humans are benefited by whatever gives them pleasure, fulfils their desires, or contributes to something describable as their "happiness." **Perfectionism**, by contrast, equates the human good with knowledge, achievement, love, virtue, and other states that it values apart from any connection to happiness. What matters is not how enjoyable someone's life is but how far it develops human potentials or realizes "spiritual values." But the debate between welfarism and perfectionism, prominent though it has been in Western ethics, seems less important for an issue such as climate policy. It seems likely that, in this policy area, the acts that turn out to benefit and harm humans will be roughly the same on welfarist, perfectionist, and indeed all plausible theories of the human good.

If we confine ourselves to the uncontentious principle that we should consider the effects of our actions on humans living in our own country now, what follows for the choice between adaptation and avoidance? This principle—call it the humans-here-and-now principle—does not count some of the largest harms threatened by global climatic change: that a rise in global temperatures may damage the environment, killing individual organisms and destroying ecosystems, does not matter in itself, since only effects on humans have intrinsic ethical significance. And many of the effects on humans do not get counted either. There is a substantial time-lag between the release of greenhouse gases into the atmosphere and the resulting increase in temperature. Partly because of this, the largest effects of global climate change are projected to occur several decades into the twenty-first century, when most of the humans living today will no longer be alive. And those who will be alive—future generations—do not have ethical standing on the humans-here-and-now principle, so effects on them are also irrelevant. At the same time, this principle does count many of the harms involved in choosing avoidance. If reducing the use of fossil fuels has economic costs, these will be felt initially by humans existing today, and the losses in **welfare** or perfection they may suffer are ethically significant. Given its restricted concern for consequences, the humans-here-and-now principle has a tendency to favour adaptation over avoidance—since it ignores many of the former's effects while counting the latter's, it has a bias towards letting climatic change occur.

It is not that this principle allows no arguments for avoidance. If humans today want the environment to be preserved or future generations to flourish, then, according to some welfarist theories, they will be harmed by future events that prevent these desires from being fulfilled. And according to some perfectionist theories, if humans today are pursuing goals whose achievement requires the flourishing of future generations—if, for example, they are trying to preserve and pass on some human tradition—there is again an indirect here-and-now reason to prevent warming. But these here-and-now arguments cannot have great weight: even if humans today have some future-oriented desires and goals, they have many more directed mainly at the present.

The more serious here-and-now arguments for avoidance appeal to consequences other than ones directly concerning climate. The use of chlorofluorocarbons, for example, not only contributes to greenhouse warming but also damages the ozone layer, creating health risks for humans in the very short term. Especially since chlorofluorocarbons are easily replaceable, this last fact gives us a here-and-now ethical reason to eliminate them, a policy that happens, as a side-effect, to reduce global climate change. Other avoidance measures can be justified on economic grounds. Increasing the efficiency of heating and lighting systems or the fuel efficiency of automobiles and electrical generating plants can save money while, on the side, reducing emissions of greenhouse gases. This, again, supplies a here-and-now reason for these measures. . . . To justify more avoidance we would need to adopt a more controversial ethical principle, such as one extending the concern for consequences, and ethical standing, to humans in future generations and/or humans in other nations.

Consequences: Humans at Other Times and Places

A concern for humans in future generations reflects the ethical idea that the temporal location of a harm or benefit—the time when it occurs—has no bearing on its ethical significance. Goods and evils in the future will be just as real as ones today and ought to count as much in our ethical deliberations. . . . This idea is central to the concept of "sustainable development," which "meets the needs of the present without compromising the ability of future generations to meet their own needs."[2] To care about sustainability is to care about future humans as well as about those now alive.

Like the here-and-now principle, a concern for future generations can take different forms. A maximizing principle tells us to produce the greatest good possible for humans in all generations, with future interests counted equally against those in the present. Egalitarian principles tell us to aim at equality between generations. Thus, in one formulation, each generation is to leave its successors a total range of resources and opportunities that is at least as good as its own. . . . Finally, what we called satisficing principles require each generation to allow its successors to be, not as well off as possible, nor even as well off, as they, but at least reasonably well-off.

A parallel extension of concern to humans in other countries reflects the idea that the spatial location of a good or evil—the place where it occurs—does not matter ethically: benefits and harms far away are as real as ones close by and should figure as much in our deliberations. . . . If we maximize or satisfice with respect to the good, we should include effects on distant humans in our calculations of consequences; if we are egalitarians, we should accept a principle of equality between nations.

. . .

What of extending concern to humans in other countries? This may strengthen some arguments for avoidance. To here-and-now claims about energy efficiency in our country we can add similar claims about energy efficiency in other, especially developing, countries. . . . And future generations in these countries are likely to be among those most seriously harmed by global climatic change. They live on low-lying islands or coastal plains or depend on industries such as farming or fishing that can be destroyed by small changes in the environment, and their local economies lack the resources to pay for the expensive adaptation measures that climatic change would require.

But humans-everywhere principles also magnify the ethical costs of avoidance. Humans in developing countries have a low quality of life, and any ethical principle that counts their interests will recognize an ethical demand to improve that quality of life. This improvement seems likely to require further industrialization, which, even given the most efficient technologies, will probably involve increases in greenhouse gas emissions from developing countries. To forbid these countries this industrialization in order to protect future generations' interest in a healthy environment is to do those countries' citizens a serious harm, that of perpetuating an indefensibly low standard of living; but to allow their industrialization is to place very serious burdens on developed countries. If greenhouse gas emissions will increase in the developing world, the reductions required in wealthier countries to ensure an overall decline in emissions are very large indeed. Some sacrifices by developed countries do not raise serious ethical objections: when the well-being of (most of) their citizens is already so high, a small decrease is not ethically troubling. But what is contemplated in the face of increased emissions from developing countries is a large decrease, and that may be a substantial objection to wholesale avoidance.

This is, for many, the central dilemma of climate policy, and indeed of environmental policy generally: how to weigh against each other the interests of developing countries in a higher quality of life, based on further industrialization, and the interests of future generations in an unravaged environment. The dilemma is especially pressing for egalitarians, who must try to balance the competing claims of equality among nations and equality among generations. . . .

Consequences: The Environment Valued for Itself

Despite their extension beyond the here and now, the principles discussed in the last section confine ethical standing to humans. If changes in the environment matter ethically it is only indirectly, because of their effects for good or ill on human lives. . . .

A more radical environmental view rejects this assumption and extends ethical standing to parts of the environment. This environment-centred view directs us to care for the **natural** world around us, not just as a means to better human lives, but as an **end in itself**. This marks a radical break with much of traditional Western ethics, which has emphasized the lordship of humans over nature. It is a reforming view, and far from universally accepted, but it too comes in less and more radical forms.

The less radical environment-centred principles are modelled on our ethical concern for humans. This latter concern is individualist, treating individual humans as the bearers of ethical value and any social or global good as merely an aggregate of the goods of individuals. Individualist environmental principles extend this approach to the environment, finding intrinsic value in the lives of individual non-human organisms. How far these principles extend standing depends on what the good in general consists in. Welfarists equate the human good with, for example, pleasure and the absence of pain, and will value the same states of feeling in nonhumans. This extends concern to mammals, who may also be capable of desires and satisfactions, and to organisms as far down the developmental scale as (perhaps) arthropods. But it does not include lower beings such as mollusks, insects, and plants, who lack the capacity for feeling. Perfectionists equate the human good with states such as knowledge and achievement, which they value apart from any connection to happiness. At the deepest level, many perfectionists equate the human good with the development of properties **essential** to or distinctive of human nature. . . . Their environmental **ethic** will therefore extend standing to all beings with a nature that can be developed to varying degrees, that is, to all living things. . . .

The rationale given for individualist environmentalism is ethical consistency. If we value a state such as freedom from pain in humans, it is arbitrary and "speciesist" not to value it also in non-humans. We do not accept the racist view that the interests of whites count more than those of blacks even though there is no ethically relevant difference between them. In the same way, it is argued, we should not accept a view that gives ethical weight to a state in humans but no weight to a qualitatively similar state in non-humans.

Nonetheless, individualist environmentalism is criticized as insufficiently radical to capture the real intrinsic values in the environment, which reside not in individual organisms but in wholes such as species and ecosystems. It is argued, for example, that individualism cannot account for the importance of preserving biodiversity, or a large number of biological species. Biodiversity has value for humans, and there may therefore be indirect reasons to preserve it even on a human-centred view: humans can enjoy a varied environment, and the preservation of rare species may lead to benefits in the future, such as the discovery of new medicines. But some environmentalists claim that there is value beyond this—intrinsic value—in a rich and varied natural world, and that individualism cannot account for this value. If we have a choice between saving the last members of an endangered species and a slightly greater number of members of a populous species, individualism will tell us to prefer the latter. Because it counts only the interests of individuals, it cannot recognize the special environmental value in groups. . . .

Those who urge this objection espouse a more radical, **holistic** environmental ethic, which takes the bearers of intrinsic value to be wholes such as ecosystems or the entire biosphere, and which grants individuals ethical significance only as contributing to valued properties of these wholes. (Holistic principles can either be added to human-centred and individualist ones or, on the most radical view of all, can supplant them entirely.) The classic statement of this holistic view is that of Aldo Leopold: "A thing is right when it tends to preserve the integrity, stability, and beauty of the biotic community. It is wrong when it tends otherwise."[3] Ethical standing belongs not (or not just) to individual organisms but to the interrelated wholes they compose.

Adopting either environment-centred principle, the individualist, or the holist, would push the ethically acceptable climate policy closer to avoidance. The new principle would not see any significant additional costs in avoidance, since the bad effects (if any) of this policy fall almost entirely on humans: it is they whose quality of life may decline as greenhouse emissions are reduced. And the principle does see additional costs in adaptation: the harms this policy causes to the environment matter not just because of their effects on humans but also in themselves, as affecting a natural world that has ethical standing in its own right. The chief worry here is the threatened rate of climatic change. There is nothing in itself environmentally objectionable about change: those who value diversity should prefer a world where, through history, forms of life succeed each other to one where species and ecosystems are eternally fixed. But the rate of warming projected for the next century given adaptation is faster than any in the last ten thousand years, and forms of life that could adapt to a slower warming may be destroyed by one this rapid. This will be bad both on an individualist environmental view—where individual animals will suffer or find their natural life-activities impossible—and on a holist view, where complex and fragile ecosystems, such as in the Canadian Arctic, will disappear.

. . .

Consequences: Further Applications

Principles about consequences are relevant not only to the broad choice between adaptation and avoidance but also to other aspects of climate policy. In fact, some writers on ethics, known as **consequentialists**, hold that consequences are all that is relevant to any ethical evaluation, in any area: what is right is always, for example, what produces the most good possible. For maximizing consequentialists, once we have chosen a climate policy, the right mechanism for implementing it is the one that is most efficient, that is, that produces the greatest benefits at the least cost. Similarly, the right division of the policy's costs is the one that makes those costs smallest. Those people (or beings) should pay for the policy who are best able to pay, or who will be harmed least by paying, whatever their or others' responsibility for the problem the policy addresses.

The implications of these further consequentialist ideas depend on economic and sociological facts about the efficiency of different policy mechanisms and the impacts on people of different divisions of their costs. However, **consequentialism** tends to imply that avoidance in particular ought often to be implemented in developing countries with its costs borne by developed countries.

The rationale for the first part of this implication is efficiency. It is often more cost-effective to bring new industrial facilities in developing countries up to the highest technological standards of efficiency than to attempt expensive retrofits of existing plants in the developed world. The most efficient policy, therefore, will often operate in developing countries.

The implication about the bearing of costs rests, given a maximizing principle, on the thesis of "diminishing marginal **utility**": that the contribution an extra unit of wealth or income makes to a person's quality of life, in welfarist or perfectionist terms, gets smaller the more wealth or income the person has. Where an extra thousand dollars can make a large difference to the happiness or human development of a person who is starving, it may not be noticed by one who has millions. Given diminishing marginal utility, the overall consequences of a climate policy will be better if its economic costs are borne by those who are wealthiest rather than by those who are poor. And this claim is strengthened if our consequentialist principle is egalitarian or satisficing. On an egalitarian view, we have an extra reason to equalize people's levels of well-being; on a satisficing view, losses by those whose lives are above a threshold of reasonable well-being have no ethical significance.

The second implication also holds for a policy of adaptation. If global temperatures rise, adaptive measures should be implemented where they need to be—where environmental damage is greatest. But it is again best if the costs of these measures are borne by those who are wealthiest and thus best able to pay. This meets the general consequentialist standard that what is right is always what produces the best outcome overall.

Rights: Constraints

Though some writers on ethics endorse consequentialism, many reject it. They agree that an act or policy's having good consequences is one consideration in favour of it, but they deny that this is the only relevant consideration. Sometimes, they argue, "the end does not justify the means"; other times the act with the best overall consequences is wrong because it violates an independent ethical rule constraining the ways we may permissibly act in pursuit of valuable goals. Often these constraining rules are formulated in terms of **rights**: we have a duty not only to promote good consequences but also to respect rights. What is ethically right is no longer the act with the best consequences, but the one with the best consequences and that does not violate any rights.

To say that a being has rights is to say more than that it has ethical standing. If a being has ethical standing, its interests are weighed equally against the similar interests of other beings in the calculation of good and bad consequences. But the result of this calculation may be that it is best overall if the being's interests are harmed: this may most further the interests of the group as a whole. This last implication is blocked by the granting of rights. If a being has rights, it has certain interests that it is wrong to damage even if the effect of doing so is best for all beings taken together. According to an absolutist rights view, the infringement of rights can never be justified by the appeal to consequences, "though the heavens fall." According to a non-absolutist view, avoiding a major disaster can justify infringement. On any rights view, however, an act whose overall consequences are only somewhat better than the alternatives is ethically wrong if it infringes a right.

It is widely accepted that humans have rights, such as the right to life. For example, if the only way to save the lives of five patients who need organ transplants is to kill an innocent person and divide his organs among them, most people would say that the killing is wrong even though, by saving five lives at the expense of one, it has overall good consequences. And the right to life surely constrains ethically acceptable climate policies. It may be that, in the face of massive population growth, killing some excess humans would have overall good consequences, but such killing is ethically ruled out. . . .

There would be very strict constraints on climate policies if there were strong property rights, or rights to make choices about the objects one owns. **Libertarians** believe in such rights and argue that government interference with citizens' property (for example, compulsory taxation to finance a welfare system) is ethically equivalent to robbery. . . . According to this view, a coercively backed avoidance policy, involving legally enforced emissions ceilings or a carbon tax, would be ethically unacceptable. The government could exhort its citizens to restrain their greenhouse emissions, and perhaps organize a plan enabling them to do so, but could not force anyone to participate in the plan. Any avoidance measures would have to be chosen voluntarily by individuals. . . .

Some writers extend rights such as the right to life to at least some higher animals. . . . but this is more controversial. Imagine that a herd of elk has grown too large for its habitat, so food is in short supply and a population crash is threatened. If the individual elk had the right to life, it would be wrong to cull the herd to reduce its numbers to an ecologically sustainable level. Yet many of us, including many who are deeply committed to environmental values, think culling is right. Although it harms some individual elk, it is in the interests of the herd as a whole, and that seems primary.

Even more controversial is the idea that ecosystems or environmental wholes have rights. This implies that it is wrong to interfere with an ecosystem even to give it more holistic value: more life or more biodiversity. Thus, it would be wrong, according to this view, to implant life on Mars because doing so would violate Mars's "integrity" as a dead planet.[4] This is very hard to believe. If environmental wholes count in ethics—and this is itself a radical view—they do so only in the evaluation of consequences. The rights that constrain our pursuit of good ends belong only to humans or, at the very best, to humans and some higher animals.

Rights: Compensation

Rights have a further ethical function: to require that compensation be paid to those whose rights have been infringed. Sometimes compensation is owed when a rights-infringement was ethically wrong and therefore constituted a rights-violation: if a thief steals and damages your property, he must compensate you for the damage. At other times compensation is owed even though the rights-infringement was all-things-considered acceptable. Thus, it may be ethically acceptable for the government to expropriate your property provided that it pays you adequate compensation. Cases of this second kind place an additional constraint on the pursuit of good consequences: a policy that harms some individuals may be right but only if those individuals are compensated. This imposes a constraint because the policy-plus-compensation may have less good consequences than the policy-without-compensation, as it will do, for example, if the compensation is owed to the rich and the money would do more good if given to the poor. And even if the policy-plus-compensation has the best consequences, a principle about rights strengthens the ethical grounds for compensation: those who have been harmed should be paid not just because this is good for them or for the world, but because it is owed them as a matter of right.

Claims about compensation have been prominent in recent discussions of climate policy, especially concerning the division of the costs of avoidance. For example, developing countries have argued that because the developed countries bear the main responsibility for degrading the global environment, they should carry the main burden of repairing the environment. This is in effect a claim to be paid compensation by those who caused harms to the environment.

In this unrestricted form, the claim is unsustainable. Someone owes compensation for harming another only if he or she knew or should have known at the time of acting that the harm would result, and in the early years of industrialization, in the nineteenth and early twentieth centuries, no one could have known the effects of, for example, carbon dioxide emissions on global temperatures. More recently, however, the developed countries have known of the risks of global climate change yet have continued to emit greenhouse gases, and the same will be true in the future if there is a conscious choice of adaptation. Both recent and future emissions will involve knowledge of the harms they may cause. Is there, then, or will there be a claim to compensation for these harms?

Even this claim requires further defence, since not every harm to another involves an infringement of his or her rights. If I outdo you in fair economic competition, reducing your income and lowering the value of your assets, I make you worse off but do not owe you any compensation. It must therefore be shown by ethical argument that, for example, the earth's atmosphere is not unowned but is the joint property of all humans, so that actions that increase its temperature damage something over which other humans have rights. If this can be shown, those who damage the atmosphere must compensate its other owners. This means that an ethically acceptable climate policy must include such compensation: to the extent that it harms some individuals, it must include compensation payments to those individuals. And this in turn means that the ethically acceptable policy is probably closer to pure avoidance. If the acceptable mix of adaptation and avoidance is not the one with (simply) the best consequences, but the one with the best consequences once compensation has been paid to those harmed by its adaptation component, there is pressure on the mix to slide towards avoidance.

. . .

There are difficult issues about when compensation is owed, but most views assume they turn only on the rights of humans. Just as it is hard to believe that non-humans have rights that can constrain an acceptable climate policy, so it is hard to believe that they have rights that call for compensation within such a policy. If a mix of adaptation and avoidance harms some animals, that may be a bad consequence and something it would be desirable to prevent. But it does not call for compensation if, counting all interests equally, the mix has the best result possible.

Conclusion

To evaluate climate policies ethically we need to combine empirical facts about the threat of global climate change with ethical principles. Two kinds of principle are relevant. The first kind concerns the consequences of acts or policies, and explains what consequences count ethically for and against them. The second kind specifies rights, which either rule out certain means to good consequences or require compensation for those knowingly harmed by others' actions.

. . .

. . . Even the least controversial principles about consequences concerning present and future humans give us substantial reasons to pursue avoidance, that is, to change our present practices so the largest changes in global temperatures are prevented. In implementing this policy we must respect basic **human rights**, but if we accept the least controversial claim about compensation we have a further reason for avoidance. If we knowingly do what causes global climate change, we will owe compensation to those harmed by the warming; if we want to avoid paying the compensation, we must prevent the warming from occurring.

Notes

1. L.W. Sumner, *Abortion and Moral Theory* (Princeton: Princeton University Press, 1981).
2. World Commission on Environment and Development, *Our Common Future* (Oxford: Oxford University Press, 1987), p. 43.
3. A. Leopold, *A Sand County Almanac* (New York: Oxford University Press, 1970), p. 262.
4. C.P. McKay, "Does Mars Have Rights? An Approach to the Environmental Ethics of Planetary Engineering," in Donald MacNiven, ed., *Moral Expertise: Studies in Practical and Professional Ethics* (London: Routledge, 1990).

Bjørn Lomborg

Perspectives on Climate Change

AV = author's view; ~AV = not the author's view

Lomborg makes many empirical claims in this reading, which he backs up with citations. These can be found in original, at www.climatechangefacts.info/ClimateChange Documents/lomborg_testimony.pdf.

Introduction

Climate is back on the agenda, thanks to a large degree to . . . Al Gore.[1] The climate discussion was strong in 1992 when it was put on the agenda by the Earth Summit in Rio[2] and through the Kyoto Protocol agreed in 1997.[3] Gore deserves applause for making global warming cool again.

However, in this presentation I will move beyond recognizing the importance of global warming and ask how we should view it, deal with it, and put it in perspective.

I will make four basic points.

1. Global warming is real and man-made. This point has been made in many places, but perhaps most strongly and convincingly by the IPCC (Intergovernmental Panel on Climate Change). . . .
2. Statements about the strong, ominous, and immediate consequences of global warming are often wildly exaggerated, as I will show below.
3. We need a stronger focus on smart solutions rather than excessive if well-intentioned efforts.
4. We need . . . to put global warming in perspective. Climate change is not the only issue on the global agenda, and actually one of the issues where we can do the least good first.

Let us be frank. Al Gore and the many people he has inspired have good will and great intentions. However, he has got carried away and . . . show[s] only worst-case scenarios. This is unlikely to form the basis for a sound policy judgment. The problem is compounded in that if we follow Al Gore's recommendations, we will likely end up choosing very bad policies to solve the many problems [that] we agree need attention.

In short, following Gore's logic, with its good will and fine intentions, will actually end up costing millions of lives.

Global Warming Is Real and Man-made

I would argue that our best information comes from the UN Climate Panel, the so-called IPCC. . . . [The] standard prediction for the coming hundred years from the medium scenario of the 2007 IPCC report . . . [indicates] that over the [twenty-first] century global mean temperatures will increase about 2.6°C (4.7°F) with a span of 1.8–4.0°C.

The total cost of global warming is anything but trivial, about 15 trillion dollars. Yet it is only about 0.5% of the total net worth of the twenty-first century, about 3000 trillion dollars.

Consequences [Are] Often Vastly Exaggerated

Global warming is being described in everyday media in ever more dire terms. The IPPR [Institute for Public Policy Research] think tank (which is strongly in favor of CO_2 cuts) in 2006 produced an analysis of the UK debate. It summarized the flavor thus:

> Climate change is most commonly constructed through the alarmist repertoire—as awesome, terrible, immense, and beyond human control. This repertoire is seen everywhere and is used or drawn on from across the **ideological** spectrum, in broadsheets and tabloids, in popular magazines and in campaign literature from government initiatives and environmental groups. It is typified by an inflated or extreme lexicon,

incorporating an urgent tone and cinematic codes. It employs a quasi-religious register of death and doom, and it uses language of acceleration and irreversibility.[4]

~AV This kind of language makes any sensible policy dialogue about our global choices impossible. In public debates, the argument I hear most often is a variant of "if global warming is going to kill us all and lay waste to the world, this has to be our top priority—everything else you talk about, including HIV/AIDS, malnutrition, free trade, malaria,[5] clean drinking water may be noble but utterly unimportant compared to global warming." AV Of course, if the deadly description of global warming were correct, the **inference** of its primacy would also be correct, but as we will see, global warming is nothing of the sort. It is one—but only one—problem of many . . . we will have to tackle through the twenty-first century.

. . .

Heat and Cold Deaths

Very often, we only hear about the heat deaths but not the cold deaths—and sometimes this is even repeated in the official literature, as in the US 2005 Climate Change and Human Health Impacts report, where heat is mentioned 54 times and cold just once. We need to know just how much more heat deaths we can expect compared to how many fewer cold deaths.

Much has been made of the heat wave in Europe in early August 2003, which killed 35,000 people, with 2000 deaths in the UK. Yet, each year more than 25,000 people die in the UK from cold. It can be estimated that every year more than 200,000 people die from excess heat in Europe. It is reasonable to estimate that each year about 1.5 million people die from excess cold in Europe. This is more than seven times the total number of heat deaths. Just in this millennium Europe [has] lost more than ten million people to the cold, 300 times the iconic 35,000 heat deaths from 2003. That we so easily forget these deaths and so easily embrace the exclusive worry about global warming tells us of a breakdown in our sense of proportion.

. . .

Sea Level Rise

In its 2007 report, the UN estimate that sea levels will rise about 34.5 cm over the rest of the century. While this is not a trivial amount, it is also important to realize that it is certainly not outside the historical experience. Since 1850 we have experienced a sea level rise of about 29 cm, yet this has clearly not caused major disruptions. Sea level rise is a problem, but not a catastrophe. Ask a very old person about the most important issues that took place in the twentieth century. She will likely mention the two world wars, the cold war, the internal combustion engine, and perhaps the IT revolution. But it is very unlikely that she will add: "oh, and sea levels rose."

It is also important to realize that new prediction is lower than the previous IPCC estimates. The new span is 18–59 cm (midpoint 38.5 cm), down from 9–88 cm in 2001 (midpoint 48.5 cm). This continues a declining trend from the nineties (where the first IPCC expected 67 cm), and the 80s, where the US EPA projected several meters.

But this information is much less troublesome than what we often hear from global warming advocates. ~AV Al Gore has perhaps made their point most forcefully in his book and film. In a very moving film clip he shows us how large parts of Florida, including all of Miami, will be inundated by twenty feet of water. He goes on to show us equally strong clips of San Francisco Bay being flooded, the Netherlands being wiped off the map, Beijing and then Shanghai being submerged, Bangladesh . . . made uninhabitable for sixty million people, and even how New York and its World Trade Center Memorial will be deluged.

AV How is it possible that one of today's strongest voices on climate change can say something so dramatically different from the best science . . . ? The IPCC estimates a foot, Gore tops them twenty times. Well, technically, Al Gore is not contradicting the UN, because he simply says: "If Greenland melted or broke up and slipped into the sea—or if half of Greenland and half of Antarctica melted or broke up and slipped into the sea, sea levels worldwide would increase by between eighteen and twenty feet. . . ."[6] He is simply positing a hypothetical and then in full graphic and gory detail showing us what—hypothetically—would happen to Miami, San Francisco, Amsterdam, Beijing, Shanghai, Dhaka, and then New York.

. . .

Yet, take an overview of the simulations of Greenland sea level contributions. None are higher than 3mm/year by the end of the century, whereas Gore's claim . . . would have to be around 120mm or 40 times higher than the very highest model estimate. The IPCC estimate that Greenland is expected to contribute 3.5 cm over the century by itself. . . . This means that Gore's claim is 174 times higher than the IPCC. . . . It is unlikely that such an approach will lead to good policy initiatives.

Hurricanes

Stronger and more frequent hurricanes have become one of the standard exhibits of the global warming worries. ~AV The solution offered is invariably CO_2 cuts and Kyoto.

With the strong 2005 hurricane season and the devastation of New Orleans by Katrina, this message has reverberated even more powerfully. Al Gore spends twenty-six pages on showing pictures of the suffering from New Orleans and names every single hurricane in 2005.

AV So has global warming caused stronger and more frequent hurricanes, and what will happen in the future? Let us here use the latest **consensus** statement from the UN World Meteorological Organization [WMO] (parent organization for the IPCC), which is more recent and more specific but generally in agreement with the 2007 IPCC report. It makes three strong and specific points.

1. Though there is evidence both for and against the existence of a detectable anthropogenic [human-caused] signal in the tropical cyclone climate record to date, no firm conclusion can be made on this point.

They basically tell us that the strong statements of humans causing more and stronger hurricanes (or tropical cyclones as researches call them) are simply not well supported. We just don't know as of yet. When Al Gore tells us that there is a "scientific consensus that global warming is making hurricanes more powerful and more destructive" it is incorrect.[7]

2. No individual tropical cyclone can be directly attributed to climate change.

The strong statements on hurricane Katrina are simply not supportable.

This brings us to the third and perhaps most important WMO consensus point. In reality, we don't really care about hurricanes as such—what we care about is their damage.

Do they end up killing people and cause widespread disruption? And with global warming, will they kill and disrupt even more? The answer is—perhaps surprisingly—that the whole hurricane debate is somewhat tangential to this important question.

3. The recent increase in societal impact from tropical cyclones has largely been caused by rising concentrations of population and infrastructure in coastal regions.[8]

~AV . . . [T]he US cost of hurricane damage has increased relentlessly over the past century, and it seems to provide ample underpinning for Gore's "unmistakable economic impact of global warming." AV Yet, just comparing costs over long periods of time does not make sense without taking into account the change in population patterns and demography as well as economic prosperity. There are many more people, residing in much more vulnerable areas, with many more assets to lose. In the US today, the two coastal South Florida counties, Dade and Broward, are home to more people than the number of people who lived in 1930 in all 109 coastal counties stretching from Texas through Virginia, along the Gulf and Atlantic coasts.

. . .

We have to ask what it is we want. Presumably our goal is not to cut CO_2 emissions per se, but to do good for humans and the environment. We want to help the people who are potential victims of future Katrinas, Charleys, and Andrews. But how can we best do that?

. . .

If society stays the same—no more people living close to the coast, no more costly and densely built neighborhoods—and climate warms causing somewhat stronger hurricanes, the total effect will be less than a ten per cent increase in hurricane damages. To put it differently, if we could stop the climatic factors right now, we would avoid ten per cent more damage in fifty years' time.

On the other hand, if climate stays the same—no more warming—but more people build more and more expensive buildings closer to the sea, as they have done in the past, we will see an almost five hundred per cent increase in hurricane damages. To put it differently, if we could curb societal factors right now, we could prevent five hundred per cent more damage in fifty years' time.

So if we want to make a difference, which knob should we choose first—the one reducing damage by less than ten per cent or the one reducing damage by almost five hundred per cent? The difference in efficiency between the climate knob and the societal knob is more than fifty times.

This seems to suggest that policies addressing societal factors rather than climate policies will do . . . much more good first.

Malaria

~AV Al Gore writes: "Mosquitoes are profoundly affected by global warming. There are cities that were originally located just above the mosquito line, which used to mark the altitude above which mosquitoes would not venture. Nairobi, Kenya, and Harare, Zimbabwe, are two such cities. Now, with global warming, the mosquitoes are climbing to higher altitudes. . . ."[9]

AV Yet WHO and researchers have documented that malaria epidemics happened in Nairobi many times between WWI and the 1950s. The town's first medical officer, Dr. DE

Boedeker, wrote that even for the early ivory and slave caravans, Nairobi "had always been regarded as an unhealthy locality swarming with mosquitoes."[10]

Like most stories there is at core some truth to the claim that malaria will increase with temperature, but it is a small part compared to richness and health infrastructure.

How much does global warming matters to malaria? One way to get an upper limit on the importance of global warming is to look at the projections of populations at risk. These models show an extra almost 300 million people will be living in areas that could harbour malaria in the 2080s because increasing temperatures expand the area where the parasite can multiply. These models also tell us what will happen without climate change. Here, they project an increase from 4.4 billion in 1990 to 8.8 billion people at risk in 2085. The total population at risk will thus be 9.1 billion out of a population of 10.7 billion.

But notice the proportions: 8.8 billion will be at risk from malaria in 2085 due to social factors, whereas 0.3 billion will be at risk due to global warming. Thus, even if we could entirely stop global warming today (which we can't), we would only change malaria risk in 2085 by 3.2%. More realistically, with the Kyoto Protocol, including the US and Australia, and committing everyone to constant emissions throughout the rest of the century, would reduce malaria risk by 0.2% in 80 years. . . . With a stringent climate policy "there is little clear effect even by the 2080s . . .."[11]

. . .

Smarter Policies

The current raft of policies that are either enacted or suggested are costly but have virtually no effect.

Take the Kyoto Protocol, which even if it had been successfully adopted by all signatories (including the US and Australia) and even if it had been adhered to throughout the century, would have postponed warming by just five years in 2100 at a cost of $180 billion annually, see Figure [1].[12]

In the first real commitment since Kyoto in 1997, the EU announced in March 2007 that they would **unilaterally** cut emissions to twenty per cent below 1990-levels by 2020. This would mean a twenty-five per cent cut of emissions from what they would otherwise have been in 2020. Yet the effect on temperature would be smaller than Kyoto . . . , postponing warming by the end of the century by about two years. The cost would be about ninety billion dollars per year in 2020. Thus, we see the same pattern from both the well-established Kyoto protocol and the new EU minus-twenty per cent decision—that they have fairly small impact at fairly high cost.

This is also the case for Al Gore's public commitment to tackle global warming. ~AV In [a] . . . speech [at] New York University, he explicitly said that he would eliminate payroll taxes and substitute them with pollution taxes, principally a CO_2 tax. AV Yet he never actually say[s] how much this would cost or how much good it would do.

If one calculates the impact of such a promise, it shows that payroll taxes (social security) in the US amounted to $841 billion in 2006. With the US emitting about six gigatonnes[13] of CO_2, this means a tax of $140 per tonne of CO_2, and a tax on gas at about $1.25 per gallon. In one respected model, the annual economic cost amounts to about $160 billion for the US economy in 2015. This would cut emissions to about half in 2015 and about twenty-five per cent in 2105. Yet, since the US will make up an ever smaller amount

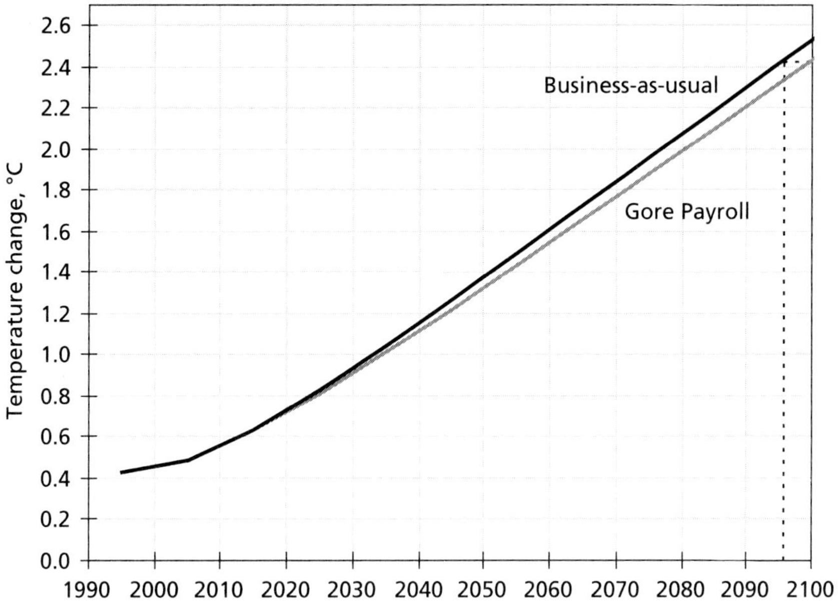

Figure 1

The expected increase in temperature with business-as-usual and with the Kyoto restrictions extended forever. Broken line shows the temperature for the business-as-usual scenario in 2095 is the same as the Kyoto temperature in 2100 (2.42°C).

Source: Nordhaus, W.D. (2006). RICE model. Retrieved 27 November 2006, from www.econ.yale.edu/~nordhaus/homepage/dice_section_vi.html

of the total CO_2 emitted throughout the century, the total effect in 2100 will be a reduction of global temperature by 0.1°C [see Figure 1]. Essentially, what Al Gore is suggesting is that the US carries through a Kyoto-type restriction all by itself.

This is why the major peer-reviewed economic cost-benefit analyses show that climate change is real, and that we should do something but our cuts should be rather small. . . .

. . .

The trick probably lies in understanding that what matters is not whether we cut a little now, but whether we eventually cut a lot. So maybe we should try going a different way.

Right now we could get all the world's energy from solar cells taking up very little (and otherwise useless) space. The equivalent of 2.6% of the area of the Sahara. Why don't we? Because it would be horrendously costly. But solar energy has come down in price about fifty per cent per decade over the past thirty years. Even at a much lower pace, it will probably become competitive before mid-century for many uses, and before the end of the century for most uses. If we invested more in research and development (R&D) this development would probably go faster. Likely, such an investment would do much more good than Kyoto ever could, and be much cheaper.

And of course, solar power is but one—if very promising—opportunity. We have wind, that is already competitive some places, as in Denmark. We have carbon capture, fusion and fission, energy efficiency, biomass, and biodiesel. It is hard to tell which will work best, but maybe we shouldn't. Maybe we should let **nations** search out these opportunities for the long term benefit for the world.

My proposal for tackling global warming in the long run is that all nations commit themselves to spending 0.05% of GDP in R&D of non-carbon emitting energy technologies. This approach would cost about twenty-five billion dollars per year, seven times cheaper than Kyoto and many more times cheaper than a Kyoto II.[14] It would involve all nations, with richer nations naturally paying the larger share. It would let each country focus on its own future vision of energy needs, whether that means concentrating on renewable sources, nuclear energy, fusion, carbon storage, or searching for new and more exotic opportunities.

Such a massive global research effort would also have potentially huge innovation spin-offs (a bit like NASA's going to the moon also gave us computers and velcro). Because the costs are low and there will be many immediate innovation benefits, countries do not have to be ever more strongly cajoled into ever more restrictive agreements. They will partake because it involves them in a strong, science-based endeavor. They will partake, because it is a smart thing to do.

And most importantly, it will likely have a much greater impact on the long-term climate.

Global Warming [Is] Only One of Many Issues

Global warming is not the only issue we need to tackle. This especially holds true for the third world. It is obvious that there are many other and more pressing issues for the third world, such as almost four million dying from malnutrition (underweight), three million from HIV/AIDS (unsafe sex), 2.5 million from indoor and outdoor air pollution, more than two million from lack of micronutrients (iron, zinc, and vitamin A) and almost two million from lack of clean drinking water.

Even if global warming exacerbates some or more of these problems, it is important to point out that the total magnitude of the problems is likely to far exceed the contribution from climate change. Thus, polices to reduce the total problems will have much more leverage than policies that only try to address the global warming part of the issues. Again, we have to ask if there are better ways to help than by cutting CO_2.

We have to ask ourselves: what do we want to do first? Do we want to focus on cutting CO_2, at fairly high costs and doing fairly little good a hundred years from now? Or would we rather want to fix some of the many obvious problems in the world, where we could do a lot more good and do it now?

In the so-called Copenhagen Consensus[15] process, we asked this general question to some of the smartest economists in the world: where would you spend extra resources to do good first? Experts put forward their best solutions [for] climate change and communicable diseases, . . . conflicts, education, financial instability, **governance** and corruption, malnutrition and hunger, population migration, . . . sanitation and water, and subsidies and trade barriers. But they didn't just say their proposals would do good—they said how much good they would do and how much they would cost.

A panel of top-level economists, including four Nobel Laureates, then made the first explicit global priority list ever, shown in Table 1.[16] It divided the world's opportunities into very good, good, and fair according to how much more good they would do for each dollar spent, and bad opportunities where each dollar would do less than a dollar worth of good.

Table 1
Global priority list from Copenhagen Consensus

		Challenge	Opportunity
Very Good Opportunities	1	Diseases	Control of HIV/AIDS
	2	Malnutrition	Providing micro-nutrients
	3	Subsidies and trade	Trade liberalization
	4	Diseases	Control of malaria
Good Opportunities	5	Malnutrition	Development of new agricultural technologies
	6	Sanitation and water	Small-scale water technology for livelihoods
	7	Sanitation and water	Community-managed water supply and sanitation
	8	Sanitation and water	Research on water productivity in food production
	9	Government	Lowering the cost of starting a new business
Fair Opportunities	10	Migration	Lowering the barriers to migration for skilled workers
	11	Malnutrition	Improving infant and child nutrition
	12	Malnutrition	Reducing the prevalence of low birth weight
	13	Diseases	Scaled-up basic health services
Bad Opportunities	14	Migration	Guest worker programs for the unskilled
	15	Climate	Optimal carbon tax ($25–300)
	16	Climate	The Kyoto Protocol
	17	Climate	Value-at-risk carbon tax ($100–450)

Source: Bjørn Lomborg, ed., *Global Crises, Global Solutions* (Cambridge, NY: Cambridge University Press, 2004), 606.

Preventing HIV/AIDS turns out to be the very best investment humanity can make—for each dollar it spends saving lives it will do about forty dollars' worth of social good. For twenty-seven billion dollars, we can save twenty-eight million lives over the coming years.

Malnutrition kills almost 2.4 million lives each year. Perhaps even more dramatically, it affects more than half the world's population, by damaging eyesight, lowering IQ, reducing development, and restricting human productivity. Investing twelve billion dollars could probably halve the incidence [of malnutrition] and [the] death rate, with each dollar doing more than thirty dollars' worth of social good.

Ending first world agricultural subsidies and ensuring free trade would make almost everyone much better off. Models suggest that benefits of up to $2400 billion annually would be achievable, [with] half of that benefit accruing to the third world. In achieving this, it would be necessary to bribe first world farmers, but the benefits of each dollar used would do more than fifteen dollars' worth of social good.

Finally, malaria kills more than a million each year. It infects about two billion people each year (many several times) and causes widespread debilitation. Yet, an investment of thirteen billion dollars could cut [the] incidence by half, protect ninety per cent of newborns, and cut deaths of under-fives by seventy-two per cent.

At the other end of the spectrum, the Nobels placed climate change opportunities, including Kyoto at the bottom under the heading "bad opportunities," underlining what we saw above, namely that for each dollar spent, we would end up doing much less than a dollar worth of good for the world.

But the Copenhagen Consensus did not just ask top economists. We asked eighty young college students from all over the world, with seventy per cent from developing countries, with equal gender representation, and from arts, sciences, and social sciences. After five days independently inquiring the experts in all the areas, they came to a surprisingly similar result as the Nobels. The placed malnutrition and communicable diseases on top, climate change next to last.

In 2006 we asked a wide range of UN ambassadors to make their priority list after two days of intensive debates. Besides the three biggest countries China, India, and the US, countries as diverse as Angola, Australia, and Azerbaijan participated, along with Canada, Chile, Egypt, Iraq, Mexico, Nigeria, Poland, South Korea, Somalia, Tanzania, Vietnam, Zimbabwe, and many others. They came out with a quite similar list, placing communicable diseases, clean drinking water and malnutrition at top, with climate change towards the bottom.

This should make us stop and pause. None of these forums have said that climate change is not real or not important. But they ask us to consider, whether we would do better by addressing the real and pressing needs of current generations that we can solve so easily and cheaply, before we try to tackle the long term problem of climate change where we can do so little for so much.

To put it very bluntly, the Kyoto Protocol would likely cost at least 180 billion dollars a year and do little good. UNICEF[17] estimates that just seventy to eighty billion dollars a year could give all Third World inhabitants access to the basics like health, education, water and sanitation. More important still is the fact that if we could muster such a massive investment in the present-day developing countries this would also give them a much better future position in terms of resources and infrastructure from which to manage a future global warming. What would we rather do first?

Notes

1. Al Gore is a former Vice President of the United States, and is currently an author and environmental activist. His book *An Inconvenient Truth: The Planetary Emergency of Global Warming and What We Can Do About It* (Emmaus: Rodale Press, 2006) was also released as a film documentary the same year. Much of this reading is a response to this film documentary. [Editor]
2. The United Nations Conference on Environment and Development (UNCED), or Earth Summit, was a United Nations conference held in Rio de Janeiro in June 1992. Two hundred and fifty-five governments

(more governments than there are member states of the UN) assembled to address issues such as water scarcity, public transportation, and alternative energy sources to replace fossil fuels. [Editor]

3. The Kyoto Protocol is an established agreement among 191 UN member states participating in the United Nations Framework Convention on Climate Change environmental treaty. Although Canada initially signed and ratified the treaty, it withdrew from the Kyoto Protocol in 2011. [Editor]
4. Ereaut, G., & Segnit, N. (2006). Warm Words: How are we telling the climate story and can we tell it better? Institute for Public Policy Research Retrieved 20-1-07, from www.ippr.org.uk/members/download.asp?f=/ecomm/files/warm_words.pdf&a=skip
5. Malaria is a mosquito-borne infectious disease affecting humans and animals. The disease causes headaches, fevers, muscular pain, and dry cough, and severe cases may result in coma and death. [Editor]
6. Gore, *An Inconvenient Truth*, p. 196.
7. Gore, p. 92.
8. WMO-IWTC. (2006a). Statement on Tropical Cyclones and Climate Change. 6th International Workshop on Tropical Cyclones of the World Meteorological Organization Retrieved 18-12-06, from www.wmo.ch/web/arep/press_releases/2006/iwtc_statement.pdf
9. Gore, p. 173.
10. P. Reiter, "Dangers of Disinformation Pseudoscience," *International Herald Tribune* (12 January 2007).
11. N.W. Arnell, M.G.R. Cannell, M. Hulme, R.S. Kovats, J.F.B. Mitchell, R.J. Nicholls, et al., "The Consequences of CO_2 Stabilisation for the Impacts of Climate Change," *Climatic Change* 53, 4 (2002): 440.
12. T.M.L. Wigley, (1998), "The Kyoto Protocol: CO_2, CH_4 and Climate Implications," *Geophysical Research Letters* 25, 13 (1998): 2285–2288.
13. A gigatonne (Gt) is 1 billion tonnes (1,000,000,000 tonnes). [Editor]
14. Kyoto II is the extension of the Kyoto protocol beyond 2012. [Editor]
15. The Copenhagen Consensus is a project established in 2004 by Bjørn Lomborg, whose goal is the advancement of global **welfare** through the theory and application of welfare economics. [Editor]
16. B. Lomborg, ed., *Global Crises, Global Solutions* (Cambridge, NY: Cambridge University Press, 2004) p. 606.
17. The United Nations Children's Fund (UNICEF) is a United Nations fund that provides humanitarian assistance to children and mothers in developing countries. [Editor]

Thomas Homer-Dixon

The Great Transformation—Climate Change as Cultural Change

AV = author's view; ~AV = not the author's view

. . .

The climate change problem is getting worse. Leading scientists tell us that carbon sinks around the world appear to be saturating and that the Arctic is changing much faster than was expected. With respect to variables such as sea-ice loss in the Arctic basin, we are at least twenty and perhaps even fifty years ahead of model predictions. And when we look at the proposed technical, institutional, and economic solutions that are part of the current international climate change dialogue, they seem radically insufficient in light of the problem's rapidly changing character. They don't seem to offer much prospect of getting us close to where we need to be with anything like the speed we need to get there.

Real solutions, I believe, ultimately reside at the level of culture broadly defined—that is, at the level of our deep values and our deep beliefs about how the world around us works. ~AV Now, one might say: "Well if that's the case, then solutions will be beyond reach, because these things change only over generations." AV But I don't think we should listen to that counsel of despair. I'm convinced that in our world today—partly because of the remarkable communication technologies we have available to us and partly because of the extraordinary analytical capability available to people around the world—cultural change can happen far faster than it has ever happened in human history.

. . .

At its core, the climate problem is fundamentally an energy problem. But it's an energy problem in ways a lot of people don't recognize. Most people think it's an energy problem because the carbon released from the combustion of fossil fuels significantly drives climate change. Of course that's true, but it's also an energy problem because we are probably close to the peak global output of conventional oil.

Even conservative experts now acknowledge that . . . a peak in conventional oil output has arrived for non-OPEC[1] [Organization of Petroleum Exporting Countries] countries. The world increasingly depends for its oil-production "surge capacity" on OPEC countries. But that extra capacity is not infinite. Sometime within the next ten years we will see the peak in total output of conventional oil—we may be seeing it now—and a steady decline after that. This change will sharply boost our use of coal. As oil drillers have to go farther into more hostile natural environments to drill deeper for smaller pools of lower quality oil, they will have to work harder for every extra barrel. Oil's "energy return on investment"—that is, the amount of oil energy obtained for every unit of energy invested to get that oil—will steadily drop, which will make coal progressively more attractive.

. . .

Human beings deal with their problems, mainly, by applying energy to them. They create more complex technologies and **institutions** that require more energy to invent, implement, and maintain. Just at the time when we are going to need enormous amounts of energy to cope with increasingly difficult problems like climate change, we're entering a transition from a world of abundant, cheap energy to a world of scarce and much more expensive energy. In particular, we will need a lot of energy to address climate change: we are going to have to rebuild coastal infrastructures, move people away from coastlines, drill deeper for water, move water from newly wet areas to newly dry areas, desalinize water along coast lines, and pump billions of tons of carbon dioxide underground. All of that activity will demand huge amounts of energy right at the time when energy is becoming much more scarce and much more costly.

For the most part, our policymakers do not grasp the significance of this fundamental contradiction. It means, I believe, that we are entering a time of enormous turbulence, in which instabilities of various kinds will develop in global systems. There will be crises, including systemic breakdowns of economies and agricultural systems. Sometimes whole societies will succumb as converging climate, resource, and economic stresses produce internal instability and violence.

It may be a time of crisis, but it doesn't have to be a time of catastrophe. It's in times of crisis that human beings are often most creative and ingenious and that they pull together most effectively to solve their problems. I am convinced that we won't really address the climate change problem until it produces some major shocks or instabilities that mobilize broad populations.

. . .

This evening I will focus on what I think are four essential components of the coming great transformation. . . . The transformation must incorporate:

- a cognitive transition,
- an economic transition,
- a political transition, and
- a **normative** transition.

I will spend a few minutes talking about each.

The Cognitive Transition

The cognitive transition will help people better understand the implications of complexity and in turn help societies better cope with complex problems like climate change. By complexity I mean something technical, and I want to spend a bit of time explaining the term.

Most fundamentally we need to move from believing our world is composed mainly of machines to understanding that it's composed largely of complex systems. When I explain this idea to my students, I take into class an old mechanical windup clock that sits on the mantle in my office. I note that I can disassemble the clock into its component parts—its bushings, springs, cogwheels, and screws, and I can understand how all the bits and pieces work. I can understand exactly how they fit together. And when I put the parts back together, if the clock isn't working properly—and, by the way, it means something to say that the clock isn't working properly—I can point to one or two parts where the problem resides. Something is bent, or something is not on the right place. In other words, I can have a very accurate and complete understanding of this machine.

Many of the challenges we face in the world today arise in significant part because we think the world is composed mainly of machines like this clock, instead of recognizing that it's composed largely of complex systems. Machines like my clock can be taken apart, analyzed, and fully understood. Ultimately, they are no more than the sum of their parts. They exhibit "normal" or "equilibrium" patterns of behavior, according to how we define "normal" for that particular machine. Most fundamentally, they show proportionality of cause and effect. Small causes cause small effects. Big causes cause big effects. And because of these characteristics we can often predict and manage the behavior of machines very precisely.

I believe that this kind of understanding has been as at the root of disasters such as the collapse of the huge cod fishery off the east coast of North America in the 1980s and early 1990s. That fishery was the most productive ecological system in the world. It produced more biomass annually than any other ecological system. Today it's gone. Many very smart Canadian scientists were in charge of managing a significant portion of that fishery, and they thought they understood how it worked really well. Based on this understanding, they estimated the fishery's annual "sustainable" yield—the total mass of cod, in hundreds of thousands of tons, that could be harvested each year without damaging the productivity of the underlying resource. But it turned out that many other factors affected the fishery's behavior and productivity, like changes in ocean temperature and salinity, variations in seal predation, and increasingly heavy harvesting beyond Canada's exclusive economic zone by foreign factory trawlers. In the context of these other factors, Canadian extraction was far too large, and the system flipped from one equilibrium to another.

Complex systems like that cod fishery are ultimately more than the sum of their parts. They have what specialists call "emergent" properties: when their parts are put together, things happen that one wouldn't expect even with the complete knowledge of each individual part. They can flip from one pattern of behavior to another—that is, they have multiple equilibriums. They show disproportionality of cause and effect: small causes can cause enormous effects, but sometimes really big changes in the system don't seem to produce any effect at all. This is what specialists mean by nonlinear behavior.

As we found with the cod fishery, systems exhibiting these characteristics can't be easily managed, because their behavior can't be easily predicted. Going back to a distinction made originally by Frank Knight—a leader of the department of economics at the University of Chicago in the 1920s through 1940s and one of the most prominent American economists of the time—we need to distinguish between risk and uncertainty. We also need to recognize that as our world in many respects becomes more complex—or as we increasingly perturb complex systems Earth's climate—we're moving from a world of risk to a world of uncertainty.

In a world of risk we have data at hand on which we can base probabilistic judgments about what pathways a system we're interested in—such as an economy, an ecology, or Earth's climate—might move along in its future behavior and about what the costs and benefits of moving along those pathways might be. In a world of true uncertainty, we don't have data to make such judgments. . . .

. . .

Notice that I'm suggesting that many of the causes of the crisis lay at the level of people's perception of the world's most basic features. That's why I call this first transition we must make a cognitive shift: It's a shift in our deepest worldview—that is, in what philosophers of science call the "**ontology**" we use to understand the building blocks of the world around us.

Climate change is an example of what specialists sometimes call a "wicked problem." Such problems almost always emerge from systems that are complex in the way I have defined the term here. These systems tend to have three defining characteristics: high uncertainty and nonlinear behavior, which I've already discussed, and time lags of indeterminate length in response to perturbations. These time lags might be short or they might be long, and one usually doesn't know how they're operating in the system. I'll illustrate these three characteristics with specific reference to climate change.

Let's look at uncertainty first. Although our climate models do give us a fair amount of certainty about what might happen in the short term, as we go further out in this century uncertainty increases rapidly. Figure 1 shows an illustration from the most recent IPCC [Intergovernmental Panel on Climate Change] report[,] . . . a set of superimposed bell curves representing probability distributions. Each curve is a probability distribution generated by a general circulation model using the IPCC's A2 emission scenario. Researchers entered the A2 emissions figures into a general circulation model and then ran the model repeatedly to generate a probability distribution of likely temperatures. On the right of the figure, we see a set of superimposed probability distributions for 2090 to 2099.

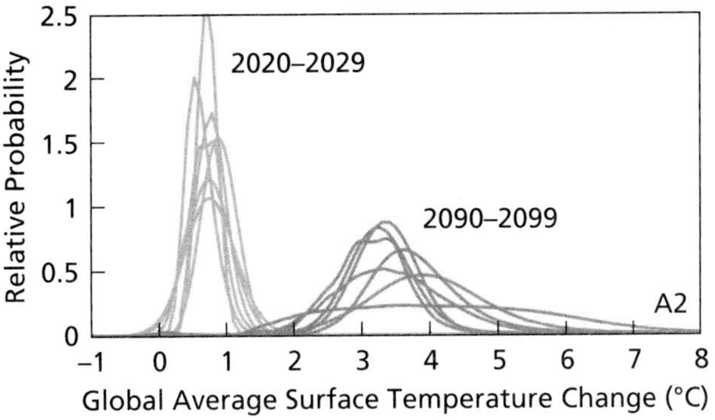

Figure 1

Global Average Surface Temperature Change

For the 2020 to 2029 time frame, we have a pretty good consensus about what the average warming is likely to be—somewhere just under one degree Celsius. The probability distributions are tall and narrow. But as we move to the end of the century they flatten out. The distributions develop what statisticians call "fat tails," and they seem to have particularly substantial fat tails on the high side.

There's a vigorous debate in the economics community right now . . . over the implications of this uncertainty. . . . [I]f we take these models' findings seriously—that is, if we accept that there's an indeterminate but nonetheless significant possibility of a warming of four, five, six, or even seven degrees Celsius this century—then we should be doing everything we can to avoid that outcome. Put simply, avoiding a fat tail outcome should drive public policy.

Yet almost all our discussions about the economic costs of climate change this century assume that we will get something like the mean predicted warming of about three degrees. They resolutely ignore the possibility that we might end up in a fat tail.

Discussion of fat tails brings us to the Arctic. I mentioned earlier that climate change seem to be happening faster than expected in the Arctic, where developments put us twenty to fifty years ahead of model projections—a reflection, again, of uncertainty in our understanding of the climate system.

. . .

Finally, there is the matter of time lags—something that few people outside the scientific community adequately grasp. Our climate and energy systems are replete with lags. There is, for instance, the lag between changes in our emissions of carbon and the climate's response, which might be as long as centuries. We also have lags between policy decisions to change our energy infrastructure and the actual completion of this change. The shift to a zero-carbon world economy is going to take at least a century. . . .

In a situation of high uncertainty and long time lags, we have great scope for procrastination. But procrastination isn't a solution, because if we don't deal with underlying trends and rising stresses, at some point the system we're dealing with will likely go nonlinear—it will probably flip to another state. At that point, it's very likely that we won't be able to get back to the system's previous state.

. . .

The Economic Transition

. . .

I am going to be controversial: ~AV There is a common argument, which often comes under the label of the "environmental Kuznets curve," that as poor societies become wealthier (conventionally, as their aggregated GDP [**gross domestic product**] increases) the amount of damage they cause to the environment at first increases and then at some point starts to decrease (see Figure 2).

When we look at the historical data for wealthy countries in Europe, North America, and Asia, this "inverted U" relationship indeed holds for certain pollutants such as sulphur dioxide and lead. AV But if we examine data for what I think is the best proxy measure of total human load on the environment—carbon dioxide output—the relationship looks more like that shown in Figure 3. For any modern economy in aggregate, as wealth has

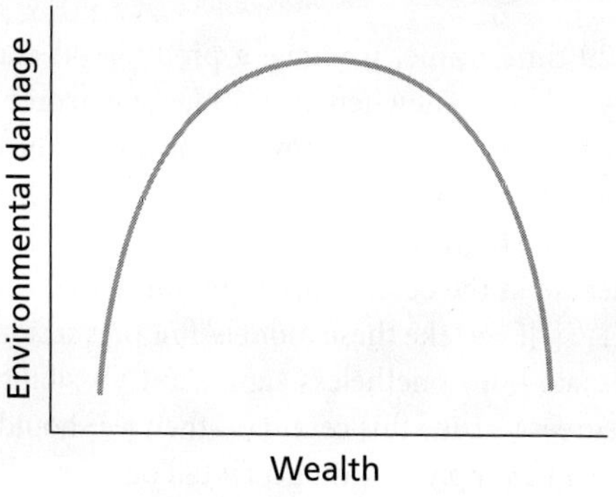

Figure 2

What Conventional Economists Hoped Would Happen

Growth Reduces Environmental Damage

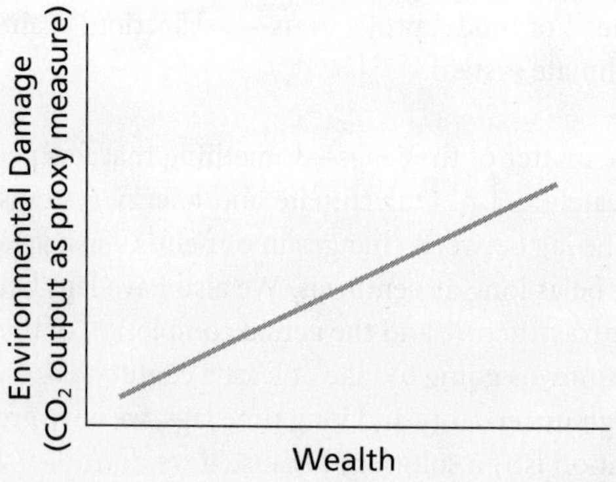

Figure 3

What Really Happened

Growth Increases Environmental Damage

increased total carbon dioxide output has increased steadily too—maybe not as fast as wealth has increased, but still significantly nonetheless. When we look at the data for carbon dioxide, we don't see anything approximating an environmental Kuznets curve.

So, what is going on here? Why is it that we commonly hear one story from conservative economists about the environmental Kuznets curve and yet observe another story when we examine CO_2 output?

I believe that the missing part of the story is economic growth. As our economies grew fast in rich countries in the 1960s, 70s, and 80s, we invested in end-of-pipe environmental solutions: We cleaned up our power plants, our sewage outfalls, and to a large extent the emissions from our car tail pipes. But this was just the visible stuff—the stuff that was accumulating in our cities' air, that we could see in our streams, rivers and lakes, and that was palpable to people. As citizens became wealthier in our democracies, and as they started to be concerned about their natural environment, they turned to their politicians and said: "Fix this mess. It could be making us sick. We don't like the look of it. It smells. Clean it up."

In almost all cases, the end-of-pipe solutions that our societies adopted involved higher energy consumption, and because most of our energy comes from fossil fuels, higher energy consumption meant higher carbon dioxide output. For instance, the catalytic converters we plugged onto the ends of our car tail pipes lowered our cars' overall gas mileage. We had cleaner urban skies but emitted more CO_2.

Still, rich countries managed to improve their efficiency quite remarkably over this period of time—efficiency defined in terms of the amount of energy or material used per dollar of GDP. Rates of improvement of two per cent a year were common. Over a period of thirty years, these improvements added up to a very substantial change. Between 1970 and 2000, rich countries saw gains in many cases of forty per cent or more in material and energy efficiency.

But economic growth swamped all these improvements, which meant that these societies' total environmental impact, if we use a measure like total emissions of carbon dioxide, steadily increased. Efficiency improvements of two per cent a year were overwhelmed by real economic growth of three per cent a year or more. And because we got rid of all the visible problems—the visible pollution in our rivers and our streams and our lakes, and the pollution in the air over our cities—we couldn't see the extra environmental load we were putting on the environment and on the planet. . . .

So we need to ask: Why are we so deeply committed to economic growth? Here we come to some profound cultural issues. We have internalized four equivalencies in our cultures and our societies, in part because they are backed by a fair amount of evidence.

1. Growth equals solvency. After the Second World War, all the deeply indebted countries that had fought that war grew out of their debt. In the same way, we often use growth to ease the burden of household debt: if our household incomes and wealth rise over time, our debt becomes a smaller proportion of that wealth, and payments on the debt a smaller fraction of income. . . . In all kinds of ways, both explicitly and implicitly, we associate growth with maintaining solvency over time.
2. Growth equals freedom. This equivalency probably dates back as far as the Renaissance[2] with the development of modern notions of social, intellectual, and scientific progress. It became even more deeply embedded in Western

cultures during the Enlightenment.[3] Today, some conservative economists, such as Benjamin Friedman at Harvard University, cogently argue that the only way we can be truly free is to live within societies that experience continual economic growth.

3. Growth equals happiness. There's an association in our minds between wealth and happiness: if we get wealthier, we're happier. Researchers argue about whether this relationship actually holds. The evidence is interesting and complex, but there's enough of it to support the claim that there is—especially at lower incomes—a strong correlation between wealth and happiness. Beyond a level of around 20,000 dollars per year per capita the relationship likely starts to weaken, as every extra dollar of income produces diminishing returns (that is, as people's basic needs are satisfied).

And then there's what I believe is the most persuasive and culturally powerful equivalency.

4. Growth equals peace. This is a lesson we learned in the 1930s: an economic collapse leads to the rise of political extremism and horrible outcomes like the Second World War. John Maynard Keynes[4] understood this relationship and gave us tools to maintain perpetual economic growth. How ironic that the man regarded by many people on the left as the icon of **liberal** economists gave us the tools to destroy the planet's environment. And today in this time of economic crisis, the world's central bankers and policy makers are using every single Keynesian tool in their tool kit to sustain consumption. It seems that the only way we can reduce humankind's load on the natural environment is to have an economic collapse.

. . .

What's the alternative [to economic growth]? Whatever the alternative, I expect it will involve the notion of resilience. . . . Resilient people, institutions, and societies can withstand shocks without catastrophic failure. In a complex, tightly coupled world exhibiting increasingly frequent and severe system shock, the balance of economic and social investment, I argue, should go towards increasing resilience rather than towards increasing efficiency, productivity, and growth.

. . .

. . . [R]esilience means putting aside and protecting reserves; loosening coupling in food, energy, economic, and other systems vital to our well-being; increasing redundancy of critical components in these systems; increasing the diversity of entities and procedures across these systems; and decentralizing decision making. Decentralizing is key because it allows for . . . "safe-fail experimentation"—that is, experimentation that takes place at the local level and doesn't produce cascading failures outwards if it doesn't work. Cascading failure is like a row of dominoes falling over, and it's exactly the phenomenon we have lately seen in the world economy. Tightly coupled systems are prone of such failures.

All of these changes would maximize flexibility in response to an uncertain and rapidly changing world. When we don't really know what is going to happen in a world of unknown unknowns, we need to be able to respond in a wide range of ways to new contingencies.

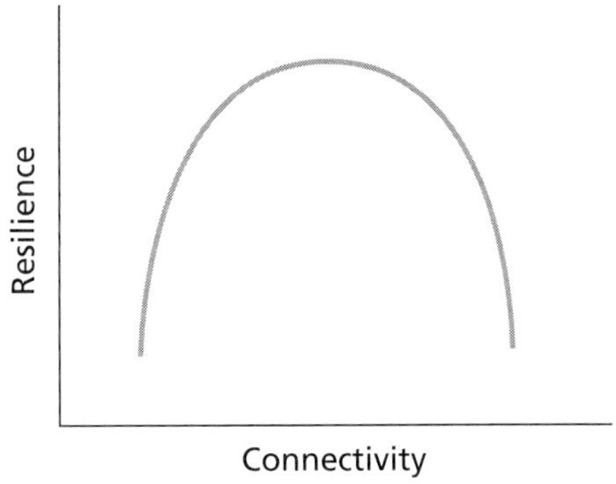

Figure 4

Connectivity and Resilience

I also argue, controversially, that there is an inverted U-relationship between connectivity and resilience (see Figure 4). I disagreed with the inverted U we saw in the case of the environmental Kuznets curve, but here I think the representation is quite accurate. In a complex system, resilience (the capacity to withstand catastrophic shock) can increase up to a point as connectivity in the system rises. In a food system for instance, we don't want all the food producing regions to be disconnected from each other. The food system in aggregate needs some internal connectivity so that a producing region affected severely by disease or a drought can reach out to draw the food it needs from the rest of the network.

But beyond a certain point, represented by the top of the inverted U, the risk of cascading failures starts rising. Greater connectivity in the network actually reduces resilience. This is a profound critique, I would argue, of dominant notions of globalization and of the economic benefits of rising global inter-connectivity. In the last two or three decades, rich countries have shared the deep culturally embedded presumption that the more connectivity we have in the world, the better off we all are. I suggest, in response, that we're too far up the connectivity continuum now and that we are seeing the negative results in the form of phenomena like our recent economic crisis.

. . .

The Political Transition

. . .

The real political challenge here is the following: we need democratic mobilization to increase the power of our publics relative to special interests that are blocking change. This challenge is the same across all today's economic, political, and social systems, and it's the main reason why we aren't making progress on climate change. It's true in Canada, for instance, with Alberta's tar sands. Canada has an abysmal national policy on climate change because tar sands companies reach right into Canada's federal cabinet to block any kind of meaningful climate policy. Politicians in Ottawa don't have the political capacity to push back.

This kind of political gridlock is visible all over the world. We can address the problem only through a reinvigoration of democracy, in the process getting beyond purely procedural democracy and, perhaps, engaging in some kind of open-architecture process of democratic problem solving.[5]

. . .

Any form of open-architecture democracy will face four specific challenges: winnowing, cumulation, preventing hijacking, and managing experts. First, any ideas put forward or solutions to problems that are suggested in the democratic discussion—and there are going to be a multitude of them within any real democratic space—somehow have to be winnowed those down to a few that **merit** further conversation and focused investment of resources. Then, second, we need to take these remaining suggestions and improve them over time, which is a process of cumulation. Wikipedia, interestingly enough, cumulates very well: in general, the encyclopedia's entries steadily improve over time as people contribute to them. Third, the process must not be hijacked by special interests that are extremely vocal and can focus their resources to block solutions. Fourth, and perhaps most fundamentally, we need to manage experts effectively.

Now, I guess I qualify as something of an expert, and there are many experts in this room. But I'm increasingly convinced that unless the general public is an integral part of the process of solving our climate change and energy problems—that is, I'm convinced that if these problems remains fundamentally technocratic challenges addressed by experts—they probably won't get solved. Our communities of experts cannot generate a sufficient stream of creative ideas fast enough. More importantly, without the involvement of large democratic communities in their development, any proposed solutions, especially those that require significant sacrifice, will not be legitimate enough to be widely accepted. Experts need to contribute ideas and knowledge to the democratic discussion, listen very carefully and respond constructively, but not stand in the way or occlude debate in any way. Unfortunately experts do stand in the way far too often.

. . .

The Normative Transition

I come finally to the normative transition. This will be in some respects the deepest cultural shift. We need to shift our common understanding of value and to expand the scope of what we mean by "we."

. . .

[By "we" I mean] our notion of collective identity and community. Anatol Rapoport was one of the twentieth century's great mathematical psychologists. . . . [He said,] "The moral development of a civilization is measured by the breadth of its sense of community." That statement has stayed with me for many years now, because I think it's profoundly true.

. . .

. . . I have visited sixty countries or so and traveled extensively in several dozen. In these countries, as one does when one travels, I've talked to people about their concerns. And I have learned one vitally important thing. Across all our world's divisions of race, ethnicity, religion, language, caste, and class, and even across the world's divisions among civilizations that some people insist tear us apart, all people care about their kids. And people actually want more or less the same thing for their kids. Parents say: "Well, we'd like a world, a future, in which our children are safe and secure and in which they can flourish as human beings." People use slightly different language depending on their culture, but the sentiment is basically the same everywhere.

Now, if we can agree on this fundamental point across all of these societies, we have the basis for a common conception of community that will allow us to address our monumental common problems. We're not going to start making the difficult choices about who is going to give up what—or about how wealth and resources might be transferred from one place to another—unless we think of ourselves as part of one "we."

I think it's possible. But we have to remember our children. And if we do, it's conceivable that in 100 or 120 years we'll live on a substantially warmer planet, a planet that has lost thirty per cent or more of its biodiversity, with coastlines that are receding, but one on which, nonetheless, we have achieved a **modus vivendi** among ourselves—the silver lining, in a sense, of climate change—and created a more prosperous world, by some definitions, and a more humane world certainly, a world in which our children and grandchildren can flourish as we have in our lives.

Notes

1. The Organization of the Petroleum Exporting Countries (OPEC) is an intergovernmental agreement among twelve oil-producing countries, whose stated goals are the safeguarding of member state interest, price stability, and consumer satisfaction. As of 2012, OPEC member states collectively hold approximately seventy-five per cent of the world's crude oil reserves and forty per cent of the world's crude oil production capacity. [Editor]
2. The Renaissance was a European cultural movement that spanned the fourteenth to seventeenth centuries. This period involved unprecedented advancements in technology and art, including the introduction of the printing press to Europe, a renewed interest in Ancient Latin and Greek literature and philosophy, the development of linear perspective, and the scientific method. [Editor]
3. The Enlightenment was a European cultural movement between the seventeenth and eighteenth centuries, and was marked by an increased degree of scientific exploration, religious scepticism, individual liberty, and democracy. [Editor]
4. John Maynard Keynes was a British economist widely recognized as the most influential economist of the twentieth century. His contributions to understanding of the causes of economic expansion and recession (the business cycle) have helped shape the economic policies of modern Western countries. [Editor]
5. Procedural democracies focus on free and fair voting as the core political act: citizens vote for representatives who enact rules and authorize individuals to carry out their policies.

Vandana Shiva

Soil Not Oil: Environmental Justice in an Age of Climate Crisis

AV = author's view; ~AV = not the author's view

The climate crisis is at its roots a consequence of human beings having gone astray from the ecological path of living with justice and sustainability. It is a consequence of forgetting that we are earth citizens. It is acting like we are kids in a supermarket with limitless appetites for consumption and falsely imagining that the corporations that stock the supermarkets have unlimited energy warehouses. The real problem is the conflict between the economic laws that have reduced the planet and society to a supermarket where everything is for sale and the ecological laws that maintain the planet's ecological functions and social laws that distribute nature's goods and services equitably. The real problem is a global economy that has created a planetary ecological imbalance.

If these are the real problems, then the real solution cannot be replacing fossil fuels with other non-sustainable sources to power the same systems. The real solution must be to search for right living, for well-being, and for joy, while simultaneously reducing consumption. In Indian philosophy, right living is "dharma"—the bridge between resources, *arth*, and human needs, *kama*. Dharma is therefore based on the sustainable and just use of resources for fulfilling needs. Ecological balance and **social justice** are intrinsic to right livelihood, to dharma. "Dharanath dharma ucyat"—that which sustains all species of life and helps maintain harmonious relationship among them is "dharma." That which disturbs the balance of the earth and her species is "adharma."

Equity is about fair share. There are currently two **paradigms** of equity. ~AV One sets the overconsumption and waste of rich industrial societies as the model and measure of being human, being developed. Equity is presented as the entire world being pushed to that level of resource and energy consumption. However, this version of equity would need five planets. This non-sustainable paradigm inevitably produces **inequity**. Shall we choose a non-sustainable paradigm in which we affirm an equal right to pollute or a sustainable paradigm in which we affirm an equal responsibility to *not* pollute?

AV Earth Democracy and ecological equity recognize that because the planet's resources and capacity to renew resources are limited, a reduction in energy and resource consumption of the rich is necessary for all to have access to land and water, food and fibre, air and energy. In an ecological paradigm, what works against Gaia works against the poor and works against future generations, and what works for Gaia works for the poor and for the future.

We need to define equity on the same ecological parameters locally and globally. If communities in India are resisting displacement and uprooting, if they define and experience their lives in the forest or small farms as the terms of their material and spiritual well-being, respecting their rights and freedoms is the first step toward equity. Equity needs to be grounded in the earth, in people's struggles and movements, not dropped in as an abstraction from remote conference halls. Those who would uproot farmers say the life of a peasant is "undignified." Those who would uproot indigenous people define life in a forest as "below the **dignity** line." Dignity is an experience and consequence of self-organization and sovereignty, of sufficiency and satisfaction.

I have never found working the soil or lighting a wood fire lacking in dignity. It is disposability that robs people of their dignity and selfhood. That is why movements against displacement are so intense and widespread in contemporary India.

Real solutions will come from breaking free of the crippling world of mechanistic assumptions, industrial methods of producing goods with high energy and resource costs, and market mechanisms that make high-cost products appear cheap on supermarket shelves.

~AV The eco-**imperialist** response to the climate crisis is to grab the remaining resources of the planet, close the remaining spaces of freedom, and use the worst form of militarized violence to exterminate people's rights and people themselves when they get in the way of an insatiable economy's resource appropriation, driven by the insatiable greed of corporations.

AV There is another response—that of Earth Democracy.

Earth Democracy recognizes that if the survival of our species is threatened, maintaining our ability to live on the planet is the only intelligent response. Chasing economic growth while ecosystems collapse is a sign of stupidity, not wisdom. Earth Democracy calls for a systemic and inclusive response to the climate crisis, not the fragmented and self-serving response that corporations and rich countries are making. Earth Democracy allows us to break free of the global supermarket of commodification and consumerism, which is destroying our food, our farms, our homes, our towns, and our planet. It allows us to re-imbed our eating and drinking, our moving and working, into our local ecosystems and local cultures, enriching our lives while lowering our consumption without impoverishing others. In Earth Democracy, everything is interconnected. To address the pollution of the atmosphere, we do not have to limit ourselves to changes in the atmosphere. We can change agriculture; we can change the way we design buildings and towns; we can change the way we shop.

In Earth Democracy, solutions will not come from the corporations and governments that have raped the planet and destroyed peoples' lives. Solutions are coming from those who know how to live lightly, who have never had an oil addiction, who do not define the good life as "shop till you drop," but rather define it as looking after the living earth and their living community. Those who are being treated as disposable in the dominant system, which is pushing the planet's ecosystems to collapse and our species to extinction, carry the knowledge and values, the cultures and skills, that give humanity a chance for survival.

To mitigate and adapt to climate change we need to stop the assault on small farmers and indigenous communities, to defend their rights to their land and territory, to see them not as remnants of our past but as the path for our future.

Earth Democracy begins and ends with Gaia's laws—the law of renewability, the law of conservation, the law of entropy, the law of diversity. In Earth Democracy, all beings and all peoples are equal, and all beings and all communities have rights to the resources of the earth for their sustenance.

In Earth Democracy, the solution to the climate crisis begins with the cultures and communities who have not contributed to it.

Earth Democracy is based on equal rights of all beings to ecological space, including atmospheric space. The atmosphere is an ecological **commons**. Climate justice demands that this commons not be enclosed by a handful of polluters. Climate justice also demands that people be compensated for the impact of climate chaos caused by the actions of others. But above all, climate justice demands that every person, every community, every society have the freedom to create and defend economies that cause no harm to the climate or to other people.

To prevent climate chaos and to avoid further increases in emissions we must stop the coercion of trade **liberalization** and rewrite the rules of trade to favour the local.[1] WTO[2] rules and World Bank[3] structural adjustment programs are robbing sustainable local economies and sustainable communities of their freedom to be sustainable. Compelling them to import food from thousands of miles away and preventing them from having safeguards that protect the local are—in terms of climate change—ecological crimes.

Earth Democracy generates a radical shift in our paradigms and in our patterns of production. It offers real solutions to resource exhaustion, peak oil, climate change, disposability of people, and the erosion of democracy.

Climate Change and the Two Carbon Economies: Biodiversity v. Fossil Fuels

Reductionism seems to have become the habit of the contemporary human mind. We are increasingly talking of climate change in the context of "the carbon economy." We refer to "zero carbon" and "no carbon" as if carbon exists only in fossilized form under the ground. We forget that the cellulose of plants is primarily carbon. Humus in the soil is mostly carbon. Vegetation in the forests is mostly carbon. It is living carbon. It is part of the cycle of life.

The problem is not carbon *per se*, but our increasing use of fossil carbon that was formed over millions of years. Today the world burns four hundred years' worth of this accumulated biological matter every year, three to four times more than in 1956. While plants are a renewable resource, fossil carbon for our purposes is not. It will take millions of years to renew the earth's supply of coal and oil.

Before the industrial revolution, there were 580 billion tons of carbon in the atmosphere. Today there are 750 billion tons. That accumulation, the result of burning fossil fuels, is causing the climate change crisis. Humanity needs to solve this problem if we are to survive. It is the other carbon economy, the renewable carbon embodied in biodiversity, that offers the solution.

Our dependence on fossil fuels has broken us out of nature's renewable carbon cycle. Our dependence on fossil fuels has fossilized our thinking.

Biodiversity is the alternative to fossil carbon. Everything that we derive from the petrochemical industry has an alternative in the realm of biodiversity. The synthetic fertilizers and pesticides, the chemical dyes, the sources of mobility and energy, all of these have sustainable alternatives in the plant and animal world. In place of nitrogen fertilizers, we have nitrogen-fixing leguminous crops and biomass recycled by earthworms (vermi-compost) or microorganisms (compost). In place of synthetic dyes, we have vegetable dyes. In place of the automobile, we have the camel, the horse, the bullock, the donkey, the elephant, and the bicycle.

Climate change is a consequence of the transition from biodiversity based on renewable carbon economies to a fossil fuel-based non-renewable carbon economy. This was the transition called the industrial revolution.

While climate change, combined with peak oil and the end of cheap oil, is creating an ecological imperative for a post-oil, post-fossil fuel, postindustrial economy, the industrial paradigm is still the guiding force for the search for a transition pathway beyond oil.

That's because industrialization has also become a cultural paradigm for measuring human progress. We want a post-oil world but do not have the courage to envisage a postindustrial world. As a result, we cling to the infrastructure of the energy-intensive fossil fuel economy and try and run it on substitutes such as nuclear power and biofuels. Dirty nuclear power is being redefined as "clean energy." Non-sustainable production of biodiesel and biofuel is being welcomed as a "green" option.

Humanity is playing these tricks with itself and the planet because we are locked into the industrial paradigm. Our ideas of the good life are based on production and consumption patterns that the use of fossil fuels gave rise to. We cling to these patterns without reflecting on the fact that they have become a human addiction only over the past fifty years and that maintaining this short term, non-sustainable pattern of living for another fifty years comes at the risk of wiping out millions of species and destroying the very conditions for human survival on the planet. We think of well-being only in terms of human beings, and more accurately, only in terms of human beings over the next fifty years. We are sacrificing the rights of other species and the welfare of future generations.

To move beyond oil, we must move beyond our addiction to a certain model of human progress and human well-being. To move beyond oil, we must reestablish partnerships with other species. To move beyond oil, we must reestablish the other carbon economy, a renewable economy based on biodiversity.

Renewable carbon and biodiversity redefine progress. They redefine development. They redefine "developed," "developing," and "underdeveloped." In the fossil fuel paradigm, to be developed is to be industrialized—to have industrialized food and clothing, shelter and mobility, ignoring the social costs of displacing people from work, and the ecological costs of polluting the atmosphere and destabilizing the climate. In the fossil fuel paradigm, to be under-developed is to have non-industrial, fossil-free systems of producing our food and clothing, of providing our shelter and mobility.

In the biodiversity paradigm, to be developed is to be able to leave ecological space for other species, for all people and future generations of humans. To be underdeveloped is to usurp the ecological space of other species and communities, to pollute the atmosphere, and to threaten the planet.

We need to change our mind before we can change our world. This cultural transition is at the heart of making an energy transition to an age beyond oil. What blocks the transition is a cultural paradigm that perceives industrialization as progress combined with false ideas of productivity and efficiency. We have been made to believe that industrialization of agriculture is necessary to produce more food. This is not at all true. Biodiverse ecological farming produces more and better food than the most energy- and chemical-intensive agriculture. We have been made to falsely believe that cities designed for automobiles provide more effective mobility to meet our daily needs than cities designed for pedestrians and cyclists.

Vested interests who gain from the sale of fertilizers and diesel, cars and trucks, have brainwashed us to believe that chemical fertilizers and cars mean progress. We have been reduced to buyers of their non-sustainable products rather than creators of sustainable, cooperative partnerships—both within human society and with other species and the earth as a whole.

The biodiversity economy is the sustainable alternative to the fossil fuel economy. The shift from fossil fuel-driven to biodiversity-supported systems reduces greenhouse gas emissions by emitting less and absorbing more CO_2. Above all, because the impacts of atmospheric pollution will continue even if we do reduce emissions, we need to create biodiverse ecosystems and economies because only they offer the potential to adapt to an unpredictable climate. And only biodiverse systems provide alternatives that everyone can afford. We need to return to the renewable carbon cycle of biodiversity. We need to create a carbon democracy so that all beings have their just share of useful carbon, and no one is burdened with carrying an unjust share of climate impacts due to carbon pollution.

Notes

1. While the term "liberalization" usually means to make something less restrictive, Shiva here associates liberalization with the imposition of European values and economic systems. She sees globalization and unchecked international commerce as an attack on the rights to life and **self-determination** of **indigenous** peoples and ecologies. [Editor]
2. The World Trade Organization (WTO) is an international organization that supervises and mediates the liberalization of international trade. [Editor]
3. The World Bank is an international financial institution that provides loans to developing countries for the purpose of building and maintaining **public goods** and infrastructure. [Editor]

Discussion Questions

1. Hurka argues that, even on the view that only "humans here and now" matter morally, we have some reasons for avoidance (mitigation). What are his reasons for this claim? Do you think they are good reasons? Why or why not?
2. Lomborg argues for a form of adaptation rather than mitigation. He believes rich countries should invest billions of dollars in research to make green energy sources more efficient and affordable. What are his reasons for this claim? Do you think they are good reasons? Why or why not?
3. The economic transformation Homer-Dixon argues for involves replacing the view that economic growth is the engine that powers society with what he calls "resilience." What does he mean by this term? What are his reasons for the necessity of this transformation? Do you think they are good reasons? Why or why not?
4. Homer-Dixon says the normative transformation is the deepest one: we need to expand who "we" includes. What does he think grounds this expansion of moral concern? Do you think his arguments are **sound**? Why or why not?
5. Hurka gives different reasons than Homer-Dixon's for expanding the scope of our moral concern. What are his reasons in favour of a "humans-everywhere" scope? Do you think his arguments are better, worse than, or as good as Homer-Dixon's? Why?
6. Shiva rejects technological and economic solutions to climate change and other forms of environmental destruction. Instead, she argues that only biodiversity and lower-tech ways of living can save the planet. What are her reasons for this view? Do you think they are good reasons? Why or why not?
7. Both Homer-Dixon and Shiva say we need to change how we think about the environment. What sorts of changes do they propose? Are their views compatible? Why or why not? Do you agree with one, both, or neither?

Suggested Readings and Websites

♣ = Canadian source or author

Donald Brown, Nancy Tuana, et al. "White Paper on the Ethical Dimensions of Climate Change." University Park, PA: Collaborative Program on the Ethical Dimensions of Climate Change and Rock Ethics Institute, Pennsylvania State University, n.d. [Describes "relevant facts, ethical questions, and preliminary ethical analyses" in the climate change debate.]

Copenhagen Consensus Center. www.copenhagenconsensus.com/CCC%20Home%20Page.aspx [Think tank created by Bjørn Lomborg; focusses on "the international community's effort to solve the world's biggest challenges and on how to do this in the most cost-efficient manner."]

♣ Coward, Harold, and Thomas Hurka, eds. *Ethics and Climate Change: The Greenhouse Effect*. Waterloo, ON: Wilfred Laurier University Press, 1992. [The first book in English on the ethics of climate change.]

♣ Friedmann, S. Julio, and Thomas Homer-Dixon. "Out of the Energy Box." *Foreign Affairs* 83, 6 (2004): 72–83. [Friedmann and Homer-Dixon argue in favour of carbon sequestration, injecting CO_2 "into old oil or gas fields, unminable coalfields, or deep, briny aquifers."]

♣ Greenpeace Canada. www.greenpeace.org/canada/en/, and Greenpeace International, www.greenpeace.org/international/en/ [Founded in Vancouver in 1971, Greenpeace "uses non-violent, creative confrontation to expose global environmental problems," in order to work toward "a green and peaceful future."]

Guggenheim, Davis. *An Inconvenient Truth*. [Academy Award-winning documentary about former US Vice-President Al Gore's attempts to publicize the dangers of global warming.]

♣ Homer-Dixon, Thomas. "Terror in the Weather Forecast." *New York Times*, 24 April 2007. [Argues that climate change is a "threat multiplier" that will cause political instability, particularly in hard-hit poor countries.]

Intergovernmental Panel on Climate Change. www.ipcc.ch/

♣ Morito, Bruce. "Ethics of Climate Change: Adopting an Empirical Approach to Moral Concern." *Human Ecology Review* 17, 2 (2010): 106–16. [Argues ethicists should be "stand-in interpreters" who help communities "identify, categorize and evaluate their values" as they come to terms with effects of climate change.]

♣ Westra, Laura. *Environmental Justice and the Rights of Indigenous Peoples: International and Domestic Law Perspectives*. London: Earthscan Publishers, 2007. [Argues the effects of environmental degradation on Aboriginal peoples are forms of environmental injustice that should be heard by Canadian and international courts.]

Glossary

The words in this glossary are defined context-sensitively, that is, according to their meanings in context in the readings. Many words have additional meanings not given here; a good dictionary, whether online or hard copy, is a great help.

Words or phrases in the definitions in boldface are defined elsewhere in this glossary.

a-: (prefix) Not, negation; e.g., "atheoretical" means "not theoretical," "asocial" means "not social."

a priori: Concerning or referring to knowledge acquired through reason, rather than from observation. A priori knowledge is often contrasted to **empirical** knowledge.

ableist: Involving discrimination and prejudice in favour of able-bodied people.

abolition: The act of getting rid of laws, customs, practices, etc. This is the noun form of the verb "to abolish."

abolitionist: A supporter of abolition; historically, a supporter of the abolition of slavery throughout the Western world.

aboriginal: Describing people whose ancestors were the first to settle a land, and usually whose descendants continue to live on the land to this day.

Aboriginal and treaty rights: Part II of the *Constitution Act, 1982* (Part I is the ***Charter***) "recognize[s] and affirm[s]" Aboriginal and treaty rights. Roughly, Aboriginal rights are rights that Aboriginal people exercised prior to European contact and that have not been **extinguished** by treaties or laws. Treaty rights are rights that arise from treaties between Aboriginal people and the Canadian government.

Aboriginal peoples: (in Canada) First Nations peoples, the Métis, and the Inuit. "Peoples" is plural to indicate that there were many separate **nations** in Canada before European contact.

abounds with: Is full of.

abrogate: To officially deny or do away with.

absolute: Without exceptions, restrictions, or limits.

abstract, to: To separate, or to consider something separately from its context, or to consider the general characteristic of a kind of thing rather than the factual instances of any one thing.

abstraction: The state of being **abstract**.

abuse of process: The use of the legal process or any part of the **administration of justice** to perform an illegal action or accomplish an unlawful **end**.

academy: The **institutions** of higher learning, teaching, and research in Western society.

accede: To agree or consent.

accidental: Describing a characteristic of something that is not **essential** to its nature, that could be otherwise. See also **distinction between essence and accident**.

accord: To be in agreement (with something); to officially grant or give.

accord: (noun) A formal agreement, often between two or more **nations** or countries.

active euthanasia: Intentionally causing the death of another person, (supposedly) for their own good.

actor: A person or corporate body, such as a government or a corporation, that takes action or participates in a process.

actus reus: (in the criminal law) A crime. Punishment for a crime requires both a criminal act and intent to commit the act (***mens rea***).

ad hoc: For a specific purpose and without general application, often improvised, or even made up for a particular case.

adherent: A follower of a belief or religion.

adjudicate: To judge; to settle a dispute or disagreement.

adjudicator: One who acts as a judge.

administrative detention: The arrest and detention of individuals by the **state** without warrant or trial.

administrative law: The branch of law that deals with government laws and policies, and disputes involving how the laws and policies have been applied.

administration of justice: In criminal law, a term that references the totality of activities involved in the identification, investigation, arrest, and trial of people suspected of crime.

adversarial: Involving opposed parties or **interests**, as in a trial.

affirmative action: A set of laws or policies created to promote **substantive equality of opportunity** and to eliminate discrimination, particularly in education and employment.

age of majority: The age at which a person legally becomes an adult. This age varies for different purposes, such as voting, driving, getting a job, signing a contract, or drinking.

agency: Having the power to act according to one's desires or will. See also **moral agency** and **moral agent**.

agent: Someone who can act according to his/her desires or will. See also **moral agency** and **moral agent**.

alien: (noun) A person of foreign origin; (adjective) foreign; unusual.

alienate: In law, to transfer a right or property to someone or something else.

alienation: In law, the transfer of a right or property from one person or entity to another.

all and only or **all or only**: These phrases refer to the precision of a claim, term, group, etc. The most precise philosophical claims are broad enough to apply to *all* the cases we want to include (they do not omit any relevant cases), and yet narrow enough to apply *only* to those cases (they do not include any irrelevant cases). See also **necessary**, **sufficient**, and **necessary and sufficient**.

allopathic medicine: Mainstream Western medicine.

ameliorate: To improve or make better.

amnesty: Forgiveness or pardon for past offences.

amoral: Not concerned with or related to ethical considerations; neither moral nor immoral.

analytic: Concerning reason or analysis.

analytical: Characterized by reason or analysis, usually by breaking something down to its **constitutive** parts and carefully considering their relationships.

anarchism: The belief that social and political liberty require the **abolition** of all government.

anarchist: One who endorses the principles of **anarchism**.

anarchy: A state in which a group of people exist without effective **governments**. **Anarchists** consider anarchy necessary for social and political liberty. **Political realists** believe it describes international relations, because there is no international body with the power to enforce law. In common use, anarchy has negative associations with lawlessness and civil war.

Anglicize: To make into or similar to English.

Anglification: Becoming more, or more like, English.

animist: A follower of animism, which is the belief that some or all plants, animals, and natural objects possess souls or spirits.

anomie: A state of society or individuals in which there is a breakdown or lack of social responsibility or **norms** which tie individuals and their communities together.

anti-colonial movement: The organized effort to promote and bring about **decolonization**.

apartheid: The legal and political practice of keeping racial and economic groups segregated from one another. In South Africa, until 1994, apartheid enforced the segregation of blacks and whites in matters including residence, education, medical care, and other public services.

appellant: (in law) A person or organization making an appeal (a request to a higher court to reverse the decision of a lower court).

applied ethics: The branch of ethics that examines real-world moral and/or political issues, like **multiculturalism**, assisted suicide, and animal rights.

arbiter: A judge.

artifact: A thing constructed or shaped by human beings.

ascription: The act of ascribing; an assignment or judgment.

asset: Any good or useful quality, person, or thing.

assisted death: The act of helping a person to voluntarily end her/his life. See also **assisted suicide**.

assisted suicide: The act of helping a person to voluntarily end her/his life. The death is assisted but ultimately brought about by the person undergoing the death. Assisted suicide differs from euthanasia, in which one person ends another's life, either through some action or omission, supposedly for the other person's own good. See also **physician-assisted suicide**, **active euthanasia**, and **passive euthanasia**.

assurance: A guarantee, certainty.

asymmetrical federalism: A form of **federal** government in which powers between the subunits (in Canada, provinces) are not identical. For example, Quebec has power over pensions (the Quebec Pension Plan as opposed to the

Canada Pension Plan) and increased control over immigration, powers that are normally reserved for the federal government.

atomism: A description and understanding of people, their behaviour, and their relationships in terms of **self-interest**, or their individual beliefs, values, motivations, etc., rather than in terms of their group membership, or the shared experience of those with whom they share significant relationships.

atomistic: Having to do with **atomism**.

attenuated: Weakened or reduced.

attribute: (noun) A characteristic, quality, or feature of something.

Auditor General: In Canada, an office held by a single person, appointed by the **Governor General**, who performs the role of an auditor for the financial operations of the Canadian **federal government**.

autonomous: Characterized by **autonomy**.

autonomy: Self-rule (auto = self, nomos = custom or law): being able to run one's own life; liberty. Autonomy may also refer to the **sovereignty** of a **nation** or a state.

axiomatic: Self-evident, appearing true without further evidence.

band council: The governing body of a particular group of Aboriginal people. It usually consists of a chief and group of elected councillors who deal with issues concerning education, roads, water and sewage, and other **public goods**.

to **beg the question**: This is a technical term in philosophy. It means that a claim is circular, by assuming in a **premise** most of, or a crucial element of, what needs to be demonstrated. For example, suppose the question is, "What is a fair distribution procedure for social resources?" An answer that begins by assuming the current distribution is fair and then determines a procedure for future distribution begs the question, because *whether* the current distribution is fair is part of what must be examined. If the current distribution is unfair, then following a fair procedure from now on might only maintain, or even worsen, the current unfair situation. *"Begging the question" does not mean that another question "begs" to be asked.*

beneficence: An action or practice that promotes health and well-being. This is a fundamental **tenet** of medical ethics taught to all medical students.

benevolence: Good will or charitableness.

benign: Harmless; neutral.

bicameral: A **parliamentary system** which divides **legislative power** between two bodies. In Canada, legislative power is divided between the Senate, a group of 105 people appointed by the **Governor General** on the advice of the Prime Minister, and the House of Commons, comprising 305 elected representatives.

bioethics: A branch of **applied ethics** dealing with moral issues in medicine.

blastocyst: A structure formed after the fertilization of an **ovum**. It is characterized by an outer layer of cells that houses an inner cell mass which constitutes the embryo in its earliest stage of development.

BNA Act: The *British North America Act, 1867*, made by the British Parliament, created the **dominion** of Canada. The BNA Act specified a **federal system of government** for Canada, and determined **federal** and provincial areas of responsibility and **jurisdiction**.

brief: A written legal document submitted to a court, containing arguments relevant to a case.

burden of proof: The obligation to prove one's claims. In criminal cases, the Crown has the burden of proof—it must prove beyond a reasonable doubt that the accused committed the crime; the defence does not have to prove the accused person's innocence. In **civil** cases, the burden of proof rests on the **plaintiff**, the person alleging that a wrong was committed. In philosophy, the burden of proof rests on a person making an argument in favour of or against a position.

byzantine: Complicated or inflexible. Refers to the Byzantine Empire, the eastern half of the Roman Empire whose capital was Byzantium (modern-day Istanbul). It survived the fifth-century collapse of the western half of the Roman Empire, and lasted until it was conquered by the Ottoman Turks in the fifteenth century. It is remembered for complex, pointless bureaucracies.

calculus: Any method of calculating values to arrive at a definite solution or outcome.

Canadian Charter of Rights and Freedoms: See ***Charter***.

capabilities: What people are able to do and be in their society. In general, a society whose citizens are able to do more things and take on more roles that they consider meaningful is better and freer than one in which they have fewer meaningful options. ("Meaningful" here is subjectively defined, from each individual's perspective.)

capital: Money and property available for, or directly involved in, maintaining and expanding a business or industry.

care ethics: A kind of **normative ethics** that focuses on the **norms** and standards of caring relationships.

categorical imperative: Kant's formulation of the moral law, which states that we ought to do something only if we can generalize from our conduct and say that everyone ought to do the same thing in similar circumstances. Categorical means "**absolute**, without exceptions" and an imperative is a command, so the "categorical imperative" is an exceptionless command; it applies to everyone, always and everywhere.

cede: To surrender or give over.

centrist liberal: Someone whose political views combine aspects of both **conservative** and **egalitarian liberalism**. The main centrist liberal positions in Canada are **progressive conservatism** and **welfare state liberalism**.

cetaceans: the biological order that includes dolphins and whales.

Charlottetown Accord: A number of proposed amendments to the ***Canadian Charter of Rights and Freedoms*** submitted in 1992. Its intent was to secure Quebec's agreement to the ***Charter*** and to resolve **jurisdictional** disputes between the **federal government** and the provinces. It was defeated that same year in a **referendum**.

Charter: Canada's **constitution**. Its full name is the ***Canadian Charter of Rights and Freedoms***.

charter: An instrument that acts as evidence or the **foundation** for a contract.

checks and balances: The separation of political powers in order to prevent political power from being usurped and to protect the rights of citizens. In Canada, the **legislative** and **executive powers** are combined in **Parliament** but the **judiciary** is a separate branch of power.

civic: Concerning the nature of citizenship, or belonging to a city or **nation**.

civic republican: Someone who advocates **civic republicanism**.

civic republicanism: A political theory which encourages active and publicly spirited citizenship. Civic republicanism promotes political participation and public deliberation because these are believed to be shared common goods which have **intrinsic worth**.

civil: Concerning citizens. (in law) Concerning the rights of individual citizens relevant to non-criminal legal proceedings, such as divorce and breach of contract.

civil code: The entire body of laws which inform a system of **civil law**. Quebec re-wrote its civil code in 1994.

civil law: A system of law used in Quebec, and in most non-British European countries and their colonies. In the civil law, the state creates the entire body of laws at once. The idea is that the laws must be published—made known—before they can apply to people. The laws are designed to cover all possible legal outcomes. Judges apply the law to particular cases to reach decisions. Quebec uses a civil law system for legal matters concerning the family, inheritance, property, contracts, and so on. Contrast with **common law**. (Note: In common-law systems the civil law refers to private law, the law of contracts and **torts**, as opposed to public law, which includes criminal, administrative, and military law.)

civil libertarian: An advocate for the supremacy of individual rights and liberties in political policy and decision making.

civil liberties: The basic liberties that any **democratic** government should guarantee, such as freedom of expression, religion, and association, and the right to life, liberty, and security of the person. In Canada, these liberties are guaranteed by section 2 of the ***Charter***, Fundamental Freedoms, and sections 7–14, Legal Rights.

civil rights: The political rights enjoyed by citizens. These rights usually concern protections against various forms of discrimination, and protections for **civil liberties**.

civil rights movement: In the US, the social and political movement by African Americans for equal rights. Two famous results of the struggle were the *Civil Rights Act of 1964*, which outlawed discrimination against racial, ethnic, and religious minorities, and women, in the workplace and public facilities, and the *Voting Rights Act of 1965*, which prohibited discrimination of the same kind in political elections.

civility: The way citizens should conduct themselves in public and how they should treat one another. Civility includes the mutual obligation to treat others as equal citizens, to overcome prejudice and discrimination, and to participate in political discussions with openness to **dissenting** or minority opinion.

claimant: A person who makes a legal or moral claim.

clan: A traditional social unit characterized by a grouping of close-knit, interrelated families.

clarion: Loudly ringing.

classical liberal: Someone who advocates **classical liberalism**.

classical liberalism: A political doctrine first developed in the nineteenth century that advocates limited government, **constitutionalism**, the **rule of law**, and **liberal individualism**.

climate change: Long-term changes in weather patterns caused by **greenhouse gases**. **Global warming** and the increase in the frequency and severity of extreme weather phenomena are two aspects of climate change.

clitoridectomy: The surgical alteration or removal of the clitoris.

codify: To write down, organize, or formally authorize in a system of law or morality.

coerce: To force another to do something.

coercion: The act of forcing someone to do something, often through the threat of violence.

coercive: In a manner characterized by **coercion**.

cognitive: Having to do with thinking, understanding, remembering, etc.

cognizable: Understandable.

cognizant: Understanding.

collective rights: Rights belonging to a group rather than individuals. These rights may include protection from other groups, to ensure the group's existence despite the political actions of the larger society. In a **liberal democracy**, collective rights must not conflict with liberal principles.

colonial: (noun) A person who lives under **colonialism** whose cultural group is a subordinated or conquered nationality; (adjective) characterized by **colonialism**.

colonialism: A process in which one **nation** establishes colonies within the territory of another nation. The colonizing nation claims **sovereignty** over the colonized territory, and governs the colony for the benefit of the colonizers, often at great expense to the local people.

command responsibility: A doctrine under which commanding officers are morally and legally accountability for war crimes committed by their subordinates. If a commanding officer knows that subordinates are conducting human rights violations or war crimes but fails to intervene, then that officer is held to account for these actions with at least as much moral and legal severity as those subordinates who literally carried out the violations or crimes.

common law: Law made by judges, based on **precedent** and custom. Judges consult court decisions reached in older, similar cases to determine how to apply the law in specific cases. In some cases, a judge may **strike down** a law, **read in** a missing portion of the law, or **read down** a wrongly included portion of the law. In common-law systems, judges are supposed to both interpret and make the law. People who complain about "judge-made law" misunderstand our legal system. Contrast with **civil law**.

commons: A good that belongs to and can be used by everyone, and that should not or cannot be divided. A public park, the atmosphere, and the oceans are commons.

Commonwealth: An international political organization of fifty-four member states, almost all of which were originally British colonies.

communal identity: The parts of a person's identity that come from cultural membership. Language, nationality, religion, tradition, family life, and life goals may all be shaped by a communal identity.

communism: A radical form of **socialism** in which all land and industry are **state**-owned, and money and private property are abolished (but personal property is retained). **Communist** governments aim to establish classless, moneyless, **egalitarian** societies.

communist: (noun) A supporter or advocate of **communism**; (adjective) characterized by or in agreement with **communism** and its goals.

communitarian: Concerning or like **communitarianism**.

communitarianism: A political philosophy that emphasizes interconnections between individuals and the community. Communitarians believe culture is inextricably "embedded" in the identities of individuals, so that someone born in Canada, for example, will always remain at least partly Canadian, even if she/he leaves the country permanently. Communitarianism is compatible with **liberalism** if it recognizes the importance of individual **autonomy**, and incompatible if it does not.

compatriot: A fellow citizen.

competent: Able to understand and appreciate relevant information and the consequences of any actions or decisions.

complementary: Serving as support or adding something without taking anything away.

conceit: A fanciful idea.

concrete: Concerning the particular or factual existence of something. Contrast with **abstract**.

condition: To accustom, sometimes through hardship.

confederacy: A state of **confederation**, or a **union** of people or groups in alliance. See also **federal system of government**.

confederation: The **union** of people or groups in alliance, or the process of creating a **federal system of government**.

consciousness: Mental awareness, such as thoughts, feelings, and desires. Compare with **self-consciousness**.

consensus: An opinion or decision reached by everyone in a group.

consequentialism: A kind of **normative ethics** that focusses on the consequences of actions or policies.

consequentialist: Someone who believes in **consequentialism**.

conservative: Someone who promotes maintaining (that is, conserving) existing **institutions** and customs, and who resists change.

conservative centrist: A liberal who is economically **conservative** but socially egalitarian, who believes government should both promote free enterprise and ensure that social inequalities do not become too great.

conservative liberal: Someone who believes the main or even only function of government is to protect private property and maintain a **free market**. Taxation is justified mainly or only for these purposes (which includes police and military protection, a fair court system, and **democratic** government); everything else should be left to individuals.

consonant: Agreeing or in accordance (with something).

constitution: A document that spells out the principles on which a **nation** is grounded and by which it is to be governed. The ***Canadian Charter of Rights and Freedoms*** is part of our constitution. The constitution is the supreme law of Canada; all legislation and court decisions must conform to its principles.

Constitution Act, 1982: The act that gave Canada an independent **constitution**. Part I of the *Act*, sections 1–34, is the ***Canadian Charter of Rights and Freedoms***. Part II (section 35) lays out "Rights of the **Aboriginal** Peoples of Canada." Section 52 in Part VII states that "The Constitution of Canada is the supreme law of Canada, and any law that is inconsistent with the provisions of the Constitution is, to the extent of the inconsistency, of no force or effect."

constitutional: In line with the **constitution**. A law or policy that is constitutional does not violate any part of the constitution. See also **unconstitutional**.

constitutionality: The degree to which a law does not conflict with provisions or principles of a constitution.

constitutionalism: The principles of a **constitutional** government.

constitutionalize: To make by a **constitution**, or to provide with a constitution.

constitutive: A necessary part.

context of choice: The historical, cultural, social, political, and economic factors which determine the opportunities available to individuals in a society.

contingent: Something that is conditional, that may or may not be the case; not necessary.

contrive: To make or create, sometimes by trickery.

controverted: Contested, argued against.

conversable: Capable of speech.

converse: Reverse or opposite direction or order.

conversely: On the other hand; in an opposite way.

corollary: A conclusion that follows immediately or easily, with little or no further proof.

correlate: To demonstrate the significant relation of two things to each other.

cosmopolitan: International; composed of people or ideas from around the world.

coup d'état: An illegal overthrow of a state government.

covenant: An agreement or promise.

creed: A system of principles or belief.

crime against humanity: Persecution, murder, torture, genocide, ethnic cleansing, rape, and other crimes committed as part of a widespread attack on a civilian population.

criterion: The singular form of "criteria."

critique: A detailed, well-thought-out evaluation or judgment about an issue.
cross-appeal: To appeal the other side's appeal.
culpable: Legally responsible.
cultural commitments: The obligations, responsibilities, and social roles of individuals that come from their membership in a cultural community. Cultural commitments may be chosen or imposed, **egalitarian** or **inegalitarian**, restrictive or expansive.
cultural imperialism: An aspect of **imperialism** emphasizing its cultural aspects or outcomes. Cultural imperialism usually involves a dominant society imposing its values on a subordinate society.
curricula: the plural form of "curriculum."
de facto: According to practice, but not necessarily according to law. See also **de jure**.
de jure: According to law. See also **de facto**.
decolonization: The process of undoing the effects of **colonialism**.
decolonize: To undergo a process of **decolonization**.
deliberative democracy: A form of democracy in which open discussion (deliberation) is central to decision making. Deliberative democracy is compatible with **representative democracy**, but shifts emphasis away from decision making based on voting to decision making based on discussion. According to deliberative **democratic** theorists, a democratic decision is legitimate only if it arises from deliberation among all affected people, and not just from voting.
démarche: A diplomatic or political initiative.
demobilization: The act of changing troops from active to standby status, or of discharging soldiers from military service.
democracy: A system of government in which citizens hold political power, exercising it either directly through participation and **referenda**, or through elected and appointed representatives.
democratic: Characterized by political equality among citizens and **popular sovereignty**.
denizen: A resident.
deontological: Concerning **deontology**.
deontology: In **normative ethics**, deontology is a theory which proposes that the morality of an action should be judged on the basis of the action's adherence to a principle, rule, or law, for example, "treat each person as an **end rather than a means**," or "respect other's rights." "Deontology" comes from the ancient Greek words *deon* (duty) and *logos* (science), roughly translating to "the science of duties."
derogable: (of a law, regulation, or right) Legally can be limited under certain circumstances. See **non-derogable**.
determinant: A cause or influence. Not to be confused with **determinate**.
determinate: Precisely defined or concluded. Not to be confused with **determinant**.
dialectic: Contradiction and conflict. For Kant, a method of exposing contradictions; for Hegel, the process of reconciling contradictions.
dialectical: Characteristic of a **dialectic**; contradictory.
differentiated citizenship: A conception of citizenship which enforces different legal rights for different cultural groups of people. In a **liberal democracy**, differentiated citizenship usually exists to accommodate group or **communal identities**.
dignity: Inherent value and worth.
diploid: In humans, a cell containing all forty-six chromosomes (twenty-three from each biological parent).
diplomatic assurance: The legally binding promise not to torture detainees who are scheduled to transfer from the custody of one government to another.
discourse: A method of communicating ideas, whether through conversation, writing, art, performance, architecture, etc.
disenfranchise: To deny a person or group the right to political participation, including but not limited to the right to vote. See also **disenfranchisement**.
disenfranchisement: Denying a person or group the right to political participation, including but not limited to the right to vote. Disenfranchisement may result from laws that specifically target certain groups for exclusion, or it may result from less obvious forms of oppression and subordination, such as making participation difficult or impossible in practice.
disinterested: Without bias or selfish motives.
dispensation: An exemption or freedom from a duty or obligation.
dissent: (in law) To disagree with the majority opinion.
dissent: (in law; noun) Disagreement with the majority opinion.

distinction between essence and accident: Essence describes the central characteristics of something that makes it what it is, and without which it would not be that thing. Accident describes the non-central characteristics of something, without which the thing retains its **essential** character. For example, the essence of a chair is that it is a human-made object designed for the purpose of sitting. The accidents of a chair might include that it is constructed from wood and has armrests. The material the chair is made from and the presence or absence of armrests does not make an object any more or less a chair, so these are not essential to what defines a chair as a chair.

distributive justice: A principle for the fair distribution of material or economic benefits for the members of a society. Distribution might be based on criteria such as welfare, desert, and free exchange.

docket: A list of court cases.

doctrinal: Relating to a doctrine.

doctrine of double effect: A set of criteria used to argue for the moral permissibility of actions whose consequences are ordinarily immoral. According to the doctrine of double effect, an action with normally immoral consequences is morally permissible if (a) the act, under normal circumstances, is morally permitted; (b) the immoral consequence is an unintended effect of the permitted act; and (c) the good of the act outweighs the immorality of the consequence.

dominion: (verb) The right to rule; (noun) rule, authority; a self-governing member of the Commonwealth.

double effect: See **doctrine of double effect**.

due process: The conducting of legal proceedings according to established rules for the protection and enforcement of legal rights. Due process requires that governments respect the legal rights of individuals.

economies of scale: Factors that make the average price of items fall as the volume of production increases. For example, it might cost $100 to make twenty copies of a book but only $500 to make a thousand copies. The cost per unit drops from five dollars to fifty cents.

ectopic: Outside the uterus.

egalitarian: (noun) Someone who promotes greater social and political equality than currently exists in her/his society; (adjective) characterized by or in agreement with the promotion of greater social and political equality than currently exists in her/his society.

egalitarian centrist: A liberal who supports a partially free-market economy, with government controls (e.g., **progressive taxation**, minimum wage laws, laws banning child labour) to prevent inequality from becoming too great. The difference between egalitarian centrists and **egalitarians** is how much government management of the economy they support, and how much equality they think government should maintain. On both issues, egalitarian centrists support a lesser role for government than egalitarians do.

egalitarian: Someone who believes a liberal society must balance **substantive liberty** and **substantive equality**. Governments must not only protect citizens' rights and freedoms, but also promote their well-being by fostering a society in which everyone has the opportunity to live a life that they consider worthwhile.

egalitarian: (noun) Someone who advocates **egalitarianism**; (adjective) characterized by egalitarian principles.

egalitarianism: Any political **doctrine** which promotes and aims for social and political equality.

egoist: A self-centred person who is concerned only with his/her own **interests**.

embargo: A government restriction, usually concerning freedom of trade or mobility of people.

empirical: Provable with evidence, by numerous observations or by experiments.

empirically: In an **empirical** manner.

employment equity: A Canadian term coined by Supreme Court Justice Rosalie Abella for policies designed to ensure that members of **equality-seeking groups** have fair access to jobs and benefits.

encroach: To overstep proper boundaries.

encroachment: A gradual taking over, or slow movement beyond proper limits.

end: A desired goal, purpose, or outcome.

end in itself: Something that is valued for its own sake, rather than as a **means to an end**.

end rather than a means: An **end** is the goal or purpose of a thing, and a **means** is a way of achieving an end. As a **deontological** principle, "treating people as ends rather than as means" requires that people be treated with the **dignity** and moral consideration owed to rational beings—their end—and not used as means to achieve some other goal.

engender: To produce or cause.

the **Enlightenment**: A European cultural movement between the seventeenth and eighteenth centuries, notable for increased interest in scientific exploration, religious scepticism, individual liberty, equality of all people before the law, and **democracy**.

entail: (logic) To have as a **necessary** consequence.

epistemological: Concerning matters of knowledge and how knowledge is gained.

epistemology: The branch of philosophy that studies the validity, scope, and methods of knowledge.

equality rights: Rights to social goods that maintain or promote equality, such as education, old age pensions, or health care.

equality-seeking group: A phrase used by the Canadian government to designate women, members of visible minorities, **Aboriginal** people, and people with disabilities. Some philosophers and activists include other groups as well, such as poor people, refugees, colonized people, and lesbian/gay/bisexual/transgendered/queer people.

equality-seeking movement: A political movement for equality by members of a **disenfranchised** group.

equitable: Fair, just, reasonable, or **impartial**.

equity: The quality of being fair, just, reasonable, or **impartial**.

essence: The central characteristics of something that makes it what it is, and without which it would not be that thing.

essential: Describing a characteristic that is necessary to a thing, or constituting the **essence** of something; the opposite of **accidental**. See also **distinction between essence and accident**.

ethic: A moral theory or a system of moral values.

ethical: Concerning morality; morally good or correct.

ethics: The philosophical study of the moral principles that do or should guide human action.

ethnocultural: Describing an ethnic group with a distinct culture, or the specific culture of an ethnic group.

eugenics: The practice of trying to improve humans genetically, most commonly by reducing the reproduction of those with traits considered "undesirable."

Eurocentric: Refers to the belief that Europe and Europeans are the centre; usually derogatory.

exceptionalism: The belief that a **nation** or culture is superior to others in important ways.

exculpatory: Acting or tending to clear of guilt or blame.

executive: The **executive power**, or executive branch of government.

executive power: The branch of government that **administers** the law. In a **parliamentary system**, as we have in Canada, both the executive power and the **legislative power** belong to **Parliament**. (In some countries they are separated; in the US, for example, the President has executive power and Congress has legislative power.) See also **legislative power** and **judiciary**.

exercise jurisdiction: To carry out authorized functions or powers.

exigencies: Urgent circumstances.

existential: Referring to the ideas of a set of philosophers who believed that philosophy must begin not only with the thinking subject, but with the whole human being—thinking, acting, feeling, and so on.

external reviewer: An expert who participates in the review of a project, department or organization, who is not involved in that project, department or organization.

extinguish: (in law) To nullify a right, ownership, etc.

extinguishable: Capable of being nullified.

extirpate: To uproot or destroy.

extirpation: removal, destruction.

extradition: The legal surrender of a person to the legal **jurisdiction** of another **state** or government authority.

extrajudicial: Outside of the authority or **jurisdiction** of a court, government, or **state**.

extraordinary rendition: Secretly and **extrajudicially** transferring a suspected terrorist from one country to another, generally to a country known to violate human rights and due process of law.

factory farming: The mass production of animals for food, commonly involving crowding, confinement, pain, and distress for the animals.

fallacy: An error of reasoning that is usually the result of intentional or unintentional mistakes or presumptions. An argument that includes a fallacy may have a true conclusion, but the conclusion will not logically follow from the **premises**. For example, to argue that most

Canadians speak English based on knowing one or two English-speaking Canadians involves a true conclusion, but it uses too small a sample in order to reasonably draw this conclusion (this specific example is a **hasty generalization**).

false dichotomy: A **fallacy** in which someone claims there are two and only two alternatives, when in fact there are more than two. "You're either with me or against me" is a false dichotomy, because it is possible for others to be neutral about the speaker or to have no opinion at all.

federal: Concerning a form of government in which there is one central government and several regional governments.

federalist: Someone who advocates a **federal** union in which there is a central government and several subordinate sub-units.

federal court: The national court of a country with a **federal system of government**. In Canada, the Federal Court is a trial court that hears cases under federal law, such as judicial review of immigration decisions, Aboriginal law matters, and claims against the federal government itself.

federal government: The central government in a **federal system of government**.

federal system of government: A form of government in which political power is split between a central government and several regional governments. In Canada, the **federal** (central) government and the provincial and territorial governments have political power, though both also give some power to other authorized bodies (e.g., **Aboriginal** peoples and municipalities).

federalism: A political system that involves the **union** of smaller political units into one overarching political organization. Federalism divides **sovereignty** between a central government and regional governments (in Canada, provinces) that make up the **federal** union.

federation: The organization of smaller political units such as provinces or territories into a larger political **union**.

female circumcision: Partial or total removal of the external female genitalia for non-medical (cultural) reasons; also known as female genital mutilation.

feminism: The movement that advocates social, economic, political, and/or spiritual equality between women and men.

feminist: Someone who advocates social, economic, political, and/or spiritual equality between women and men.

fiduciary: (noun) Someone who is in a position of trust or confidence with respect to someone else; (adjective) based on trust and confidence.

fiduciary relationship: A relationship in which one party, the **fiduciary**, is in a position of trust with respect to the other, and where the fiduciary is required to use its rights and powers for the benefit of the other.

fifth column: A group that secretly aids a foreign enemy or invading army.

First Nations: A term that refers to the **Aboriginal** peoples of Canada. It does not include the Métis or Inuit.

fora: Plural of "forum."

formal equality: Applying the same rules to everyone who is similarly situated. "First come, first served," merit-based systems, and "one person, one vote" are forms of formal equality. See also **substantive equality**.

formal equality of opportunity: A principle of distribution in which advantageous positions are open to everyone, and are distributed strictly according to set criteria such as merit (e.g., grades), a fair competition (e.g., a game), or an **impartial** procedure (e.g., "first come, first served"). See also **substantive equality of opportunity**.

formal liberty: Freedom from interference. Formal liberty exists when individuals are able to do what they want without interference from others or the state, as long as they do not harm others. ("Harm" includes physical harm, **coercion**, fraud, and breaking contracts. It does not include emotional or psychological harm, or harm to oneself.) See also **substantive liberty**.

foundation: The reasonable support or explanation for something, or the set of principles serving as the reasonable support or explanation for something.

foundational: Describing something to serve as a **foundation**.

free market: An economic system in which prices, wages, and the distribution of economic and material goods are determined by unrestricted or minimally regulated competition and contract among individuals and businesses.

free rider: Someone who enjoys more of their fair share of something, or enjoys it without the associated costs. The cost of the free rider's enjoyment is usually passed on to and paid by others who pay their fair share, but must pay more because of the free rider.

fundamentalism: The strict adherence to a religious, **ideological**, or political set of beliefs.

fundamentalist: (noun) A religious believer who interprets the writings of her/his sacred texts as literal truth, and who advocates strictly following the fundamental, traditional principles of the religion; (adjective) characterized by strictly following the fundamental, traditional principles of a religion.

gamete: A reproductive cell prior to fertilization; a sperm or **ovum**.

GDP: Gross domestic product, the market value of all final goods and services produced within a country in a given period. The calculation takes into consideration the total spending of consumers, investors, and government, income from exported goods and services, and expenses from imported goods and services. Unlike gross national product (**GNP**), gross domestic product calculates market value by way of location (the country), rather than by ownership.

gender: The social classification of male and female individuals; the social attribution of particular traits or roles to the different sexes, such as the claim that women are nurturing caregivers and men are tough warriors, often with little evidence of connection to **sex**.

gender-neutral: Free of, or applied without, reference to **gender**.

genocide: The attempt to wipe out an entire people, race, ethnicity, etc.

global warming: The rise in the average temperature since the nineteenth century, caused by human-made **greenhouse gases**. In the past century, the earth's mean temperature has increased 0.8 degrees Celsius. Two-thirds of the temperature increase has occurred in the last thirty years.

GNP: Gross national product, a measure of the market value of all the products, services, and property owned and produced by the residents of a country in a single year. Unlike **GDP** (gross domestic product), gross national product calculates market value by the citizenship of owners and producers, rather than by the country in which they are produced.

good, the: Used in **consequentialism** to refer to the moral consequences that people should aim for, such as the greatest good for the greatest number. See also the **right**.

governance: The act or process of governing.

Governor General: The representative of the Crown (Queen Elizabeth II) in Canada. The Governor General's duties are largely ceremonial.

greenhouse gases: Gases that trap heat. Some greenhouse gases are necessary; without them, the earth would be too cold to sustain life. But carbon dioxide and other greenhouse gases that are by-products of industrialization, urbanization, and intensive agriculture have increased dramatically, contributing to **climate change**.

group recognition: The political recognition of a cultural group's special status in order to preserve its **autonomy** and distinct cultural identity in the presence of a dominant culture. Group recognition may grant political powers to the cultural group, such as rights of representation in legislative bodies, or forms of **self-government**.

gross domestic product: See **GDP**.

gross national product: See **GNP**.

haploid: A cell containing only half (one set) of the full number of chromosomes of an organism. Haploids are sex cells (sperm and **ovum**).

hasty generalization: A kind of **fallacy** in which a conclusion is made about a large group of people or things on the basis of an unrepresentative sample of that group. For example, concluding that everyone supports policy *X* because your friends do is a hasty generalization; people you are not friends with may have different views. Generalizations must be based on representative samples to be credible.

have a right against, to: To have a claim to moral and/or legal protection from certain people doing certain things. For example, everyone has a right against everyone else that they not be assaulted; an individual who orders and pays for something has a right against the seller that the product be delivered as promised.

hegemony: Cultural or political dominance.

hermeneutic: Concerning a method of interpretation or explanation.

hijab: A traditional female Muslim headscarf that covers the hair but leaves the face exposed.

holistic: Considering something as a whole whose parts are interdependent rather than independent.

homologous: Similar in kind.
homology: A state of being **homologous**.
horizon: The range or limit of knowledge or understanding.
human rights: A form of **natural rights**, grounded in the **inherent** or natural **dignity** or worth of human beings, which asserts that humans possess certain **liberty rights** (such as the right to free speech, freedom of the press, and freedom of religion) and/or **equality rights** (such as the right not to starve or the right to maintain their language or culture). Proponents of human rights say they exist regardless of whether a particular society or government recognizes or enforces them.
identity politics: Political arguments or activities based on the shared experience of injustice by members of a marginalized group. Group members often proudly claim identities that are or were socially stigmatized, re-envisioning them as positive.
ideological: Characteristic of an **ideology**; usually derogatory in philosophy.
ideologue: A follower or advocate of an **ideology**; usually derogatory.
ideology: A body of ideas that underlie the beliefs and **interests** of members of a group or **nation**. In philosophy, "ideology" usually means false, narrow, and/or **self-interested** beliefs and ideas.
illiberal: Contrary to **liberal** principles.
immiscible: Incapable of being mixed into a homogeneous solution, as with oil and water.
immunity: (law) A legal freedom or exemption from a duty or obligation.
impartial: Without bias; fair. An impartial theory, system, standard, or person treats everyone or everything fairly or judges everyone or everything by the same standard. Courts aims at **impartiality**.
impartiality: The state of being unbiased or fair.
impartially: In an **impartial** manner; fairly.
imperial: Like an empire or an emperor.
imperialism: The policy of creating and maintaining an empire, involving political control or **sovereignty** over foreign **nations**. See also **colonialism**.
imperialist: Characterized by **imperialism**.
imperialistic: Characterized by **imperialism**.
in accord with: According to, in agreement with.
in camera: (Latin) In private, in a room.
in their own right: Depending on nothing but themselves; with consideration to nothing else but themselves.
in virtue of: Because of or due to.
incommensurability: The state in which two or more things are so different from each other that comparison or common measure is impossible.
incommensurable: So different (from something) that comparison or common measure is impossible.
incommunicado: Without the capability or right to communicate with others.
incumbent: (adjective, usually with "on" or "upon") Obligatory; imposed as a duty.
Indian Act: A Canadian law that primarily regulates the legal status of First Nations people, and, controversially, punished certain actions with loss of status. For example, if an Indian woman married a non-status Indian man, she would lose her Indian status. Since 1985, this and other discriminatory provisions have been revoked.
indigenous: Native to or originating in the place it resides; sometimes refers specifically to **First Nations**, Inuit, and Métis peoples.
individualistic: Characterized by an emphasis on the needs, **rights**, and **autonomy** of individuals, often in opposition to an identifiable group or society in general.
inegalitarian: Opposed to **egalitarian** principles.
inequity: Unfairness, injustice.
infer: (in logic) To conclude from **premises**.
inference: A conclusion reached on the basis of a **premise** that is known or assumed to be true.
infibulation: The surgical removal of the clitoris, the **labia minora** and part of the **labia majora**, and sewing together the two sides of the vulva, leaving only a small opening for menstrual blood and urine.
injunction: A warning; a command or order.
institution: A formal organization or commonly practised tradition within a society which guides the cooperative behaviour, expectations, and values of members of the society.
institutionalization: To make into an **institution**.
institutionally complete: Describes a self-sufficient society, one which does not depend on the **institutions** of another society for its continued existence. An institutionally complete society has its own distinct traditions, values, social and

legal practices, homeland, language, and its own means for delivering education, medical care, and other **public goods**.

intellectual disability: Below-average intellectual ability involving difficulty in reasoning, thinking abstractly, and adapting and learning quickly.

inter-: (prefix) Between or among; e.g., "international" involves two or more nations.

interdelegation: The act of assigning political powers to two or more levels of government.

interest: An **end** that a person or organization believes is good and worth pursuing. In law, a **right**, claim, or **privilege** that a person may have legally enforced.

internal colonization: A theory which describes the subordination of a group or groups by a dominant group in the same **state**. The difference between internal colonization and traditional **colonialism** is the source of the oppression. **Colonial** control is imposed from outside the **state**, whereas internal colonial control originates from within the state.

internecine: Mutually destructive.

interrelated: Mutually and reciprocally (not distantly) related.

intra-: (prefix) Within, inside; e.g., "intrastate" means something occurring within the boundaries of a state.

intrinsic worth: Having (moral) worth just **in virtue of** being the sort of thing it is (human, rational, autonomous, etc.), and not for any particular attribute like age, race, or shoe size.

inure: To become familiar with and used to something distasteful or immoral.

invidious: Unfairly or offensively discriminating.

inviolable: Describes something that it is morally impermissible to act against or transgress. A right is inviolable if transgression of the right is always wrong.

inviolability: The state of being **inviolable**.

Islamist: A supporter of Islamic **fundamentalism**.

jeremiad: A long and mournful complaint.

judiciary: The branch of government that interprets law, as well as the **constitution** if there is one. See also **executive power** and **legislative power**.

juridical: Legal, concerning law.

jurisdiction: The limits or extent of an authority's control. Political jurisdiction may be measured either by geographic limits, such as national borders, or by the extent of the **state's** or **sovereign's** power. Legal jurisdiction is a court's authority to hear a case and issue a judgment.

jurisdictional: Having to do with a **jurisdiction**.

jurisprudence: The science or philosophy of law.

just war theorist: An advocate of **just war theory**.

just war theory: An ethical theory concerning war. Just war theory argues that some but not all wars are morally justified. It has three parts. *Jus ad bellum* conditions address reasons for resorting to war, *jus in bello* conditions address how to fight wars, and *jus post bellum* conditions concern how to end wars and restore peace.

l/g/b/t/q: Lesbian/gay/bisexual/transgendered/queer, sometimes written as LGBTQ. Some writers prefer l/g/b/t/t/q, lesbian/gay/bisexual/transgendered/transsexual/two-spirited/queer.

labia majora: The two outer folds of skin that form the external boundaries of the female genitals.

labia minora: The two folds of skin on either side of the vaginal opening, situated between the **labia majora**.

laissez-faire: A political and economic doctrine that opposes government interference in the affairs of individuals and their property, or that supports no more than a necessary minimum of interference.

left, the: In Canadian politics, "the left" or "left-wing" indicates **egalitarian** parties, individuals, and views; some egalitarians are also **socialists**.

legislative power: The capacity to make laws; also, the law-making branch of government. See also **executive power**, **judiciary**, and **Parliament**.

lexical order: An order of priority for a list of items. Lexical ordering determines that items lower on the list may be restricted or interfered with for the sake of items higher on the list, but items higher on the list cannot be restricted or interfered with for the sake of items lower on the list.

liberal: (noun) Someone who advocates **liberalism**; (adjective) characterized by liberal principles.

liberal democracy: A system of government combining the values and practices of liberalism and democracy. The citizens of liberal democracies enjoy individual freedom, equality under the law, and participation in political decision-making.

liberal democratic: Characterized by the values and practices of **liberal democracy**.

liberal-democratic values: The combination of the liberal commitment to freedom and equality with the **democratic** practice of political participation. Liberal-democratic values include individual freedom, political and legal equality, tolerance among citizens, the willingness to work together, participation in the political process, and responsibility for one's choices and the demands they **impose** on others.

liberal individualism: A system of values that advocates for the political freedom and equality of all individuals in a society, and **privileges** these values over other competing concerns, such as **communitarian** values.

liberalism: A political theory that advocates individual freedom and equality, usually in combination with **rights** and **democracy**.

liberalization: To make less restrictive.

libertarian: Someone who advocates **maximizing** liberty, and who thinks government should protect only individual freedom and private property. Libertarians favour a minimal state that ensures fair procedures (the **free market**, fair **civil** and criminal courts, and police and military protection). Anything more is an unjust limitation of liberty, they say.

liberty rights: Rights to freedom, to be free of interference from the **state** or other people. Liberty rights include rights to free speech, protest, and freedom of religion, and rights against arbitrary detention or torture.

liminal: Pertaining to or at a threshold; borderline.

linguistically deficient: Lacking the ability to communicate ideas and thoughts effectively through the use of language, or through the use of an official language in a **state**.

litigation: To do something or pursue a goal using the justice system.

machismo: Exaggerated manliness, strength, or power.

Magna Carta: (Latin) The "Great Charter," an English political charter drafted in 1215. It is the first of its kind to set legal limits to the exercise of political power. For example, it prohibits punishment and imprisonment without **due process**.

male captus bene detentus: (Latin) Wrongly captured, rightly detained; a controversial legal doctrine that determines that a person may be detained and undergo trial in spite of illegal arrest.

manslaughter: Killing unlawfully but without malice or deliberation. For example, a driver who kills someone while driving recklessly may be charged with manslaughter—the recklessness makes the killing unlawful, but the driver did not intend to hurt or kill anyone.

market economy: An economic system in which prices, wages, and the distribution of material goods (what things are purchased by whom) are determined by those directly involved in the transactions. Ideally, every person is a voluntary participant in the economy. In a **welfare state**, laws guarantee certain rights and liberties to citizens, which may limit the market to ensure legal **equity**.

marginalization: The process or state of being positioned on the margins of society, usually with a substantial loss of social or economic status and power.

marginalize: To position at, or force to the margins of, society, usually with a substantial loss of social or economic status and power for the marginalized person or group.

masculinist: Describing values, beliefs, or attitudes of those who advocate male superiority.

-**maximize**: To aim to create the greatest total—the maximum—of something, such as **welfare** or liberty.

means to an end: Something valued or used for achieving a purpose or goal.

mens rea: (in the criminal law) Criminal intent. Punishment for a crime requires both a criminal act (*actus reus*) and intent to commit the act.

mental competence: The capacity to reason, deliberate, understand, and choose. Legally, mental competence is situation-specific—competence or incompetence with respect to one situation or decision (say, accepting or refusing treatment) does not mean competence or incompetence with respect to other situations or decisions (say, the ability to control one's own finances). In general, adults are assumed to be competent unless proven otherwise.

to **merit**: To deserve or to qualify for something.

meritocratic: Characterized by a system of reward which permits unequal outcomes based on merit. Greater rewards go to those who earn them through greater ability and achievement. Grading is a meritocratic system.

metaethics: The branch of **ethics** that examines the presuppositions and beliefs of ethical thought and practice, such as whether moral judgments are objective or relative. The prefix "meta-"

means "behind," so metaethics is behind—that is, it grounds—ethics.

metaphysical: Having to do with the nature of existence or reality.

metaphysics: The branch of philosophy that deals with the nature of existence or reality. The prefix "meta-" means "behind, beneath," so metaphysics is behind or beneath—that is, it grounds—physics.

misrecognition: The failure to understand or respect a group or member of a group as different but equal in dignity and value.

modernity: Referring to the modern age, from about 1500 on, but especially associated with the **Enlightenment** (seventeenth and eighteenth centuries), which was characterized by grand, all-encompassing theories that attempted to apply to all people, in all times and places.

modus vivendi: (Latin) Way of living; a phrase describing a state of agreement, peace, or end to hostilities between two or more parties whose opinions, beliefs, or goals differ.

moral agency: Having the capacity to make moral decisions and act morally, and thus to be held morally responsible.

moral agent: Someone who is capable of making moral decisions and acting morally, and who can be held morally responsible. See also **moral patient**.

moral luck: Occurs when we assign someone moral responsibility for an action or its consequences, despite the fact that significant aspects of the act or consequences are beyond the person's control.

moral patient: A person or other being that is not capable (or not fully capable) of acting morally and who cannot be held (fully) morally responsible, but who is still the object of moral concern and action. Children, people with moderate to severe **intellectual disabilities**, people with severe mental illnesses, and perhaps fetuses and some animals are moral patients. See also **moral agent**.

moral pluralism: An ethical view containing more than one theory or principle, none of which dominates the others. See also **pluralism**.

moral relativism: The belief that there is no universal standard of morality; morality differs between various times and cultures, and there is no external standard by which to judge one form better or worse than another.

moral standing: The status describing something as worthy of moral consideration.

moral status: The moral position or value of individuals or classes of individuals. Individuals with **moral standing** figure, or ought to figure, in moral deliberations.

moral vegetarianism: Being a vegetarian for moral reasons, as opposed to religious, health, or other reasons.

morally relevant: Something that makes or ought to make a difference in our moral deliberations. For example, having committed a wrongful act is morally relevant to being blamed for the act, while shoe size and (in principle) race are not morally relevant to blame.

mores: The customs and practices that embody the central values of a group or society.

multicultural: Concerning **multiculturalism**.

multiculturalism: The political policy of promoting and preserving different cultures and cultural identities within a single **nation** or society.

multinational: Comprised of two or more **nations**.

nation: A large group of people who share a common culture and history, or a large group of people organized under a single **state** government, or a large group of people who occupy the same region and mutually identify one another as legitimate residences of that region.

Nation of Islam: A Muslim religious movement founded in Detroit, Michigan, in 1930, whose stated goals are the spiritual, mental, social, and economic improvement of African Americans in the United States and all of humanity. Malcolm X was a member of the Nation of Islam.

nation-state: A **state** in which most of its citizens share the same culture, language, traditions, and so on.

national identity: A sense of belonging to a **nation** and others who share the same history, language, customs, institutions, and territory. National identity usually emphasizes the positive aspects of a nation, and downplays the negative, less favourable elements of a nation's history and practices.

nationalism: Preference for, loyalty to, or commitment to one's **nation**; patriotism.

nationalist: Someone who promotes the **interests** of her/his **nation**.

nationalistic: Describing something **nationalist** in nature.

natural: Existing in nature, independent of human beings; when applied to human beings, it refers to an inborn trait such as instinct or eye colour. "Natural" is frequently a problematic term, often used to mean "good" or "unchangeable," when in fact it is neither. Cancer is natural but not good, and most bad eyesight is natural but now easily corrected with a pair of glasses.

natural property: A characteristic that is inherent or naturally occurring in a thing. For example, a natural property of a circle is that every point of its circumference stands at an equal distance from its centre.

natural rights: **Rights** that exist independently, regardless of whether a particular government recognizes or upholds them. See also **human rights**.

Nazi: An advocate of **Nazism**.

Nazism: A national **socialist** political **ideology** of Germany in the first half of the 20th century. Nazism both promoted and put into practice ethnic **nationalism**, **imperialism**, the permanent division of society into social and economic classes, and **totalitarianism**.

necessary: (in logic) A condition or set of conditions that must be fulfilled for something to be the case or for an event to occur. For example, someone must be a Canadian citizen to vote in Canada; only citizens are eligible to vote. Something may be necessary without being **sufficient**, though; for example, Canadian citizens younger than eighteen may not vote.

necessary and sufficient: (in logic) A condition or set of conditions that must be fulfilled for something else to be the case and whose fulfillment guarantees that the second thing is the case. Being (a) a citizen, (b) who is eighteen or older, and (c) who wants to vote are necessary and sufficient for being able to vote in Canada; these are **all and only** the conditions necessary to vote. See also **necessary**, **sufficient**, and **all and only**.

necessary condition: A condition that must be met in order for something else to be the case. See also **necessary**.

negative rights: Rights that protect people from external interference, such as a right against assault. Usually contrasted with **positive rights**.

neo-conservative: Someone who favours minimal government, and who thinks the main function of government should be to support and promote private enterprise. Also called **neo-liberal**.

neo-liberal: A **neo-conservative**.

neonate: A newborn infant.

NGO: A non-governmental organization that is legally recognized as a non-profit organization, operates independent of a government, and pursues a social aim such as humanitarian aid and encouraging the observance of **human rights**. Although NGOs are often financed by governments, they necessarily exclude government representatives from membership in the organization.

niqab: A full Muslim veil that covers the hair and face, exposing only the eyes.

non-culpable: Not legally responsible.

non-derogable: (of a law, regulation, or right) Cannot legally be limited or suspended under any circumstances. Non-derogable rights may be **absolute** (without exceptions or limits) or non-absolute. The right not to be tortured is both non-derogable and absolute. Freedom of religion, on the other hand, is non-derogable but non-absolute: the government cannot forbid holding any religion, but it may restrict some practices of some religions, such as polygamy or snake-handling.

non-refoulement: A principle of international law which forbids surrendering a victim of persecution (for example, a refugee) to his/her persecutor (for example, a **human rights**–violating government).

nonmaleficence: An ethical principle that asserts that one should not cause harm deliberately. This is a fundamental **tenet** of medical ethics, taught to all medical students.

norm: A moral rule or principle shared by members of a cultural group or community to which each member is expected to conform.

normative: Concerning **norms**, value judgments, or **prescriptions**. For example, a normative claim is a claim about the way something should be.

normative ethics: The branch of ethics that examines the moral rules or principles we use to guide our conduct (e.g., "**maximize** the good" or "respect rights"), develop our character (through virtues such as honesty and generosity), and maintain our relationships (by caring for others in various ways).

normative prototype: A **norm** which describes how something should be or how a kind of relationship should be understood and achieved.

normatively: In a **normative** manner.

notwithstanding clause: Section 33 of the ***Charter***, which allows a **federal** or provincial government to retain a law that violates section 2 (the fundamental freedoms) or sections 7 to 15 (individual rights), "notwithstanding" (that is, in spite of) what the *Charter* says. Such a law is valid for only five years, after which the government must re-enact the legislation. This clause was added to maintain the **supremacy of Parliament**.

Oakes test: The test for applying section 1 of the ***Charter***, which says the rights and freedoms in the ***Charter*** are "subject only to such reasonable limits **prescribed** by law as can be demonstrably justified in a free and **democratic** society." The test requires answering four questions, in sequence: (1) Does the law fulfill a "pressing and substantial objective"? (2) Is the law rationally connected to this objective? (3) Does the law impair the right or freedom as little as possible? (4) Are the effects of the law proportionate to its objective? A law is saved only if the Court answers "yes" to all four questions. A negative answer to any question stops the process; the law is not a "reasonable limit," and the remaining questions need not be answered. (Named after the first case in which the Supreme Court used a section 1 analysis.)

observant: Strictly following law or tradition.

obtain, to: To be accepted or customary.

ontologically: In the manner of **ontology**.

ontology: A branch of **metaphysics** dealing with the nature of being, existence, and reality.

Order in Council: A regulation or law made by the Cabinet and not **Parliament**. Orders in council are often but not always made under the express authority of an act or legislation—that is, the legislation is worded generally and the specific regulations under the act are made by orders in council. They are usually considered "subordinate legislation."

orthodox: Relating to the traditional or **fundamentalist** practices of a religious faith.

os sacrum: In vertebrae, a triangular formation of fused bones at the base of the spine.

pace: With all due respect to.

pacifism: The belief that war is never, or almost never, justified.

pacifist: An advocate of **pacifism**.

palliative care: End-of-life care for a patient who has accepted that she or he is dying, which focuses on keeping the patient comfortable but not prolonging life.

pan-: All of a group.

pan-Canadianism: Concerning Canadian **nationalism**, or anything that is relevant to Canada as a whole.

pantheism: A kind of religion in which everything is believed to embody or be a tangible expression of the creator.

pantheistic: Referring to **pantheism**.

paradigm: (noun) A range of concepts, values, and practices that either serve as a model for understanding the world or constitute the shared worldview of a community; (adjective) serving as a model or typical case.

paramilitary: Refers to civilians trained and operating like a military, but not as part of the official armed forces.

paradigmatic: Concerning a typical example.

paradigmatically: In the manner of a typical example.

parliament, Parliament: The body that makes and administers law in a **parliamentary system**. When capitalized, it refers to the **federal** legislature of the particular **state** under discussion (in this textbook, usually Canada).

parliamentary system: A form of government in which the **legislative** and **executive powers** are combined in one body. In Canada, **Parliament** both makes and administers the law.

passive euthanasia: Allowing someone to die when the death could be prevented or postponed, (supposedly) for the person's own good.

paternalism: Forcing adults to do what is (supposed to be) good for them against their wills.

patriarchal: Characteristic of **patriarchy**.

patriarchalism: See **patriarchy**.

patriarchy: A social, legal, or political system which subjects women to the rule of men. In such a system, men as a group exercise control over women as a group, and individual men exercise control over individual women in their family life.

patriate: To bring home.

patriation of the Constitution: From 1867 to 1982, Canada was governed by the *British North America Act*, which was subject to British law. During this time, only the British Parliament could make changes to the Canadian constitution. In 1982 the *Constitution Act, 1982* was passed, which gave Canada an independent **constitution** and thus ultimate control over its government. This event is often described as the patriation or **repatriation** of the Canadian constitution because it marks the significant political change which "brought home" (patriated) or "brought back home" (repatriated) Canada's constitutional powers from England to Canada.

peers: People of equal social or legal standing.

people: A community with a common culture, history, religion, etc. The plural "peoples" is often used to denote the existence of many distinct cultures, as in "the **Aboriginal** peoples of Canada." (The Iroquois and Dene are as different as the French and Iranians.)

persistent vegetative state: A long-lasting coma resulting from brain damage, in which involuntary activities like breathing continue. Most doctors have believed that persistent vegetative states were permanent and that no conscious activity occurred. However, that view has been challenged recently. Some people recover from persistent vegetative state, and others have exhibited clear evidence of consciousness in clinical trials.

personhood: A term for **moral standing** or **moral status**.

petty workers: People whose wages are so low that they must live from paycheque to paycheque with little or no disposable income.

pharmacare: Having prescriptions funded by the government, as part of medical care.

phenomenon: The singular form of "phenomena."

physician-assisted suicide: A form of **assisted suicide** in which a physician provides a patient with the means of committing suicide.

plaintiff: The person who brings a civil suit in a court.

plebiscite: A process in which a proposal is voted on by citizens, who decide the matter through direct voting. Also called a **referendum**.

pluralism: Combining or containing more than one theory, principle, belief, way of living, etc., none of which dominates the other(s). See also **moral pluralism**.

pluralist: A person, group, or society that accepts and/or promotes more than one theory, principle, belief system, way of living, etc., none of which dominates the other(s).

pluralistic: Of or relating to **pluralism**.

plurality: More than one.

plurality opinion: In law, the opinion from a group of judges which is not shared by the majority of the judges, but receives more support than any other opinion.

polis: A state or society, especially one where there is a sense of community.

political realism: A political theory which describes countries as rational, competitive, **self-interested actors** that seek to further their own security and survival. This theory is used to explain international relations, particularly regarding war, peace, and economic cooperation and competition. The theory assumes an **adversarial** relationship among **states**. Since states are considered self-interested, **political realists** argue that a country may do whatever it considers necessary to protect itself and its **interests**.

political realist: An advocate of **political realism**.

polity: A **nation** or society.

popular: Having to do with the people, especially the common people.

popular sovereignty: The view that governments are created by and for the people.

populism: A political doctrine that supports the values and beliefs of the average citizen, or the political strategy of appealing to the values and beliefs of average citizens in hopes of achieving political reform.

positive rights: Rights to certain sorts of social goods, such as education or health care. Usually contrasted with **negative rights**.

postcolonial: Describing the relationship that exists between Europeans and former colonies, usually critical of the colonizers. Postcolonial attitudes vary depending on the **nation**, but usually include attempts to introduce alternative forms of theory that do not rely solely on the language and understanding of Europeans, and the assertion of cultural and political **self-determination**.

post-imperial: Describing a state of affairs existing now or in the future following the end of **imperialism**.

postmodern: Characteristic of **postmodernism**. Sometimes an author uses it only to mean "contemporary."

postmodernism: A set of theories that are critical of grand, overarching theories that characterized the **Enlightenment**, that aimed to apply to all people, in all times and places. The problem, according to postmodernists, is that the grand theories usually fail to apply universally; instead, they apply only to a **privileged** subset of people. Postmodernists favour local, fine-grained theories that apply to specific people in specific times and places. (The Enlightenment is sometimes considered the beginning of the modern era, hence the name "*post*modernism," meaning after the modern era.)

postmodernist: an advocate of **postmodernism**.

potentiality: The capacity or ability to come into existence.

potlatch: A cultural, political, and economic system used by many Pacific Coast First Nations. A potlatch affirmed changes of status (marriages, births, etc.) and political power. The person holding the potlatch gave gifts to everyone who attended. This affirmed the gift-giver's political power, by showing that she/he was rich and powerful enough to give significant gifts. The Canadian government outlawed potlatches in 1884. This restriction was removed in 1951. Potlatches continue to this day, though they tend to be less elaborate than they were prior to European contact.

practical wisdom: The ability not only to know what you ought to do morally, but also to know how to do it well—sensitively, honestly, and so on. Practical wisdom combines knowledge of the good with the skill to apply that knowledge appropriately and consistently. Like any skill, it must be practised for a long time before we can say that someone even possesses it, much less that she/he possesses it to a high degree.

pragmatic: Concerning practical considerations, often in opposition to theoretical or ethical considerations.

preanalytically: In a way that takes place before careful analysis.

precautionary principle: The ethical duty to prevent harm to others, even in the absence of conclusive scientific evidence. The **burden of proof** shifts to those who argue a policy or action is not harmful. The duty becomes stronger as the amount or likelihood of harm increases.

precedent: A legal decision, grounded on a particular set of facts and evidence, that determines how all similar cases must be decided in the future.

preconceive: To form a belief without knowledge or experience of the thing that is believed.

pre-contact: Concerning the time before Aboriginal people had made any contact with European people.

premise: A statement that an argument is based on or a conclusion is drawn from.

prepuce: A fold of skin covering the **clitoris**.

prescribe: To require. (Do not confuse with **proscribe**.)

prescription: A moral or legal rule or requirement, or setting up a moral or legal rule or requirement.

presumption of innocence: The assumption that an accused person is innocent until proven guilty beyond a reasonable doubt in a court of law.

prima facie: At first glance, what appears to be the case before closer inspection.

primary good: A term coined by John Rawls for a social good necessary to pursue one's conception of the good life. Primary goods are all-purpose means for people to pursue their ends, whatever they are. They include things like rights, liberties, opportunities, a reasonable amount of material goods, and the social bases of self-respect.

principal: First in importance or significance.

principles of natural justice: Some legal principles are considered "natural," that is, part of the natural order and self-evident to anyone with good judgment and practical wisdom. The best-known principles of natural justice are the right to present one's case in court and the rule that no one can judge in his/her own case.

private sphere: The sphere in which we live our day-to-day lives. It always includes individuals and the family. Sometimes it includes businesses (e.g., private property) and social **institutions** such as clubs and religious organizations. Contrast with the **public sphere**.

privilege: A special right or advantage available exclusively to one person or social group, in some cases resulting from the social disadvantages experienced by another social group.

privilege: To give special consideration or an advantage to someone or something.

procedural: Having to do with procedures. Refers to rules or processes, rather outcomes or distributions. In procedural justice, we design a set of fair procedures, and as long as they are applied fairly, whatever results from those fair procedures is just. Courts use procedural justice—as long as procedures have been applied fairly, we say the outcome is just. Contrast with **substantive**.

proceduralist: Describes a political system which emphasizes **procedural** commitments over **substantive** ones; that is, a system that has no overarching aim, other than procedural fairness.

progressive taxation: A tax system in which those with more income are taxed at higher rates than those with less income.

proscribe: To forbid. (Do not confuse with **prescribe**.)

protocol: Customs, regulations, and laws.

proviso: A condition or restriction.

prudence: Governing oneself by reason, sound judgment, care, and foresight.

prudential: Characterized by **prudence**.

public good: (philosophy) A good that is shared and beneficial for all of society. In this sense, education is a public good. An educated population is believed to contribute positively to the cultural, economic, and political well-being of society, and is therefore a good that is shared and mutually beneficial. (economics) A good that is non-excludable and non-rivalrous. In this sense, clean air is a public good: it is non-excludable because I cannot prevent you from accessing clean air and you cannot prevent me from accessing it; it is non-rivalrous because my breathing the air does not prevent you from breathing the same air.

public health: The science and practice of promoting and protecting the health of a society. Because of the direct role that health plays in both individual and communal well-being, many **liberal** societies have enacted public health policies in order to advance equality and **social justice**.

public sphere: The political sphere; the sphere in which we live our lives as citizens. It always includes the **state** and society at large. Sometimes it includes businesses and social **institutions** such as clubs and religious organizations. Contrast with the **private sphere**.

queer: A broad term which refers to all sexual and gender minorities that do not identify as heterosexual. Although the word can be used as a slur, many activists involved with **equality-seeking groups** and movements have adopted the word and made it positive.

question-begging: See **beg the question**.

rational: Capable of exercising reason; the capacity to make sense of the world by establishing evidence and verifying facts, and to act according to one's beliefs about the world.

rationality: The capacity to act rationally.

re-inscribe: To reestablish, or to be **codified** again as part of a legal system or doctrine.

read down: To interpret a law or policy in a way that restricts its scope of application. The substance of the law or policy remains, without the portion(s) that violate the ***Charter***.

read in: To interpret a law or policy in a way that broadens its scope of application, so the law or policy applies to people or situations previously excluded by it.

realpolitik: See **political realism**.

recapitulation: The act of summing up or restating a number of points.

recognition: The acknowledgment of something as important and worthy of consideration.

redress: To make right, to correct for.

reductionism: The view that complex phenomena—ideas, data, and so on—can be explained by analyzing them in terms of their simplest components, sometimes to the point of minimizing or distorting the original phenomena.

reference question: A question asked by the federal or a provincial government, requesting the court's opinion on an important legal matter.

referenda: Plural form of **referendum**.

referendum: A process whereby a proposal is accepted or rejected by a population who decide the matter through direct voting. Also called a **plebiscite**.

referent: Something that is referred to.

reflexive: (adjective) Something is reflexive when people's actions and ideas affect the very actions or ideas they are developing. Self-fulfilling prophecies are reflexive: sometimes predictions cause people to change their behaviour and bring about the prediction. Feedback loops are also reflexive: feedback and self-correction allow a system to adjust and change from one output to a more desired one.

refoulement: Returning a refugee or other victim of persecution to her/his country of origin.

regime: A ruling system.

relational: Concerning the significant connections among people in a community or society.

religionist: A religious person.

render: To give over.

repatriate: To return to one's own **nation** or country. In Canada, the act of repatriating is often made with reference to the **patriation of the Constitution**.

repeal: To officially annul or cancel a law.

representative democracy: A form of **democracy** in which citizens elect representatives who **enact** laws and policies on their behalf.

republic: A form of government in which the people hold power (as opposed to a king, dictator, or ruling class), and exercise their power through elected representatives.

republican: One who supports a government in which the people hold ultimate political power.

restorative justice: A system or practice of criminal law that centres on rehabilitating criminals, restoring victims' sense of security and wholeness, and repairing community relations.

retribution: Deserved punishment for a moral wrong-doing.

retributive justice: A system or practice of criminal law that centres on the delivery of deserved punishment for criminals.

rhetoric: The use of language for the purpose of persuasion.

rhetorical: Persuasive or convincing, but not necessarily true. A statement or question may be rhetorical if it is intended to evoke a certain idea or **inference** without the expectation of a response from the listener or audience.

rhetorically: Making a point without expecting a response.

right: (noun) A valid, enforceable claim, either against everyone (e.g., the right not to be assaulted) or against a specific person (e.g., the right of minor children to be maintained by their parents).

right, the (1): Used in **deontology** to refer to the principles or rules that underlie moral conduct (such as Kant's **categorical imperative** or **rights theory**); usually contrasted with the **good**. (2) Used in Canadian politics to refer to **conservative** parties, individuals, and views.

rite: A religious ceremony.

rive: To break apart or split.

rule of law: A system in which every person, **institution**, and official, public or private, as well as the government itself, is subject to the law.

salience: Standing out as important or meaningful.

salient: Important or meaningful.

sanction, to: To socially or legally approve.

sanction: (law) A penalty or reward. (international law) Actions taken by one or more **states** against another to force the targeted state to comply with certain standards or rules; a penalty imposed by one or more states on another.

sanctity of human life theory: The theory that human life is sacred or of such high value that it should always be treated as an **end rather than a means**. Because proponents of the theory generally take **absolute** stances on what is and is not a violation of the sanctity of human life, they are usually pro-life on the issue of abortion, and oppose assisted suicide and stem cell research.

sanguine: Optimistic, positive.

SARS: Severe Acute Respiratory Syndrome, a viral disease which causes severe flu-like symptoms, and in severe cases respiratory failure and death.

schism: A separation into groups or factions, usually in opposition to one another.

secede: To withdraw from a **state** in order to establish an independent state or **nation**.

secession: The act of withdrawing from a **state** in order to establish an independent state or **nation**.

secessionist: A supporter or advocate of **secession**.

secular: Not having to do with religion.

secularize: To change something from a religious symbol, meaning, or practice into a **secular** symbol, meaning, or practice.

security certificate: In Canada, a legal tool for detaining and possibly deporting a foreign national or permanent resident who the federal government considers a danger to national security. The accused and her/his lawyer may not see the evidence against her/him; they see only a summary provided by a judge.

seigneurial system: A form of landownership in Quebec in which a *seigneur* (landowner) leased land to a *censitaire* or *habitant* (tenant). The *seigneur* could establish courts of law and mills; the *habitant* could farm, hunt, fish, and cut wood, and owed the *seigneur* rent, a portion of crops grown, and a few days of work a year. It was abolished in 1854.

self-consciousness: The ability to reflect on and evaluate one's thoughts, desires, hopes, fears, etc. See also **consciousness**.

self-determination: The ability of a person or group to determine its own future without external interference.

self-determining: Describing a person or group that can determine its own future without external interference.

self-governing: Independent, capable of **self-government**.

self-government: The political independence and **sovereignty** of a **nation**, **sub-state** group, or society. Self-government may include different forms of political authority, ranging from municipal-like powers to **secession** and political independence.

self-interest: Any individual's action, belief, or way of being that primarily serves the individual's well-being without regard to others. Many theories that attempt to describe and explain human behaviour assume self-interest to be either a primary motivation behind human action, or the only motivation.

self-rule: **Self-government**.

semi-: (prefix) Partially, in part, incomplete; e.g., semicircle means an incomplete circle.

seminal: Original, fundamental, or of great importance.

sentience: The capacity to experience pleasure and/or pain.

sentient: Having the capacity to experience pleasure and/or pain.

separatist: Someone who advocates that her/his **nation secede** from the larger **nation-state** and become **sovereign**.

sex: The biological classification of individuals as male or female based on their reproductive organs. See also **gender**.

sexual politics: The relations of men and women considered in terms of personal, social, political, and economic power inequalities.

simpliciter: Plainly, without qualification.

siren call: Anything that leads toward danger by way of charm or false appearances.

social conservative: Someone who believes government should promote religious values and the traditional family.

social democracy: A system of government combining the values and practices of egalitarianism and democracy. Social democracies aim to reduce economic and social inequalities, in order to **maximize** individual freedoms and maintain a healthy **democracy**.

social democrat: An **egalitarian** liberal who believes **democracy** is undermined if economic or social inequalities become large enough that some individuals, corporations, or groups gain unequal access to government. Governments must manage the economy to maintain equality and democracy, then. The difference between social democrats and **egalitarian centrists** is how much management of the economy they support, and how much equality they think government should maintain; on both issues, social democrats support a greater role for government than egalitarian centrists do.

social democratic: Characterized by the values of **egalitarianism** and **democracy**.

social inequality: Group-based inequality in social status and income, such as sexism, racism, ableism, large economic inequalities, religious discrimination, and so on.

social justice: Fair distribution of social benefits and burdens to the members of a society. It may include protecting and enforcing of **rights**, equality of opportunity, assuring a baseline for individual autonomy, safeguarding individual self-respect and its preconditions, and equitable access to social, economic, and political influence or power.

socialism: A system of government in which many or most of the major industries of a society are collectively owned, usually by the government itself. The aims of socialist systems are usually **egalitarian**, and involve the **equitable** distribution of material goods, the equalization of opportunities, and the fair organization of society's institutions.

socialist: An advocate or supporter of **socialism**.

socialize: To place in the control or under the regulation of government.

socially constructed: Created socially, not naturally. A social construct is "social" in the sense that it is not created by any one individual, but rather by a group or a whole society. It is "constructed" in the sense that it is a human **artifact**, and not something occurring in nature. Social constructs arise from a society's **institutions**, and may be the intentional or unintentional result of laws, traditions, and **norms**.

solidarity: A state of mutual support, or a **union** of **interests** and goals.

solipsism: Extreme self-centredness. (philosophy) The view that only the self can be proved to exist.

sound: (of an argument) Without defects in reason or evidence.

sovereign: (noun) The group or individual with supreme power in a **state**. (adjective, adverb) Having supreme power; independent, **self-governing**.

sovereigntist: (in Canada) Someone who supports Quebec's right to **sovereignty**, independence, and **self-government**.

sovereignty: Having supreme political power, usually in a **state**.

sovereignty association: The political independence (**sovereignty**) of Quebec, combined with some political and economic ties to Canada.

specious: Appearing to be correct or true but really incorrect or false.

squatters' rights: Rights gained by people who continuously occupy unused or unowned property for a certain amount of time. Not all societies recognize squatters' rights, and they usually put further conditions on these rights, in addition to continuously occupation. In some societies, squatting is illegal.

state, the: The government; political society.

state of nature: A concept from political philosophy which describes a hypothetical condition prior to the creation of government and political society. The state of nature is usually described as a culturally and technologically primitive period in human development. In social contract theory, political society is legitimate only if it arises, or could arise, from the actions and choices of individuals in a state of nature.

statutory: Concerning or enacted by a law.

stay (charges, proceedings): To delay charges or the legal process in a trial. Stayed charges are suspended for a period of time or indefinitely. Staying charges is not the same as dropping them. When charges are stayed, the accused person still has a police record.

strike down: (of a law or policy) To declare **unconstitutional** and therefore of no force or effect.

stipulate: To specify a requirement or condition of something.

straw man argument: A form of **fallacy** where the author attacks only a very weak argument against her/his position, figuratively knocking down a straw man rather than a real one.

sub-: Under or below, e.g. a sub-unit is a smaller part of a larger unit, or a whole.

subjection: Being under the rule, power or authority of another.

substantive: Refers to what the outcomes, distributions, etc. in fact are, rather than the rules and processes that brought them about. Contrast with **procedural**.

substantive equality: Equal life chances. Substantive equality exists when all citizens have equal chances of living lives they consider worthwhile and equal chances of prospering or suffering, as the case may be. Substantive equality underlies the Canada Pension Plan and Old Age Security; they ensure that everyone is able to retire at some point without being destitute. See also **formal equality**.

substantive equality of opportunity: A level playing field. Substantive equality of opportunity exists when every qualified person has equal access to desirable social positions, services, and opportunities available in the society. See also **formal equality of opportunity**.

substantive liberty: Equal ability to exercise freedom. Substantive liberty exists when all citizens are equally able to be **agents** in their own lives, and can choose among equally good or bad alternatives, as the case may be. Substantive liberty underlies public education; it ensures all citizens have access to at least a decent range of choices. See also **formal liberty**.

sub-state: Smaller than, and usually within, a **state**.

subversive: Characterized by the attempt to **subvert**.

subvert: To undermine or change in a manner characterized by conflict or disagreement.

suffice: To be adequate or meet the requirement for something.

sufficient: (in logic) A condition or set of conditions which, when they are fulfilled, guarantees that something else is the case. For example, (a) being twenty years old, (b) having been born in Canada, and (c) wanting to vote is sufficient for being able to vote here—everyone with those characteristics is qualified to vote. However, something may be sufficient but not **necessary**: neither being twenty nor having been born in Canada is necessary to being able to vote. See also **necessary** and **necessary and sufficient**.

sufficient condition: A condition that, if fulfilled, guarantees something else is the case. Being a Member of Parliament is a sufficient condition for being able to vote in Canada. All Members of Parliament, but not only them, may vote in Canada. See also **sufficient** and **all and only**.

suffrage: The right to vote in political elections.

sui generis: (Latin) One of a kind, unique.

Sun Dance: A religious ceremony practised by many First Nations and Native American peoples, especially from the Prairies.

supersede: To replace or take the place of something.

supra-: Greater or above, e.g. a supra-unit is larger than the smaller units of which it is made up.

supranational: Describes an institution or organization whose influence or relevance extends beyond national borders.

supremacy of Parliament: The claim that Parliament is, ultimately, the highest political authority in the land. Parliament can overturn **judicial** decisions by changing the law or, if a law is found **unconstitutional**, it can amend the ***Charter*** or invoke the **notwithstanding clause**.

systemic discrimination: Discriminatory policies and practices that are part of the formal or informal structure of an **institution** or society.

table: To submit a bill, regulation, legislation, etc. for consideration by a legislature.

tacit: Unspoken, implied.

tacitly: Quietly or silently.

tariffs: Taxes or duties.

temporal: Having to do with time.

temporally: Concerning the **temporal** nature of a thing.

tenet: A belief or principle. (Not to be confused with "tenant," which is an occupant.)

tenuous: Weak or feeble.

theological: Religious.

thesis: A point of view that is argued for.

tort: A wrongful act that injures a person's body, property, reputation, etc., which entitles the injured person to compensation.

total tax-to-GDP ratio: The ratio of tax collection against the **gross domestic product** (GDP). A total tax-to-GDP ratio of one hundred per cent would indicate that the market value of all goods and services produced within a country in a given period has been taxed away; a ratio of zero would indicate no taxes whatsoever.

totalitarianism: A form of government with a one-party state that exercises control over every aspect of life. Contrast with **democracy** and **liberalism**.

totemic symbol: The representation of an animal, plant, or natural object that stands in a special relation to a **clan** or family, and is often regarded as the ancestor or guardian of the clan or family.

transcend: To go beyond.

transgendered: A person whose socially assigned **gender** and biological **sex** do not match; someone who is born one sex but who identifies with the other sex and gender.

transnational: Reaching beyond the **interests** or borders of a single **nation** or country.

treat as an end and not merely as a means: to treat someone with **dignity** and moral consideration, and not to use her/him only as a stepping stone to achieve a desired goal.

treaty rights: Rights guaranteed by a treaty. See also **Aboriginal and treaty rights**.

triage: The process of sorting patients, or casualties in a battle or disaster, into categories to determine priority for treatment.

tribunal: A committee or group who have the authority to judge on certain matters.

Trojan Horse: A **subversive** or destructive group that is secretly planted behind enemy lines. In Greek mythology, Greek men hid within a large wooden horse which was accepted as a victory trophy by the city of Troy. The Trojans pulled the horse into their city, and at night the Greek men emerged from the horse and destroyed the city.

tyranny of the majority: A problem in democracies in which the lawful preferences, practices, or enacted policies of a political majority oppress a political minority. Most democracies address this problem by introducing measures to protect the **rights** of minorities.

unassimilable: Not capable of assimilation. A group which is unassimilable resists absorption into another group and retains its distinct group identity.

unconstitutional: Violating one or more sections of a **constitution**. See also **constitutional**.

unconstrained: Without restriction.

underdetermine: To contain too little evidence to draw a determinate (specific) conclusion or to support a specific belief, theory, or view. That is, the evidence available supports at least two plausible conclusions, beliefs, theories, or views (generally, multiple plausible conclusions etc.).

unilateral: Involving only one side; not mutual.

unilateralism: The policy or doctrine of acting on one's own, without consulting others.
unilaterally: On one's own, without consultation.
unilingual: Speaking only one language.
union: The act or state of uniting or combining two or more things.
Union Jack: The flag of the United Kingdom.
universalism: A universal application of something to all members of a group.
usurpation: The wrongful exercise of authority or the wrongful taking of **sovereignty**.
utilitarian: In accordance with **utilitarianism**; a supporter or advocate of **utilitarianism**.
utilitarianism: A form of **consequentialism** that defines "good" as that which improves **welfare** and "bad" as that which reduces welfare, and that says we should aim to produce the greatest good for the greatest number.
utility: Happiness or **welfare**; the **good** at which **utilitarianism** aims.
utopia: A fictional, perfect society.
valorization: The act of fixing the value of something artificially.
valorize: To fix the value of something artificially.
vaunt: To brag or praise.
vegan: A vegetarian who uses no animal products, whether for food or clothing.
viability: When the fetus/unborn child is capable of living outside the womb.
viable: Capable of success; capable of living.
vindicate: To provide justification, or to excuse from blame.
virtue ethics: A kind of **normative ethics** that focuses on people's motives or character as **moral agents**.
vis-a-vis: In relation to.
vicissitudes: Changes; ups and downs.
vitiate: To weaken or disqualify.
want: A lack of something desirable or important.
ward: A person under the legal protection of another.
warrant, to: To provide justification for an argument, belief or action.
watershed: A turning point, an event of significance.
welfare: How *well* individuals *fare* (do).
welfare state: A form of government in which the **state** takes responsibility for social and economic security, through pensions, employment insurance, minimum wage laws, universal healthcare, etc.
zoonotic: Concerning diseases or infections that can be transmitted from animals to humans.

Credits

Grateful acknowledgement is made for permission to reproduce the following:

LOUISE ARBOUR "Crimes Against Women under International Law," (Stefan A. Riesenfeld Award Lecture, 28 February 2002), *Berkley Journal of International Law* 21 (2003): 196–212. © 2003 by the Regents of the University of California. Reprinted from the Berkley Journal of International Law 21 Berkeley J. Int'l L. 196 (2003). By permission of the Regents of the University of California.

FRANCOISE BAYLIS, NUALA P. KENNY, AND SUSAN SHERWIN "A Relational Account of Public Health Ethics," *Public Health Ethics* 1, 3 (2008): 196–209.

BENJAMIN L. BERGER "The Cultural Limits of Legal Tolerance," from *Canadian Journal of Law and Jurisprudence* 21, 2 (2008): 245–77. Used by permission of Benjamin Berger.

JOHN BORROW "'Landed' Citizenship: Narratives of Aboriginal Political Participation," *Citizenship in Diverse Societies*, Will Kymlicka and Wayne Norman, eds. (Oxford University Press, 2000): 326–42. By permission of Oxford University Press.

ED BROADBENT "Equality is the Core Value of Democracy," *The Monitor* (1 February 2010), www.policyalternatives.ca/publications/monitor/equality-core-value-democracy

JOSEPH H. CARENS AND MELISSA S. WILLIAMS "Islam, Immigration and Group Recognition," *Citizenship Studies* 2, 3 (1998): 475–500.

Chaoulli v. Quebec (Attorney General), [2005] 1 S.C.R. 791, 2005 SCC 35, http://scc-csc.lexum.com/scc-csc/scc-csc/en/item/2237/index.do

MARCEL CHAPUT *Why I Am a Separatist*, Robert Taylor, trans. (Toronto: Ryerson, 1961).

Charkaoui v. Canada (Citizenship and Immigration), [2008] 2 S.C.R. 326, 2008 SCC 38 http://scc.lexum.org/en/2008/2008scc38/2008scc38.html

STEVEN L. DAVIS "The Least Harm Principle May Require that Humans Consume a Diet Containing Large Herbivores, Not a Vegan Diet," *Journal of Agricultural and Environmental Ethics* 16, 4 (2003): 387–94.

ROMÉO A. DELLAIRE Remarks and Questions, Carnegie Council for Ethics in International Affairs (New York, 29 January 2003).

ROMÉO A. DELLAIRE "The Lessons of Rwanda," *Refugee Survey Quarterly* 23, 4 (2004): 19–27.

LOUIS A. DELVOIE "Terrorism: Global Insecurity or Global Hyperbole?," *Canadian Military Journal* 6, 4 (2005-2006): 103–4, www.journal.forces.gc.ca/vo6/no4/views-vues-eng.asp. Reprinted with the permission of the Canadian Military Journal as originally published in the CMJ Vol. 6, No. 4, (Winter 2005-2006) issue.

MONIQUE DEVEAUX "Conflicting Equalities? Cutural Group Rights and Sex Equality," *Political Studies* 48, 3 (2000): 522–39.

SUE DONALDSON AND WILL KYMLICKA *Zoopolis: A Political Theory of Animal Rights (Overview)*, accessed 19 January 2015, http://www.academia.edu/2394382/Sue_Donaldson_and_Will_Kymlicka_Zoopolis_A_Political_Theory_of_Animal_Rights_An_Overview_ © Will Kymlicka and Sue Donaldson. Used with permission.

JOCELYN DOWNIE *Dying Justice: Decriminalizing Euthanasia and Assisted Suicide in Canada*. © University of Toronto Press, 2004. pp. 89–132. Reprinted with permission of the publisher.

FRASER, DAVID "Animal Ethics and Animal Welfare Science: Bridging the Two Cultures," Applied Animal Behavior Science 65 (1999): 171–89.

CATHERINE FRAZEE "Affidavit of Catharine Frazee, Intervener, Ginette v. Attorney General of Canada," No. 400-17-002642-110. Used with the permission of Catherine Frazee.

TRUDY GOVIER AND WILHELM VERWOERD "How Not to Polarize 'Victims' and 'Perpetrators,'" *Peace Review* 16, 3 (2004): 371–7. Copyright © 2004 Routledge.

THOMAS HOMER-DIXON "The Rise of Complex Terrorism," *Foreign Policy* 128 (2002): 52–62.

THOMAS HOMER-DIXON "The Great Transformation—Climate Change as Cultural Change," speech in Essen, Germany (June 2009), www.homerdixon.com/2009/06/08/the-great-transformation-climate-change-as-cultural-change/ © Thomas Homer-Dixon. Used with permission.

THOMAS HURKA "Proportionality and Necessity," *War: Essays in Political Philosophy*, (Cambridge University Press, 2008): 127–44. Reprinted with the permission of Cambridge University Press.

THOMAS HURKA "Ethical Principles," *Ethics and Climate Change: The Greenhouse Effect*, Harold

Coward and Thomas Hurka, eds. (Wilfrid Laurier Press, 1993): 23–38.

Tasha Kheiriddin and Adam Daifallah "Vision Wanted: Tax Cuts Aren't Enough," excerpt from *Rescuing Canada's Right: Blueprint for a Conservative Revolution*, (John Wiley and Sons, 2005): 187–200. © 2005 by Tasha Kheiriddin and Adam Daifallah. Published by HarperCollins Publishers Ltd. All rights reserved.

Will Kymlicka "Being Canadian," *Government and Opposition* 38, 3 (2003): 357–85. Copyright © 2003 Will Kymlicka. Published by Government and Opposition Limited and Cambridge University Press. Reprinted with the permission of Cambridge University Press.

Diane Lamoureaux *L'amère patrie. Féminisme et nationalisme dans le Québec contemporain* (Les Éditions du remue-ménage, 2001): 159–67. (Trans. by Karen Wendling and Hannah Peck.)

Bjørn Lomborg "Perspectives on Climate Change," Statement to the Subcommittee on Energy and Air Quality joint hearing with the Subcommittee on Energy and Environment of the Committee on Sceince and Technology, March 2007, www.climatechangefacts.info/ClimateChangeDocuments/lomborg_testimony.pdf

Odette Madore "The Canada Health Act: Overview and Options," reproduced with the permission of the Library of Parliament, 2014.

Don Marquis "Why Abortion is Immoral," *Journal of Philosophy*, LXXXVI, 4 (April 1989): 183–202.

Brian Orend "Justice After War," *Ethics and International Affairs* 16, 1, (2002): 43–56.

Tom Regan from "The Moral Basis of Vegetarianism", *Canadian Journal of Philosophy* 5, 2 (1975): 181–214. Copyright © Canadian Journal of Philosophy, reprinted by permission of Taylor & Francis Ltd, www.tandfonline.com on behalf of The Canadian Journal of Philosophy.

John Roberts abridged version of "Liberalism: The Return of the Perennial Philosophy", *Searching for the New Liberalism*, Howard Aster and Thomas S. Axworthy, eds.(Oakville, ON: Mosaic Press, 2003): 3–21.

Hugh Segal "Advancing the 'Canadian Ideal'", *Queen's Quarterly* 111, 1 (2004): 51–6. Used by permission of Hugh Segal.

Ayelet Shachar "Faith in Law? Diffusing Tensions Between Diversity and Equality," *Philosophy and Social Criticism* 36, 3–4 (2010): 395-411. Reproduced by permission of SAGE Publications Ltd., London, Los Angeles, New Delhi, Singapore and Washington DC. Copyright © Sage Publications, 2010.

Susan Sherwin "Abortion," *No Longer Patient: Feminist Ethics and Health Care*, (Temple University Press, 1992): 99–116. Used by permission of Temple University Press. © 1992 by Temple University. All Rights Reserved.

Susan Sherwin "Theory versus Practice in Ethics: A Feminist Perspective on Justice in Health Care" from *Philosophical Perspectives on Bioethics*, Joseph Boyle and Wayne L. Sumner, eds. © University of Toronto Press 1996. pp. 187–209. Reprinted with permission of the publisher.

Vandana Shiva "Soil not Oil: Environmental Justice in an Age of Climate Crisis," South End Press, 2008.

L.W. Sumner "Abortion", *Health Care Ethics*, Donald Van de Veer, ed., (Temple University Press, 1987): 162–83.

Supreme Court of Canada *Rodriguez v. British Columbia (Attorney General)*, [1993] 3 S.C.R. 519, http://scc-csc.lexum.com/scc-csc/scc-csc/en/item/1054/index.do

Charles Taylor "Shared and Divergent Values," from *Options for a New Canada*, edited by Ronald L. Watts and Douglas M. Brown, © University of Toronto Press 1991, published in association with the Institute of Intergovernmental Relations, Queen's University and the Business Council on National Issues, pp. 53–76. Reprinted with permission of the publisher.

Judith Jarvis Thomson "A Defense of Abortion", *Philosophy and Public Affairs* 1, 1 (1971): 47–66. Reproduced with permission of Blackwell Publishing Ltd.

James Tully "A Just Relationship between Aboriginal and Non-Aboriginal Peoples of Canada," *Aboriginal Rights and Self-Government*, Curtis Cook and Juan D. Lindau, eds. (McGill-Queen's University Press, 2000): 39–71.

Index